SEVENTH EDITION

CONTEMPORARY AMERICAN SPEECHES

A Sourcebook of Speech Forms and Principles

RICHARD L. JOHANNESEN

Northern Illinois University

R. R. ALLEN

University of Wisconsin

WIL A. LINKUGEL

University of Kansas

KENDALL/HUNT PUBLISHING COMPANY
2460 Kerper Boulevard P.O. Box 539 Dubuque, Iowa 52004-0539

Cover and interior photos courtesy of the Bettmann Archive

Library of Congress Catalog Card Number: 91–75652

ISBN 0–8403–6519–5

Printed in the United States of America
10   9   8   7   6   5   4   3   2

CONTENTS

1

WHY STUDY SPEECHES?

2

THE ANALYSIS OF SPEECHES

=========================== **3** ===========================

SPEECHES THAT INCREASE UNDERSTANDING

=========

=========================== **4** ===========================

SPEECHES THAT AFFIRM PROPOSITIONS OF FACT

=========

5

SPEECHES THAT AFFIRM PROPOSITIONS OF VALUE

6

SPEECHES THAT CREATE CONCERN FOR PROBLEMS

7

SPEECHES THAT AFFIRM PROPOSITIONS OF POLICY

8

SPEECHES THAT INTENSIFY SOCIAL COHESION

ALTERNATE TOPICAL CONTENTS*

*Asterisked speeches are "paired" speeches that present differing views on essentially the same general topic.

===================== CONCERNS OF WOMEN =====================

===================== CONCERNS OF MINORITIES =====================

===================== THE POLITICAL PROCESS =====================

TECHNOLOGY AND THE ENVIRONMENT

CONTEMPORARY MORALS AND VALUES

PREFACE

This edition, like the first six editions of *Contemporary American Speeches,* is dedicated to the belief that acquisition of speaking skills is best achieved through three complementary lines of study: *theory,* from which the student may gain a basic understanding of the speech act; *example,* through which the student may evaluate precept in the light of real and varied instances of public discourse; and *practice,* in which the student may apply rhetorical principles to the creation of speeches. This book is primarily designed to contribute to the second of these lines of study, *example.*

Teaching by example is an ancient practice. Isocrates used the study of speeches as one of his principal teaching devices. Cicero, himself an assiduous student of speeches, advocated the study of Greek and Roman speech models to all aspiring orators. Quintilian said, "It is from . . . authors worthy of our study that we must draw our stock of words, the variety of our figures and our methods of composition." Chauncey Goodrich noted that "He who would teach eloquence must do it chiefly by examples." Edmund Burke studied Demosthenes; Daniel Webster studied Burke; and Woodrow Wilson studied Webster.

In producing a seventh edition of *Contemporary American Speeches,* we again faced the critical question of which speeches to retain and which ones to replace. As we have done with earlier editions, we approached this problem by surveying as many users of the previous editions as we could, asking them to tell us which speeches they found especially useful and which ones they felt could be discarded. We have also been guided by our own teaching experience, noting those addresses that generated much student discussion and comprehension of speech principles.

For our purpose, *contemporary* includes the sixties and seventies with significant emphasis on the eighties and nineties. We have added 36 new speeches and retained only 13 from the sixth edition. Only six of the speeches are from the sixties and seventies, 16 are from the eighties, and 27 are from 1990–1991. Three speeches have continued through all seven editions: Martin Luther King's "I Have a Dream," Douglas MacArthur's "Farewell to the Cadets," and John F. Kennedy's "Inaugural Address." Each category of speeches includes one student speech.

Compared to past editions we have significantly increased the diversity of "voices" represented. Certainly the political spectra of Democrat-Republican and liberal-conservative are represented. Thirty-seven percent of the speakers are women compared to 20 percent in the sixth edition. Twenty-six percent of the speakers are African American, Hispanic American, and Native American compared to 15 percent in the sixth edition.

As a new feature for this edition, we have "paired" speeches that present differing viewpoints on essentially the same general topic: Mario Cuomo and Phyllis Schlafly on what values should be taught in the public schools; Russell Train and Virginia Postrel on the values central to the environmental movement; Diane Ravitch and Molefi Asante on multiculturalism in education; Faye Wattleton and Jerry Falwell on legalized abortion; Sam Nunn and George Bush on war with Iraq; Patricia Schroeder and Colin Powell on the best policy for stationing American military forces at home and abroad; and Mario Cuomo and James Pinkerton on the proper roles of federal, state, and local governments.

We have also revised some of the chapter essays. Although the basic thrust and sub-stance of each essay remains the same, we have sought to improve some of our explanations of basic concepts. Each essay develops criteria that the student may use in exploring and evaluating the speeches. The suggestions "For Further Reading" at the end of each chapter have been updated as well.

The introductory headnotes that precede each speech provide background information and pose thought provoking suggestions and questions to stimulate student analysis of each address. In some headnotes, even more than in previous editions, we undertake at length our own analysis of a speech to illustrate some of the ways in which a rhetorical critic might describe, interpret, and evaluate important elements of the speech.

Whether the teacher chooses to emphasize speech forms or speech principles, this book should prove useful. As in previous editions, we have included an Index of Rhetorical Principles which notes the passages in each speech that best illustrate the major speech principles discussed in modern speech textbooks.

This book also can serve as the core textbook in a course in Contemporary Public Address. While we have continued to emphasize speech forms and principles, in this edition more than in previous editions we have included speeches by well-known speakers. And always we have sought speeches that typify current public scrutiny of some of society's most pressing questions. The speech forms themselves assure coverage of the spectrum of contemporary public address. Knowledge, facts, values, problems, and policies have always been rhetoric's essence. At the same time, ceremonial address continues to be a vital form for social cohesion.

We again wish to acknowledge our indebtedness to the many people and sources who have given us permission to reprint speeches in this book. *Vital Speeches of the Day* continues to be an important source for representative speeches on current issues. We are also grateful for the recommendations that have been so thoughtfully provided by colleagues.

R. L. J.
R. R. A.
W. A. L.

President George Bush talks to children at an East Harlem elementary school.

CHAPTER 1

WHY STUDY SPEECHES?

Only as the constant companions of Demosthenes, Cicero, Burke, Fox, Channing, and Webster can we hope to become orators.

Woodrow Wilson

The primary purpose of *Contemporary American Speeches* is to present a collection of speeches for student analysis and evaluation. Just as Woodrow Wilson considered the study of speeches essential to his personal development as a speaker, we hope that this chapter will stimulate your thinking about the importance of such study in your own intellectual life.

WE STUDY SPEECHES TO INCREASE OUR KNOWLEDGE OF HUMANITY

One of the purposes of a college education is to encourage students to ponder the nature of their own humanity. In most degree programs, students are encouraged to engage in liberal studies as a complement to the sequence of professional courses that leads to specialized careers. A professional person is, after all, a person: a lawyer is a person who practices law, a teacher is a person who teaches, a doctor is a person who practices medicine, a scientist is a person who studies the physical world in which we live. Through liberal studies, students are encouraged to develop insights regarding the potentialities and limitations of the human condition. Through such knowledge, a system of values should emerge that provides the basis for future decisions, both professional and personal.

Students may take varied paths in their efforts to understand what it means to be human. Each liberal study holds such promise—and rightfully so. Nothing thought or made or done by people is alien to the student in search of human understanding. Emerson said: "Raphael paints wisdom; Handel sings it; Phidias carves it; Shakespeare writes it; Wren builds it; Columbus sails it; Luther preaches it; Washington arms it; Watt mechanizes it." In each of these studies, students may find evidence of the creative struggle of human beings with their environment. And from each of these studies, students may gain insights into their own lives.

In the liberal arts tradition, speeches deserve to be studied because they are a unique form of human expression. No other artifact of social life reflects the same exact process. A painting encompasses the elements of thought and form; yet a speech is composed of language. A poem embraces thought, language, and form; yet a speech is conveyed by sound. Theatre makes use of thought, language, form, and sound; yet a speech is at once more urgent and real, more literal and spontaneous. A speech is a unique product of human creativity; it calls for special understanding as does a painting or a poem, a statue or a scroll.

Speeches have a quality that makes them especially deserving of study by students in search of human understanding; speeches are highly transparent. They are the product of human beings in dynamic confrontation with ideas and audiences. In speeches, students will find men and women articulating the noble ideals of our civilization and making enlightened judgments on the great social, moral, and political issues of our own and other times. In speeches, students will also find men and women degrading our common humanity and concocting themes of hatred and bigotry. In speeches, the potentialities and limitations of the human condition are clearly reflected.

WE STUDY SPEECHES TO DERIVE STANDARDS FOR THE CRITICAL APPRAISAL OF PUBLIC DISCOURSE

Few will question the claim that the quality of our public dialogue is not what it might be. In lecture halls, we have grown accustomed to speakers who are dull, disorganized, and unclear. In chambers of social decisionmaking, we have come to accept as the norm under-developed ideas expressed in careless language and sloppy speech. And even at moments of public ceremony, we expect speeches that are trite and mundane when what is called for is an inspiring rearticulation of our social purpose and identity.

As members of audiences, we have come to demand too little of those who address us. Through the study of speeches, we may develop higher standards for the public dialogue. We may come to demand more of those who address us, both in terms of the merit of their ideas and their means of public expression.

The study of speeches offers a broad familiarity with the crucial issues of humanity. Our communion with the past, the freedom of our citizens, the quality of our private and public life, our hopes for the future—all of these are evident in the public dialogue. Through an awareness of the significant issues of our own and other times, students may come to reject trivial issues and petty thoughts as unworthy of public attention.

Through the study of speeches, students may also acquire insights regarding the habits of intellect through which responsible speakers examine, test, and temper ideas. Through such knowledge, they may appraise the worth of a speaker's critical processes. They may test the sufficiency of the speaker's proof. They may deny the specious inference and the faulty deduction. They may reject simplistic answers to complex social questions.

But the enlightened critic must not stop here. Public discourse does not exist in a social vacuum. It is not soliloquy, but purposive address seeking to impart to its hearers some knowledge or interpretation, some value or course of action. Public discourse always seeks to influence the hearer and to change his or her behavior—whether cognitive or overt. If ideas are to have social utility, they must be transformed from private conceptions into meaningful public statements. Speakers must so develop and project their thoughts that direction is given to those who listen. They must choose from a complex of elements those most likely to give energy and vitality to their ideas in a particular public context.

Through the study of speeches, students will come to realize that speakers can adapt ideas to audiences in meaningful and socially productive ways. While recognizing the short-comings of the public intellect, they will know that speakers have made complex ideas clear. While recognizing that speakers have exploited public avarice and ignorance in achieving personal power, they will know that other speakers have fostered social excellence. While recognizing that speeches have embodied appeals to low motives and base instincts, they will know that oratory has sometimes inspired audiences to act in accord with the noble ideas of humanity.

The dimensions of rhetorical choice are numerous. In Chapter 2, you will be introduced to thirteen questions which will guide your study of the means speakers employ in rendering their ideas clear, persuasive, and memorable. As you apply these questions to speeches, you will develop an increased appreciation for the artistry which undergirds effective public communication. As you witness speakers conveying the essence of significant thoughts with skill and integrity, you will have cause to reject other speakers whose expressions are feeble, whose appeals are base, whose strategies are unethical, and whose purposes are suspect.

WE STUDY SPEECHES TO ENLARGE AND DEEPEN OUR UNDERSTANDING OF RHETORICAL THEORY

The student of speech, faced with a body of precepts set forth in a contemporary basic public speaking textbook, will often fail to assign importance to the ideas expressed. The text, it may seem, is too firm in its adherence to inviolate rules, too committed to the perpetuation of useless names and distinctions, and too verbose in the expression of common sense. Any body of principles divorced from the context that gave it being may seem drab and useless. But if these principles are viewed in their proper context, they tend to become meaningful and even intellectually stimulating.

Rhetorical theory was born of the attempt of people to systematize their observations of the purposive and dynamic public interactions of other people. In the fifth century B.C. the first body of rhetorical precepts emerged from Corax's observations of the attempts of his fellow citizens of Syracuse to give social order to a society newly emerged from tyranny. In the centuries that followed, countless other people recorded their observations of identifiable speech principles. While those who followed owed a great debt to those who preceded them, each generation of theorists sought to redefine and reconceptualize the art of speaking in a manner consistent with their own perceptions of public address as it occurred in their own cultures and in their own times.

Authors of modern public speaking textbooks must also acknowledge their debt to the great rhetorical tradition. Their task, however, is not the perpetuation of "the intellectual faults of eminent men." Rather, they seek to test and temper the principles of the art of public communication. They must blend with the old the particular insights of the new—insights gleaned from the scholarship of their own and related disciplines, insights gathered from their own judicious observation of public discourse. Building on the rhetorical philosophies of the past with a knowledge of the present, modern theorists seek to create not a memorial to the past but a structure consistent with the needs and realities of the present. Such work is vital and meaningful, not drab or devoid of intellectual stimulation.

Is it strange that what is bright with intellectual challenge in process often seems boring in product? Not really. The excitement of the intellectual search for precepts by one person is easily lost when relegated to a body of generalizations for the consumption of another. It is not that the theory is bad; it is just that theory alone, divorced from the world from which it was abstracted, is inadequate.

Would it not be best, then, for the student of speech to seek out his or her own precepts? Not really. The perceptive student, skilled in listening to popular instances of communication and afforded such great examples as Burke, Churchill, and Roosevelt, could derive his or her own theory of speech. But at what expense of time? At what expense to progress? Each student would have to begin anew the quest for order and meaning, as helplessly alone as if no one else had ever walked the same path.

While the problem is not fully solved by presenting the student with the generalizations of another's mind, concisely arranged, neither is it fully solved by presenting the student with a body of speech masterpieces, past and present, with the caution to keep "an open mind and vigilant eye." The study of a public speaking textbook is, like the study of examples of public discourse, one important element in the training of the student of public speaking. Preference for one should not lead to a discarding of the other. A public speaking textbook is a body of generalizations drawn from the author's contemplation of the long tradition of rhetorical theory, the scholarship of the day, and his or her own perceptions of human communication. It exists not to inhibit but to stimulate. Intelligent students will put the precepts of a textbook to the pragmatic test of actual public life. They will realize, as did Quintilian, that "rhetoric would be a very easy and small matter, if it could be included in one short body of rules, but rules must generally be altered to suit the nature of each individual case, the time, the occasion, and the necessity itself. . . ." By testing the generalizations of a textbook in the light of real and varied instances of public discourse, students will learn to challenge, question, and compare and, ultimately, develop for themselves a theory of speech that is both comprehensive and personal.

WE STUDY SPEECHES TO DEVELOP AN APPRECIATION FOR EMINENCE IN PUBLIC ADDRESS

In 1852, Chauncey Goodrich, Professor of Rhetoric at Yale College, reviewed his teaching philosophy in the preface to his work *Select British Eloquence.* He wrote:

> My object was not only to awaken in the minds of the class that love of genuine eloquence which is the surest pledge of success, but to aid them in catching the spirit of the authors read, and, by analyzing passages selected for the purpose, to initiate the pupil in those higher principles which (whether they were conscious of it or not) have always guided the great masters of the art, till he should learn the *unwritten* rules of oratory, which operate by a kind of instinct upon the mind, and are far more important than any that are found in the books.

This passage has merit today for students who would be more than followers of blueprints. It recommends that students develop an appreciation for eminence in public address, a love of eloquence, by looking beyond textbook principles to the unwritten rules of the art. It suggests the importance of developing a sense of the rightness, or the strength, or the felicity of a thought or an expression through exposure to speeches. Such an appreciation of eminence serves to inspire students to seek in their own works only the highest level of excellence.

Students who have come to acquire this appreciation for eminence will reject trivial subjects. They will understand that a concern for significant ideas has been at the heart of great oratory since ancient times. Demosthenes spoke for the freedom of a city. Churchill spoke for the survival of a nation. Roosevelt spoke for the freedom of man. Kennedy spoke for peace in a divided world. Rhetorical eminence presupposes worthy ideas to express, ideas that merit the attention and efforts of the speaker and the concern of the audience.

But rhetorical excellence also requires eloquence in expression. Given significant ideas, great public address demands an expression that renders the idea in a striking and compelling way, giving it life and vitality. Stephen Spender once wrote a poem called *I Think Continuously of Those Who Were Truly Great*. As public speakers, students may find great inspiration from the speeches of people who surpassed the ordinary and achieved new heights in skillful and effective communication.

The dimensions of rhetorical excellence are diverse. Some speakers are models of eminence in delivery. Billy Graham, to whom charisma is often attributed, is a model of both vocal and physical involvement and intensity. Barbara Jordan, who captured the spirit of the 1976 Democratic Convention, is known for her vocal precision and overall dynamism. Paul Harvey, with his distinctive oral style, has captivated generations of Americans via radio. Student speakers, finding inspiration in the delivery of able speakers, may seek in their own delivery the same sense of dynamism and involvement.

Students may also gain inspiration from those who use language in lively and memorable ways. The history of public discourse is rich with examples of language which illuminated thoughts in compelling ways: Roosevelt dispelled panic with the expression, "The only thing we have to fear is fear itself"; Churchill imparted strength with the expression "This was their finest hour"; Kennedy inspired dedication with the expression "Ask not what your country can do for you—ask what you can do for your country"; Martin Luther King generated hope with the expression "I have a dream." Students who are exposed to eminence in language usage may acquire an intimate sense of the rightness, appropriateness, and artistry of language that will help them to give greater force to their own ideas.

In the study of speeches, students may also find eminence in ordering ideas, marshalling supporting materials, and enlisting the emotions of audiences. Having acquired an appreciation for eloquence, students may demand more of themselves at those moments when they give public expression to their ideas.

CONCLUSION

The study of speeches can play an important role in the intellectual development of contemporary college students. Through such study we may expect to *increase our knowledge of humanity, to derive standards for the critical appraisal of public discourse, to enlarge and deepen our understanding of rhetorical theory,* and *to develop an appreciation for eminence in public address.*

For further reading

ON SPEECH AS A HUMANE STUDY

Linkugel, Wilmer A., and Johannesen, Richard L. "The Study of Masterpieces of Public Address." *Southern Speech Journal,* Summer 1960, pp. 289–97. Presents the rationale for the scrutiny of noted speeches in the classroom.

Nichols, Marie Hochmuth. *Rhetoric and Criticism.* Louisiana State University Press, 1963. Chapter 1 analyzes rhetoric and public address as a humane study—as a study of people making enlightened choices in a rhetorical context.

Walter, Otis. *Speaking Intelligently.* Macmillan, 1976. Chapter 1 examines the role of rhetoric as a force in the growth of civilization.

Wilson, John F., Arnold, Carroll C., and Wertheimer, Molly. *Public Speaking as a Liberal Art.* 6th ed. Allyn and Bacon, 1990. Chapter 1 examines speech as a liberal study showing people apprehending truths about themselves and their environment and communicating them to others.

ON THE CRITICAL ANALYSIS OF SPEECHES

Cathcart, Robert. *Post Communication: Rhetorical Analysis and Evaluation.* 2nd ed. Bobbs-Merrill, 1981. A brief but very useful treatment of speech criticism.

Walter, Otis M., and Scott, Robert L. *Thinking and Speaking.* 5th ed. Macmillan, 1984. Chapters 11 and 12 present advice on analysis of speeches and arguments.

Wilson, John F., Arnold, Carroll C., and Wertheimer, Molly. *Public Speaking as a Liberal Art.* 6th ed. Allyn and Bacon, 1990. Chapter 11 presents a methodology for the critical appraisal of speeches.

ON RHETORICAL THEORY

Aristotle. *Rhetoric.* The definitive ancient treatise on the art of rhetoric.

Clark, Donald Lemen. *Rhetoric in Greco-Roman Education.* Columbia University Press, 1957. Chapter 2 explains what the ancients meant by rhetoric. Chapter 4 presents the five ancient rhetorical canons of invention, organization, style, delivery, and memory. Chapter 5 discusses how the ancients used speech models for study and emulation.

Golden, James et al., eds. *The Rhetoric of Western Thought.* 4th ed. Kendall/Hunt Publishing Company, 1989. A collection of original and reprinted essays that trace the development of theories of rhetoric from Greco-Roman times to the present.

Wilson, John F., Arnold, Carroll C., and Wertheimer, Molly. *Public Speaking as a Liberal Art.* 6th ed. Allyn and Bacon, 1990. Appendix A presents an overview of the historical development of rhetorical theory.

ON EMINENCE IN PUBLIC ADDRESS

Bryant, Donald C. *Rhetorical Dimensions in Criticism.* Louisiana State University Press, 1973. Chapter 6 explores the concept of "eloquence" in discourse.

Osborn, Michael. *Orientations to Rhetorical Style.* Science Research Associates, Modcom Modules in Speech Communication, 1976. A 35 page booklet that discusses the significance, techniques, and abuses of language choices in discourse.

Jamieson, Kathleen Hall. *Eloquence in an Electronic Age.* Oxford University Press, 1988. Assesses the functions, forms, and quality of contemporary American public address.

Wilson, John F., Arnold, Carroll C., and Wertheimer, Molly. *Public Speaking as a Liberal Art.* 6th ed. Allyn and Bacon, 1990. Chapter 9 discusses the nature of oral and written style, resources of language, and criteria of effective style.

Rich Scobee and Kathie Krause, children of astronaut Francis Scobee, June Scobee, the astronaut's widow, Nancy Reagan, President Ronald Reagan, Jane Smith, widow of astronaut Michael Smith, and two of Smiths' children, Scott and Alison, listen to a memorial service for the seven dead astronauts killed in the 1/28/86 shuttle explosion.

THE ANALYSIS OF SPEECHES

Because communication is a powerful force, we need profound and searching insight into communications—into their truth or falsity, their wisdom or stupidity, their profundity or emptiness, into their subtle greatness or disguised and hidden meanness. Since we need such insights, we need critics of rhetoric and communications. In a democratic society, rhetorical criticism is especially important, for in a democracy, all individucals must understand and judge what they hear and read. Therefore, we all must be, at times, our own rhetorical critics.

Otis M. Walter and Robert L. Scott

This book is a collection of speeches that exemplify the major forms and principles of public address in contemporary American society. A rationale for the study of speeches has been presented in the preceding chapter; it thus remains for us to place in perspective the underlying philosophy and the procedural patterns for the use of this book.

THE ART OF RHETORIC

Rhetoric is a term with varied and vague meanings today. Major dictionaries, reflecting the popular confusion, list numerous definitions. Among those commonly cited are the following: the speech of stereotyped politicians—empty, misleading, insincere, and highflown; an oratorical display or exaggeration; highly figurative language, commonly called "purple patches"; the art of prose writing; and, originally, the art of oratory. *Rhetoric, oratory,* and *eloquence* all come from roots meaning *to speak.* Quintilian, the Roman schoolmaster, placed the art of rhetoric at the center of his educational system. Aristotle thought that rhetoric had the capacity to prevent the triumph of fraud and injustice, to instruct popular audiences, to help persons see both sides of an issue, and to help provide a dignified and distinctive means of self-defense.

As used in this book, *rhetoric* is the art of selecting, adapting, and communicating ideas primarily through verbal means to achieve a desired response from a specific audience. The rhetorical act involves making choices related to both the matter of communication—what subjects may be chosen, what issues they embrace, and what values they embody—and the manner of communicating perceptions in order to produce a desired effect. It is important to the welfare of a democratic society that both of these types of choices be enlightened and ethical. Interest in the effectiveness of rhetorical techniques must not outstrip concern for their ethical use. Ethical judgments about rhetorical means employed to achieve ends or judgments of the ethics of the ends cannot be escaped. Each of us must decide for ourself the ethical balance point between our own idea in its pure form and that idea modified to achieve maximum impact on the specific audience.

In seeking to define the nature of rhetoric, theorists have identified those dimensions common to all instances of public discourse. First, there is a person with an idea and a speech purpose—the *speaker.* Governed by personal physical, intellectual, and experiential characteristics, the speaker seeks to choose, structure, and present the message so as to elicit a desired response. Next, there is the *audience,* whose members see the rhetorical context through individual lenses. They may view the speaker as expert, trustworthy, and of good will, or they may set up emotional blocks to the message because the speaker's image and reputation strike them unfavorably. They may view the speaker's thesis as interesting, wise, accurate, and of unquestionable merit, or they may erect barriers to the message because the speaker's ideas run contrary to the beliefs, attitudes, and values that their personal experiences have dictated to them. Finally, there is the *situation* in which the speech occurs: a place—a college classroom, the United States Senate, an ancient synagogue, or London's Hyde Park; a time—fourth century Athens, twentieth century Washington, before lunch or after, November 22, 1963, December 7, 1941; an occasion—a prep-school commencement, a Rotary Club meeting, a Presidential inaugural, a murder trial, a United Nations Security Council meeting, a business association luncheon, or a scientific conference.

In addition to the dimensions of speaker, audience, and situation, speech theorists have identified four variables common to the speech itself. In attempting to promote a desired response, the speaker makes choices about each of these four variables. Through the process that rhetoricians call *invention,* or the discovery and selection of the central idea and its supports, the speaker utilizes appropriate evidence, reasoning, and appeals to audience motives and values to substantiate the message. The remaining three variables relate to transmission of the idea. The speaker selects relevant patterns of *organization* to provide structure and design. Furthermore, the speaker employs impelling symbolization through *language* best suited to himself or herself, to the subject, to the audience, and to the situation. Finally, the speaker uses *delivery* to get the idea across to the audience. Whether he or she uses the impromptu, extemporaneous, manuscript, or memorized methods of delivery, the speaker employs both voice and body to reinforce the meaning and feeling embodied in the message.

Standard speech textbooks contain general principles on these dimensions and variables as they pertain to all types of speeches. By including these principles, these books seek to provide a foundation for purposive and responsible public address that you may use as a guide for your speaking behavior. We will not discuss all of these principles. Rather, we will present examples of speeches illustrating them. Additionally, the introduction to each chapter will focus on the nature of the constraints that influence the speaker's choices in adapting principles to that speech form.

THE FORMS OF SPEECHES

Since ancient times, scholars have sought to classify those social contexts that give rise to public discourse. They have done so in order to understand the nature of the rhetorical act and to formulate principles by which it might be taught. In 336 B.C. Aristotle saw men in law courts trying to secure justice concerning past actions. Accordingly, he identified one class of speeches as *forensic.* In a second instance, he witnessed men deliberating about problems and the best courses of action for their solution. He saw statesmen in the political assembly giving counsel and advice about the practicality and desirability of future policies. He saw men in legislative chambers seeking to exhort or dissuade those who could decide future action. These speeches he classified as *deliberative.* Finally, he observed men at ceremonial gatherings praising the virtuous and eulogizing the noble dead. At other times he beheld men launching vitriolic attacks against others at public gatherings. These speeches of praise and blame he labeled *epideictic.*

As Aristotle profited from appraising the speeches of his day, so too may the modern scholar of rhetoric profit from an examination of contemporary speeches. As we survey twentieth century public address, we see people in public gatherings translating technical information into popular terms; we see others describing an experience or event. At other times we see people publicly probing for definitive meanings, searching for the causes of natural and social phenomena, dispelling stereotypes, and seeking out the implications of things and events. We classify such speeches as attempts to increase *understanding*. In other situations, we see lawyers seeking decisions on the guilt or innocence of their clients, politicians asking for acceptance of what they validate as facts, and citizens arguing over the "real" cause of something. These speakers are *affirming propositions of fact*. On some occasions, we witness speakers urging adoption of new standards for human behavior, and we see drama and literary critics applying criteria to art forms to establish a judgment about their quality. When people seek to formulate or change human values or to apply standards as measurements of quality, we label their efforts *affirming propositions of value*. In some instances, we observe speakers seeking to make people vitally aware of problems that hinder personal and social fulfillment. These persons are *creating concern for problems*. In still other situations, we see persons advocating programs for the solution of perplexing problems and for the ultimate betterment of society. This effort we call *affirming propositions of policy*. Finally, we see speakers on ceremonial occasions asking for a unity of spirit or for a reenergizing of effort or commitment. When a person urges increased dedication to the existing values of a group, we label that purpose *intensifying social cohesion*.

SOME GUIDELINES FOR ANALYSIS OF SPEECHES

As a type of rhetorical criticism, the analysis of speeches is not a fool-proof, mathematically precise act of description and calculation. An act of criticism is, by its very nature, an act of persuasion and argument. As a critic you apply standards, make claims, and offer support for those claims. As a critic you argue for the reasonable probability, not absolute certainty, of your descriptions and judgments. In addition, your own beliefs and predispositions will influence your selection and application of a framework for criticism. Such influential factors would include your assumptions about the nature and sources of reality and truth, the ways in which humans derive reliable knowledge, the basis of ethics, and the capacities that mark the essence of human nature. In turn the critical framework that you employ will focus your analysis *toward* some aspects while at the same time deflecting your attention *away from* other aspects. And another critic employing a different critical perspective might reasonably describe and evaluate a particular speech differently than you.

Each of the remaining chapters in this anthology is introduced by a brief essay setting forth guidelines for analyzing the speeches which illustrate that form. At this point we will limit ourselves to suggesting some potential general dimensions and questions for use in judging speechmaking.[1]

Our suggestions are not intended as a definitive statement on speech criticism. They simply are some starting points for possible use in assessing speeches inside and outside the classroom. We do not view this set of guidelines as the only method or the "best" method of speech analysis. Other useful approaches for the criticism of speeches are described in some of the Sources for Further Reading at the end of this and subsequent chapters.

Obviously, in assessing a specific speech, each dimension or question would not be of equal importance. You might, for instance, consider reasonableness and ethicality more crucial than language and delivery. The criteria you use for evaluation should be those particularly appropriate for both the general speech form and the specific speech. Furthermore, consider how dimensions and questions may point to an interaction of factors. How might a listener's value system influence her or his perception of what is reasonable? Or how might a speaker's attitude toward an audience influence that speaker's credibility or perceived ethicality?

As you analyze a particular speech, you may find that some aspects of it are so prominent and worthy of note that they "invite," indeed they "demand," your critical attention. Aspects of a speech may be noteworthy, for example, because they are so frequent, so obvious, so unique, so subtle, so probably effective, so superbly handled, so poorly done, or so detrimental to effectiveness. Based on the general nature of the speech and the rhetorical aspects that invite your critical attention, you probably will select for use only some of the following dimensions or questions.

In presenting an oral or written analysis of a speech, the quality of your criticism will be improved if you discuss *both* strengths and weaknesses; criticism is not solely the making of negative judgments. In addition, quality is improved by specifying, explaining, and justifying the lines of inquiry, framework for analysis, or standards for evaluation you will utilize.

1. To what factors in the immediate occasion or more general relevant situation does the speaker seem to be responding?

Speechmaking is situationally motivated and a speaker makes choices of communicative ends and means in response to a set of circumstances and to a specific audience. Hence, it is well to begin an analysis of most speeches by discussing the societal milieu,

1. Some of the following material is adapted from the contributions of Richard L. Johannesen for *Principles and Types of Speech Communication,* Seventh Edition, by Alan H. Monroe and Douglas Ehninger, pp. 245–47, 249–57, 453–63. Copyright © 1974, 1967, 1962, 1955, 1949, 1939, 1935 by Scott, Foresman and Company.

the nature of the physical and ideological setting, and the probable causes that led up to the speech. How might factors in the occasion or prevailing ideological climate have influenced the speaker's purpose and/or methods? To what in particular does the speaker seem to be responding: To a problem, opportunity, lack of information, duty, challenge, ceremonial obligation, attack, issue, or routine invitation?

What is the nature and significance of the specific audience addressed by the speaker? Consider the relevance of such matters as size, age, sex, occupation, educational background, memberships in organizations, ethnic background, and knowledge of the subject of the speech. Is the primary audience the one physically present, or is it perhaps one to be exposed "second-hand" through the various mass media, or is it one "observing" a confrontation between a speaker and audience? Are there any secondary audiences intended for the message?

Sometimes the impact of a speech is influenced by such factors in the occasion as time of day, room acoustics and seating arrangement, preceding and following speeches, and audience customs and expectations. Clearly the expectations for a presidential inaugural address and for a political rally speech differ. Depending upon the role the audience expects a speaker to fulfill (such as leader, advisor, expert, lecturer, intruder, spokesperson for them or others), they may expect different evidence, appeals, proposals, language, and delivery. How adequately a speaker handles questions and answers in a forum period after the speech may influence audience perceptions of the speech.

The speech may play a role in some larger campaign of communication or in the activities of a particular social movement. Is the speaker a spokesperson in behalf of some group or other person and thus probably less free to voice entirely his or her own viewpoint? Is the speech a major effort to be supplemented by other modes of communication? Is it one in a planned series of addresses on the subject? Is the central communication thrust on this subject being carried out through other modes and channels with this speech as only a minor part of the total program? What influence might presentation via radio and/or television have on the impact of the speech?

2. What seem to be the speaker's general and specific purposes?

Typical general purposes are to entertain, to present information and increase understanding, to reinforce existing beliefs and values, to change values and beliefs, and to secure overt action. Consider whether the speaker's intent seems to be identification and agreement, shock and arousal, or confrontation and alienation. What more concrete outcome does the speaker seem to want from his or her audience? What exactly does the speaker want the audience to believe, feel, or do? Does the specific purpose seem appropriate for the subject, audience, and occasion?

Given the audience and relevant circumstances, probe whether the speaker's purposes appear realistic and achievable. Remember that countermessages from other communicators, or unexpected and uncontrollable events, may work on listener's minds to weaken the impact of the speaker's message. Remember, also, that some situations are not altered very easily through public speech. No matter what is said to some audiences, for instance, they may refuse to modify their strongly held beliefs, values, and actions. And some audiences may believe, accurately or inaccurately, that they do not possess the power, authority, skill, money, or facilities to adopt the speaker's idea.

3. How does the speaker capture and sustain audience attention and interest?

No matter how sincere the speaker's intent, no matter how sound her or his reasoning, no matter how worthwhile the message, if the audience's attention is not aroused at the outset and maintained throughout, the speaker's efforts are doomed to failure. If no one listens, belief and action cannot be influenced as the speaker hopes. In the content, language, and delivery of the speech, are such interest-factors as conflict, suspense, familiarity, novelty, humor, action, curiosity, and concreteness capitalized on? Is interest heightened through such means as narration of a story, vivid description, analogy, contrast, hypothetical and factual examples, and extended illustrations?

4. How does the speaker strive to insure that the audience clearly understands the message as intended?

Assess the probability that listeners will know exactly what the speaker is asking of them and concretely how to help implement that idea or proposal. Judge whether ideas are presented accurately and clearly and whether extremes of complexity and simplification are avoided. If ambiguity seems employed intentionally, what factors in the subject or occasion might account for or even justify it? How adequately does the introductory portion of the speech gain attention, challenge the audience, lead smoothly into the topic, or create goodwill for the speaker and topic? How adequately does the conclusion summarize basic ideas, convey a sense of completion, leave the listeners in an appropriate mood, or stimulate acceptance of the central belief or action sought? Consider what patterns of organization the speaker uses to foster unity and clarity: chronological, spatial, problem-solution, general-to-specific or vice versa, cause-effect, examination of alternatives, and so forth. If the speech lacks clear structure, is this apparently due to speaker ineptness or may there be some justification for it?

To promote understanding, how does the speaker utilize such devices as repetition, restatement, transitions, internal summaries, parallel phrasing, numerical "sign-posts," itemization, association with the familiar, examples and illustrations, questions and answers, statistics, and definitions. Some definitions are "objective" in the sense that they report widely accepted, noncontroversial meanings current with experts or with the public.

Other definitions are "persuasive" in the sense that the speaker is asking the audience to accept her or his particular meaning as the correct or appropriate definition for a concept which is subject to challenge or controversy. How does the speaker employ audiovisual aids and vocal-physical delivery to increase understanding? If appropriate, how adequately does the speaker answer such standard questions as who, what, where, when, why, and how?

5. To what degree might listeners perceive the speaker's proposal (idea, belief, policy) as sound and reasonable?

Bear in mind that accepted standards of reason, logic, and soundness may vary from one audience to another, from one culture to another, or between fields of discourse (such as politics, religion, natural science, law, historiography). As a critic you may wish to apply to the message some "universal" or "traditional" tests of soundness for evidence and reasoning. But also consider whether such tests are appropriate for the specific speech situation or subject matter. Furthermore, an audience may not make a sharp distinction between so-called logical and emotional appeals. For instance, a set of statistics showing a high probability of listeners being stricken with some form of cancer during their lifetime may be perceived by them as both logical and emotional; for them it simply is a reasonable item of support.

Assess how adequately the speaker employs evidence and reasoning to demonstrate that his or her proposal actually will work, will solve the problem, will be efficient, and will not be too costly. Is the proposal feasible despite such potential limitations as minimal time, personnel, or finances? Evaluate the soundness of the factual examples, expert testimony, literal analogies, statistics, and cause-effect reasoning the speaker employs. Is the speaker's idea consistent with the relevant beliefs and attitudes of the audience? If not, is such inconsistency seemingly due to speaker ineptitude or planned to serve some persuasive function? Is there a legitimate connection between the speaker's idea or purpose and the audience's relevant needs, motives, goals, and emotions? Are listeners made to "feel" a personal stake in the outcome? Has the speaker exaggerated the connection or appealed to irrelevant needs?

What premises or fundamental beliefs are verbalized by the speaker as underpinnings for further argument? Implicitly undergirding the speaker's ideas, are there any unstated assumptions, any unspoken basic beliefs, values, premises, or stereotypes? Are such unstated assumptions probably omitted to avoid scrutiny by the audience or because the speaker and audience already share the assumption? Consider in what ways the spoken and unspoken assumptions reflect the speaker's conception of reality, truth, dependable knowledge, goodness, religion, or the essence of human nature. What might be the intended function or unintended impact of omission of an expected idea or of silence on a controversial issue?

6. To what degree do the speaker's ideas harmonize with the audience's relevant values?

A value, for our purposes, is defined as a conception of "The Good" or "The Desirable." Honesty, fairness, honor, efficiency, progress, economy, courage, safety, prudence, and patriotism all are examples of possible values for persons. In numerous speeches throughout his two terms as president, Ronald Reagan stressed a cluster of "traditional" American values: family, neighborhood, work, patriotism, peace, and freedom. A value may function either generally, as a goal motivating our behavior, or specifically, as a standard we use to assess the acceptability of means to accomplish ends. We might, for instance, recognize that a policy or solution is efficient and economical, but reject that program for being dishonest and inhumane. Frequently dominant personal or group values are reflected in slogans or mottos: "Liberty, Equality, Fraternity"; "Duty, Honor, Country"; "Law and Order"; "Law and Order with Justice"; "Freedom Now"; "All Power to the People"; "Peace with Honor."

Values are not proved or disproved in quite the same way as "factual" matters. We measure the length of a table with a ruler to demonstrate that it is indeed one meter long. But it is difficult, if not impossible, to measure precisely degrees of beauty, courage, and honesty. And proposed measures of freedom, progress, or efficiency often themselves are controversial. As a culture or subculture develops, a given value becomes accepted as functional for that group. Naturally, the values which predominate often vary from one culture to another. One culture may hold punctuality as a basic value, for example, while another deems being on time of little importance. We develop our own individual value systems in the context of larger cultural and subcultural value systems.

Usually we *rank* the values we hold into a rough *hierarchy* so that some values to which we are committed take precedence over others. In fact, in *The New Rhetoric,* philosopher Chaim Perelman argues that a "particular audience is characterized less by values it accepts than by the way it grades them." Note also that in a specific situation several audience values may come into conflict, thus forcing a choice of one value over another in making a decision. The audience may continue to believe in both values, but temporarily set one aside in favor of the other. For instance, a speaker may advocate in a given situation adherence to honesty over efficiency, patriotism over self-concern, economy over education, or humaneness over frankness.

A warning is in order. A speaker often overtly appeals to a seemingly potent value to which the audience *says* it is committed. But do not assume that the audience always will *act* in accordance with the declared value. In a particular instance the audience may perceive some other value as more important; they may not *apply* the value appealed to and to which they in general are devoted.

In assessing the various value appeals of a speaker, consider the general approach used. Is the aim to get listeners to adopt a new value to replace an outmoded one, perhaps through a redefinition of the meaning we should have for the original value-word? Is the speaker urging acceptance of her or his value judgment of something as an accurate and appropriate judgment? In what ways does the speech function to reinforce and reenergize values already held by the audience? Is the speaker creating concern for a problem by showing that relevant audience values are being threatened or violated? Is the speaker advocating adoption of a policy or solution in part because it harmonizes with or fosters relevant audience values? By exploring such questions, you can move toward an understanding of specific techniques through which a speaker attempts to link an idea or proposal to potent audience values.

7. To what degree is the speaker perceived as a credible source on the subject?

The positive or negative perceptions that listeners have of a speaker's personal qualities play a major role in determining whether they will accept his or her information, arguments, or proposal. Ancient Greek and Roman rhetorical theorists called this concept *ethos* and identified its three major elements as good sense, good character, and good will. Contemporary communication scholars use such labels as source credibility, image, and reputation to describe audience attitude toward the speaker; they have identified expertness and trustworthiness as the two most potent dimensions of speaker credibility. Listeners assess a speaker's *expertness* by making judgments about competency, experience, and knowledge of the subject. *Trustworthiness* is a quality audiences attribute to a speaker whom they perceive as honest, dependable, sincere, fair, and similar to them in values, beliefs, and background. Researchers have identified a moderately influential dimension, often called *dynamism,* rooted in how alert, energetic, firm-minded, and interesting an audience considers a speaker. And informed observation would suggest that listeners evaluate a speaker's *good will* toward them by judging her or his friendliness, likability, and concern for them.

Ethos is variable rather than static. A speaker's credibility might vary from one audience to another, from one decade to another, or from one subject to another. Different cultures or subcultures may prize different personal qualities as constituting positive *ethos,* or an audience may perceive different qualities as relevant on different topics. The *ethos* attributed to a speaker by listeners will fluctuate during presentation of the speech as the audience judges use of evidence and reasoning, motivational appeals, language, structure, and vocal-physical delivery. Sometimes speakers directly attempt to foster positive *ethos* with an audience by overtly mentioning experiences or qualifications as marks of their expertise or by quoting or indicating associations with persons whose *ethos* with the audience already is high. A speaker's *ethos* level at the conclusion of the speech is an outcome of interaction of her or his reputation (prior audience knowledge of speaker's views, accomplishments, associations, and personality) with the audience's assessment of how well the speaker performed during the speech itself.

Although high *ethos* will not guarantee speaker success, markedly low source credibility usually thwarts a communicative effort. No matter how *actually* sound and ethical are a speaker's program, information, arguments, and appeals, if the audience *perceives* the speaker as incompetent, unethical, untrustworthy, bored, overly nervous, or aloof, then her or his message probably will have little of the desired impact.

8. What attitudes toward his or her audience does the speaker seem to reveal?

A speaker's attitude toward an audience reflects his or her view of the listener's personal worth and abilities as well as an indication of the speaker's orientation or stance toward the audience. First, attempt to isolate how the speaker's attitude orientation is revealed in communicative choices, strategies, and techniques. Such reflections may be inferred from verbal and nonverbal elements such as word choice, level of abstraction, types of examples, specificity of analysis, emphasis given to items, vocal pitch and quality, facial expression, and directness of eye contact.

Second, attempt to identify the attitudinal stances characteristic of all or parts of the speech. Is the attitude that you perceive probably the one perceived by the audience, the one intended by the speaker, and a sincere index of his or her "real" view? Are any of the speaker's attitudinal stances especially ethical or unethical? Our discussion later in this chapter of question #13 on ethical standards for assessing public discourse may help you consider this issue. Your efforts may be aided by considering to what degree the speech reveals one or more of the following attitude clusters: (1) respect, equality, understanding, honesty, genuineness, concern for audience welfare and improvement, sincerity, openness to new views, trust, selflessness, empathy, helpfulness, humility; (2) prudence, moderation, indifference, aloofness, unconcern, apathy, disinterest, blandness, coldness; (3) objectivity, neutrality; (4) self-aggrandizement, ego-satisfaction, personal "showing off," pretentiousness; (5) superiority, domination, exploitation for personal gain, deception, insincerity, dogmatism, coercion, facade, judgmentalism, arrogance, contempt, condescension, possessiveness, selfishness; (6) aggressiveness, abrasiveness, hostility, nonconciliation, insult, derogation, curtness; (7) inferiority, supplication, pleading, deference; (8) defensiveness, competitiveness, fear, distrust, suspicion; (9) conciliation, consensus, cooperation, identification.

Third, explore in what ways the speaker's attitude toward the audience seems to reflect personal philosophy; beliefs about human nature, society, reality, values, and ethics are some elements of such a philosophy. Does the attitude reflect optimism or pessimism toward human capabilities and potential? Does the speaker see humans as capable of reflective self-decision or only of being coerced or dominated? An attitude might indicate a belief that reality and knowledge are perceived and attained with certainty or with much relativism and uncertainty. Attitudes of cynicism, duplicity, and domination may stem from a commitment to the end justifying the means.

Fourth, probe how the speaker's attitude toward an audience relates to her or his purposes and motives. Does the attitude revealed appear to reinforce or to thwart achievement of the speaker's intended purpose? Is there any verbal and nonverbal inconsistency between the speaker's attitude and the apparent intended meaning of the speech? Does a perceived attitude of insincerity, unconcern, or superiority contradict words proclaiming sincerity, concern, or equality?

Finally, attempt to assess the influence of the speaker's attitudinal stance on the effects or consequences of the speech. Does the attitude seem appropriate for the speaker, subject, audience, and occasion? What effects might the speaker's attitude have on the audience's beliefs, feelings, and actions? Listeners' perception of a speaker's attitude toward them may influence their estimate of expertness, trustworthiness, goodwill, and similarity to them. Attitudes of dominance, superiority, or aloofness, for example, may contribute to people's doubts about the speaker's sincere concern for their welfare.

9. In what ways does the speaker's language usage contribute to clarity, interest, and persuasiveness?

Consider whether the language is appropriate for the speaker, audience, subject, and occasion. Examine the communicative function served by stylistic resources such as repetition, restatement, rhetorical question, comparison, contrast, parallel structure, antithesis, alliteration, analogy, metaphor, imagery, personification, or narration. Do any stylistic devices seem ornamental or "added on" primarily for "showing off"? What does the speaker's language reveal about him or her personally or about the speaker's view of the audience? How do language choices compare with those the speaker reasonably might have made? What stylistic alternatives seem available to the speaker and why might the speaker have made particular choices? If the speaker's language is militant and abrasive, why might this choice have been made? If obscene words are used, what might be their intended function and actual impact?

Why might the speaker rely heavily on one particular stylistic device? If use of metaphors is a major stylistic characteristic, are they largely trite and overly familiar, or are they fresh and insightful for that particular audience? Might the audience have expected to be addressed in familiar, even stereotyped, metaphorical images? If there is a dominant or thematic metaphor woven throughout the speech, what might be its significance? What functions might be served by a speaker's heavy reliance on "god terms" and "devil terms," on value-laden concepts with intense positive or negative meanings? In what ways are names, labels, and definitions employed to channel perceptions—to direct attention toward or away from both relevant and irrelevant aspects of persons and programs? Remember, also, that public tastes in rhetorical style vary from era to era and even between different audiences in the same era. For the particular speech you are analyzing, consider what might be the most appropriate standards of stylistic judgment.

10. In what noteworthy ways does the speaker's delivery of the speech contribute to clarity, interest, and persuasiveness?

Do nonverbal elements of speech presentation reinforce or conflict with the speaker's verbal meaning? Does the speaker's vocal and physical delivery convey one meaning while his or her words convey another? If so, which would the audience probably believe and why? Does the manner of delivery seem appropriate for the speaker, subject, audience, and occasion? Examine the roles of loudness, vocal pitch, vocal quality, pauses, and rapidity in the presentation. How do the speaker's posture, gestures, facial expression, and eye contact help or hinder effectiveness? Are there any distracting mannerisms of vocal or bodily delivery that hinder audience attentiveness or comprehension? Explore also the communicative functions of various nonverbal cues accompanying the speech. Examine the possible intended and unintended implications of music, flags, banners, salutes, emblems, lapel pins, mode of dress, and pictures of family or revered persons.

11. What rhetorical strategies seem noteworthy because of their frequent use, apparent function in the speech, or probable effectiveness?

This line of inquiry obviously builds upon insights and questions from previously suggested guidelines for analysis. But such a scrutiny of concrete strategies will aid you as practitioner and critic of public discourse to see more clearly how others have approached different audiences and situations. The strategies briefly explained here are not offered as an exhaustive list but only as some possibilities. Strategies typical of discourse about values, problems, and solutions are discussed briefly in later chapters which focus on that type of speechmaking.

In the *this-or-nothing* strategy the speaker evaluates leading alternative solutions to a problem, shows in turn why each is unworkable or inappropriate, and finally presents his or her policy as the only sound remaining choice. *Visualization* involves painting a vivid word picture of the positive consequences of adopting or negative results of rejecting a proposal. Sometimes speakers use the *scapegoat* technique wherein they shift all responsibility or blame for problems or faults afflicting their own group onto the shoulders of some other person or group depicted as the embodiment of evil. As a variation of scapegoating, a *conspiracy* appeal claims that the cause of problems facing the group resides in a powerful, widespread, organized, secret effort of some other person or group.

The strategy of *persuasive definition* finds a speaker offering the audience her or his particular meaning as the correct or appropriate definition for a concept which actually is open to challenge or controversy. A speaker might employ *association* to emphasize values, beliefs, experiences mutually held with the audience and/or with persons and programs esteemed by the audience. *Disassociaion* involves the speaker's repudiation of relationships with or favorable views toward undesirable people, ideas, or policies. In a strategy of *differentiation,* the speaker avoids guilt or responsibility by arguing the rationale that the action or belief under attack is different or unique from some other state of affairs which may be open to condemnation. Finally, there is a strategy of *transcendence* in which speaker and audience, or opposing groups, are to submerge, at least temporarily, differences of opinion or policy in the name of some commonly agreed upon higher value or goal: national security, political party unity, victory, humanitarianism, or national honor.

12. As best you can determine, what are some of the effects or consequences of the speech?

Often it is very difficult to determine exact and certain causal connections between a specific speech and later outcomes. And an effect may be the result of a number of rhetorical and nonrhetorical events. Remember, too, that a speech may have consequences never intended by a speaker; these, also, can be scrutinized. You may attempt to assess the effects of a speech by noting the impact on the immediate audience, the long-term impact on the policies and ideology of society-at-large, the impact on persons in positions of public opinion leadership, the influence on experts, and the reactions of news media reporters. You might also explore whether the speaker's aim has been achieved, whether the speaker's ideas have been verified by later historical events, or whether the audience's expectations have been met. Sometimes virtually nondetectible shifts in audience attitudes and beliefs may occur, such as from a favorable to a strongly favorable position. Finally, you may want to consider the influence of the speech on the *speaker.* Did it enhance or lower the speaker's reputation? How did the speech affect the speaker's subsequent rhetoric and actions? Did the speaker in any way become trapped by his or her own rhetoric? When speakers publicly become "locked in" to a position, later modification may be difficult.

13. What ethical judgments seem appropriate regarding the speaker's purposes, arguments, appeals, and strategies?

Ethical judgments focus on degrees of rightness and wrongness in human behavior. A speech is designed by one person (sometimes with the aid of a speechwriter or speechwriting team) to influence the lives of other persons. And a speaker makes conscious choices concerning specific ends and communicative techniques to achieve those ends. Potential ethical issues regarding means and ends seem inherent in any act of speechmaking. But how those issues are to be faced and resolved (by speaker, listener, and critic) is not clearcut.

Traditional American textbook discussions of the ethics of public speaking, argumentation, and persuasion often include lists of standards to be applied in assessing the ethicality of an instance of discourse. What follows is Johannesen's synthesis and adaptation of a half-dozen or so typical traditional lists of ethical criteria for public discourse.[2] Such ethical criteria usually are rooted in a commitment to values deemed essential to the health and growth of our political-governmental system of representative democracy. Obviously other cultures and other governmental systems may embrace basic values that lead to quite different standards for public discourse.

Even within our own society, the following criteria are not necessarily the only or best ones possible; they are suggested as general guidelines rather than inflexible rules, and they may stimulate discussion on the complexity of judging the ethics of communication. Consider, for example, under what circumstances there may be justifiable exceptions to some of these criteria. Also bear in mind that one difficulty in applying these criteria in concrete situations stems from differing standards and meanings people may have for such key terms as: distort, falsify, rational, reasonable, conceal, misrepresent, irrelevant, and deceive.

1. Do not use false, fabricated, misrepresented, distorted, or irrelevant evidence to support arguments or claims.
2. Do not intentionally use specious, unsupported, or illogical reasoning.
3. Do not represent yourself as informed or as an "expert" on a subject when you are not.
4. Do not use irrelevant appeals to divert attention or scrutiny from the issue at hand. Among appeals that commonly serve such a purpose are: "smear" attacks on an opponent's character; appeals to hatred and bigotry; god and devil terms that cause intense but unreflective positive or negative reactions; innuendo.
5. Do not ask your audience to link your idea or proposal to emotion-laden values, motives, or goals to which it actually is not related.
6. Do not deceive your audience by concealing your real purpose, by concealing self-interest, by concealing the group you represent, or by concealing your position as an advocate of a viewpoint.
7. Do not distort, hide, or misrepresent the number, scope, intensity, or undesirable features of consequences or effects.
8. Do not use "emotional appeals" that lack a supporting basis of evidence and reasoning, or that would not be accepted if the audience had time and opportunity to examine the subject themselves.
9. Do not oversimplify complex, gradation-laden situations into simplistic two-valued, either-or, polar choices.
10. Do not pretend certainty where tentativeness and degrees of probability would be more accurate.
11. Do not advocate something in which you do not believe yourself.

2. For example, see the following sources: E. Christian Buehler and Wil A. Linkugel, *Speech Communication for the Contemporary Student* (Harper and Row, 1975), pp. 30–36; Robert T. Oliver, *The Psychology of Persuasive Speech,* 2nd ed. (Longmans, Green, 1957), pp. 20–34; Wayne Minnick, *The Art of Persuasion,* 2nd ed. (Houghton Mifflin, 1968), pp. 278–287; Henry Ewbank and J. Jeffrey Auer, *Discussion and Debate,* 2nd ed. (Appleton-Century-Crofts, 1951), pp. 255–258; Wayne Thompson, *The Process of Persuasion* (Harper and Row, 1975), Ch. 12; Bert E. Bradley, *Fundamentals of Speech Communication,* 4th ed. (Wm. C. Brown Company Publishers, 1984), pp. 20–29.

To assess the degree of ethicality of specific *appeals to values,* consider the following questions that are rooted in standards central to ethical communication in our representative democracy: honesty, relevance, accuracy, fairness, and reasonableness. To what degree do the value appeals serve as relevant motivational reinforcement for a point or proposal that has an independent basis in reasonable evidence? To what degree do the value appeals serve a legitimate function of promoting social cohesion, of reinforcing audience commitment to ideas they already believe? With what degree of appropriateness are the consequences of commitment to the values clarified? To what degree do the value appeals serve as substitutes, as pseudoproof, for the factuality of an assertion? To what degree do the value appeals divert attention from more fundamental, pressing, or controversial matters? To what degree do the value appeals seem to promote, intentionally or not, unreflective stimulus-response reactions when the occasion demands reflective judgment?

What are the ethical implications of the *power relationships* urged or reinforced? In what ways do the language, structure, evidence, and arguments in the speech attempt to alter or reinforce power relationships? What persons, groups, ideas, or institutions are given legitimacy, approval, rights, superiority, or status either overtly or because their role is unquestioned? Which are directly or indirectly delegitimized, disapproved, trivialized, or denied rights? What relevant ones are ignored or dismissed as insignificant because they are not mentioned or taken into account?

We now turn to a list of some questions that we hope will stimulate your examination of various ethical issues as you assess a particular speech. To what degree should ethical standards for judging speeches be relative, flexible, and situation bound, or universal, inflexible, and absolute? Should there be different ethical standards for speechmaking in different fields such as politics, business, education, and religion? Should ethical standards for communication directed at children be higher than for messages aimed at adults? To what degree should ethical standards for public communication differ from or be similar to those appropriate for interpersonal and small group communication?

To what degree, if any, does the worthiness of the speaker's end justify the employment of communication techniques usually deemed ethically suspect? Does the sincerity of the speaker's intent release him or her from ethical responsibility for means and effects? Under what circumstances might intentional use of ambiguity be considered ethical? Should "tastefulness" and "tactfulness" be included or excluded as *ethical* criteria for assessing speeches? To what degree and for what reasons might we consider the use of "sexist" and "racist" language as unethical?

CONCLUSION

Sonja K. Foss, a contemporary rhetorical critic, reminds us: "We live our lives enveloped in symbols. How we perceive, what we know, what we experience, and how we act are the results of our symbol use and that of those around us. . . . One of the ways we can use to discover how symbols affects us is rhetorical criticism. We engage in the process of rhetorical criticism constantly and often unconsciously, but with some formal training we can become more adept and discriminating in its practice."

By focusing on contemporary American speeches, this book necessarily focuses on one particular kind of rhetorical practice. Speeches still form a significant portion of our communication environment, an environment constantly bombarding us with data, appeals, reasons, and judgments. Whether a speech seeks to create understanding, to advocate or reinforce values and value judgments, to resolve "factual" disputes, to generate concern for problems, or to secure acceptance of solutions—that speech seeks a specific response from a specific audience. Thus such speeches inherently involve some degree of "persuasive" intent, some degree of conscious concrete influence.

As responsible citizens in a representative democracy, we are expected to develop skills in communicating our ideas and choices on matters of personal and public concern. Also we are expected to become discerning consumers of communication, to become perceptive evaluators of messages we receive. We have a social responsibility to become intelligent and ethical speakers and listeners. Part of this responsibility has been summarized forcefully by a contemporary rhetorical critic, Karlyn Kohrs Campbell: "Never has the need to understand the nature of persuasive discourses and to develop techniques and standards by which to analyze and evaluate them been more crucial. . . . In short, we shall have to become working rhetorical critics."

For further reading

ON THE ART OF RHETORIC

Brockriede, Wayne. "Dimensions of the Concept of Rhetoric." *Quarterly Journal of Speech*, February 1968, pp. 1–12.

Foss, Sonja K., Foss, Karen A., and Trapp, Robert. *Contemporary Perspectives on Rhetoric*. 2nd ed. Waveland Press, 1991. A thorough exploration of the implications for rhetorical theory of the works of Kenneth Burke, I. A. Richards, Richard M. Weaver, Stephen Toulmin, Chaim Perelman, Ernesto Grassi, Jurgen Habermas, and Michel Foucault.

Johannesen, Richard L., ed. *Contemporary Theories of Rhetoric: Selected Readings*. Harper and Row, 1971. An anthology including the works of Kenneth Burke, I. A. Richards, Richard M. Weaver, Chaim Perelman, Stephen Toulmin, and Marshall McLuhan.

ON THE ETHICS OF RHETORIC

Jaksa, James A., and Pritchard, Michael S. *Communication Ethics: Methods of Analysis*. Wadsworth Publishing Co., 1988. Includes chapters on moral reasoning, the principle of veracity, and procedures for justifying ethical judgments.

Johannesen, Richard L. *Ethics in Human Communication*. 3rd ed. Waveland Press, 1990. Explores varied perspectives, issues, and examples to foster skill in assessing degrees of ethicality.

Larson, Charles U. *Persuasion: Reception and Responsibility*. 5th ed. Wadsworth, 1989. Includes a chapter by R. L. Johannesen on "Perspectives on Ethics in Persuasion."

ON THE FORMS OF SPEECHES

Allen, R. R., and McKerrow, Ray E. *The Pragmatics of Public Communication.* 3rd ed. Kendall/Hunt Publishing Company, 1985. Chapters 7–9 discuss informative, persuasive, and ceremonial speeches.

Campbell, Karlyn Kohrs, and Jamieson, Kathleen Hall. *Deeds Done In Words: Presidential Rhetoric and the Genres of Governance.* University of Chicago Press, 1990. Examines such forms of presidential discourse as inaugural addresses, state of the union messages, farewell addresses, and war rhetoric.

Walter, Otis M., and Scott, Robert L. *Thinking and Speaking.* 5th ed. Macmillan, 1984. Chapters 6–10 discuss speeches that deal with problems, causes, solutions, values, and definitions.

ON THE INVENTION OF SPEECH IDEAS

LeFevre, Karen Burke. *Invention as a Social Act.* Southern Illinois University Press, 1987. Examines invention as an interactive process involving the individual rhetor, small numbers of collaborators, and society-at-large.

Corbett, Edward P. J. *Classical Rhetoric for the Modern Student.* 3rd ed. Oxford University Press, 1990. Chapter 2 contains intensive discussion of the discovery of arguments

McCroskey, James C. *An Introduction to Rhetorical Communication.* 5th ed. Prentice-Hall, 1986. Chapter 9 offers suggestions on invention.

Wilson, John F., Arnold, Carroll C., and Wertheimer, Molly. *Public Speaking as a Liberal Art.* 6th ed. Allyn and Bacon, 1990. Chapters 4–6 examine the basic processes of invention, including some general thought lines to aid the speaker in finding appropriate ideas and arguments.

Winterowd, W. Ross. *Contemporary Rhetoric: A Conceptual Background with Readings.* Harcourt, Brace, Jovanovich, 1975, pp. 39–162. Twelve essays focus on invention.

ON THE CRITICAL ANALYSIS OF SPEECHES

Andrews, James R. *The Practice of Rhetorical Criticism.* 2nd ed. Longman, 1990. This textbook presents standards and sample analyses of public addresses.

Campbell, Karlyn Kohrs. *Critiques of Contemporary Rhetoric.* Wadsworth, 1972. Chapters 1–3 consider in some detail the process of rhetorical criticism.

Johannesen, Richard L. "Attitude of Speaker Toward Audience: A Significant Concept for Contemporary Rhetorical Theory and Criticism," *Central States Speech Journal,* Summer 1974, 95–104.

Brock, Bernard L., Scott, Robert L., and Chesebro, James, eds. *Methods of Rhetorical Criticism: A Twentieth Century Perspective.* 3rd ed. Wayne State University Press, 1980. An anthology of essays illustrates varied approaches to the theory and practice of rhetorical criticism.

Cooper, Martha. *Analyzing Public Discourse.* Waveland Press, 1989. Of special interest are Chapters 7–9 on ethics, ideology/propaganda, and freedom of speech.

Foss, Sonja K. *Rhetorical Criticism: Explorations and Practice.* Waveland Press, 1989. Presents critical methods that focus on context, message, or rhetor. Types of criticism illustrated are: neo-Aristotelian, generic, feminist, metaphoric, narrative, fantasy theme, pentadic, and cluster.

Hart, Roderick P. *Modern Rhetorical Criticism.* Scott, Foresman/Little, Brown, 1990. Describes the rhetorical and critical perspectives; presents forms of criticism that analyze situations, ideas, argument, structure, and style; illustrates specialized forms of criticism (role, cultural, dramatistic, ideological).

Rybacki, Karyn, and Rybacki, Donald. *Communication Criticism: Approaches and Genres.* Wadsworth, 1991. Chapters 3–7 cover various methods and perspectives for criticism and Chapter 8 focuses on the rhetoric of public speaking.

Major James N. Rowe pays a courtesy call on President Nixon at the White House. Major Rowe escaped from the Viet Cong on 12/31/68 after five years of captivity.

CHAPTER 3

SPEECHES THAT INCREASE UNDERSTANDING

Because information can change society, and because the amount of information doubles every eight years, our culture, if it is to become enriched and improved by its information, needs speakers and writers to digest and assimilate information and to present it to us with clarity.

Otis M. Walter

THE NATURE AND IMPORTANCE OF SPEECHES
THAT INCREASE UNDERSTANDING

Americans have long valued the broad diffusion of knowledge. This value is founded on the premise that our social and political systems function most effectively when all citizens possess the knowledge that is the basis for intelligent decision making. Without affirming or denying this premise, one can note the diverse institutions that pay tribute to its worth. Our vast system of public education, the media of mass communication, and public and private agencies for information dissemination all justify their existence, at least in part, by the premise.

In contemporary America, the broad diffusion of knowledge is becoming increasingly difficult. Alvin Toffler, in his popular book *Future Shock* observes:

> Today change is so swift and relentless in the techno-societies that yesterday's truths suddenly become today's fictions, and the most highly skilled and intelligent members of society admit difficulty in keeping up with the deluge of new knowledge—even in extremely narrow fields.[1]

In response to this challenge, Otis Walter, in the quotation that headnotes this chapter, calls for a generation of communicators who can digest and assimilate the explosion of knowledge and render it useful for others who must know. As the rate of new knowledge continues to accelerate, and as local, national, and world problems become increasingly complex, speeches that increase understanding must continue to grow in number and significance.

Speeches that serve this function may be of different kinds. Lectures, intelligence briefings, reports of research findings, treasurers' reports, the happy chef show, and the evening TV weather report are all instances of this genre. Whenever speakers seek to create in the minds of their listeners an understanding of an event, concept, phenomenon, object, process, or relationship, they may be viewed as seeking to increase understanding.

In certain instances, increasing understanding is a speaker's *primary* speech purpose. A professor of history, for example, may be totally content if his students understand the major forces which contributed to the beginning of the Civil War. A computer systems engineer may be fully satisfied if installation procedures are understood by technical personnel. An accountant may be adequately rewarded if a company's executive officers understand the implications of a new federal tax regulation.

In other instances, increasing understanding is a speaker's *ancillary* purpose. For example, a sociologist may describe an event in order that he may urge social reform. A civil

1. Alvin Toffler, *Future Shock* (New York: Bantam Books, 1971), p. 157.

rights leader may narrate a story of social injustice in order to elicit a greater commitment to social tolerance. A senator may explain a piece of legislation as a prelude to urging its adoption.

From the perspective of the audience, it is often difficult to determine the extent to which a speech increases understanding rather than serving some other major purpose. Audience members listening to the same speech may come away feeling informed, persuaded to a new point of view, or even inspired to recommit their lives to cherished values. But a speaker who purports to increase understanding, whether as a primary or an ancillary purpose, should be expected to meet several fundamental criteria.

CRITERIA FOR EVALUATING SPEECHES THAT INCREASE UNDERSTANDING

Four general criteria are especially important for evaluating speeches that seek to increase understanding. Failure to satisfy any of these four will seriously restrict the speaker's communication of information.

1. Is the information communicated accurately, completely, and with unity?

Because genuine understanding by an audience is the speaker's goal, an *accurate, complete,* and *unified* view of the subject must be presented. Wilson, Arnold, and Wertheimer have expressed this criterion in this way:

> The tests that listeners apply when talk seems intended to be predominantly informative are these: (1) Is the information *accurate?* Listeners want information that is true to fact in both detail and proportion. (2) Is the information sufficiently *complete?* Does the speaker cover the *whole* subject adequately? (3) Is the information *unified?* We want information that "hangs together" to form a whole of some sort. If we're to understand a wheel, we must understand not just that there are a hub, some spokes, and a rim, but we must understand also how their arrangement in relation to one another enables the wheel to *turn.* Speakers trying to inform need to pay special attention to how facets of the explained subject "fit together" to form or create the explained thing as a totality. If an explanation meets the three tests we have just given, listeners experience the satisfaction of "having been informed."[2]

Given a specific body of knowledge to impart, a speaker must select those items of information that an audience must have to gain understanding. These items must then be arranged in a unified sequence and expressed in an undistorted manner.

2. John F. Wilson, Carroll C. Arnold, and Wertheimer, Molly, *Public Speaking as a Liberal Art,* 6th ed. (Boston: Allyn and Bacon, 1990), pp. 190–191.

2. Does the speaker make the information meaningful for the audience?

It is not enough that speakers know the essential components of a truth. In seeking to increase understanding for a particular audience at a particular time, they must transform their perceptions of facts and concepts into symbols that evoke understanding in those who listen. Even a highly motivated audience may lack the substantive, linguistic, and conceptual skills essential to understanding an idea presented in its pure form. Speakers must be faithful to both the integrity of the truth they seek to impart and to the demands of the particular audience they address.

These demands need not be incompatible, as an example will demonstrate. Let us assume that you wish to clarify the reasoning processes of induction and deduction to an audience of laborers who have come to your campus. You know that *induction* is a method of systematic investigation that seeks to discover, analyze, and explain specific instances or facts in order to determine the existence of a general law embracing them, whereas *deduction* is a process by which a particular conclusion about an instance is drawn from the application of a general law. In appraising your audience, you recognize that, although these terms are meaningful to you, they represent an unfamiliar level of conceptual abstraction to your audience. The rhetorical problem is clear; the solution is not.

In 1866, Thomas Henry Huxley faced exactly the same problem. The rhetorical choices that he made in explaining these processes to a group of English workingmen in his speech entitled "The Method of Scientific Investigation" are demonstrated in the following paragraphs.

> Suppose you go into a fruiterer's shop, wanting an apple—you take one up, and, on biting, you find it is sour; you look at it, and see that it is hard and green. You take another one and that too is hard, green, and sour. The shopman offers you a third; but, before biting it, you examine it, and find that it is hard and green, and you immediately say that you will not have it, as it must be sour, like those you have already tried.
>
> Nothing can be more simple than that, you think; but if you will take the trouble to analyze and trace out into its logical elements what has been done by the mind, you will be greatly surprised. In the first place, you have performed the operation of induction. You found that, in two experiences, hardness and greenness in apples went together with sourness. It was so in the first case and it was confirmed by the second. True, it is a very small basis, but still it is enough to make an induction from; you generalize the facts, and you expect to find sourness in apples where you get hardness and greenness. You found upon that a general law, that all hard and green apples are sour; and that, so far as it goes, is a perfect induction. Well, having got your natural law in this way, when you are offered another apple which you find is hard and green, you say, "All hard and green apples are sour; this apple is hard and green, therefore this apple is sour." That train of reasoning is what logicians call a syllogism and has all its various parts and terms—its major premise, its minor premise, and its conclusion. And, by the help of further reasoning, which, if drawn out, would have to be exhibited in two or three other syllogisms, you arrive at your final determination. "I will not have that apple." So that, you see, you have, in the first place, established a law by induction, and reasoned out the special conclusion of the particular case.

In this instance, Huxley chose to impart only a very basic understanding of the processes of induction and deduction by showing them to be inherent in a commonplace happening familiar to the workers who comprised his audience. He chose not to treat the subtleties of form and fallacy. Did he compromise the integrity of the truth in order to win popular understanding? Most critics think not. Although he simplified these processes, he did not misrepresent them. His illustration accurately portrays their essential nature. And it is complete in the sense of comprehensively demonstrating the specific purpose of the speech: to show that "there is not one here who has not in the course of the day had occasion to set in motion a complex train of reasoning of the very same kind, though differing of course in degree, as that which a scientific man goes through in tracing the causes of natural phenomena." Finally, his speech possesses unity in providing a systematic development through which the listener may gain a clear grasp of the total meaning.

In giving meaning to the knowledge that he wished to present, Huxley chose to move from a simple illustration to a complex generalization, to develop a common understanding of a process before attaching labels to it, and to use periodic summations of what had been discussed. Martin Luther King, in his speech "Love, Law, and Civil Disobedience," utilized definition to amplify the various meanings of the concept of love. Other speakers have used restatement and repetition, clarity of organization, factual and hypothetical examples, synonyms and negation, comparison and contrast, analogies and statistics, description and narration, photographs and films, blackboards and diagrams, questions and answers, meaningful gestures and movement, and varied patterns of rate and pitch.

3. Does the speaker create audience interest in the information being presented?

Because understanding is the goal of the speech designed to increase understanding, the speaker must create in the audience a reason for concentrating on the information that is being transmitted. Creating this interest is not always easy. Often the speaker must explain technical, detailed, and abstract concepts to an apathetic audience. In seeking to do so, the speaker can capitalize on the interest factors in content, language, and delivery. *Concrete* and specific terms and illustrations have more interest value for most listeners than vague generalities or abstract concepts. *Conflict* in the form of disagreements, threats, clashes, and antagonisms capture and hold an audience's attention. *Suspense* and *curiosity* in building to a climax, anticipating a conclusion, or asking intriguing questions can be used. Description or narration focusing on activity and movement capitalizes on *action*. The new, unusual, or unexpected reflect the *novelty* factor. On the other hand, listeners are also interested in things that are "close to home" and *familiar*. When carefully and appropriately used, *humor* may increase interest while explaining or highlighting a main point.

As a study of the choices that one speaker made, let us again return to Huxley's illustration. In appraising his audience, Huxley realized that, for average English workingmen of his time, the scientific method represented an esoteric construct of little interest or significance to all but the disciples of science. By making his individual audience member "you," the chief participant in his illustration, by choosing a familiar environment as the setting, and by selecting such suspense words as "suppose" and "you will be greatly surprised" as major transitional devices, he gave to his material a sense of vitality, realism, suspense, and urgency that it did not naturally possess. Huxley chose a hypothetical illustration for this purpose; others have selected metaphors, narratives, comparisons, contrasts, real and figurative analogies, and specific examples. Thus, a speaker who is inventive need not worry about losing the audience even when an unusual or difficult subject is involved.

4. Does the speaker show the audience that the information is important?

Beyond presenting information that is accurate, complete, unified, meaningful, and interesting, speakers must also get their audiences to feel that they should make such knowledge a permanent part of their storehouse of data. In order to do so, speakers might clarify the relation of the information to the wants and goals of their audiences. They might point out ways in which the information can be used or applied, where this new knowledge fits within the context of information already considered worthwhile by the audience, and, if appropriate, where and how the audience can obtain additional information on the subject.

Given the vast array of information that may be communicated, the critic has a right to question the quality of the information that the speaker chooses to present. Student speakers often err by selecting speech topics that are trivial and lacking in real information value. Gruner, Logue, Freshley, and Huseman, in *Speech Communnication in Society,* recall

> . . . a dreadful speech by a young man who spoke on and demonstrated how to use two simple types of can openers, one being the elementary "church key" type for opening beverage cans. Disappointed by his low grade he compained, "Well, the speech *did* contain information, didn't it?" The instructor replied: "Not for this audience; I'm sure they already know how to open cans." The instructor's reply could be paraphrased: "You instructed no one."[3]

An effective speech of this form presents information that is worth having to an audience that lacks such knowledge.

---

3. Charles R. Gruner, Cal M. Logue, Dwight L. Freshley, and Richard C. Huseman, *Speech Communication in Society* (Boston: Allyn and Bacon, Inc., 1972), p. 179.

CONCLUSION

Increasing understanding is one of the primary and ancillary functions that speeches serve. When speakers try to fulfill this purpose, they must be aware of the constraints that govern their speech behavior. They must choose information that is worth knowing. They must present the information with *accuracy, completeness,* and *unity.* They must be aware of the demands that varied audiences impose on the choices they make in giving *meaning, interest,* and *importance* to a body of knowledge. In other words, they must be faithful to the integrity of their perception of truth while adapting to the demands of their audiences.

For further reading

Allen, R. R., and Ray E. McKerrow. *The Pragmatics of Public Communication.* 3rd ed. Kendall-Hunt Publishing Company, 1985. Chapter 7 discusses the nature, types and development of speeches to inform.

Hart, Roderick P.; Friedrich, Gustav W.; and Brooks, William D. *Public Communication.* 2nd ed. Harper and Row, 1983. Chapter 5 is devoted to reducing the complexity of information.

Lucas, Stephen. *The Art of Public Speaking.* 3rd ed. Random House, 1989. Chapter 13 presents guidelines for speaking to inform about objects, processes, events, and concepts.

Netter, Gwyn. *Explanations.* McGraw-Hill, 1970. Chapters 2–6 explore the main variations of explanation used in discourse: definitional, empathetic, scientific, and ideological.

Osborn, Michael, and Osborn, Suzanne. *Public Speaking.* 2nd ed. Houghton Mifflin, 1991. Chapter 12 examines the functions, types, and structure of speeches to increase inderstanding.

Verderber, Rudolph F. *The Challenge of Effective Speaking.* 8th ed. Wadsworth, 1991. Chapters 8–12 examine demonstration, description, definition, and reporting.

Walter, Otis M. *Speaking to Inform and Persuade.* 2nd ed. Macmillan, 1982. Chapters 2–4 present an extremely useful discussion of imparting knowledge, including selection of main ideas and use of supporting material.

The Information Age: Technology and Computers
David F. Linowes

Unquestionably electronic technology, computers in particular, impact heavily on our lives. Computer programming is gaining in sophistication so rapidly that it is difficult to even imagine its ultimate capabilities. It seems appropriate that the first speech in this edition of *Contemporary American Speeches* should explore the information age and depict some of the phenomenal advances of artificial intelligence. David F. Linowes, Professor of Political Economy and Public Policy, University of Illinois, delivered an address on this topic to the White House Conference on Libraries and Information Services at the Krannert Center for the Performing Arts, Urbana, Illinois, October 27, 1990. In his speech he detailed the numerous ways that the "new information" is impacting on human life and he makes one appreciate that we have no idea as to where it will end. He even suggests that home computer terminals may make going to school obsolete!

Linowes depends heavily upon startling information and the implications of such information to generate interest in his subject. Beginning with an analogy between the Industrial Age and the Information Age, he moves to information about the extent of artificial intelligence. Of the key questions identified in Chapter 3 concerning speeches to increase knowledge, the second one, "Does the speaker make the knowledge meaningful for the audience?", seems particularly important in assessing and learning from this speech. We ask you to make a careful study of the ways the speaker uses to achieve meaningfulness. Ironically, a speech on new technologies and the information explosion can readily overwhelm an audience with too much information, given too quickly, without ample illustration. Do you find information overload in this speech? If so, why? If not, how does Linowes make it possible for the audience to follow him closely throughout?

——— This speech is reprinted by permission from *Vital Speeches of the Day,* January 1, 1991, pp. 168–171.

———

1 In this Information Age information is inextricably linked to electronic technology. Computers in particular. That combination is causing a profound revolution in every aspect of our lives.

2 Just as the machine had become the extension of a person's limbs and muscles during the Industrial Revolution, so is the computer becoming the extension of one's mind and memory during the Computer Revolution, spawning the Information Age. Technology we currently have in place is 100 years behind what has already been developed. Pushing these developments is the fact observed by Walter Wriston that 85 percent of all the scientists who have ever lived are alive today. The time between the realization of an idea and its arrival in the marketplace is now the shortest it has ever been in history—usually just a few months. In contrast it took gunpowder almost 200 years to move from laboratory to use in artillery.

3 During the past 20 years—during our lifetime—we have learned more about the human brain than in the rest of history. With that new knowledge, the brain is being re-created in computers.

4 This ultra-sophisticated software or "artificial intelligence" is being used to solve complex mathematical problems and to make medical diagnoses. Researchers at IBM and Texas Instruments are using artificial intelligence to analyze geographical formations, to design new biological genes, and to read, digest and answer correspondence.

5 Computers are being programmed to duplicate the decision-making process of leading experts in given fields. These "expert" programs are designed by programming all known information on a given subject into the computer. Programmers then interview recognized experts in the field to determine how they process information to form judgments. That process is then also programmed into the same computer.

6 Stanford researchers have developed a program called "Eurisko" that enables a computer to develop its own theories and ideas once it is given the principles of a discipline!

7 In the coming decade people will talk to computers the same as they do with one another. A number of computers already allow communication in written English. To give computers fluency, researchers at the University of Illinois, Yale, and IBM are programming the machines with two types of knowledge. First they instruct the computer on rules of grammar and syntax. Then they give the computer some knowledge about the world.

8 During the next decade the Japanese Ministry for International Trade and Industry expects to have a thinking computer. It will understand natural speech, read written language, and translate documents. The machine will draw inferences and make its own judgments. It will learn by studying its errors.

9 The computer is being educated! It is acquiring unorganized and unrelated facts, what we commonly recognize as "information." It is being taught knowledge, i.e., extensive facts in a particular field just as any specialized professional. And, through "Artificial Intelligence" it is acquiring wisdom, i.e., knowledge of people and human life so as to produce sound judgments. All of this adds to the mountains of information that is being amassed, processed, classified, and stored for retrieval.

10 How a person communicates his knowledge determines how he thinks, the pace at which he thinks, what he thinks, and the amount and complexity of knowledge he is able to develop. When writing was first invented information was limited to a person's memory. As it evolved to writing with pencil and paper, knowledge was stimulated. Printing quickened the pace. Now we have a quantum leap into electronic writing. Speeds of calculations and projections—trillions of calculations a second—are beyond the dreams of the wildest science fiction writers. Computers even are acquiring the ability of psychological reasoning, making decisions based on emotional understanding.

11 It took from the time of Christ to the mid-eighteenth century for knowledge to double. It doubled again 150 years later, and then again in only 50 years. Today it doubles every 4 or 5 years. More new information has been produced in the last 30 years than in the previous 5,000.

12 Some look askance at this avalanche of information. Arguing that our computing ability has reached the point where computers give us more information than we can possibly use. They argue we have reached the point of "negative information" where we are being bombarded with so much data that useful information is actually reduced instead of increased.

13 In the United States, the dissemination of information is a major economic force. About 1,000 specialized periodicals come out each year, and 1,000 new book titles are printed each day. The entire contents of a 250,000-page encyclopedia can now be stored on a single compact disk.

14 Our laws and institutional mores have not been adequate to deal with these challenges. Information has always been essential to a democracy. It is an observed fact that the economic, political, and social strength of the United States depends on people's ability to acquire and use information. And, Michael C. Maibach of Intel Corporation significantly observes that the critical components of manufacturing today come from the mind and not the ground. Integrated circuits, for example, are made from two of the earth's most common substances oxygen and sand.

INFORMATION AND LEARNING

15 Nowhere is the clash between technological development and societal impact more acute than in the field of education for education involves information and communication. In order for information to be communicated it must be available. In principle, the computer offers the prospect of enormous strides in the learning ability of everyone in society. In practice, the implementation of widespread computerized learning is posing a number of severe problems which are only just being recognized by educators and policy-makers.

"GOING TO SCHOOL" MAY BE OBSOLETE

16 If education can be successfully accomplished through computer programs linked to information bases and individual terminals, why not educate students at home? Already home computers are a major industry. There is no technical barrier to the fulfillment of a complete educational experience from a computer in one's own living room.

17 In the long term, the school building or campus and even the concept of "going to school" may increasingly become obsolete. Over a decade ago some of the more imaginative educators were speaking of eliminating the "social addiction" to attending school. Proposals have been made for a deschooled world that would replace formal classes with networks of "learning exchanges." Instead of confining formal learning to the classroom, students would be taught wherever they might be, at home, the work place, or at the playground by giving them access to centralized information networks. People of any age who wanted to learn something would go to a reference library counselor.

18 Just as the inventions of writing and the printing press necessitated a reformulation of pedagogic philosophy and technique, so the current advances will require the same careful re-examination of means, purpose, and policy in education.

19 Those in education expressing concerns about the onslaught of the computer into the halls of learning should recall that 2,400 years ago when writing was invented the educators of that day were alarmed for fear that writing would diminish the student's interest in learning. They argued students would refuse to memorize information anymore because the information would always be available to them on a written surface.

PRIVACY

20 The continuous tension between bureaucratic values and democratic control has been complicated in recent years by information technology's application to the agencies of government. As sophisticated computer and communications equipment has been introduced into public agencies, so information has become far easier to collect, store, manipulate, and disseminate. On the one hand, this has enhanced the management, decision-making, and analytical capabilities of government organizations. However, the advantages that contemporary data-processing techniques have brought are offset by certain dangers.

21 The immense capability to control vast quantities of personal information on individual citizens has generated a worldwide concern about the potential for bureaucratic surveillance and about the consequent erosion of personal privacy.

22 Data on almost any given subject is instantly available. Information companies which serve as libraries of giant computer warehouses can analyze a topic or person in seconds, running searches for newspaper and magazine stories or anything else.

23 Along with expanded information services, comes the potential for abuses. Plagiarism, parading borrowed work as original, and insufficient or incomplete research are enhanced by the new technology. Also, personal privacy becomes invaded in new and unexpected ways. The subject of an electronic inquiry, for instance, can be victimized by the increased ability to manipulate video images as well as the factual elements of the public record.

24 Most Americans have no idea of the scope of personal, sensitive information about all of us now being accumulated and maintained in massive computer memories, never to be destroyed. They are held by business corporations, banks, insurance companies, government agencies, even schools and religious organizations.

25 People would be surprised at how easy it is for others to obtain information we assume is confidential.

26 This personal information is used not only as a tool for those who make organizational decisions, but it is marketable for a variety of commercial and political purposes, and even as an instrument of surveillance and possible abuse.

27 The gradual realization of these dangers over the last twenty years has motivated most Western democracies to provide an all embracing policy response in the form of "privacy" or "data-protection" laws. Not the United States.

28 We do not have adequate national public policy privacy protection legislation. Such broad legislation would establish "fair information principles" designed to minimize intrusiveness in the collection of personal information: to maximize fairness in its use; and to provide reasonable and enforceable expectations of confidentiality of that data.

INFORMATION AND DEMOCRACY

29 It is widely believed that the balance of power in our society is becoming more and more dangerously weighted in favor of large institutions—government and business alike. A chief reason is that they are the ones with the information about people, and the people don't know it.

30 The phenomenon of individuals demanding an increasing number of services from all institutions continues to grow at a never-ending pace. From the government the public expects social security, unemployment compensation, guaranteed mortgage loans, and all levels of welfare. From business, the public expects credit cards which give instant credit approval any place in the world, and the ability to make plane reservations in matters of minutes for any kind of trip to anywhere. Libraries themselves are being called upon to render more and more personal and community services. The public is demanding faster user service within a library, and networking across libraries.

31 Administrators responsible for furnishing these services must satisfy themselves of an individual applicant's eligibility by getting more and more personal, often sensitive, information. Thus, increasing quantities of confidential data are being injected into institutional mainstreams, never to be destroyed.

32 In the political arena, computerized information has given pressure groups the power to influence candidate selection and important legislative issues as never before.

33 By pressing a key, a clerk obtains your profile that includes voting history, address, family composition, model of car, neighborhood characteristics, ethnic group, and even indication of sexual orientation. The candidate then targets you with either a telephone call or a direct mail message.

34 GOP headquarters in Washington maintains voter lists with millions of names and relevant personal information in its computers.

35 Observing the extent to which personal information is used in the election process, arch Republican Richard Viguerie, pioneer in the use of computerized information on behalf of conservative candidates and issues, describes what is occurring as "manipulative politics"; and admits it is "scary."

36 Some people believe space-age information technology is "driving politics underground."

IMPACT ON INSTITUTIONS AND NATIONS

37 The problems of information combined with technology are not problems confined to the United States; but, in fact impact on relations between countries. For instance, some nations want to create electronic barriers to halt the flow of information. They consider information within a country a national resource, much like copper or oil. If information does cross their borders electronically, they want to charge a tariff on it.

38 The lack of controls over information transmission for processing or use in another country leaves developed nations concerned and developing nations alarmed. Economic data, government data, data from home offices of multinational corporations are beamed through the sky in the normal course of business. Technology in the United States has advanced so far that many developed countries, and especially Third World countries, lag hopelessly behind.

39 Economic, social, and military information are being bandied about the far corners of the earth at the speed of light by way of satellites. There are over 3,000 communication satellites in space, and their numbers are increasing each year. These satellites are over 20,000 miles up in the sky, moving at the same speed as the earth. A combination of three of them can reach every person on the globe.

40 Once computer and telecommunications facilities are established by multinational corporations or by government agencies there is no technological means presently in existence to prevent their use for other purposes. All information has become inextricably intertwined. Information needed to conduct commercial and government affairs is no different from news for newspapers or that used by subversive groups. Information often moves from country to country with the speed of light over various routes depending on the availability of computer time and open telecommunications facilities. Authorities or their librarians today have no way of controlling what information is being beamed into and out of their nations.

DEVELOPING NATIONS

41 Have-not nations are of the conviction that divisions are widening between nations possessing sophisticated information and those that do not, creating greater disparities than have the differences in material wealth. It is this recognition that gives rise to many of the problems we are having with developing nations today and it will continue, even intensify.

42 In time, economic exploitation, they argue, can be overcome but disparities between information-rich and information-poor societies based on continually advancing sophisticated technology and knowledge, can never be balanced.

43 The flood of new knowledge, coupled with the negative tide of information flow, make it impossible for them to catch up and become self-sufficient, resulting in a new and more sinister form of colonialism. This perspective embitters relationships between us and the have-not nations and will increase in the future.

NATION-STATE

44 Some studies of history point to the possible disintegration of the nation-state as we know it. The rise of the nation-state occurred shortly after the invention of the printing press making it possible to transmit information to large groups of people over broad geographic areas. The printing press was invented about 1455 and was widely used throughout Europe by 1487. The nation-state, using the printed word as the basic communication medium for its laws and edicts, followed immediately, coming into being in Europe around 1500.

45 Communication today no longer depends on the physical distribution of the printed word. Satellites send information to all people of all nations instantaneously in their own languages. The impact of evolving technology transmitting all kinds of information is now creating what centuries of war and statesmanship could not establish, namely, One World. The question is "Whose world will it be?"

NEW ISSUES

46 The transfer of information into and out of a nation, without the knowledge or permission of the authorities in the jurisdiction, raises a number of issues that in years prior to this Information Age were barely perceptible, if they existed at all.

47 Many sites are transfer stations for information. Whose laws have jurisdiction when data is in a country only for retransmission? For example, if data is transmitted by a Polish national by way of an American satellite to a British library in a split-second, whose laws control and when? And, do we know when a split-second host government intercepts that information for its own purposes? We do not.

MASTER DATABANKS OF INFORMATION

48 Business, government, and other institutions increasingly are establishing and maintaining huge databanks of valuable information coming from all parts of the globe accessible by personal terminals. This same information is needed by a broad universe of people—educators, researchers, students, government officials, the general public. Could not a Master Databank of Information be created linking the various independent databanks into a cooperative project for all to access under the auspices of the libraries in a region? What a great challenge and opportunity this could be for librarians, educators and museum curators. Librarians joining with computer industry executives could point the way.

NATIONAL PUBLIC POLICY AGENDA FOR INFORMATION AND LITERACY

49 To expedite such developments the Secretary of Education working with libraries and educational institutions could design a National Public Policy Agenda for Information and Literacy to promote expanded learning environments for everyone. Mayors and governors together with libraries, local schools, and museums could serve as catalysts and stimulants for bringing together industry, school and home to promote adoption of appropriate programs.

50 The exciting developments in the applications of electronics to information pose dramatic and vital challenges—challenges we as a nation and librarians as a profession must continue to respond to, but with increasing focus and vigor.

An American Prisoner of War in South Vietnam
James N. Rowe

For more than five years Major James N. Rowe was a prisoner of the Viet Cong. He was captured by the enemy when he was a Special Forces advisor in 1963 and was held prisoner in the Mekong region and the U Minh Forest. He devised a cover story about himself that kept the enemy from executing him, a fate which befell several others imprisoned with him. His cover story held up until 1968, when the enemy found out he had lied. Major Rowe felt that they received a biographical sketch with complete information about him and his family from the Peace and Justice Loving Friends of the National Liberation Front in America. This information put him on the list for execution. But on December 31, 1968, circumstances conspired that allowed Major Rowe to escape. A heavy American air strike shook up the guards. One of the Viet Cong groups panicked when United States gunships came into the area, and Major Rowe took advantage of the confusion. He was picked up by an American helicopter pilot who almost mistook him for a member of the enemy because he was wearing the pajama-like garb of the Viet Cong. The beard that Major Rowe had grown during his imprisonment permitted the helicopter pilot to identify him as an American a second before pulling the trigger.

Major Rowe delivered his speech at the U.S. Army General Staff and Command College at Leavenworth, Kansas. The audience consisted primarily of students of the college—mostly majors and lieutenant colonels of the American Army, some Navy and Air Force personnel, and a significant number of Allied officers attending the college. [More information about Major Rowe's experiences can be found in his book, *Five Years to Freedom* (Boston: Little, Brown, 1971).]

This speech by Major Rowe is a personal narrative used to impart knowledge about Viet Cong prison camps and what an American prisoner of war lives through. In assessing the speech you will thus want to ask how well Major Rowe tells his story. Does he make effective use of suspense? Imagery? Action? Anecdotes? Is he able to organize his narrative effectively so it can easily be followed? How well does he draw increased understanding with general application from his story?

Major Rowe delivered this address extemporaneously and used no notes. The manuscript you are about to read is a transcript of an audio-tape recording. The extemporaneous style of Major Rowe is thus very apparent. What difficulties do you encounter in reading a speech with genuine oral style? You may want to discuss the statement "Good speeches don't read well."

On April 21, 1989, Col. "Nick" Rowe was assassinated by communist terrorists on the streets of Manila, the Philippines.

This speech is printed by permission of Major James N. Rowe.

1 The American prisoners of war are particularly close to those of us in the military, because the prisoners of war are members of the military. It could be any one of us, and I was one of those prisoners of war. I am Major Nick Rowe; I spent 62 months as a prisoner of the Viet Cong in South Vietnam. The issue of the prisoners of war has come to the forefront in our nation; and in bringing this issue to the forefront, we have found that it's not that American people don't remember, or that they don't care, it's that most of the

people in our country don't know. And those of us who have come out feel that we have a particular duty, because we are speaking for 1,600 men who have no voices. So this afternoon I would like to bring you some insight into the prison camps and some insight into what an American prisoner of war lives through.

2 I was a Special Forces advisor in 1963 in Phuoc Hoa. I was in a camp approximately in this area and I was captured very near there in October of 1963. Shortly after capture, I was moved down in the Mekong region; I stayed in this region until January of 1965, when I was moved into the U Minh Forest. I stayed in the U Minh Forest from January 1965 through December of 1968, when I escaped. The camp I was held in was on canal 21 and canal 6. I was approximately fourteen kilometers from our old district capital. I was that close to Americans, and yet they couldn't get to me nor could I get to them. This is the most frustrating thing about being an American prisoner in South Vietnam.

3 The conditions that an American lives under are those that are structured by his captors, and there are several new aspects of captivity. It is not the Hogan's Heroes concept that many people have, because in South Vietnam and in North Vietnam, we found that an American prisoner of war is not a military prisoner, he is a political prisoner; and the Communists are dealing with American prisoners of war based on the Pavlovian theory— stimuli and response—the manipulation of human behavior. These are parameters that we have never dealt with before and are not prepared to deal with. The American prisoners find themselves being manipulated and being made more pliable by the Communists using principles that we have read about in Koestler's *Darkness at Noon,* perhaps in *1984;* these types of things that are never reality. But in prison camps in South Vietnam and in North Vietnam and in Laos, it is reality. An American prisoner of war has two main purposes for the Communists. First of all, propaganda; because in an age of ideological conflict, the most important thing is political opinion, and formation of political opinion, and this is done through propaganda. What more effective source do the Communists have for propaganda than an American prisoner of war? Through coercion, manipulation, or force, to cause that man to condemn our society, our government, our actions throughout the world; and then, as a representative of our system of government and our society, for him to confess to crimes against humanity. Think of the impact of this propaganda in either a Communist or nonCommunist country when contrasted with the same propaganda coming from a Communist source.

4 The second purpose of an American prisoner of war is that when the Communists finally do decide to negotiate, what better blue chip do they have to lay down on the table than an American prisoner of war, trading American lives for political gain—this is why they take an American prisoner of war. When I was captured, there were three of us, two of us Special Forces and one MAAG advisor, who were with a strike force company when we were overrun; all three of us were wounded and were taken prisoners. The other strike force wounded were shot by the VC. And yet an American was of value. In captivity we found, first of all, that we were political prisoners. We weren't military prisoners. This was

typified during the initial interrogations. I was one of the first American officers captured in the Mekong Delta, and they really didn't know what to do with us. The first cadre who came in were hampered by the decided lack of ability to speak English, so they brought in a journalist-by-trade who spoke English, and used him as an interrogator. They had an S-2 who stayed across the canal from our camp in a cadre hut, and he was responsible for the interrogation. But since he couldn't speak English, he would write his questions down in Vietnamese, give them to this journalist, the interpreter, who would then translate them into English and come down to my cage. I was in the low-rent district right behind the camp, about thirty meters behind the camp, and he would come down and would sit down and ask me the questions. Anything I said he would write down verbatim. Then he would take the answers back and translate them from his Vietnamese-English dictionary back into Vietnamese to take to the S-2. Well, the first thing I discovered there was that he could deal with a large number of American prisoners, because the S-2 is in one place with the interpreter doing the legwork for him. And he got nothing for it.

5 About four to five weeks, six weeks, seven weeks, and the S-2 got upset, but he was apparently prevented from doing any more than threatening us. And when this little interpreter would come down and threaten, he would say, "I can kill you, I can torture you, I can do anything I want"; then he'd wince. So we knew he wasn't really serious; and I decided after a period of time, that since he had so much flexibility, it would be better to try and see if anything could be done to play with him, I had him come down one day, and I said, "Well, all right, Plato, I am ready to talk." We had nicknames for all of them, and he was very philosophical, so we nicknamed him Plato. I said, "All right, Plato, I am ready to talk." He beamed, pulled out extra paper and a new ballpoint pen, and sat down. I gave him four pages on the theory of laminar flow. This was to include calculus, integrated differential. I gave him pressure formulas—the weights, dams, storm gutters—the aerodynamic principles of air flow. I almost failed mechanical fluids at West Point, so it wasn't really that good anyway, but he copied it down verbatim. Everything I said he copied down, checking on spelling, and he took it back to his hut, and spent the next five days translating it from English into Vietnamese, coming down every day to check on the formulas and things like that; and I said, "Drive on, Plato, you are in good shape." Well, when he finished, he had a great volume, almost like *Khrushchev Remembers.* He took all of this great volume of paper over to the S-2. The enemy are very stoic individuals, and although I was thirty meters behind the camp, I soon heard screams from the S-2's hut. Not more than two minutes later, here came Plato scurrying down this little log walk with the S-2 right behind him. Obviously, the S-2 found out in a very short period of time what Plato had been doing, and it had erased his ability to deal with other American prisoners. Had the S-2 had the ability to deal with me as he wished, there wouldn't have been a tree high enough in the area for him to string me up to. But, I was a political prisoner, and the political cadre said no. Interrogation is secondary, indoctrination is primary. If they lose you through interrogation, they lose you for indoctrination; and so that was when we established what was of primary importance.

6 In dealing with an American prisoner of war their philosophy is that you can take any man and if you control the physical, you do not necessarily control that man; but if you can control and manipulate his mind, you will control the physical and the man. So this is what their target is, not necessarily physical torture, because they realize that indiscriminate physical torture can alienate a man, and once you have done that, he identifies you with the enemy, and you will never indoctrinate him. They will use physical torture, but they use it only to amplify the mental pressure. We found that a bruise will heal, a broken bone will heal, a wound will heal, but if they push you over the line mentally, or they break your spirit, then you are not coming back. That was the big battle. And that was what we had not been prepared for.

7 One of the first things that came up, and I will bring this up here because it is very important to members of the military, was the Code of Conduct. The Code of Conduct to me was a series of pictures in an orderly room. I had read them. I had gotten the T.I. and E. classes on Code of Conduct; it really wasn't that clear. I knew that I was supposed to give my name, my rank, my serial number, my date of birth, and then I thought I was supposed to shut up. This is the way it usually comes down to the troops. But this is a fallacy, because if you don't know the Code of Conduct when you're captured, the Communists will teach it to you. Because they teach our Code of Conduct to their cadre. And then they tell you while you're there, go ahead and follow it, but you will die if you do. They'll let you make your own decisions. What they are doing here is one of the first steps in breaking down a man's will to resist, because generally speaking, an individual feels if he goes beyond name, rank, serial number, and date of birth, he is a traitor. I know I felt it right at first. And this is the first question that comes up in a man's mind. What about the Big Four? How long do I last? Well, you hang onto the Big Four as long as you can, but the next line says, "I will evade answering further questions to the best of my ability." It does give you credit for having basic intelligence. And this is what a man does. Fortunately, I went to West Point, and they teach you ambiguity; this is one of the things that really comes in handy. When you get a B.S. degree from West Point, that is exactly what it is. I liked English up there, and that is where they teach you to say the same thing 25 different ways. So this is what the American is doing. He is hedging, working for a way to get around, or get under, or get through. But if an individual goes in thinking, if I break from name, rank, serial number, and date of birth, I am a traitor, the first thing they are going to do is instill a guilt complex into him that will beat him into the ground. I know, because we had an individual who felt, initially, that anything beyond name, rank, serial number, and date of birth, was a violation of a punitive article of the uniform code of military justice. Now, this is where a man feels, all right, I have broken; and then they say, "Well, you have broken once, you are going to be punished, you might as well go all the way." Once they've got their finger in that crack, you're in trouble. And they teach our Code of Conduct as a punitive article, if you don't know it before you go in, find out about it now and find out exactly what it is. Because they are going to tell you and they are going to try to convince you that it is a punitive article, once you violate anything, once you go beyond name, rank, serial number, and date of birth, you have violated the Code of Conduct and you are going to be punished. Then they have their foot in the door. And they say, "Drive on, because you are going to be punished anyway. Why not get out sooner and go home?" This is the thing that a person has to be aware of. Remember that the code says, "I will make no statements disloyal to my country, its allies, or detrimental to their cause." And that's the thing that you have to remember. But as far as name, rank, serial number, and date of birth, you hold it as long as you can, but they are going to move you off of it at one point or another. They have developed all types of evasive techniques. We are training our people now, finally, to include a calculated breakdown, where you plan ahead what you are going to say, and then you dole it out a little bit at a time over an extended period, buying time to escape.

8 The other thing I used is a cover story; and in this case, I realized I wasn't the bravest person, so I decided to devise something which would allow me to say, "I don't know," rather than "I can't tell you" or "I won't tell you." So, I employed first of all the old artillery kiss formula, keep it simple, stupid. Then I built a cover story that would allow me to say, "I don't know"; and in that cover story, I graduated from the United States Armed Forces Institute in Washington, D.C., as an engineer; I went there for four years, and gave them three years of service back. It was 1963 and I was ready to go be a civil engineer. Since I studied engineering, I was assigned to the Adjutant General. I went to Fort Belvoir afterward, and studied bridge building and house building and road building, and then I went to civilian seminars throughout the nation, again engineering subjects; finally I was assigned to a Special Forces attachment because of my outstanding capabilities as an engineer, and because they needed civil affairs project people. So this was my cover story which allowed me over the period of time to tell them, "I don't know," to a great volume of things, and to hide behind it.

9 So, what they are trying to do initially is find out who is this person that they have, what are his capabilities? And they come out with a very neat form, it is entitled, "Red Cross Index Data Card"; the first thing it says, military information: name, rank, serial number, and date of birth. And you think, great, that is what it is supposed to be. But they have a heavy dotted line; under it, it says, "Who did you train with in the United States, what was your unit in the United States, when did you come to Vietnam, who did you come with, how did you come, when did you land, where did you serve in Vietnam, what operations did you go on?" They want to know your educational background, your political background, your religious background; they want to know your mother, your father, your wife, your children; educational, religious, and political backgrounds for all of them; your hobbies and your sports. Then they give you four sheets of paper and they want a short biographical sketch. Now they are going to try and build a picture of this American. And they've taken American prisoners of war from Korea, from North Vietnam, and from South Vietnam. They try to fit these people into some sort of category, based on their background, the psychological category if you will, and this is column A. They've got different categories; column B is different environmental situations of the stimuli that have been applied to these different groups of Americans. In column 3, are the reactions they have gotten from them. So if they get a new man, and they can categorize him, then they just look to column 3 to find out what they want him to do, and then they come back to column 2 to find out what they have to do to him to get him to do it. This again is stimuli and response.

10 Now, in the camp, the physical conditions in South Vietnam with the Viet Cong are primitive. I was in the U Minh Forest, the camps were temporary at best. You had two to three feet of standing water during the rainy season; in the dry season it sank out, and you were hunting for drinking water. We had two meals of rice a day, and generally we got salt and nuoc mam with them. We did get infrequent fish from the guards, but always the castoff that the guards didn't want. If we got greens, it was maybe one meal's worth every two or three months. Immediately vitamin deficiency and malnutrition were a problem. This is a thing you are going to fight the whole way through. And you are fighting on two sides. You are fighting a physical survival, and you are fighting for mental survival. The physical survival is just staying alive. We found that we had to eat a quart pan of rice each meal, two meals a day, just to stay alive. We found that if we could put down everything we had, and I think the most difficult thing initially was the nuoc mam. It is high in protein value, but the VC don't have that much money to spend on nuoc mam. You don't get Saigon nuoc mam. Theirs is called ten-meter nuoc mam. You can smell it within ten meters, and it is either repulsive or inedible, depending on how long you have been there. But this was the type of thing you are eating for nutritional value, and not for taste. So you are fighting on that side.

11 Disease, this is always present. Dysentery, beri-beri, hepatitis, jaundice, lac—which is a fungus infection, I had all those while I was in. I had about 85 percent of my body covered with lac. And you find that depending on your political attitude, there is either very little medication or no medication.

12 This is another thing which was disturbing, as if your political attitude determines whether you will get medication and what your treatment will be. And you are either re-actionary or progressive, or somewhere in between. You find that it is not a military type thing, it is purely political. And again, we are not prepared for this. The Geneva Convention, international law, the VC say, we don't recognize them. The only law you are subjected to is our law. And if you ever want to go home, you are going to have to be a good POW, and it is based upon your good attitude and behavior as prisoner and your repentance of your past misdeeds. That last one is a hooker, because that is a confession. So they set up perimeters, and they set up this dirty little world that they keep you in; then they throw the mental pressure on top of this.

13 Indoctrination, this is where they take an individual's beliefs, and his faiths, and his loyalties, and they challenge them, because they have to break all of these before they can influence him. This is where thought correction comes in, because thought correction is nothing more than creating confusion and doubt in a man's mind and filling the void that follows with answers to the questions that you have created for him. If you will take a man as an island, with little bridges running to the mainland, and his faiths, his beliefs, his loyalties, his ethics, his standards, are all these little bridges that link him to something, to his place in the universe. If they can cut these, then they are going to turn that man inside himself, and they are going to make him fight himself. And that's exactly what they want him to do. Because as soon as you compromise one of your beliefs, as soon as you compromise one of your loyalties, just to survive, then you are condemning yourself for it. That is exactly what they want. Because this is the pressure that doesn't stop. Physical torture, as soon as they stop it, you've got relief. But mental torture is something that will last 24 hours a day, and you do it to yourself.

14 One of the most vital things that came up was when men in the camp were asked, "Do you have a wife, do you have a family?" A couple of them answered, "Yes, we've got wives, we've got families." And the first thing that was asked was, "Do you think of your wife very often, do you think of your children, do you think of your family?" In an off-hand manner, we would respond, "Well, yah, we do, we are concerned, but we can't do anything about it." Then the guard would walk off. It didn't bother the individual for a couple of days, but pretty soon he started to think, and he began to wonder, "Is my wife all right, are my children all right, do they have enough money, are they sick, are they provided for?" and this was beginning to bother them, because they didn't know. Then the guard came down, and a little bit later, he would toss in another one; he would say, "How long does it take a woman in the United States to get a divorce after her husband is missing in action? Would your wife do this?" And of course, the immediate comment was, "No sweat. Not with my wife. She is going to hang in tight." Then he goes back to his cage at night, where he is by himself, and he lays there in that mosquito net, and he starts to think, and they give you plenty of time to think, and he begins to wonder, "Will she? What is it? What's the story? What's happening back there?" And he doesn't know. Next they go one step further, after he is going up the wall over these two questions, maybe a week later, he will come back, and he will say, "What is this we hear about immorality in your country? We read much about immorality. Do you know what your wife is doing?" And again, the first answer that comes out of the prisoner's mouth is what he believes, "My wife is straight, there's no problem." But then he goes back to his cage at night, and he begins to wonder: "I've been gone four years, I've been gone three years, what is happening back there?" You talk about frustration and anxiety, this is what does it to a man. This is a very subtle thumbscrew that they put on his mind, and then he tightens it down. And they don't even have to touch him. Because he doesn't know and he is in a prison camp. Now this works constantly. There is no getting away from these, and these are just everyday things.

15 Then you have the threats, and you find that anxiety comes in. When Plato said, "I can kill you, I can torture you, I can do anything I want," it really didn't mean anything. But in 1965, they moved us into the U Minh Forest and we met Mr. Hi. Mr. Hi was a political cadre, he was in charge of indoctrination, interrogation, and proselytizing of the enemy troops. He was a professor of English in Saigon before he joined the Revolution. We called him Mafia, and he fitted his name. Because when Mafia said I can kill you, I can torture you, I can do anything I want, he meant it. We met him in March 1965, Captain Humbert "Rock" Vercase and I both failed the initial interrogation indoctrination, we both went to punishment camps. I stayed in a starvation camp for six months, Rocky Vercase was executed in September of 1965. That was Mafia's lesson. When he said I can kill you, I can torture you, I can do anything I want, he meant it. And that was a lesson to all the American POW's. It was an entirely new ballgame. Here was a political cadre who was in charge of our lives; he could take us and he could do anything he wanted to with us. This is a hard lesson to learn. This was the new concept beginning in 1965, and this is what exists now.

16 The threat of violence, the anticipation of violence, the anxiety that goes with it, sometimes, in fact most of the time, is far more devastating than what follows. This is what they are doing. They'll take a man and they'll threaten and then they will watch him run himself up and down the ladder worrying about what is going to happen to him. This is the thing—when they get hold of your emotions, and they can run them up and down the scale like a yoyo; then they've got you ricocheting off the wall; and this is exactly what they want. Because now they've got you fighting on both fronts. They've got you fighting to stay physically alive, and they've got you fighting to maintain your sanity. At that point you're becoming pliable. Because they're dangling this carrot in front of you that says, "Comply, and go home." And they toss in a few extras. One of the cadre told me in 1968, "Merely because the war ends is no reason for you to go home. If your attitude is not correct, you may rest here after the war." And ties that in with something he said a few months before, "We are here to tell you the truth of the situation today, and if you do not believe us, we will tell you tomorrow. And if you do not believe us tomorrow, we will tell you the day after, and the day after, until one day, if you don't die first, you'll believe us, and then you can go home." And so you have that carrot dangling in front of you which is "Going Home," and that is something you really want to do, because the environment is so oppressive that you want to get out of it, and yet what he is telling you is that there is no way out except our way.

17 Well, there is a way, initially, and that's escape, but that's hard. I tried three times and failed, and a fourth time it took a B-52 strike, and Cobras and light observation helicopters to get me out, which is a rotten way to do it, but it worked. But this is the only other way an American has out at the immediate time. The people in the prison camps in North Vietnam are not so fortunate. Like Bob Frishman said one time, "You know, even if you do get out of the camp, where does a round-eye go in downtown Hanoi wearing striped pajamas?" So this is one thing that the prisoners in North Vietnam don't even have to hope for. The prisoners in South Vietnam have this to look forward to, if they are strong enough to do it. But generally speaking, you are kept so physically weak that you can't.

Yet you keep trying. So you are closed in on from all sides, and they seem to give you the only way out. But to take their way means you are going to compromise everything you believe in.

18 Now there have been individuals who have done this without really believing it, just going along to get out. The cases are very few, and I think the Communists have found that the Americans are probably the most insincere group of people they have ever come in contact with. The only thing is when a man comes out, if this has actually happened, when he finds that freedom is something of a hollow thing, because he has given more to get that freedom than it was worth. He's got to live with himself the rest of his life. This is one thing people have to think about. I found, for myself, that under this pressure, you find that there is a tight, hard little core inside of everybody, and it is basically faith, a person with a faith in God. This is something they can't challenge, because they don't believe in God. You find that if you can attach your belief to something far above and beyond this dirty little world they've got you in, then you have an opportunity to remove yourself from it. Their understanding of faith or of God is purely ritual and dogma. They've studied our ritual. For instance, every Christmas, they'd come down, like Mafia would come down, and he gave me a candle. He said, "According to our policy, the Front respects the religious beliefs of the POW. Take this candle, go to your net, and burn it for Midnight Mass." And I said, "Look, Mafia, I'm a Protestant, I've already had my little service, and I really don't need a candle, I don't have Midnight Mass." He stuck the candle out and said, "Take it to your net and burn it, we respect your religious beliefs." So I took the candle, I went to my net, and I burned it, for a couple of minutes. This is what they understand about religion. But you find it's a very personal and a very simple communication between one man and his God. And that's all it requires. This is essential, because it removes you from this imprisonment. And you find, I think more importantly, that the Communists have stripped you of everything that identifies you. They strip you of your rank, your position, your money, of status, anything which allows you to identify yourself with material means, to identify yourself as a human being. They are trying to dehumanize you; you might as well be a handful of mud that they pick up off the ground. But faith in God is something that identifies you far more clearly than anything material that we have right now. Once you establish that, then you'll never lose your identity.

19 The second thing was faith in our country and faith in our government. And this they did attack very well. Initially, their Communist propaganda sources were not really effective because it was a Vietnamese writing for American consumption. When Radio Hanoi, the Radio Liberation, and all their bulletins and papers came across, they were using Webster's 1933. The words were either obsolete or obsolescent. I had to look some of them up when I got home to find out what they meant. What they are sending out is things that you will not accept because they are so far out. Like we lost 3,247 aircraft over North Vietnam, which includes five B-52's and three F-111A's. And they said one of the F-111A's was shot down by a girls' militia unit in Haiphong. So we read that and said, "Okay, fine, that's great." The next thing they came up with was that we lost more tanks and artillery than we actually had in Vietnam. Another one they came up with, two of the ones that I really liked, they said that the VC platoon in the Delta had defeated a South Korean company in hand-to-hand combat. I read through that and I sort of scratched my head on that one. The next thing they came up with was during the Tet offensive in 1968, a VC girls' militia squad in Hue, they were called the Twelve Daughters of the Perfume River, which flows through Hue, had defeated a Marine batallion. The first thing I asked the cadre was, "Well, was this hand-to-hand combat, too?" But you know, we read this, and it really didn't affect us.

20 But then, in 1966 and '67, they started dropping all their sources, and we started getting the Congressional Record, magazines, newspapers, articles from the United States. This is what really turned out to be the greatest morale-breaker in the camp. The fact that we were sitting here defending our country and our government and our system, not only against the Communist political cadre, but against individuals right within our own government. And it is difficult to defend yourself when somebody in your own government is calling you an aggressor. This was the greatest weapon that they had. I think this was the thing that was most devastating to my morale personally, because there was no way that I could contest it. This was coming from my country. How do you explain dissent to Communist cadre who have never had the right to dissent in their whole lives? It was something they couldn't understand. And yet even in this context one of the cadre said, "Very soon the people in your country will decide that your coming to Vietnam was a mistake. And at that time those of you who have died here will have died a useless death. And those who lead the Revolution in your country will be the heroes and the saviors. Why should you rot in a jungle prison camp when you can return to your home, join the Revolution, repent of your crimes, and live with your family?" And you sit there and you say, "Why?" And then you begin to evaluate; and I found that no matter how many negatives they came up with, on our side, we always had more positives than the system that they were advocating. And there was always a chance for change within our system, whereas in the system they offered there was no chance for change. We got everything about the demonstrations, the riots, and the anti-war movement. I looked at the groups, the photographs of the college students carry VC flags, the American flags being desecrated, and the one thing I thought of was, well, what if these people did this in Czechoslovakia, or Hungary, or Communist China? And I thought, "Thank God they are in the United States and they've got the right to do it." But it was disturbing to me, because nobody wants to die for nothing.

21 The other thing that came up was a faith in the other American POWs. You find that these are the only friends you've got. The communist cadre are going to try to convince you that they are your friends, but you learn rapidly that all they are doing is exploiting you, they're using you as a tool. When you see an American prisoner giving up his meager ration of fish, just so another American who is sick can have a little bit more to eat, that is sacrifice. Because when you don't have anything and you give it up, or you have very little and you give it up, then you're hurting yourself, and that is true sacrifice. That's what I saw in the prison camp.

22 So those were the three things that I found were a sort of a basis for survival in this environment that's structured to break you down. The one thing they're finding out is that the American prisoners are first of all physically tougher than they ever expected. They read our society as materialistic, as being soft, as being apathetic, and yet they're finding that once they put these prisoners in this situation, and it's a battlefield just like any other, except it's more terrifying because you're fighting in the mind, they are finding that the American prisoners are hanging on. Everybody who has come out has said the same thing— there's three faiths, and these are the three things that stand strong. But the thing is, how long can these people hold up? In my camp, there were eight of us total over the five-year period. Contrary to the VC claims for humanitarian treatment, in my camp alone, out of eight of us, three died of starvation and disease, one was executed, three were released, one of whom was dying, and I escaped before I was executed. This is actuality. This is the fact contrasted with the promise.

23 Since my wife and I have been around the country, the one thing that civilians are asking is "Why doesn't the military do something for its own people? Why don't they do something to help those men?" We're starting. We just got a letter from Fort Knox the other day in Fort Campbell, and both of them are starting a Concern for POW drive; the whole posts are turning out. This is the type of thing that needs to be done, because it could be any one of us, and it could be any one of the military families of men on this post. I had one individual that told me on one occasion, "Why should we do it, when we've got too much other to do, the Red Cross, the Officers' Wives' Club, the various things that we have to do?" and the only thing I could think of was "Just pray to God that your husband doesn't get captured some day, and you have to ask somebody else for help." I think this is the saddest commentary, that the families and loved ones of these men have to go out and seek help, not only from the military community, but from the civilian community, for their husbands, and their fathers. This is to me something that needs to be changed, and it's not so much that the people don't care, it is just that most people don't know.

24 I'm thankful for the opportunity I had to come today, to perhaps enlighten you a little bit as to what does happen inside the camps. Thank you.

The Future of Black Politics: From the Margin to the Mainstream
Eddie N. Williams

Eddie Williams is the President of the Joint Center for Political and Economic Studies. The Center is "organized to provide, on a nonpartisan basis, research, public policy analysis, and information programs for black and other minority elected and appointed officials." The Center also monitors elections throughout the country and collects and disseminates statistical data of all aspects of black political participation.

Williams delivered this address on "The Future of Black Politics" at an annually sponsored institute by the Public Affairs Council at Pomona, California (January 7, 1991). The Council is a nonpartisan professional organization of corporate public affairs executives. The Council exists to encourage members of the business community to be active, informed participants in political affairs. Its members are to provide thoughtful leadership in terms of corporate citizenship and social responsibility.

What attempts at audience adaptation do you see in this address? You may want to begin with the introduction and ask how Williams seeks to fulfill the goal of a good speech introduction? For example, how does he attempt to make his subject important to the audience and, in that sense, build a need to listen? How does he relate the rest of the address to the audience?

When we talk about the "strategic design of a speech" we commonly think of a persuasive address. Nevertheless, informative speeches are designed strategically in terms of an audience as well. Make a careful study of the flow of ideas in this speech and try to determine how the speech is strategically unfolded for the audience. How does Williams make use of the technique of numbering points?

The conclusion of this speech is of special interest. Call to mind what you know about speech conclusions and assess Williams' conclusion.

This speech is reprinted by permission from *Vital Speeches of the Day,* March 15, 1991, pp. 348–350.

1 The beginning of a new year is a tempting time to peer into the future, and the prospect of a new century just nine years from now is enough to bring out the futurist in all of us.

2 For Americans who advocate social change or who merely accommodate to it, the year 2000 has come to symbolize the dramatic demographic changes that are transforming our nation. From a country that used to think of itself as almost entirely European in heritage, we have become a nation whose diversity reflects a mosaic of all the people of the world.

3 As leaders of the business community—indeed, as the eyes and ears of your companies—you are certainly familiar with the increasing diversity of your markets and your work forces. The inevitability of demographic change, as well as some of the implications of that change, was underscored in the Hudson Institute's report for the Labor Department on *Workforce 2000.* By the beginning of the next century, four out of every five people entering the American work force will be minorities, women, and immigrants. One in every

three Americans will be a racial minority. In fact, in the next century the phrase "racial minority" may become less meaningful because no racial, ethnic, or color group will comprise an absolute majority of Americans. In many political jurisdictions today we already find a majority of minorities, and it is clear that the nation as a whole is headed in that direction.

4 And, as you know so well, this changing America will be facing growing competition in a complex and ever-changing world economy. Just one year from now, the countries of western Europe will be coming together as a common economic entity. Meanwhile, the economic powerhouses of the Pacific—Japan, Korea, Taiwan, and Singapore—will continue to be formidable competitors.

5 Looking at our changing nation and the changing world in which we live, one fact is clear: America will need the talents and productive skills of every worker, every student, and every citizen if we are to prosper and prevail in the twenty-first century. As the United Way of America would say, we must bring out the best in all of us—those who have been locked out of economic and social opportunities as well as those who have always enjoyed such opportunities.

6 America's continued success—and perhaps even America's continued survival—will depend on our ability to resolve the great historic question that our country has wrestled with since its founding: Will this nation fulfill its promise of justice for all—its promise of a fair opportunity to participate in the economic, political, and social life of our society?

7 The subject which I will discuss today—the evolution of black politics—is central not only to the future of black Americans but of all Americans and indeed to the future of our nation. And it is directly relevant to your businesses. In a democratic society politics is not only the key to governance but to opportunities and resources as well. And to the extent that blacks and others who are disadvantaged master the art of politics, especially in an era of increasing diversity, they not only enhance their own life chances but they also help the nation to fulfill its promise of both liberty and justice for all.

8 During the quarter century since passage of the Voting Rights Act, the growth of black political power has been both a barometer of change and a strategic weapon in the continuing struggle for full equality.

9 By virtually any measure, since 1965, blacks have made giant strides toward full participation in the political process.

- We and our allies have torn down all of the official obstacles to voting; eliminated most of the devices that dilute our votes; and have opened up elected offices at every level of government—except the presidency.
- In relative voting terms, we have narrowed the gap between blacks and whites—from over 12 percentage points to about 4 points.

- From less than 500 black elected officials in 1965, there are now more than 7,400 officials. In the capital of the old confederacy, L. Douglas Wilder serves as governor. In our nation's two largest cities—New York and Los Angeles—and in Philadelphia, Detroit, Washington, D.C., and more than 300 other cities across this country, black men and women serve as mayors. In the aftermath of the 1990 elections, there are now 26 black members of the U.S. House of Representatives, including the first black republican in more than half a century.
- In fact, so far only the presidency and vice presidency have eluded blacks. The 1984 and 1988 Jesse Jackson presidential candidacies, the Wilder and Dinkins elections, and the selection of Ron Brown as Democratic National Chairman and Bill Gray as House Majority Whip—all suggest that the nation's highest offices may not be beyond reach.

10 The road to these offices may also be paved with political successes at the state and local levels where black influence is growing significantly.

11 With the election last November of William Jefferson to the New Orleans congressional seat previously held by Lindy Boggs, blacks now hold every congressional seat in the nation with a black majority. And similar trends are coming to a crest at every level of politics, from school boards, to city halls, to state houses. These trends will continue as the black population becomes more concentrated in political jurisdictions. But this is old news.

12 What is new today, however, is the historic breakthrough blacks are beginning to make in predominantly white political jurisdictions. This is today's big news: the mainstreaming of black politics has enormous implications for the nation's political process, for the vitality of our society, and for the competitiveness of our economy.

13 There are important precedents for the kind of politics we see emerging today. More than a century ago, blacks held statewide offices in the south, during reconstruction. A quarter century ago, a black republican, Edward Brooke, made headlines and history when he was elected to the United States Senate from Massachusetts. Another milestone came in 1973, when Tom Bradley won election as Mayor of Los Angeles, a city whose electorate is less than 20 percent black.

14 Mayor Bradley may have become the contemporary role model for a new breed of black elected officials whose base is in the black community but who can also win the support of whites, Latinos, Asian-Americans, Jews, and other segments of our diverse society.

15 The Bradley model became even more salient when he almost won the governorship of California in 1982.

16 The dawn of the 1990's brought more examples of this new breed of political leader: Wilder, Dinkins, Mayor Norman Rice of Seattle, Mayor John Daniels of New Haven—the list keeps growing. And even in North Carolina, Harvey Gantt won 35 percent of the white vote despite Jesse Helms' racial demogoguery. And now, a black legislator, Daniel Blue, Jr., is heavily favored to be elected Speaker of the North Carolina House of Representatives.

17 Just as a quarter century ago, when the cutting edge of the civil rights movement shifted from protest to politics, we are now witnessing the beginning of an equally momentous change—from the margins to the mainstream of the American political system. Today, blacks are no longer limited to the periphery of the political system. After more than a century of struggle, they have gained access to the political system; after decades of painstaking organizing, they have built a formidable base in predominantly black communities; and now, they are building coalitions across racial lines, winning public offices in predominantly white jurisdictions and capturing leadership positions that can influence the full spectrum of public policies—from civil rights and human services to economics, foreign policy, and national security.

18 What we are witnessing as we approach the 21st century is a shift from the politics of marginality to the politics of mainstream; from the politics of access to the politics of opportunities and from the politics of rights to the politics of resources. It is this dramatic process of evolution that promises to shape the future of American politics as the demographic profile of the nation continues to change.

19 While this evolutionary process is still unfolding, I believe there are already three generalizations that can be drawn about the emerging black politics.

20 First, and perhaps foremost, it is a politics of inclusion, a politics that reaches across the barriers of race, ethnicity, and color. It is a politics that encompasses the protection of basic rights, to be sure, but it also envisions the achievement of other hopes and aspirations in the context of pursuing the larger goals of the nation as a whole. In the words of Louis Martin, the godfather of black politics, it is a politics that "draws the larger circle."

21 This is the kind of inclusiveness that characterized the campaigns of Wilder, Dinkins, Bradley, and Gantt. The Jackson presidential candidacy also evolved into a more inclusive mode in 1988. You will recall that while Jackson continued to stress his concern for the disadvantaged of America, he called for policies that addressed the entire electorate. He campaigned against factory closings and farm foreclosures; he marched in picket lines in urban ethnic neighborhoods and opened campaign headquarters in rural Iowa; his staff included Hispanics and Jews, Asian Americans and southerners. He carried Michigan and he made strong showings in Vermont, Hawaii, Maine, and Wisconsin—states with relatively small black populations.

22 The second generalization we can make about the new black politics is that it differs in tone and temper from the politics of the '60s. While it remains firmly grounded in moral values, it is no longer a politics based primarily on civil rights laws and moral suasion. Yes, the issues of access to employment and health care are as morally compelling as the issues of access to voting rights and public accommodations; but there is room for honest disagreement and principled compromise on the policy issues of the 90's in ways that there was not on the issues of the 60's. Thus, these new priorities are pursued not only with appeals to conscience but also with appeals to enlightened self-interest. They are not characterized by non-negotiable demands but by the give-and-take of traditional politics.

23 Third, the emerging black politics is increasingly the politics of a new generation. Of course, many of our political pace-setters are indeed veterans of the struggles of the 60's. But, increasingly, black political leaders—both those with multiracial constituencies as well as those in heavily black jurisdictions—will be men and women who proudly proclaim their gratitude to the civil rights movement but who were born too late to participate in it. When the Voting Rights Act was passed in 1965, for example, Congressmen Mike Espy of Mississippi and Alan Wheat of Missouri were teenagers. Understandably, this new generation of leadership will have a different style, a different vocabulary, and even different priorities from the generations that preceded it.

24 The emerging black politics is oriented not only to the historic conflicts between blacks and whites but to the changing relationships among the varied hues of our increasingly multi-ethnic environment. All across this country, from California to New York, and from Chicago to Miami, it is increasingly important for African-American politicians not only to consolidate their base among blacks and to reach out to whites but also to build support among Latinos, Asian-Americans, and other politically prominent segments of an ever-more-variegated society.

25 While all political leaders should reach out to every group within our society, such outreach is particularly important for black political leaders whose traditional bases in central cities are increasingly being integrated by Latinos and Asians. Despite differences in heritage and culture, all these groups share common concerns like job opportunities, better schools, affordable housing and health care, and safe streets.

26 Reaching out to other minorities means that blacks must make an effort to speak their language—in policy terms to be sure, but, sometimes, even literally, especially in states like California, Florida, and Texas.

27 Black politicians are challenged to show the same cultural sensitivity to other minorities that we ask them and white politicians to show to us. Latinos and Asians may share some of blacks' specific concerns as minorities with issues such as discrimination in education and employment, but they may not relate to all the specific slogans and symbolism of the civil rights movement. Thus, new political styles and pragmatic coalitions are needed to achieve mutual goals in the era of multiracial and multicultural politics.

28 These three generalizations contain, I think, some of the most salient features of the kind of mainstream black politics that I see emerging today. Whether mainstream strategies will in fact become the dominant thrust of black political empowerment in the years ahead or will give way to some other approach, including—quite possibly—a reversion to protest politics, will depend, in large measure, on two factors. One is how mainstream politics plays in the larger black community; and the other is whether it leads to significant improvements in the social and economic status of the black population.

29 To be sure, there is a lively, healthy, and sometimes confrontational debate within the black community today about the consequences—and the costs—of this evolution in black politics. A few influential blacks question whether the prize is worth the price. They see "mainstream politics" as a device for distracting black public officials from black concerns and for coopting the black electorate in a national political system that often ignores their hopes and aspirations.

30 From a black perspective, each of these dangers is real; but none need be inevitable.

31 First—and most importantly—these trends need not amount to what Howard University Professor Ron Walters has provocatively called "the death of black politics."

32 Predominantly black constituencies will continue to exist, and they will continue to elect effective and aggressive leadership in the tradition of Adam Clayton Powell, Shirley Chisholm, and Richard Hatcher. And these officials can always be relied on to articulate the black agenda in its boldest form.

33 But, the trends that I have described today serve to increase, rather than compromise, black political power, while allowing for expanded black representation beyond constituencies with heavy black majorities. Indeed, many of the forerunners of what has been called "crossover" politics—including Harold Washington, Tom Bradley, Douglas Wilder, and David Dinkins—all had their roots in the politics of overwhelming black communities. And—as Governor Wilder has demonstrated once again in his eloquent criticism of President Bush's veto of the Civil Rights Act—"crossover politics" most certainly need not mean abandoning the black community.

34 Second, the inalienable right to protest need never be sacrificed to the expediencies of politics.

35 I think black people in America are stronger, not weaker, because there is a black governor of Virginia, black mayors in 300 cities, and black public officials at virtually every level of government.

36 We haven't forfeited the right to picket the city halls of New York, Los Angeles, Philadelphia, or Detroit, any more than labor and industry forfeit the right to protest the actions of public officials they helped to elect. Yes, we can still fight city hall—even when one of our own is sitting in the mayor's chair!

37 A third factor that commends mainstream politics is that, framing black demands in non-racial terms may be shrewd salesmanship, not "selling out."

38 As Jesse Jackson explains so effectively, the majority of black Americans have the same needs as the majority of Americans of every race: good jobs at good wages; health insurance for our families; decent, drug-free schools for our children—these priorities have universal appeal. They are more likely to be achieved by a broad-gauged policy coalition.

39 In short, what we see on the horizon is not the death of black politics but its growth and maturation.

40 The question for the future is not only whether black political leaders will seek to appeal to the larger society, but also how the larger society will respond.

41 And, as business leaders, as community leaders, and simply as citizens, you as well as I have a vital interest in how that question is resolved.

42 As I indicated at the beginning of these remarks, today more than ever America needs the talents and productive skills of all of its people. Our future will depend, to a considerable extent, on how successfully we can enlist the participation of all our people in the economy and in the political system and on how well we help them achieve their version of the "American Dream."

43 Thus America, and especially the corporate and political sectors, should see in the mainstreaming of black politics an opportunity to further integrate blacks into the economic and political mainstreams of our society. This means aggressively identifying ways to pursue our mutual interest.

44 Mutual enlightened self-interest is the key. Across the barriers of race, ethnicity, color, and station, we must take the time to identify the critical junctures where our various interests intersect. In most cases this is likely to be the point at which the national interest is paramount.

45 For some of you in the business community, black politics is an alien, sometimes threatening phenomenon. It should not be. It is as American as apple pie. All that is different is the profile of the people seeking a fairer share of the opportunities and resources of our society. Through the politics of inclusion, they are addressing issues that are vital not only to black Americans but to all Americans.

46 As we enter an era of dramatic demographic changes in the labor force, in the electorate, and in our multicolored and multicultural society, we are all being challenged to appreciate the fact that the politics of democracy is the politics of diversity.

47 Looking to the future, I am reminded of these lines from a poem by James Russell Lowell:

New occasions teach new duties;
Time makes ancient good uncouth;
They must upward still and onward
Who would keep abreast of truth."

Inventors, Invention and Innovation
Robert M. White

Robert M. White, President of the National Academy of Engineering of the United States, delivered this speech as the Inventors Day Address to the Allied Signal Corporation, Morristown, New Jersey, April 18, 1990. The National Academy of Engineering is a private, honorary organization; its members are elected in recognition of their distinguished and continuing contributions to engineering. The Academy, along with the National Academy of Sciences, advises the federal government through the National Research Council. Allied Signal Corporation is a company whose operations are conducted in three business areas: aerospace, automotive, and engineered materials. The company's products are used by numerous industries in textiles, construction, plastics, telecommunications, and so forth.

White's goal in this address is to increase understanding of the importance of the innovative process to invention. He begins the speech with a past-present introduction concerning American invention, and then notes that presently America's leadership in invention is challenged by other nations, especially by the Japanese. He begins the body of the speech by defining invention (6–7). Here you may want to analyze his approach to definition, and identify other approaches to definition a speaker may use. He next broadens the discussion to the contexts in which inventions tend to occur (8–12). This is critical to developing the importance of his subject to the listening audience. By paragraph 13 he approaches "need to listen" directly when he tells the audience that "invention can make entire industries and companies obsolete." You may want to discuss the importance of relating ideas and information to the audience in speeches that have as their goal to increase understanding. For one thing, the speaker must make the audience appreciate the significance of the information presented.

You may want to discuss how White leads listeners to an appreciation of the importance of innovation to invention and gets them to understand their possible roles in innovation. Can you identify any special rhetorical techniques that he uses in this process? How does he use praise for the audience in achieving his purpose?

This speech is reprinted by permission from *Vital Speeches of the Day,* July 15, 1990, pp. 593–596.

1 I welcome this opportunity to join with you and the Allied Signal community to honor inventors and invention. Let me begin by saying that I believe invention—and inventors—are as critical to the advancement of our nation's economic growth in the 1990s as they were in what we sometimes think of as the Golden Age of Invention in the 1890s. In his book *American Genesis,* author Thomas Hughes states that "inventors, industrial scientists, engineers, and system builders have been the makers of modern America." Looking back over the past hundred years of American history, and looking around this room today, one has to agree with him.

2 In terms of invention, the past century has been like no other in history. In one century—only a moment in historical time—inventors have given the world the automobile, the airplane, the earth-orbiting satellite, the radio, the television, and countless other wonders. From noninvasive medical diagnostic systems to new pharmaceuticals to microchips and space shuttles, perhaps more progress has been made in the past century in raising the standard of living everywhere than has been made in all the preceding centuries. Our inventions have even permitted man to reach beyond the earth to other extraterrestrial bodies.

3 The productivity of some individual inventors during these years was awesome. Some became folk heroes, lionized and celebrated. The output of the giants of the early years of this century—Edison, Bell, Tesla, Wright, Sperry—was prodigious. A thousand patents for Edison, 350 for Sperry. This kind of productivity is hard to match. However, that kind of productivity can still be found. Indeed here at Allied Signal I'm told there are individuals who can chalk up as many as 300 patents to their credit.

4 But today, some point to the fact that the Japanese are now filing more U.S. patents than Americans—that American ingenuity is running out of steam. There's no question that the numbers have changed as other nations have recognized the central role of invention in economic success. But the number of patents awarded is not the sole measure of the health of the creative enterprise. Indeed scientific discovery and invention are not a problem in this country. We do very well. Discovery and invention now take place throughout the world as scientific and engineering capabilities grow in many countries. Despite recent progress, the problem in the United States has been in the rapid translation into quality products and services—in short, the process of innovation.

5 Let us step back for a moment and examine the role of invention historically to give us some perspective on our problems. In the landscape of human thought, inventions are the peaks. They support all social progress. Their roots lie deep in the subsoil of a fostering institutional, cultural, or social framework, without which they are as unlikely as an Everest without its foothills.

6 Invention is more than the development of useful and productive devices, although these are vital for material progress. Instead, it is a manifestation of the creativity in all human activities. The invention of the Gothic arch permitted the soaring cathedrals of the Middle Ages and the Renaissance. The paintings of Monet and Pissarro brought us the glories of impressionism. Our daily lives are uplifted by the songs of Irving Berlin and the symphonies of Betthoven.

7 In short, invention is where you find it. And so it is in industry. Whatever the function, whether in research and development, design, production, or distribution of goods and services, inventions are at the root of new products and processes and also the source of the economic success of companies. Inventions are the lifeblood coursing through the heart of industrial competitiveness.

8 One cannot overemphasize the importance of the context in which invention occurs. These contexts can be cultural, social, economic, or organizational and managerial. Civilizations and societies rise and fall in large measure on their ability to provide a context in which invention leads to innovation—the process by which invention is translated into useful building blocks for social development. Paper was a Chinese invention of the second century and the basis of a widely diffused culture of learning and social achievement that in turn translated to a civilization of the highest achievements. The compass and the quadrant, and later the chronometer and sextant, were great inventions of the age of global exploration, which led to the hegemony of the West over much of the world.

9 Great waves of economic progress have periodically changed the face of society related to the times of great outbursts of invention. The inventions are so sweeping that they completely transform the institutions of society, the general welfare of people, the economies of nations, and the fate of individual industries. These periods of innovation correspond to shifts in the locus of economic and political leadership among nations.

10 Those who have studied the process have identified three major cycles of invention leading to modern times. The first was associated with the development of textile manufacturing, the factory system, and steam power from about 1750 to the middle of the next century. The second embraced the development of railroads and iron and steel technology from about 1850 to about the turn of the century. The first half of this century has been characterized as the era of electrical power, the internal combustion engine, the automobile, and the growth of the chemical industry. We are now in a fourth cycle, dominated by new technologies of electronics, computers, semiconductors, aerospace, pharmaceuticals, biotechnology, materials, and yes, nuclear power.

11 It is interesting to note that the full implications of inventions at the time of their development were frequently not understood either by the inventors or by companies or industries that were vitally affected. The steam engine was invented in Britain to pump water from coal mines. Only much later did steam power become the basis for railroad transportation systems, the generation of electricity, the powering of factories, and the social and economic revolution caused by them. In fact railroads when first put into operation were visualized only as overland ways to connect canal transportation systems.

12 It is also interesting to note that inventions that displace existing technologies are frequently developed outside the industry providing the services with the old technology. Carriage makers did not participate significantly in the development of the internal combustion engine and the automobile. Stagecoach companies did not participate in the development of the steam engine and modern railroads, that supplanted them. The makers of vacuum tubes, the principal elements of electronic systems until two decades ago, failed to participate significantly in semiconductor development, the backbone of modern electronic systems. John Mayo, executive vice president of AT&T Bell Laboratories, calls these "killer" inventions.

13 The lesson for companies is that invention can make entire industries and companies obsolete. For this reason one of the central concerns of managers must be the potential of inventions to outflank their business and render it obsolete. Keeping abreast of inventions everywhere and their potential for affecting company futures becomes a sine qua non for management of all companies. And today when discovery and invention take place throughout the world as science and engineering knowledge diffuse globally, this becomes an even more important and more difficult task.

14 Invention is a many-splendored thing. It can be the logical extension of progress in basic science. Research in solid-state physics led to the invention of the transistor by Bardeen, Brattain, and Shockley. It can proceed from practical needs as did the invention of the integrated circuit by Kilby and Noyce, who were seeking a more efficient and productive system for the manufacture of solid-state circuits. It can occur serendipitously. Any of you who has seen the G.E. television commercial with the cat kicking over a beaker at night in a closed laboratory to create Lexan knows what I mean. Inventions can occur because of a management determination to achieve a specific objective. Quality control techniques in Japan flowed from the persistence of Deming and the determination of Japanese management to make quality the hallmark of their production.

15 Inventors themselves are not very good at predicting the consequences of their work either. Marconi, the discoverer of radio communications, visualized it only as a means of communicating where it was difficult to put wires—hence the term "wireless." He never visualized the broadcast industry. Bob Noyce, the coinventor of the integrated circuit recently commented that at the time of invention neither he nor Jack Kilby imagined the full implications of a new "information society." What the past tells us is that invention and its translation into products, processes, and services are the key to changing the rules of the game. And with ever-shortening product life cycles, the rapid conversion of scientific discovery and invention is the surest way to competitiveness for successful corporations.

16 It was inevitable that industry, recognizing the central value of invention and its translation into products and processes for the market, would move to systematize the process. The distinguishing mark of successful modern industry is its dedication to the process we now call technological innovation. The innovation process itself spans and integrates all of the functions of a modern corporation, from basic research to marketing. For the innovation process to work, all links in this process have to work together.

17 Hiroshi Inose, a Japanese Foreign Associate of the U.S. Academy of Engineering, currently Director General of the Japan Center for Science and Information Systems, reflected on the essence of the process as seen in Japan. In a recently published paper, he wrote

> . . . the necessary condition for a technological innovation to be accomplished successfully is that something new must be introduced to either one or more of the phases of the innovation process, namely, basic research, application research, development, design, production, marketing, distribution and consumption. However, this is not enough. The sufficient condition for successful innovation is that, responding to the introduction of the novel feature, all the links of the process are to function properly to control relevant phases so that the whole process can adjust itself organically and dynamically to provide better products or services.

18 I do not for a moment suggest that the United States is unsuccessful in the innovation process; many of our companies and industries continue as world leaders. It's just that in too many areas we are being bested by our competitors. We all now are well aware that the America that invented the transistor, the integrated circuit, color television, industrial robots, the video recorder, and plain paper copiers has seen great markets ceded to others who have made the innovation process work for them. To paraphrase something Roland Schmitt said at last year's Inventors' Day: "America gets the gold medal for invention, but others get the gold."

19 Because all companies operate in an increasingly integrated global economy, they have found that they can prosper only if their vision is global. The "not invented here" syndrome is a prescription for competitive failure in this new global economy. In a recent paper entitled "The Quiet Path to Technological Preeminence" in the *Scientific American* Robert Reich caught the issue and the need well (and I quote):

> This quiet path back to competitiveness depends less on ambitious government R&D projects aimed at specific technology areas such as supercomputers or high-temperature superconductors than on improving the process by which technological insights—wherever they may be discovered around the globe—are transformed by American workers into high-quality products.
>
> The first step in rapid assimilation of new technologies is to discover what they are. American firms are often slow to learn of a new technological insight achieved elsewhere— whether it is a breakthrough invention, a more efficient method of fabricating and assembling products or a new way of organizing production and distribution. Some American researchers and engineers, whose formal education and early job experiences occurred when the U.S. was far ahead of other nations in developing and using technology, are simply skeptical of foreigners' abilities; anything 'not invented here' is considered of little value.

20 The motivation and sources of innovation are numerous. Recently, the Academy of Engineering completed a major study, *Profiting From Innovation,* in which it examined various ways companies move ideas to the market.

21 The first type of innovation is "technology-driven" innovation. This is what many consider the "classic" case of a bright, new idea that grows into a major commercial success. While we all dream of such sudden success, it rarely happens overnight. This type of innovation, our study found, typically takes 15 to 20 years to go from initial idea to final product. The risk, of course, is that the market will change or evaporate.

22 The second kind of innovation is what we call "product or production driven." Through many quick, incremental improvements, one races to make an existing product better, cheaper, more reliable, or more attractive. The time frame here is not measured in years, but in weeks or months, and the greatest risk is that your competition will get there first. The Japanese have amply demonstrated their ability to move from sufficiency of design toward perfection of design—while the product is on the market.

23 The third type of innovation we've identified is the "market-driven" innovation. Here, you perceive a need in the marketplace—a gap—and you work to find a technological fix. It requires close communication with, and a thorough understanding of, the market. The risk is that the technological fix you pursue will not be the right one, or that the competitor will find a better one before you do.

24 You may be wondering: in all of this talk of racing to the market and knowing the end user, where does the individual inventor fit in? It is simply that every idea starts in a single mind, which nurtures it and brings it to fruition. In fact, the need has never been greater for ideas and the ability to recognize their worth. While today's environment for independent inventors is not so easy as it was a hundred years ago, it is much easier for the corporate inventor.

25 In 1890, the state of the art—levers, screws, and wedges—was simple and inexpensive. Today, the complexity and cost of instrumentation and other technological support for many devices and products has escalated beyond the means of the independent inventor. This intensive capitalization has created a formidable hurdle to the independent inventor and made it increasingly difficult to go it alone. People still do, of course—the members of our own Academy include Wilson Greatbatch, Arnold Beckman, Bill Hewlett, and Dave Packard. It's not impossible—but the corporation (or the university or the government) offers an advantage.

26 But too often our corporate inventors view their company's organizational structure as an obstacle to be overcome, instead of an asset to be employed. Where they should find support, they frequently find resistance—to change, to new ideas, to the challenges that come with an increasingly global economy. Discouragement drives these potential innovators into "going along to get along," and finally into lethargy, their creative energy blocked by bureaucratic barriers.

27 And this is a challenge to our companies, our universities, and our government to provide the supporting technological and economic environment that will enable the creative juices to flow. We need to leverage the talent of our individual inventors. If innovation is to thrive, we will have to give the inventors a special place in our organizations. Instead of snarling the inventors in red tape, we must use the organizational structure to provide them the freedom to dream. In February, we were pleased to have President Bush at The Academy's first Charles Stark Draper Prize ceremony. In his remarks, he commented that (and I quote): "only men who are free create the inventions and intellectual works which make life worthwhile."

28 Individual freedom can have enormous power when the support of the organization is behind it. There are dozens of examples of what is possible. Wallace Carothers of Du Pont was, as you all know, a brilliant but moody man who, left to himself, might well have lost his way. Under the aegis of a large, supportive organization, which looked after his needs and gave him the freedom necessary to pursue his vision, he gave the world moistureproof cellophane, neoprene, and nylon.

29 And while it may be immodest, I must return to the two recipients of our First Draper Prize. Jack Kilby and Bob Noyce, the inventors of the integrated circuit, must rank with the great inventors of a century ago if we consider the revolution that their chip touched off. What's more, they were working in large companies—which understood their needs and worked with them to make the integrated circuit a commercial reality. Their work proves what can be done when the bureaucracy, if you will, frees inventors to pursue their vision.

30 A structured environment offers great advantages—to relieve the day-to-day pressures of business and the law. It concentrates expertise from dozens of disciplines at the inventor's fingertips. This is vital when the inventions of the day are space shuttles and automated manufacturing lines.

31 It's been said that lab specimens and humor perish when you dissect them. I think that we can add invention to that list—the inventor's inner world is a private one. But innovation is a different story, and we may be able to renew it by taking the process apart and putting it back together again. The American system has worked wonders—and can work wonders again. Our institutions can protect and nurture the spark of innovation. We have in the United States some of the best schools, some of the best companies, and some of the best workers in the world. What we need is not more creativity—we need more freedom to *be* creative.

32 Product life cycles are shortening. Competition, as you well know, is intensifying. With the opening of new markets in Eastern Europe and in the Soviet Union, there will be great opportunities ahead for those who can capitalize on them. If we let our people go to work—if we can get a product into the marketplace before we test and refine it to death, we will succeed.

33 All I have to do to confirm that invention and innovation are alive and well is to look around this room. Each of you who are recognized today for your contributions to invention should be very proud. But the very fact that you *have* succeeded and that you are here today means that many others have succeeded too, by providing the kind of supportive environment in which your ideas could bear fruit.

34 The historical record suggests that the rush of technology will not slow. If you look at the Academy's recent list of the ten outstanding engineering achievements since 1964, you will see what I mean. In 1964, when our Academy was founded, there were no commercial applications of satellites, of lasers, of genetic engineering. No one had played a compact disc or flown in a jumbo jet.

35 It was our inventions and these institutions that made those things possible. As we look toward a new millennium, we will need to develop and incorporate new advances into the political and ethical foundations of a new world in which Berlin Walls and Cold Wars don't loom so large. We will need the creativity of our inventors—people like you. And we will need our corporations and our universities and our government to turn your creations into applications.

36 Once again, I congratulate each of you. You are the advance scouts of technology, and your hard work, vision, and knowledge will become an even greater asset in the years to come. I urge each one of *us* to support you, to protect and nurture that creative spark of invention, and to work on turning invention into innovation. There are great challenges ahead; an inventive nation like our own has, in my opinion, the world's best chance for meeting them and advancing human welfare in the process.

37 Thank you for your kind attention.

Virtual Reality: Immersion in an Artificial World
Steve Harris

This speech was written by Steve Harris, a junior majoring in Economics and International Relations at the University of Wisconsin–Madison. On April 26, 27, and 28, 1991, he delivered this speech at the National Forensic Association Tournament held on the campus of Marshall University in Huntington, West Virginia.

Mr. Harris begins his speech with a hypothetical illustration of virtual reality in action. He names the hero of his illustration "Rifstorc Nurthmuson" a name invented by Jaron Lanier, President of VPL Research. He clothes his hero in Datasuit, Dataglove, and Eyephones. What mood does this illustration create for the speech that follows? Does it effectively capture the attention of the audience?

Effective informative speeches are usually characterized by sound organization, strong transitions, and clear supporting or expository materials. What pattern of organization is used to structure the main ideas in this speech? How does the speaker signal his transition from one major component to the next? Each of the three main points in this speech is supported by well defined subpoints. Identify the subpoints of each main point and the pattern(s) these subpoints reflect. What kinds of verbal supporting materials (expository devices) are used to amplify the speaker's ideas? Do these materials (devices) offer a clear and vivid view of the subject addressed? Mr. Harris concludes his speech in an effective and forceful manner. Where does his conclusion begin? What concluding devices are used?

This speech is printed by permission of Steve Harris, who wishes to express appreciation to William Cosh and Kathryn Olson for serving as his coaches.

1 Rifstorc Nurthmuson's Macintosh computer alerts him to a hazardous waste emergency. He quickly pulls on his Datasuit and Dataglove, and slips his Eyephones over his eyes in order to enter Virtual Reality. Rifstorc tele-operates a robot located at the site of the accident through his Datasuit and glove. These devices calculate every motion he makes, right down to each finger and knuckle. These motions are transmitted to the robot who performs exactly the same movements as Rifstorc. He sees what the robot sees through his Eyephones, giving him the illusion that he is actually cleaning up the toxic mess. As Rifstorc "experiences" the accident site and begins the cleanup, the robot follows his actions and actually does the work.

2 Virtual Reality promises to revolutionize the computer industry. As *Forbes* magazine of February 5, 1990 states, "according to the visionaries and futurists who abound in Silicon Valley, Virtual Reality is where the computer user of the 21st century will telecommunicate, design, and do research." In order to appreciate how this technology will affect our lives, today we will examine what Virtual Reality is, what its capabilities are, and what future applications it may hold.

3 Author Stewart Brand notes in Compute magazine of October 1989, that yesterday's Virtual Reality was the movie theater—the creation of an artificial world. He writes about today's technology, "Virtual Reality is as much of an immersion in an artificial world

as you can get without piping it into your nervous system." We'll now look at the intricacies of Virtual Reality or VR, look at its concepts, and examine its technical components. Compute magazine of the same month defines Virtual Reality as the creation of artificial worlds of experience. It continues, "Virtual Reality devices place you inside a controlled hallucination—the ultimate simulation." In fact, many people have found the experience so compelling, they compare VR to drugs. This coupling was further advanced by a Wall Street Journal article entitled "A Kind of Electronic LSD?"

4 Virtual Reality's basic technology stems from a revolution in how we control computers. According to *Business Week* of February 20, 1989, most computers are manipulated through a keyboard and several cumbersome command keys. Virtual Reality surpasses the mouse in ease of operation by allowing you to control computer functions through your own movements and gestures. Virtual Reality allows you to control computers more naturally. "If you let people manipulate spatial things, you're taking advantage of something they already knew before they knew the word computer," says Paul McAvinney, chairperson of Sensor Frame Corporation, a VR research company. Another company developing this technology is VPL Research located in Silicon Valley, California. They are actively involved in producing hardware equipment used in controlling Virtual Reality software. The VR system already developed by VPL utilizes two pieces of high tech equipment. First is a pair of goggles, called Eyephones, that resemble a scuba mask. But you can't see through Eyephones, because a miniature televison screen is positioned over each eye. These screens bombard the user with a 3-dimensional image. A plastic cube on top of the Eyephones headpiece transmits data to a computer, via a cable running out the back, about the wearer's position in space. The cable runs from the headpiece to an ordinary personal computer.

5 The second piece of equipment is called a Dataglove. *Rolling Stone* magazine of June 14, 1990 describes it as an average spandex rubber glove with several fiber optic cables wired to it. These cables are connected to the same computer as are the Eyephones to communicate where your hand is in space. *Forbes* magazine of February 5, 1990 explains that as the hand is flexed, the light flow along each finger changes enough to be read by a sensor, which in turn transmits these data to the computer. As you make a motion with your hand, the computer shows you what you're doing in the computer environment through your Eyephones. What you see is a disembodied hand on the tiny television screens inside your Eyephones. In essence, you see your motions take the form of a computer generated hand that can manipulate computer generated objects. Not only confined to grabbing objects, the Dataglove also signals the computer to move in the computer generated environment. If you point to the left, the computer pans that direction, as seen on the Eyephones. Point up and you can fly. David Churbuck, writing for *Forbes* in the February 5, 1990 edition, claims to have first grabbed a fish and then pulled it over his head. He states, "I'm inside a hollow fish with two eyes at the far end." Virtual Reality has simplified computer use beyond imagination. Although its technology is unique and revolutionary, it is still simple. Work is being done to perfect a full Datasuit, that will measure every motion of every part of the body. Then this technology will become truly amazing.

6 Turning now to VR's capabilities and limitations, we find that the implications of this technology are staggering. People now have the power to create quickly and easily. Molecular engineers can "pick up" and view a single molecule from all directions. They can reach in and sculpt or mold objects directly on a screen, without typing in commands one at a time as was needed previously. As mentioned in the *Futurist* of May/June 1990, architects can tour a building with a client in Virtual Reality, moving walls and doorways with ease before plans are committed to paper. A surgeon can practice surgical techniques with such a system. The computer would simply read the doctor's hand motions and display the effect on the body organ being resected.

7 But Virtual Reality will certainly not leave the average consumer behind. In fact, *Business Week* of February 20, 1989 claims that Mattel, Inc. has contracted with VPL Research to provide a $75 version of the Dataglove for use with its Nintendo Videogame system. But Virtual Reality's uses extend much further than toys. People will soon be able to take instant vacations anywhere in the world with the help of fiber optics. The *Wall Street Journal* of July 10, 1990 states that fiber will provide remarkably crisp audio and video in order to transport you to another time or place. Not only limited to a Caribbean beach, the president of VPL, Jaron Lanier, claims that programs can be developed to allow us to experience life in ancient Egypt or over the rainbow in the land of Oz.

8 All of these features, however, are not yet possible. In order for a person to virtually travel to another place, computer software must first be created containing information such as the location of buildings and the appearance of landscape. Another cosmetic problem mentioned in the *Utne Reader* of March/April 1990 is that it cannot yet perfectly simulate reality. When you pick up a virtual baseball, you can see on your Eyephones that you are grasping it, but you cannot actually feel the baseball in your hand. As reported in *Forbes* of February 5, 1990, researchers are developing a method to provide tactile feedback, so the user can touch and feel computer generated objects. In addition, 3-dimensional sound and eye tracking are features being developed. Eye tracking will enable wearers to pan and zoom in response to eye movement instead of head movement. But VR's limitations extend beyond non-perfect reality simulations. The picture provided by the program software is described in *Maclean's* magazine of June 4, 1990 as "crude, Saturday morning cartoon quality." Also, the computer is not powerful enough to keep up with your movements. As a result, you see a jerky movement in Virtual Reality. Although a more advanced, powerful computer would solve the previous problem, the research companies have rejected it based on cost. Currently, according to *Maclean's* of the same date, the Eyephones cost over

$11,000, the Dataglove $10,500, and the entire package about $267,000. So although Virtual Reality's capabilities are amazing, its limitations are significant and being diligently overcome at the VR development labs of VPL Research, Sendor Frame, and Autodesk, Inc.

9 The possible future applications for Virtual Reality have the potential to alter almost all aspects of life. The *Utne Reader* of March/April 1990 mentions a few applications. Wearers could perform ultra-precision work with the aid of robots, such as cleaning up after a nuclear disaster without endangering human life. NASA intends to develop a VR system to enable a technician to repair spacecraft and satellites from earth. Medicine will also be transformed by Virtual Reality. A doctor in one country could perform surgery in another by donning Virtual Reality hardware connected to a robot. *The Futurist* of May/June 1990 states that VR could be used for "internal surgery." A microrobot would be swallowed by the patient and would perform surgical work from the inside, while being guided by a human surgeon seeing the inside of the patient through Virtual Reality. If plans for a full Datasuit become realized, Wimbledon could take place in Virtual Reality. *Forbes* magazine of February 5, 1990 claims that if Boris Becker and Ivan Lendl were placed in Datasuits and Eyephones, Wimbledon could take place in both Sweden and Germany.

10 But let's get back to reality. Plans are already underway by General Electric, NASA, and the Army to develop a helicopter training simulator. The system uses fiber optics to create amazing video displays. Its life-like images of simulated crashes can make promising pilots physically ill. Another realistic application down the line may make business more efficient. The *Wall Street Journal* of July 10, 1990 states that costly business travel could be reduced if companies used Virtual Reality for teleconferencing. In fact, large meetings may one day be possible with every member in a different part of the country. Using fiber optics, you could see a life-like image of everyone and hear them with crystal clarity. *Rolling Stone* of June 14, 1990 quotes an Autodesk Corporation document as saying, "It is quite likely that the technology will supplant commuting." Although these futuristic applications may seem far-fetched, most researchers predict that many of the statements here will be fully realized within the next decade.

11 Virtual Reality is an extraordinary, new technology that may very well change our lives. While its more amazing applications may be realized only in future years, for now VR devices such as the Dataglove and Eyephones allow us to manipulate computers more naturally. Virtual Reality's capabilities affect science, art, medicine, and space exploration. One day, systems based on today's technology may alter our lives completely. Eventually, Rifstorc Nurthmuson, in addition to getting a better name, may become more than just a scenario character and begin saving real lives using Virtual Reality.

A debate taping between Middletown, New York Mayor Earl Moody, State Senator Ricard Stout, Dr. Paul Tillett, and Joan Konner—Dean of Graduate School of Journalsm, Columbia University.

CHAPTER 4

SPEECHES THAT AFFIRM PROPOSITIONS OF FACT

Matters of fact…are very stubborn things.

Matthew Tindal

THE NATURE AND IMPORTANCE OF SPEECHES THAT AFFIRM PROPOSITIONS OF FACT

There are instances of discourse when a speaker tries to prove to the satisfaction of an audience that a proposition of fact is, in reality, true. While the preceding chapter was concerned with the art of interpreting established knowledge or original inquiry for the *enlightenment of an audience,* the present chapter is devoted to the principles involved in *establishing an alleged truth in order to win agreement.* Earlier, the primary task for the speaker was to help an audience understand an event, process, concept, or inquiry; in this chapter, the speaker's efforts are directed toward seeking approval of the "facts" that are presented. In the previous speech form, the speaker might publicly analyze, "What is the present state of space exploration?"; in this chapter, the speaker seeks to gain acceptance of a conclusion: "The American program of space exploration is without military significance."

The social environments that produce speeches affirming factual propositions are diverse. A district attorney may seek to establish the guilt of a labor leader charged with misuse of union funds. The president of a liberal arts college may try to convince the board of regents that faculty salaries are not equal to those of competing schools. A state legislator may attempt to prove to his or her constituency that the condition of state highways will deter expansion of the tourist industry. While in certain instances the affirmation of a proposition of fact is the sole purpose of a persuasive speech, at other times a speaker may affirm a fact as a means of affirming a value, creating concern for a problem, or gaining acceptance for a course of action. On the whole, matters of fact are more commonly argued in relation to one of those ends than they are as separate entities.

In the quotation opening this chapter, Matthew Tindal expresses an awareness that matters of fact are not self-evident. In the common vernacular, the term *fact* connotes an incontrovertible truth. Thus the novitiate to the advocate's art seeks to stifle further argument by asserting, "It's a fact"—by which it is meant, "It is uncontestable truth." But "Matters of fact . . . are very stubborn things." Were all facts self-evident, there would be no such thing as a proposition of fact because the term *proposition* implies a statement about an unsettled or controversial state of affairs.

What, then, is a proposition of fact? A proposition of fact may be defined as a statement (a sentence with assertive content) that may be affirmed or denied through tests of *existence, occurrence,* or *causality.* The fact in question may concern an individual, an event, a process, a condition, a concept, or even a policy. Whatever the fact to be judged, however, the advocate is primarily interested in gaining listener acceptance that something was, is, or will be true. Consider these examples:

Proposition A: The Great Depression was caused by excessive speculation on the stock market.

Proposition B: The Japanese attack on Pearl Harbor was precipitated by United States failure to provide military safeguards.

Proposition C: The sightings of flying saucers are real events.

Proposition D: Marijuana smoking is harmless.

Proposition E: The nuclear family as we know it will utlimately become obsolete.

Proposition F: The absence of the player reserve clause will ultimately cause the demise of major league baseball.

Although these six propositions differ substantially in subject matter, they are all legitimate factual propositions. Propositions A and B concern matters of past causality. Propositions C and D concern matters of present existence and causality. Propositions E and F concern matters of future occurrence and future causality respectively.

Whatever the subject matter and tense of a factual proposition, its proposer is interested in gaining audience acceptance of an alleged truth. The following section identifies the criteria that are especially relevant for evaluating speeches that affirm propositions of fact.

CRITERIA FOR EVALUATING SPEECHES THAT AFFIRM PROPOSITIONS OF FACT

Because propositions of fact treat supposedly verifiable or predictable phenomena, the tests of speeches affirming such propositions are strongly concerned with the logical sufficiency of the affirmation.

1. *Has the speaker adequately assessed the proof requirements of the factual proposition?*

Implicit in a proposition of fact is the assumption that there are reasonable criteria with which to judge the truth of alleged events, states of being, causal relationships, and so on. Proof requirements are often field dependent; that is, they differ from one area of knowledge or profession to another. For example, the affirmation of a proposition of medical fact may require that standards on the observation and clinical diagnosis of patients be met. The affirmation of a proposition of historical fact, on the other hand, may require that standards relevant to sound historical research be met. Lawyers, behavioral scientists, chemists, mathematicians, and astronomers have all devised standards by which certain types of phenomena are to be judged. When talking to a specialized group about a specialized topic, the speaker can expect that the proposition will be judged by the special proof requirements established by that profession as a modus operandi.

In the world of ordinary discourse, the criteria by which propositions of fact are judged are less well defined and less rigorous. However, even the popular proposition of fact demands that the speaker employ responsible standards of assessment. If popular speakers fail to support their assertions or if they support them with emotional appeals and shallow truisms, they will be criticized for their faulty interpretation of the responsible proof requirements of their propositions. Enlightened lay critics do not excuse the maxims and pseudo-arguments of modern mass media advertisements even though they are aware of the logical permissiveness of the American consuming public.

2. *Has the speaker offered acceptable arguments in support of the proposition of fact?*

Given that a speaker demonstrates awareness of the general proof requirements of a particular factual proposition, the next question to be raised is "Has the speaker offered relevant arguments—reasons for belief—in support of the proposition of fact?" Imagine, for example, that a district attorney seeks to affirm the proposition that "a labor leader is guilty of misusing union funds." Imagine, further, that our barrister has recognized that the particular proof demands that must be met are those of the bar rather than the public forum. We may then question whether the arguments that are selected support the conclusion that the labor leader is guilty of misusing union funds. We might expect, for example, that it would be argued that (1) the labor leader in question did spend union funds on nonunion activities, (2) legal precedence makes the misuse of union funds a criminal offense, and (3) the expenditure of the funds in question is classifiable as a misuse in light of legal precedence. Should our lawyer fail to offer any of these arguments or should irrelevant nonlegal arguments be offered in their place, we may deny that a convincing case in support of the proposition has been made.

In the world of everyday discourse, the specific argument or arguments necessary for the establishment of a factual proposition are largely dependent on the criteria of sufficiency employed by the listener/critic receiving the argument. As an enlightened critic the listener should consider the possible reasons that make the argument advanced questionable. Assume, for instance, the following argument:

Proposition (claim):   Capital punishment is not an effective deterrent to crime.

Reason (justification):   The states that have capital punishment have more serious crimes than the states that do not have capital punishment.

Will you accept this argument? What possible exceptions or reservations to this argument might you legitimately raise? Should you note that there are serious differences between the states that have capital punishment and those that do not, you are well on your way to discrediting the argument. Should you know that the capital-punishment states are highly populated urban areas, while the noncapital-punishment states are essentially rural and less populous, you may raise one important reservation to the argument. Should you know that the states with capital punishment have a higher incidence of poverty, unemployment, and racial antagonism, you may raise another serious reservation.

Thus, in evaluating an argument, the critic must ask whether there is cause to question the sufficiency of it. If there are reasonable reservations and if the speaker has failed to refute them, the argument may be denied.

3. *Has the speaker provided adequate evidence in support of arguments?*

In some fields of argument, the nature of adequate evidence is carefully specified. For example, the rules of evidence of the American bar are rather carefully specified. In the courtroom, there are rules governing the admissibility and inadmissibility of evidence. Historians, scientists, and behavioral scientists also have some clear notion of what constitutes sound evidence and what does not.

However, in the world of ordinary discourse, evidential requirements are less well known and less well defined. Perhaps the most distinctive characteristic of ordinary arguments on propositions of fact is the reliance of the speaker upon secondary information and uncontrolled, unsystematic observation. Thus, the popular speaker often bases arguments on the *testimony* of others, well-known or verifiable *specific instances,* and *statistical data.* Sometimes speakers use a *literal analogy* or describe a *cause-effect relationship.*

In using *testimony,* the speaker draws evidence from the statements of others. One interesting example of testimonial evidence occurred in the championship debate at the National College Debate Tournament at West Point in 1960. John Raser of San Diego State College sought to prove that "Eventually the public and the nation always get their way in national policy." Having stated what he hoped to prove Mr. Raser went on to say:

> Now that sounds like a strong statement, but I've got more than a few people who tell me it's true. . . . I'd first like to turn to Robert H. Jackson, the former Supreme Court Justice, who should know if anyone does. He said, in *Vital Speeches* in October 1953, that "The practical play of the forces of politics is such that judicial power has often delayed but never permanently delayed the persistent will of substantial majorities." In other words, the majority always gets its way. Let's turn to some more support. Professor Jack W. Peltason, University of Illinois . . . [in] his book *The Federal Courts and the Political Processes,* states, "In almost every decision in which the judges have imposed a check on Congress in the name of the Constitution, in one way or another Congress eventually has

Congress in the name of the Constitution, in one way or another Congress eventually has done what the judges told them they could not do and should not do." . . . Let's turn to further support of this idea that judges can't really thwart national policy. James MacGregor Burns, and the same man, Jack Walter Peltason, told us that, in their joint effort, *Government by the People,* published in 1954, "Judges have no armies or police to execute their laws; they have no authority to levy taxes to support their activities. In the long run they must adapt themselves to the nature and demands of government by the people." Now what do we draw from this? Simply that the Supreme Court does not thwart national policy because always eventually the policies which the people apparently want and always the policies which Congress endorses eventually are put into effect.

In this example, a college debater uses three pieces of testimony to support his point, In evaluating a speaker's use of testimony, the critical listener should employ some of the popular tests of testimonial evidence: (1) Was the source of the testimony in a position to observe? (2) Was the source of the testimony competent to observe? (3) Was the source of the testimony biased? (4) Was the source of the testimony qualified? (5) Was the source of the testimony consistent with other sources and with himself or herself on previous occasions? and (6) Is the testimony sufficiently recent?

In using *specific instances* as evidence, the speaker provides well-known or verifiable examples that demonstrate the truth of the proposition or of a claim leading to the proposition. An excellent example of the use of specific instances can be found in a speech delivered by Richard Nixon well before his catastrophic involvement in the Watergate affair. As vice president under Dwight Eisenhower, Nixon visited Russia, and during his stay there delivered an important "Address to the Russian People." In an effort to prove that United States efforts to assure peace had been thwarted by the Soviet government, Nixon effectively drew upon a series of specific instances.

> . . . It is possible that many of you listening to me are not aware of the positive programs the United States has proposed which were designed to contribute to peace. Let me tell you about just a few of them and what happened to them:
>
> We had a monopoly on the atomic bomb when on June 14, 1946, we submitted the Baruch plan for international control of atomic energy. What happened? It was rejected by the USSR.
>
> At the Summit Conference in Geneva on July 21, 1955, President Eisenhower made his offer of open skies aerial inspection. What happened? It was rejected by the USSR.
>
> On May 1, 1958, the United States offered an Arctic aerial inspection plan to protect both nations from surprise attack. What happened? It was rejected by the USSR. I realize that your government has indicated reasons for its rejection of each of these proposals. I do not list these proposals for the purpose of warming over past history but simply to demonstrate the initiative our government has taken to reduce tensions and to find peaceful solutions for differences between us.

An equally good example of the use of specific instances occurs in a speech by Phyllis Jones Springen on "The Dimensions of the Oppression of Women."

> An infuriating example of unequal pay for equal work concerned a New Jersey manufacturer. Their chief financial officer was a woman paid $9,000 a year. When she left, they had to pay a man $20,000 a year to do her job. When he left they hired another woman at $9,000. When she left, they hired a man at $18,000. According to the recruiter, they were all good at the job.

In evaluating specific instances used as evidence in support of factual propositions, the critic should raise such questions as these: (1) Were a sufficient number of instances presented? (2) Were the instances presented typical instances? and (3) Are there any negative instances that should be accounted for?

In using *statistical data,* the speaker draws evidence from studies that have surveyed large numbers of cases and reported data numerically. In a speech, Charles Schalliol seeks to demonstrate that "The increasing size of our metropolitan areas is compounding our air pollution problem" by citing relevant statistics.

> Since 1940, our population has grown by 50,000,000, the use of energy had quadrupled, disposable income has increased 60%—yet—our air supply remains the same. In such a setting air pollution is a murderer. According to Edward Parkhurst, a noted health authority, death rates are "consistently higher in the central cities of 50,000 and over than in places under 10,000 and in rural areas in nonmetropolitan districts." The Census Bureau further establishes that life expectancy is three years greater in the rural states than in the urban states.

In evaluating a speaker's use of statistics, the enlightened critic asks: (1) Do these statistics come from a reliable source? (2) Are these statistics based on a reliable sample? and (3) Were these statistics accurately and completely reported? (4) Are they presented in a meaningful form?

In demonstrating a *literal analogy,* the speaker typically compares two things or instances that belong to the same category or classification (two nations, people, corporations, etc.) to show that because the two actually are similar in several major relevant elements, something known to exist in the first instance probably exists (or will exist) in the second. You might contend, for example, that because England and the United States are similar in language, general economic system, and general political system, and because so-called "socialized medicine" is working in Great Britain, it probably would work in the United States. In evaluating the soundness of a speaker's literal analogy, the critic could ask some of the standard questions: (1) Are the known elements of both actually similar enough? (2) Are the known similarities actually relevant to the issue-at-hand? (3) Are significant relevant differences ignored? (4) Does the element assumed to exist in the first instance but unknown in the second actually exist in the first? (5) Do essential points of similarity outweigh essential points of difference?

In asserting a *cause-effect relationship,* the speaker contends that one factor (or set of factors) directly contributes to the occurrence of another factor (or set of factors); in some sense the first causes (or will cause) the second. As a variation, a given effect or circumstance is described as the result of a certain cause. Sometimes use of words such as "because," "due to," or "if . . . then" can alert us to possible cause-effect arguments. Jenkin Lloyd Jones, in a speech titled "Let's Bring Back Dad: A Solid Value System," suggests a number of cause-effect relationships, including the following. At one point he describes "neo-Socialist" university professors who are "hostile" to the free enterprise business system "because they have never had any experience with it." At another point he asks concerning some Black families, "Why are our ghetto societies in such chaos? Because the man walks off when it gets tough." Jones concludes the speech by predicting a cause-effect relationship:

> . . . If enough American dads were to resolve to become partisan dads, unashamed to hold moral standards, willing to take the time to communicate values, then the chances of raising a new generation that would live in the agony of social chaos, or worse yet, lose their liberties for generations yet to come, will be substantially diminished.

To assess the soundness of any asserted cause-effect relationship, the critic could inquire: (1) Might there be multiple causes, several significant contributing and interrelated influences, rather than just the one asserted? (2) Might there be a chain or sequence of causal factors to consider, not just the asserted one as the immediate cause? (3) Is the speaker confusing a causal connection either with *chronology* (one thing simply happened after another) or with *correlation* (two things vary together in predictable ways, but *both* may be the effects of some unknown cause)? (4) Might there be additional positive or negative effects to consider other than the single effect identified? (5) Can the asserted cause-effect relationship be supported by evidence such as scientific studies, expert testimony, or other factual examples of the relationship?

CONCLUSION

In certain instances of persuasive discourse, speakers seek to prove to the satisfaction of their audiences that given propositions of fact are really true. When evaluating such speeches, the critic should consider *whether the speaker has adequately assessed the proof requirements of the factual proposition, whether acceptable arguments in support of the proposition of fact have been offered, and whether adequate evidence in support of the argument has been provided.*

For further reading

Cooper, Martha. *Analyzing Public Discourse.* Waveland Press, 1988. Chapter 3 examines issues of fact, value, and policy and Chapter 6 discusses standards for sound evidence and reasoning.

Gronbeck, Bruce, et al. *Principles and Types of Speech Communication.* Scott, Foresman/Little, Brown, 1990. Chapter 7 on finding and using supporting materials discusses specific instances, illustrations, statistics, and testimony. Chapter 17 on organization and critical thinking discusses claims of fact, value, and policy and explores the nature and evaluation of evidence and reasoning.

Lucas, Stephen E. *The Art of Public Speaking.* 3rd ed. Random House, 1989. Chapter 6 discusses supporting ideas with examples, statistics, and testimony. Chapter 9 examines questions of fact, value, and policy in persuasion and the use of evidence and reasoning.

Osborn, Michael, and Osborn, Suzanne. *Public Speaking.* 2nd ed. Houghton Mifflin, 1991. Chapter 6 explains the use of supporting materials such as facts, testimony, examples, and narrative. Chapter 14 discusses evidence, proof, and sound argument.

Rieke, Richard D., and Sillars, Malcolm O. *Argumentation and the Decision Making Process.* 2nd ed. Wiley, 1984. Chapter 5 examines use of factual instances, statistics, and expert testimony and notes the field-dependent nature of some standards for sound argument.

Toulmin, Stephen, Rieke, Richard, and Janik, Allan. *An Introduction to Reasoning.* 2nd ed. Macmillan, 1984. This book presents a framework for analyzing the soundness of arguments and stresses that criteria for sound evidence vary among fields of discourse such as law, science, the arts, and business.

Warnick, Barbara, and Inch, Edward S. *Critical Thinking and Communication: The Use of Reason in Argument.* Macmillan, 1989. Chapters 3–5 discuss claims of fact, value, and policy and types of evidence and reasoning.

Problem Students: The Socio-Cultural Roots

D. Stanley Eitzen

Professor Eitzen, of the Department of Sociology at Colorado State University, delivered the following address to the Public School Teachers of Pueblo, Colorado, at the University of Southern Colorado in Pueblo, February 21, 1990. Professor Eitzen is known for his interest in the possible impact of the sociocultural environment upon the quality of life. In another recent address, for example, he expressed concern for the possible impact of overemphasizing competitiveness in sports on our nation's youth.

In this address he first argues "that the children of this generation manifest more serious behavioral problems than did the children of a generation ago (3)," and then he searches for causality by answering the question, "What accounts for this difference?" Since the speech is tightly organized, be sure to observe Eitzen's organizational approach carefully. The topic is stated in the third paragraph, and the four principle issues of the speech, or as Eitzen calls them, social forces, are forecasted. Even in the development of the principle issues, Eitzen tends to enumerate subpoints.

Eitzen has two important tasks in addressing his proposition of fact. First, he must demonstrate the factual quality of each of the social forces he addresses and then he must show that those forces *cause* the effect he contends. You will want to analyze his use of documentation in establishing each of his points; does he rely on statistics or testimony, for example, and how adequate is the evidence he uses? This is a good time for you to thoroughly review rules of evidence. Next analyze if he establishes probable causality: does he demonstrate that these social forces actually produce children who are problems in school? Or, expressed differently, are these social forces the reasons why children misbehave in school? What problems does a speaker confront in trying to establish causality?

This speech is reprinted by permission from *Vital Speeches of the Day,* May 15, 1990, pp. 476–480.

1 Although I suspect that many of your pupils are a joy to work with at least some of the time, some, I'm sure, are not. Some children are angry, alienated, and apathetic. A few are uncooperative, rude, abrasive, threatening, and even violent. Some abuse drugs. Some are sexually promiscuous. Some belong to gangs. Some are sociopaths. The question we address this morning is why are some children such heavy duty problems to themselves, to their parents, to us, and to the community? Is the answer biological—a result of flawed genes? Is the source psychological—in warped personalities? My strong conviction is that children, with very few exceptions, are *not* born with sociopathic tendencies. These problem children are socially created.

2 Now you might say, here we go again, a bleeding heart liberal professor is going to argue that these problem kids are not to blame, the system is. Well, you are partly right. I am politically liberal and as a social scientist I embrace a theoretical perspective that focuses on the system as the source of social problems. However, I do recognize that while human actors are subject to powerful social forces, they make choices and must be held accountable for those choices. But I also believe that it is imperative that we understand the social factors that influence behavior and propel a disproportionate number of children in certain social categories to act in deviant ways.

3 I'm going to argue that the children of this generation manifest more serious behavioral problems than did the children of a generation ago. What accounts for this difference? There are four social forces that I believe account for this difference in the youth of today compared to those 15 years ago—the changing economy, the changing racial and ethnic landscape, changing government policies, and changing families. These structural changes occur within a cultural milieu, combining to create the problem people we face today. It is imperative that we understand this socio-cultural context of social problems, for only then will we be successful in understanding troublesome youth and in attacking the sources of their problems.

THE CHANGING ECONOMY

4 I begin with the assumption that families and individuals within them are shaped fundamentally by their economic situation, which, of course, is tied directly to work. I want to consider two related features of the changing economy in this section: (1) the structural transformation of the economy; and (2) new forms of poverty.

5 *The transformation of the economy.* We are in the midst of one of the most profound transformations in history, similar in magnitude and consequence to the Industrial Revolution. Several powerful forces are converging in the United States that are transforming its economy, redesigning and redistributing jobs, exacerbating inequality, reorganizing cities and regions, and profoundly affecting families and individuals. These forces are technological breakthroughs in microelectronics, the globalization of the economy, capital flight, and the shift from an economy based on the manufacture of goods to one based on information and services. I want to focus here on the significance of the last two of these.

6 The term capital flight refers to the investment choices to maximize profit that involve the movement of corporate monies from one investment to another. This takes several forms: investment overseas, plant relocation within the U.S., and mergers/buyouts. These investment choices, which are directly related to the shift from manufacturing to services, have had dramatic and negative impacts on communities, families, and individuals. I don't need to dwell on this since you have experienced this firsthand here in Pueblo with the collapse of the local steel industry. Across the country this has meant the loss of millions of good paying industrial jobs as plants shut down and the jobs moved to other localities or the companies shifted to other types of work. Similarly, there has been a dramatic downward tug on organized labor and wages. Between 1981 and 1986, for example, one-half of all unionized workers were forced to take wage cuts, accept two-tiered pay agreements, and other concessions. Although many new jobs have been created as we shifted to a service economy, as Presidents Reagan and Bush are fond of reminding us, by far the majority of these jobs are "bad" jobs with much lower pay and fewer benefits than the jobs in manufacturing that were lost.

7 To illustrate the consequences of the economic transformation, let's do a brief historical comparison. There is a common argument pertaining to the economy that "a rising tide lifts all boats." From 1950 to 1973 this alleged truism held as the average standard of living for families steadily increased. But since 1973 the opposite has occurred. To keep the boat metaphor, after 1973, the water level was not the same for all boats, some boats leaked severely, and some people were without boats at all. The following facts comparing life before and after 1973 make this point forcefully.

8 First, the standard of living (controlling for inflation) for most families declined. Real weekly wages dropped 14 percent between 1973 and 1986. During those same years the already low real wages for black men in poor areas dropped 50 percent.

9 Second, many families escaped this decline by having both spouses work. In the 1950s the average family consisted of three children and one paycheck. In the 1980s the average family had one or two children and two paychecks.

10 Third, in 1970 mortgage payments of homeowners took 17.9 percent of family income. In 1986 it took 29 percent of median family income for these payments. Thus, the decline of a basic tenet of the American Dream—home ownership.

11 Another pillar of this Dream is to send your children to college, but this is less likely now than it was a generation ago. In 1970 the average annual cost of attending a private college amounted to about 30 percent of the median family income. In 1986 this cost had jumped to 40.4 percent of the median family income and by then this was likely to come from the incomes of *two* wage earners, rather than one back as it was in 1970.

12 Finally, the level of inequality has risen—that is the rich are getting richer and the poor poorer. The income gap between the richest 20 percent and the lowest 20 percent of Americans is greater today than at any time since the federal government began keeping such statistics. At the upper end, the wealth of the richest 1 percent increased from 27 percent of the total in 1973 to 36 percent in 1987. Thus, it appears that President Reagan's "trickle down" economics did not.

13 These statistics have real and sometimes disturbing consequences, which might be reflected in your classrooms. This is the first generation in American history to have more downward social mobility than upward mobility. Downward mobility is devastating in American society not only because of the loss of economic resources but because self-worth is so closely connected to occupation. Individual self-esteem and family honor are bruised. Those affected feel the sting of stigma, embarrassment, and guilt. Moreover, this ordeal impairs the chances of the children as children and later as adults to enjoy economic security and a comfortable lifestyle. Some families find successful coping strategies to deal with their adverse situations. Others facing downward mobility experience stress, marital separation and divorce, depression, high levels of alcohol consumption, and spouse and child abuse. Children, so dependent on peer approval, often find the increasing gap in material differences between themselves and their peers intolerable. This may explain why some try to be "somebody" by acting tough, joining a gang, rejecting authority, experimenting with drugs and sex, and running away from home.

14 *Poverty.* One especially unfortunate consequence of capitalism is that a significant proportion of people—currently about 13 percent—are officially poor (of course, many additional millions are just above the government's poverty line, but poor nonetheless). Poverty in the 1980s declined for some categories—whites and the aged—and *increased* for others—racial minorities, fully employed workers (the working poor), households headed by women, and children.

15 There is an important historical distinction regarding the poor. Before 1973 the poor had hope to break out of poverty because jobs were generally available to those willing to work, even if the prospective workers were immigrants or school dropouts. The "new poor," on the other hand, are much more trapped in poverty because of the economic transformation. Hard physical labor is rarely needed in a high-tech society. Moreover, those few available jobs now have low wages and few, if any, benefits or hope of advancement. This undercuts the workingclass, especially blacks, Hispanics, and other racial minorities who face the added burden of institutional racism.

16 The consequence is that poverty is more locked in for this generation. Now a relatively permanent category of the poor—the underclass—has emerged. These people have little hope of making it economically in legitimate ways. This explains, in part, their overrepresentation in the drug trade and other criminal activities. Their hopelessness and alienation, moreover, help us understand their overuse of alcohol and other drugs. All of the above stem from the lack of stable and well paying jobs. A further consequence of this is that it undermines the stability of families.

17 Poverty is especially costly to children. They are more likely to be born with low birth weight, receive little or no health care, live in substandard housing, be malnourished, and be exposed to the health dangers of pollution. Let me provide one example of this last point. Poor children are much more likely than others to be exposed to lead from old paint and old plumbing fixtures and from the lead in household dust. Sixteen percent of white children and 55 percent of black children have high lead levels in their blood, which leads to irreversible learning disabilities and other problems. Children exposed to lead have an average IQ four to eight points lower and run four times the risk of having IQs below 80 than do unexposed children.

THE CHANGING RACIAL LANDSCAPE

18 American society is becoming more racially and ethnically diverse. Recent immigration (legal and illegal) especially by Latinos and Asians accounts for most of this change. If current trends continue, Latinos will surpass blacks as the most populous racial minority by the year 2020. In some areas of the country, most notably California, the new immigration has created a patchwork of barrios, Koreatowns, Little Taipeis, and Little Saigons. This has also created competition and conflict over scarce resources including battles over disputed turf among rival gangs, intense rivalries between members of the white working class and these people of color. Moreover, communities, corporations, and schools have had difficulty providing these peoples with the services they require because of the language and cultural barriers.

19 We are currently experiencing a resurgence of racial antipathy in the U.S. This is evidenced in various forms of racial oppression and overt acts of racial hostility in communities, in schools and universities, and in the workplace. We can expect these hateful episodes to escalate further if the economy worsens.

20 Racial minorities, especially blacks, Native Americans, and Latinos are also the objects of institutional racism, which keep them disadvantaged. They don't fare as well as the racial majority in schools, in performance on so-called "objective" tests, in job placement and advancement, and the like. They are negatively stereotyped and stigmatized. Their opportunities in this "land of opportunity" are drastically limited. They are blamed for their failures, even when the causes are structural. Is there any wonder that a disproportionate number of them are "problem" people?

CHANGING GOVERNMENT POLICY

21 One of the reasons that the disadvantaged are faring less well now than a generation ago is that government policies are less helpful to them now. At the very time good jobs were lost and jobs were harder to obtain, the government reduced various forms of aid

to those negatively impacted. During the Reagan years, for example, government programs designed for the economically disadvantaged shrunk by $51 billion. The policies of the Bush Administration continue this tradition of neglect. With regard to education (recall that Bush wants to be known as the "education president") President Bush wants to eliminate illiteracy and emphasize Head Start—both noble goals—but without new taxes to fund them. This sounds like empty rhetoric to me. Even with the additional $500 million the President seeks for Head Start (the cost of one-half of a Stealth Bomber) the program will miss 25 percent of the nation's eligible 4-year-olds. If we are serious about increasing the success ratio for disadvantaged youth, we should accept the argument of *The New York Times* in a recent editorial:

> Why stop at 4-year-olds? The Bush proposal . . . doesn't allow for better salaries for instructors or broader programs. Most important, it doesn't allow for Head Start to enter a poor child's life as soon and as often as possible. Ideally, Head Start would be all day, all year and so generously funded it could include all eligible children.

22 Obviously, President Bush is not willing to go this far. We should, however, insist on it. In the meantime, poor children fall further behind and may become all the more mired in a permanent underclass. The bitter irony is that these disadvantaged youth will end up as society's losers and most Americans will blame them for their failure.

THE CHANGING FAMILY

23 A number of recent trends regarding the family indicate the lessening of family influence on children. Let me note a few of these trends. First, more and more families include two primary wage earners. This means, in effect, that more and more women are working outside the home. Over 50 percent of mothers with a child under 6 work outside the home and about 70 percent of mothers with children between 6 and 17 are in the workplace. This means, among other things, that more and more children are being raised in families where parents have less and less time for them. It also means that more and more preschool children are being cared for by adults who are not their parents. This is not necessarily bad, but it can be.

24 Second, although the divorce rate has declined slightly since 1981, it remains at a historically high figure. Over one million children each year experience their parents' divorce, compared to about 300,000 a year in 1950.

25 Third, it is estimated that 60 percent of today's 5-year-olds will live in a single parent family before they are 18 (90 percent of them will live with their mothers, which means with their mothers' incomes, which are decidedly lower than their fathers' incomes).

In terms of school behaviors, research has shown that children from one-parent families differ significantly from the children of two-parent families: (1) they are less likely to be high achievers; (2) they are consistently more likely than two-parent children to be late, truant, and subject to disciplinary action; and (3) they are more than twice as likely as two-parent children to drop out of school.

26 Fourth, about 3 million children between 5 and 13 have no adult supervision after school. One study has found that these latchkey children are twice as likely to use drugs as those who come home from school to an adult.

27 These trends indicate widespread family instability in American society—and these have increased dramatically in one generation. Many of the children facing such unstable situations cope successfully. Others do not. Rejection from one or both parents may lead some to act out in especially hostile ways. Low self-esteem may lead to sexual promiscuity. Alcohol and drug abuse may be another response. Whatever the negative response, I believe that we can conclude that the victims of family instability are not completely to blame for their misbehaviors.

THE CULTURAL MILIEU

28 The structural changes I have noted occur within a cultural milieu. I will address only two aspects of culture here—American values and the messages sent by the media. Let's begin with values. The highly valued individual in American society is the self-made person—i.e., one who has achieved position, money, and privilege through his or her own efforts in a highly competitive system. Economic success, as evidenced by material possessions, is the most common indicator of who is and who is not successful. Economic success, moreover, is commonly used to measure self worth.

29 Competition is pervasive in American society and we glorify the winners. What about the losers? How do they respond to failure? How do we respond to them? How do they respond to ridicule? How do they react to the shame of being poor? How do the children of the poor respond to having less than their peers? How do they respond to social ostracism for "living on the other side of the tracks?" They may respond by working harder to succeed, which is the great American myth. Or, alternatively, they may become apathetic, drop out, tune out with drugs, join others who are also "failures" to fight the system that has rejected them, or they may engage in various forms of deviance to obtain the material manifestations of success.

30 The other aspect of culture I want to address briefly is the messages of the media, particularly those from television, the movies, and advertising. These media outlets glamorize, among other things, materialism, violence, drug and alcohol use, hedonistic lifestyles, and easy sex. The messages children recieve are consistent: they are bombarded with ma-

terialism and consumerism, what it takes to be a success, the legitimacy of violence, and what it takes to be "cool." Let me illustrate the power of the media:

- 3-year-olds watch about 30 hours of television a week. By the time an American child graduates from high school, she or he will have spent more time in front of the tube than in class.
- Between the ages of 2 and 18, the average American child sees 100,000 beer commercials on television.
- Young people see some 12,000 acts of televised violence a year. A study by the University of Pennsylvania's Annenberg School of Communication revealed that children watching Saturday morning cartoons in 1988 saw an average of 26.4 violent acts each hour (up from 18.6 per hour in 1980). Two of the conclusions by the authors of this study were that: (1) children see a mean and dangerous world in these cartoons where people are not to be trusted and disputes are legitimately settled by violence; and (2) children who see so much violence become desensitized to it.

31 The powerful and consistent messages from television are reinforced in the movies children watch, as well as the toys that are made for them, and the computerized games such as Nintendo that so many find addicting.

32 Given these strong cultural messages that pervade society, is it any wonder that violence is widespread among the youth of this generation? Nor should we be surprised at children using sex, alcohol, tobacco, and other drug use as ways to act "adult." Moreover, we should not be puzzled by those youth who decide to drop out of school to work so they can buy the clothing and car that will bring them immediate status.

CONCLUSION

33 This generation is clearly different from earlier ones. Its members manifest problems that are structural in origin. Obviously, these social problems cannot be solved by the schools alone, although the community often blames the schools when these problems surface. Since the problems are structural, the solution requires changes at that level. The government must create jobs and supply job training. There must be an adequate health care delivery system, rather than our current system which rations care according to ability to pay. There must be massive expenditures on education to equalize opportunities among states and communities that differ in resources. There must be pay equity for women. And,

finally, there must be an unwavering commitment to eradicating institutional sexism and racism. Such a strategy will, among other benefits, strengthen families, and give children resources and hope.

34 The government must also exert more control over the private sector. In particular, corporations must pay decent wages and provide adequate benefits to their employees. Also, corporations contemplating a plant shut down or dramatic layoff must go beyond the present 60 days notification so that communities and families can plan appropriate coping strategies.

35 These proposals are laughable in the current political climate where politicians are timid and the citizens seemingly only interested in reducing their tax burden. The political agenda for meeting our social problems requires political leadership that is innovative and able to convince the public that sacrifices now to help the disadvantaged will have long term benefits to all. Such leadership will emerge from a base of educated citizens who will work to challenge others to meet societal goals.

36 At the community level we must reorder our priorities so that human and humane considerations are paramount. This means that community leaders must make the difficult decisions required to help the disadvantaged secure adequate jobs, job training, health care, housing, and education. Schools must be committed to educate all children. This requires a special commitment to invest in the disadvantaged with extra resources, assigning the most creative and effective teachers to them, and providing the necessary preschool foundation to children through programs such as Head Start. Most important, all children must believe that the school and community want them to succeed, thus creating a positive self-fulfilling prophecy.

37 Last week Roger Wilkins presented a visual essay on the PBS series Frontline entitled "Throwaway People." This essay examined the structural reasons for the emergence of the black underclass in Washington, D.C. in this past generation. His conclusion is appropriate for us to consider.

> If [the children of the underclass] are to survive, America must come back to them with imagination and generosity. These are imperiled children who need sustained services to repair the injuries that were inflicted on them before they were born, adults need jobs, jobs that pay more than the minimum wage, that keep families together, that make connections with the outside world, and the strength to grow. We can face the humanity of these people and begin to attack their problems, or we can continue to watch the downward rush of this generation, in the middle of our civilization, eroding the core of our conscience and destroying our claim to be an honorable people.

38 You are confronted daily with unacceptable behaviors by students. Obviously, these must be handled. I hope that this discussion will assist all of us in understanding the complex sources of these objectionable and seemingly irrational behaviors. We must begin with an understanding of these problem children. And, from my vantage point, such an understanding begins with social factors. Most important, we must realize that social and economic factors have battered down certain children, increasing their likelihood of failure and of behaving in ways that we deplore.

39 Everyone needs a dream. Without a dream you become apathetic. Without a dream you become fatalistic. Without a dream and the hope of attaining it, society becomes the enemy. We educators must realize that some of our youth act in antisocial ways because they have lost the dream. Moreover, we must realize that we are partly responsible for destroying the dream of children, especially disadvantaged children. We are part of a noble profession whose goal is to increase the success rate for *all* children. That's our goal. Let's do it!

Women in the Marketplace: Have Women in Journalism Made a Difference?

Joan Konner

Joan Konner, Dean of the Columbia University School of Journalism, delivered this speech at the New Jersey Press Women's Association Luncheon, Paterson, New Jersey, May 5, 1990. The speaker achieves considerable interest value through personal anecdotes. The introduction, for example, is highly personal, and then after Konner states her topic to the audience (3) and gives a few examples of historic women pioneers in journalism (5), she returns to a fairly lengthy personal anecdote (7–18). Discuss what the possible impact is in terms of interest and credibility of the speaker's personal involvement. You may want to take time to review theoretical thoughts concerning personal involvement in public address. Is it possible that since the speaker herself is dean of a nationally known school of journalism she enacts her basic proposition so as to give a kind of credibility to her argument? What is meant by rhetorical enactment of the argument?

Konner makes heavy use of examples in developing her thesis that women in journalism have made a difference. How effective is this in establishing factual credibility? The speech is also interesting in that the speaker argues that a shift in values supports her basic proposition. Once more, we have an issue of causality. As a minimum, causality arguments must seem plausible, if not probable or certain. What is your critical evaluation of the causality in this instance? This speech is reprinted from *Vital Speeches of the Day*, September 15, 1990, pp. 726–728.

1 Good afternoon. Thank you very much for inviting me. I am pleased to have the chance to address the New Jersey Press Women's Association for several reasons. One, I grew up in New Jersey. Paterson is my hometown. My children and my grandchildren still live here. My first job was in New Jersey in the Bergen *Record,* where I enjoyed one of the best jobs in this business . . . and the New Jersey Press Women's Association was, I believe, at least in part, responsible for the opportunity I was given at the *Record* so early in my professional life. I had worked at the newspaper only a short time when you gave me my first award in this business for a feature story I wrote for the Women's Page.

2 Shortly thereafter I became assistant editorial page editor, and an editorial writer and columnist, working for the best boss—teacher, mentor, friend—I ever had in this business, Bill Caldwell. I always credited the award with helping to call attention to my work. The award was a silver plate. I still have it. Also, it was second prize, so I always tried harder. I thanked you then, but I'm pleased to have the opportunity to thank you again today.

3 I'm going to talk about: "Have Women in Journalism Made a Difference?" Actually, that title isn't quite right. It should be: "Are Women in Journalism Today Making a Difference?" but for those of you who were drawn here by the first title, the short speech is "Yes."

4 There have been great women journalists since the beginning, and their work has, indeed, made a difference.

5 Margaret Fuller, Leonel Campbell O'Bryan aka "Polly Pry", Elizabeth Cochrane Seaman aka "Nellie Bly", Anne O'Hare McCormick, Dorothy Thompson, and others. They were pioneers and we all have benefitted from their accomplishments.

6 The slice of this subject I'd like to consider today is the impact of increased numbers in all media as a result of the most recent chapter in the women's struggle for equality, in our society, in our time.

7 I'll start with an anedocte. It goes back to the late 60s or early 70s. It must have been that one of my children was ill that day because it was a weekday and I was home.

8 I always tried to follow a piece of advice I picked up when I was a student at the Columbia Graduate School of Journalism. The school had a ritual for the women students in the class at the end of the school year. A panel of women journalists was invited to discuss how to manage home and career.

9 One of the panelists, if I recall correctly, was Betsy Wade of the New York *Times,* who advised:

> When you're sick, go to work, because when your children are sick, you're going to have to stay home and you can't be absent for both.

10 Such was the balancing act of women who worked in the newsroom at the time, and I'm not sure that it's much changed today.

11 In any case, I was home, and I was watching a morning program on WNBC-TV where I worked at the time as a documentary producer.

12 Barbara Walters was the host and the program was called "For Women Only." About a year later, the name was changed to "Not For Women Only," one of the early achievements of the women's movement.

13 The guest on the program that day was Clare Booth Luce, and they were talking about the time Mrs. Luce served in Congress.

14 Mrs. Luce said it was the worst experience of her professional life, and further, she thought that women would never become a strong presence in Congress.

15 "Why?" Barbara Walters asked.

16 Mrs. Luce replied, "because women do not have the instinct for the jugular, and men do."

17 Barbara Walters replied: "We'll learn."

18 I remember thinking that wasn't the point at all. We weren't supposed to be trying to become like men. We were supposed to be trying to get into the decision-making roles so that we could change the way business is done to the advantage of both sexes. What's the point of women getting into the positions of power if, in the process, we have to turn ourselves into killers, psychologically, at least, with an instinct for the jugular? Aren't those killer values the ones we are trying to change?

19 That's still the question today when we ask: Are women in journalism, especially now that there are more of us, some of us in positions of leadership, making a difference? Given the impact of the media in shaping our social, political, and economic life, are we seeing changes not only in numbers in the newsrooms, but in the agenda and priorities of society?

20 I suggest the answer is "yes," but it is only beginning.

21 Here is one recent example, a story reported on the front page of The New York *Times* on Sunday, March 25, 1990.

22 The *Times* reported on an article in another newspaper, the Des Moines, Iowa, *Register,* written by the editor, Geneva Overholser. Ms. Overholser wrote that by withholding the names of victims of rape, the press did more than protect their privacy. It also compounded the stigma, and she urged that victims of rape speak out and identify themselves.

23 "As long as rape is deemed unspeakable—and is therefore not fully and honestly spoken of—the public outrage will be muted as well," she wrote.

24 Nancy Ziegenmeyer, a rape victim, read the article and shortly afterward decided to tell her story publicly. What followed was a five-part front-page series reporting the experience in graphic detail in defiance of journalistic tradition. The series still sparks debate about rape and journalistic propriety.

25 The *Times* wasn't the only one to report on the *Register's* series. Subsequently an episode of ABC's "Nightline" was devoted to it, and that was followed by an entire editorial page of *USA Today* carrying several columns, not only opinion about the coverage of Nancy

Zeigenmayer's story but another column giving a graphic account of a rape told in the first person by a senior editor of that newspaper who also identified herself by name—Karen Jurgensen. The headline was: "I was another nameless victim." The ripple effect, in which the courage of one woman editor begins to have an impact on the handling of a serious issue in other news media. You probably know the most often quoted definition of news: It comes from the editor who said: "News is what I say it is." In these cases, the editorial sensibility, and judgment, of a woman editor was different, the published story was different, and it is producing a change. There are other examples, some just that obvious, and others much subtler.

26 But before I go on with anecdotal evidence about changes of sensibility in the news, let's look at some statistics: I have seen some of this association's communications.

27 You are clearly following the documentary evidence about numbers of women employed in the newsroom. But I'd like to review just a few because despite some good news, the situation is still discouraging. In television, where statistics can be seen in the flesh: The number of female network correspondents increased by only six percent from 1975 to 1989. In 1974, women reported 9.9 percent of the stories on network news. In 1984, they accounted for 10.2 percent. In February 1989 women were responsible for 15.7 percent, according to a study conducted by the Communications Consortium for a conference on "Women, Men and Media" held last year.

28 The print statistics don't look much better. In March '89, women accounted for 27 percent of the front page bylines in 10 major American newspapers. *USA Today* was at the top. The New York *Times* was at the bottom.

29 Clearly, there is an upward trend, but slow. And when you consider that women comprise 52 percent of the population and that more than half of today's journalism students are female, the disproportion is considerable. Salary statistics reinforce the finding.

30 When you get to management ranks, the percentages dwindle to near imperceptibility. As of 1989, females constituted just three percent of television station presidents and vice presidents, six percent of newspaper publishers and 8 percent of radio presidents and vice presidents. Women hold about 25 percent of middle management jobs. The prediction that once we got in we would work our way to the top hasn't yet come true.

31 But let's look at how far we've come. Take television again: Some of the stories seem funny now . . . almost. Pauline Frederick, for example, became the first female full-time network correspondent for NBC in 1953. The story goes that she was reluctant to accept an assignment to cover the candidates' wives at the 1948 political conventions for television because she didn't know what to wear, and there was no one to tell her how to do her makeup. She ended up doing her own and the wives, too.

32 The FCC started requiring affirmative action plans for women to be filed with license renewal applications in 1971—the forced entry into a male-dominated establishment which was met with a good deal of resistance.

33 In 1974 Susan Peterson arrived to take up her assignment as a correspondent at the London Bureau of CBS and found her desk near the door next to the receptionist. Her male colleagues all had offices.

34 Before women could become members of the National Press Club, they were allowed in for important speeches but they had to sit in the balcony, and the rules permitted questions to be asked only from the floor.

35 Few male assignment editors were willing to take the risk of sending the first woman out to cover a priority hard news story. Those who did were pleasantly surpised. A 1971 story in *Newsweek* drew attention to a new breed of reporters, "tough young women" like Gloria Rojas, Pia Lindstrom and the 25-year-old Connie Chung "who can cover hard news on an equal basis with men." In that same story Reuven Frank of NBC said:

> I have a strong feeling that audiences are less prepared to accept news from a woman's voice than from a man's.

36 Flash forward from there to 1976 when Barbara Walters gets the first million dollar contract to move to ABC from NBC . . . Reuven Frank gets his comeuppance.

37 1981: Christine Craft sues Metromedia and wins a half a million dollars because she was demoted for being too old, too unattractive, and not deferential enough to men.

38 1989: Diane Sawyer goes from CBS to ABC for $1.6 million; Connie Chung goes from NBC to CBS for between 6 and 7 hundred thousand. Mary Alice Williams goes from CNN to NBC for $500 thousand.

39 But stars, salaries, and statistics alone do not tell the story.

40 We shouldn't mistake quantity for quality, and the quieter history includes the accomplishments of many women off-camera in television newsrooms as well as many more in newspapers and magazines throughout the country. For one, the remarkable *Ms.* magazine, which legitimized women's issues by producing a serious magazine about them. It no doubt can take the credit for the greater seriousness of women's magazines in general, and for leading the way to the changing definition of news generally—the inclusion of domestic and workplace issues like battered wives, child abuse, and maternity leave, in so-called hard-news; values and quality of life stories; stories about children, health, education, social trends, community, and the environment—not only on the front page, but on every page and on television news as well.

41 Last fall the Columbia Journalism School Alumni chose the topic "Is News Getting Too Soft?" for its annual fall meeting. The subject, and the title, were picked by one of the men. Of course. "Hard" and "soft" are terms only a man would have invented. It goes with the sports metaphor of most news. Who's winning? Who's losing? In politics, business, culture. Who's up? Who's down? If you're winning, you're "hard" news. If you're losing, you're a "soft" feature for the inside pages.

42 I didn't know exactly what the title—"Is News Getting Too Soft"—meant. It turned out there was concern about changes brought about by different perspectives in the newsrooms—from women and minorities—that are beginning to alter the definition of news.

43 Soma Golden, national editor for The New York *Times,* an alumna of our School, gave her analysis of the change in the front page of her paper. On a given day in 1959 there were 18 stories, all hard news. On the same day in 1969, there were 23 stories, again all hard news. By 1979, the format had changed so there were fewer stories, but even so, what was called "new" news stories made it to the front page along with hard news. In 1989, the trend continued with as many as three "new" news stories mingled with dateline news. A new story was a series on care of the elderly or Public School 94 in the Bronx or an analysis of social trends. The position of these stories in The *Times* tells us that the distinction between soft news and hard news is blurring.

44 Is this happening because there are more women in the newsrooms?

45 Probably, but who knows? Clearly a shift of values and priorities is taking place.

46 Are women better equipped to cover this "new" news? It is possible we are. The psychologist Carol Gilligan, in her book, "In A Different Voice," described a difference between the moral development of men and women.

47 Women, she says, develop an ethic of care, an empathy based on their identification with the primary parent, usually the mother. Women define themselves in terms of relationship and responsibility.

48 Men develop an ethic of justice as they separate from the mother. They define themselves in terms of difference, position and hierarchy. If we accept this, then I think we can assume the responsibility that comes with our capacity to adopt a broader perspective and show the human, caring side of the news.

49 The feminine sensibility is growing everywhere in our culture today—in literature, in art, in history, politics, and the media. It coincides with concerns about the environment, a growing awareness of Mother Earth, as our life support system. There is talk of the Saia principle, of world view that says we are all part of one living body. We find the principle expressed in the mythology of the Goddess, in which there is also a revival of interest today. The Goddess was worshipped for thousands of years in agrarian, egalitarian societies in which there was a love of life, of nature and beauty.

50 There seems at this time to be a greater hunger in the American culture for the values of the goddess—the values of life, generation, and creation. There seems to be a growing reverence for nature, for a collective spirit, and relationship based on the awareness of the interconnectedness of life. We are becoming more concerned that our competitive Western culture that developed along the lines of the Darwinian principle of the survival of the fittest may have been a life-supporting pattern for one period of human evolution but it may no longer be a life supporting pattern for another—this one. Human intelligence creates systems to protect human life. Today those very systems are threatening it—industrial development which threatens the environment; nuclear weapons that threaten all of life. In such a world, those with a wider perspective and greater awareness are turning out to be the fittest.

51 We are coming around a bend, and we realize there is a need for other values, values of collaboration, community, care. These are the values that used to belong to the private sphere of home and family. But we are beginning to see these values in the workplace and in public life as well. One hypothesis is that women, as they succeed in the marketplace, retain what is valuable from what used to be considered the domestic sphere and bring that wider perspective into view. It does seem some of us—women and men—have had enough of the instinct for the jugular. I think that women in positions of power—in politics, public service, and the media—are helping to make that difference.

The Truth About Savings and Loan Institutions: State and Federal Bungling
Theo H. Pitt, Jr.

Theo H. Pitt, Jr., is Chairman and President of the Pioneer Savings Bank and Chairman of the U.S. League of Savings Institutions. He delivered this address June 28, 1988, at the Third Regulatory Policy Conference of the U.S. League of Savings in Washington, D.C. The League exists to serve the savings institution business and the public interest by furthering thrift and home ownership. It also strives to improve the statutes and regulations affecting the savings institution business.

Pitt opens his speech by referring directly to the listeners in the room, praising them as "successful managers" who "make it possible for American families to realize the dream of home ownership." Praise of the audience is a technique speakers commonly use in beginning their speeches. Review other types of speech openings and try to discern which approaches seem best suited for what situations. Why would praise for the audience be especially effective in this instance?

In all probability Pitt is addressing a sympathetic audience. How would that affect the proof requirements for the speech? It may not be the amount of proof the speaker offers the listeners that is most critical but accurate detection of what is required for the immediate audience that matters the most. In other words, careful audience analysis may be integral to the concept of proof.

Speeches dealing with propositions of fact emphasize logic and evidence, but are not necessarily void of emotional appeals. Striking the right emotional chord is often every bit as important as documentation. What role does emotional appeal play in this speech?

Pitt's speech tends to merge with the "create concern for problems" category of this book. The speaker in this case attempts to establish fact about how the problem occurred. Since problem speeches are grounded in fact, what differences in emphasis do you see between the two forms of address?

This speech is reprinted by permission from *Vital Speeches of the Day,* September 1, 1988, pp. 674–676.

1 As I look around this room this afternoon I see people who have devoted their working lives to the savings and loan business—successful managers who can be proud that, day in and day out, they deliver on the promise that is the savings institutions charter: To make it possible for American families to realize the dream of home ownership.

2 Ours is a worthy, necessary pursuit and one that has made this nation the best-housed of any in the world.

3 And because I believe this so strongly my words today will be directed in part to those who question our commitment to home ownership . . . to those who would eliminate our system of specialty lending institutions . . . to those who neglect to consider that what is at stake in dealing with the so-called "Savings and Loan Crisis" is this nation's long-standing commitment to home ownership as a national priority.

4 Headline hunters and headline writers hammer at the theme that the savings and loan business is in crisis.

5 Ladies and gentlemen, if I make one point today I want it to be this:

6 The savings and loan business is *not* in crisis, thank you. The savings and loan business is comprised of nearly 3,200 institutions, the overwhelming majority of which are earning profits.

7 But you don't read or hear about those institutions. What you read and hear about is that aggregate first-quarter losses for our business amounted to $3.8 billion.

8 What you *don't* read about is that $3.7 billion of the $3.8 billion in net losses is attributable to a mere 50 institutions . . . fifty institutions representing about one and one-half percent of the total number of savings institutions.

9 What you *don't* read about is that $3 billion of those losses—$3 billion of the $3.8 billion—were attributed to a mere 20 institutions—less than one percent of the total number of savings and loans—primarily in the Southwest.

10 What you *don't* read about is that 2,774 solvent institutions, holding 90 percent of total industry assets, reported first-quarter profits . . . and that the percentage of profitable institutions rose to 69 percent from 65 percent, quarter to quarter.

11 Yet the self-appointed "experts" on our business—and I place quotation marks around the word "experts"—conveniently ignore the positives, preferring instead to use the negative numbers to smear us all.

12 And they run about town, red-faced and screaming that the savings and loan business is in "crisis" . . . that the savings and loan business needs "bailing out."

13 I'll give them credit for one thing. They have the terminology right. The words "crisis" and "bailout" are appropriate, but not in the context in which they're being applied.

14 There's no crisis in the savings and loan business at large, so let them stop talking about "bailing out" the savings and loan business.

15 The problem rests within one government agency—the FSLIC—which finds itself under pressure to fulfill the contract which 54 years ago yesterday the Congress of the United States wrote with the American people.

16 It's the FSLIC that needs bailing out, and in actual fact that bailout has been in progress for nearly three years now.

17 And who's doing the bailing? It's not the American taxpayer. It's the savings and loan business—you and I and our savings institutions.

18 You and I have paid a special tax in excess of $3 billion since 1985 to bail out the government-run FSLIC, despite the fact that our healthy institutions had nothing to do with the problems that have been visited upon that agency.

19 Our healthy institutions are having to make good on government's contract with the American people.

20 I'd just like to take a little time here today to offer my view of how this situation developed.

21 As most of you well know, the overwhelming majority of our business is strong and operating at a profit. Less than one-sixth of our institutions are in trouble.

22 Economic conditions have played a major role in this, most obviously in the Southwest . . . in the energy, farming and primary commodity producing regions which have experienced economic depression.

23 There also have been cases of poor management. And, yes, some institutions' problems can be traced directly to blatant wrongdoing. But thankfully, the scoundrels and the bad managers have been driven out of the business.

24 Those that got in trouble because of fraud or mismanagement were invited to do so largely as the result of a poorly planned, poorly executed deregulation process—at both the state and the federal levels.

25 The Administration plunged headlong into deregulation in the early years of this decade. They went at it with a vengeance. And they went at it in a lopsided fashion.

26 For years we had sought authority for federally chartered institutions to engage in variable-rate lending. But we were blocked time after time. We needed that variable rate lending authority to prepare ourselves for interest-rate deregulation. But we were denied it.

27 Instead, we got interest rate deregulation first. And we got it at a time of rampant inflation and rate volatility. Our cost of funds skyrocketed beyond the earnings capabilities of our government-dictated, government-enforced, fixed-rate mortgage portfolios.

28 It wasn't until three years after the start of interest-rate deregulation that we were fianlly granted the authority to engage in variable-rate mortgage lending.

29 We who are operating healthy institutions didn't do the mismanaging. The mismanaging was done by people here in Washington. And their mismanagement cost us $12 billion . . . yes, $12 billion in capital lost to deregulation alone.

30 Rate deregulation wasn't the only miscalculation being made here in Washington. It was obvious to all but those in a position to do something about it that a deregulated marketplace would require a larger federal police force. The regulatory body needed more and better qualified people.

31 The Bank Board asked for more staff and authority to pay them at levels comparable to those of other financial regulators. We supported the Bank Board in this effort.

32 But the Office of Management and Budget and the Office of Personnel Management said "No." They wouldn't let the Bank Board hire the supervisors and examiners that were so crucially needed, even though not one nickel of the money would have come from the taxpayers.

33 Thus the OMB and the OPM laid out the welcome mat for the high fliers. They said: "Come on in. No one's watching." And come they did . . . and they ran amuck in the absence of government supervision.

34 Meanwhile, back in certain state capitals, some legislatures saw fit to expand the investment authority of their state-chartered institutions far beyond the traditional housing-finance mission of savings institutions.

35 Take a look at those states where the S&L problems are in highest concentration—and I say this even though my own institution is state-chartered. What you'll find are state legislatures which sanctioned the broadest range of nontraditional lending activity.

36 But these state legislatures had a safety net. If their judgment was wrong, A Federal agency—the FSLIC—would take the fall for their imprudence.

37 One has only to recall the former Empire Savings and Loan Association of Mesquite, Texas, to find a text-book example of how these failings at the state and the federal levels converged to produce disaster . . . a disaster that cost the FSLIC nearly $200 million.

38 I'm going to read a little from a 1984 report from the House Government Operations Committee. This passage says it all, and I quote:

> Empire's failure . . . culminated a frustrating and ineffectual Federal and State
> supervisory experience with the institution since (the controlling officer) acquired control.
> Although (the controlling officer) failed to file the required notice of change of ownership,
> nothing was done by the (Bank Board) about this significant omission until shortly before
> the institution failed.
>
> Although the Bank Board's regular supervisory examination of Empire as of October 7,
> 1982, disclosed 'significant examination factors rated as either material deficiencies or
> requiring immediate forceful supervisory action,' no effective supervisory action was taken
> by the (Bank Board) until late 1983.
>
> Even as late as August 1983, when a special limited examination took place revealing
> virtual chaos, the (Bank Board) allowed an additional 7 months to pass before it closed
> Empire in March 1984.
>
> During this period deposits and consequently FSLIC's exposure grew significantly.

39 The committee found a number of reasons for this supervisory fiasco . . . communications failures between state and federal regulators . . . bureaucratic rigidity and an insufficient number of trained and experienced examiners.

40 Fortunately, these problems have since been corrected. But the corrections were late in coming.

41 These sorts of failure by government at all levels went on for far too long, and as a result, we are in the position of having to pull Uncle Sam's chestnuts from the fire.

42 We, the healthy institutions, are required to pick up the tab for those that failed—whether they were victims of unmanageable regional economic trauma, of financial skulduggery, or of governmental bungling.

43 We the healthy are in the ironic position of having to pay not only for the errors of our competititors, but the errors of state and federal government as well.

44 Up to now the business has been able to do this . . . to bail out the FSLIC, and hence all those in government and formerly in our business who contributed to the FSLIC's problems. But there is a limit to how much we can contribute without endangering the whole system.

45 As I said earlier, we've paid out an extra $3 billion since 1985 in special assessments—$3 billion from our bottom line.

46 That means that you and I are trying to stay competitive with our local commercial bankers and credit unions while—at the same time—paying 2½ times as much as they are paying for deposit insurance coverage.

47 Last year's FSLIC recapitalization law authorized an industry-funded mechanism to put more money into the FSLIC. No taxpayer money was involved.

48 You remember the debate over this recapitalization question. It focused on the amount of the recapitalization bonding authority—how much and for how long. The compromise was struck at $10.8 billion over three years.

49 Despite what some say, we weren't debating the size of the *problem*. In reality, no one really knew its size then, and they still don't know.

50 Frankly, the more important question in our minds was how much more we as a business could afford to pay. We already were paying the special assessment. Paying off the FSLIC bonds is an obligation on top of all others.

51 We focused on the special assessment, and Congress agreed that it should be phased out as part of our willingness to shoulder the responsibility for the $10.8 billion in FSLIC bonds.

52 Unfortunately, our fears of last year are being realized. The Bank Board has revealed it intends to continue the full special assessment through fiscal 1995, in spite of the phasedown Congress advised.

53 Using Bank Board numbers, this means our business will contribute $11.5 billion in extra premiums between now and then—an amount equal to one-third of the industry's current GAAP capital.

54 On top of this, the Bank Board's numbers show that the Board expects to build up a huge FSLIC obligation separate from the borrowing authority authorized by Congress.

55 They are doing this through the issuance of notes which, though they may be backed by receivership assets, nevertheless will be in amounts which far exceed the borrowing limits set by Congress. The interest bill on these bonds and notes—a bill which you and I will have to pay—will reach about $1.5 billion a year.

56 I'm going to wind up here, but I want to emphasize first that today's financial environment is riskier than ever.

57 The ultimate protection against risk is capital. In our case, that capital is being drained away as quickly as we build it.

58 Assessments in excess of what we can prudently pay deplete our capital and jeopardize the safety and soundness of the entire financial system.

59 Just as the ballooning federal debt will be an enormous burden to our children, the ongoing and staggering FSLIC debt could seriously weaken this nation's healthy institutions.

60 What looms before us is the prospect of "Vampire Economics" . . . a prescription for FSLIC's problems that would drain away our capital, the very life blood of our system of depository institutions.

61 I believe this nation needs and wants a system of deposit-taking institutions with a special commitment to housing finance.

62 And I am not alone in that belief. The people have said that . . . people from all age groups and from all of our society's economic levels. . . . And they've said it quite emphatically in the days since last October's Wall Street collapse.

63 We've seen our deposit inflows run positive and at record levels for the past seven months.

64 The people are voting when—in the face of all the negative press our business receives—they continue to entrust their savings to our safe keeping.

65 That's as solid a vote as anyone could ask for, and this nation's policy makers would be wise to take note of it.

66 But unfortunately we have reached a point in this debate where the accumulation of misrepresentations and material omissions regarding our healthy savings institutions is approaching what the physicists call "critical mass."

67 It threatens a run-away chain reaction of misbegotten public policies and legislation which would jeopardize national priorities and values.

68 At stake is our nation's commitment to home ownership as a national priority. Somehow this, and the crucial role our savings institutions play as the largest source of housing credit as well as the largest holders of mortgage-backed assets, has been lost in the clamor.

69 We managers of healthy savings institutions have every right to be angry. We are paying for problems we did not create. Our integrity and our management capability are being questioned. We are painted as guilty by association. The very continuation of the industry to which we have devoted our working lives is under assault.

70 That's why we're angry. But the homebuying public should be angrier still, for the threat to them in the form of lost opportunity for home ownership is real and present.

71 As we are beseiged, so is this nation's traditional commitment to home ownership beseiged.

72 We were created to serve as an instrument of public policy, the basic premise of which is that a well-housed society is a stable one. That policy has served this nation well, and our role in its pursuit is as valid today as it has ever been.

73 We want to continue in that role. We want to continue to make our major contribution to home ownership . . . and we will do that, so long as we are not overwhelmed by our contribution to the resolution of the errors of others.

Human Resource Management Issues in the '90s
Christine D. Keen

One of the most frequently heard terms in American business in the past decade has been human resource management, for many think that proper management of human resources is the key to an effective business enterprise. It is thus that the Society for Human Resource Management, consisting of human resource, personnel, and industrial relations executives, attempts to promote the advancement of human resource management. In this vein, Christine D. Keen, Issues Manager for the Society for Human Resource Management, delivered the following address to its National Conference at Atlanta, Georgia, June 25, 1990.

This tightly organized, factual prediction speech, which begins with a quotation from Yogi Berra and ends with one from Shoshana Zuboff, consists of two sections, the first being devoted to three predictions about today's Baby Boomers (1–24) and the second consisting of four scenarios for the changing times (25–33). A speaker wishing to predict must make the predictions seem both plausible and probable. To do this the speaker must look to present trends that seem to be deviating from the past and discern those trends that are the most likely to develop. Examine how Keen uses data from the present to support her predictions. Are all her predictions sufficiently developed to be both plausible and probable? Can you offer different predictions and different scenarios? Of what use are such attempts at predictions?

This speech is reprinted by permission from *Vital Speeches of the Day,* October 1, 1990, pp. 752–754.

1 When asked about an upcoming series, Yogi Berra supposedly once said, "I try never to make predictions, especially about the future." But I've never been very good about following commonly accepted wisdom, so that's exactly what I'm going to do. I'm going to chance some predictions about how the workplace may change over the next 10 or 15 years.

2 Let me start by asking you a question: how many of you were born sometime between 1946 and 1964? You're the Baby Boom generation, and during the '90s the work force and the work place will come to be dominated by the Baby Boomers—demographically, hierarchically, and psychologically. The Boomers already make up 55 percent of the work force, but during the '90s they will be moving into senior management. They will be policy-setters, and their attitudes and philosophies will govern the workplace.

3 I think we could see three broad trends developing over the next ten years which have, at their root, the differences between the Baby Boomers and the generation which preceded them.

4 First, we are seeing a shift toward putting more importance on family relationships and less on work. During the '70s and '80s the Boomers deferred marriage and children in order to develop their careers. They were ambitious and worked long and hard. But the restructurings of the last several years have taught them an important lesson: you cannot rely on your job as your source of self-validation. If all you've got is your career, when you lose your job, you lose your sense of self.

5 Consequently, the Boomers are now shifting from "In Search of Excellence" to "in search of meaning." They are seeking non-career avenues of self fulfillment, including family relationships, volunteer work and the personal growth movement. Not too surprisingly, the birth rate is rising again: last year there were more babies born in the U.S. than in any year for the past 25. The fertility rate went up 2 percent, which means, in layman's terms, women are having more children.

6 And perhaps even more revealing, we are starting to hear more comments—from men and women—like "unless I'm inventing a cure for AIDS or something, my work is not worth missing my kinds grow up." Or "I married you for you, not for your paycheck." Don't get caught in the trap of thinking this is just a "women's thing." Men may not articulate it, but a recent study of employees at Fortune 500 companies showed men were three times as likely to cite children as a reason for leaving a position as women were.

7 During the '90s we may see parents—male and female—scaling back their devotion to their jobs or dropping out of the traditional 9 to 5 work force entirely.

8 Where are they going to go? This brings me to my second broad trend: the emergence of the independent work force.

9 We are moving toward a point when we may have individual contracts with each of our employees. Employees may, in fact, become more akin to independent contractors, negotiating schedules, responsibilities, and rates of pay. We are already seeing a trickle-down effect, for example, from the severance contracts we gave senior executives in the '80s—more middle managers are now insisting on similar written guarantees.

10 Likewise, many companies are broadening their experiments with flextime. A hospital in Dallas, for example, is using a "work three, get one free" approach to recruiting nurses. The nurses work nine months a year, get to choose any three months they would like off, and have benefits for a full year. (This approach has, by the way, increased employment inquiries by 100 percent.)

11 Meanwhile, some European companies are taking the flextime approach to its logical conclusion. Whereas flextime generally lets you choose which 8 hours a day you want to work, and the compressed work week lets you choose which 40 hours a week you want to work (say, four 10 hour days), European companies are pioneering the flexyear: an employee chooses which 2000 or so hours he or she wants to work during the year.

12 The computer, the modem and the fax machine are allowing employees to choose not just when but where they work.

13 Further, the independent employee wants to determine his or her compensation package—not just the money, but the benefits. Flexible or cafeteria benefit plans have, in part, appealed to this desire. The '90s, though, could go in one of two opposite directions: a smorgasbord of mandated and optional benefits or no benefits at all.

14 Congress is actively interested in the possibility of taxing the value of employee benefits as income. Already, tuition assistance benefits are taxed in many cases, and the new child care bill awaiting President Bush's signature contains a provision taxing the value of employer-provided child care benefits for couples with a household income of $70,000 or more. Are benefits going to be an effective recruiting tool if their value is taxed. Perhaps companies would be wiser to get rid of their benefits entirely and compensate employees with more cash—after all, that's more the way we compensate consultants and independent contractors in the first place.

15 Further, the movement toward an independent work force may be accelerated by the Boomers' emphasis on independence and self-reliance. More outplaced middle managers are choosing to chuck corporate life entirely and go into business for themselves than ever before. Half of a recent graduating class of MBAs said they expect to work for themselves one day. Moonlighting is at its highest level in 30 years. Two factors will be feeding the entrepreneurial urge of the independent employee during the '90s; career plateaus and inheritance.

16 The Boomers are plateauing earlier than the previous generation. This is true for a couple of reasons: (1) there are more Boomers and fewer middle management positions for them to aspire to, and (2) much of the job growth over the last 15 years has been in small firms which often do not have the well-developed corporate ladder larger firms might. Second, in another 10 years the Boomers are expected to have more of the necessary capital to invest in their own businesses—not because of any saving they did, but because they will have inherited their parents' considerable assets.

17 How are you going to respond to the challenges and opportunities posed by the independent work force?

18 My third broad trend for the '90s and beyond is a complete redefinition of employment rights and responsibilities.

19 The Boomers do not share their parents attitudes about the role of business in society. "Big business" still carries a negative connotation. This generation doesn't think twice about targeting the deep pockets of business if they think they've been wronged. And they think they've been wronged a lot.

20 The Boomers tend to believe they should not have to waive their Constitutional rights in order to make a living. They believe in rights to privacy, due process, and freedom of speech in the workplace. They believe employees should not be fired without a good reason. They believe in meritocracy—the best should be rewarded without regard for age, gender, race, position, or seniority.

21 The ramifications of these attitudes will reverberate throughout the workplace. We can reasonably expect more concern about testing, for example. Polygraphs are all but gone, and there is movement afoot to ban psychological testing as well. Drug testing is still a thorny subject, and genetic testing could be a powder keg in the '90s.

22 We can also expect more erosion of employment-at-will doctrine. We may see more whistleblowing and more challenges to separation agreement waivers.

23 We will definitely see a call for a more equitable sharing of the benefits and burdens of the company's success and failure. That means linking pay more clearly with individual performance. It may mean generous severance compensation if the termination is not related to performance. It could even mean demands for reform of exorbitant CEO pay packages.

24 These three trends—the renewed emphasis on family, the independent work force and the redefinition of rights and responsibilities—may apply to some but certainly not all of your work force during the '90s. I'd like to sketch very quickly for you four other scenarios to watch for during the '90s.

25 First, the official bilingual or multilingual workplace. Immigration levels are at their highest levels this century, and for most of these immigrants, English is a second language—if they know it at all. We may see the development of a bilingual or multilingual workplace out of necessity or out of government intervention.

26 At Digital Equipment Corp.'s Boston plant, for example, 350 employees speak 19 different languages. Company announcements are printed in English, Chinese, French, Spanish, Portuguese, Vietnamese and Haitian Creole. Other companies are finding they need to teach employees English or teach managers Spanish.

27 Some people apparently feel employers are not reacting to this problem quickly enough on their own. A new law in Iowa requires all business to hire interpreters if 10 percent or more of their workplace speaks no English. This is the first law I am aware of which requires accommodation of a language handicap.

28 In the second scenario, tuition assistance for dependents becomes to the late '90s what child care was to the mid '80s. Tuition has been outpacing inflation for the last 10 years, and federal support for financial aid has halved since 1980. The leading edge of the baby boomlet—the children of the Baby Boomers—will be 13 this year. It was the birth of these same children which turned child care into a political issue and ushered in employer-provided child care benefits.

29 The Boomers have high expectations of their kids. Eighty-six percent expect their kids to go to college. Yet only 54 percent are saving for it. As was the case with child care, employers could be asked to come up with the rest.

30 In the third scenario, employers may step up dramatically their importation of skilled workers because the domestic work force cannot meet the demands for quantity or quality. Canada, for example, which currently has a higher national unemployment rate than the U.S., could be one pool to tap in the '90s (Canadians tend to be well educated, speak English, and free movement of labor may be encouraged by the U.S.-Canada free trade agreement.)

31 Finally, we may see a resurgence of unions during the '90s. Organized labor has spent much of the last decade reinventing itself to appeal to a changing work force. They have been successful in capitalizing on mainstream family issues such as health care, child care, parental leave and housing affordability. Unions have a rising approval rating among the general public, particularly among younger people, and have a rising rate of victory in union elections.

32 Women, minorities, immigrants, service sector workers and even white collar workers are being targeted by organized labor in an attempt to reach out to pockets of the work force which do not typically join unions. Employers should not be too sure that their work force is immune to the charms of a repositioned labor movement, particularly if workers feel their interests are at odds with management's—and evidence is that feeling is growing.

33 Issues for the '90s—the good, the bad and the ugly. How things develop over the next 10 years depends in large part on how we respond today. I read a quote from Shoshana Zuboff, a Harvard business school professor, a few months ago: "The future creeps in on small feet." Here at SHRM we are trying to not only track the footprints; we're trying to help you head them off.

Plutonium 238:
NASA's Fuel of Choice
Jenny Clanton

Jenny Clanton delivered this speech at a contest of the Interstate Oratorical Association in Salem, Oregon on May 6 and 7, 1988. A student at Southeastern Illinois College at Harrisburg, she was one of two students representing the State of Illinois in this annual intercollegiate event. She was awarded first place among the 37 contest participants.

Ms. Clanton advances the factual claim that NASA's use of plutonium 238 is unsafe. The first two main points in this speech, paragraphs 6 through 8 and paragraph 10, seem informative since they explain the nature of plutonium and consider NASA's assurances. To what extent can "mere" information be persuasive for an audience?

What specific arguments are advanced by Ms. Clanton in paragraphs 11 through 14 in support of her claim? What kinds of evidence are used to support each of the arguments? Does this evidence pass conventional tests of sound evidence? What central emotional appeal emerges in paragraph 14? Does this appeal help prepare the audience for the "call to action" appearing in paragraph 19?

This speech is reprinted by permission of the Interstate Oratorical Association from *Winning Orations,* 1988, pp. 24–27.

1 On January 28, 1986, the American Space Program suffered the worst disaster in its more than 30 year history. The entire world was shocked when the space shuttle Challenger exploded seconds after lift-off, claiming the lives of seven brave astronauts and crippling our entire space agenda. I suppose the oldest cliché in our culture, spoken on battlegrounds and indeed virtually anywhere Americans die, is "We must press forward, so we can say they did not die in vain." Rest assured. They didn't. The deaths of our seven astronauts probably saved the lives of untold thousands of Americans.

2 For, you see, if the O-rings had not failed on January 28, 1986, but rather on May 20, 1987, the next scheduled shuttle launch, in the words of Dr. John Gofman, Professor Emeritus at the Univeristy of California at Berkeley, you could have "kissed Florida goodbye."

3 Because the next shuttle, the one that was to have explored the atmosphere of Jupiter was to carry 47 lbs. of Plutonium 238, which is, again, according to Dr. Gofman, the most toxic substance on the face of the earth. Dr. Helen Caldicott corroborates Dr. Gofman's claim in her book, *Nuclear Madness,* when she cites studies estimating one ounce of widely dispersed Plutonium 238 particles as having the toxicity to induce lung cancer in every person on earth.

4 Today, when you leave this room, I want you to fully understand just what impact NASA's plans could have on this planet. I want you to become cynical. I want you to be a little scared. I want you to become angry. But most of all, I want you to begin to demand some answers.

5 To move you in this direction I would first like to explore with you just what plutonium is and what could happen if it were released in our atmosphere. Second, let's consider NASA's argument for the safety of the plutonium as used in the shuttle program. And finally, I want to convince you that NASA's conclusions are flawed.

6 So now, let's turn our attention to the nature of plutonium. Plutonium is a man-made radioactive element which is produced in large quantities in nuclear reactors from uranium. Plutonium is a chemically reactive metal which, if exposed to air, ignites spontaneously and produces fine particles of plutonium dioxide. These particles, when dispersed by wind and inhaled by living organisms, lodge in the lungs. Lung cancer will follow sooner or later. Once inside the human body, plutonium rests in bone tissue, causing bone cancer. Plutonium 238 is so poisonous that less than one *millionth* of a gram is a carcinogenic dose.

7 Last July, *Common Cause* magazine contacted Dr. Gofman at Berkeley and asked him to place Plutonium 238 in perspective. Before I share Dr. Gofman's assessment, please understand he's no poster-carrying "anti-nuke." Dr. Gofman was co-discoverer of Uranium 233, and he isolated the isotope first used in nuclear bombs. Dr. Gofman told Karl Grossman, author of the article "Redtape and Radio-activity" that Plutonium 238 is 300 times more radioactive than Plutonium 239, which is the isotope used in atomic bombs.

8 Dr. Richard Webb, a Nuclear Physicist and author of *The Accident Hazards of Nuclear Power Plants,* said in a similar interview that sending 46.7 lbs. of Plutonium 238 into space would be the equivalent of sending five nuclear reactors up—and then hoping they wouldn't crash or explode.

9 Dr. Gofman's final assessment? It's a crazy idea, unless—unless shuttle launches are 100 percent perfect. Which is just about what NASA would have liked us to believe, and at first glance NASA's guarantees are pretty convincing.

10 NASA estimates the chance of releasing Plutonium into the environment, because of the possibility of a malfunction of the space shuttle, at .002%—that's not quite 100% perfect, but it's awfully close. NASA and the Department of Energy base their reliability figures on three factors: 1) the Titan 34D launch vehicle and its high success rate, 2) Energy Department officials in the March 10th *Aviation Week and Space Technology* magazine explain that the Plutonium would be safely contained in an unbreakable, quarter-inch thick iridium cannister which would withstand pressures of over 2,000 pounds per square inch, and 3) in that same article, NASA explains there is "little public danger" because the Plutonium on board would be in the form of oxide pellets, each one-inch in diameter. If you'll remember, the danger of Plutonium is in fine particles.

11 Now, let's take a second glance. One month later, the April 28th issue of *Aviation Week and Space Technology* reported that two of the last nine Titans launched have blown-up. Two failures in nine trips is great in baseball, but not when we're dealing with nuclear payloads. That same article estimates loss of orbiter and crew, not at .002% but at 1 in 25.

12 With odds on the launch vehicle reduced to 1 in 25, the dual questions arise: just how breach-proof is that cannister and, in a worst case scenario, what could happen if the pellets of 238 were released? For the answers to those questions we go to Dr. Gary Bennett, former Director of Safety and Nuclear Operations, who not only answers those questions, but also explains why NASA is so insistent on using Plutonium.

13 Last July, Dr. Bennett told *Common Cause* that there is concern within NASA and the Department of Energy that an explosion aboard the Galileo spacecraft, a Titan or other rocket, would, in turn, set off an explosion of the booster rockets. Bennett admitted that government tests in 1984 and 1985 determined that if the shuttle exploded, and then the booster rockets exploded, there would be a likelihood of breaching the iridum cannister. The Plutonium would then be vaporized and released into the environment; and there goes Florida.

14 But why would NASA take such a risk? It's really quite simple. On the one hand, Plutonium 238 is the one fuel that would enable space exploration beyond the limit of Mars. Without it, distant space exploration must wait for research to develop an equally effective, safe fuel. On the other hand, a worst case scenario would create the worst nuclear accident in history. In short, NASA weighed exploration now against the chances for disaster and opted to take the risk. The only problem is, I really don't like the idea of someone risking my life without consulting me—and I hope you don't either. By the way, there is evidence that NASA and the Department of Energy have projected some pretty horrible figures. Under the Freedom of Information Act rules, Karl Grossman was able to obtain agencies' estimates for the number of lives lost in a major accident. The only problem there is, every reference to the number of people affected is blanketed out with liquid paper and the term Exempt #1 is written over the deletion. James Lombardo of the Energy Department explains the white-outs were necessary for—you've got it—national security reasons. I would contend the national security would be threatened by mass anger over the callousness of the Energy Department, and justifiably so. Representative Edward Markey agrees, and when he was head of the House sub-committee on Energy, Conservation and Power, he uncovered most of the information I share with you today.

15 In a telephone interview last August, I asked Congressman Markey three questions: Why hasn't Congress done anything? What should be done? What can we do to help?

16 His answer to the first question was quite interesting. You may remember that shortly after the shuttle exploded and just when Congress was showing some interest in a thorough investigation of the space program, another larger, even more dramatic accident occurred—Chernobyl. The attention to Chernobyl as it related to our own power industry captured not only the attention of most Americans, but of Congress as well. Consequently, most of our nuclear experts are involved in working with Congress and the nuclear power industry.

17 And while Congress is focusing on one facet of the nuclear question, NASA and the Department of Energy are receiving much less attention. Which is why Congressman Markey helped found Space Watch.

18 Representative Markey is of the opinion that hysteria accomplishes nothing, but that all space flight should be halted until either Plutonium 238 can be made safe, which is highly unlikely, or until an alternative fuel can be found. The burden of proof should be on NASA to prove a fuel safe, and not on the public to prove it dangerous.

19 This is where you and I come in. First, if by now you are sufficiently scared or angry, contact Space Watch through Representative Markey's office. Then, keep abreast of developments and exert pressure through your elected officials if Congress does nothing to interfere with NASA's plans. Send your objections not only to your own legislators, but to Representative Markey as well. Allow him to walk into the House with mailbag after mailbag of letters in opposition to NASA's unbridled desire to go to Jupiter. We have a friend in Congress who solicits help. The least we can do is give it to him.

20 One last thought: as of November, Plutonium 238 is *still* NASA's and the Department of Energy's fuel of choice. Dr. Bennett's last words in that July interview were, "I think you should understand there's a degree of risk with any kind of launch vehicle." But isn't that the point?

New York Governor Mario Cuomo drives home a point during his keynote address at the 1984 Democratic National Convention.

CHAPTER 5

SPEECHES THAT AFFIRM PROPOSITIONS OF VALUE

Values are the light by which we see our world; they are the bases of our choices; they help determine which problems, causes, and solutions we believe are important; they give our civilizations their distinctive hues. ...Therefore, we must understand how to analyze values and how to persuade others to accept them if we are to make intelligent speeches.

Otis M. Walter and Robert L. Scott

THE NATURE AND IMPORTANCE OF SPEECHES THAT AFFIRM PROPOSITIONS OF VALUE

The centrality of values to human existence and to the communication process is acknowledged by Richard M. Weaver, a rhetorical theorist and critic, and by Kenneth Boulding, social critic and economist. In his *The Ethics of Rhetoric,* Weaver contends, "It is the nature of the conscious life of man to revolve around some concept of value. So true is this that when the concept is withdrawn, or when it is forced into conflict with another concept, the human being suffers an almost intolerable sense of being lost." Boulding, in *The Image,* argues:

> . . . The value scales of any individual or organization are perhaps the most important single element determining the effect of the messages it receives on its image of the world. If a message is perceived that is neither good nor bad it may have little or no effect on the image. If it is perceived as bad or hostile to the image which is held, there will be resistance to accepting it.

On the other hand, when a message reinforces a value that is cherished, auditors are likely to be receptive to the position being advanced.

During the past three decades, values have been very much in conflict in American society. Activists have questioned war as a legitimate method of resolving international disputes, poverty as a necessary consequent of a complex economic order, and civil obedience as an unquestioned obligation of responsible citizenship. Americans of all ages have become more compellingly aware of their own values. Some have sought to translate new values into working political and economic practices. Others, threatened by the aggressiveness of reformers, have reasserted their own traditional values as the appropriate way for civilized community life. Hopefully this continuing dialogue about values will meet Richard Weaver's test of public discourse in its finer moments: " . . . Rhetoric at its truest seeks to perfect men by showing them better versions of themselves, links in that chain extending up toward the ideal. . . ."

Not all propositions of value, however, concern the crucial issues of modern social existence. While some speakers affirm propositions related to war or peace, prosperity or poverty, and human love or bigotry, others affirm propositions of value related to artistic excellence, academic achievement, or even, via the mass media, the taste of colas and toothpastes. Propositions of value pervade all facets of human life.

Recall that in Chapter 2 a value was defined as a conception of "The Good" or "The Desirable" which functions sometimes as a goal motivating our behavior and sometimes as a standard for evaluating means to achieve ends. You may wish to reread the comments in that chapter explaining the line of critical analysis that asked: "To what degree do the speaker's ideas harmonize with the audience's relevant values?"

Somtimes speakers urge adoption of a new value, or adoption of a new perspective through redefining an old value. Some speakers aim to reinforce and reenergize audience commitment to values already held. Often speakers offer their value judgment of something (such as a book, film, play, or speech) as valid for audience belief. On occasion a speaker must defend his or her character and reputation against criticism. Such a speech of personal defense aims at refuting negative value judgments concerning the speaker's honesty, integrity, ethics, morals, and public responsibility.

Speakers also affirm values in speeches not primarily devoted to values. A speaker presenting information to enhance audience understanding will show that the information is valuable because it is relevant and useful. To generate listener concern about a problem, a speaker must show that the situation threatens or violates basic relevant audience values. To secure audience acceptance of a policy as a solution to a problem, a speaker must show that the policy is consistent with or enhances central audience values. And, contrary to the popular notion, "facts" do not "speak for themselves." *Humans* present and interpret matters agreed upon as factual in light of their own related values.

Whatever the particular proposition of value, the advocate seeks listener agreement that something meets or does not meet a specific value standard. Unlike the proposition of fact, which is affirmed or denied through tests of existence, occurrence, or causality, the proposition of value is affirmed through tests of *goodness* or *quality*. A value standard may be applied to an individual, an event, an object, a way of life, a process, a condition, or even to another value. Consider the following examples:

Proposition A: Modern art is rubbish.
Proposition B: Sexual chastity before marriage is an outmoded value.
Proposition C: Winston Churchill was a great man.
Proposition D: War is immoral.
Proposition E: A speaker who uses primarily emotional appeals is unethical.
Proposition F: Civil disobedience always is bad.
Proposition G: President Reagan was irresponsible in his handling of the Iran-Contra Affair.

These propositions of value differ in subject matter being valued or devalued. However, each affirms or denies something measured against standards rooted in listener values. Like all propositions of value, those noted above include a word or words that imply a value dimension—"is rubbish," "is an outmoded value" "was a great man," "is immoral," "is unethical," "is bad," "was irresponsible." Because the meanings associated with such evaluative terms are deeply rooted, saturated with emotion, and wrapped in tradition, the task of the advocate seeking to affirm a proposition of value frequently is an incredibly difficult one. And equally difficult is the task of judging such speeches.

CRITERIA FOR EVALUATING SPEECHES
THAT AFFIRM PROPOSITIONS OF VALUE

1. Has the speaker demonstrated or is it assumed by the audience that he or she is a person of high credibility with respect to the proposition being advocated?

When the speaker leaves the realm of empirically verifiable fact and enters the realm of culturally-based and often abstractly-defined values, the assessment by listeners becomes increasingly dependent on their perceptions of the speaker's expertness and trustworthiness. In stressing the potency of speaker ethos, Aristotle wrote: "As a rule we trust men of probity more and more quickly about things in general, while on points outside the realm of exact knowledge, where opinion is divided, we trust them absolutely."

Listeners tend to believe statements about values and value judgments made by speakers they admire and respect. But different audiences and cultures value different qualities in speakers. A college professor of economics arguing that American advertising is unethical may be considered an expert by an audience of high school sophomores, a starry-eyed idealist by an audience of business people, and an extreme liberal by an audience of college Young Republicans.

Although most communication scholars agree that the speaker who is considered by an audience as highly credible has an advantage over the speaker whose ethos is low, they do not always agree on the exact factors determining speaker prestige. In *Principles of Speaking,* for example, Hance, Ralph, and Wiksell list *competence,* which "grows out of a combination of mental ability, know-how, intelligence, understanding, experience with the subject, and knowledge"; *good character,* which is "made up of honesty, integrity, sincerity, fairness, and similar qualities that meet the standards of listeners"; and *good will,* which "consists of friendliness, likeableness, rapport, warmth, and being 'in' with the audience." In *The Art of Persuasion,* Minnick includes confidence and poise, physical energy, sincerity and conviction, mental alertness, intelligence and knowledge, fairness and justice, self-discipline, even temper and restraint, sympathy and understanding, decisiveness, dynamism, and similarity to audience values and beliefs. For further discussion of the importance of source credibility, you may want to read again in chapter 2 the line of critical inquiry which asked: "To what degree is the speaker perceived as a highly credible source on the subject?"

Among the questions you may wish to ask about the advocate of a proposition of value are these: Is the speaker a person who embodies the qualities of character, intelligence, and experience most admired by the audience? Does the speaker's life demonstrate commitment to the value she or he advocates or applies? Does the speaker have the training and experience to qualify for making the value judgment expressed?

2. Has the speaker advanced acceptable criteria for the assessment of the proposition of value?

The criteria for assessing a proposition of value differ from those for assessing a proposition of fact. The criteria for the latter are essentially empirical or quasi-empirical, whereas those for the former are steeped in feelings and related values. For example, consider the following proposition:

Proposition of fact: Capital punishment is not an effective deterrent to crime.

Proposition of value: Capital punishment is morally bad.

In the first case, widely accepted criteria for judgment involve tests of empirical reality. Has capital punishment led to a reduction in serious crimes in states where it has been tried? Do states with capital punishment have lower rates of serious crimes than equivalent states that do not have capital punishment? Have carefully controlled, systematic studies demonstrated that potential criminals consider the consequences of their crimes before committing them? In the second instance, the criteria for judgment are rooted in earlier value commitments. Is the taking of human life, for whatever cause, contrary to values fundamental to the Judeo-Christian ethic, to human decency, or to communal life?

In attempting to gain acceptance of a proposition of value, a speaker has a number of rhetorical options available for stressing the appropriateness of his or her value criteria. The speaker can show that the value standards used or values advocated are consistent with other values already held by the audience. The speaker might show that the value advocated has produced desirable consequences in the past when adhered to; this involves using *another* value standard to demonstrate "desirability." Sometimes speakers use examples and testimony to show that "good" persons generally have accepted the advocated value and "bad" or less desirable persons have rejected it. Or the value being advocated may be *contrasted* with its undesirable opposite (disvalue) or with a less desirable value. And some speakers offer to an audience a *hierarchy* of values by verbally indicating that the value advocated or defended is *better than* other specific values. Finally, a speaker might argue that socially undesirable consequences will result from continued adherence to old, outmoded values.

Speakers need not fail when their value judgments run counter to the values of the audience. When in 1932 Franklin D. Roosevelt spoke to San Francisco's Commonwealth Club, a group of businessmen with conservative economic values, he began with a careful historical review of the values that had produced industrial America. Then he pointed out that these values had served the nation well but were no longer consistent with our best national interest. In 1886, Southerner Henry W. Grady, in an address to members of the New England Society, sought to erase their long-standing hositility toward the South by praising the spirit of Lincoln and by urging commitment to national values rather than to regional loyalties. Admittedly persuading about values is a complex task, but it is one that a perceptive and sensitive speaker can accomplish to some degree.

In evaluating a speech affirming a proposition of value, the enlightened listener must carefully consider the criteria for judgment that he or she is being asked to accept. Is the value advocated for acceptance or application clearly and exactly specified? Does the speaker demonstrate that the value is reasonable and relevant for the subject at hand? Is the value or value judgment only asserted or implied without clear and reasonable support or demonstration? To what degree do the value appeals serve a legitimate function of promoting social cohesion, of reinforcing audience commitment to ideas they already believe? With what degree of appropriateness are the consequences of commitment to the values clarified? To what degree do the value appeals serve as substitutes, as pseudoproof, for the factuality of an assertion? To what degree do the value appeals divert attention from more fundamental, pressing, or controversial matters? To what degree do the value appeals seem to promote, intentionally or not, unreflective stimulus-response reactions when the occasion demands reflective judgment?

3. Has the speaker presented a fair view of what is being evaluated?

It should be apparent that a speaker may be eminently qualified to judge and may have acceptable criteria of judgment in mind and yet may have a distorted view of what is being judged. Propositions of value usually are emotion-laden and a speaker's bias may impair her or his ability to depict fairly the object being judged.

Propositions of value often depend on the previous acceptance or establishment of a proposition of fact. Thus the critic must consider whether the advocate has met adequate criteria for the assessment of fact that portrays what the advocate is judging. Should the speaker be intersted in evaluating an event, we first must be assured that the event has been portrayed accurately. Similarly, should the speaker wish to assign a value to a work of art, a belief, an individual, an institution, an action, or another value, we should inquire about the accuracy with which the object being judged is described. Faced with an object described in two-valued, either-or, no-middle-ground terms, the critical listener must consider whether such a description is accurate and adequate for the situation.

CONCLUSION

The climate of public debate in America during the late 20th Century reflects "an unwillingness, if not a psychological inability, to make and defend judgments of better and worse." Emmanuel Mesthene, a professor of philosophy, elaborates on his view by condemning the widespread hesitancy to "argue a position or justify an action on the basis of judgments of relative worth, whether of morality, of art, of individuals, or of institutions." To what extent do you agree with his contentions? Are value judgments or advocacy of values far too rare in contemporary public discourse?

No matter how frequently we are exposed to value-oriented messages, and because values play such an important role in decisions related to individual and social well-being, the enlightened listener/critic must consider carefully the evaluative messages received each day. In assessing speeches that affirm propositions of value, the critic should consider (1) *whether the speaker is a person of high credibility with respect to the proposition being advocated,* (2) *whether the speaker has advanced acceptable criteria for the assessment of the proposition, and* (3) *whether the speaker has presented a fair view of what is being evaluated.*

For further reading

Andersen, Kenneth E. *Persuasion.* 2nd ed. Allyn and Bacon, 1978. Chapter 11 probes the influence of a persuader's credibility.

Condon, John C., and Yousef, Fathi S. *An Introduction to Intercultural Communication.* Bobbs-Merrill, 1975. Chapters 3 and 4 examine the functioning of values in various non-American cultures and between different cultures.

Bradley, Bert E. *Speech Communication: The Credibility of Ideas.* 5th ed. Wm. C. Brown, 1988. Chapter 6 examines the elements of speaker credibility: competence, trustworthiness, similarity, attraction, and sincerity.

Ehninger, Douglas, and Hauser, Gerard. "Communication of Values." In Carroll Arnold and John Bowers, eds. *Handbook of Rhetorical and Communication Theory.* Allyn and Bacon, 1984, Chapter 4.

Fisher, Walter R. "Toward a Logic of Good Reasons." *Quarterly Journal of Speech,* December 1978, 376–384.

Harrell, Jackson; Ware, B. L.; and Linkugel, Wil A. "Failure of Apology in American Politics: Nixon on Watergate." *Speech Monographs,* November 1975, 245–61. Analyzes Nixon's first two Watergate speeches from the perspective of the bases of political authority and the theory of apology.

McEdwards, Mary G. "American Values: Circa 1920–1970." *Quarterly Journal of Speech,* April 1971, pp. 173–80. Illustrates how basic American values have remained relatively constant.

Mesthene, Emmanuel G. "On the Importance of Judging Between Better or Worse." *National Forum,* LXIX (Summer 1979): 4–8.

Rieke, Richard D., and Sillars, Malcolm O. *Argumentation and the Decision Making Process.* 2nd ed. Scott, Foresman, 1984, Chapter 6. After explaining the nature of values, the authors describe in detail six traditional and nontraditional American value systems.

Rokeach, Milton. *The Nature of Human Values.* Macmillan, 1970. A theoretical discussion of what values are and an empirical description of major contemporary American value commitments.

Sillars, Malcolm O. *Messages, Meanings, and Culture: Approaches to Communication Criticism.* Harper/Collins, 1991. Chapter 7 considers criticism of values in discourse.

Walter, Otis M. *Speaking Intelligently.* Macmillan, 1976, pp. 131–49, 228–30. The author focuses on the functioning of values in public discourse aimed at problem-solving.

Walter, Otis M., and Scott, Robert L. *Thinking and Speaking.* 5th ed. Macmillan, 1984. Pages 95–97 survey some contemporary American values and Chapter 10 discusses persuading about values.

Ware, B. L., and Linkugel, Wil A. "They Spoke in Defense of Themselves: On the Generic Criticism of Apologia." *Quarterly Journal of Speech.* October 1973, 273–83. Examines the rhetorical strategies and tactics available to speakers in defending their personal character against negative value judgments.

Warnick, Barbara, and Inch, Edward S. *Critical Thinnking and Communication: The Use of Reason in Argument.* Macmillan, 1989. Chapter 8 discusses advocating and opposing value propositions.

Weaver, Richard M. *The Ethics of Rhetoric.* Regnery, 1953, Chapter 9. Weaver's discussion of "ultimate terms" in the rhetoric of the era illuminates the persuasive potency of values and disvalues as they appear in the form of societal "god terms" and "devil terms."

The Watergate Affair
Richard M. Nixon

Early morning, June 17, 1972, five employees of the Committee to Reelect President Nixon were arrested as they attempted to burglarize the Democratic National Headquarters in the Watergate office and apartment building in Washington, D.C. High officials of the Nixon Administration quickly became involved in covering up the details of the incident. For some time, little real information concerning the incident was available. Hearsay and rumor, however, were rampant. By the Spring of 1973 investigations revealed that top presidential officials participated in the cover-up. In early April, John Dean, former Presidential counsel, was dismissed, and shortly thereafter top aides, H. R. Haldeman and John Ehrlichman, resigned their positions on the President's staff. These actions were the immediate exigency that precipitated President Nixon's first Watergate apologia.

An apology is a speech of personal defense. The questioning of a person's moral nature, motives, or reputation is qualitatively different from the challenging of that individual's policies or ideas. An attack upon a person's character, upon his or her value as a human being, seems to demand a direct response that seeks to purify the speaker's personal image. The resulting address seeks to prove a proposition of value.

As President Nixon addressed the nation via national television on the evening of April 30, 1973, he did so against the backdrop of tradition. Socrates, Demosthenes, Martin Luther, Sir Thomas More, Edmund Burke, Sam Houston, Adlai Stevenson, and President Truman all, at one time or another, sought to purify their personal images from charges of wrongdoing. Nixon himself was no novice to this type of speaking. He had delivered his famous "Checkers" speech on national television in the 1952 election when he was charged with possessing an illegal campaign fund. Success had crowned his efforts on that occasion. Dwight Eisenhower kept Nixon on the ticket as a direct result of his apologetic appeal. But now, April 30, 1973, Richard Nixon once more faced the nation as he gave his first Watergate apologia.

Apologetic discourse commonly involves four main strategies: denial, bolstering, differentiation, and transcendence. Strategies of *denial* seek to negate alleged facts, sentiments, objects, or relationships and can easily be imagined to be important to speeches of self-defense. Denial is obviously useful to the speaker only to the extent that a negation does not constitute a known distortion of reality. When a speaker *bolsters,* he attempts to identify himself with something the audience views favorably. Bolstering thus reinforces the existence of a fact, sentiment, object, or relationship. Strategies of *differentiation* are divisive in that they seek to divide the speaker from a fact, sentiment, object, or relationship. A speaker may, for example, do as Senator Edward Kennedy did in his "Chappaquiddick" speech when he sought to differentiate his erratic behavior immediately after the accident that proved fatal to Mary Jo Kopechne from that of his usual behavior when his faculties are functioning more normally. *Transcendental* strategies psychologically move the audience away from the particular charges at hand in a direction toward some more abstract, general view. When General Douglas MacArthur addressed the Congress in 1952 after President Truman relieved him of his Korean command for insubordination, he sought to move the rhetorical proposition to the larger context of American security in the Pacific. (For further elaboration of these strategies see the Ware and Linkugel citation in sources for further reading.)

Keep these four basic strategies in mind as you read President Nixon's first Watergate apology. Examine his uses of denial (paragraphs 4–6), bolstering (10, 12, 17, 42–47, 48, 54–55), differentiation (6, 21–23), and transcendence (31–38). In what ways and to what degree do you judge them to be effective, reasonable, and ethical? In addition, what is your assessment of the apparent function and legitimate relevancy of some of the information and appeals he presents (4, 31, 40, 53)? Is there any contradiction in Nixon's uses of the ethical premise that the end does not justify the means (27, 50–51)? For a broad analysis of presidential rhetoric that defends against charges of personal wrongdoing, see Karlyn Kohrs Campbell and Kathleen Hall Jamieson, *Deeds Done In Words: Presidential Rhetoric and the Genres of Governance* (1990), Chs. 7 and 8.

President Nixons' rhetoric on this occasion achieved limited success. The Gallup Poll showed that only about 30 percent of the public thought that he had "told the whole truth." How possible was it for the President to be persuasive in this situation? Nixon presented a series of Watergate defense speeches and statements during the spring and summer of 1973. In late July 1974, the U.S. House of Representatives debated formal articles of impeachment against Nixon. After a U.S. Supreme Court decision forced Nixon to release incriminating taperecordings of White House conversations, Nixon resigned on August 8, 1974, when he presented a nationally televised address to the nation.

President Nixon's speech is reprinted from *Weekly Compilation of Presidential Documents*, 9 (May 7, 1973), 433–438.

Good evening:

1 I want to talk to you tonight from my heart on a subject of deep concern to every American.

2 In recent months, members of my Administration and officials of the Committee for the Re-election of the President—including some of my closest friends and most trusted aides—have been charged with involvement in what has come to be known as the Watergate affair. These include charges of illegal activity during and preceding the 1972 Presidential election and charges that responsible officials participated in efforts to cover up that illegal activity.

3 The inevitable result of these charges has been to raise serious questions about the integrity of the White House itself. Tonight I wish to address those questions.

4 Last June 17, while I was in Florida trying to get a few days rest after my visit to Moscow, I first learned from news reports of the Watergate break-in. I was appalled at this senseless, illegal action, and I was shocked to learn that employees of the Re-election Committee were apparently among those guilty. I immediately ordered an investigation by appropriate Government authorities. On September 15, as you will recall, indictments were brought against seven defendants in the case.

5 As the investigations went forward, I repeatedly asked those conducting the investigation whether there was any reason to believe that members of my Administration were in any way involved. I received repeated assurances that there were not. Because of these continuing reassurances, because I believed the reports I was getting, because I had faith in the persons from whom I was getting them, I discounted the stories in the press that appeared to implicate members of my Administration or other officials of the campaign committee.

6 Until March of this year, I remained convinced that the denials were true and that the charges of involvement by members of the White House Staff were false. The comments I made during this period, and the comments made by my Press Secretary in my behalf, were based on the information provided to us at the time we made those comments. However, new information then came to me which persuaded me that there was a real possibility that some of these charges were true, and suggesting further that there had been an effort to conceal the facts both from the public, from you, and from me.

7. As a result, on March 21, I personally assumed the responsibility for coordinating intensive new inquiries into the matter, and I personally ordered those conducting the investigations to get all the facts and to report them directly to me, right here in this office.

8 I again ordered that all persons in the Government or at the Re-election Committee should cooperate fully with the FBI, the prosecutors, and the grand jury. I also ordered that anyone who refused to cooperate in telling the truth would be asked to resign from government service. And, with ground rules adopted that would preserve the basic constitutional separation of powers between the Congress and the Presidency, I directed that members of the White House Staff should appear and testify voluntarily under oath before the Senate committee which was investigating Watergate.

9 I was determined that we should get to the bottom of the matter, and that the truth should be fully brought out—no matter who was involved.

10 At the same time, I was determined not to take precipitate action, and to avoid, if at all possible, any action that would appear to reflect on innocent people. I wanted to be fair. But I knew that in the final analysis, the integrity of this office—public faith in the integrity of this office—would have to take priority over all personal considerations.

11 Today, in one of the most difficult decisions of my Presidency, I accepted the resignations of two of my closest associates in the White House—Bob Haldeman, John Ehrlichman—two of the finest public servants it has been my privilege to know.

12 I want to stress that in accepting these resignations, I mean to leave no implication whatever of personal wrongdoing on their part, and I leave no implication tonight of implication on the part of others who have been charged in this matter. But in matters as sensitive as guarding the integrity of our democratic process, it is essential not only that rigorous legal and ethical standards be observed, but also that the public, you, have total confidence that they are both being observed and enforced by those in authority and particularly by the President of the United States. They agreed with me that this move was necessary in order to restore that confidence.

13 Because Attorney General Kleindienst—though a distinguished public servant, my personal friend for 20 years, with no personal involvement whatever in this matter— has been a close personal and professional associate of some of those who are involved in this case, he and I both felt that it was also necessary to name a new Attorney General.

14 The Counsel to the President, John Dean, has also resigned.

15 As the new Attorney General, I have today named Elliot Richardson, a man of unimpeachable integrity and rigorously high principle. I have directed him to do everything necessary to ensure that the Department of Justice has the confidence and the trust of every law abiding person in this country.

16 I have given him absolute authority to make all decisions bearing upon the prosecution of the Watergate case and related matters. I have instructed him that if he should consider it appropriate, he has the authority to name a special supervising prosecutor for matters arising out of the case.

17 Whatever may appear to have been the case before, whatever improper activities may yet be discovered in connection with this whole sordid affair, I want the American people, I want you to know beyond the shadow of a doubt that during my term as President, justice will be pursued fairly, fully, and impartially, no matter who is involved. This office is a sacred trust and I am determined to be worthy of that trust.

18 Looking back at the history of this case, two questions arise:

19 How could it have happened?

20 Who is to blame?

21 Political commentators have correctly observed that during my 27 years in politics I have always previously insisted on running my own campaigns for office.

22 But 1972 presented a very different situation. In both domestic and foreign policy, 1972 was a year of crucially important decisions, of intense negotiations, of vital new directions, particularly in working toward the goal which has been my overriding concern throughout my political career—the goal of bringing peace to America, peace to the world.

23 That is why I decided, as the 1972 campaign approached, that the Presidency should come first and politics second. To the maximum extent possible, therefore, I sought to delegate campaign operations, to remove the day-to-day campaign decisions from the President's office and from the White House. I also, as you recall, severely limited the number of my own campaign appearances.

24 Who, then, is to blame for what happened in this case?

25 For specific criminal actions by specific individuals, those who committed those actions must, of course, bear the liability and pay the penalty.

26 For the fact that alleged improper actions took place within the White House or within my campaign organization, the easiest course would be for me to blame those to whom I delegated the responsibility to run the campaign. But that would be a cowardly thing to do.

27 I will not place the blame on subordinates—on people whose zeal exceeded their judgment, and who may have done wrong in a cause they deeply believed to be right.

28 In any organization, the man at the top must bear the responsibility. That responsibility, therefore, belongs here, in this office. I accept it. And I pledge to you tonight, from this office, that I will do everything in my power to ensure that the guilty are brought to justice, and that such abuses are purged from our political processes in the years to come, long after I have left this office.

29 Some people, quite properly appalled at the abuses that occurred, will say that Watergate demonstrates the bankruptcy of the American political system. I believe precisely the opposite is true. Watergate represented a series of illegal acts and bad judgments by a number of individuals. It was the system that has brought the facts to light and that will bring those guilty to justice—a system that in this case has included a determined grand jury, honest prosecutors, a courageous judge, John Sirica, and a vigorous free press.

30 It is essential now that we place our faith in that system—and especially in the judicial system. It is essential that we let the judicial process go forward, respecting those safeguards that are established to protect the innocent as well as to convict the guilty. It is essential that in reacting to the excesses of others, we not fall into excesses ourselves.

31 It is also essential that we not be so distracted by events such as this that we neglect the vital work before us, before this nation, before America, at a time of critical importance to America and the world.

32 Since March, when I first learned that the Watergate affair might, in fact, be far more serious than I had been led to believe, it has claimed far too much of my time and my attention.

33 Whatever may now transpire in the case, whatever the actions of the grand jury, whatever the outcome of any eventual trials, I must now turn my full attention—and I shall do so—once again to the larger duties of this office. I owe it to this great office that I hold, and I owe it to you—to my country.

34 I know that as Attorney General, Elliot Richardson will be both fair and he will be fearless in pursuing this case wherever it leads. I am confident that with him in charge, justice will be done.

35 There is vital work to be done toward our goal of a lasting structure of peace in the world—work that cannot wait, work that I must do.

36 Tomorrow, for example, Chancellor Brandt of West Germany will visit the White House for talks that are a vital element of "The Year of Europe," as 1973 has been called. We are already preparing for the next Soviet-American summit meeting later this year.

37 This is also a year in which we are seeking to negotiate a mutual and balanced reduction of armed forces in Europe, which will reduce our defense budget and allow us to have funds for other purposes at home so desperately needed. It is the year when the United States and Soviet negotiators will seek to work out the second and even more important round of our talks on limiting nuclear arms, and of reducing the danger of a nuclear war that would destroy civilization as we know it. It is a year in which we confront the difficult tasks of maintaining peace in Southeast Asia and in the potentially explosive Middle East.

38 There is also vital work to be done right here in America: to ensure prosperity, and that means a good job for everyone who wants to work; to control inflation, that I know worries every housewife, everyone who tries to balance a family budget in America; to set in motion new and better ways of ensuring progress toward a better life for all Americans.

39 When I think of this office—of what it means—I think of all the things that I want to accomplish for this Nation, of all the things I want to accomplish for you.

40 On Christmas Eve, during my terrible personal ordeal of the renewed bombing of North Vietnam, which after 12 years of war, finally helped to bring America peace with honor, I sat down just before midnight. I wrote out some of my goals for my second term as President.

41 Let me read them to you.

42 "To make it possible for our children, and for our children's children, to live in a world of peace.

43 "To make this country be more than ever a land of opportunity—of equal opportunity, full opportunity for every American.

44 "To provide jobs for all who can work, and generous help for those who cannot work.

45 "To establish a climate of decency, and civility, in which each person respects the feelings and the dignity and the God-given rights of his neighbor.

46 "To make this a land in which each person can dare to dream, can live his dreams—not in fear, but in hope—proud of his community, proud of his country, proud of what America has meant to himself and to the world."

47 These are great goals. I believe we can, we must work for them. We can achieve them. But we cannot achieve these goals unless we dedicate ourselves to another goal.

48 We must maintain the integrity of the White House, and that integrity must be real, not transparent. There can be no whitewash at the White House.

49 We must reform our political process—ridding it not only of the violations of the law, but also of the ugly mob violence, and other inexcusable campaign tactics that have been too often practiced and too readily accepted in the past, including those that may have been a response by one side to the excesses or expected excesses of the other side. Two wrongs do not make a right.

50 I have been in public life for more than a quarter of a century. Like any other calling, politics has good people, and bad people. And let me tell you, the great majority in politics—in the Congress, in the Federal Government, in the State Government—are good people. I know that it can be very easy, under the intensive pressures of a campaign, for even well-intentioned people to fall into shady tactics—to rationalize this on the grounds that what is at stake is of such importance to the Nation that the end justifies the means. And both of our great parties have been guilty of such tactics in the past.

51 In recent years, however, the campaign excesses that have occurred on all sides have provided a sobering demonstration of how far this false doctrine can take us. The lesson is clear: America, in its political campaigns, must not again fall into the trap of letting the end, however great that end is, justify the means.

52 I urge the leaders of both political parties, I urge citizens, all of you, everywhere, to join in working toward a new set of standards, new rules and procedures to ensure that future elections will be as nearly free of such abuses as they possibly can be made. This is my goal, I ask you to join in making it America's goal.

53 When I was inaugurated for a second term this past January 20, I gave each member of my Cabinet and each member of my senior White House Staff a special 4-year calendar, with each day marked to show the number of days remaining to the Administration. In the inscription on each calendar, I wrote these words: "The Presidential term which begins today consists of 1,461 days—no more, no less. Each can be a day of strengthening and renewal for America; each can add depth and dimension to the American experience. If we strive together, if we make the most of the challenges and the opportunity that these days offer us, they can stand out as great days for America, and great moments in the history of the world."

54 I looked at my own calendar this morning up at Camp David as I was working on this speech. It showed exactly 1,361 days remaining in my term. I want these to be the best days in America's history, because I love America. I deeply believe that America is the hope of the world. And I know that in the quality and wisdom of the leadership America gives lies the only hope for millions of people all over the world, that they can live their lives in peace and freedom. We must be worthy of that hope, in every sense of the word. Tonight, I ask for your prayers to help me in everything that I do throughout the days of my Presidency to be worthy of their hopes and of yours.

55 God bless America and God bless each and every one of you.

For the World to Live, 'Europe' Must Die
Russell Means

In the Summer of 1980, Russell Means, a member of the Ogala Lakota tribe, of the Sioux nation, addressed several thousand people during the Black Hills International Survival Gathering held on the Pine Ridge Reservation in South Dakota. This meeting was held to protest the pollution and exploitation of American Indian lands throughout the West. For most of those in his audience, Means' ethos, his level of source credibility, would be extremely high. Their perceptions of his personal qualities, such as expertness and trustworthiness, would be very positive. He co-founded the activist American Indian Movement (AIM). He organized activist groups in cities and on reservations. He played a major role in the protest occupation of Wounded Knee, South Dakota, in the Spring of 1973. In the course of his various activities, he has been injured, shot, and jailed. Although now he downplays his leadership role (par. 46), his audience would listen carefully to his advice because of their high esteem for him as a leader.

The central issue, according to Means, is the clash between two antagonistic value systems, between two opposite world views—the European and the traditional American Indian tribal. A revolution in value commitments is needed, and he offers a persuasive definition of what we should mean by the label "revolution" (par. 21, 23, 33–34).

An attack on the European-American value system comprises the bulk of Means' address. He pinpoints some of the values he feels are central to the European mind-set; step-by-step logical thinking (7); mechanical image of nature and humans (8), material gain (10); scientific despiritualization of nature and humans (11); and arrogant elevation of humans above other animate and inanimate things (29–30). The values of progress, development, victory, and freedom, all highly prized in the European cultural view, Means depicts as actually undesirable, as disvalues (12).

One major strategy used by Means to undermine European values is to describe the dangerous consequences of following such values (11–12, 24, 18–19, 25–26). Assess the soundness of the cause-effect reasoning he uses to make such arguments. Means contends very specifically that Marxism is only a different version of the European cultural tradition and, as such, is just as flawed as capitalism or Christianity (21–23, 27). As another rhetorical strategy he itemizes objectionable groups and individuals who embody the undesirable European values (38).

To a lesser extent, Means discusses a few of the specific values central to the traditional American Indian world view: the universe as complex and spiritual (7); ''being'' a good person (10); and the inter-relation of all humans and facets of nature (29–31, 40). To what degree would the speech have been strengthened by a more complete discussion of the values central to the Indian world view? Might Means' audience already have understood and assumed the validity of some key values not discussed? Means mentions a few groups that seem to embody the praiseworthy tribal value system (39). The labels Means chooses heightens the stark contrast between the antagonistic value stances: ''death culture'' (41) versus ''correct peoples'' (32). Means' fundamental belief is that the strength to resist and overturn Europeani-zation flows from commitment to traditional American Indian tribal values (5, 34).

In December 1985, along with other members of the New American Indian Movement, Means went to Nicaragua to join Indians native to Nicaragua in fighting that country's Marxist Sandinista government (*Chicago Tribune,* December 28, 1985, Sec. 1, p. 3). Means argued that the Marxist government could not deal fairly with Nicaraguan Indians because ''Marxists are racists.''

For an analysis of the broad historical and cultural context within which Means advocates Native American values, see Richard Morris and Philip Wander, ''Native American Rhetoric: Dancing in the Shadows of the Ghost Dance,'' *Quarterly Journal of Speech,* 76 (May 1990): 164–191. The clash of the Lakota and European cultures and value systems in the late 1800s in the American West is depicted vividly in the 1990 academy award film, ''Dances With Wolves,'' produced by, directed by, and starring Kevin Costner.

Reprinted with permission from *Mother Jones* magazine, December, 1980, pp. 24–38.

---

1 The only possible opening for a statement of this kind is that I detest writing. The process itself epitomizes the European concept of "legitimate" thinking; what is written has an importance that is denied the spoken. My culture, the Lakota culture, has an oral tradition, so I ordinarily reject writing. It is one of the white world's ways of destroying the cultures of non-European peoples, the imposing of an abstraction over the spoken re-lationship of a people.

2 So what you read here is not what I've written. It's what I've said and someone else has written down. I will allow this because it seems that the only way to communicate with the white world is through the dead dry leaves of a book. I don't really care whether my words reach whites or not. They have already demonstrated through their history that they cannot hear, cannot see; they can only read (of course, there are exceptions, but the exceptions only prove the rule). I'm more concerned with American Indian people, students and others, who have begun to be absorbed into the white world through universities and other institutions. But even then it's a marginal sort of concern. It's very possible to grow into a red face with a white mind; and if that's a person's individual choice, so be it, but I have no use for them. This is part of the process of cultural genocide being waged by Europeans against American Indian peoples today. My concern is with those American Indians who choose to resist this genocide, but who may be confused as to how to proceed.

3 (You notice I use the term *American Indian* rather than *Native American* or *Native indigenous people* or *Amerindian* when referring to my people. There has been some controversy about such terms, and frankly, at this point, I find it absurd. Primarily it seems that *American Indian* is being rejected as European in origin—which is true. But *all* of the above terms are European in origin; the only non-European way is to speak of Lakota—or, more precisely, of Oglala, Brulé, etc.—and of the Diné, the Miccosukee and all the rest of the several hundred correct tribal names.

4 (There is also some confusion about the word *Indian,* a mistaken belief that it refers somehow to the country, India. When Columbus washed up on the beach in the Caribbean, he was not looking for a country called India. Europeans were calling that country Hindustan in 1492. Look it up on the old maps. Columbus called the tribal people he met "Indio," from the Italian *in dio,* meaning "in God.")

5 It takes a strong effort on the part of each American Indian *not* to become Europeanized. The strength for this effort can only come from the traditional ways, the traditional values that our elders retain. It must come from the hoop, the four directions, the relations; it cannot come from the pages of a book or a thousand books. No European can ever teach a Lakota to be Lakota, a Hopi to be Hopi. A master's degree in "Indian Studies" or in "education" or in anything else cannot make a person into a human being or provide knowledge into the traditional ways. It can only make you into a mental European, an outsider.

6 I should be clear about something here, because there seems to be some confusion about it. When I speak of Europeans or mental Europeans, I'm not allowing for false distinctions. I'm not saying that on the one hand there are the by-products of a few thousand years of genocidal, reactionary, European intellectual development which is bad; and on the other hand there is some new revolutionary intellectual development which is good. I'm referring here to the so-called theories of Marxism and anarchism and "leftism" in general. I don't believe these theories can be separated from the rest of the European intellectual tradition. It's really just the same old song.

7 The process began much earlier. Newton, for example, "revolutionized" physics and the so-called natural sciences by reducing the physical universe to a linear mathematical equation. Descartes did the same thing with culture. John Locke did it with politics, and Adam Smith did it with economics. Each one of these "thinkers" took a piece of the spirituality of human existence and converted it into a code, an abstraction. They picked up where Christianity ended; they "secularized" Christian religion, as the "scholars" like to say—and in doing so they made Europe more able and ready to act as an expansionist culture. Each of these intellectual revolutions served to abstract the European mentality even further, to remove the wonderful complexity and spirituality from the universe and replace it with a logical sequence: one, two, three, Answer!

8 This is what has come to be termed "efficiency" in the European mind. Whatever is mechanical is perfect; whatever seems to work at the moment—that is, proves the mechanical model to be the right one—is considered correct, even when it is clearly untrue. This is why "truth" changes so fast in the European mind; the answers which result from such a process are only stop-gaps, only temporary, and must be continuously discarded in favor of new stop-gaps which support the mechanical models and keep them (the models) alive.

9 Hegel and Marx were heirs to the thinking of Newton, Descartes, Locke, and Smith. Hegel finished the process of secularizing theology—and that is put in his own terms—he secularized the religious thinking through which Europe understood the universe. Then Marx put Hegel's philosophy in terms of "materialism," which is to say that Marx despiritualized Hegel's work altogether. Again, this is in Marx' own terms. And this is now seen as the future revolutionary potential of Europe. Europeans may see this as revolutionary, but American Indians see it simply as still more of that same old European conflict between *being* and *gaining*. The intellectual roots of a new Marxist form of European imperialism lie in Marx'—and his followers'—links to the tradition of Newton, Hegel, and the others.

10 *Being* is a spiritual proposition. *Gaining* is a material act. Traditionally, American Indians have always attempted to *be* the best people they could. Part of that spiritual process was and is to give away wealth, to discard wealth in order *not* to gain. Material gain is an indicator of false status among traditional people, while it is "proof that the system works" to Europeans. Clearly, there are two completely opposing views at issue here, and Marxism is very far over to the other side from the American Indian view. But let's look at a major implication of this; it is not merely an intellectual debate.

11 The European materialist tradition of despirtualizing the universe is very similar to the mental process which goes into dehumanizing another person. And who seems more expert at dehumanizing other people? And why? Soldiers who have seen a lot of combat learn to do this to the enemy before going back into combat. Murderers do it before going out to commit murder. Nazi SS guards did it to concentration camp inmates. Cops do it. Corporation leaders do it to the workers they send into uranium mines and steel mills. Politicians do it to everyone in sight. And what the process has in common for each group doing the dehumanizing is that it makes it all right to kill and otherwise destroy other people. One of the Christian commandments says, "Thou shalt not kill," at least not humans so the trick is to mentally convert the victims into nonhumans. Then you can proclaim violation of your own commandment as a virtue.

12 In terms of the despiritualization of the universe, the mental process works so that it becomes virtuous to destroy the planet. Terms like *progress* and *development* are used as cover words here, the way *victory* and *freedom* are used to justify butchery in the dehumanization process. For example, a real-estate speculator may refer to "developing" a parcel of ground by opening a gravel quarry; *development* here means total, permanent destruction, with the earth itself removed. But European logic has *gained* a few tons of gravel with which more land can be "developed" through the construction of road beds. Ultimately, the whole universe is open—in the European view—to this sort of insanity.

13 Most important here, perhaps, is the fact that Europeans feel no sense of loss in all this. After all, their philosophers have despiritualized reality, so there is no satisfaction (for them) to be gained in simply observing the wonder of a mountain or a lake or a people *in being*. No, satisfaction is measured in terms of gaining material. So the mountain becomes gravel, and the lake becomes coolant for a factory, and the people are rounded up for processing through the indoctrination mills Europeans like to call schools.

14 But each new piece of that "progress" ups the ante out in the real world. Take fuel for the industrial machine as an example. Little more than two centuries ago, nearly everyone used wood—a replenishable, natural item—as fuel for the very human needs of cooking and staying warm. Along came the Industrial Revolution and coal became the dominant fuel, as production became the social imperative for Europe. Pollution began to become a problem in the cities, and the earth was ripped open to provide coal whereas wood had always simply been gathered or harvested at no great expense to the environment. Later, oil became the major fuel, as the technology of production was perfected through a series of scientific "revolutions." Pollution increased dramatically, and nobody yet knows what the environmental costs of pumping all that oil out of the ground will really be in the long run. Now there's an "energy crisis," and uranium is becoming the dominant fuel.

15 Capitalists, at least, can be relied upon to develop uranium as fuel only at the rate at which they can show a good profit. That's their ethic, and maybe that will buy some time. Marxists, on the other hand, can be relied upon to develop uranium fuel as rapidly as possible simply because it's the most "efficient" production fuel available. That's *their* ethics, and I fail to see where it's preferable. Like I said, Marxism is right smack in the middle of the European tradition. It's the same old song.

16 There's a rule of thumb which can be applied here. You cannot judge the real nature of a European revolutionary doctrine on the basis of the changes it proposes to make within the European power structure and society. You can only judge it by the effects it will have on non-European peoples. This is because every revolution in European history has served to reinforce Europe's tendencies and abilities to export destruction to other peoples, other cultures, and the environment itself. I defy anyone to point out an example where this is not true.

17 So now we, as American Indian people, are asked to believe that "new" European revolutionary doctrine such as Marxism will reverse the negative effects of European history on us. European power relations are to be adjusted once again, and that's supposed to make things better for all of us. But what does this really mean?

18 Right now, today, we who live on the Pine Ridge Reservation are living in what white society has designated a "National Sacrifice Area." What this means is that we have a lot of uranium deposits here, and white culture (not us) needs this uranium as energy

production material. The cheapest, most efficient way for industry to extract and deal with the processing of this uranium is to dump the waste by-products right here at the digging sites. Right here where we live. This waste is radioactive and will make the entire region uninhabitable forever. This is considered by industry, and by the white society that created this industry, to be an "acceptable" price to pay for energy resource development. Along the way they also plan to drain the water table under this part of South Dakota as part of the industrial process, so the region becomes doubly uninhabitable. The same sort of thing is happening down in the land of the Navajo and Hopi, up in the land of the Northern Cheyenne and Crow, and elsewhere. Thirty percent of the coal in the West and half of the uranium deposits in the U.S. have been found to lie under reservation land, so there is no way this can be called a minor issue.

19 We are resisting being turned into a National Sacrifice Area. We are resisting being turned into a national sacrifice people. The costs of this industrial process are not acceptable to us. It is genocide to dig uranium here and drain the water table—no more, no less.

20 Now let's suppose that in our resistance to extermination we begin to seek allies (we have). Let's suppose further that we were to take revolutionary Marxism at its word: that it intends nothing less than the complete overthrow of the European capitalist order which has presented this threat to our very existence. This would seem to be a natural alliance for American Indian people to enter into. After all, as the Marxists say, it is the capitalists who set us up to be a national sacrifice. This is true as far as it goes.

21 But, as I've tried to point out, this "truth" is very deceptive. Revolutionary Marxism is committed to even further perpetuation and perfection of the very industrial process which is destroying us all. It offers only to "redistribute" the results—the money, maybe—of this industrialization to a wider section of the population. It offers to take wealth from the capitalists and pass it around; but in order to do so, Marxism must maintain the industrial system. Once again the power relations within European society will have to be altered, but once again the effects upon American Indian peoples here and non-Europeans elsewhere will remain the same. This is much the same as when power was redistributed from the church to private business during the so-called bourgeois revolution. European society changed a bit, at least superficially, but its conduct toward non-Europeans continued as before. You can see what the American Revolution of 1776 did for American Indians. It's the same old song.

22 Revolutionary Marxism, like industrial society in other forms, seeks to "rationalize" all people in relation to industry—maximum industry, maximum production. It is a materialist doctrine that despises the American Indian spiritual tradition, our cultures, our lifeways. Marx himself called us "precapitalists" and "primitive." *Precapitalist* simply means that, in his view, we would eventually discover capitalism and become capitalists; we have always been economically retarded in Marxist terms. The only manner in which American

Indian people could participate in a Marxist revolution would be to join the industrial system, to become factory workers, or "proletarians" as Marx called them. The man was very clear about the fact that his revolution could occur only through the struggle of the proletariat, that the existence of a massive industrial system is a precondition of a successful Marxist society.

23 I think there's a problem with language here. Christians, capitalists, Marxists. All of them have been revolutionary in their own minds, but none of them really mean revolution. What they really mean is a continuation. They do what they do in order that European culture can continue to exist and develop according to its needs.

24 So, in order for us to *really* join forces with Marxism, we American Indians would have to accept the national sacrifice of our homeland; we would have to commit cultural suicide and become industrialized and Europeanized.

25 At this point, I've got to stop and ask myself whether I'm being too harsh. Marxism has something of a history. Does this history bear out my observations? I look to the process of industrialization in the Soviet Union since 1920 and I see that these Marxists have done what it took the English Industrial Revolution 300 years to do; and the Marxists did it in 60 years. I see that the territory of the USSR used to contain a number of tribal peoples and that they have been crushed to make way for the factories. The Soviets refer to this as "The National Question," the question of whether the tribal peoples had the right to exist as peoples; and they decided the tribal peoples were an acceptable sacrifice to industrial needs. I look to China and I see the same thing. I look to Vietnam and I see Marxists imposing an industrial order and rooting out the indigenous tribal mountain people.

26 I hear a leading Soviet scientist saying that when uranium is exhausted, *then* alternatives will be found. I see the Vietnamese taking over a nuclear power plant abandoned by the U.S. military. Have they dismantled and destroyed it? No, they are using it. I see China exploding nuclear bombs, developing uranium reactors and preparing a space program in order to colonize and exploit the planets the same as the Europeans colonized and exploited this hemisphere. It's the same old song, but maybe with a faster tempo this time.

27 The statement of the Soviet scientist is very interesting. Does he know what this alternative energy source will be? No, he simply has faith. Science will find a way. I hear revolutionary Marxists saying that the destruction of the environment, pollution, and radiation will all be controlled. And I see them act upon their words. Do they know *how* these things will be controlled? No, they simply have faith. Science will find a way. Industrialization is fine and necessary. How do they know this? Faith. Science will find a way. Faith of this sort has always been known in Europe as religion. Science has become the new European religion for both capitalists and Marxists; they are truly inseparable, they are part and parcel of the same culture. So, in both theory and practice, Marxism demands that non-European peoples give up their values, their traditions, their cultural existence altogether. We will all be industrialized science addicts in a Marxist society.

28 I do not believe that capitalism itself is really responsible for the situation in which American Indians have been declared a national sacrifice. No, it is the European tradition; European culture itself is responsible. Marxism is just the latest continuation of this tradition, not a solution to it. To ally with Marxism is to ally with the very same forces that declare us an acceptable cost.

29 There is another way. There is the traditional Lakota way and the ways of the other American Indian peoples. It is the way that knows that humans do not have the right to degrade Mother Earth, that there are forces beyond anything the European mind has conceived, that humans must be in harmony with *all* relations or the relations will eventually eliminate the disharmony. A lopsided emphasis on humans by humans—the Europeans' arrogance of acting as though they were beyond the nature of all related things—can only result in a total disharmony and a readjustment which cuts arrogant humans down to size, gives them a taste of that reality beyond their grasp or control and restores the harmony. There is no need for a revolutionary theory to bring this about; it's beyond human control. The nature peoples of this planet know this and so they do not theorize about it. Theory is an abstract; our knowledge is real.

30 Distilled to its basic terms, European faith—including the new faith in science—equals a belief that man is God. Europe has always sought a Messiah, whether that be the man Jesus Christ or the man Karl Marx or the man Albert Einstein. American Indians know this to be totally absurd. Humans are the weakest of all creatures, so weak that other creatures are willing to give up their flesh that we may live. Humans are able to survive only through the exercise of rationality since they lack the abilities of other creatures to gain food through the use of fang and claw.

31 But rationality is a curse since it can cause humans to forget the natural order of things in ways other creatures do not. A wolf never forgets his or her place in the natural order. American Indians can. Europeans almost always do. We pray our thanks to the deer, our relations, for allowing us their flesh to eat; Europeans simply take the flesh for granted and consider the deer inferior. After all, Europeans consider themselves godlike in their rationalism and science. God is the Supreme Being; all else *must* be inferior.

32 All European tradition, Marxism included, has conspired to defy the natural order of all things. Mother Earth has been abused, the powers have been abused, and this cannot go on forever. No theory can alter that simple fact. Mother Earth will retaliate, the whole environment will retaliate, and the abusers will be eliminated. Things come full circle, back to where they started. *That's* revolution. And that's a prophecy of my people, of the Hopi people, and of other correct peoples.

33 American Indians have been trying to explain this to Europeans for centuries. But, as I said earlier, Europeans have proven themselves unable to hear. The natural order will win out, and the offenders will die out, the way deer die when they offend the harmony by overpopulating a given region. It's only a matter of time until what Europeans call "a major catastrophe of global proportions" will occur. It is the role of American Indian peoples, the role of all natural beings, to survive. A part of our survival is to resist. We resist not to overthrow a government or to take political power but because it is natural to resist extermination, to survive. We don't want power over white institutions; we want white institutions to disappear. *That's* revolution.

34 American Indians are still in touch with these realities—the prophecies, the traditions of our ancestors. We learn from the elders, from nature, from the powers. And when the catastrophe is over, we American Indian peoples will still be here to inhabit the hemisphere. I don't care if it's only a handful living high in the Andes. American Indian people will survive; harmony will be reestablished. *That's* revolution.

35 At this point, perhaps I should be very clear about another matter, one which should already be clear as a result of what I've said. But confusion breeds easily these days, so I want to hammer home this point. When I use the term *European,* I'm not referring to a skin color or a particular genetic structure. What I'm referring to is a mind-set, a world view that is a product of the development of European culture. People are not genetically encoded to hold this outlook; they are *acculturated* to hold it. The same is true for American Indians or for the members of any other culture.

36 It is possible for an American Indian to share European values, a European world view. We have a term for these people; we call them "apples"—red on the outside (genetics) and white on the inside (their values). Other groups have similar terms: Blacks have their "oreos"; Hispanos have "coconuts" and so on. And, as I said before, there *are* exceptions to the white norm: people who are white on the outside, but not white inside. I'm not sure what term should be applied to them other than "human beings."

37 What I'm putting out here is not a racial proposition but a cultural proposition. Those who ultimately advocate and defend the realities of European culture and its industrialism are my enemies. Those who resist it, who struggle against it, are my allies, the allies of American Indian people. And I don't give a damn what their skin color happens to be. *Caucasian* is the white term for the white race; *European* is an outlook I oppose.

38 The Vietnamese Communists are not exactly what you might consider genetic Caucasians, but they are now functioning as mental Europeans. The same holds true for Chinese Communists, for Japanese capitalists or Bantu Catholics or Peter "MacDollar" down at the Navajo Reservation or Dickie Wilson up here at Pine Ridge. There is no racism involved in this, just an acknowledgment of the mind and spirit that make up culture.

39 In Marxist terms I suppose I'm a "cultural nationalist." I work first with my people, the traditional Lakota people, because we hold a common world view and share an immediate struggle. Beyond this, I work with other traditional American Indian peoples, again because of a certain commonality in world view and form of struggle. Beyond that, I work with anyone who has experienced the colonial oppression of Europe and who resists its cultural and industrial totality. Obviously, this includes genetic Caucasians who struggle to resist the dominant norms of European culture. The Irish and the Basques come immediately to mind, but there are many others.

40 I work primarily with my own people, with my own community. Other people who hold non-European perspectives should do the same. I believe in the slogan, "Trust your brother's vision," although I'd like to add sisters into the bargain. I trust the community and the culturally based vision of all the races that naturally resist industrialization and human extinction. Clearly, individual whites can share in this, given only that they have reached the awareness that continuation of the industrial imperatives of Europe is not a vision, but species suicide. White is one of the sacred colors of the Lakota people—red, yellow, white and black. The four directions. The four seasons. The four periods of life and aging. The four races of humanity. Mix red, yellow, white, and black together and you get brown, the color of the fifth race. This is a natural ordering of things. It therefore seems natural to me to work with all races, each with its own special meaning, identity, and message.

41 But there is a peculiar behavior among most Caucasians. As soon as I become critical of Europe and its impact on other cultures, they become defensive. They begin to defend themselves. But I'm not attacking them personally; I'm attacking Europe. In personalizing my observations on Europe they are personalizing European culture, identifying themselves with it. By defending themselves in *this* context, they are ultimately defending the death culture. This is a confusion which must be overcome, and it must be overcome in a hurry. None of us have energy to waste in such false struggles.

42 Caucasians have a more positive vision to offer humanity than European culture. I believe this. But in order to attain this vision it is necessary for Caucasians to step outside European culture—alongside the rest of humanity—to see Europe for what it is and what it does.

43 To cling to capitalism and Marxism and all the other "isms" is simply to remain within European culture. There is no avoiding this basic fact. As a fact, this constitutes a choice. Understand that the choice is based on culture, not race. Understand that to choose European culture and industrialism is to choose to be my enemy. And understand that the choice is yours, not mine.

44 This leads me back to address those American Indians who are drifting through the universities, the city slums, and other European institutions. If you are there to learn to resist the oppressor in accordance with your traditional ways, so be it. I don't know how you manage to combine the two, but perhaps you will succeed. But retain your sense of reality. Beware of coming to believe the white world now offers solutions to the problems it confronts us with. Beware, too, of allowing the words of native people to be twisted to the advantage of our enemies. Europe invented the practice of turning words around on themselves. You need only look to the treaties between American Indian peoples and various European governments to know that this is true. Draw your strength from who you are.

45 A culture which regularly confuses revolution with continuation, which confuses science and religion, which confuses revolt with resistance, has nothing helpful to teach you and nothing to offer you as a way of life. Europeans have long since lost all touch with reality, if ever they were in touch with it. Feel sorry for them if you need to, but be comfortable with who you are as American Indians.

46 So, I suppose to conclude this, I should state clearly that leading anyone toward Marxism is the last thing on my mind. Marxism is as alien to my culture as capitalism and Christianity are. In fact, I can say I don't think I'm trying to lead anyone toward anything. To some extent I tried to be a "leader," in the sense that the white media like to use that term, when the American Indian Movement was a young organization. This was a result of a confusion I no longer have. You cannot be everything to everyone. I do not propose to be used in such a fashion by my enemies; I am not a leader. I *am* an Oglala Kalota patriot. That is all I want and all I need to be. And I am very comfortable with who I am.

Teaching Values in Public Schools
Mario M. Cuomo

A lawyer by profession and Democrat by party, Mario M. Cuomo was elected Governor of New York in 1982 and re-elected to four-year terms in 1986 and 1990. Cuomo is a political liberal and a Roman Catholic and has advocated controversial positions against the death penalty and against government restrictions on abortion. On March 4, 1987 the Long Island newspaper, *Newsday,* sponsored an Education Symposium held at the State University of New York College at Old Westbury. In his address at the symposium, Governor Cuomo argued his view on another controversial topic—whether and what values should be taught in public schools.

In a broad sense this speech is about a policy—a course of action—and Cuomo does mention suggestions for implementing the policy. However, it seems clear that his main purpose is not to detail a comprehensive plan for implementing the policy. Rather his focus is on the necessity for reaching agreement about what values should be taught (par. 48). Primarily Cuomo advocates adoption of a specific system of values (27). At length he itemizes and explains these values (29–33). How clearly does he explain the values? Are there any of these values that you believe should *not* be taught in public schools? Why?

As a prelude to identifying the specific values he advocates, Cuomo uses two strategies to predispose the audience toward their adoption. He stresses the desirable consequences of living by these values when he contends that the nation has made progress when citizens have remembered and adhered to the values (11). In contrast, he stresses the undesirable consequences of not following these values. At length he accumulates a list of overwhelming problems facing Americans—problems which implicitly reflect people who never learned or have rejected the values (13–18).

Cuomo further justifies the values in two ways. First, they are rooted in revered founding documents of America (5, 28) and they derive from the Greco-Roman, Judeo-Christian, Western cultural tradition (34–36, 45). Second, they represent a consensus of the core values of American life and form the basis of "our nation's conscience" (27–28, 38).

Where and how adequately do you find Cuomo refuting the idea that public schools can be or should be value-neutral? Where and for what purpose does he associate the desirable values with revered persons? What rhetorical functions are served by the clusters of questions throughout the speech (5–6, 15–18, 49)? For what apparent purpose and how well does Cuomo use personal narrative and dialogue (19–21)? Finally, how perceptive and realistic is Cuomo's recognition of the complexity and difficulty of the subject?

The text of this speech was provided by Governor Cuomo's office in Albany, New York. (4, 7–10, 49–50).

---

1 Thank you, Mr. Johnson. Chief Judge Wachtler; Regent Matteoni; Dr. Pettigrew; Steve Isenberg; Sam Ruinsky; Charlotte Frank; Dr. Mondschein; Judge Forest; ladies and gentlemen.

2 First, let me commend Newsday for sponsoring this symposium on the occasion of two most important events—the bicentennial of the Constitution and the celebration of the Year of the Reader.

3 Second, let me say that the format of this morning's program puts me in an unenviable position. Although the Constitution is a subject I study and talk about with relish, and although the gift of literacy that I was given by PS 50 in South Jamaica is one I regard with immense gratitude, you've already heard those topics treated by Chief Judge Wachtler, Louise Matteoni and the other distinguished panel members—people much better equipped than I to discuss them.

4 Instead, then, of trying to expand on what the panelists have already said so well, let me suggest another direction in which their words on the Constitution and on literacy may lead us. It's a direction into territory that's already been explored and charted but is, nevertheless, somewhat perilous—with few sure footholds or reliable signposts and much disputed land.

5 It's the whole question of teaching values in public schools. When, finally, we use our gift of freedom to make ourselves all as literate as we should be, when we are all able to read and understand the Constitution—and the Declaration of Independence and the Federalist Papers and all the documents that order us and describe us as a people—what ultimate ideas will we find in them? What values, norms, and codes of conduct will they teach us?

6 Should we then, having found them, try to teach any of these values to children in our public schools? If so which? Or should we avoid even trying to teach any at all, for fear that we may encourage the teaching of religions, or specific orthodoxies, that will threaten our most precious gift of all . . . our freedom.

7 Difficult questions. Exactly the kind we politicians like to avoid. But I believe they are so important it would be wrong to neglect them.

8 Let me add quickly that the very idea that anyone my age should purport to talk about values—let alone teach them to our children—is a personally difficult one. How can anyone of my generation, the generation largely in control of things in recent years, talk about values and try to teach lessons that we seemed to have learned so imperfectly ourselves?

9 How could we—who have so often done the wrong thing to one another—tell students that it is *their* duty to use all that they have been given to make a better world? We who did so much to pollute and poison the environment? We who allowed drugs to become so widely available that they are now one of the most menacing threats to the future of this generation? Isn't it hypocritical?

10 Mark Twain made the same point . . . a little more gently; "To be good and virtuous," he said, "is a noble thing, but to *teach* others to be good and virtuous is nobler still—and much, much easier." That's good. Because if, as I fear, we have little right to hold ourselves out as examples, still I believe we have an obligation to try, at least, to teach the values on which our nation was founded.

11 We know that despite our personal failures, when this nation *has* remembered and acted upon those basic values, we have made progress and thrived as a people. Despite Howard Beach, Queens, and Forsyth County, Georgia, the civil rights of all citizens are more respected today than they were two decades ago. Despite some of the failures in our schools, education *is* more widely available today than ever in our history. Despite lingering discrimination, women are closer today than ever before to occupying the place they deserve in our society.

12 These are all embodiments of strong basic values on which this nation is built. I believe we must point that out to our youth. And I believe they would welcome that instruction. They need it.

13 Today's children are confronted with more complexity, more distractions, more psychological pressures, more temptations than we were. Every night prime-time television assails them with mindless sit-coms and soap operas that present ostentatious materialism and unrelenting self-gratification as the only goals worth pursuing; confronts them with "action" shows in which vigilantism is portrayed as the answer to crime, and macho heroes who live by a code of violence are glorified; with videos that demean women and make a mockery of gentleness.

14 There's another syndrome involving children today—one my generation hardly knew—that is even more menacing—and can be deadly: drugs. The statistics on the self-inflicted madness of drug abuse are frightening—hospital emergency rooms crowded; treatment centers overwhelmed; more and more victims, many of them adolescents and even pre-adolescents; a rising death toll. And the drug epidemic is only one aspect of a broader *syndrome of self-destructive activity* involving our youth: the steady rise in alcoholism and other forms of reckless abuse of their own minds and bodies . . . even teenage suicide.

15 Add to these a disgraceful school drop-out rate, and the confusing wave of adolescent pregnancy, and we're left with profoundly disturbing, fundamental questions: Have we cared enough about what happens to our children? What is it that we believe in, that we value? What *are* we teaching them? Are we sure enough about our own values to convince youngsters to live *for* something, to believe in themselves, in the significance of their own lives? To believe in believing? If so, how do we go about doing it? How do we stop the madness?

16 And there are more questions—What do we do about Aids? If in fact it is now threatening a wider and wider part of our population, do individuals have the right to engage in personal expressions of intimacy that threaten themselves with perhaps deadly illness . . . and threaten those beyond them? Is it time to surrender privacy in the name of public safety? Can a surrogate mother "own" the child she carries from an implanted seed by agreement with a man and woman who understand that she was merely hosting *their* fetus?

17 Is the Governor from a western state right to raise a question as to whether we are trying too hard to keep people alive for too long because society can't afford the costs? How do we decide if life is worth living in a society where the technology needed to make it happen is available only to the super-rich?

18 What should be the test for opening Shoreham [nuclear reactor]—economic necessity? A new chance for economic growth? The threat to health and life? How much of a threat? How important is one life? Who should decide? By what rules? By what *values?*

19 These are powerful questions that can hit one with great force. It happened to me not long ago, in a New York City schoolyard. I was there to talk to a couple of hundred ninth and tenth graders about the dangers and madness of using crack. I spoke about the beauty of life, the opportunities in their future, and the threat to all their hopes and dreams that drugs posed.

20 After I'd finished, I asked them if what I'd said made sense to them. Most of them nodded. One didn't. A boy, maybe fifteen—with a chipped front tooth who looked at me with his head half-cocked to the side, his face impassive but his skepticism showing through quite clearly. "Didn't you agree with me?" I said. "That your life is too precious to give away to drugs?" "I'm not sure," he answered. "The stuff you said sounded good but I don't really know. I'm not sure what my life is for, why we're here. I really don't understand it." I was stunned by his answer. By its simplicity. By its staggering profundity. I was at a loss. I told him he was awfully bright to be thinking about those kinds of questions, and that a lot of what life was about was looking for answers to those questions. And that if he did that with his whole mind and his heart, he'd never be sorry, and he'd discover all sorts of wonderful things as he searched. But that if he started looking for answers in three minute drug highs, all he'd ever do was cripple his searching and all he'd ever be was sorry.

21 I don't think I reached him. And I didn't leave those questions behind when I left the schoolyard. They have followed me ever since that afternoon. And they've followed me here this morning. . . . That boy's need to be told and to somehow understand that his life—and everyone's—is good. And precious. And full of purpose. That he has value. And that we have values.

22 So, setting aside the personal tentativeness I have about speaking of values, let me tell you what I think. Ideally, the primary and best source for instruction in values is the family. There are other sources. Churches and synagogues, youth organizations and community groups—all of these can project a strong sense of values as well.

23 But it's clear that today we need more. And I believe it's clear we need to turn to our public schools. Of course, schools cannot—alone—counter the messages and pressures that bombard children. It's too much to ask teachers to do single combat with all of those influences. But if schools can't be expected to do it all, they have proven in the past to be one of the best ways we have for exposing youth to the ideals and traditions—intellectual, ethical, moral—that form our common heritage.

24 Actually, asking whether schools should teach values may be the wrong question. The truth probably is that they do it, *inevitably,* whether formally or informally, deliberately or inadvertently.

25 Even when schools try to be totally silent on the question of ethics, of morals—their silence is *not* a neutral lesson. Silence teaches! Silence teaches that the choice between good and evil is not important; the difference between right and wrong, not significant; the difference between being a good or a bad citizen inconsequential. That's a very real kind of instruction.

26 Given that, it seems to me that at the very least, schools should work to make young people aware that *some* standards of virtue and decency do exist. I believe that can be done without teaching a specific religion or philosophy or instilling someone else's orthodoxy. Not easily, but nonetheless it can be done appropriately and effectively.

27 We can begin with the recognition that whether formally taught or not, at the core of every society is a set of moral values, a code of behavior, a credo. That has been so throughout history. Even here in our uniquely free society where diversity of belief is protected and cherished, there is a rough—but clear—national understanding of what is right and wrong, what is allowed and what is forbidden, what we are entitled to and what we owe.

28 We can find much of that consensus in the original documents that defined us as a people. The Declaration of Independence and the Constitution reflect values at the core of American life . . . values implicit in the concept of ordered liberty, to which the founders of our nation mutually pledged their lives, their fortunes, their sacred honor . . . and our nation's future.

29 What are those values? Here are some: An awareness of the profound ways in which we are all equal; reverence for the individual rights that issue from that equality—the rights of others as well as our own; a sense of the importance of working for a good greater than our individual goals—a common good; a respect for our system of laws, which so majestically balances individual rights and that common good; and, finally, a love for this place, America, that has dared to try to be true to these revolutionary insights and principles.

30 Now, these are real, tangible, specific values. And we can teach them to our young specifically. We can show them that: *equality, individual rights, the common good,* (or community, what I prefer to call "family,") *the rule of law,* and *love of country* aren't just pat phrases to be wheeled out and paraded on national holidays. They are some of the realities on which our national life was founded. On which we have flourished. And on which America's future will be built.

31 As we study these values—and explicate them—it becomes clear that for all the genius and daring of their ideas and actions, America's founders did not invent these basic principles.

32 In drafting this magnificent new chapter in the history of government, they drew from a deep well of wisdom and history, from philosophical, cultural, and religious traditions that stretched back thousands of years . . . traditions that yielded other values on which our own great civic values are based. Traditions that were supposed to shape us and guide us in our coming together as a nation. They include: a sense of personal worth; the importance of each individual person; the protection of one's self and others from all forms of degradation or abuse. We can call these values *dignity* and *integrity.* There are others. Real and specific values. Like: *compassion, service,* and *love of knowledge.*

33 These values are not just sweet abstractions. Nice generalities. They are not inert ethical entities, but dynamic ways of understanding human nature and purpose—ways that men and women have struggled for centuries to define and develop. As are the companion values of *responsibility* and *accountability*—the limitations on freedom created by the rights of others—and *the need for discipline and order.*

34 These are things that have been taught in places for centuries. They have guided much of the progress in this civilization. They can be formally taught again. When the great thinkers of the Greek city-states first made explicit the dignity inherent in our nature as human beings, their insights were as startling and unsettling to the Mediterranean world of their day as gene-splicing is to ours.

35 Integrity isn't something that an ancient philosopher simply stumbled over on his way to work one day. It is the fruit of a tradition of learning that produced the Book of Exodus and the Psalms. It is an idea that Virgil and Cicero, Aquinas and Thomas Jefferson grappled with . . . refining and expanding it.

36 The development of the idea that we should love our neighbors as ourselves—the golden rule used by the great philosophers to teach compassion and service—has been as crucial to the course of human history as the splitting of the atom.

37 And basic to all these achievements has been a respect for knowledge—at best a *love* of knowledge—a sense of wonder and excitement for the human enterprise. A sense of delight that comes from understanding what you didn't understand before, from stripping away some of life's mystery, unravelling some of the reasons for things. If there is anything that is the mark of a successful school—and of a successful society and civilization—it is the presence of that electric sense of wonder on which all our knowledge has been built.

38 Not all these values are written explicitly into our laws. But they are part of the consensus—sometimes spoken, sometimes unspoken—that underlies our nation's conscience. They all continue to play a crucial role in how we live, how we conceive of ourselves and of others, what we cherish, and even how we construct our hopes and ambitions.

39 To recollect these things and to recall our history, is a helpful reaffirmation of the existence of the essential understanding of values in this nation. And to do it explicitly by making a list of shared values is an exercise I recommend to teachers and school boards and community groups.

40 But simply making a list is not enough. If we're serious about it, if we really believe that a life lived according to our code of values is a more fulfilled, more fully human life, then we must find concrete ways to teach values in our schools.

41 The obvious experts on that are those among us who are teachers and education professionals. In many instances they have been doing it, and doing it well, for years. Our own Regents have included values components in the curricula they have already produced. What we need to do *now* is elaborate and expand their experience and the efforts of the other professionals.

42 Our educators remind us that a school should be a place where students have a pervasive exposure to the best we're capable of; where they learn self-esteem because they're treated as individuals with their own special dignity; where they begin to see that a community works best when each individual—their peers and those in authority—respect the rights of others, and that their actions have an effect on the community.

43 A school should be a place where students learn, as well, the necessity of discipline. Where they come to appreciate more fully that success—in the classroom, in the gym, or on the athletic field—requires self-control, practice, some measure of denying oneself immediate gratification . . . training that gradually corrects weaknesses and perfects strengths.

44 How can we accomplish all of this? To a non-professional like myself, some broad ideas occur. We know that the curriculum—especially in areas like History, Science and Literature—can be an effective instrument for transmitting values.

45 History can teach students that no man, no woman is an island . . . no people, no country either. It can teach them to see events as connected, to realize that the world is ever-changing and evolving but that the best—and the worst—of human instincts are constant. Students can be taught that our own nation's history—and our state's—is more than a jumble of dates and events. It's a continuous story built on outrageous dreams in millions of men and women—early settlers and wave after wave of those who came later—many in steerage or in chains—and who fought and struggled to make the dream they believed in come true for their children and those who would come after them. A real life struggle in which men and women gave all their talents—and sometimes their lives—to uphold freedom and equality. To eradicate racism and discrimination. To preserve the Union and the rule of law. To expand opportunity. And throughout this entire history, properly taught, it will be clear that this progress was largely guided and propelled by the values I speak of today. So teaching history *well* is a good way to teach values.

46 And we can derive powerful instruction from biography and autobiography—in all their forms. Children need heroes. We all do. We can all benefit from reading Carl Sandburg's life of Lincoln, or Dumas Malone's life of Jefferson. *A Man For All Seasons,* the dramatization of Thomas More's life; the *Diary of Anne Frank;* the monumental achievements of Eleanor Roosevelt or of Martin Luther King, Jr.—all these, and many others, can teach us about integrity and courage and steadfastness. We can learn from people admired for their willingness to devote their lives to serving others. If our teachers will point it out, literature can teach children that they're not the first ones in the world to experience fear or disappointment, failure or sorrow. It can teach them the great nobility we are capable of, at our best. And it can show them, especially as they develop intellectually, how difficult it sometimes is to resolve the conflicts among values. How patriotism doesn't always require us to march lock-step to the same drummer. How integrity can mean standing alone.

47 Beyond the curriculum, schools should offer students opportunities to apply the values we say we share. Real opportunities to serve the community and its people—younger students and older residents, the sick, the homebound, anyone in need of the help students can provide, if given the chance. There are all sorts of community organizations that will provide them the opportunity. We should get them involved. It is a common experience of people who volunteer their services that they get out of the experience more than they put in. For adolescents, particularly, one benefit may be a new sense of self-esteem . . . a new understanding of the idea of community.

48 Others are more competent than I to suggest all the specific ways to teach values. My point is that we need to be clearer about what we believe and what we value. We must overcome any reluctance to teach our values from every public pulpit, especially in our public schools. Not just talk about them, but teach them. And that work will involve everyone—the Board of Regents, school boards, teachers, administrators, parents, public officials, all the people of this state. Where it's not being done it should be. Where it's being done we should continue to do it . . . and do it better.

49 If we do all these things—if we identify our basic values and teach them throughout the curriculum of our public schools—will it answer all the hard questions? Will it make a difference? Where it counts, in the lives of our children? Would it have made a difference to the boy in the schoolyard? Will it convince some youngsters that they are too good, too valuable—that they have too much to contribute to our society—to throw it all away by using drugs? Will it keep some from committing suicide? Will we see a decline in the drop-out rate, in teenage pregnancy? Will there be diminished violence and vandalism in the schools?

50 No one can say for sure. Perhaps our efforts won't make a difference. But I believe that, unless we try, we are conceding in full view of our children—that there are forces whose evil power and sweep are too great to be met by instruction in values or by a summons to dignity and self-respect. I don't believe such a concession to hopelessness is one any of us wants to make. It would be an abdication of our responsibility as parents, as teachers, as public officials. We must value responsibility more than that.

51 And, we know, our responsibility cannot end with mere exhortation. Hard as it is to teach values, we know there are other basic needs which, if not met, make instruction too difficult. We have to invest more intelligently and more generously in our schools and our teachers. We must remember that a child who comes to school malnourished will not learn well. That lessons in self-love can be too hard to teach to a child who is abused at home. That lessons in civility will ring hollow to students who wage a daily struggle merely to survive the violence of the streets. That without the prospect of a job or of the chance to go to college if they choose, students won't be sufficiently motivated to succeed.

52 In the end, the best lesson in values is the example we give as individuals and as a society. What we do to give this generation of students—all of them—the same opportunities that most of us were given, the same chance to be everything they can be. For me as a child, that work began at home, with my parents. With momma and poppa and church and rules, and discipline learned from the hard end of a broom. But for me and probably most of you—and millions like us—it was continued and reaffirmed, fleshed out and fortified in public school.

53 I believe we need that help from our public schools today more than ever. It may be the most important thing our schools can do. I believe that as we teach literacy, we must teach the values that have made us a special people in the 200 years since we were joined together by the miracle of our Constitution.

54 Thank you for having me.

The Teaching of Values in the Public Schools
Phyllis Schlafly

By chance, less than four months after Mario Cuomo presented his speech on teaching values in public schools, Phyllis Schlafly also addressed the same topic. On June 26, 1987 she spoke at a conference sponsored by the Office of Legal Services of the New York City Board of Education and held at the Pocono Manor Conference Center in Pennsylvania.

A nationally prominent political conservative, Mrs. Schlafly organized the STOP ERA movement in the early 1970s against the Equal Rights Constitutional Amendment. In 1975 she founded the Eagle Forum which absorbed STOP ERA and undertook persuasive efforts on a broad spectrum of current issues. She earned her B.A. from Washington University of St. Louis, her M.A. from Harvard University, and her J.D. degree from Washington University Law School. A syndicated columnist and radio commentator, she is author of 12 books including *A Choice Not An Echo, The Power of the Positive Woman, Kissinger on the Couch,* and *Child Abuse in the Classroom.*

To an audience for whom her views probably were in a minority (par. 1), Phyllis Schlafly overtly attempts to clarify and strengthen her credibility—the audience's perception of such personal qualities as expertness, trustworthiness, and sincerity (2, 8–9, 16). Assess the appropriateness and probable successfulness of her approach. Also evaluate how adequately she justifies her basic premise that "anybody who spends the taxpayers' money simply has to put up with citizen surveillance" (6).

While not wanting to *impose* her religious and moral values on the public schools (2), she *defends* the constitutional right of parent and child not to have their religious and moral values attacked, belittled, and deemed irrelevant in public schools (17, 32). To underscore her argument, she offers two clear summaries—one internal (20) and one concluding (33).

Unlike Mario Cuomo who itemized the values he advocated, the values that Phyllis Schlafly advocates for adoption are imbedded in her arguments and often phrased in antithetical style where the preferred values are contrasted with disvalues or violations of values (11, 12). Among Schlafly's preferred values are: basic skills; facts; knowledge based on the great books and classics; knowledge of what society judges illegal (21); God's moral law (17); traditional family structure (24–26); and equality of treatment under the law (19, 22, 32). What other preferred values can you identify? Among the disvalues or violations of values that she attacks are: education as group therapy (11); teaching moral dilemmas that undercut religious and family values (12); "mischief-making" between parent and child (23, 26); and moral relativism (20, 23, 33).

Phyllis Schlafly's extensive use of examples and illustrations strongly invites evaluation by the rhetorical critic (8–9, 14–17, 19–31). She uses examples to attack the alleged value-free, value-neutral procedures of the Values Clarification educational method (15, 17). She employs questions to reinforce her conclusions from the examples (24–26). Consider how adequately she reassures the audience that her examples are typical or representative of many others that exist (14–16, 29).

Assess the question-and-answer period that followed the speech (35–45). To what degree and in what ways did her answers strengthen or weaken her position? Why might it have been desirable or undesirable for her to introduce the tests of truth, health, legality, and constitutionality explicitly in her speech rather than waiting for the answer period (38, 44)? Where do you believe she significantly clarified a view that actually was unclear in the speech?

Finally, compare Phyllis Schlafly's speech with the previous one by Mario Cuomo. What potential common ground, if any, appears to exist between their views? With which of the values advocated by Cuomo might Schlafly agree or disagree? Why? With what premises or positions of Schlafly might Cuomo agree or disagree? Why? Explore other points of comparison and constrast between the two speeches.

The text of this speech was provided by Phyllis Schlafly's office and is reprinted with her permission.

1 I thank the sponsors of this meeting for presenting a balanced program, and I thank you for your willingness to hear another side of the issue.

2 First, it's important to know what frame of reference I am coming from. I am not part of the religious right or a fundamentalist group trying to impose my religion on public school children. I come from a state where prayer was banned from the public schools at the time of World War I, and I am not seeking to put it back in. I am not an enemy of public schools. I had a very happy public school experience. I certainly believe in education. I come from a family where the women and men have been college graduates for more than a century. I wanted college so much that, having no money, I worked my own way through college without any aid of any type, in a grimy night job, 48 hours a week. My husband and I have financed six children through 38 years of university education at seven secular universities. So, indeed, I care about education.

3 The three lawsuits pertaining to public school textbooks that have been in the Federal Courts this year (*Smith v. Board of School Commissioners of Mobil County, Mozert v. Hawkins County Board of Education,* and *Edwards v. Aguillard*) are symptomatic of two movements which are current in our society. On the one hand, we have those people who seem to believe that the public school child is a captive of the administrators of the public schools, and that the schools can do anything they want with the children, pretty much as though they were guinea pigs. Those people seem to think that, if parents presume to interfere with or criticize curriculum, they can be called troublemakers, mischief-makers, censors, bigots—the whole host of epithets spun out by the American Civil Liberties Union and People for the American Way.

4 On the other hand, there are those of us who believe that, since the children—and they are minor *children* in public schools—are a captive audience under compulsory school laws, the authority figure must be limited and restricted by two other factors.

5 First is the power and rights of the parents. It is good constitutional law in our nation that the parents are the primary educators of their children. They have the right to safeguard the religion, the morals, the attitudes, the values, and the family privacy of their children.

6 Secondly, the schools are subject to the taxpayers and the citizens of our nation. I come from the frame of reference that anybody who spends the taxpayers' money simply has to put up with citizen surveillance. The President has to put up with it. The Congressmen have to put up with it. The state legislators have to put up with it. And teachers, school administrators and librarians have to put up with it. This is one of the penalties of being able to spend the taxpayers' money. Those who don't like other citizens looking over their shoulders and second-guessing their judgment should really go into some other line of work where they're not spending the taxpayers' money. So, we find it very distressing when schools resent parents and citizens looking over their shoulders.

7 Forty years ago it was not necessary to identify these different categories or types of rights because the public schools had a very high reputation in our land. I can remember that 40 years ago, when conservative speakers made some critical remarks about public schools, they were literally hooted down. Public schools then enjoyed a high reputation like the Post Office. They were sacred cows. Nobody could attack them and get by with it.

8 That public confidence, frankly, is no longer there. Let me explain one reason why it's no longer there. Thirty-two years ago, I was ready to enter my first child in public school, thinking that the first task of the school was to teach the child to read. We now know that there are at least 23 million illiterates in this country, adults who have been through the public schools and didn't learn how to read.

9 Well, 32 years ago when my first child was ready to start school, I discovered that the public schools didn't teach children to read. They only taught them to memorize a few words by guessing at them from the picture on the page. That is why I kept all my six children out of school until I taught them to read at home—so that they would be good readers, and so they would not be six of the 23 million functional illiterates in our country today. This is not a matter of Secular Humanism or morals, or affluence versus poverty, or anything else. No public school in my area taught children how to read. Schools only taught word guessing, which was a cheat on the taxpayers and on the children. We see the results today.

10 Thirty-two years ago I didn't know anybody else who taught her own child. Today there are about a million parents doing that because they feel cheated by the public schools.

11 In the mid-1970s something else came into the schools to use up the hours that could not be spent in reading the great books and the classics, which formerly children were able to do. This new element was best summarized and described by Senator Sam Hayakawa, who was a university president before he became a United States Senator. He called it a "heresy" in public school education. He said that, instead of teaching children knowledge and basic skills, the purpose of education has become group therapy. That's the best way to describe what has happened in the schools.

12 In public school classrooms, children are required to discuss feelings and emotions and attitudes. They are confronted with all sorts of moral dilemmas, instead of being given the facts and the knowledge they need. As a result, Hayakawa was a major promoter of a federal law passed in 1978 called the Protection of Pupil Rights Amendment, which said that schools should not give psychological testing or treatment to public school children on subjects that include family privacy, sexual and other personal matters, without the prior written consent of their parents. The purpose of this law was to prevent the schools from engaging in psychological probing, invasion of privacy, or manipulation of values.

13 The education establishment was so powerful that no regulations were issued on this law until 1984. But the parents were discovering what was happening to their children, and they didn't like it. They discovered that these psychological manipulations in the classroom constituted a continuing attack on their religion, on their morals, on their family, and even on parents. We believe that the continuing attack is so gross as to rise to the level of a violation of the First Amendment rights of parents and their children.

14 What happened is best illustrated by the classic lifeboat game presented in Sidney Simon's book on Values Clarification, and probably used in every school in this country. I had a reporter tell me that she had some variation of it at every level of elementary and secondary education. This is the game where the child is taught that ten people are in a sinking lifeboat, and the child must throw five of them out to drown. What five will you kill? Will it be the senior citizen, or the policeman, or the pregnant woman, or the college co-ed, or the black militant, or whoever? You pick *which* you will kill.

15   This "game" is played widely, in many variations—the fallout shelter, the kidney machine, starting a new race, and so forth. To explain what's wrong about this game, we have the example of the child who answered the lifeboat problem by saying, "Jesus brought another boat, and nobody had to drown." That child was creative but she got an "F" on her paper. That explains what values clarification does. It is not value neutral in any shape or form. It is a direct attack on the religion and the values of those of us who believe that God created us, and that it is not up to the child to play God and decide who lives and who dies.

16   The curriculum is filled with these moral dilemmas. The reason we know about so many of them is that, in 1984, the Department of Education conducted hearings across the country, where parents could come and describe what had happened to their own children. Those hearings had no press, but you can read much of the testimony in my book called *Child Abuse in the Classroom.* They are the authentic testimonies of parents. They told how the children were given such moral dilemmas as: stand up in class and give a good example of when it's okay to lie; write a paper on when it's all right to steal; discuss which kind of drugs you will take, how much and how many.

17   These moral dilemmas never tell the child that anything is wrong. The child is taken through all the areas of sex, with obscene descriptions, discussions, role-playing, and other psychological manipulations in the classroom. You can call this secular humanism, you can call it situation ethics, you can call it group therapy, you can call it psychological manipulation, you can call it counseling. You can call it no-name. But whatever it is, it is pervasive in the public schools, and it is a direct attack on the First Amendment rights of those who believe that God created us and that He created a moral law that we should obey. There's nothing neutral about the way values clarification is taught. The option that we should abide by God's law is never offered.

18   The Alabama textbook case (*Smith v. Board of School Commissioners of Mobile County*) finally brought out of the closet a situation that has been going on for 15 to 20 years, without media coverage or public attention. A previous speaker said how surprised he was to discover that home economics is about sex. Well, if you've been reading the textbooks, you would have known that. And that is why parents are so upset.

19   The issue in the Alabama textbook case was, simply, does the child who believes in God have the same rights in the public school classroom as the atheist?

20   In the 1985 case of *Wallace V. Jaffree,* the Supreme Court held that little atheist Jaffree had the right to be in the public school classroom and not be embarrassed when his peers said a prayer or spoke about God. In the Alabama textbook case, the U.S. District Court decision simply gave the child who believes in God the same rights as the atheist (but that decision was overturned by the U.S. Court of Appeals). I believe that the child

has a right to be in the public school classroom, and not have his religion, his morals, or his family, belittled or harassed, or told that they are irrelevant, or be presented with moral dilemmas which tell him that he can personally decide what is moral or legal.

21 We hear about teaching the child to make decisions. Of course, the child, if accosted by the drug peddler, must make a choice whether to buy or not. But it is so wrong to tell the child in class that he is capable of making a choice on an issue which the law has already decided. The schools should teach that the law has already decided that illegal drugs are bad and that he must not take drugs.

22 Since the First Amendment seems to prohibit the public schools from teaching a belief in God and His moral commandments, the school must also not be permitted to teach that there *isn't* any God, that God did *not* create the world, or that God did *not* give us His moral commandments.

23 If you look at what was involved in the textbooks in the Alabama case, you'll find textbooks saying that "what is right or wrong depends more on your own judgment than on what someone tells you to do." That's a direct attack on religion. One book tells the teacher to design a bulletin board showing conflicting values held by young people and their parents. This is mischief-making between the child and his parents.

24 Another textbook teaches that a family is a group of people who live together. That's not what a family is. A family starts with a marriage between a man and a woman. We find one textbook telling a child that, "in democratic families, every member has a voice in running the family, and parents and teenagers should decide together about curfews, study time, chores, allowances, and use of the car." Where does anybody get the idea that the school can tell the child that he's got a right to decide when he uses the car?

25 Here's another one. "Steps in decision-making can apply to something so simple as buying a new pair of shoes. They can also be applied to more complex decisions which involve religious preferences, use of alcohol, tobacco, and drugs." Where did anyone get the idea that schools can teach children that the family should be democratic and that children should participate in making such decisions?

26 Here's a quotation from another Alabama textbook: "In the past, families were often like dictatorships. One person, or two, made all the decisions." Is that mischief-making? You bet it's mischief-making.

27 Here's a quotation from another textbook: "People who have strong prejudices are called bigots. Bigots are devoted to their own church, party, or belief." That really puts your parents down, doesn't it!

28 Another textbook seems to say that it's okay if people want to experience parenthood without marrying. A long passage from another textbook says that divorce is an acceptable way of solving a problem. Then it calls on the class to role-play the circumstances that might lead the child to choose a divorce. The school has no right to attack the morals of children by telling them that divorce is acceptable.

29 Actually, the Alabama school textbooks are probably pretty mild compared to a lot of others we find around the rest of the country. In Seattle we found a textbook which said that promiscuity should not be labeled good or bad, that premarital sexual intercourse is acceptable for both men and women, that morality is individual—it's what you think it is, that homosexuality is okay, that prostitution should be legalized, that it is not deviant for teenagers to watch others performing sex acts through binoculars or windows, that alternatives to traditional marriage such as group sex and open marriage are okay, and then asks the child if he'd like to join such a group.

30 It took 18 months and finally some TV cameras, to get the curriculum committee to say the school would replace that textbook. It had been the textbook in a mandatory course in the Seattle public school system from 1978 to 1987.

31 Your New York City School Board video, "Sex, Drugs and AIDS," has been so controversial in New York that it is now being revised. But the original version has now gone all over the country. It blows my mind to think that anybody could believe it is constitutional to present a video in the public school classroom teaching children that fornication and sodomy are acceptable behavior so long as you use condoms, and telling them that homosexuality is all right, which is exactly what that video does. It is hard to believe that anybody could approve such an evil video for use in the public school classroom. The video is a direct attack on the First Amendment rights of those who believe that fornication and sodomy are wrong.

32 We want the same rights for people who believe in God and His commandments as the atheist has already established. Whatever you call it, this no-name ideology, it all boils down to an attack on religion, a war on parental rights, and a betrayal of trust. What a terrible thing it is to indicate, imply or even tell children that sexual intercourse, outside marriage, with males or females, of the same sex or the opposite sex, is okay and socially acceptable! Yet, that is widely taught in the public schools across the country.

33 The general attitude of most public school administrators, when parents make objections is: If you don't like it, take your child out and send him to a private school. That is not an acceptable answer. Our position is that the child who believes in God and His commandments has a right to be in the public school classroom without having his religion, his morals, and his family degraded, belittled, subjected to "clarification" or role-playing, or subjected to any of the psychological dilemmas that are presented by authority figures, who tell them in every possible way, overtly and indirectly, that there is no right or wrong answer, that anything the little fifth grader decides will be perfectly all right.

34 While the public schools, with their great battery of lawyers, may be able to win in the courts, and the media are clearly on their side, these cases are not increasing respect for the public schools. These cases have brought into public debate issues which should have been debated for the last 20 years.

35 Question: Whose morality are we going to be teaching in the public schools, and do you recognize that your personal morality may not be the morality of a majority of the other citizens in that community, and what would be the mechanism that you would establish in order to decide what morality should be taught in school?

36 Mrs. Schlafly: I think you heard me say I wasn't trying to impose my morality on the schools, and there wasn't anything in my remarks that could have possibly led you to believe that I'm trying to do that. I feel that the public schools can teach consensual values as indicated by the laws in this country. For example, it is a crime to lie, steal, cheat, kill, destroy property. It is against the law, in at least half the states, to engage in fornication or sodomy. At the very least, the public schools can teach that you should not do things which are illegal. Unfortunately, that is generally not done in the drug education courses. I've examined hundreds of these drug ed courses. They teach the child that we're in a drug society, that everybody takes drugs, that it's simply a question of how many you take and which kind, that it's up to you, little child, to make your own decision. This is called "critical thinking" or "decision-making skills," but they don't tell children that drugs are wrong. I see no problem with teaching children that acts are wrong when they are illegal. Schools are now telling children that smoking is not preferable. In the sex courses, schools are definitely teaching that it is wrong to have a baby, but they are not teaching that fornication is wrong. Now, there's no constitutional difference between teaching that it's wrong to have a baby and teaching that sex with unmarried teenagers is wrong. So, my answer to that question is that, if schools would simply teach the criminal law version of morality in this country, we would go a long way toward promoting civil order.

37 Question: In regard to AIDS education, what do we do? Do we live in the real world or do we live in a world of what should be?

38 Mrs. Schlafly: Anything taught about AIDS should meet four tests. It should be true, it should be healthy, it should be legal, and it should be constitutional. If any public schools teach a child that sex with condoms is safe or healthy, they are telling them something that is not true. Just wait for the lawsuits that are going to come! Sex for teenagers is unhealthy for many reasons of which AIDS is only one. As I pointed out earlier, fornication and sodomy are illegal in about half the states. I believe it is unconstitutional to teach sex-with-condoms because the children who come from homes where they believe that premarital sex is wrong have a constitutional right to be in the public school and not have that belief diminished, harassed, or taught that something that they believe is immoral is socially acceptable. The schools have an obligation to teach only that which is true, healthy, legal and constitutional.

39 Dr. C. Everett Koop told the *Village Voice* that he has already discussed sodomy with his gifted nine-year-old grandson. If he wants to do that, that is his privilege, but he has no right to discuss sodomy with our nine-year-old children or grandchildren. That's what the New York video does, and that's what some people are trying to do all over this country. We should get this teaching out of the public school classroom because it isn't legal, it isn't constitutional, and it certainly isn't healthy.

40 Question: Is the remedy, then, for a parent to be able to bar a curriculum, or do you suggest a more restrained approach that a parent should have the right to opt his child out of a program?

41 Mrs. Schlafly: A parent should not have to opt his child out of the public school classroom. The child has a right to be in the public school classroom without being embarrassed by some teacher describing how to use condoms and how to engage in sex, or role-playing what to do when you get pregnant with an illegitimate baby, or discussing conflicts with your father or your mother. The child has a right to be in the public school classroom and not be subjected to that type of teaching by an authority figure.

42 Question: 85% of public school parents in a nationwide poll indicated that the public schools should teach a family living/sex education course. How can you deny these parents who want such a program in the schools?

43 Mrs. Schlafly: The 85% doesn't impress me at all because all Gallup and Harris polls say that at least 85% of the American people want prayer in the public schools. But the Supreme Court has said no. The atheist child not only has a right not to pray, he has a right to silence everybody else in the classroom. So, when we're talking about religion or attacks on religion, the one person, apparently, can silence the rest. As I said, those who believe in God and His moral law, including about sex, have a right to be in the public school classroom without having an authority figure telling them that fornication is acceptable behavior. Whether 85% want sex education becomes totally irrelevant because I see it as an unconstitutional attack on the First Amendment rights on those who believe that discussed behaviors are wrong. Those parents who want to give their children contraceptives, that's their privilege, but the public school shouldn't do it.

44 My answer is that schools cannot appear to give social acceptance or authority acceptance to a behavior which is contrary to the faith and morals of a number of children. Whatever the school teaches must be true, healthy, legal, and constitutional.

45 You can make the same argument about drugs. Maybe half of your children are on drugs, but certainly we don't set up a room to pass out clean needles and tell them how to avoid some of the consequences. That isn't the way to teach. We should start by telling them that illegal drugs are bad and wrong and you shouldn't take them or they might kill you. The whole subject can be approached as a health measure. Furthermore, schools ought to teach that the consequences of sex fall twice as heavily on girls as on boys. The morals are the same, but the consequences are very different. It's contrary to feminist ideology to teach children that there's any difference between boys and girls. But little girls ought to be taught about the terrible price that girls pay in terms of the side effects of contraceptives, of abortion and its trauma, venereal diseases, the poverty, the cervical cancer, the emotional and psychological trauma. In all those ways, the girl pays twice as much.

A Just War
George Bush

Prior to the start of the war with Iraq on January 16, 1991, many "advocates and opponents of war resorted—at least implicitly—to the distinctions and categories of just-war thinking" (*Newsweek*, February 11, 1991, p. 47). On January 25, 1991, in an address to over 1000 delegates at the conservative National Religious Broadcasters annual conference in Washington, D.C., President George Bush explicitly and at length employed the "just war" doctrine to defend American and coalition military action. He advocates the value judgment that the war with Iraq "is a just war" (par. 8, 22) and he applies the traditional value criteria for such a war.

President Bush is speaking to a friendly audience (2, 4) and he reinforces values (3) and policy positions that he and the audience share (5–6). As he begins his argument, he employs antithetical phrasing to underscore the moral conflict involved and he describes the roots of the just war doctrine in Greco-Roman philosophy and Christian theology (8). A morally just war, the doctrine holds, should be waged only: (1) for a morally just cause; (2) when approved by a legitimate authority; (3) as a last resort when all peaceful alternatives have been exhausted; (4) when the good achieved outweighs the bad side-effects; (5) when the war is waged with just means; and (6) when there is a reasonable chance for success.

To develop his contention that the war with Iraq is a noble and just cause, Bush discusses the purposes and motivations of American military action (9–10, 13). Toward the end of the speech, he uses a quotation from Abraham Lincoln to stress again the morality of the cause (24). The President then cites twelve United Nations resolutions and the united agreement of twenty-eight nations from six continents to show that the war is approved by legitimate authority (11–12).

Bush employs a compact summary of statistics and examples to demonstrate that peaceful diplomatic efforts have been exhausted. (14–15). In contrast, in his speech to the nation on January 16 announcing the start of the war, the thrust of his argument focuses not only on exhausted diplomatic efforts but also on the failure of economic and political sanctions against Iraq. In fact the tone of that speech is very pragmatic and his rationale is not at all placed in the context of a morally just war. Bush's speech on January 16 (reprinted in chapter 7 of this book) stresses pragmatic necessity—circumstances now dictate that we have no choice but to go to war with Iraq. Why might the President have used a primarily pragmatic justification in announcing the war and a full-blown moral argument here?

That the greater good of thwarting the threat posed by Saddam Hussein can be achieved through just means with minimal bad side-effects is a contention developed through Bush's pledge to minimize casualties, act humanely, and "avoid hurting the innocent" (16–17). Finally, Bush argues that there is a reasonable chance of success—that victory can be achieved—by pledging that it will be a relatively short and decisive war (not another Vietnam) and by reminding the audience of the high quality of America's military forces (18–19).

In what ways and to what extent do you agree or disagree that Bush proved his value judgment that the war with Iraq was a morally just war? Also consider the role in war rhetoric throughout American history of what critic Robert Ivie terms "images of savagery"—images of "cunning but otherwise irrational enemies who are driven to circumvent all the restraints of international law and of human principles in order to impose their will on others." (See Robert L. Ivie, "Images of Savagery in American Justifications for War," *Communication Monographs,* 47 (November 1980): 279–294; also see Ivie, "Presidential Motives for War," *Quarterly Journal of Speech,* 60 (October 1974): 337–345.) What rhetorical functions in this speech might be served by such images as "naked aggression"; "the rape, the pillage, the plunder"; "wanton, barbaric bombing of civilian areas"; and "indiscriminate use" (9, 13–14, 17)?

This speech by President Bush to the National Religious Broadcasters was given on the morning of January 25 and was covered live only by the CNN television network. On the evening of the next day, January 26, 1991, via major network television and radio coverage, President Bush presented the annual State of the Union message to the nation. In his lengthy State of the Union speech on both domestic and international topics, Bush does indirectly and implicitly touch on some of the standards for a just war but does not explicitly and clearly apply the just war criteria. In place of the tone of morality pervading the January 25 speech, there remains in the State of the Union address a simple summary alluding to the more complex argument of the previous day: "Our cause is just. Our cause is moral. Our cause is right." The morning hour and the coverage only on CNN severely limited the exposure of the general citizenry to the explicit just war argument of Bush's January 25 speech. Why might the President have decided not to use the same explicit and overtly developed just war argument in his State of the Union address to the nation the next night?

The text of this speech is reprinted from *Weekly Compilation of Presidential Documents*, 27 (February 4, 1991): 87–89.

---

1 Thank you, President Rose, thank you, sir, and Executive Director Gustavson—all. First, let me salute your leadership of the NRB: Billy Graham and Jerry Falwell, Pat Robertson, James Dobson, Chuck Colson; and FCC Commissioners: Sikes and Duggan and James Quello.

2 This marks the fifth time that I've addressed the annual convention of the National Religious Broadcasters. And once again, let me say it is, for both Barbara and me, an honor to be back here.

3 Let me begin by congratulating you on your theme of declaring His glory to all nations. It's a theme eclipsing denominations and which reflects many of the eternal teachings in the Scripture. I speak, of course, of the teachings which uphold moral values like tolerance, compassion, faith, and courage. They remind us that while God can live without man, man cannot live without God. His love and His justice inspire in us a yearning for faith and a compassion for the weak and oppressed, as well as the courage and conviction to oppose tyranny and injustice.

4 And I'm very grateful for that resolution that has just been read prior to my speaking here.

5 Matthew also reminds us in these times that the meek shall inherit the Earth. At home, these values imbue the policies which you and I support. Like me, you endorse adoption, not abortion. And last year you helped ensure that the options of religious-based child care will not be restricted or eliminated by the Federal Government.

6 And I commend your concern, your heartfelt concern, on behalf of Americans with disabilities, and your belief that students who go to school to nourish their minds should also be allowed to nourish their souls. And I have not lessened my commitment to restoring voluntary prayer in our schools.

7 These actions can make America a kinder and gentler place because they reaffirm the values that I spoke of earlier, values that must be central to the lives of every individual

and the life of every nation. The clergyman Richard Cecil once said, "There are two classes of the wise: the men who serve God because they have found Him, and the men who seek Him because they have not found Him yet." Abroad, as in America, our task is to serve and seek wisely through the policies we pursue.

8 Nowhere is this more true than in the Persian Gulf where—despite protestations of Saddam Hussein—it is not Iraq against the United States, it's the regime of Saddam Hussein against the rest of the world. Saddam tried to cast this conflict as a religious war, but it has nothing to do with religion per se. It has, on the other hand, everything to do with what religion embodies: good versus evil, right versus wrong, human dignity and freedom versus tyranny and oppression. The war in the Gulf is not a Christian war, a Jewish war, or a Moslem war; it is a just war. And it is a war with which good will prevail. We're told that the principles of a just war originated with classical Greek and Roman philosophers like Plato and Cicero. And later they were expounded by such Christian theologians as Ambrose, Augustine, Thomas Aquinas.

9 The first principle of a just war is that it support a just cause. Our cause could not be more noble. We seek Iraq's withdrawal from Kuwait—completely, immediately, and without condition; the restoration of Kuwait's legitimate government; and the security and stability of the Gulf. We will see that Kuwait once again is free, that the nightmare of Iraq's occupation has ended, and that naked aggression will not be rewarded.

10 We seek nothing for ourselves. As I have said, U.S. forces will leave as soon as their mission is over, as soon as they are no longer needed or desired. And let me add, we do not seek the destruction of Iraq. We have respect for the people of Iraq, for the importance of Iraq in the region. We do not want a country so destabilized that Iraq itself could be a target for aggression.

11 But a just war must also be declared by legitimate authority. Operation Desert Storm is supported by unprecedented United Nations solidarity, the principle of collective self-defense, 12 Security Council resolutions, and in the Gulf, 28 nations from 6 continents united, resolute that we will not waver and that Saddam's aggression will not stand.

12 I salute the aid—economic and military—from countries who have joined in this unprecedented effort, whose courage and sacrifice have inspired the world. We're not going it alone, but believe me, we are going to see it through.

13 Every war—every war—is fought for a reason. But a just war is fought for the right reasons, for moral, not selfish reasons. Let me take a moment to tell you a story, a tragic story, about a family whose two sons, 18 and 19, reportedly refused to lower the Kuwaiti flag in front of their home. For this crime, they were executed by the Iraqis. Then, unbelievably, their parents were asked to pay the price of the bullets used to kill them.

14 Some ask whether it's moral to use force to stop the rape, the pillage, the plunder of Kuwait. And my answer: Extraordinary diplomatic efforts having been exhausted to resolve the matter peacefully, then the use of force is moral.

15 A just war must be a last resort. As I have often said, we did not want war. But you all know the verse from Ecclesiastes—there is "a time for peace, a time for war." From August 2, 1990—last summer, August 2d—to January 15, 1991—166 days—we tried to resolve this conflict. Secretary of State Jim Baker made an extraordinary effort to achieve peace: more than 200 meetings with foreign dignitaries; 10 diplomatic missions; 6 congressional appearances; over 103,000 miles traveled to talk with, among others, members of the United Nations, the Arab League, and the European Community. And sadly, Saddam Hussein rejected out of hand every overture made by the United States and by other countries as well. He made this just war an inevitable war.

16 We all know that war never comes easy or cheap. War is never without the loss of innocent life. And that is war's greatest tragedy. But when a war must be fought for the greater good, it is our gravest obligation to conduct a war in proportion to the threat. And that is why we must act reasonably, humanely, and make every effort possible to keep casualties to a minimum. And we've done so. I'm very proud of our military in achieving this end.

17 From the very first day of the war, the allies have waged war against Saddam's military. We are doing everything possible, believe me, to avoid hurting the innocent. Saddam's response: wanton, barbaric bombing of civilian areas. America and her allies value life. We pray that Saddam Hussein will see reason. To date, his indiscriminate use of those Scud missiles—nothing more than weapons of terror, they can offer no military advantage—weapons of terror—it outraged the world what he has done.

18 The price of war is always high. And so, it must never, ever, be undertaken without total commitment to a successful outcome. It is only justified when victory can be achieved. I have pledged that this will not be another Vietnam. And let me reassure you here today, it won't be another Vietnam.

19 We are fortunate, we are very fortunate, to have in this crisis the finest armed forces ever assembled, an all-volunteer force, joined by courageous allies. And we will prevail because we have the finest soldiers, sailors, airmen, marines, and coastguardsmen that any nation has ever had.

20 But above all, we will prevail because of the support of the American people, armed with a trust in God and in the principles that make men free—people like each of you in this room. I salute Voice of Hope's live radio programming for U.S. and allied troops in the Gulf, and your Operation Desert Prayer, and worship services for our troops held by among others, the man who over a week ago led a wonderful prayer service at Fort Myer over here across the river in Virginia, the Reverend Billy Graham.

21 America has always been a religious nation, perhaps never more than now. Just look at the last several weeks—churches, synagogues, mosques reporting record attendance at services; chapels packed during working hours as Americans stop in for a moment or two. Why? To pray for peace. And I know—of course, I know—that some disagree with the course that I've taken, and I have no bitterness in my heart about that at all, no anger. I am convinced that we are doing the right thing. And tolerance is a virtue, not a vice.

22 But with the support and prayers of so many, there can be no question in the minds of our soldiers or in the minds of our enemy about what Americans think. We know that this is a just war. And we know that, God willing, this is a war we will win. But most of all, we know that ours would not be the land of the free if it were not also the home of the brave. No one wanted war less than I did. No one is more determined to seize from battle the real peace that can offer hope, that can create a new world order.

23 When this war is over, the United States, its credibility and its reliability restored, will have a key leadership role in helping to bring peace to the rest of the Middle East. And I have been honored to serve as President of this great nation for 2 years now and believe more than ever that one cannot be America's President without trust in God. I cannot imagine a world, a life, without the presence of the One through whom all things are possible.

24 During the darkest days of the Civil War, a man we revere not merely for what he did but what he was, was asked whether he thought the Lord was on his side. And said Abraham Lincoln: "My concern is not whether God is on our side, but whether we are on God's side." My fellow Americans, I firmly believe in my heart of hearts that times will soon be on the side of peace because the world is overwhelmingly on the side of God.

25 Thank you for this occasion. And may God bless our great country. And please remember all of our coalition's armed forces in your prayers. Thank you, and God bless you.

Joy in Our Times
Georgie Anne Geyer

Georgie Anne Geyer is an internationally respected foreign correspondent and syndicated news columnist. She has regularly appeared as a panelist or questioner on such television news programs as Washington Week in Review and Meet the Press. In 1983 she published her autobiography, *Buying the Night Flight.* On May 7, 1989 Geyer delivered this address at the annual commencement ceremonies of Saint Mary-of-the Woods College, a small Roman Catholic liberal arts college for women located in the Indiana town of the same name.

The typical commencement speech has earned a reputation for dullness, triteness, and irrelevance. But this need not be the case. Creative and sensitive commencement speakers genuinely can praise, inspire, and challenge the graduates rather than bore them with irrelevant examples, cliché phrases, stereotyped images, and sleep-inducing platitudes. Among the expectations that an audience may hold concerning speeches that honor graduates for completion of a course of study are the following. (1) Praise for the individual and collective achievements of the class. (2) A call to use the knowledge and skill they have acquired in innovative, humane, and socially worthy ways. (3) Description of the significant challenges, problems, or opportunities facing the graduates; this may include criticism of existing societal conditions or forces. (4) Creative interweaving of realism and idealism—of telling it like it is and envisioning how it ought to be. (5) Reinforcement of commitment to values already held by the audience; or perhaps more often advocacy of a set of values to be adopted by the audience in preference to less desirable (but more currently popular) values.

Clearly Georgie Anne Geyer advocates adoption of a value (joy) and its components (risk-taking; historical and personal perspective; appropriate timing; wise choices; and love). These values are contrasted to pervasive but less desirable values such as selfishness, isolated individualism, and desperate approval of others (paragraphs 3, 4, 8, 14, 20). What assessment could you make of her speech in light of the other four commonly held audience expectations for a good commencement speech?

How adequately does Geyer clarify and justify the values that she advocates? Processes of definition are central to her persuasive effort. Among her definitional techniques are dictionary meaning, descriptive explanation, and negation (5); she also uses personal examples (11–12) and identification of elements that foster joy (15, 17, 21, 23, 28). Geyer's use of narration—of stories and illustrations—is so widespread as to strongly invite, indeed demand, the attention both of the audience and the rhetorical critic (1–2, 12–13, 16, 19, 22, 24–26). How clear, relevant, and effective are the stories she tells?

Speaker credibility is a vital factor in speeches that propose a value judgment or advocate adoption of values. In addition to the positive reputation that Geyer probably had with her audience prior to the speech, assess the appropriateness and effectiveness of sections of her speech that function to reinforce that high credibility (10, 24–26). Also consider what rhetorical functions are served—what communicative work is done—by such stylistic resources as antithesis (5, 7, 18), alliteration (28, 29), parallel structure (10, 30), and questions (4, 9, 14).

Reprinted with permission from *Vital Speeches of the Day,* August 15, 1989, pp. 666–668.

---

1 Three months ago, I walked into my condominium in downtown Washington and happened to see the great Russian/American conductor, Mstislav Rostropovich, standing at our front desk. We are proud that he lives there. He is always a man filled with life and spirit, but this day he had the most marked look of pure joy on his face that I had ever had the . . . well . . . joy of seeing.

2 After greeting me, he stood for a few minutes at the desk and repeated several times, as if in sheer wonder, "Last night, I conducted 250 cellists. . . . Last night, I conducted 250 cellists. . . ." Ladies and gentlemen, at that moment I knew that I had seen as close to a beatific joy as I have ever seen, next to certain pictures of Christ. For I discovered then that this great musician, who is a cellist, had conducted at the world conference of 5,000 cellists!

3 That magical moment—that blessed moment—made me think of our younger generation today—of your generation—and I wondered if any of them, of you, would understand that kind of joy. For when I go around to schools—and to the very best and most serious schools—what even our best young people ask me is things like, "Miss Geyer, what are they looking for out there?" In short, in place of that inner joy of Rostropovich's which knew his love for his music and for his cello, many young people of your generation instead are looking and waiting for some elusive and fickle "someone" out there to tell them what they are.

4 "What are they looking for out there?" That is one phrase that will warn you if you let it of what NOT to be thinking, even in today's often treacherous world. Some others? "How can I get ahead? What's in it for me? Let's get him." And, "How can I stop being bored? What company can I take over today? How much will I make? What's in it for me?"

5 Let us, for a moment, consider "Joy." My dictionary says that it is the emotion excited by the acquisition or expectation of good." I like that. Not the acquisition of things, or of power, or of a handsome husband, or of importance of position, but of good. It is right action, rather than merely the paltry fruit of any action. It is the magical and mystical act of discovering and finally knowing the God-given talents and the artistry that is inside yourself and nurturing and expressing them rather than trying vainly to find out what "society," whatever that is, fashionably at that moment, wants. Aristotle said that happiness is an activity that is "in accordance with virtue." Vince Lombardi, more in tune with our times, said that "happiness is winning." Donald Trump carried it to the zenith of our times' senselessness and anomie, saying that it's not "whether you win or lose, it's winning."

6 Let me say right off that I think the search for joy—and, remember, that only in America is the "pursuit of happiness" assured in the very Constitution itself—is very difficult for all Americans, young and old, today. Dr. Joseph Plummber, an authority on values, recently put out a study listing profound changes in our basic American values. He found that more people in the developed Western nations were seeking self-actualization rather than security or traditionally defined success. He found a self-fulfillment ethic, individualized definitions of success, a growing sense of limits . . . .

7 Now, this is all right so long as it is associated with principles, with "good," and with the courage to carry it through, for, as Churchill said, "Courage is the most important virtue, because it GUARANTEES all the rest." Instead, I see many Americans terrified by risk, thinking apparently that a life without risk really IS possible. We see the mother who drank half a bottle of Jim Beam whiskey every day during her pregnancy and is suing the company because her poor child is deformed. I see a remarkable amount of lack of joy, of gamesplaying instead of principle and of cases where the grand principle of equality has been debased to no more than equality of appetite.

8 And I see the warning of Alexis de Tocqueville about excessive individualism being realized. Two centuries ago the brilliant Frenchman warned of the democracy that he so admired that it held within it the seeds of its own demise. "Not only does democracy make every man forget his ancestors," he wrote, "but hides his descendants and separates his contemporaries from him; it throws him back forever upon himself alone and threatens in the end to confine him entirely within the solitude of his heart." That isolation, ladies and gentlemen, graduates and friends, is not democracy but a perverted democracy that looks to others desperately for approval, that looks not to a work one loves but to a lottery and to chance for succor, and that creates a person afraid to take the joy to live in one's time, and equally incapable of living fully either in one's own self—or in community, for the common good.

9 Amidst all the good we have in our country, our churches and our lives, nevertheless today I also find this wanting. Where is joy? What is joy? Permit me to muse, modestly, on what I have learned through living an unorthodox life, about joy.

10 So I was the first woman foreign correspondent and syndicated columnist in our time. So I had to break ground and sometimes face barriers put up against me. So I lost a number of fiances because of my love for understanding other countries, because of my liking for hotels and plane rides across the Red Seas of the world. So one of them once said in irk, "Gee Gee, the most beautfiul words in the world to you are not, 'I love you' but 'Room Service, Please.' "

11 That meant that everybody was always and is still asking me, "Didn't you feel bitter about it?" I have thought about that. Bitter? It never crossed my mind to be bitter. I was having so much fun, I was so filled with spirit and joy, I thanked God every day for the very privilege of being able to know everyone in the world and for being able to do this work I so loved. And if the Sisters of Providence will forgive me a wicked aside, I will add that the one thing your enemies can never forgive you is, not money, not even success, but having so much fun in life!

12 My joys were often the little things: Interviewing a Khomeini or a Castro, Sadat or a Duarte, yes, those were good professionally, and afterwards I felt a great sense of satisfaction for breaking through . . . But I would often experience pure joy in odd and unexpected places . . . Sitting at breakfast in Chile and quietly observing people and feeling so privileged to be there . . . being able to bring some message of truth about the world to my own people, something they didn't know . . . seeing an election in a war-torn El Salvador and watching the poor people dare everyone to go to vote . . . seeing Russia return to its own conscience—the inner conscience that was always there, waiting—as Gorbachev frees the Russian people these very days, before our eyes. . . .

13 I remember special messages that warmed me tremendously, like when I interviewed the late great Archbishop Oscar Romero of El Salvador in 1979. At one point, I asked this man, who seemed just to radiate goodness, whether it would not have been easier to have stayed out of all the fights for social justice he had entered? And his simple but profound words: "Well, I could have just stayed in the Archbishop's palace, but that would not have been very EASY, would it?" It rang so very true. It would have been immeasurably harder, just as it will be immeasurably harder for you, if you choose to live a life without the components of joy.

14 But—what are those components? And why are they so hard to come by in our "fun-loving . . . non risk taking . . . gamesplaying . . . world?"

15 —RISK TAKING. First and very important, being able to feel joy involves risk taking, and I do not mean juggling monies around frenziedly in the stock market. It means risking your popularity by taking a genuinely unpopular stand, risking your life to do what it is that YOU want to do in life. Risks are going to be there anyway. It's just street sense to take them on your terms, not theirs. In warfare, it is called being on the offensive. In life, it is called embracing life with all your heart.

16 Along these lines, I recall one spring day seven years ago when I was going to Central America—again. I just had a gut feeling that I did not want to go to El Salvador, because there had been so much fighting there. Usually I don't obey fearful feelings, having found that they pass and are not really accurate, but this time I did. So I took the plane to Nicaragua, and that week nothing at all happened in Salvador—and when I got to the Managua airport, I was standing second in line to pass through to the center of the airport . . . and the airport was blown up! I never try to second-guess fate again after that!

17 —PERSPECTIVE. What, you may ask, does perspective have to do with joy? Well, a whole lot!

18 Young people are always asking me how I "control" (a favorite word of your generation) my interviews. And I always answer, "Knowing more than they do." This is not, repeat not, a popular answer, but it is genuine and workable. I know history—so nothing surprises me. I know where things are, why and where they will be. The perspective of history—of all human life—gives me a terrifying confidence. Knowing the trajectory of mankind—its victories, its sordid defeats, its searchings for God and for meaning—I cannot be a utopian, which is dangerous anyway, but I also cannot be a pessimist. I see how far we have come, I can take joy in what we can accomplish in our lifetimes, because I know and understand the limits of what we can do.

19 Once I wrote a good friend, a Jesuit priest in Latin America, about how discouraged I was about how Latin America was going and he wrote back these very wise words, "Remember, Gee Gee, I am not responsible for the outcome, but I am responsible for my own fight." That's it. That's what I know. And that very simple perspective allows one to have joy in what one IS able to do and not to moan and mourn over not being able to do the impossible. Because we cannot be perfect, that does not mean we cannot be good.

20 Perspective comes at you from the funniest, most unexpected places. In Finland last fall, I went to see this fine artist, Bjorn Weckstrom, and he explained to me, as no one else quite has, how we have come to this point, where so many search not for deeper meaning or for joy but "to do something, just to be someone for a moment." "A hundred years ago," Bjorn said, "people were living in small communities. Everyone had an identity known by the whole village. The group created the morals, the rules . . . Even your name was taken from your father—you were 'son of . . .' Now the frames are eliminated. People are desperate, living in this super tribe. The village was an enormous security for people. In a way it gave people stability and a kind of harmony in life. The problem has been to create something new which would replace this . . . Before, it was enough to be recognized for what you do before the village. But now the borders of the tribe have been moving out. Now to be somebody you have to be on television. It is the problem of the identity of man today, the need to be someone even for a short moment. Even if man knows he's almost at the end of his rope. . . ." And, of course, the amorphous, unseen, cruelly judgmental audience of the TV is a harsh audience indeed, compared to the village—and the person never really knows, in this new audience, whether what he has done is good or not. And it really doesn't matter, for this audience more than likely has already long succumbed to the lowest value of the collective will.

21 —TIMING. Understanding the right time for an idea, for a painting, for doing something—it is critical. It is an instinct, it comes from within people in whom street sense has been blended blessedly with intellectual searching. It is critical for work and it is critical for personal relationships. Too often today, we want to rush work, rush relationships, become managing editor at 32, editor at 35 . . . And later, we wonder where we have been, or whether we've been anywhere at all.

22 I talked with a young man the other day, who happened to be a fundamentalist Christian. He spoke of how important the three years before marriage to his wife had been, when they were not making love. "We got to know each other in a way at that time that we could never have known otherwise," he told me. "When you go to bed too soon, you lose all kinds of precious levels of the development of a relationship." He was so right. The Bible has a lot about this. "There is a time to . . . and a time . . ."

23 CHOICES. I have found through life that a truly joyful person is willing to make choices on the basis of what he knows, then stick with them, and change them if he must. It is a terribly unjoyful life, not to be able to make choices, not to have the inner confidence.

24 That recalls the most interesting evening I had, four years ago, when I was asked to drive the late Clair Booth Luce to a dinner party. I was delighted, for here was one of the truly great women of our time, a woman who had done just about everything. . . . Mrs. Luce was not, repeat not, a woman you contradicted or, as I soon found out, even questioned. As soon as she got in the car, she was throwing very pointed and brilliant one-liners at me. She obviously had a message for me. In fact, she repeated it several times.

25 "You did it right." she said. "You spent 20 years doing what you do best." When I tried to remonstrate with this woman who had been ambassador, playwright, journalist, novelist, wife, mother, she disdained the suggestion. "No," she said, "I could have been a great playwright, I could have been a great playwright. . . ."

26 I am not suggesting that Mrs. Luce was right. Personally, I feel deeply what I have had to give up for what I wanted most. I am suggesting that wise people at different times in their lives realize that we all make choices, even when we think we are not making them; so, again, it is better to embrace them than to run from them. I dedicate that story to our noble older women graduates here today, who I know have had to make many, many choices and are still courageously making them, as their presence here attests.

27 And think, women of my generation—think of what we have seen! We have seen the first age when women have sought to define THEMSELVES! All through history, men have defined us. Finally, we are taking responsibility for ourselves! Easy? How could it be easy. And yet, we have finally arrived at trying to know and understand the ultimate political relationship, which is the ecstatic but endlessly bedeviling relationship between men and women and we have finally arrived at the moment, as the poet Louise Bogan puts it so beautifully, of women giving back to the world "half of its soul." Which brings me to . . .

28 —LOVE. Finally, love! There is really only one thing that I know to tell you graduates—only one thing—and that is to FOLLOW WHAT YOU LOVE! Follow it intellectually! Follow it sensuously! Follow it with generosity and nobility toward your fellow man! Don't deign to ask what "they" are looking for out there. Ask what you have inside. I was blessed—I was blessed because I knew what I loved—writing, my countries, being a courier between cultures—and I had dogged determination to follow it. Doing what you love, whether it is having children, working in a profession, being a nun, being a journalist, is all encompassing, all engrossing, it is like a very great love affair occurring every day. It is principle and creation, you know why you are here, your personal life and your professional life is all one. It is not fun, not games, not winning or losing, not making money or having your 15 minutes on television; it is what no one can ever, ever take away from you, it is . . . pure joy.

29 In closing, I would like to ask you just to look around you today . . . to relish and preserve in your mind's eye and your memory this treasured moment at this quintessentially beautiful school.

30 Never again will you graduates be at this pure moment of your existence, when all the roads are open to you. Perhaps never again will you have friends and comrades, and teachers and sisters, as pure in their friendship because no one is yet what he or she is going to become. Never again probably will your families be quite so specially proud of you.

31 So, seize the moment joyfully. Follow not your interests, which change, but what you are and what you love, which will and should not change. And always remember these golden days.

32 God bless you all, and may the gods of the winds and the seas be with you on your voyage. Thank you.

Caring for Creation: Religion and Ecology
Russell E. Train

As Chairman of the World Wildlife Fund and Conservation Foundation, Russell Train represents an organization with over 300,000 members—an organization that seeks to protect the biological resources on which human well-being depends. On May 18, 1990 Train presented this address at the closing session of the North American Conference on Religion and Ecology held in Washington, D.C. As is true of other speeches in this anthology, this speech legitimately could be evaluated from several critical viewpoints. It could, as discussed in Chapter 6, be analyzed primarily as attempting to create concern for environmental problems (paragraphs 12–14).

In our view, however, this speech primarily advocates propositions of value—it offers value judgments and advocates adoption of certain desirable values in contrast to less desirable values. After stressing that organized religion generally has been oblivious to and silent on environmental issues (3–4) and illustrating possible cooperative efforts (6), Train argues both early and late in the speech that organized religion should be the primary vehicle for instilling environmental values in people (4, 19, 22). He criticizes the value priorities imbedded in the Roman Catholic Church's birth control policies for contributing to ecological problems (11–12). Note his use of alliteration—the repetition of the same initial sound, usually a consonant, in a series of words in proximity. Often used to make an idea more memorable or to associate several positive or negative ideas, here alliteration stimulates negative associations (degrade, deface, desecrate, destroy). Train urges organized religion to readjust its value priorities to show equal concern for human and ecological issues (16). Very overtly he advocates specific values to be taught by organized religion (19) and he encourages adoption of them by describing the positive consequences of holding those values (20).

A key strategy in advocating his values and value judgments is the emphasis through diverse techniques in the interrelation and interdependence of human welfare and environmental welfare (15, 16). He develops the "web of life" metaphor (7) and presents creative twists on two common phrases: "facts of life" (9) and "right to life" (15). Train overtly employs representative examples (9 —"their number could be almost infinite") and he accumulates a lengthy list of examples to underscore the massiveness of the threats to the environment (10).

Finally, consider the role of speaker credibility in this address. In what ways might some of his statements (2, 7) strengthen or weaken his credibility with his audience?

This speech is reprinted with permission from *Vital Speeches of the Day,* August 15, 1990, pp. 664–666.

---

1 It is a privilege to address this closing event of the Conference on Caring for Creation on the subject of "Religion and the Environment." Following so many splendid speakers, it is highly doubtful that I will offer you anything very original. Anyway, someone has said that "the only secret of being original is not to reveal your sources."

2 I am neither a theologian nor a philosopher. For a good many years of my life, I was a relatively active layman in the Episcopal Church here in Washington, although something of a "backslider" in more recent years. It may have some significance that my absence from regular attendance at Sunday services dates back almost exactly to the time my wife and I purchased a farm on the Eastern Shore of Maryland. Suddenly, my weekends no longer included formal religious observance in church but instead were filled with the enjoyment of fields and woods and water, the presence of wildlife, the rhythm of the seasons. And for the past 30 years I have been part of the environmental movement, both in government and in the private sector.

3 During much of this time, I have been puzzled—to say the least—by what has seemed to me the almost total obliviousness of organized religion toward the environment. It has been nothing less than extraordinary. Here we have had one of the most fundamental concerns to agitate human society within living memory—certainly in North America and Europe and increasingly around the globe. Here we have issues that go to the heart of the human condition, to the quality of human life, even to humanity's ultimate survival. Here we have problems that can be said to threaten the very integrity of Creation. And yet the churches and other institutions of organized religion have largely ignored the whole subject.

4 Of course, a number of thoughtful persons have over the past twenty years or so explored the interrelationship of religion and the environment, of human spirituality and nature. However, until recently, organized religion has remained largely silent and on the sidelines. Yet our churches, synagogues, temples, and mosques should be a principal vehicle for instilling environmental values in our planet's people. And, believe me, it is very much a matter of values.

5 To be fair, I must point out that the organized environmental movement has on its side largely ignored the potentially central role that religion can have in bringing about a new harmony between man and nature. Hopefully, an active partnership is now arising between the environmental and religious communities. This conference will help build that partnership.

6 It was in 1986 that the World Wide Fund for Nature (formerly called the World Wildlife Fund and still so called in the United States and Canada) brought together at Assisi representatives of the five major religions of the world—Christian, Jewish, Moslem, Hindu and Buddhist—to explore the development of a single, unified statement of religious responsibility toward nature. As you know, while a single statement did not prove practical at that time, each religion did its own statement consonant with its own beliefs and traditions, and these have been published in the *Assisi Declarations*. The Assisi experience was an exciting one, and it has been highly influential in bringing different religious groups to address their responsibility toward nature. In 1988, Pope John Paul II and the Dalai Lama met in Rome to discuss issues of "world peace, spiritual values, and protection of the earth's natural environment." A number of other initiatives have and are occurring, and I will not try to enumerate them here. At long last, religion seems to be awakening to the environment. I am delighted on this occasion to acknowledge that our honored guest, H.R.H. The Duke of Edinburgh, was the principal moving force in bringing about Assisi and its continued follow-up.

7 I said earlier that I am neither a theologian nor a philosopher. Nor am I a scientist. Yet I know that our human life, its quality and its very existence, are totally dependent upon the natural systems of the Earth—the air, the water, the soils, the extraordinary diversity of plant and animal life—systems all driven by the energy of the sun. We could not exist without the support of these natural systems. Nor could any of the other forms of life with which we share the Earth. These are facts over which it seems to me there can be no argument. We are all part of a living community that is mutually dependent. All life exists in an infinitely complex set of interrelationships—truly a "web of life"—that we disturb at our peril.

8 We depend upon the air to supply us with oxygen we must breathe—oxygen that in turn is produced by the microorganisms in the surface of the ocean and by the vegetative cover of the land, particularly its tropical forests, often referred to as the "lungs of the planet." We depend for our sustenance on the productivity of the soil, whose fertility is in turn sustained by the nitrogen-fixing ability of soil bacteria. The humus essential to productive soils is of course the product of the work of other bacteria, beetles, worms, and such. (Size is clearly no measure of the importance of one's role in the planetary scheme. In fact, it is truly the little things that run the world!) Our grains and other crops, our orchards, and much of the world's forests depend for pollination and, thus, their continued existence upon insects, birds, and bats among other mammals—often highly specialized to serve the needs of a particular species of plant. The most valuable fruit crop of southeast Asia is *durian,* a $100 million-a-year crop, and it is pollinated entirely by bats. Birds and bats are responsible for eliminatng a high proportion of the world's destructive insects and weed seeds—far more than all the insecticides and herbicides we apply. Only last week, I read a news report that in Pakistan a species of owl, considered there a bird of ill omen, is responsible for controlling the rats and mice that would otherwise destroy a large part of the grain crop. A majority of our North American bird species, which provide us with such valuable (and free) services, migrate to Mexico and farther south in the winter. A number of these species are in substantial decline because of the destruction of the tropical forests on which they depend for winter habitat. And, of course, it is on the tropical forests that the entire planet depends for much of the production of oxygen and much of the sequestration of carbon which together in turn help maintain the life-sustaining quality of the global atmosphere.

9 These are a few examples—and their number could be almost infinite—to illustrate the dependence of human and other life on the natural systems of the Earth as well as the intricate interdependence of the living community as a whole. I feel it is important to be explicit about such examples because our increasingly urban population tends to take human self-sufficiency for granted and lives in almost total ignorance of the true "facts of life."

10 Given the historic tendency of the human race to put its own self-interest ahead of everything else and usually to measure that self-interest in the near term rather than the long term, it is probably not surprising that the natural systems of the Earth are under such dire threat today. You are no doubt familiar with the litany of environmental threats. A partial one would include the destruction of tropical forests, the loss of productive soils, the spread of deserts, declining supplies of fresh water, the depletion of ocean fisheries, the pervasive pollution of air, land and water, the accelerating extinction of species, the likelihood of global warming, and the depletion of the life-protecting stratospheric ozone layer. It should be pointed out that, in the case of stratospheric ozone depletion, which could have a catastrophic impact on life on Earth, the cause is purely and simply human technology— our refrigerants, air conditioners, fire extinguishers, spray propellants, etc. Finally, overarching all the other environmental threats, of course, is the burgeoning human population. And here again we clearly have no one to blame but ourselves, and here it is not so much our technology as the lack of its use.

11 As critical and seemingly intractable as environmental problems are today with 5.3 billion people on the face of the Earth, these problems will be compounded exponentially as we move inevitably to 11.3 billion and very likely to 14 billion by the end of the next century. And yet, Pope John Paul is reported to have declared last week in Mexico:

> If the possibility of conceiving a child is artifically eliminated in the conjugal act, couples shut themselves off from God and oppose His will.

12 Personally, I find it difficult to accept that it is the will of God that humanity should degrade, deface, desecrate, and ultimately, perhaps, destroy His Creation on Earth. Yet that is the course on which we are embarked. Almost every significant threat to the environment is contributed to and compounded by human numbers. Moreover, whatever other adverse impacts on the natural environment may result from the growth in sheer human numbers, such growth is necessarily accompanied by a reduction in space for other species, in the opportunity for other forms of life. Natural ecosystems do not have the capacity to absorb infinite numbers of species.

13 To me, the most grievous assault on the Earth's environment is the destruction of species—both plant and animal. It is the destruction of life itself, life which has evolved over hundreds of millions of years into a diversity of forms that stagger the imagination, life of a beauty and complexity that fill one with awe and wonder, life in which the Creation is surely manifest.

14 Some scientists today estimate that there are up to 30 million species of life on the Earth. Twenty to 30 percent of these are projected to vanish forever over the next very few years due in large part to human action and especially to the destruction of tropical forests. The eminent biologist, E. O. Wilson, has said: "The sin our descendants are least likely to forgive us is the loss of biological diversity."

15 We hear much today about the "right to life" and the phrase as normally employed seems to extend only to human life, as if the rest of life is somehow irrelevant. I have tried to develop the point that human life cannot exist in isolation from other forms of life, that our existence is, in fact, dependent upon those other forms of life. We are, indeed, part of a community of life and our apparent dominance as a species should not be permitted to obscure that fact. Putting it bluntly, anthropocentrism is simply irrational. And yet that is the thrust of much of our traditional religious thought and teaching, particularly in the West.

16 I do not suggest that the Christian church abandon its concern for humanity but that it give at least equal time to the rest of God's Creation and do so not as a concern that is separate and apart, but as one that recognizes that the welfare of any part, including the human part, is inseparable from the welfare of the whole; that it is the community as a whole for which we must necessarily care. We really have no other option in this regard. If we truly care for the human condition, then we must necessarily care for the rest of Creation on which humanity's well-being and even existence so clearly depend.

17 It is not enough in my mind to say that we should act as good stewards of the Earth. Stewardship suggests that we have a management responsibility and that smacks too much to me of the same anthropocentrism that has gotten us into trouble in the first place. After all, the planet got along very well indeed for a very long time without our managerial assistance. Indeed, you might say that the Earth has been a far better steward of the human race than vice versa. If the living community of the Earth operated on a democratic basis, I have no doubt the other members would quickly vote us out.

18 There is no doubt that humanity is now the dominant species on the Earth although there is no assurance that this is a permanent status. After all, *homo sapiens* has only been here about 250,000 years, a blink of the eye in evolutionary terms. Humanity today holds the fate of most other life in its hands, a reality that is awesome and should be humbling. Unfortunately, we are more apt to feel such power a mark of our success. I am afraid we have our values pretty much backwards in this regard.

19 And here it is, it seems to me, that the church should define its special role in environmental matters. In my own experience, family, school, and church were the principal transmitters of values in my early life. The church will seldom have the expertise and, thus, the credibility to involve itself in the increasingly technical and complex debates over environmental issues, whether involving clean air, toxic wastes, tropical forests, etc., but it does have the credibility and the historic mission of articulating and teaching values to society. The church should assume a major responsibility for teaching that we humans, individually and collectively, are part of the living community of the Earth that nurtures and sustains us; that humanity as well as all life depends for its very being upon the healthy functioning of the natural systems of the Earth; that all living things, including humans, are interdependent; that we have the duty, collectively and individually, to care for God's Creation and that in it lie all the creative possibilities for life now and in the future. These are precepts that could provide the substance for an Eleventh Commandment: Thou shalt cherish and care for the Earth and all within it.

20 Of course, adoption of such a set of values would require a fundamental change in the way we look at the world around us and at our relationship with it. Such values would be decidedly human values, not self-centered but providing positive guidelines for creative human outreach to the world and all within it. Such values would provide a logical framework within which human society can address the entire range of environmental problems facing the planet. And these values would provide the essential spiritual energy for effective action to address these problems.

21 And so it seems to me that the major challenge to religion as it addresses the environment is to give leadership to human understanding and acceptance of these essentially ecological values. It should do so in the curriculum of its seminaries, in the liturgy of its services, in its preaching from the pulpit, and in its teaching of the young. I suspect that a contributing factor in the failure of religion up to now to address these matters is that the clergy has not felt at home with them. Basic courses in ecology should be required in the seminaries and, as a matter of fact, throughout our education system. After all, ecology is nothing more than Creation at work.

22 Over the past twenty years, we have seen concern for environmental values institutionalized throughout much of our society—in government at all levels, in business, in the professions, in international agencies, in citizen environmental action, among other areas. It is now high time for the oldest human institutions of all, our religions, to make concern for nature—Caring for Creation—a central part of their doctrine and practice. I firmly believe that doing so could help revitalize society's commitment to religion, particularly among the young, and would help establish these fundamental values on which the future of the Earth and of ourselves so clearly depends.

The Environmental Movement: A Skeptical View
Virginia I. Postrel

"To a large degree, however, green ideology is not about facts. It is about values, and the environmental movement is about enforcing those values through political action." This argument highlights the central theme developed by Virginia I. Postrel in her speech to the City Club of Cleveland on June 19, 1990. As editor of *Reason Magazine,* she addressed an audience of men and women in leadership roles in the businesses and industries of Cleveland. *Reason Magazine* is published by the Reason Foundation which has as its goal the promotion of individualist philosophy and free market economic principles.

In taking a "skeptical view," Postrel identifies and attacks the central value underlying the "green" ideology of most environmental activists (7, 14–15, 29). Stasis or sustainability is the core value in a static view of "an ecosystem that has reached an unchanging climax stage." The values that a speaker advocates or condemns should be presented accurately and fairly. To what degree do you believe Postrel does so? Note that she is sensitive to the complexity of ideologies (11–12) and wants to demystify the green ideology (9–10).

Postrel's major strategy in attacking the core value of the green ideology is presentation of multiple undesirable consequences of adhering to that value (17). Green values, she contends, typically are enforced through government policies—often a single prescribed solution (18, 29). Green ideology overemphasizes both a crisis mentality (26–28) and feelings of guilt/sin (31–32). In the name of simplicity, green ideology promotes regression rather than progress (35–37). And most undesirable of all, green ideology leads to extreme and radical programs for remaking human nature (41–43, 47–48, 51–52). Note how effectively she uses alliteration to associate the environmental movement with a negative concept: "environmentalists tolerate totalitarians in their midst."

Postrel's extensive use of quotations invites evaluation by a rhetorical critic. What type of person does she typically quote? What persuasive functions do such quotations seem to serve? Evidence to prove a point? Illustration to clarify a point? Would you question her use of any of the quotations? If so, on what grounds?

Often through contrast and antithesis, Postrel advocates a desirable value system to guide concern for the environment (19–20, 49). Her ideology embodies individual choice in pollution control, a dynamic and growth-oriented view, governmental encouragement of innovation, and the "common" or "ordinary" desire for a cleaner world through "tradeoffs," but not at all costs (7, 50).

Compare Virginia Postrel's speech with the previous one by Russell Train. Explore the ways in which the value systems advocated by them may be similar or clearly in conflict. Would Postrel probably condemn the values advocated by Train (19)? Why? Would she probably categorize the World Wildlife Fund as representative of the green movement? Note her statement: "Grassroots activists criticize the 'Gang of 10,' the large, well-funded environmental groups."

This speech is reprinted with permission from *Vital Speeches of the Day,* September 15, 1990, pp. 729–732.

---

1 On Earth Day, Henry Allen of The *Washington Post* published a pointed and amusing article. In it, he suggested that we've created a new image of Mother Nature:

> A sort of combination of Joan Crawford in *Mildred Pierce* and Mrs. Portnoy in *Portnoy's Complaint,* a disappointed, long-suffering martyr who makes us wish, at least for her sake, that we'd never been born.
>
> She weeps. She threatens, She nags. . . .
>
> She's a kvetch who makes us feel guilty for eating Big Macs, dumping paint thinner down the cellar sink, driving to work instead of riding the bus, and riding the bus instead of riding a bicycle. Then she makes us feel even guiltier for not feeling guilty enough.
>
> *Go ahead, use that deodorant, don't even think about me, God knows I'll be gone soon enough, I won't be here to see you get skin cancer when the ozone hole lets in the ultraviolet rays . . .*

2 I think all of us can see that Allen is on to something. There's a lot of truth in his picture of the new Mother Nature.

3 The question is, Where did this New Mother Nature come from? And how does this picture of nature affect—even warp—the way we deal with environmental issues?

4 Americans have historically been a can-do people, proud of our Yankee ingenuity. We believe in solving problems. Based on our history, you'd expect to see us tackling environmental problems the way John Todd took on sewage sludge.

5 Todd is an environmental biologist who became concerned about the toxic sludge that comes out of sewage plants. Based on his biological research, he realized that the sludge could be cleaned up by mixing it with certain microbes. The microbes would metabolize it and produce clean water. Todd now has a pilot plant in Providence, Rhode Island, and he estimates that such a system could handle all of that city's sludge with 120 acres of reaction tanks—a modest number.

6 Now, if you're like me, you think this is great. Here is a bona fide environmental problem. An ingenious man with an environmental conscience has come along, put his ingenuity and training to work, and *solved the problem.* But rather than applauding Todd's solution, many of his friends in the environmental movement have stopped speaking to him. "By discovering a solution to a man-made offense," writes Gregg Easterbrook in *The New Republic,* "he takes away an argument against growth."

7 Todd's practical environmentalism has run up against what I refer to as "green" ideology. This ideology is distinct from the common desire for a cleaner world—that's why it can lead people to condemn solutions like Todd's. It is also different from the traditional doctrines of either the left or the right: It combines elements from each with a values system of its own.

8 This green ideology underlies many of the environmentalist critiques and policy recommendations that we see today. Now, I'm not suggesting that environmentalists are engaged in some sort of grand conspiracy or are governed by some lockstep system of thought. What I *am* suggesting is that if you want to understand a political movement, it's a good idea to read its theorists and find out who its intellectual heroes are.

9 Green ideology is not mysterious. Anybody can go to the library and read the books that define it.

10 Green ideology is not some fringe theory cooked up in California. Like many important ideas in American history, it is largely imported from Britain and Germany. It is, increasingly, one of the most powerful forces in our culture. We may even adopt parts of it without realizing their origins. To be informed citizens, we ought to know something about it.

11 First of all, a caveat. Ideologies are messy. They tend to associate disparate ideas in unexpected ways. What's more, people who share the same general ideological viewpoint rarely agree on everything. No two conservatives or liberals or libertarians or even Marxists believe exactly the same thing. And political movements are almost always riven by internal conflict (you should read some of the things the abolitionists said about each other).

12 The environmental movement is no different. Purist greens who distrust political compromise berate Washington-based groups that lobby for legislation. The Green-Greens, who aren't leftist, attack the Red-Greens, who are. Grassroots activists criticize the "Gang of 10," the large, well-funded environmental groups.

13 And perhaps the biggest *philosophical* split is between "deep ecology" and other forms of environmentalism. Deep ecologists advocate a mystical view of the natural world as an end in itself, not made for human beings. They criticize traditional conservationism, as well as leftist "social ecology," for emphasizing the environment's value to people.

14 Most environmental activists—the rank and file—combine some of each outlook to create a personal viewpoint. They can do this because, deep down, the greens aren't as divided as they sometimes like to think.

15 Every ideology has a primary value or set of values at its core—liberty, equality, order, virtue, salvation. For greens, the core value is stasis, "sustainability" as they put it. The ideal is of an earth that doesn't change, that shows little or no effects of human activity.

Greens take as their model of the ideal society the notion of an ecosystem that has reached an unchanging climax stage. "Limits to growth" is as much a description of how things *should* be as it is of how they are.

16 That is why there is no room in the green world for John Todd and his sewage-cleaning microbes. Todd hasn't sought to stop growth. He has found a way to live with it.

17 The static view has two effects on the general environmental movement: First, it leads environmentalists to advocate policies that will make growth hard on people, as a way of discouraging further development. Cutting off new supplies of water, outlawing new technologies, and banning new construction to increase the cost of housing are common policies. And, second, the static view leads environmentalists to misunderstand how real environmental problems can be solved.

18 Consider how we regulate air pollution. Since the 1977 Clean Air Act, Americans spend some $30 billion a year just to comply with the 1977 Clean Air Act—with very little to show for it. Current policy dictates *specific technologies*—for example, smokestack scrubbers for coal-burning power plants. The plants can't just use cleaner coal. And cars have to have catalytic converters. If someone comes up with a cheaper or more efficient way to get the same result, the government says, Sorry. We've picked our one true technology. You can't sell yours.

19 Now, for decades economists have suggested that we take a different approach to regulating pollution. Set an overall allowable level, they say, then let companies decide how to achieve it. Let them buy and sell permits that regulate the amount of pollution they can emit: If you wanted to build a new plant, you'd have to buy some permits from somebody else who was closing their plant or reducing their pollution. The economy could grow without increasing the total amount of pollution. Companies woud have to pay a price for the pollution they put out. And plant managers would have an economic incentive to adopt—or even develop from scratch—pollution-saving technologies.

20 Most environmentalists, however, hate, loath, and despise this whole idea. They call it a "license to pollute." Emissions trading treats pollution as a cost, a side effect to be controlled, rather than an outright evil, a sin. It allows growth. And it lets individual choice, not politics, determine exactly which technologies will be adopted to control pollution. It takes a *dynamic* view, rather than a static one. Over time, it assumes, people will come up with better and better ways to deal with pollution. And, it assumes, we ought to *encourage* those innovations.

21 People rarely adopt a new technology because it makes life worse. But nowadays we tend to pay more attention to the dangers or pollution from new technologies. We take the old technologies' disadvantages for granted. So, for example, we forget that the automobile actually made city life cleaner.

22 By creating a market for petroleum-derived gasoline, the car also encouraged the production of heating oil and natural gas—much cleaner fuels than the coal people used to use to heat homes and businesses. And, thanks to the automobile, cities no longer have to dispose of tons of horse manure every day.

23 Extrapolating from his own time, a British writer in 1885 described the future of London:

> It is a vast stagnant swamp, which no man dare enter, since death would be his inevitable fate. There exhales from this oozy mass so fatal a vapour that no animal can endure it. The black water bears a greenish-brown scum, which forever bubbles up from the putrid mud of the bottom.

24 Clearly, modern environmentalists have no monopoly on dire predictions of disaster. From this particular fate we were saved by the automobile.

25 A dynamic view sees the pluses of change as well as the minuses. And it appreciates how new, unforeseen technologies or social changes can allay current problems.

26 By contrast, the environmental movement has been built on crisis. Around the turn of the century, Americans were terrified of the growing lumber shortage. A 1908 New York *Times* headline read: "Hickory Disappearing, Supply of Wood Nears End—Much Wasted and There's No Substitute." Actually, as prices rose, the railroad—the major consumers of wood—did find substitutes. And more-efficient ways of using wood.

27 Meanwhile, however, Gifford Pinchot used the specter of a "timber shortage" to get the U.S. Forest Service started. There was, of course, no such shortage, unless you take the static view. And a growing number of both economists and environmental activists now see Pinchot's legacy of central planning and federally managed forest lands as an economic and enviromental disaster.

28 Contrary to the doomsayers, both past and present, people have a knack for innovating their way out of "crises"—if they have both the permission and the incentive to do so. So we find that people developed petroleum as whale oil became scarce, that farmers turn to drip irrigation as water prices rise, and that drivers bought fuel-efficient cars when gas prices went up.

29 To a large degree, however, green ideology is not about facts. It is about *values,* and the environmental movement is about enforcing those values through political action. Green politics, write British greens Jonathon Porritt and David Winner, "demands a wholly new ethic in which violent, plundering humankind abandons its destructive ways, recognizes its dependence on Planet Earth, and starts living on a more equal footing with the rest of nature. The danger lies not only in the odd maverick polluting factory, industry, or technology, but in the fundamental nature of our economic systems. It is industrialism itself—a 'super-ideology' embraced by socialist countries as well as by the capitalist West— which threatens us."

30 If we look around, we can see the effort to remake "violent, plundering humankind" in a number of current initiatives. Take recycling. On one level, it seems like common sense. Why waste resources? That's certainly true with aluminum, which takes huge amounts of electricity to make in the first place and very little energy to recycle. But then there's glass. Both making glass in the first place and melting it down for recycling take about the same amount of energy. The only other thing new glass takes is sand—and we have plenty of that. Unless you're worried about an imminent sand crisis, there's little reason to recycle glass. It doesn't even take up much room in landfills.

31 But, of course, glass—like other forms of packaging—is convenient. Getting people to recycle it is a way of reminding them of the evils of materialism and the folly of convenience. As Jeremy Rifkin's little booklet *The Greenhouse Crisis: 101 Ways to Save the Earth* advises shoppers: "Remember, if it's disposable and convenient, it probably contributes to the greenhouse effect." On a scientific level, this is ridiculous. But as a value statement it conveys a great deal. Convenient disposable products are the creations of an affluent, innovative, industrial society that responds to consumer demands. In a static, green world, we would forego incandescent lighting for fluorescent bulbs and clothes dryers for clothes lines. We would give up out-of-season fruits and vegetables, disposable diapers (of course), free-flowing shower heads, and other self-indulgent pleasures.

32 If green ideology is guilt transformed into politics, we might wonder why people adopt it. Partly, I think green ideology appeals to many people's sense of frustration with modern life. Technology is too complicated, work too demanding, communication too instantaneous, information too abundant, the pace of life too fast. Stasis looks attractive, not only for nature but also for human beings.

33 E. F. Schumacher put it this way in *Small Is Beautiful,* a central work of green theory. "The pressure and strain of living," he wrote, "is very much less in, say, Burma than it is in the United States, in spite of the fact that the amount of labour-saving machinery used in the former country is only a minute fraction of the amount used in the latter."

34 Jeremy Rifkin describes the green coalition as "time rebels," who "argue that the pace of production and consumption should not exceed nature's ability to recycle wastes and renew basic resources. They argue that the tempo of social and economic life should be compatible with nature's time frame." Rifkin, therefore, can't stand computers. They go too fast.

35 To slow economy and society to the approved *adagio,* the greens have some fairly straightforward prescriptions: Restrict trade to the local area. Eliminate markets where possible. End specialization. Anchor individuals in their "bioregions," local areas defined by their environmental characteristics. Shrink the population. Make life simple again, small, self-contained.

36 It is a vision that can be made remarkably appealing, for it plays on our desire for self-sufficiency, our longing for community, and our nostalgia for the agrarian past. We will go back to the land, back to the rhythms of seedtime and harvest, back to making our own clothes, our own furniture, our own tools. Back to barnraisings and quilting bees. Back to a life we can understand without a string of Ph.D.s.

37 "In living in the world by his own will and skill, the stupidest peasant or tribesman is more competent than the most intelligent workers or technicians or intellectuals in a society of specialists," writes Wendell Berry, an agrarian admired by both greens and cultural conservatives. Berry is a fine writer; he chooses words carefully; he means what he says. We will go back to being peasants.

38 These are, of course, harsh words. And we aren't likely to wake up as subsistence farmers tomorrow. But an economy, like an ecology, is made up of intricate connections. Constantly tinkering with it—cutting off this new technology here, banning that product there—will have unintended consequences. And sometimes, one suspects, the consequences aren't all that unintended.

39 Take electricity. Environmentalists, of course, rule out nuclear power, regardless of the evidence of its safety. But then they say coal-powered plants can cause acid rain and pollution, so they're out, too. Oil-fired plants release greenhouse gases (and cost a bundle, too). Hydroelectric plants are no good because they disrupt the flow of rivers.

40 Solar photovoltaic cells have always been the great hope of the future. But making them requires lots of nasty chemicals, so we can expect solar cells to be banned around the time they become profitable. Pretty soon, you've eliminated every conceivable source of electricity. Then your only option is to dismantle your industry and live with less: the environmentalist warning of impending shortages becomes a self-fulfilling prophecy.

41 And, make no mistake about it, many environmentalists have a truly radical agenda. "It is a spiritual act to try to shut down DuPont," says Randall Hayes, director of the Rainforest Action Network. From the appealing ads his group runs to solicit donations to save the rainforests, you'd never guess he had that goal in mind.

42 And consider the remarkably frank book, *Whatever Happened to Ecology?,* by longtime environmental activist Stephanie Mills, recently published by Sierra Club Books. Mills garnered national attention in 1969, when she delivered a college commencement address entitled "The Future Is a Cruel Hoax" and declared she'd never have children. The book traces the evolution of the environmental movement and of her ideas since then. Today, she and her husband live on a farm in northern Michigan, where they pursue their bioregionalist ideal of "reinhabiting" the land by restoring some of its wildness and blocking future development. A journalist, not a theorist, Mills speaks not only for herself but for the intellectual movement of which she is a part. Her words are chilling:

> We young moderns resort to elaborate means of getting physical experience. Yogic practice, fanatical running, bicycling, competitive sports, bodybuilding. All of these recreations are voluntary and may not cultivate the endurance necessary for the kind of labor required to dismantle industrial society and restore the Earth's productivity.

Are voluntary . . . the endurance necessary . . . the labor required . . . dismantle industrial society. The prose is pleasant, the notions it contains disturbing. She continues:

> One summer afternoon a few days after a freak windstorm, I made a foray out to buy some toilet paper. (Every time I have to replenish the supply of this presumed necessity, I wonder what we're going to substitute for it when the trucks stop running.)

43 *When the trucks stop running.* There is a history of the future buried in those words, fodder for several science-fiction novels—but no explanation of when and why the trucks will stop. Or who will stop them.

44 People don't want to be peasants: The cities of the Third World teem with the evidence. And certainly, the typical subscriber to the *Utne Reader* (a sort of green *Reader's Digest* with a circulation of 200,000 after only six years of publication) doesn't envision a future of subsistence farming—much less the hunter-gatherer existence preferred by deep ecologists. More to the reader's taste is, no doubt, the cheery vision offered by Executive Editor Jay Walljasper.

> It's 2009. Nuclear weapons have been dismantled. Green publications have huge circulations. Minneapolis has 11 newspapers and its own currency ("redeemable in trout, walleye, or wild rice"). Sidewalk cafés sell croissants and yogurt. A local ordinance decrees a 24-hour workweek. Cars are nearly nonexistent (a delegation from the "People's Independent Republic of Estonia" is in town to help design better ski trails for commuters). Citizens vote electronically. The shopping mall has become a nature preserve.

45 Walljasper is clearly having fun—after all, he puts Aretha Franklin's face on the $10 bill—and he doesn't consider any of the tough questions. Like how all those magazines and newspapers exist without printing plants or paper mills. How the Estonians got to town without airplanes or the fuel to run them (Jeremy Rifkin specifically names the Boeing 747 as the kind of product that can't be produced in the small-is-beautiful factories of the coming "entropic age.") How the chips to run the electronic voting got etched without chemicals. Where the chips were made. How a 24-hour workweek produced the sustained concentration needed to write software or the level of affluence that allows for restaurant croissants.

46 And, above all, Walljasper doesn't explain why after millenia of behaving otherwise, humans simply gave up wanting *stuff*. If the Walljasper of 2009 still overloads on reading material, why should we assume that people whose fancy runs toward fast food and polyester (or fast cars and silk) would be struck with a sudden attack of bioregionally approved tastes? How *exactly* did that shopping mall disappear?

47 "The root of the solution has to be so radical that it can scarcely be spoken of," says movie director and British green John Borrman. "We all have to be prepared to change the way we live and function and relate to the planet. In short, we need a transformation of the human spirit. If the human heart can be changed, then everything can be changed."

48 We have heard this somewhere before—in, for example, the promise of a "New Soviet Man." People are forever seeking to change the human heart, often with tragic results.

49 The greens want people to give up the idea that life can be better. They say "better" need not refer to material abundance, that we should just be content with less. Stasis, they say, can satisfy our "vital needs." They may indeed convince some people to puruse a life of voluntary simplicity, and that is fine and good and just the thing a free society ought to allow. Stephanie Mills is welcome to her organic farm.

50 But most of us do not want to give up 747s, or cars, or eyeglasses, or private washing machines, or tailored clothing, or even disposable diapers. The "debased human protoplasm" that Stephanie Mills holds in contempt for their delight in "clothes, food, sporting goods, electronics, building supplies, pets, baked goods, deli food, toys, tools, hardware, geegaws, jim-jams, and knick-knacks" will not happily relinquish the benefits of modern civilization. Many ordinary human beings would like a cleaner world. They are prepared to make sacrifices—*tradeoffs* is a better word—to get one. But ordinary human beings will not adopt the Buddha's life without desire, much as E. F. Schumacher might have ordained it.

51 At its extreme, green ideology expresses itself in utter contempt for humanity. Reviewing Bill McKibben's *The End of Nature* in the *Los Angeles Times,* National Park Service research biologist David M. Graber concluded with this stunning passage:

> Human happiness, and certainly human fecundity, are not as important as a wild and healthy planet. I know social scientists who remind me that people are part of nature, but it isn't true. Somewhere along the line—at about a billion years ago, maybe half that—we quit the contract and became a cancer. We have become a plague upon ourselves and upon the Earth. It is cosmically unlikely that the developed world will choose to end its orgy of fossil-energy consumption, and the Third World its suicidal consumption of landscape. Until such time as Homo sapiens should decide to rejoin nature, some of us can only hope for the right virus to come along.

52 It is hard to take such notions seriously without sounding like a bit of a kook yourself. But there they are—calmly expressed in the pages of a major, mainstream, Establishment newspaper by an employee of the federal government. When it is acceptable to say such things in polite intellectual company, when feel-good environmentalists tolerate the totalitarians in their midst, when sophisticates greet the likes of Graber with indulgent nods and smiles rather than arguments and outrage, we are one step farther down another bloody road to someone's imagined Eden.

53 Thank you.

Time Theft: The Silent Thief
Karen Kimmey

This speech was given by Karen Kimmey, a student at Arizona State University, at the Interstate Oratorical Association Contest at Menomonie, Wisconsin on May 4 and 5, 1990. She placed first among the thirty-nine contest participants.

Ms. Kimmey advances the evaluative proposition that stealing time on the job is socially unacceptable. In her introduction, she highlights the social significance of her claim by the use of loaded language such as ''work place crime,'' ''ripping us off,'' and ''employee theft.'' Does this language strategy effectively relate the speaker's evaluative proposition to her audience?

In supporting her proposition, the speaker advances three related lines of argument: time theft is pervasive, time theft is socially harmful, and time theft must be eradicated. The second line of argument, paragraphs 11 through 18, is primarily responsible for supporting the evaluative judgment that time theft is socially unacceptable. How many discrete charges of social or moral wrongs can you identify? How does the speaker invite the audience's emotional involvement with her charges? Were you convinced that time theft is morally and socially wrong?

This speech is reprinted by permission of the Interstate Oratorical Association from *Winning Orations* 1990, pp. 4–8.

1 Susan was your typical office employee: punched in on her timecard, spent eight hours at her desk, got paid fairly well for her time, and left without snagging so much as a pencil to take home with her. Yet she was deliberately stealing from her employer every day. You see, while being paid for her work in financial services, she was busy running three personal businesses from her desk—selling exercise equipment, video cassettes, and designer clothing over the phone—all on company time.

2 Yes, employee theft has once again become a hot issue. But it has taken a new and even more harmful twist. While so much has been said about merchandise and supply theft, we've failed to recognize a form which, according to Dunn's *Business Month,* is three times more costly, making it what June, 1988 *Nation's Business* calls the "number one work place crime." This crime is the employee theft of our most precious commodity, time, which has reached epidemic proportions. This common practice is aggravating negative working conditions, harming U.S. competitiveness, and ripping us off to the tune of 170 billion dollars every year. Although you may never before have put a name to it, we are all directly affected by time theft. As employees, professionals, consumers, and Americans we literally cannot afford to ignore this problem.

3 So today, we will initially learn exactly what time theft is and recognize the many ways that it threatens us. And finally, we will learn how to put an end to this great American rip-off.

4 Back in the 1970s we were all inundated with facts regarding employee theft. There were probably even a few orations on the subject. It was easy to recognize theft when it was something tangible. But how does one steal something as elusive as time? Well, according to a 1988 Robert Half International study, the nation's largest employer, which conducted an extensive inquiry into the matter, there are more ways to steal time than there are hours in a work week. The study outlines the more common culprits: constantly socializing, making excessive personal phone calls, taking those few extra minutes on lunch or coffee breaks, and habitually arriving late or leaving early.

5 Sound familiar? Chances are if you've ever held a job, you've either slipped into one of these indiscretions or certainly know someone who has. But we have taken the art of goofing off to new heights. According to the *Entrepreneur,* March 1988, the average employee now wastes 4.5 hours every week.

6 This figure primarily reflects the basically honest employee. But as *Nation's Business,* June 1988, explains: the greatest damage is done by those who steal time calculatingly and consistently, deliberately ripping off employers, co-workers, and eventually all of us! For those professional time thieves the methods we've discussed are only the beginning.

7 An October 24, 1988 edition of the *Nightly Business Talk* revealed several new techniques. For example, with many buildings now forbidding smoking, employees are wandering outside to light up several times every day, adding up to approximately two hours per week per smoker. Talk about money going up in smoke.

8 Another new device of thievery is the office computer. Financial consultant, Michael Nolan, tells of one marginal employee who was not quite ready to be fired but certainly [was] not a top worker. But all of this changed when the firm computerized; the formerly listless employee began to spend hours in front of his computer and management was encouraged, until they discovered he had become so familiar with the computer that he had created a game program and was spending his previous hours on the job playing "black jack."

9 Meanwhile, at a Kansas City Corporation, two more computer terminal operators were also seemingly quite busy. Their supervisor discovered they were actually quite busy using the electronic mail to exchange romantic messages.

10 Viewed independently, these incidents seem harmless enough. But add to them the Long Island, New York supervisor who was caught punching employee timecards an hour late so they could collect overtime. Then realize that for every example I've given, thousands of millions of others are doing the exact same thing. This gives us a glimpse of just how pervasive time theft has become.

11 But what's the harm? It's certainly humorous, and almost inspirational, to hear these stories of the poor employee beating the system. They work hard; they deserve to get something back.

12 We heard these excuses before. We heard them offered as realizations for outright employee theft. We didn't accept them then, and we cannot accept them now.

13 For as *Nation's Business,* June 1988, states, "Employees who willfully squander their paid working hours are just as guilty of stealing from their employers as they would be if they took money or materials."

14 And herein lies the first harm to arise from time thievery—an overall loss of integrity and pride in the work place. It has become socially acceptable for employees to cheat on their jobs. As a result, morale decreases and incentives disappear. In today's workaholic society, this is especially oppressive as dedicated employees work harder to pay for the shortcomings of the system and of fellow workers.

15 It may be possible for you to overlook a flawed employment system. But as educated leaders, we simply [cannot] ignore the incredible financial desperation which time theft is creating for our economy.

16 A July 20th, 1989, industry-wide press release warns that time theft "saps productivity and erodes profits." A year ago the price tag for this loss of productivity equaled $170 billion—170 billion which, to put [things] into perspective, equals the current value of the entire U.S. automobile industry. Financial experts warn that 1989's losses have easily topped 200 billion. Quite a price to pay for a few hours off of work!

17 And who's picking up the tab? We all are. First, any of us who work for a corporation, even a nonprofit, like a college or university, pay through a decrease in revenues which leads to cuts in our salary, job loss, even bankruptcy. Second, we pay through higher consumer prices and lower quality goods and services. We pay with our taxes for theft in all levels of government. Most frighteningly, we pay as a nation. It is no secret that the U.S. is losing much of its competitiveness in the world market. It seems we're always trying to find an outside source on which to blame our economic woes. But this is likely the first time we've realized that our $170 billion enemy is our own American value system. In a November 16, 1988 report, Robert Half himself warns that "Time theft is a serious threat to the American economy." If time theft continues unchecked, the U.S. could well be on its way to committing economic suicide.

18 By now, I hope that you have begun to view time theft for the massive scandal that it really is; I hope that you've become a little angry about this $170 billion bill that you're being forced to pay. Because the time has come for you to stop paying.

19 While we never can completely eradicate time theft, there are many steps we can take to cut down on the absurd amount of time which is stolen every day. Because we as individuals are the source of this problem, we also are the ultimate solution.

20 The first step is obvious. Don't steal time! As college students, and underpaid forensics coaches, we all must work. While none of us can be 100% productive we must resist the urge to take "goofing off" too far. You may not think you make a difference but as the Cincinnati *Enquirer,* January 1, 1990, pointed out, that 4.5 hours every week adds up to 6 weeks every year. Viewed in this light our efforts indeed become significant.

21 On a larger scale, there are many steps that businesses can implement. By becoming aware of the facts surrounding time theft, managers can significantly increase their own profits. For example according to the Houston *Chronicle,* December 4, 1988, the most likely times for thievery are the first and last hours of the workday. Employers should schedule more structured tasks to occupy these hours. But as the *Wall Street Journal,* May 30, 1989, points out, simply tightening rules is counterproductive; thus managment must be guided by moderation and consideration in establishing policies.

22 But we can't stop here, simply addressing the symptoms of time theft. We must work together to correct the flaws in our economic system which leave employees dissatisfied.

23 Supervisors must create, and we must demand of them, an integrated and rewarding work environment. Andrew Sherwood, chairman of the nation's largest human resources consulting firm, offers some tangible means of doing this by suggesting rewards for top performers and encouraging employee involvement in company operations through means such as profit sharing. Above all, he advises each of us to communicate the following: "Time is our company's most valuable asset and stealing it can threaten the existence of this company and our jobs."

24 Finally, as a society we must begin to view time theft as socially unacceptable and foster a return to the not so old adage of "A day's work for a day's pay." For we cannot afford to continue on our present course for even just one more year. The responsibility for stopping this silent thief is ours. But if we choose to continue to ignore this problem, it may be the most expensive mistake we'll ever make.

Farm labor leader César Chávez speaks to a group of supporters.

CHAPTER 6

SPEECHES THAT CREATE CONCERN FOR PROBLEMS

The speaker must awaken those who sleep or are indifferent; he must help others see the unnoticed danger, and understand it; he must direct us away from the false and petty problems that set us off course.

Otis M. Walter and Robert L. Scott

THE NATURE AND IMPORTANCE OF SPEECHES
THAT CREATE CONCERN FOR PROBLEMS

Human existence in society gives rise to problems that threaten the perpetuation of the group and the welfare of its members. A problem might be described as a defect, difficulty, barrier, need, threat, state of dissatisfaction, or undesirable situation that people perceive as necessitating removal, rectification, or solution. The ability of groups and individuals to perceive and understand the nature and importance of the problems confronting them is one measure of a society's maturity and strength. If a society is unable to comprehend the significance of its problems, it has little chance of solving them.

Speakers often address audiences for the primary purpose of creating concern for problems. Whereas speeches advocating values are designed to develop value standards and value judgments in the minds of listeners, speeches trying to create concern for problems focus on specific social situations calling for remedial action. The mayor of a large city, for example, may seek to arouse public concern over the urban conditions that breed crime or riots. A sociologist may attempt to create concern for senior citizens on welfare. A politician may try to arouse sympathy for the plight of the American Indian.

Sometimes a speaker focuses on a problem as a prelude to advocating specific programs or policies as solutions for that problem. In any case, we face potential personal and public problems at virtually every turn: alcoholism, drug abuse, racial conflict, unemployment, suicide, pollution and abuse of the environment, violence as a way of life, discrimination against women, political deception, economic inflation, deceptive or harmful advertising, automobile accidents, and rising crime rates.

While the proposition of fact asserts that something is true or false and the proposition of value asserts that something has or lacks merit, the speech attempting to create concern for a problem asserts that specific social conditions should be perceived or defined as problems. Consider the following examples:

Proposition A: Racial unrest is Boston's most impelling community problem.

Proposition B: The unrestricted sale of firearms is cause for public alarm.

Proposition C: All parents should be concerned by the increased availability of hardcore pornography.

Proposition D: Student drug usage is a serious campus problem.

Proposition E: The depiction of violence on television programs oriented toward children merits public concern.

Proposition F: The increasing rate of traffic fatalities on Highway 12 warrants action by the state legislature.

Although the speech that creates concern for a problem usually depends on the affirmation of subsidiary propositions of fact and value, the basic purpose of such a speech is to invite attention to a problem needing solution.

CRITERIA FOR EVALUATING SPEECHES THAT CREATE CONCERN FOR PROBLEMS

1. Has the speaker presented a compelling view of the nature of the problem?

The philosopher John Dewey emphasized the importance of this criterion when he wrote: "The essence of critical thinking is suspended judgement; and the essence of this suspense is inquiry to determine the nature of the problem before proceeding to attempts at its solution." To depict compellingly the nature of a problem, a speaker must prove that a certain state of affairs, a concrete set of circumstances, actually does exist. The nature is explained by focusing on the major elements of the problem and on its symptoms or outward manifestations.

Naturally a complete view of a problem includes a thorough exploration of the causes (the contributing influences) which combine to produce the state of affairs. Some problems are rooted in defective structures, personnel, or policies; other problems stem from inadequate goals, standards, and principles; still others derive from "outside" threats, opponents, or enemies. Remember, also, that social problems seldom are the result of a single cause. Rather, although one contributing factor may be described as the primary or the immediate cause, several contributing factors usually combine in primary-secondary and immediate-remote relationships. Finally, a compelling view often stems from describing the intensity and/or the widespread scope of the problem.

In exploring the nature of a problem, speakers may assume the role of social informant. When they do, the success of their speeches is governed, in part, by the same constraints imposed on speakers seeking to increase understanding. They must choose those supporting materials that best demonstrate the nature of the problem: analogy and illustration, expert testimony and factual example, description, definition, and narration. Their messages are subject to the same criteria suggested in Chapter 3: Is the information communicated accurately, completely, and with unity? Does the speaker make the information meaningful for the audience? Does the speaker create audience interest in the information presented? Has the speaker shown the audience that the information is important?

In a speech called "Mingled Blood," Ralph Zimmerman, a college student and a hemophiliac, chose to use definition and description to illuminate the nature of hemophilia:

> What is this thing called hemophilia? Webster defines it as "a tendency, usually hereditary, to profuse bleeding even from slight wounds." Dr. Armand J. Quick, Professor of Biochemistry at Marquette University and a recognized world authority on this topic, defines it as "a prothrombin consumption time of 8 to 13 seconds." Normal time is 15 seconds. Now do you know what hemophilia is? . . .

What does it really mean to be a hemophiliac? The first indication comes in early childhood when a small scratch may bleed for hours. By the time the hemophiliac reaches school age, he begins to suffer from internal bleeding into muscles, joints, the stomach, the kidneys. This latter type is far more serious, for external wounds can usually be stopped in minutes with topical thromboplastin or a pressure bandage. But internal bleeding can be checked only by changes in the blood by means of transfusion or plasma injections. If internal bleeding into a muscle or joint goes unchecked repeatedly, muscle contraction and bone deformity inevitably result.

Along with increasing understanding about a problem, speakers also may affirm propositions of fact related to the problem. When speakers seek to prove propositions of fact in developing a compelling view of the problem, their efforts are subject to the same criteria suggested in Chapter 4: Has the speaker adequately assessed the proof requirements of the factual proposition? Has the speaker offered acceptable arguments in support of the proposition of fact? Has the speaker provided adequate evidence in support of the arguments?

2. Has the speaker shown the significance of the problem for the specific audience?

In addition to gaining an understanding of the nature of the problem, an audience must also be convinced that the problem has significance for them individually or collectively. Thus, value judgments must augment factual demonstrations. To demonstrate that juvenile delinquency is extensive, a factual state of affairs must be established. To demonstrate that juvenile delinquency poses a threat or is an undesirable situation, a judgment must be made in light of societal value standards. When a speaker affirms a proposition of value in showing the significance of a problem, the criteria suggested in Chapter 5 usually are relevant: Has the speaker demonstrated, or is it assumed by the audience, that he or she is a person of high credibility with respect to the proposition? Has the speaker advanced acceptable criteria for the assessment of the proposition? Has the speaker presented a fair view of what is being evaluated?

A problem is not really a problem to an audience until they perceive it as such. A situation may exist, and the audience even may know that it does, but in their eyes it remains nothing more than a lifeless fact until they view it as something that threatens or violates their interests and values. The members of an audience who have just been informed that many American Indians endure substandard economic, educational, and health conditions may greet this knowledge with indifference. Although they may accept the situation as actual, they have not perceived it as a problem for themselves, either as individuals or as members of society.

In the background of public debate on societal issues are values which, according to Robert B. Reich, in his book, *Tales of a New America* (Times Books, 1987, p. 6), often are unstated, disguised, or taken for granted. These values, typically embodied in narrative "morality tales," influence when we "declare a fact to be a problem, how policy choices are characterized, how the debate is framed." Reich emphasizes: "Public problems don't exist 'out there.' They are not discrete facts or pieces of data awaiting discovery. They are the consequences of our shared values. Without a set of common moral assumptions we would have no way of identifying or categorizing problems and their possible solutions." Clearly a problem is "created" for an audience through their own perceptual processes. An audience labels something as a problem only when they perceive a strong link between a situation (real or imagined) and their relevant basic values which they see as undermined or threatened by that situation. Speakers and listeners employ values as standards to "define" something as a problem.

What approaches could a speaker use to show the significance of a problem? Ralph Zimmerman concluded that for many listeners it is sufficient to show that the problem brings danger, degradation, or suffering to those who directly experience it. Thus he depicted hemophilia as a source of suffering for those afflicted by it:

> I remember the three long years when I couldn't even walk because repeated hemorrhages had twisted my ankles and knees to pretzel-like forms. I remember being pulled to school in a wagon while other boys rode their bikes, and being pushed to my table. I remember sitting in the dark empty classroom by myself during recess while the others went out in the sun to run and play. And I remember the first terrible day at the big high school when I came on crutches and built-up shoes carrying my books in a sack around my neck. . . . And how well I remember the endless pounding, squeezing pain. When you seemingly drown in your own perspiration, when your teeth ache and bombs explode back of your eyeballs; when darkness and light fuse into one hue of gray; when day becomes night and night becomes day—time stands still—and all that matters is that ugly pain.

Although the most hardened pragmatist might state that the problem is of little social importance because when Zimmerman spoke in 1955 there were only 20,000 to 40,000 hemophiliacs in the United States, most Americans, committed to the worth of the individual human, would agree with Zimmerman that "if society can keep a hemophiliac alive until after adolescence, society has saved a member."

Guided by the actual nature of the problem and by relevant standards of ethics, a speaker may choose from a variety of potential strategies to create audience concern. Here we present a few such strategies, some adapted from the writings of Otis M. Walter. To show that the problem directly or indirectly harms the audience addressed (economically, socially, morally, physically) is an approach often used. Sometimes the problem is described as a unique, immediate, and pressing one demanding speedy recognition, diagnosis, and treatment; or it is described as an important contemporary manifestation of a timeless, continuing, larger problem always faced by humanity. Awareness of the problem may be emerging only gradually in the public consciousness and an audience might be urged to be in the vanguard of citizens concerned about it. On the other hand, the audience might be asked to join large numbers of fellow citizens who already recognize the problem.

Through use of historical examples, a speaker could argue that the failure of past societies to recognize the same or a similar problem caused them harm. Often this argument is embodied in an analogy to the decline and fall of the Roman Empire. The ways in which the problem contributes to or interacts with other societal problems could be demonstrated. If the problem is now in the embryonic stage, audiences could be warned that if it is not treated it will steadily worsen and perhaps become unsolvable. On occasion, a problem of concern for those affected takes on added significance when shown also to be working for the political or psychological advantage of our opponents or enemies. If the audience and the people harmed by the problem both have similar goals, values, needs, and fears, the audience could be made to feel that they might just as easily have experienced the problem themselves ("There but for the grace of God go I"). A speaker could show that the problem is acknowledged as vital by those whom the audience regards highly, such as public officials, statesmen, religious leaders, or experts on the subject.

The harmful economic, political, social, religious, or moral consequences of leaving the problem unsolved could be stressed. The problem could be shown as one of physical survival or security; or it could be shown as a problem threatening the enhancement or growth of the human spirit. A problem becomes of concern when it causes our society and its institutions to function at less than normal expected effectiveness. Sometimes the problem legitimately is described as stemming from conflict between an accepted but outmoded belief or value and existing circumstances. Finally, a speaker usually must secure audience perception of the problem as a high priority one—more crucial than most other problems faced by them or society.

CONCLUSION

In *Constructing the Political Spectacle,* Murray Edelman, a political scientist, reminds us: "Problems come into discourse and therefore into existence as reinforcements of ideologies, not simply because they are there or because they are important for wellbeing. They signify who are virtuous and useful and who are dangerous or inadequate, which actions will be rewarded and penalized." Problems, continues Edelman, "constitute people as subjects with particular kinds of aspirations, self-concepts, and fears, and they create beliefs about the relative importance of events and objects." Edelman concludes that problems "are critical in determining who exercise authority and who accept it. They construct areas of immunity from concern because those areas are not seen as a problem."

In our society people often seek to generate concern about problems, both great and small. At certain times the speaker's sole purpose is to set the stage for private thought or public discussion. At other times the speaker seeks to arouse interest in a problem to prepare the audience for accepting a specific solution. In either case, the speaker must present *a compelling view of the nature of the problem* and *the reasons that it is significant for the particular audience.*

For further reading

Dewey, John. *How We Think*. D. C. Heath, 1910, pp. 72–74. Concisely explains the importance of understanding the nature of problems.

Edelman, Murray. *Constructing the Political Spectacle*. University of Chicago Press, 1988. Chapter 2 probes the symbolic construction and ideological bases of social problems.

Jensen, J. Vernon. *Argumentation: Reasoning in Communication*. Van Nostrand, 1981. Chapter 4 suggests potential lines of argument basic to presenting the nature of a problem.

Walter, Otis M., and Scott, Robert L. *Thinking and Speaking*. 5th ed. Macmillan, 1984. Chapters 6 and 7 focus on suggestions for persuading about problems and causes.

Walter, Otis M. *Speaking Intelligently*. Macmillan, 1976, Chapters 2, 3, 4, and pp. 216–21. An exploration of the nature of societal problems and causes of such problems, along with suggested strategies for persuading about problems and causes.

African Americans and Social Justice

John E. Jacob

On March 13, 1990, John E. Jacob, President and CEO of the National Urban League, addressed an audience of about 100 professional social workers, students and teachers of social work, and others interested in human resource development at the Catholic University of America in Washington, D.C. The occasion was the celebration of the 50th anniversary of the founding of the journal, *Social Thought,* which is affiliated with Catholic Charities U.S.A. and with the Catholic University. Jacob has a graduate degree in social work and professional experience as a social worker. The National Urban League is a voluntary non-partisan community service agency of civic, professional, business, labor, and religious leaders with a staff of trained social workers and other professionals. The Urban League aims to eliminate racial discrimination and to assist black citizens and other economically and socially disadvantaged groups. Thus Jacob was speaking to a friendly audience that already acknowledged his high credibility by asking him to speak on this significant occasion.

John Jacob's rhetorical task was to create concern for a problem—lack of economic and social justice for black Americans and other minorities (par. 6)—and to provide the motivational groundwork for a variety of actions. While most of his audience probably already agreed in general terms that the problem existed, his challenge was to provide a *compelling view of the problem* and to show the *significance of the problem for his particular audience.* Throughout the speech, he relates the problem to the values and professional interests of the audience (1, 10) and to persons and documents revered by them (2, 14, 38).

At the outset of the speech, he identifies the values that are being threatened or violated—that allow the existing circumstances to be defined as a problem (1–3). He employs contrast to illustrate how goals and actuality historically have been in conflict (4–5). And he uses treatment of African Americans as a reality test, as a litmus test, of the degree to which the values have been actualized in American society for the many, not the few (3, 5, 9).

Jacob demonstrates the scope, intensity, and elements of the problem for those directly affected through use of statistics (6, 15–18), representative examples (7), and expert testimony (12). For this particular audience, should he have provided more information on how the research study he mentions was conducted (15)? Why? Also note that Jacob addresses the scope of the problem and the justification for widespread concern by arguing that it is "a national problem affecting all of us" because it involves not only values of fairness and justice but also pragmatic economic self-interest of all Americans (24, 35–36). Consider where and how adequately Jacob discusses contributing causes of the problem such as individual attitudes (racism, lack of willpower) and systemic-institutional inadequacies of structure or policy. Where and how overtly does Jacob take into account black and other minority *women* in describing the dimensions of the problem?

Jacob utilizes refutation of opposing arguments as a major persuasive strategy (10–11, 20, 29, 37). How reasonably developed and adequately supported are his refutations? His use of two stylistic resources also is noteworthy. Parallel structure or parallel phrasing of a series of ideas is used to associate examples and for contrast (10–11, 20, 38). Antithesis is the phrasing of two opposing or competing items into sharp, terse contrast with one item of the pair given clear preference of the other. Jacob frequently uses antithesis to crystalize value judgments (2, 9, 11, 38) and sometimes reinforces the antithesis by using a "not this . . . but that" construction (21, 39).

To demonstrate that all is not hopeless in the face of massive problems, Jacob offers evidence throughout for optimism that slow but significant positive change is possible (8, 26–27, 32–33). To what degree do you believe he is realistic or idealistic in this optimism? Why? Finally, as might be expected of the President of the National Urban League, he periodically reminds his audience of the programs and policies of the Urban League in fighting the problem (15, 26–27, 32–33).

The text of this speech was provided by John Jacob's office at the National Urban League.

---

1 It is a great honor to be asked to deliver your *Social Thought* lecture. For fifty years, *Social Thought* has been a valuable forum for important issues of social work, social welfare, and simple justice. It has pioneered in tying such public policy issues to underlying principles of religious values and a fair, just, society. So I am happy to preface my remarks today with a tribute to an important journal that has had a positive impact on America. The application of religious principles to issues of social justice places the workings of a society in a moral context, which is central to the survival of that society.

2 In recent years, issues related to fairness have been relegated to the back of the bus, while issues of economic efficiency are in the driver's seat. Nearly one hundred years ago, Pope Leo XIII addressed the imbalance in his encyclical, Rerum Novarum. Implicit in that document is the conviction that a truly just society is both fair and productive—that the workings of a free enterprise economy and the burning need of working people for dignity and sustenance can be mutually supportive.

3 Today, we in the United States are grappling with the same issues. We are still trying to build a wealthy and productive society rooted in fundamental values such as justice and fairness. The measure of our success in that effort has to be the state of African Americans. For the condition of African Americans has always been the rock of reality upon which the moral state of our society has foundered.

4 To cite a very few examples: The Constitution proclaimed the right of life, liberty and the pursuit of happiness for all men. But African Americans were subjected to slavery, and that same Constitution defined them as three-fifths of other Americans. In the 1890s,

America was the haven for Europe's poor and dispossessed. Immigration swelled as millions left poverty and repressive homelands for the land of liberty. But African Americans were shamelessly exploited in conditions of peonage and apartheid.

5 Let us leap forward to our own times. In the 1950s and early 1960s, the United States was seen as a just society, in contrast to the brutality of communist countries. But African Americans in many parts of our nation had fewer rights than citizens of totalitarian dictatorships abroad. Today, many Americans are under the illusion that we have finally reached a stage in our history in which we can say that we are indeed a just society. Unfortunately that is an illusion. And the reality test to be applied to such claims is the condition of African Americans—the historic litmus test of our society's fairness.

6 Let me briefly run through a few facts that indicate racial justice and social justice are far from being characteristics of our society.

- Half of all African American children are growing up poor.
- Over a third of all African Americans are poor—two million more blacks became poor in the past dozen years.
- One out of every four young black men are either in prison, on probation, or on parole—more than the proportion of young African Americans in college today.
- Almost two million African American workers are jobless—over eleven percent of the black work force, and a rate two-and-a-half times that for whites.
- Black family income is only 58 percent that of whites; the typical African American family earns less than the government itself says is needed for a decent but modest living standard.
- African American households have less than one-tenth the wealth of white-households.

7 And racism is still alive and well. In recent months we have seen such incidents as letter bombs sent to civil rights activists and judges . . . the case in Boston, where a false accusation that a black man committed a terrible crime was accepted without question by the police, public officials, and citizens . . . and the torching of a black family's home in Brooklyn, New York. While such incidents are highly publicized, many, many others are not. Nor are the daily slights and hurts dished out to African Americans in daily life and in the workplace.

8 Many, if not most, Americans prefer to ignore the presence of inequality and racism. They focus on those African Americans who have entered the mainstream. And their accomplishments are gratifying. To see a Douglas Wilder in the governor's mansion of the state that pioneered massive resistance to desegregation is inspiring. To see top corporate executives such as A. Barry Rand at Xerox and Ken Chennault at American Express is gratifying. And to see literally hundreds of thousands of African American judges, doctors, lawyers, managers, and other professionals is extraordinary. Most of those individuals would not have been allowed in the front door just a generation ago.

9 At the same time, however, the measure of America's progress toward a just society is not by the achievements of the few but by the condition of the many. It is hard for African Americans to celebrate the inroads made by people who still face limits on their aspirations because of race—especially when the majority of black people are in a crisis situation.

10 That situation was worsened by the orgy of greed and selfishness in the 1980s—a time when the investment banker, not the social worker, was America's hero. It was a time when America's vast middle class—which had been created and nurtured by government programs like the GI Bill, subsidized mortgages, and tax breaks—turned against the needs of the poor. And it was a time when government withdrew from social concerns. While the Reagan Administration threw money at the Pentagon, it said that you can't solve social problems by throwing money at them.

11 While it said we were a colorblind society, it implemented policies that had severe racial impacts and worsened poverty for African Americans and other minorities. And while it proclaimed the health of American democracy, it weakened society's social fabric with policies that encouraged inequality and class conflict.

12 One living legacy of the Reagan Administration is today's Supreme Court. Once, African Americans looked to the Court for protection of our rights. Today, the Court appears to be an aggressive opponent of our rights. In a recent address, Justice Harry Blackmun said, and I quote: "these are indeed somber and sobering times for those interested in pressing and enhancing basic civil rights. The last term of your Supreme Court attests to that fact." Among other things, Justice Blackmun was referring to the Court's rulings that reduced the legal protections against discrimination in the workplace.

13 The Court's rulings send a terrible message to America, a message that says: "we're drilling loopholes into anti-discrimination laws and you don't have to worry about the consequences of violating the rights of minorities." Congress can reverse that message by passing the Civil Rights Act of 1990, which corrects the Court's misguided rulings in some key cases. We cannot have a just society that places the burdens of proving discrimination on the victims of discrimination . . . that prevents those victims from seeking legal redress . . . that refuses to punish those who illegally discriminate. But that is the society we will have unless the Civil Rights Act of 1990 is passed.

14 Today's battleground should not have to be the legal one—because past laws and court decisions constructed a sound framework to protect civil rights and the legal aspects of equal opportunity. Rather, we need to address the economic and social issues that prevent so many African Americans from enjoying equal opportunity. Those issues are central to the values we find in the Church's teachings, in Pope Leo's encyclical, and in such important contributions to contemporary debate as the Bishops' pastoral letter on Economic Justice for All. A just society cannot allow gross disparities based on race, yet that is what our society does.

15 The National Urban League has taken as its theme, racial parity by the year 2000. Today, African Americans are far from parity. To measure just how far, we did a research study that asked: How far behind are we and how long will it take to catch up? Unemployment was one important issue we looked at. We found that black unemployment has grown worse since 1967. The conclusion—at the current rate of change, African American workers will *never* reach parity with white workers. We'll just slip further behind.

16 Next, we looked at earnings. For black men, it will take 73 years at the current rate of progress to close the racial gap in earnings. What about family income? Back in 1967, black family earnings were about 59 percent of white family earnings. In 1985, they were down to about 57 and a half percent. No progress. Family income is becoming more unequal, and unless that changes, there will *never* be black-white parity.

17 What about poverty? Black family poverty is triple the white rate, and it will take 169 years at the current rate of change for black and white families to have the same poverty rate.

18 The one economically important area where the gap appears to be closing faster is education. If we continue to improve our high school graduation rates at the same pace that held between 1967 and 1985, in 16 years black and white high school graduation rates will be equal. For college completion rates, it will be 40 years.

19 There's a lot more to our study—but the conclusion is inevitable. Our society is far from reaching parity, and in several crucial indicators will never reach it unless there is strong, positive action by government, the private sector, and the voluntary sector.

20 We often hear that such a massive national effort is unaffordable. But I can't buy that—I can't believe that a trillion dollar federal budget cannot accommodate the programs America needs. I can't believe there's not enough money available for housing—not when Secretary Jack Kemp tells us the bill for HUD's past mismanagement will be over $2 billion, and when we give people tax writeoffs for vacation homes. I can't believe there's not enough money to train everyone without marketable skills—not when the General Accounting Office says the Pentagon has $30 billion in *excess, unusable* spare parts all over the world. And I can't believe we can't afford to assure poor children access to food and to health care—not when the bill for bailing out the savings and loan industry is expected to come to $200 billion or so.

21 Somehow government always finds the money for what it wants to do—whether to throw it at the Pentagon or to cut taxes for the affluent. But when it comes to poor people and programs that help poor children get the opportunities to move out of poverty, we're told the government can't afford it. We've got to be about the business of helping people to understand that the issue today is not inadequate resources but inadequate will and inadequate priorities.

22 And I believe the time is ripe for such an effort to be successful. There are several reasons for my optimism.

23 First, there are signs that the nation is waking from a decade-long time of irresponsibility and greed. The get rich quick, look out for number one, selfishness of the 1980s is passing. We see signs of this everywhere—in the highly publicized troubles of some of the leading actors in the boom times of the '80s . . . in the new concerns political leadership is showing about the nation's real problems . . . in the growing community activism of citizens. Put simply, the party is over. America is coming to understand that an awful lot of people were never invited to the party and now it is time to pay attention to their needs. As the era of excess and selfishness ends, we should enter a new era of concern about our social problems, poverty and racial inequalities.

24 Second, the demographic revolution is making itself felt. As the proportion of young people in the population shrinks, the proportion of disadvantaged young people is larger. What once looked like a marginal problem confined to minorities or isolated groups can now be seen as a national problem affecting all of us. Only fifteen percent of new entrants to the work force in the 1990s will be white males. Minorities will make up a third of all new workers. If we continue to have minority children growing up poor, suffering bad health and housing conditions, dropping out of school, and failing to get the skills this country needs—we can look forward to a sharp decline in America's standard of living. So arguments of fairness and justice have to be joined with appeals to the self-interest of people whose futures depend on how well other people's children do in life.

25 That leads me to the third reasons for my optimism—the economic revolution. We are now in a competitive global economy in which national wealth and power derive from human resources, not from natural resources. It is an economy driven by information and knowledge, requiring high skills levels and communications abilities. Combine that with the demographics, and it is apparent that unless all our children get the schooling they need in this brave new world, America is going to wind up a third-rate economic power. That's clear to the people who run our economy, too. It's behind the whole school reform movement, and the effort to get our schools to function at a higher level for all our children.

26 The Urban League is part of that effort. Our Education Initiative is a movement-wide programmatic thrust in which every single Urban League affiliate targets creative education programs at disadvantaged youngsters and their families. Well over 150,000 children and their parents participate in some 300 Education Initiative programs run by our 113 local Urban Leagues. We are getting parents involved in their childrens' schooling . . . introducing elementary school children to math and science . . . encouraging higher aspirations and college goals . . . and we are implementing other programs aimed at raising our children's achievement levels.

27 At the same time we are trying to get the message across that school success cannot take place in a vacuum. Many of our children have multiple problems unrelated to the school building. They are in poor, single-parent families and go to school hungry and poorly clothed. They have illnesses that go untreated and impede learning. They live in substandard housing and have no place to study or to do homework.

28 So we have to tell policy-makers and the public that school reforms aren't enough. We've got to be concerned with the whole child and meet that child's needs in the total context of the factors affecting him or her. We have to tell America that it will not be able to compete unless our long-neglected human resources are developed through child care, child services, education, job training, and employment opportunities.

29 Finally, a window of opportunity is opening that suggests we can afford to make human resource investment a priority after all. That window of opportunity is popularly known as the peace dividend. There are plenty of people who will tell you that the peace dividend doesn't exist. Don't believe them. The peace dividend exists, all right.

30 What is in doubt is whether we as a nation have the common sense and the responsibility and the political will to use it in the right way. Over the past decade we poured over two trillion—yes, trillion—dollars into military spending. Currently, the Pentagon budget is at $300 billion. But a funny thing happened on the Pentagon's way to the Treasury—the Cold War ended. Uncle Sam is all dressed up in battle gear—without anyone to fight. And if you don't have anyone to fight, you don't need an $80 billion Stealth bomber program or a Star Wars program that could run into the hundreds of billions of dollars. Many defense experts say that we can ensure national security at half the current spending levels. That would mean spending $150 billion on defense each year—releasing another $150 billion for other purposes.

31 What shall we do with those savings . . . with that peace dividend? According to public opinion polls, most Americans want to use it to resolve social problems such as drugs and homelessness. They're not looking for another round of tax breaks. They are concerned with the social problems they see all around them, and view the peace dividend as an opportunity to do something positive about them.

32 That means we must come up with sound, positive proposals and marshall national support to make them happen. The National Urban League was one of the first national organizations to seize upon the changed global realities to develop a blueprint for social change in the 1990s.

33 We have called on Congress and the Administration to implement the peace dividend by framing a national security program that converts current military spending to investments in our future. We support using the peace dividend for deficit reduction and for funding a national Urban Marshall Plan that revitalizes our cities and draws America's poor and minority people into the mainstream. Assuming an ultimate annual peace dividend in the range of $150 billion, we suggest that up to two-thirds be applied to reducing the federal budget deficit. Economists say that would bring interest rates down to 4–5 percent, sparking healthy economic growth, job creation, and increased tax revenues.

34 The remainder of the peace dividend—at least a third, or $50 billion—would be applied to the Urban Marshall Plan. The Urban Marshall Plan would tackle such deep problems as poverty, lack of access to health care, Depression-level unemployment among minorities, a shortage of affordable housing, and others that rob us of the skills and energy of millions of people who can contribute to a productive economy. The Urban Marshall

Plan is not a catch-all for social programs, however worthy. We should broaden and expand those programs, including food stamps and other social welfare programs, outside the umbrella of the Urban Marshall Plan. The Urban Marshall Plan can get maximum support if it is seen for what it is—an investment program that develops human resources and has a clear future economic payoff for the nation.

35 There was a time when a good argument could be made for an Urban Marshall Plan on the grounds of simple fairness and equity. That still holds true, especially after a decade of growing income inequality and escalating poverty. But in the 1990s, that solid argument is joined by one that transcends economic philosophy or class interests. It is simply that the U.S. will not be able to compete in this changed world unless it harnesses the productive energies of all of its people, most especially the core of its future workforce—young minorities locked into poverty and underachievement.

36 So I believe that we have a window of opportunity in the 1990s to forge ahead with great gains for all our Americans. A nation worried about its economic competitiveness will have to abandon its racism and tolerance of poverty and inequality. The alternative is a painful slide into a decline that hurts all of us—rich and poor, white and black.

37 There will be those who say an Urban Marshall Plan is a fantasy and racial parity a distant dream. But this is a time of miracles. Who would have thought that the Berlin Wall would crumble, that the Soviet Union would tilt toward democracy, that a free Nelson Mandela would be negotiating an end to apartheid? But that is all happening. There is a worldwide movement toward freedom and democracy, and the force of that movement will shake America as surely as it has shaken other nations. It is the task of all who are concerned with social justice, who work to heal the wounds inflicted by a callous society, who wish to make our society's values more humane . . . to work for racial parity and for public policies that close the gap between the races.

38 We need to move from ministering to the needs of individuals to changing the system that brutalizes people. We need to harness the tremendous productive capacity of our system to invest in people and their needs, and thus ensure the continued prosperity of the system. We need to bring to bear on America's social and economic problems the concerns and values that inspired Pope Leo's encyclical and the Bishops' Letter.

39 For America's salvation lies not in its military arsenal nor in its material possessions, but in the goodness of a moral society that lives up to its ideals of liberty and justice for all. Those ideals have not been realized. But through a long and tortuous past full of dreams and struggles, we have come closer to them. I believe that achieving them can be within our grasp. I believe that America, for all of its faults and for all of the terrible things it has done and is doing to its minorities and its poor, can stay on the positive path of change.

40 My belief is that of the late, great Whitney M. Young, Jr., whose belief in America and its promise of parity, fairness, and justice was summed up in these words: "I do have faith in America—not so much in a sudden upsurge of morality nor in a new surge toward a greater patriotism—but I believe in the intrinsic intelligence of Americans and of the business community. I do not believe that we forever need to be confronted by tragedy or crises in order to act. I believe that the evidence is clear. I believe that we as a people will not wait to be embarrassed or pushed by events into a posture of decency. I believe that America has the strength to do what is right because it is right. I am convinced that given a kind of collective wisdom and sensitivity, Americans today can be persuaded to act creatively and imaginatively to make democracy work. This is my hope, this is my dream, this is my faith."

What Does America Have to Do to Compete?
Lee A. Iacocca

If it is possible for a corporate executive to become an American hero, then Lee Iacocca achieved that unlikely status in the early part of the 1980s. The legend began when Iacocca labored for a dollar a year at Chrysler in 1980 and was credited with pulling the automobile company back from the economic brink. When it looked like Chrysler Corporation might go under, Iacocca, in a bold move, convinced the government that his corporation was needed as competition for Ford and General Motors and persuaded Washington to guarantee loans made by banks to his automobile company. The scheme worked and Chrysler came back strongly. The newspapers often referred to the action as the Chrysler "bailout." Iacocca capitalized on this notoriety and produced an autobiography that made the best-seller list and stayed there for some time. Next, he turned up in TV commercials for Chrysler, and gave straight talk pitches for his product.

As the 1980s unfolded, Iacocca remained at the Chrysler helm as a worsening economy and questionable attempts at diversification again placed the company in jeopardy. Throughout this period he was a vocal opponent of United States trade policies and Japanese trade practices that placed American industry at a competitive disadvantage.

On March 22, 1989, Iacocca addressed a gathering at the National Association of Manufacturers in Washington D.C. While the NAM and Iacocca would appear to be on the same side of the economic/political aisle, the NAM had opposed the government loan guarantees to Chrysler ten years earlier. For this reason, he begins his speech by expressing some reservations he has about addressing the NAM on the tenth anniversary of the Chrysler loan-guarantee debate. To what extent does he defuse the hostility of the past? How does he do so?

Iacocca advances a problem claim in this speech: that present governmental policies and practices are prejudicial to the best interests of American corporations and the public at large. In advancing this claim, a vast array of problems are identified. Speeches that address a wide range of problems are often called Jeremiads—named after the old testament prophet Jeremiah who lamented the depravity of the children of Israel. Do broad-based treatments of problems, such as this one, serve a useful social function or are they merely calamity howling?

Iacocca is known for his vibrant speaking style. What is it about his language that produces an animated effect? He is also known for his ability to relate to his audience in a direct and personal manner. Through what devices or strategies does the speaker promote a sense of community with his audience?

This speech is reprinted from a manuscript provided by the office of Lee A. Iacocca and is reprinted with the permission of the author.

1 Thank you, Dick (Heckert), and good afternoon to all of you.

2 I appreciate the introduction and the reception. I've learned that you never know what to expect when you come to Washington. In fact, I gotta tell you, I feel a little like John Tower being invited back to lunch in the Senate dining room.

3 You see, when I was in town 10 years ago looking for some loan guarantees to save Chrysler, NAM was telling everybody on the hill, "Don't give him a dime." I know it wasn't personal—there was a *principle* involved.

4 I can tell you now, that *hurt*. But, of course, everybody knows that I'm not the kind of guy who holds a grudge! (At least not for over 10 years at a time—so here I am.)

5 And then, of course, I remember running into Sandy Trowbridge at the Lack Placid Olympics not long afterward. He'd just taken over as head of NAM, and he said, "Lee, the whole fleet of Plymouth Horizons (60 of them) we just bought for our field force are all running great!"

6 That really impressed me, and I had a lot of encounters like that. You see, we found that a lot of people who opposed government help for Chrysler *in principle* were still rooting for us, and actually *helped* us later on. They didn't really want to see a great old company go bankrupt and 600,000 people lose their jobs. But there was this *principle* involved!

7 Well, this year is the tenth anniversary of the whole Chrysler loan-guarantee debate. I don't want to open any old wounds, but I think we should all remember what almost happened. Chrysler was going down for the third time, and for the sake of *principle* some purists were saying, "Let her sink. It will be a good example of free enterprise at work."

8 At about the same time, if you'll recall, we were sending dollars to Latin America by the boatload. (Those were *smart* loans, of course, while Chrysler's was a *bailout*.) And in the spirit of good old-fashioned American entrepreneurship, we deregulated the S&Ls and said, "Hey, you guys go do your own thing. And don't worry, we'll back you up all the way."

9 I guess there were some *principles* involved there, too.

10 Well, let me abbreviate history for just a minute. In fact, Chrysler never did take a dime of federal money. We just asked the government to co-sign a few notes. In return, when we paid those notes off seven years early, the federal treasury made almost $350 million *profit*.

11 What happened to all those *safe* loans to Latin America? They're still on the books—about $70 billion worth—with a lot of embarrassing asterisks next to them.

12 And how about those great bastions of free enterprise, the S&Ls? A one hundred billion dollar blunder that will come right out of taxpayers' pockets. (That's you and me.)

13 Now, I didn't come here today just to say "I told you so," or to talk about some of our double standards in this country. I think (at least I *hope*) we're *all* a little smarter in 1989 than we were in 1979. In fact, helping Chrysler *was* a dangerous precedent back then—unless you happened to look at the consequences of letting us die. Moving away from our tried and true principles in this country *is still* dangerous—*unless* sticking to them *blindly* winds up taking us over a cliff.

14 I keep telling people what we need here in Washington are a few more Chrysler "bailouts." I don't mean underwriting every failing business that comes along, but I do mean breaking some old rules and traditions if that's what it takes in order *to compete.*

15 You see, I'm a *businessman,* not a *politician.* All I've ever done in my life is manage a business, and every day I ask myself, "What do I have to do to compete?" And every time I come to *this* town, I try to get people here to ask the same question: "What does *America* have to do to compete?"

16 And you're all business people, too. What would *you* like to see happen? What would help *you* compete? How about interest rates at 8 percent instead of 12? Would that help? I'm building a new research center and a new plant right now—at a billion dollars each—let me do them at 8 instead of 12 and watch how competitive I get. But it won't happen as long as the government is spending a half billion bucks a day more than it takes in . . . as long as we've got 2.6 trillion dollars of debt on our backs (with interest alone running over $200 billion or 15 percent of our total budget) . . . and as long as my competitors in Japan are paying less than one-third what I am for capital.

17 And, how would you like to compete with the same *rules* for everybody? Example: Toyota and Nissan want to come here and compete with me, so they sign up a Chrysler dealer and put their logo right next to mine. But I'm trying to sell in Japan, right now, and I'm prohibited by law from using their dealers so I have to start a whole new distribution network of my own. And yet every day, it seems, I read about another Japanese tycoon saying that we Americans aren't *trying* hard enough, or just don't *understand* the Japanese market.

18 Or how about *taxes*? Would a few changes in the tax code help you compete? The individual rates have come down, sure, but only because *business* people like you and me picked up $120 billion more of the load. (And only *American* business, by the way— Toyota got a better deal than I did.) We're out of sync with everybody else because we tax mostly savings and investment while they tax consumption. After 74 years we finally changed the tax code, and maybe made it a little *fairer* (not simpler, mind you). But it did not cut the deficit or make us more competitive in trade—our two biggest problems. So why do we make the trip?

19 Oh, and a full third of those taxes go for defense—about $1,200 for every man, woman and child in America compared with $150 in Japan. Imagine how competitive we'd suddenly get if *they* were defending *us*! (Or at least helping out.)

20 And here's one that hits all of you—how would you like to compete without this albatross around your necks called runaway health care costs? For me, it's $700 a car, and still going up at twice the rate of inflation. Other countries put those costs in their taxes, but we put them into the price of our products. That's not very healthy for competing with the other guys.

21 Or, how about if we'd just stop suing each other at the drop of a hat? Would that make us more competitive? Japan graduates ten engineers for every lawyer, and we graduate ten lawyers for every engineer. Does that tell you something? They train people to build a better mousetrap, and we train people to *sue* the guy with the mousetrap. So who's the smart guy?

22 I could go on, but we are getting less and less competitive in this country, and some of the biggest reasons don't have anything to do with what we do on the factory floor; they have to do with policies here in Washington. I should say *lack* of policies, because I honestly don't know what our game plan is on some of these issues—if we have one at all.

23 We are groping—and I mean really *groping*—for solutions, starting with what to do with our debt load. I was on the National Economic Commission that unceremoniously folded its tent three weeks ago. We worked hard for almost a year and agreed on only one major thing—that deficits are *bad for the country*!

24 Pretty profound—huh? (That makes us geniuses, right? I expect to get my Nobel Prize in the mail any day now.)

25 We listened to every reputable economist, including Paul Volcker and Alan Greenspan, who told us that a credible whack at the budget (say $30–40 billion a year for four years) would drop interest rates a couple of points almost overnight.

26 We split up because we couldn't agree on a little *sacrifice* to take that whack. We were worried about what the voters might say to a little nickel or dime tax on a gallon of gas. That might cost you $100 a year. (Just *whispering* the word "taxes" in *this* town *today* is like quoting the Satanic Verses to the Ayatollah. You could get a contract put out on you.)

27 Actually, we were asking the wrong question. We should have been asking, "How would you like to see your mortgage payments go down a couple thousand dollars a year? And, how would you like to lower your car payments, and your credit card payments?" And imagine the magic it would weave on South American debt repayments, and on the S&L insolvencies and bailouts—you name it. Hell, most of all, that $200 million interest bill on our national debt would drop like a rock. We should have told the American people about some of those things. And we certainly should have told them that high interest rates are the most insidious taxes of all (make no mistake about it).

28 I was on the NEC as a *businessman,* concerned about *competing.* That was what was so frustrating. Those deficits have made us, by far, the biggest debtor in the world. And if you look back in history you'll find that in this world it's always the guy *holding* the IOUs who calls the shots. He's the guy in the best shape to *compete.* Debtors cannot be leaders—economically, militarily, or any other way.

29 We're groping on the budget deficit, and groping on the other big deficit, too—the trade deficit. Japan is eating our lunch, and yet here in Washington it seems everybody is heading off in different directions. No coordinated policy at all.

30 At Commerce and the Special Trade Representative's office, they'd like to level the playing field a little, but the State Department doesn't want to ruffle any feathers . . . the Pentagon wants to keep Japan on our side in case the Russians act up . . . and Treasury is scared to death the Japanese won't show up at the bond auctions next Tuesday. Everybody in town has his own agenda with Japan, but the United States of America has none! We got an 1,100 page trade bill last year, but nobody seems to know how to use it.

31 I grew up believing protectionism—the old classic kind where you shut yourself off from the rest of the world—was pretty dumb, and I still do. But somewhere along the line we stopped being idealists and started being patsies. I don't want to close off the American market, and I don't want to toss out the idea of free trade. But I want to *use* the American market to make damn sure that trade is free for *Americans* for a change.

32 If that means using market access as a weapon to open up foreign markets to us and *defend* free trade, what's wrong with that?

33 I'd like to see trade policy and national competitiveness elevated to the same rank and importance as national security!

34 Now, I said that we can't get our act together when it comes to Japan, but let me tell you, *they have a plan,* and the clout to make it work. The Political Action Committee that represents Japanese auto dealers in this country gave $2.6 million to congressional campaigns last fall. That's more than General Motors, Ford, Chrysler, and the United Auto Workers gave, put together.

35 Last year alone, the Japanese paid more than $100 million to their lobbyists and other agents in this country. And do you know where a big chunk of that dough goes? To hire away our own trade negotiators! About one third of the senior people in the U.S. Trade Representative's office in recent years have left to work for foreign governments and companies.

36 Think about it. If a CIA agent quit one day and hired on with the Russians the next, we'd throw him in the slammer. But when our trade negotiators defect to the Japanese, nobody bats an eye! This really is a very strange town!

37 Well, the budget . . . trade . . . the tax code . . . all the rest of them—these are competitiveness problems we could solve, and solve *fast,* if we just had the political will to do it, and, of course, some coherent policies and good dedicated people to carry them out.

38 But let me tell you about our biggest problem of all. And this one can't be solved overnight. It's going to take a long time, but I guarantee you, without solving it, forget *ever* being able to compete. (Nothing else will matter.) What I'm referring to is the absolutely crummy job that we're doing in this country in education. We're just not giving our kids the tools they'll need to compete, and we'll pay a stiff competitive price for that for a lot of years to come.

39 We're turning out high school graduates who will have a hard time even *understanding* the problems, let alone tackling them. Somebody did a study (oh, hell, we're always doing studies). Seventy-five percent of our high school students don't known what *inflation* is . . . 66 percent don't know what *profits* are . . . and 55 percent don't have a clue as to what a government *budget deficit* is. (So the size has no meaning to them.)

40 Hell, 600,000 of our graduates last year could barely read their diplomas. (I couldn't read *mine* either, but it was in *Latin*. Theirs were in *English*.)

41 Sure, we have some great schools . . . and plenty of dedicated teachers. Many of our high school graduates are as well prepared as you'll find anywhere. But when you talk about competing as a nation, you compete on the basis of your *averages*. How does the *average* U.S. student stack up? That's what determines how competitive we'll be.

42 Well, ours are now dead last among industrialized countries in math and science. Is there any doubt that we'll fall flat on our faces trying to compete in a high tech world when we're turning out students who are dead last in math and science? And they're near the bottom in reading, too.

43 I'll bet you didn't know this: you and I and all the rest of American industry are spending more money teaching remedial math to our employees than all the grade schools, high schools, and colleges in this country spend on math education—*combined*!

44 Hell, I'm in the business of building *cars* not teaching remedial math!

45 We spend $117 million a year at Chrysler on training, and almost ten percent of it goes to teaching people the three R's they didn't learn in school.

46 At Motorola, they found that it costs $200 to train an American worker in statistical process control. Teaching the same technique to a Japanese worker costs 47 cents. Basically, all they have to do over there is hand the guy the book. We can't do that here because there's a good chance our guy can't read it.

47 Functional illiteracy in Japan runs at about 5 percent. Here it's between 20 and 30 percent, depending on whose figures you use.

48 We used to write our training material at Chrysler at the 9th to 12th grade reading levels. But we found we were out of sync because a lot of the people in the plants were only reading at the sixth grade level. So we had to translate everything into sixth grade reading because that's all some of them could handle.

49 Sometimes even sixth grade is too tough. On one of our assembly lines, we had a button on a computer labeled with three simple words: "bad hood fit." We had to replace it with *graphics*—a picture of a hood.

50 Now remember, in Detroit we draw our workforce from a city where the high school drop-out rate is 50 percent . . . the daily school attendance rate is about 75 percent . . . and where less than 30 percent of the school budget actually goes to basic education. (The other 70 percent is for administration and "support" services.) I've got over 91 percent of my people designing, building, and selling cars. Imagine if I only had *30 percent* doing that and 70 percent was pure overhead. How long would I last? Could *you* stay in business that way?

51 It goes without saying that we as manufacturers have a huge stake in education. Would you believe maybe *survival*? I know what factory workers in Japan and Korea can do. I've seen them. I also see what we're getting from our schools, and I'm scared. Everybody can get the same technology today, but if you don't have people who are smarter than the robots they work with, the game is over. You are simply not going to compete.

52 We employers have to get more involved in education. And I don't mean spending more time teaching our own people how to read or do long division, either. We've gotta go to the core of the problem and help our schools turn out the kind of people we need to run our plants.

53 And just throwing money at the problem isn't enough. We'll spend $328 billion on education this year, more than for any other public service, including national defense. And we spend a lot more of our GNP on education than any of our overseas competitors—including Japan and Germany.

54 So we deserve more productivity and efficiency for the billions in tax dollars that we're already putting into education.

55 We also have to demand higher standards. The first thing some youngsters flunk these days is life itself. That's because they've been passed from one grade to another, and eventually graduated, even though they've been failing at every step. The only problem is, nobody's told them. In attempting to shield these kids from failure, we've guaranteed it. You know what that is (we hear a lot about it these days), it's called *malpractice*. Malpractice in the *schools*.

56 Now, for some youngsters today it's already too late. They're so far behind they may never catch up. We can do a patch job on some, but we really need to make sure that we don't blow another crop. That means starting *now* with the K through 6 kids. Just like in our plants—"Do it right the first time!" We can't keep trying to make repairs at the end of the assembly line.

57 More than anything else, we have to find ways to help teachers themselves do their jobs. We're asking a helluva lot of them right now. We're asking them to be cops, and social workers, and surrogate parents, and drug counselors, and psychologists. And we're making them do all that alone.

58 I talked to the National Education Association a couple of weeks ago in San Diego. I found that only 25 percent of parents ever visit their children's schools. Let me ask you—could you turn out a quality product if you never even got to *talk* to the suppliers that send you your raw materials? I couldn't!

59 I have to get my suppliers involved in my business or I can't fit together those 12,000 parts that make a car. If you can't get the parents involved, I don't know how you fit all the parts together into that complex mosaic called a human being!

60 But that's what we're asking those teachers to do. It's not fair, is it?

61 The schools themselves, of course, are our *major suppliers*. We can't just get mad at the quality of what they're sending us. We have to work with them to fix that quality.

62 Like a lot of other companies, we're trying to do that at Chrysler. And we're doing it as hard-headed *business* people who understand it's a responsibility we have to take on in order to help ourselves *compete*.

63 One thing we're trying to do is create a better awareness in this country of just how big our education problems are.

64 Starting next Monday night, we're sponsoring a five-part **PBS** series entitled "Learning in America" with Roger Mudd (an ex-teacher, by the way) as the host. It's an in-depth look at what we're doing wrong in this country, some of the things we're doing right and, most important, whether or not our schools are preparing our kids to *compete*.

65 Secondly, we've just made a half-million dollar grant to the National Board for Professional Teaching Standards. This is a new organization, just over a year old. Dick Heckert is on the board. The aim is to create for the first time a set of national standards and an accreditation process for teachers that will help give the teaching profession the stature it deserves.

66 In Japan, teachers are up on a pedestal, like they were here when I was a kid. They're among the highest paid of all Japanese professionals, and in prestige they're right up there next to "king" (or Emperor)—not only respected, but revered. Boy, they've really got their priorities straight.

67 Then—and this may be the most lasting contribution we can make—we just provided the largest grant in history, $2.1 million, to Reading Is Fundamental. That's a program I've been involved in since it began.

68 I've learned that the average primary school student in this country spends only seven or eight minutes a day actually reading. Maybe that's our whole problem, or at least the root of it. Reading really *is* fundamental to everything else.

69 And we have to start young. The problems are in the early years. Our universities and graduate schools are still magnets for the best and the brightest from all over the world (would you believe 60 percent of engineering Ph.D.s in this country go to foreign students?). So we must be doing something right at that level. But nobody is lining up to come and enroll in our kindergartens. *That's* where we're falling down—we're failing our *own* kids, right from the start.

70 Now, we know that everything we're doing at Chrysler to support education is really just a drop in the bucket, because it's such a huge problem. We've searched for a few ways to help, and I hope every company in this room looks for ways to get involved, too.

71 President Bush, who'll be here tomorrow, says he wants to be the "Education President." I think every one of us ought to do everything we can to help him get his wish. I talked to Mrs. Bush last night, and I have a strong feeling that with that lady by his side on this issue, he stands a good chance of making education the brightest of his thousand points of light.

72 I sure hope so. The kids entering first grade next fall will be the first high school class to graduate in the 21st Century. We should focus on that class. We've already let some of the older kids down, but this class will tell how well America will be able to compete in the 21st Century.

73 You know, the Year 2000 is already getting a magic ring to it. Everything seems to be pointing to it—the Dawn of the Third Millenium. But I hope we don't look past the decade of the nineties. Because what we do between now and the end of *this* century will determine what kind of country we're going to be in the *next* one.

74 Some people like to say that we've lost the competitive edge we once had because Americans have gone soft. I don't believe that for a minute. But I do think we're living in the past. We're still living in the so-called "American Century." And we think its going to go on and on.

75 Well, I hate to tell you, but it's *over*. The Asians and the Europeans have an equal say now. And that's not all bad. In fact, that's what American policy has tried to do over the last 45 years—help build a world where people are competing in the marketplace instead of on the battlefield.

76 But that means we're going to have to learn to *compete* in a world that we no longer *dominate*. I don't think we've fully realized yet what that means.

77 It means that *competing* has to become the main policy goal in this city, and across the country.

78 I was glad to read last week that President Bush has appointed Vice President Quayle, who'll be up here in just a few minutes, to head a new White House task force on competitiveness. I can't think of a more *challenging,* or more *important,* role for the number two man in our government than to lead the effort to get us more competitive.

79 And I, for one, am glad to see that America's economic competitiveness is getting that kind of top priority treatment by the new administration.

80 Just about everything we do in this country, right or wrong, has an impact on our ability to compete. We need a broad-based solution to our competitiveness problem. And it has to be led from the highest levels.

81 Because competitiveness is a *national* problem. We're not just competing with foreign engineers and workers, we're competing against their schools, and their trade policies, and their health care systems, and all the other factors that go into this issue.

82 That will take leadership . . . it will take involvement . . . and it will also take a willingness to challenge a few old ideas, and maybe even to bend a sacred principle or two when they get in the way of our ability to compete.

83 Ten years ago, some men and women of both parties up on Capitol Hill had the courage and the vision to bend a few principles and vote to give Chrysler a chance to compete. Dan Quayle, by the way, was one of them.

84 Now that he's our new competitiveness czar, I hope he'll be able to convince some others in this town that we aren't betraying anything this country has ever stood for by doing *whatever it takes* to give our kids the chance to compete in this new world.

85 But we sure betray *them* . . . those kids . . . if we *don't*.

86 Thank you very much. It's been good to be back. And Sandy, I hope you're still buying our cars! Good day.

Pesticides Speech
César Chávez

Noted speakers—whether they are presidents of large corporations, heads of public service organizations, major government officials, or leaders of social movements—frequently are called upon to speak on the same general topic to numerous but varied audiences. Politicians during major campaigns often face the same demand. One approach such speakers sometimes take is to present a "generic" speech—a speech containing the same general information and arguments regardless of audience but with opportunities in the speech for a modest amount of concrete adaptation to each specific audience. For one discussion of such generic or "stock" political campaign speeches, see Judith S. Trent and Robert V. Friedenberg, *Political Campaign Communication* (Prager, 1983), pp. 171–177.

This speech by César Chávez is a generic speech. It contains standard or basic arguments on the topic suitable for diverse audiences and occasions with two places noted for specific audience adaptation: "insert names" (1) and "insert additional pitches" (18). There are no mentions in the text of the speech of a specific audience or occasion. The text simply is dated 1-9-90 and labeled as "Pesticides Speech for Cesar Chavez." Other texts of speeches presented by Chávez provided by his office indicate specific audiences and occasions and some of the speeches make numerous adaptations to the audiences.

César Chávez was born in 1927 in Arizona and in 1962 in California founded the National Farm Workers Association (later called United Farm Workers of America). This was a labor union noted for its aggressive but nonviolent advocacy of the rights and safety of migrant farm workers. In numerous social protest efforts spanning four decades, Chávez often has utilized the pressure tactic of consumer boycott of the purchase of farm produce such as lettuce or grapes. Although in this speech he does urge adoption of a policy—the boycott of table grapes—and he does indicate its potential effectiveness (15–18), the bulk of the speech primarily aims at creating concern for a problem rather than describing in detail a program of action.

In presenting a compelling view of the problem, Chávez answers the question—Why grapes?—by demonstrating the scope of the problem. He employs statistics to show how widespread the problem is (4, 10) and argues that the problem threatens farm workers, their children, and consumers (5–6, 10). Statistics such as 800 percent and 1200 percent above normal index the intensity of the problem (8–9). Expert testimony is used in several places, including use of so-called "reluctant" testimony from grower and government sources (2, 6, 14). What are the causes of the problem? Chávez clearly identifies two: grape grower greed (2–3, 12, 18) and inaction and misaction by state and federal governments (12–14). For Chávez, government "is part of the problem."

Chávez attempts to generate audience concern for the problem by vividly depicting the danger, degradation, and suffering of people who directly experience the problem. First, he lists the general physical harms: "cancer, DNA mutations, and horrible birth defects" (6). Second, and at length, he "humanizes" the "technical" problem of pesticides with examples of real people and groups (7–11). Note his skillful use of alliteration to make his argument memorable: "*children* are dying . . . *slow, painful, cruel* deaths in towns called *cancer clusters*" (8) And note his use of parallel phrasing to summarize his point (11).

Of special interest to the rhetorical critic is Chávez's strategy of associating the pesticides and policies he condemns with so-called "devil terms" that carry intense negative force because they represent violations of fundamental human values. He establishes associations with nerve gas (6–World War I German use and use by Saddam Hussein against Kurds in Iraq in 1988); with agent orange (6–a chemical with harmful physical side-effects used to strip leaves from trees during the Vietnam War); with killing fields (10–allusion to the 1984 film of the same name that depicted mass slaughter of Cambodian civilians by Communist terrorists); and, sarcastically, with Idi Amin (Uganda's bloody dictator) and Adolph Hitler (13). How adequately and legitimately do you believe that he establishes these associations?

In what ways and to what degree might the lack in a generic speech of arguments and appeals specifically intended for a specific audience lessen Chávez's, or any speaker's, ability to create concern for the problem she or he describes? Here recall the discussion of the second suggested criterion for evaluating speeches that create concern for problems: Has the speaker shown the significance of the problem for the specific audience? In addition, are there any ethical issues involved in the use of generic speeches? If so, what might they be and on what grounds? For a brief analysis of Chávez's rhetoric during the 60s and 70s, see John C. Hammerback and Richard J. Jensen, "The Rhetorical Worlds of César Chávez and Reies Tierina," *Western Journal of Speech Communication,* 44 (Summer 1980): 166–176.

The text of this speech was provided by President César Chávez's office at the national headquarters of the United Farm Workers of America.

---

1 Thank you very much, I am truly honored to be able to speak with you. I would like to thank the many people who made this possible for their kindness and their hospitality. (insert names)

2 Decades ago, the chemical industry promised the growers that pesticides would create vast new wealth and bountiful harvests. Just recently, the experts learned what farm workers, and the truly organic farmers have known for years. The prestigious National Academy of Sciences recently concluded an exhaustive five-year study which showed that by using simple, effective organic farming techniques, *instead of pesticides,* the growers could make *more money,* produce *more crops*, and *protect the environment*!

3 Unfortunately, the growers are not listening. They continue to spray and inject hundreds of millions of pounds of herbicides, fungicides, and insecticides onto our foods.

4 Most of you know that the United Farm Workers have focussed our struggle against pesticides on table grapes. Many people ask me "Why grapes?" The World Resources Institute reported that over three hundred thousand farm workers are poisoned every year by pesticides. Over half of all reported pesticide-related illnesses involve the cultivation or harvesting of table grapes. They receive *more* restricted-use application permits, which allow growers to spray pesticides known to threaten humans, than *any* other fresh food crop. The General Accounting Office, which does research for the U.S. Congress, determined that *34* of the *76* types of pesticides used *legally* on grapes pose potential human health hazards and could *not be detected* by current multi-residue methods.

5 My friends, grapes are the most dangerous fruit in America. The pesticides sprayed on table grapes *are killing America's children.* These pesticides *soak* the fields, *drift* with the wind, *pollute* the water, and are *eaten* by unwitting consumers. These poisons are designed to kill life, and pose a very real threat to consumers and farm workers alike.

6 The fields are sprayed with pesticides like captan, a fungicide believed to cause cancer, DNA mutation, and horrible birth defects. Other poisons take a similar toll. Parathion and phosdrin are *"nerve gas"* types of insecticides, which are believed to be responsible for the majority of farm worker poisonings in California. The growers spray sulphites, which can trigger asthmatic attacks, on the grapes. And even the growers own magazine, *The California Farmer,* admitted that growers were *illegally* using a very dangerous growth stimulator, called *Fix,* which is quite similar to *Agent Orange,* on the grapes.

7 This is a very technical problem, with very *human* victims. One young body, Felipe Franco, was born without arms or legs in the agricultural town of McFarland. His mother worked for the first three months of her pregnancy picking grapes in fields that were sprayed repeatedly with pesticides believed to cause birth defects.

8 My friends, the central valley of California is one of the wealthiest agricultural regions in the world. In its midst are clusters of children dying from cancer. The children who live in towns like McFarland are surrounded by the grape fields that employ their parents. The children contact the poisons when they play outside, when they drink the water, and when they hug their parents returning from the fields. *And the children are dying.* They are dying *slow, painful, cruel* deaths in towns called *cancer clusters.* In cancer clusters like McFarland, where the childhood cancer rate is *800 percent* above normal.

9 A few months ago, the parents of a brave little girl in the agricultural community of Earlimart came to the United Farm Workers to ask for our help. Their four year old daughter, Natalie Ramirez, has lost one kidney to cancer and is threatened with the loss of another. The Ramirez family knew about our protests in nearby McFarland and thought there might be a similar problem in their home town. Our union members went door to door in Earlimart and found that the Ramirez family's worst fears were true. There are at least *four* other children suffering from cancer and similar diseases which the experts believe were caused by pesticides in the little town of Earlimart, a rate *1200 percent* above normal. In Earlimart, little Jimmy Caudillo died recently from leukemia at the age of three.

10 The grape vineyards of California have become America's Killing Fields. These *same* pesticides can be found on the grapes you buy in the store. Study after study, by the California Department of Food and Agriculture, by the Food and Drug Administration, and by objective newspapers, concluded that up to *54 percent* of the sampled grapes contained pesticide residues. Which pesticide did they find the most? *Captan,* the same carcinogenic fungicide that causes birth defects.

11 My friends, *the suffering must end. So many* children are dying, *so many* babies are born without limbs and vital organs, *so many* workers are dying in the fields.

12 The growers, and the supermarket owners, say that the government can *handle* the problem, can *protect* the workers, can *save* the children. It *should,* but it *won't.* You see, agribusiness is *big business.* It is a *sixteen billion* dollar industry in California alone. Agribusiness contributed very heavily to the successful campaign of republican governor George Deukmajian. He has rewarded the growers by turning the Agricultural Labor Relations Board into a tool for the growers, run by the growers. The governor even vetoed a bill that would have required growers to warn workers that they were entering recently sprayed fields! And only *one percent* of those growers who *are caught* violating pesticide laws were even fined in California.

13 President Bush is a long-time friend of agribusiness. During the last presidential campaign, George Bush ate grapes in a field just *75 miles* from the cemetery where little Jimmy Caudillo and other pesticide victims are buried, in order to show his support for the table grape industry. He recently gave a speech to the Farm Bureau, saying that it was up to the *growers* to restrain the use of dangerous pesticides.

That's like putting *Idi Amin,* or *Adolph Hitler,* in charge of promoting *peace* and *human rights.*

14 To show you what happens to pesticides supposedly under government control, I'd like to tell you more about captan. Testing to determine the acceptable tolerance levels of captan was done by Bio-Tech Laboratories, later found *guilty* of falsifying the data to the E.P.A. The tolerance level set was *ten times* the amount allowed in Canada. Later, government agencies tried to ban captan, but were mysteriously stopped several times. Finally, the government banned captan on 42 crops, but *not on grapes.* Even the General Accounting Office found that the government's pesticide testing is wholly inadequate. The government is *not* the answer, it is part of the problem.

15 If we are to protect farm workers, their children, and consumers, we must use *people power.* I have seen many boycotts succeed. The Reverend Martin Luther King Junior, who so generously supported our first fast, led the way with the bus boycott. And with *our* first boycott, we were able to get DDT, Aldrin, and Dieldrin banned, in our first contracts with grape growers. Now, even more urgently, we are trying to get deadly pesticides banned.

16 The growers and their allies have tried to stop us with *lies,* with *police,* with *intimidation,* with *public relations agencies,* and with *violence.* But *we cannot be stopped.* In our *life and death struggle* for justice, we have turned to the court of last resort: the American people.

17 At last we are winning. Many supermarket chains have stopped selling or advertising grapes. Millions of consumers are refusing to buy America's most dangerous fruit. Many courageous people have volunteered to help our cause or joined human chains of people who fast, who go without food for days, to support our struggle. As a result, *grape sales keep falling.* We have witnessed truckloads of grapes being dumped because no one would stoop low enough to buy them. As demand drops, so do prices and profits. This sort of economic pressure is the only language the growers understand.

18 We are winning, but there is still much work to be done. If we are going to beat the greed and power of the growers, we must work *together. Together,* we can end the suffering. *Together,* we can save the children. *Together,* we can bring justice to the killing fields. I hope that you will join our struggle, for it is *your* struggle too. The simple act of boycotting table grapes laced with pesticides is a powerful statement the growers understand. *Please, boycott table grapes.* For your safety, for the workers, *we must act,* and *act together.* (insert additional pitches)

19 Good night, and God bless you.

Keeping Our Balance in the 90s: Women at Work, Women at Home
Rosalyn Wiggins Berne

On October 4, 1990, Rosalyn Wiggins Berne presented this speech during FOCUS Women's Week at the University of Virginia in Charlottesville. Rosalyn Wiggins Berne is a Research Assistant at the Olsson Center for the Study of Applied Ethics in the Darden Graduate School of Business Administration at the University of Virginia. Berne seeks to create concern for a problem—the problem for contemporary American women of achieving an individually appropriate balance or integration between work and home, career and family.

She creates a compelling view of the nature of the problem in varied ways. Statistics reveal the scope and intensity of the problem (7, 17). Elements of the problem are more mental than physical (9): "unclear role definition, guilt, lack of support, and the emotional stress inherent in a life of multiple, conflicting responsibilities." Lengthy contrasts between past eras and the present sharpen the view of the problem (4–6, 10, 12–13).

Berne describes a variety of causes as contributing to the problem. Unsupportive husbands, employers, and societal values significantly contribute to the problem (13, 22–26). Extremely important in her analysis of causal factors are unrealistic expectations and models (14–21). Note throughout the speech her stress on "reality" as she structures the audience's perception of the problem. Identify any points at which you disagree with her presentation of "reality." What might be a more adequate view of "reality"? To what degree is she contending that what *is* necessarily *ought* to be accepted rather than changed?

In what ways and now adequately does Berne show the significance of the problem for her specific audience? Apply suggestions from the discussion of this criterion in the theoretical section that begins this chapter.

What rhetorical functions are served, and how adequately, by Berne's quotations from Anne Morrow Lindberg (3, 12, 32) and by her own extended personal narrative (29–31)? Finally, consider the ways in which she uses stylistic and structural choices to reinforce the description of the problem. Note the choice of vivid and intense language (6, 9): difficult; burdensome; hectic, fragmented; complex. She skillfully combines metaphorical imagery and antithetical phrasing (9, 13): the privilege of choice is bitter sweet; that dream also has elements of a nightmare. And parallel phrasing accumulates and associates various elements of the problem for added force (21): the reality is; we will wonder or question why.

This speech is reprinted with permission from *Vital Speeches of the Day*, November 1, 1990, pp. 40–46.

1 I happened to mention to our new baby sitter that I would be speaking to you this evening. After explaining the topic she looked puzzled, and so I turned the discussion and asked if her own mother worked outside of the home while they were growing up. She paused, and replied, "Well, I guess so. In those days, we didn't have no running water so she was hulling water from down at the well. And we heated in the stove, so she was carrying wood up to the house. She had all the washing, and tending to the chickens and garden and all, so I guess you could say she always worked." Our baby sitter is 40 years old. "Those days" for her were not so long ago. I realized after listening to her that my

words to you this evening will not apply to all women. The subject addresses the lives of women who have a choice. And while in theory we all have choice, some of us have virtually none.

2 My reflections this evening are the result of a fairly extensive review of recent literature on the subject, interviews I conducted with twenty women, and my own personal and professional experiences.

3 In 1954 Ann Morrow Lindberg wrote *Gifts From the Sea,* in which she said,

> What a circus act we women perform every day of our lives. It puts the trapeze artist to shame. Look at us. We run a tight rope daily, balancing a pile of books on the head. Baby carriage, parasol, kitchen chair, still under control. Steady now! This is not the life of simplicity, but the life of multiplicity that the wise men warn us of. It leads not to unification but to fragmentation. It does not bring grace, it destroys the soul. And this is not true only of my life, I am forced to conclude; it is the life of millions of women in America. I stress America, because today, the American woman more than any other has the privilege of choosing such a life.

4. Thirty-five years ago, when these words were printed, the world was an entirely different place. The roles of men and women were clearly defined. And while there were certainly women pioneers forging their way into the professions, most women knew without a doubt that their primary responsibility lay with the family. If they needed for financial reasons to earn wages outside of the home, they did so. The primary focus, however, was not on our personal development but rather on the woman's commitment within the home. Well-to-do women who ventured forth in pursuit of careers, were not taken seriously, but considered a novelty; kind of cute. In those days, women were encouraged to marry so that they would be cared for, and to marry well meant finding a husband who made it so one did not have to work. Middle income women who did work did so out of economic need, risking the stigma that their husbands were not succeeding well enough to afford for them to stay at home. But, whether we worked for pleasure or necessity, women still, first and foremost, were mothers and wives. That was a time when childbirth meant a return to the home from our jobs and, in most cases, we stayed at home with our young at least until they were school aged. Women worked conscientiously out of personal and societal obligation to sustain their responsibilities to the family and community. It was within that environment that Lindberg wrote of the fragmentation and multiplicity of a woman's life. Imagine what she might say if she were writing today.

5 Today, when on a weekday, I walk my son to the neighborhood playground, where we find empty swings, quiet benches, and solitude. Thirty-five years ago, that same park would have been filled with the sound of playing children, crying babies, and chatting women whose discussions would have leant support to one another for the lives they were living. Not today. Today, most children play in day care centers, or in the backyards of baby sitters' homes.

6 Life now is significantly different from the days when our mothers pushed strollers to the park. As far as I can tell, it is a much more complicated world, especially for American women. Not only have we got a pile of books on our head dealing with family and home, but both arms are filled as well dealing with our careers. Today, over 80 percent of wage earning women are also mothers and managers of the home. Whether this lifestyle is chosen out of economic necessity, economic preference, or out of a desire for career advancement and intellectual fulfillment, the choices have been made. And with these choices, we have inherited difficult and burdensome consequences.

7 Consider the following statistics: The number of working women with children under age 1 increased 70 percent during the past decade. Seventy-three percent of employed women are of child-bearing age, and women with children under 6 are the fastest growing segment of the workforce. The number of divorced, widowed, or separated working women with children under 18 years of age increased 76 percent between 1971 and 1982. In 1984, 11 million men and 6 million women were the only wage earners in their families. Among all American families, nearly 1 out of 5 is maintained by a woman, with ⅓ of them having incomes below the poverty line. Today, fewer than 9.9 percent of U.S. households consist of a man working outside the home and a woman at home taking care of the household and children.

8 This is the reality, but it is also a reality that women have greater opportunities than ever before for achieving economic and professional success. The opportunities are greater to define our roles as individuals and women. We have much more freedom of choice in career, mate, offspring, and life-style. Thirty-five years ago, it would have been difficult and in many cases impossible for our mothers to become MBA's; M.D.'s; C.P.A.'s; clergy; electricians; computer technicians; dentists and newscasters.

9 However, the privilege of choice is bittersweet. Because, with choice, comes the natural obligation and desire to choose. Although our choices have brought us freedom, they have also brought us hectic, fragmented, complex, lives. The problem isn't hard work. Hard work is not new to women. On the contrary, in many ways life was much harder in the past. The stress we bear today is a different beast from the pain we carried in the past. Today's burden is more mental than it is physical; it is more a matter of unclear role definition; guilt; lack of support and the emotional stress inherent in a life of multiple, conflicting responsibilities.

10 In the past, only very few women had, and exercised the choices open to us today. Now, more women are equal or major wage earners in the household. As the cost of living soars, two incomes per family are required to sustain the quality of life given us by our parents, so there is pressure on women to earn a living as well as to be a homemaker. Today, the breadth and complexity of a woman's role expands far beyond what our parents would have imagined as they began their adult lives, 30, 40 and 50 years ago.

11 The concern is not about having choices. In fact, most women if asked would say they are grateful to the women of the past whose sweat, and devotion, and tears have created the opportunities we relish today. Most of us enthusiastically embrace the opportunities that exist. Technology has given us time our grandmothers never had. The problem is that we have filled that time in the exercise of our new found options, and are attempting to handle husbands, children, community work, shopping, laundry, house repairs, cooking, political leadership, PTA, *and* careers. Careers in which women demand to be treated equally with men, which has meant working the same 50 and 60 hour weeks that men put in at the office in order to succeed at the level that men do. As women today we drive cars, and tractors, and ships, and shopping carts. We wear overalls and tailored suits and aprons and maternity clothes. We carry brief cases, and shopping bags, and chain saws, and bricks, and vacuum cleaners, and calculators, and ledgers, and babies.

12 Thirty-five years ago, Anne Morrow Lindberg wrote:

> To be a woman is to have interests and duties, raying out in all directions, from the central mother-core, like spokes from the hub of a wheel. The pattern of our lives is essentially circular. We must be open to all points of the compass, husband, children, friends, home, community; stretched out, exposed, sensitive like a spider's web to each breeze that comes. How difficult for us, then, to achieve a balance in the midst of these contradictory tensions; and yet, how necessary for the proper functioning of our lives.

13 This she wrote a generation ago in a changing and yet traditional society. Today, however, we function in the midst of radical social change, in a transition of rapidly shifting roles, responsibilities, and expectations. Expectations from others, and expectations self imposed. Women's diverse interests and aspirations have few, if any natural limits . . . which is a dream many mothers worked for their daughters to realize. But that dream also has elements of a nightmare for a number of reasons. For one, we are functioning amidst change, in a social-economic structure which is not yet adapted to embrace the roles we are attempting to assume. It is a nightmare because many employed mothers feel like they are going at it alone. Far more adapted to the working world than it is to working women who are mothers, most of us function with very little understanding from our employers, who have never before been asked to share any interest or responsibility in the family, or in our dual responsibilities to work and home. Far more adapted to the working world than men are to the world of child care and home management, women may have to accept that most men simply are not inclined to do as much as we do in upkeep of the home. Dual career couples and single mothers in the work force face the difficult task of finding child care and then often worry about the quality of care that we do arrange. Many of us have the added responsibility of caring for our aging parents. Employed women are in need of more flexible work options and yet want to excel in the work force. How many of us are there still fighting for equal pay and comparable worth? While adjusting to the changes, and carrying the myriad of responsibilities, many women are beginning to ask whether what we are attempting is even possible. Possible, at least, without the major sacrifices which seem to accompany the choice to pursue this lifestyle.

14 Eighty percent of the women in the work force are mothers and spouses who have chosen, for whatever reason, to assume multiple and competing roles. While this choice makes for a stressful, imbalanced life, the benefits are apparent. Women are experiencing greater economic gains, greater independence, and the enhanced sense of self-worth which comes from making valuable contributions in the work force. But something is wrong. Each of the twenty-two women I spoke with, and nearly all of the literature on the subject I reviewed, indicated a deep and prevalent discontent with trying to do it all.

15 Perhaps what we need to do as individuals and as couples is to think realistically beyond the benefits about what these decisions mean in sacrifices. We should ask ourselves, for example, honestly, do we in some way sacrifice our children's well being when we choose full-time demanding careers? One local resident thinks so and expressed his concerns recently in a newspaper editorial. He writes . . .

> I firmly believe that many of the problems we are now experiencing with our children stem from the fact that we as a society no longer value motherhood. To be a mother and to stay at home at least for the first four years of your child's early development has taken on a stigma that labels women, especially college age women, as something less than a whole person. Our priorities in this country have shifted so that now we place more value on earning large sums of money or on self-centered goals related to career-advancement. No longer do we value as our greatest asset the one thing that can truly bring us happiness— our children. The concept of people sacrificing today for the tomorrow of their children has become quaint and out of date. Who in today's world would suggest that women reassume the lifetime role of homemaker. But unless women and men at all economic levels of society become more willing to participate regularly in the development of their children, even if it means personal sacrifice, nothing the government can do will succeed in solving our long term slide into a third rate country.

16 Could he be correct? It is certainly a concern most employed mothers have, conscious or unconscious. It's no wonder so many of us struggle to find a sense of balance when so much seems to be riding on our decisions. But what of the other side? The side which asks why must it be the woman who gives up the option to pursue a career?

17 Having children almost necessarily means a woman will sacrifice some degree of career success. Most women have found re-entry into the work force to be very difficult after an extended maternity/child rearing leave. And executive women with children truly forgo the ultimate reach for the top of the corporate ladder. Though 90 percent of male executives have children, only 35 percent of their female counterparts are parents. In a 1986 survey of the 413 women that the largest U.S. companies identified as corporate officers, the typical woman was a 44-year-old white protestant who was married, childless, and spent fewer than 10 hours a week on home making tasks. These women believed that motherhood must be foregone to succeed.

18 Do we sacrifice healthy relationships with our husbands? Perhaps not. One recent study revealed that the highest level of marital satisfaction is found among dual career couples. On the other hand, husbands of fully employed mothers may feel an extra burden as well. They too come home to a household of chores waiting to be done. It is more work for both husband and wife at the end of a dual-career work day.

19 Whether the compromise is child-rearing, marriage, career, or simply self-nurturing and preservation, sacrifice is unavoidable. At home mothers have shared with me that given current social patterns, it is emotionally difficult to feel fully valued and personally fulfilled while homemaking full time. Fully employed mothers have shared that it is simply unrealistic, in today's culture, to think that we can excel in a work force that rewards excessive time commitments, and at the end of the day, to be energetic and enthusiastic for their children; cheerful and loving for their husbands.

20 The scenario of the perfect career, wife, and mother is a brutal myth. It is the myth of Clare Huxtible, wife on the popular T.V. Cosby show. Clare Huxtible—a successful lawyer, who returns home at the end of a day in court to a beautiful, clean, orderly house, to greet happy, well adjusted, smiling children. She is a devoted and loving wife with an adoring, supportive husband. Clare Huxtible; woman with a beautiful physique, a radiant smile, and a demeanor always relaxed and in control. There she is, greeting us every Thursday night at 8:00—the epitome of perfect grace; representing the perfect balance so many of us desperately aspire to achieve. The reality is, she does not, and cannot exist.

21 Anyone who has pursued this path knows—something has to give, and does. The reality is that good day care is costly, and very difficult to find. The reality is that ambitious full-time employed mothers are ahead of society at large which has yet to adapt to their presence in the work force. As long as this is the case, most women are going to feel pain and frustration. We will wonder why our employers don't understand that sick babies have to stay home with someone, and that someone is us; we are going to question why it is so difficult to find a good paying part-time job, comparable to our skills and abilities; and we're going to wonder why we feel a constant sense of falling short; in effect *why we're trying to do it at all.* In fact, a recent and increasingly common trend is that employed women who are mothers are leaving the work place, and returning to traditional family roles—a trend which has its own sacrifices and rewards.

22 Women in the work force, mothers at home, women doing both, husbands, fathers, employers, and legislators . . . are all in transition—slowly responding to rapidly changing roles, expectations, and responsibilities of both women and men. Most men are having to rely on the role model provided by their own fathers who functioned in an entirely different world. But, these role models can no longer be relied upon, so men also are forging through new, untreaded territory.

23 An interesting article appeared in the *Chicago Tribune* which was captioned "Men Dragging Feet on Helping Working Wives in the Home." The article opens

> There she is, Ms. America. Dressed for success. Briefcase in one hand, preschooler clutching the other. On the fast track at work. Super mom at home. The woman who has it all. 1990's model. What she also has is most of the housework and child care—and a husband who is far more skilled at evading his fair share than she is at cajoling or bargaining or gently persuading him to do it.

24 The writer proceeds to say that men's underlying feelings about taking responsibility at home have changed much less than women's feelings have changed about forging some kind of identity at work.

25 Employing organizations are also using dated models; models based on the right-to-work ethic, where devotion to the job comes first, and family is cared for by someone else whose responsibility it is to do just that. But demographics are beginning to force the issue, and employers are having to look hard at the growing work force of women. For it's now a widely understood projection that by the year 2000, 61 percent of new entrants to the work force will be women. This means that change is inevitable. Tax breaks for employers who offer family leaves, job-sharing, part-time work, and flexible hours may be necessary costs for doing business.

26 Society lags as well. I believe we need to revalue homemaking and child care so that women and men who choose this role will have sufficient social support, and so employed men will be more comfortable assuming and sharing previously "female" roles. Marriage needs to evolve so that work-sharing couples can become role models of the future. Perhaps we also need to ask whether we can raise our children with values of equitable responsibility within the home and the work place. Wouldn't it be helpful if we taught our sons to cook, and clean, and change the diapers with a sense of satisfaction and esteem? Shouldn't we also teach our daughters to stop apologizing for self imposed failures and to stop nurturing unrealistic standards of success and self imposed guilt? Guilt about being out there while someone else cares for our children. Guilt about dusty window sills. Guilt about being too fatigued at the end of the day to give "quality time" to our husbands and children.

27 How can women find balance in the 90s? Personally, I do not think it is possible as long as we choose to assume multiple and conflicting, socially unsupported roles. What we can do is what women have always done: to bend, adjust, persist, and respond to the demands of each individual moment, then pause briefly for rejuvenation.

28 Can we have it all? Yes. If we can be satisfied with giving less than 100 percent, or even 85 percent to everything we do. If we can live with the sense that nothing receives our full and devoted attention. If we can compromise our standards and expectations.

29 There was a time, not so long ago, that I aspired to have it all, and worked very hard in pursuit of it. Let me take a few minutes, by way of summary, to share with you a bit about my personal quest for balance and perfection.

30 In October of 1989, 6 months pregnant, I left my position as Director of Admissions at the Darden Graduate School of Business Administration to assume the position of Assistant Vice President of Administration for the University of Virginia. At the time, I was also a part-time Ph.D. student in Ethics. I don't know whether it was ego or just pure foolishness, but I was truly convinced that I could be mother to a newborn, graduate student, and spouse, and do all three well. I worked very hard at this vision. I took four weeks maternity leave, returning energetically back to work. And then one day, the day care center teachers walked six children, including my son Ari, up to the Rotunda where my office was located. I nursed Ari, and then handed him back to the care provider. As they walked away—my baby, five other children and two adults—tears began to stream from my eyes, and then an overwhelming sense of grief swelled up inside of me. I realized that I had fallen in love with our son, and that someone else, someone I didn't even know, was raising him. All at once, my goals, dreams, and values came crashing in on one another, and I began to doubt the decisions I had made. After two weeks of painful soul searching and discussions with my husband, it was clear to me that I should find a way to spend more time with Ari. Luckily, my former employer, an ardent supporter of professional working mothers, hired me back into a flexible position which supports my professional, scholarly, and maternal needs.

31 The decision to leave a full-time, lucrative, fairly responsible position, in exchange for a life of mothering and low-keyed work was absolutely the right decision for me. But it might not have been for another woman. It is an individual choice, and in my opinion, it is not inherently, morally a right or wrong choice, just a choice. But mine, and those of countless other women today, was not a choice without pain and some sorrow over the sacrifices made. Who knows what the ramifications are for my future career. But for now, I gladly take the smaller paycheck, and the lesser status for many wonderful hours at home with the family, and a saner, more balanced daily life.

32 Lindberg concluded her book by saying, "we cannot have all the beautiful shells from the sea." Perhaps this is the reality for women in the 90s.

Men and Women Getting Along: These Are Times That Try Men's Souls
Bernice Sandler

On March 26, 1991 Bernice Sandler spoke to several hundred students and faculty at Illinois State University in Normal, Illinois, at a meeting sponsored by the university's Women's Studies Program. Since 1971 Bernice Sandler has been Director of the Project on Status and Education of Women of the Association of American Colleges. Among the many awards received by Sandler are the Women Educators award for activism and the Anna Roe award from Harvard University. The Association of American Colleges promotes "humane and liberating learning," improves public understanding of the value of a liberal education, and explores issues affecting women in higher education.

In a style that relies on informal and colloquial language, Bernice Sandler creates audience concern for the problem of peer harassment on campuses of women by men, especially sexual harassment (6). Even before she identifies her specific topic, she alerts the audience to the difficulty of discussing such a sensitive topic (2–4). She employs a broad range of rhetorical resources to stimulate audience concern. Occasionally she places the problem in the broader context of peer harassment of ethnic groups and of gays and lesbians (5–6, 35). She defines the problem by discussing the range of its manifestations (7), by straightforward explanation (16), and by stressing the role of language choice in our definitions (40). In addition to respect, humaneness, and equality, what other values does she depict as being threatened or violated?

To illustrate the nature and scope of the problem, Sandler profusely employs examples (8–10, 17–18, 21–22, 25–28). Sometimes these examples stem from her personal experience (31–33, 39). In evaluating her use of examples, consider whether a sufficient number of examples was presented, whether the examples were typical instances, and whether there are counter-examples that should be taken into account. At one point she contends that "when things have a name, you know that they are not unusual occurrences, but that they happen often, in many places at many times" (9). To what extent do you accept this argument as an index of the typicality or representativeness of examples?

In order to elaborate one important dimension of the problem, she often illustrates the differing perceptions of the same behavior held by women and men (11, 15, 18, 23–24, 35, 42). How effective would this approach probably be? Why? Another rhetorical resource used to support her analysis is statistics (13–14, 21, 24, 40). How adequately does she substantiate the source and credentials of the research "studies" she draws upon? Or does she seem to assume that the audience simply will rely on her own credibility and honesty? Sandler attempts to avoid over-generalizations (11–12) and to draw careful distinctions (16). How adequately do you believe she does so?

As means of connecting the problem to the experience of her audience, she uses statistics (40), a hypothetical example (41), and a lengthy series of final questions that skillfully underscore the value choices facing the students, especially the men (46). Note particularly her adept use of "role reversal" examples to encourage men to empathize with the problem from the perspective of women (17, 19). A rhetorical critic immediately should note as important her extensive use throughout the speech of questions to provoke thought, as transitions or forecasts, or to underscore conclusions. How well do you believe she employs questions to serve these or other functions?

At length Bernice Sandler analyzes the major causes or "reasons" for the problem (36–42). And at various points she discusses the effects of the problem (12, 39, 43–45)—effects which in one way or another reflect devaluation or debasement of women. Consider how adequately she recognizes multiple and interrelated contributing causes, avoids confusing a causal connection with either chronology or correlation, recognizes both immediate causes and a chain or sequence of causes, explores major relevant effects, and employs sound evidence to support her arguments on causes and effects.

Finally, examine her strategy of dispelling sexual "myths" that unfortunately too often are used to justify sexual harassment (20, 21, 29–30). In what ways is this also an exploration of causes that contribute to the problem? And note that Sandler condemns the "it's just in fun" rationalization used as an excuse.

The text of this speech was provided by Bernice Sandler.

---

1 As everyone knows, the word "men" applies to women as well, and surely these are times that try women's souls as well. Since the days of Adam and Eve, men and women have had trouble getting along. Scholars—psychologists, sociologists, philosophers—indeed almost everyone has some opinion as to what the problems are. So when I venture into this territory, it is with some trepidation because everyone has opinions about what the problems are and what needs to be done, if anything.

2 I want to start off with a question. Do you remember when it was ok for the boys to tease the girls? People laughed—at least the boys laughed. The girls may have been uncomfortable, but nobody took this kind of teasing too seriously. In fact many people thought of it—some still do—as cute, as "boys will be boys," and as natural, normal, behavior.

3 Well, it is not okay anymore. And when big boys do it—men—in this institution or in the workplace, it may well be illegal in many instances. And so tonight, I'm going to talk about some of the negative aspects of men and women getting along. It is not an easy subject to talk about, and many of you may not like or agree with what you hear.

4 It's a subject that is hard for me to talk about, because most of the time I like to joke around, and it's hard for me to joke about this subject. But I hope you will listen and give some thought to this not only because it is important but also because it ultimately relates to what you want to get out of your college experience, and how you will relate to people who are not like you.

5 Ideally the college experience as a whole should help students not only acquire knowledge but also build skills and confidence, learn how to make good choices in life, and particularly how to handle differences, including those of race, class, gender and sexual orientation. All too often, colleges and universities fail in helping men and women meet the challenge of learning to get along. College is a lot more than just going to classes. The social learning that happens outside of the classroom is just as important as what happens inside. The wide range of experiences you have with friends and acquaintances is not only complementary but critical to what you will be learning in the next few years.

6 There is a darker side to campus life, often unnoticed, or if it is acknowledged, it is ignored or brushed off as "normal behavior." That darker side is peer harassment, whether it is men harassing women, men and women harassing gay and lesbian students, women harassing men, but particularly the harassment of women by men students, and that is what I'm going to be talking about tonight. That's the darker side of campus life: peer harassment. For too many students the relationships between men and women are not always positive. Too many women experience hostility, anger, and sometimes even violence from male students.

7 Peer harassment covers a wide range of behaviors. At one end of the scale, peer harassment consists of so-called teasing, sexual innuendos, even obscenities—a sort of sexual bullying, both physical and verbal, often made in the guise of humor. At the other end, is explicit sexual harassment, up to and including sexual aggression, with rape as the most extreme form of peer harassment. Let me give you some examples, both serious and mild, of what I mean, although even mild ones can seriously affect a woman.

8 A woman raises something about women's issues in a class. The men in the class hiss and laugh at her. She is effectively silenced, even though theoretically in a classroom students are supposed to feel free to bring up any issues.

9　Here is another example. A lot of things happen in cafeterias. A group of men regularly sit at a table facing the cafeteria line. As the women go through the line the men loudly discuss the women's sexual attributes—size of breast and how she would act during intercourse—and then they hold up cards, rating each woman from 1 to 10. It's called "scoping", and when things have a name, you know that they are not unusual occurrences, but that they happen often, in many places at many times. Some women do not come to the cafeteria unless they can find a friend and pretend that they don't hear the men; other women skip meals altogether if the men are there.

10　Here is another example. A fraternity pledge approaches a woman student he has never seen before, and bites her on the breast, a practice called "sharking." And another. A group of men simultaneously expose themselves, or in another variation they simply surround a woman, demand that she bare her breasts, and do not allow her to leave the circle until she has done so.

11　I want to be sure that you all understand that not all men harass women students. And certainly not all women students experience this behavior. But just as certainly, on every campus, there are too many men treating women in ways that are disrespectful. That is an old-fashioned word, but I don't know what else to call this behavior, behavior that is invasive and can only be described as emotional and psychological harassment. Often however, the men do not describe their behavior this way. They are just having a good time. If a woman doesn't like it and she takes offense, the men probably say, "She just doesn't have a sense of humor." Yet to the woman, such behaviors can poison her college experience.

12　These behaviors are not universal; they don't occur all the time. And while men can also be harassed by women—that's the subject of another talk—not tonight—women are the majority of the peer harassment victims. What is interesting is that even though the women are harassed by men because they *are women,* not all women recognize these behaviors as harassment. Nevertheless, when these experiences occur again and again, and when they are either unnoticed, ignored by faculty and administrators, or even condoned by other students and some college officials, men and women alike receive the message that women are not to be treated with respect—that women can be treated with disdain and it does not matter to anyone.

13　How much of a problem are we talking about? Well, there have been a few studies—not many—but from the best information we have, somewhere between 70–90 percent of women students have experienced some behavior from male students to which they reacted negatively. 70–90 percent! In contrast, sexual harassment of women students by faculty and staff has a far lower incidence. 20–30 percent of women undergraduates report some form of sexual harassment from someone in authority, with only two percent reporting actual threats or bribes for unwanted sexual activity.

14 Additionally, widespread harassment of women by fraternities has been documented on virtually every campus that has examined fraternity life in the last five years. There is also another group of men that are likely to harass women. Anyone want to guess? Yes. Athletes—and not the swimming team, not the golf team, but the football and basketball teams, occasionally rugby, wrestling, or lacrosse.

15 Much of peer harassment is sexual harassment. In general, sexual harassment involves unwanted sexual attention, and there are a lot of men who think that all women want this and are flattered by any kind of sexual attention, especially if a woman does not indicate any displeasure about the behavior. You see this at construction sites, where, when a woman walks by, the men show their "manliness" by hooting and hollering at her, but this happens elsewhere as well. Now why doesn't the woman indicate any displeasure? Why doesn't she just say "Hey guys, knock it off. I don't like this." Sometimes she thinks if she says anything like that the behavior will get worse. Her strategy is to ignore it because she really wants the behavior to stop; in contrast, his perception is that she must really like it because she didn't say anything.

16 All sexual attention is not sexual harassment. Certainly when men and women are together, sexual attraction is possible, and people will express that attraction. Sexual attention becomes harassment when it is persistent or unwanted or personal boundaries are crossed. What may be appropriate in a continuing relationship is inappropriate coming from a stranger or new acquaintance as in the following examples:

17 Inappropriate personal remarks such as comments about a woman, her body, or sexual activities. Comments such as "You've got great breasts" from a stranger are not perceived as compliments because they depersonalize women—they reduce women to being *only* a sexual object. Her breasts become the most important part of her and it ignores her individuality or humanity. If you are a male person, try to think how you might feel if the first thing someone said to you after being introduced—say, you're a swimming star at a swimming meet, and the first thing someone said when they met you was "you've got a great penis."

18 Unwanted touching or kissing. Women have had their breasts grabbed or have been hugged and kissed by people they did not know well, especially at parties. Sometimes people say that women "ask" for this behavior. "Look at the clothes she wore." This is a good example of how men's clothing and women's clothing are seen very differently. Now women wear clothing to be in style and for their self-esteem, but men, when they see women's clothing, often assume that she is looking for sex. She could be wearing tight pants or loose pants, lowcut clothes or a high neck, ruffles, short skirts, long skirts, short sleeves, long sleeves—indeed whatever a woman wears may be viewed by some men as a sexual invitation. A woman could be wearing an old burlap potato sack and there will be some guy who'll look at her and say "Wow—this is the sexiest potato sack I've ever seen and she obviously wants to have sex, and she obviously wants to have sex with me."

19 Interestingly, men's clothing does not communicate that at all. You're on a campus, and I'm sure you all have seen guys wearing jeans that are so tight that you can surely see the size and shape of the sexual apparatus. But a guy would be shocked if some woman—or man—came up to him and—grabbed—his penis, and when he said, "Hey what's going on here?" the person responded, "well, look at the way you're dressed. You're asking for it."

20 Women's clothing does not communicate a sexual invitation. It does communicate "I am a woman" but it doesn't give anyone else permission to grab or touch. It doesn't signal what a woman wants or what she will do. This is what I call the clothing myth and it essentially views sexual harassment, and to some extent rape, as an extension of biological drives. "She was so beautiful, I just couldn't help myself." It ignores the issue of power which I'll talk about later, but it also shifts the responsibility for the harassment or the rape to the victim. *She* is the one that is causing the men to harass her. It's her fault, not his. The women are causing the men to harass them.

21 Another example is persistent sexual attention. Asking a woman for a date or sex repeatedly, even if the woman has said no. Here we see the operation of another myth, that a woman says "no" when she really means "yes." So there is no way a woman can say "no," and many men feel it incumbent upon themselves to turn that "no" into a "yes." Someone did research on this and it turns out that most women have never said "no" when they meant "yes," and of the 15 or 20 percent that had said "no" when they meant "yes," almost all of these had said "no" when they meant "yes" only one time. So it is a relatively rare phenomenon for women to say "no" whey they really mean "yes."

22 Another thing that happens are requests for sexual activity, such as men shouting obscene sexual invitations through an open dormitory window. This, like other forms of harassment, tells a woman that her individuality doesn't matter. She is being viewed only in terms of her sexuality.

23 Now, sometimes when sexual harassment or rape occurs, the man involved says, "well she asked for it." And when you ask questions about this, he usually refers to her clothing or her behavior. A woman smiled; he views it as a sexual invitation. A woman talked to him; and he views it as a sexual invitation. Indeed men often mistake a woman's friendliness as a sexual invitation.

24 Someone did a study on this. They taped several conversations of men and women talking to each other, and then showed the segments to a group of men and women and asked them to decide for each segment whether the woman was being friendly or was "coming on" to the guy. The women who view the video say for each segment, "she's being friendly, she's being friendly, she's being friendly." The men, in contrast, say "She's coming on to the guy, she wants to have sex with him, she's coming on strong." So we have a misperception here. Women are more likely to see friendliness and men are more likely to see sexual invitations. Think of how this affects the relationships between men and women.

25 Another example is a sexually demeaning climate, such as leaving pornographic materials in a woman's mailbox or in front of her dormitory door. Sometimes there are sexist posters or pictures or bumper stickers. At one fraternity party there was a poster on the door which said "No fat chicks allowed." Since 75% of young women believe that they are overweight, at least 75 percent of the women were offended.

26 Sexist graffiti can be on desks and walls, in library carrels or on cafeteria tables. Often the graffiti may also be racist or anti-semitic, or offensive to gays and lesbians. The graffiti can stay for years, often offending generations of students because most institutions ignore it. Syracuse University has one of the few programs to periodically examine the campus for graffiti and remove it. The only other example I know of graffiti being removed occurred at Brown University, where on the wall of the women's restrooms, women have begun to write the names of male students who have raped women students. These names are removed each day.

27 Let me give you an example of offensive graffiti. One university has a "free expression tunnel" which connects both sides of the campus which is divided by a railroad track. There is a painting of a Raggedy Ann doll, mutilated and bruised, with blood streaming between the doll's legs, and the statement, "I raped Raggedy Ann." What do women feel when they walk by this several times daily? And what do men feel as they see it? And is this the kind of free expression we should be encouraging?

28 Other examples of the chilly climate for women are wet T-shirt contests, activities focussing on women's sexuality, showing pornographic movies as fundraisers—that happen's at a lot of campuses—or petty hostility toward women, such as throwing things at women, heckling women, pouring drinks over women's heads or inside their clothing. All of these give men and women a message—a message that women don't count except as sexual objects, that friendship with women is not possible, and that women are natural objects of scorn and derision.

29 Now a lot of these activities are seen as fun, and if someone doesn't think so, they are accused as having no sense of humor. That's the worst thing you can say about someone, no sense of humor.

30 Now humor is important, it can be used to relax people and lighten them up. But humor has other functions. It can also be used to enhance group solidarity, to define the outsider, in this case women, and to discuss subjects that are taboo. So rather than discuss gender and sexuality, we find it easier to joke about them instead. And it can also be used to express anxiety and anger and discomfort and resentment, in this case, against women.

31 I've become very interested in humor in recent years, especially when I noticed that all of the so-called locker-room jokes are demeaning to women. So I began to think there must be jokes demeaning to men and I began to seek out these jokes—not because I'm interested in demeaning men—some of my best friends are men—but because I'm curious about the uses of humor. I have been collecting for several years, and I must tell you, jokes demeaning men are quite rare—I have about ten, and some of these are variations on the others. I'm not talking about jokes which demean some men, such as Scotsmen and hillbilly men but jokes which demean men as a group.

32 And there is a difference between the jokes that demean men and the ones that demean women. The jokes that demean women demean them in all sorts of roles, activities, and behaviors. The jokes that demean men are very limited. They deal with sexual performance and size of the reproductive organ. I'm not sure what these differences mean, but they are interesting, and I also have to tell you that I can't yet tell these jokes in public. If you know of any and want to tell them to me, I'll be glad to add them to my collection.

33 A few years ago the first of my daughters got married, and I was very happy about the forthcoming marriage, I like the young man, etc. But as the time for the wedding approached, I found myself becoming more and more uncomfortable. I finally realized what it was. I, who had been a fairly likeable person, was about to become a mother-in-law, the kind of person who is often ridiculed in jokes. I could see that I was entering a dangerous stage of my life. And again I said, there are a lot of mother-in-law jokes ridiculing women, so where are the father-in-law jokes. I'm even offering a reward of $25 for a father-in-law joke, because I don't think there are any.

34 Now what do these jokes about women tell us? They tell us that there is anger against women, anxiety, and perhaps even fear. I don't understand all of the dynamics about mother-in-law jokes but probably the mother-in-law is a stand-in for anger against one's own mother, one's spouse, or all women.

35 Similarly racist humor, ethnic humor, jokes about JAPS (the Jewish America Princess), jokes about Black women or other ethnic women are not simple fun, for too often what passes for humor is humor at the expense of someone else. What the men see as friendly fun is often viewed by the women as harassment, even though they may not use that term to define it. The men are having a good time with each other. This is how they build solidarity with each other, by being nasty to women.

36 Now since most men are nice guys, what is going on here? People who might not heckle people of another race may have no difficulty in engaging in the same behavior if the object of their disrespect is female. Well, there are a lot of reasons why, and here are some of them.

37 At a very early age, boys learn to use girls as what the sociologists call a "negative reference group." In other words, the boys define themselves by comparing themselves favorably to girls, the lesser group, the females. After all, what is the worst thing you can call a little boy? A sissy—which says he is acting like a girl. By teasing girls a boy begins to feel good about himself—he is "better" than they are, and teasing them makes him feel like a "real boy." Moreover, by putting down girls and females he can get closer to his buddies. They can all put down the girls, and feel better and bigger than the girls. Harassment, and even sexual assault, can be, for many men, the way in which they show other

men how "manly" they really are. We see this in its extreme in the case of gang rape, where psychologists have noted that the men are not raping for sexual reasons but are really raping for each other. This is how they show their friends how strong, how virile, how manly, how wonderful they are. This is how they strengthen the bond with their brothers. They need to be one of the boys and they find it difficult to go against the group. Harassment, whether it is gang rape or heckling women, is used by some men as a way to bond with their brothers.

38 For some men, harassment and sexual abuse expresses their need to show power over women. In that sense it is something like the bully syndrome—the men feel better and stronger by picking on someone they perceive as weaker than themselves, the women. Some men think primarily in stereotypes, so that they may be uncomfortable with women who have minds of their own. Some men may be angry at feminism, or angry at a particular woman, or at all women in general. Harassment, after all, is simply a milder form of assault. It tells women that men can intimidate them at will.

39 Alcohol and drugs can play a role by lowering people's inhibitions and creating an atmosphere where hurtful and even violent behavior, even a gang rape, can be seen as amusing. Pornography, easily available on most campuses, often portrays situations in which women are weak and treated badly, where women enjoy rape, pain, and humiliation, where violence against women is often an integral part of the scenario. Violence toward women, whether in pornography, movies, music videos and TV, promotes a perception of women as outsiders, as people who are less than human, as people who are objects for men to exploit, manipulate, and harm. Additionally, men in groups are often more prone to bad behavior— in a group, such as a fraternity, or as part of an athletic team, a man may do things that he might not otherwise do, because he is afraid of the hostility of the other men. The peer pressure is very strong. One of the things we need to do is to teach men how to stand up to other men when they are behaving badly, and to say "don't do that." I myself know of several attempted gang rapes that were stopped, simply because one man was strong enough to say something like "Hey guys, cut it out. Let her alone."

40 Moreover, peer harassment sets the stage for rape. Rape is merely the extreme form of peer harassment. The men who intimidate women are most likely to commit assault on women. Remember earlier I told you that 70–90% of women experience some form of peer harassment. I want to give you the figures for acquaintance rape, when one person forces or intimidates another to have intercourse and where both parties know each other. If you ask the men "Have you ever raped a woman?", most will say "No." But if you ask the question, "Have you ever forced or intimidated a woman to have sexual intercourse with you, between 10–15% will say yes. For women, the figures are more striking. Somewhere between 15 and 25% of undergraduate women have been raped by someone they know. They don't all call it rape, but if you ask them if anyone has ever forced or intimidated them to have sexual intercourse when they did not want to, that is when you get these 15–25% figures. How many is 15–25% of the women on this campus? That is a lot of women. Peer harassment makes it possible.

41 Other factors: Men are generally socialized in our society to be dominant, and that plays a role in peer harassment. Women have been socialized to play a secondary role, so that men are trained to talk, and women are trained to listen. Who has the most power in our society? Who has the most money? The best jobs? Look at our Supreme Court, our Congress, your own institution. Who holds most of the administrative posts? If you do not believe that men have more power, think of the following. You are walking alone on a dark street—it doesn't matter what sex you are. You see six women on the corner. Are you frightened? Same scenario, next night. You are walking alone on a dark street, and you see six men on the corner. Are you frightened? Who has more power in our society—men or women?

42 There are many stereotypes about women being weaker and passive, although these stereotypes interfere with our view of women as equals. We like to think of men and women, at least intellectually, as equals. But in reality, sexual relations—especially those that occur in a context of sexual harassment, sexual teasing and joking to show power, sexual bullying, and sexual assault—these occur within an implicit power relationship where one person, usually the male, has the power to intimidate and cause harm to the other— usually a woman—through physical and social means. Most men are not conscious of their power to intimidate women, although they may use that power often. In contrast women often recognize the power of men. Men and women have very different perceptions of the relationship between the sexes. Just the other day I read a chilling quotation by the author, Margaret Atwood. I found the quotation in some materials put out by a Wisconsin group called Men Stopping Rape. This is the quotation that the men chose to include in their materials. "Why are you afraid of women?" I asked a group of men. "We're afraid they will laugh at us," replied the men. "Why are you afraid of men?" I asked a group of women. "We're afraid they'll kill us," replied the women." End of quote. The quote shows how men and women view each other very differently and that men are not aware of the power that they hold and how they use that power.

43 It makes it difficult for women to say "Stop that, it bothers me." It makes it difficult for women to report harassment and sexual intimidation. Some women are frightened of retaliation. Some may believe that nothing is going to happen, so why bother? Some women begin to believe that this is the way men are, and nothing can change them. Others don't know about or trust their institution's grievance procedure. And sad to say, some women collude in the harassment and intimidation. They have accepted the ideology that any kind of sexual attention is flattery. They may be angry about feminism in part because they have implicitly accepted the myths of men's domination and power—the myths, the beliefs, and the attitudes that support sexual harassment and intimidation that make women believe that they caused the harassment. They may have seen films like "Animal House" and other media which make them believe that this is the way you have a good time. They may not want to antagonize men because they want to be liked and they are fearful of men being angry at them.

44 Peer harassment makes women feel less than equal. They may feel uncomfortable and annoyed. They may feel embarrassed, humiliated or degraded. They may feel disgusted, they may feel helpless, angry, unsure of how to respond. They may feel insulted, and they may be fearful of violence. They may also feel guilty and blame themselves, as if they did something that caused the men to act so badly. The cumulative effect of repeated harassment can be devastating. It reinforces self-doubt, and affects a woman's self-esteem, and even her academic experience. It makes coeducation less equal for women. It makes some women angry at men, and it may make it more difficult for some women to trust men.

45 Peer harassment also affects men. Peer harassment teaches men that relationships based on power are better than those based on intimacy and friendship. It makes it difficult for a man to form a healthy and satisfying relationship with a woman because it is hard to be committed to someone for whom he and others have so little respect. When men view women as objects to be demeaned and scorned, men find it difficult to relate to women as equal human beings—much less as friends or potential romantic partners or as co-workers. Even a man's friendship with other men will be shallow if the way to friendship with his brothers is to ridicule women rather than [build] a friendship based on shared feelings.

46 Let me end with some questions and then we can have some discussion. You are at the beginning of your adulthood. How do you want to relate to members of the other sex while you are in college? How do you want to relate both personally and professionally when you finish college? Do you want to be able to be friends and colleagues? Can you respect someone who is different from you? Can you have a relationship of equality or must it be based on power? Do you want a relationship where sex exists for its own sake and is not for intimacy or caring or sharing? Do we want men to continue to believe that the way to get points with their peers and the way to feel good about themselves and their sexuality is to dominate, to use and exploit women? Do we want men and women to believe that relationships with the other sex that are based on power are better than relationships based on mutual respect and intimacy?

47 The world is changing. The relationships between men and women are changing. Increasingly women are labeling forced sexual activity as rape, and calling peer harassment by name. The days of "boys will be boys" are fast disappearing as young men and young women are learning that the new world is a world in which men and women recognize that whatever their differences, they are equal, and that they must share a world in which they can work together, a world in which men and women are no longer adversarial, a world in which women and men can be friends.

48 Let me close with something that is characteristic of the new mood of women. It is "a newly discovered Biblical revelation," which was discovered in the Middle East by a woman archeologist, of course, assisted by women staff. You'll probably recognize the paraphrase, and it goes like this:

> And they shall beat their pots and pans into printing presses
> And weave their cloth in protest banners.
> Nations of women shall lift up their voices with nations of other women,
> Neither shall they suffer discrimination anymore. [By Mary Chagnon]

49 That may sound apocryphal, but I suspect it may yet prove to come from the book of Prophets, for what women are learning is the politics of power and the politics of change, and the campus and the nation, and the world shall never again be the same.

Do You Think You Know Me?
Peggy Dersch

Peggy Dersch delivered this speech in a college oratorical contest when she was a student at Southeast Missouri State University. She was coached by Tom Harte.

This is an unusual speech and therefore this brief introductory statement will not divulge the main thrust the speaker develops. We will simply present a series of topics and questions you may want to keep in mind as you read the speech and discuss it in class.

• The speech begins situationally. Why do situations tend to be effective interest-getting introductions?

• Identify key interest factors in this speech. What about the use of dialogue? Parallelisms in paragraph 5? The element of surprise? The use of examples? Direct involvement of the audience? What techniques does the speaker use to involve the audience?

• The speaker states her purpose in paragraph 6. Observe how she briefly delineates her purpose to clarify the thrust of her speech.

• Speech textbooks commonly advise speakers to show personal involvement with the topic, or, at the very least, show a relationship with the topic. How important is this in terms of establishing personal credibility?

• Has the speech affected your attitude towards the speaker's subject? Could the same results have been achieved with a different approach?

This speech is reprinted by permission of the Interstate Oratorical Association from *Winning Orations,* 1980, pp. 60–63.

1 It was winter, 1976. A news item concerning the attempted rape of an eight-year-old child was reported on WABC-TV in New York City. Following the news, the station's weather announcer, Tex Antoine, began his report by reminding viewers of what he called an ancient proverb; "Confucius once say: If rape is inevitable, relax and enjoy it!" After enough protest calls, station officials required Antoine to offer a public apology. He said simply, "I regret making the statement." And then he added, "I didn't realize the victim was a child."

2 The ignorance about rape displayed by Tex Antoine is not uncommon. In Chicago, Illinois, Gallant Greetings Corporation produced and distributed a birthday card. On the front was a disheveled woman with a wide grin across her face. The inscription read, "Birthdays are like rape." Then you open the card the message continued. "When it's inevitable—enjoy . . . enjoy . . . ." There was a space to sign your name, and then the final phrase, "Happy Day!"

3 Jokes about rape are not difficult to find. But the truth is, rape is no laughing matter. When we consider the fact that every night of the year, in fact every 14 minutes day and night all year long a woman is forcibly raped, we realize that rape is a very serious matter.

4 But you don't have to share the ignorance of a Tex Antoine or the Gallant Corporation to be guilty of misunderstanding the nature of the crime of rape. As a matter of fact, all of us, everyone in this room, is a victim of stereotype. We are all prejudiced against the rape victim. I know, and I intend to show you.

5 Now, let me assure you this is not just another speech on rape. In fact, let me make a few things clear about my intentions before I go any further. First of all, don't get the idea I'm out to accuse anyone of being apathetic or unconcerned. I'm not. Don't expect me to shock you with the latest probability figures showing that everyone in this room will be raped within the next ten days. I'm not. Don't think I'm trying to repulse you with brutal accounts of a victim's experience or horrifying stories of courtroom battles. I'm not.

6 My purpose is simply this: to make everyone here think more critically about how he views the crime of rape. You see, this is not a speech on rape, but on the attitudes we all have toward it—attitudes which are frequently as serious a problem as the act of rape itself.

7 Rape is an unusual crime. Some of us, like Tex Antoine, make a joke of it; others of us cry about it; and still others choose not to talk about it at all. But whatever our response to rape, one thing remains constant and is a factor which separates rape from any other crime in the book: we see the rapist as a criminal, but we tend to see the rape victim that way too. Society attributes at least part of the blame to the victim herself. We see her somehow at fault.

8 I suppose there are lots of reasons for this. Some of us choose to believe that deep down women secretly want to be raped—that they ask for it. You might think this attitude is outdated but it still survives, even in our courts of law.

9 Let me give you an example. In Dane County, Wisconsin, Judge Archie Simonson let a 15-year-old boy off with only probation for raping a 16-year-old girl in the stairwell of their high school. His explanation? "I'm trying to say to women—stop teasing. . . . Whether women like it or not, they are sex objects." You probably recognize this statement for the ignorance it represents. But even those who reject the notion that the victim invited the attack may still fall for the view that she didn't resist hard enough.

10 "Why didn't she fight back?" we say. "You can't hit a moving target." So common is this myth that even rape victims themselves believe it. I recently read a magazine article about one such victim; her name is Linda Rogers. She recalled: "Before the rape, I would have been surprised that a victim might feel guilty. Yet I did—not that I had invited the rape, but that I should have been able to prevent it."

11 Her feelings might be easier to understand when we examine what is currently being taught in criminology courses. For example, here's what one of the most widely used criminology textbooks, Daniel Glasner's *Adult Crime and Social Policy,* has to say: "To force a woman into intercourse is an impossible task in most cases if the female is conscious and extreme pain is not inflicted."

12 And this text is not unusual. According to Dr. Gail Wisan, professor of sociology at George Washington University, each of today's 13 most popular criminology texts, all of them published since 1970 and over half since 1975, include similar examples. Is it really any wonder that so many hold the attitudes they do? Now, of course, not everybody believes that women want to be raped or that they don't try hard enough to resist an attack. But even though we know that, we may still subconsciously feel that somehow, some way, a woman brings rape on herself.

13 Social psychologists call this the "just world hypothesis"—a belief that bad things just don't happen to good people—or, in other words, good women don't get raped. But whatever the logic or reasoning behind it, however you explain the tendency to view the rape victim as a criminal herself, the perception exists, and its effects are devastating. For example, one rape victim called a Boston Hospital follow-up counselor and explained: "I am having problems with my family. No one wants to have anything to do with me. My grandmother doesn't want me to tell my brother and I want him to know. She says it is a shame on the family. No one is talking with me. They won't even say hello to me. Even my husband is ashamed of me."

14 And the effects can be more than just psychological. A friend of mine who worked one summer in a rape crisis center in St. Louis, Missouri, told me about Sandy, a 14-year-old girl who was raped two years ago. The only girl from a large religious family, she was considered an outcast by her parents. In their own words, she had been "violated" and, therefore, was unmarriageable material. Today, at age 16, Sandy is a runaway.

15 Too often peoples' attitudes about rape and their perception of the victim do as much damage as the rapist himself. And more of us than we'd like to admit harbour these attitudes.

16 Now perhaps many of you at this point are saying to yourselves, "Not me—I don't feel that way." Maybe you're right. But maybe you're wrong. Unless I'm mistaken, everyone in this room is subject to ill-conceived attitudes about rape victims. All of us, even you, are victims of a stereotype. And I think I can prove it to you.

17 Most of you have never met me before, yet even so you have been developing just in these few minutes an idea of what I'm like, so that by now you have some notion or image of me, Peggy Dersch. Now let me tell you something about myself that you don't know. At the age of 13 I was violently and forcibly raped in the home of a friend. (Don't worry, I'm not going to recount any details for you. I promised I wouldn't, remember?)

18 Already your impressions of me are beginning to change, aren't they? Just in these last few seconds your image of me has been altered by two words—rape victim.

19 If you were to meet me again I'm almost sure you'd act differently than you would have ten minutes ago. And if I happened to be wearing shorts or a t-shirt you might even raise an eyebrow or sneer. Why? Because I'd be asking for trouble. You see, when a woman is labeled "rape victim," ordinary behavior is reinterpreted in sexual terms. Any attractiveness in dress or figure is held against her.

20 Is there anyone in this room who can honestly say that his impression of me has not changed just a little? Is there anyone who can honestly say he doesn't see me as a little cheapened, a little less wholesome? I've seen it happen before. I have just labeled myself rape victim, and Peggy Dersch the rape victim is different from the Peggy Dersch you knew before, isn't she?

21 I could be wrong. My point may be totally erroneous. But I can tell you this. In a survey taken in July of last year, 25% of those responding said they believed they'd be treated by their family and friends as though they were partly to blame if they were raped. Even though many said their families would be sympathetic, all of the respondents expressed a feeling that the rape victim is still considered at fault, either for having led someone on or for not having resisted more. In a word, many considered her "cheapened" by the experience.

22 Now please don't misunderstand; I'm not asking you for sympathy and I'm not casting blame or trying to make you feel guilty. And I'm not saying that we haven't done a great deal already to lift the "veil of shame" around the subject of rape. But it's still there. So I only ask you to level with yourself; think for a moment whether you are truly free of the prejudice against rape victims which abounds in our society. Do you somehow look down upon me and others like me, even though you know better? Don't be surprised or ashamed if you do. The attitude is quite common. And until all of us, individually and collectively as a society, can come to grips with that attitude, we will make little progress against what may well be the most reprehensible crime of all. I ask you to consider how you would act if your sister, or daughter, or wife, or someone else you love were raped. How would you treat her? And how are you going to treat me?

Faye Wattleton, President of Planned Parenthood Federation of America.

CHAPTER 7

SPEECHES THAT AFFIRM PROPOSITIONS OF POLICY

...I have suspected for some time that the key division of this society, given the awesome rate of change and what it has done to tradition and values, is not a classic ideological or economic split, but how people react to change. Whether they welcome it, merely accept it, or, as in many cases, feel deeply threatened by it.

David Halberstam

THE NATURE AND IMPORTANCE OF SPEECHES
THAT AFFIRM PROPOSITIONS OF POLICY

Whenever people have been free to choose their personal or collective destinies, speakers have arisen to advocate courses of action. When a President of the United States stands before a television camera to encourage popular approval of a Supreme Court ruling, he or she is proposing a course of action. When a legislator stands at the rostrum of a state senate to recommend adoption of a new taxation program, he or she is advocating a policy. When a social reformer urges the abolition of capital punishment, a union official the rejection of a contract, a theologian an end to doctrinal conflict, or politicians a vote in their behalf, they all are engaged in the affirmation of policies.

Listeners and speakers would benefit from holding a *process view,* rather than a static view, of life. Such a view assumes that change, process, and coping with change are normal rather than exceptional phenomena. There is no "status quo," no static existing state of affairs, to defend. Present policies and programs always evolve, modify, and change to some degree. The choice is not between change and nonchange. The choices center on how to manage the speed, degree, and direction of inevitable change. Solutions and policies never are entirely permanent. No sooner has a program been instituted than the conditions which necessitated it have altered somewhat and new conditions have arisen, thus at least partly rendering the program obsolete.

Although a society's problems have been clearly illuminated, that society will not grow and prosper unless effective courses of action are advocated and undertaken. Some critics of contemporary American society argue that advocates today too seldom conceive and present effective policies. The blunt evaluation in 1951 by William G. Carleton, a professor of political science, still seems remarkably applicable to much public discourse today:

> American speeches . . . for the most part have ceased seriously to examine fundamental policy, to discuss first principles, to isolate and analyze all the possibilities and alternative courses with respect to a given policy. . . . The result is that speeches today are rarely intellectually comprehensive or cogently analytical.

One reason for this shortcoming is the complexity of propositions of policy. The call to take action or change policy is made up of a number of intermediate claims involving all of the intellectual and rhetorical operations identified in the preceding chapters. For example, a speaker who is trying to demonstrate that "It is necessary for the federal government to subsidize the higher education of superior students" might first affirm the proposition of fact that "Many qualified high school graduates are unable to attend college for financial reasons," the proposition of value that "The development of the nation's intellectual resources is socially desirable," and the problem-centered claim that "The loss of intellectual resources constitutes a significant contemporary social and economic problem."

Speakers try to win acceptance of facts and values and create concern for problems on the basis that they are *true, good,* or *significant.* Speakers advocate policies in belief that they are *necessary* and/or *desirable*. You might note that in the phrasing of propositions of policy, the term *should* (meaning it is necessary or desirable that) appears with great frequency.

Although many persuaders urge *adoption* of a new policy or course of action, in *Perspectives on Persuasion,* Wallace Fotheringham suggests other important categories of action that speakers may seek. In addition to adoption, speakers may defend *continuance* of an existing policy, urge *discontinuance* of an existing policy, or seek *deterrence* by arguing against adoption of a proposed policy. Sometimes speakers urge retention of the basic principles or structure of an existing policy along with *revision* of means and mechanisms of implementing that policy.

All of the following assertions may be classified as propositions of policy:

Proposition A: The negative income tax should be adopted.

Proposition B: The United States should continue its support of the United Nations.

Proposition C: The use of marijuana should be decriminalized.

Proposition D: Federal regulation of the print mass media should not be adopted.

If speakers have been intellectually shallow in affirming propositions of policy, at least a portion of the blame must rest with the audiences who place too few demands on the speakers' rhetorical behaviors.

CRITERIA FOR EVALUATING SPEECHES THAT AFFIRM PROPOSITIONS OF POLICY

Although propositions of policy may call for continuance, discontinuance, deterrence, and revision in addition to adoption, the criteria that follow are written for the speech seeking adoption. The criteria can be made applicable to the other kinds of propositions of policy through modest rephrasing.

1. Has the speaker demonstrated or is it readily apparent that a need exists for a fundamental change in policy?

Because programs for action are responses to problems, the critic first should consider whether a legitimate problem exists. Among the subquestions the evaluator will wish to consider are the following:

- Are there circumstances that may legitimately be viewed as a problem?
- Is the present policy to blame for such problems?

• Is the problem sufficiently severe to require a change in policy, or may it be met through repairs, adjustments, or improvements in the present program?

In establishing a need for a fundamental change in policy, the speaker may affirm a series of propositions related to facts, values, and problems, each of which may be tested by the listener against criteria developed in earlier chapters.

2. Has the speaker provided a sufficient view of the nature of the new policy or program?

If a speech affirming a proposition of policy is to have maximum impact, the audience must know exactly what is to be done and how to do it. A sound, well-rounded policy usually encompasses not only the basic principles to guide the course of action but also the specific steps, procedures, or machinery for implementing that policy.

When the speaker describes the nature of a policy, he or she seeks increased understanding and should be assessed by the same criteria outlined in Chapter 3: Has the speaker made the policy meaningful to the audience? Has the speaker explained the policy in a sufficiently interesting way? Has the speaker shown the audience that the information is important?

3. Has the speaker demonstrated that the new policy will remedy the problem?

If the speaker is to be successful, the audience must believe that the policy will solve the problem and that it realistically can be put into operation. Among the questions that the listener should raise are the following:

• Can the policy be put into effect?
• Is the policy enforceable once it has been instituted?
• Will the policy alleviate the specific problem or problems described by the speaker (by removing the basic causes, or by speedily treating symptoms of a problem the causes of which are unknown)?

In response to such questions, a speaker will affirm one or more propositions of fact by advancing varied arguments. Speakers may argue that the proposed course of action has worked effectively elsewhere in similar situations; that analogous policies have succeeded in remedying similar problems; that experts attest to its ability to solve the problem. The best expert testimony is that which supports the specific program advocated, not just the general principle of the policy. Through word pictures and descriptions the audience should be made to vividly visualize the desirable consequences that will follow if the solution is adopted, and the undesirable consequences that will occur if it is not adopted.

4. Has the speaker demonstrated that the new policy is advantageous?

In addition to showing that the policy will alleviate the problem, the speaker should demonstrate that the policy will produce significant additional benefits and should indicate clearly how the advantages will outweigh any possible disadvantages. A speaker who advocates federal economic aid for public education could show that this policy would not only ease the immediate shortages of facilities and equipment but also would have the additional benefit of helping to equalize educational opportunity throughout the nation. The speaker might stress that the possible remote defect of federal interference in local educational matters is far outweighed by definite immediate advantages and benefits. To demonstrate such benefits, the speaker should employ appropriate examples, statistics, analogies, and expert testimony.

Because people characteristically resist new courses of action in favor of traditional policies, the speaker often will find it wise to recognize in advance and deprecate relevant major policies and arguments that run counter to the proposed policy. Beyond providing adequate reasons for adopting the proposed policy, the speaker frequently must refute alternative programs and opposing arguments. An advocate might directly refute opposing arguments with evidence and reasoning; or show that the arguments, while true in general, really are irrelevant to the specific proposal at hand; or show that the arguments have only minimal validity and are outweighed by other considerations.

People also judge the advantageousness of policies on the basis of personal values and goals. An audience of business people may judge a program partly by the effect it will have on corporate profits. An audience of clergy may judge a policy by its consistency with spiritual values. An audience of minority group members may judge a proposal by the contribution it will make to equality of opportunity. An audience of laborers may judge a program by its effect on their wages. No matter who composes the audience, the speaker advancing propositions of policy must recognize that the values, wants, and goals of listeners influence their evaluation of courses of action. An advantageous policy not only removes the causes of a problem but also harmonizes with such values as efficiency, speed, economy, fairness, humaneness, and legality.

In evaluating speeches affirming propositions of policy, the listener could ask such questions as these:

- Does the policy have significant additional benefits?
- Do the advantages of the policy outweigh its disadvantages?
- Does the policy have greater comparative advantages than other relevant policies?
- Can the policy be experimented with on a limited basis before full-scale adoption is undertaken?
- Is the policy consistent with relevant personal and societal values?

In responding to these questions, the capable speaker will affirm a cluster of evaluative and factual propositions. Such propositions may, in turn, be evaluated in terms of the criteria proposed in earlier chapters.

Although the advocate may sometimes find it wise to fulfill each of the four major criteria in detail, at other times he or she may deem it unnecessary to meet all of them. Speakers may neglect to elaborate on the need or problem because they know the audience already shares their concern for it. A detailed statement of policy may be avoided because the speaker believes it sufficient to show that a general course of action is in some ways superior to one currently pursued. A persuader may avoid mentioning the negative effects of a proposal because its defects are not major. An arguer may pose a theoretical ideal and demonstrate the superiority of the proposal in light of that ideal. Concerning the appropriateness and ethicality of such choices of emphasis as just described, a critical listener may reach judgments differing from the speaker's. But whatever the constraints imposed by audience, setting, and subject, the speaker affirming a proposition of policy must demonstrate to the audience that the proposed course of action is necessary, desirable, and beneficial.

CONCLUSION

In a free society people often assemble to consider courses of future action. In evaluating such speeches, the listener/critic may raise numerous questions that cluster around the following four criteria. *Has the speaker demonstrated, or is it readily apparent, that a need exists for a fundamental change in policy? Has the speaker provided a sufficient view of the nature of the new policy or program? Has the speaker demonstrated that the new policy will remedy the problem? Has the speaker demonstrated that the new policy is advantageous?*

For further reading

Carleton, William G. "Effective Speech in a Democracy." *Vital Speeches of the Day,* June 15, 1951, pp. 540–44.

Gronbeck, Bruce E., et al. *Principles and Types of Speech Communication.* 11th ed. Scott, Foresman, 1990. Chapter 9 explains the nature and uses of the "motivated sequence" structure (attention, need, satisfaction, visualization, action) that is especially useful in speeches advocating policies.

Fotheringham, Wallace C. *Perspectives on Persuasion.* Allyn and Bacon, 1966. Chapters 3 and 11 examine the major goals of persuasive discourse and some undesirable action responses by audiences.

Jensen, J. Vernon. *Argumentation: Reasoning in Communication.* Van Nostrand, 1981. Chapter 5 explains potential lines of argument basic to presenting solutions, policies, and programs.

Leys, Wayne A. R. *Ethics for Policy Decisions.* Prentice-Hall, 1952. Chapters 1, 12, and 22. Pages 189–92 list the critical questions relevant to policy decisions developed in 10 major systems of ethics.

Newman, Robert P., and Newman, Dale. *Evidence.* Houghton Mifflin, 1969. Chapters 1–3 present guidelines for analyzing propositions of policy.

Walter, Otis M., and Scott, Robert L. *Thinking and Speaking.* 5th ed. Macmillan, 1984. Chapter 8 presents suggestions for persuading about solutions to problems.

Walter, Otis M., *Speaking Intelligently.* Macmillan, 1976. Chapters 1 and 5 and pp. 222–24. The author stresses the necessity of high-quality problem-solving for societal survival and growth and suggests strategies for persuading about solutions and policies.

Warnick, Barbara, and Inch, Edward S. *Critical Thinking and Communication: The Use of Reason in Argument.* Macmillan, 1989. Chapter 9 discusses advocating and opposing policy propositions.

The Feminization of Power
Eleanor Smeal

Eleanor Smeal served as President of the National Organization for Women (NOW) from 1977 to 1982, a period that included a major but unsuccessful effort by that feminist organization to secure passage of the Equal Rights Amendment to the Constitution. From 1982–1985 Judy Goldsmith, whose strategies and tactics on women's issues were more moderate, served as NOW's president. In July of 1985 Smeal again was elected president, vowing to return to more aggressive approaches. The press frequently characterized her defeat of Goldsmith as one of militancy and confrontation over compromise and moderation. In a number of her speeches during 1985, she voiced anger and urgency through her exhortation, "It's time to raise hell" (*Washington Post National Weekly Edition,* August 5, 1985, p. 12; *Chicago Tribune,* August 18, 1985, sec. 2, pp. 1, 4; *Washington Post National Weekly Edition,* December 9, 1985, pp. 6–8). In a sense Smeal spoke in the tradition of Mary E. Lease of Kansas, a populist orator of the 1890s, who exhorted discontented farmers to "raise less corn and more hell."

On July 8, 1987, Eleanor Smeal spoke to an audience of journalists and other members at the National Press Club in Washington, D.C. The National Press Club may host 80 or more speakers each year on diverse public issues. Smeal's primary purpose is advocacy of a long-range program of the "feminization of power," a power strong enough for women in leadership roles at all levels of politics to "forge a new reality" of dignity and decency (29–30, 52–53). Earlier feminist anger now must be channeled more effectively. It is time to attack the "conventional wisdom" in concrete ways, time to "organize the outrage" (29, 48).

Smeal uses several lines of argument and varied persuasive tactics to show the need for her policy, to create concern for the problem. The scope of the problem is widespread. Seemingly everywhere "scandal is the order of the day" in all major institutions of public life (1, 19). In an introductory way, she quickly mentions examples from the current news with which the audience would be familiar (2–5). To show that violations of fundamental values are basic to the problem, she contrasts morality espoused with morality practiced and uses antithetical phrasing to underscore value contrasts (6–8, 16–17, 29). A sense of magnitude and intensity of the problem comes through itemization of instances in lengthy lists (7–8). Smeal locates part of the need for her policy in what she sees as a stance of timidity and moderation among Democratic Party leaders as the 1988 elections approach (20–25). Her references to what she said previously when she addressed the National Press Club in September of 1985 function in two ways (11–15, 26–28). First, she further clarifies dimensions of the problem. Second, her credibility is enhanced by snowing that her predictions and promises came true. How effectively do you feel that she uses these references to her previous comments?

Smeal explains the nature of her proposed program by describing three elements. First, feminist candidates would focus on a wide range of public issues, not just on so-called "women's issues" (32). Second, she will lead a "Feminization of Power" tour of the nation, starting on Labor Day and concentrating on states with presidential primaries (33, 46). Third, the strategy of "flooding the ticket" from top to bottom with feminist candidates will be promoted (34). To what degree do you feel that she has clearly explained her program? Smeal argues that her policy is desirable at that moment because the next few years are an opportune time to implement the course of action (36–39).

How workable and practical is her policy? Through literal analogy she demonstrates the "feminization of power" in two other nations and the example of Florida demonstrates the effectiveness of the "flooding" strategy (31, 35). She contends that grass roots support among women is growing (40–42). Again she uses antithetical phrasing, this time to stress that women are fed up with the scandals (40, 42–43). Smeal employs evidence from public opinion policy to show support on fundamental issues (47). Evaluate the soundness of evidence and reasoning used by Smeal in support of her policy.

Her concluding arguments are an attack on President Reagan's nomination of Robert Bork for a position on the Supreme Court and a proposal to start impeachment hearings against Reagan (49–50). How clearly and justifiably does she fit these arguments into her proposed policy of "feminization of power"?

As President of the Fund for the Feminist Majority, in 1000 Eleanor Smeal launched a campaign for the "feminization of power" in the legal profession. This new effort built upon continuing Feminist Majority campaigns to empower women to attain leadership positions in politics and in higher education.

The text of this speech was provided by the national office of the National Organization for Women.

---

1 In business, in the church, in high government, in the military, scandal is the order of the day.

2 The Vatican bank officials cannot leave the Vatican because Italian authorities will arrest them for bank fraud.

3 The PTL Club mess of illicit sex, fraud, and greed would provide comic relief if so many had not been taken for so much.

4 The internecine electronic ministry wars make the hostile take-overs of the corporate world look almost civilized. Wall Street is rocked by arrests for illegal trading and drug deals.

5 The Wedtech incident gives new meaning to the concept of affirmative action minority set-asides. Who could have believed Meese and company, who have repeatedly attacked legitimate affirmative action to end discrimination against women and minorities, were willing to use it for their own ends?

6 Some 100 plus officials of the Reagan administration have resigned or are hanging on under a cloud of impropriety. This administration which promised to return the nation to old-fashioned morality and balanced budgets has instead established a *high level of crook of the month club* and has made the U.S. the fastest-growing debtor nation.

7 Padded expense accounts, questionable honoraria, perjury, fraud, wife beating, conflict of interest, bending regulations for industrial polluters, fraudulent financial dealings, using government employees to work on private business, obstructing justice, creating crushing national debt while hypocritically advocating a balanced budget—this is the morality of the supply-siders.

8 But all of this pales before the revelations of the Iran-Contra scandal: clandestine arms shipments; covert wars; arms trades for hostages, diverting of arms sales monies to the Contras, to their own pockets and for their own ends; a new triangular trade: arms for drugs to profits for more arms; profiteering, altering, shredding, and theft of classified documents; all the while denials—denials—denials to the American people.

9 I believe the American people have had enough.

10 I believe the time has come to say not only what is—but what we must do.

11 When I appeared before the Press Club two years ago, I expressed the outrage of the feminist movement that we, as women fighting for women's rights, were being systematically scapegoated for all the ills in American society.

12 But if I thought it was bad then it is worse now.

13 Hear the words of retiring Marine Command General Paul Xavier Kelly who, when asked if allegations that marines in Moscow allegedly traded national secrets for sex or if Marine Lt. Col. Oliver North's behavior indicated a lack of moral fiber in the Marine Corps, replied that moral deterioration is nationwide.

14 Said Kelly, "American mothers who work and send their children to 'faceless' centers rather than stay home to take care of them are weakening the moral fiber of the Nation."

15 I have to say P. X. Kelly's remarks immediately called to mind a joke that made the rounds here when the Tower Commission's report was released: What is the difference between a Child Care Center and the National Security Council? Answer: The Child Care Center has adult supervision.

16 This is becoming a sad town. Only the wags and cartoonists are having a field day. But even they may see tough times as more and more the absurd becomes real.

17 As the powers that be define morality, they in fact create a world of immorality: where the feminization of poverty goes unchecked; where arms dealers get richer and child care workers get poorer; where war, military budgets, hunger, and inequality are the order of the day.

18 A world amok.

19 A nation struggling for its soul against a backdrop of smiling cynical corruption and immorality in the highest offices of its government, its industry, its religious institutions.

20 The conventional wisdom in Washington continues to say we must "wait out the times."

21 Democrats are advised to play it cool.

22 The big prize—the Presidency—will fall into their laps if they just wait it out.

23 The Democratic mainstream is still counseling their party to move to the Right to win in 1988 and that means, of course, to keep women's issues at arm's length.

24 The Democratic Leadership Council, composed of so-called moderates, including at least four current presidential candidates (Gephardt, Gore, Babbitt, and Biden), and led by former Virginia Governor Charles Robb, has released a 1988 agenda.

25 This DLC agenda takes *no* position on abortion, an obvious desertion of the current national Democratic platform which endorses a pro-choice position, including support for medicaid funding. The DLC advocates a strong defense policy (a code word for no substantial change in defense spending), while emphasizing "mutual obligations" (code word: workfare) in welfare reform policies.

26 In 1985 I stood before you at the National Press Club and warned of the fascist tendencies of the New Right in America. Only this weekend we learned that some of the President's advisors have operated a secret, shadow government that drafted a contingency plan for the suspension of the U.S. Constitution.

27 In 1985 I said it was time to challenge the Right Wing and pledged that feminists would go back to the streets to push the cause of women's rights. In 1986 we did just that with eight major marches, the largest bringing 125,000 people to this city's streets to keep abortion and birth control safe and legal.

28 Did it help? You bet. Eight months later we defeated anti-abortion referenda in four states and the anti-abortion movement is now in disarray.

29 It's time again to challenge the conventional wisdom. It's time to be bold. To organize the outrage. And it's time—long overdue—to encourage feminist women, and men, to take power. If the feminization of poverty is ever going to be stopped, we must have a *feminization of power.*

30 It's time for women to take the reins of power. I mean real *power*—power to forge a new reality. To restore dignity and decency to America's leadership.

31 Far-fetched? Cory Aquino and the Filipino women and men led a bloodless revolution against all odds—and the housewife is now the President of that struggling democracy. In Norway, a woman is prime minister and 36% of the parliament are women because the people wanted a national house-cleaning.

32 It's time for women—for feminists—to lead, not to be confined to what others have labeled "women's issues," but to spread out on a whole range of interconnected issues affecting our lives—our nation—yes, our world. It's time to expand the vision of the feminist movement and to change the national debate.

33 To help make this happen, I will not run for the Presidency of NOW but will launch a massive "Feminization of Power" tour, organized by a new entity—the Fund for the Feminist Majority.

34 In the year ahead I will devote my full time to injecting the feminist agenda into the 1988 elections and to recruiting feminist candidates to flood the ticket—from top to bottom.

35 How does this work? The strategy of "flooding the ticket" with feminist women candidates will secure electoral gains for women more rapidly. In Florida, for example, the flooding the ticket strategy in 1982 resulted in more than doubling the number of women in the state legislature. Today, Florida—with 20.6% women in its state legislature—has a higher percentage of women among its state lawmakers than the national average and more than any state in the South.

36 Why is this so important to do at this time? Three major reasons. After Watergate (1974), some 103 new members of Congress were elected—the most new members since 1949, and more than twice the number of new members in 1984. I believe that the Iran-Contra scandal, perceived already by a majority of Americans as more serious or as serious as Watergate, will help to produce even more changes in 1988.

37 When the 101st Congress convenes in 1989, we want at least half the new members to be feminist women. If that were so, we would have the possibility of tripling the number of women in Congress—now we're talking about real change—and finally real representation for women. But lest we think the job would be done, even if we tripled the number of women, there would only be 69 women out of 535 members of Congress.

38 The second reason is a little more long term. The most number of open seats at both the state legislature and Congressional levels occur usually after reapportionment every ten years. Reapportionment of state and Congressional districts occurs after the 1990 census. In 1982, there were 81 new members of Congress and 21 newly created seats without incumbents. If we are able to be ready for the opportunity created by reapportionment, we must begin now.

39 Many ask me if the Equal Rights Amendment can pass and when it will pass. Of course it will pass. If Constitutional equality for women is going to be approved in the decade of the 90's, we must change the faces in Congress and the state legislatures and we must do it now.

40 But the third reason we must act now is even more urgent. We can't take any more—and should not take any more—of what is happening to this nation, either at the state and local level or at the national level.

41 I believe the change is bubbling up from the people, especially women. For example, in California activist women are determined to change the state legislature, which despite the majority wishes, has once again restricted abortion rights for young girls and poor women.

42 Another example is the Presidential race. The most excitement for U.S. Representative Patricia Schroeder, the most senior woman in Congress, who is currently testing the Presidential waters, is from the grass roots. Talk about a perfect biography at a time like this. One of the principal authors of the post-Watergate Ethics Act, a senior member of the House Armed Services Committee and House Judiciary Committee, author of the Family and Medical Leave Act, and courageous enough to call military contractors the "real welfare queens." That's right, feminist women don't mean business as usual. But we do mean business.

43 We will challenge those who would continue business as usual and who ignore the pressing needs of women, men, and children. We will run for office in unprecedented numbers. We will no longer accept limited strategies of "husbanding" our resources, of targeting narrowly, of thinking too small, and of accepting the lesser of two evils. We will not be *reasonable* in a world that assaults our dreams and our goals with irrational, unreasonable, and despicable attacks.

44 We will not condemn another generation of feminists to fight for the obvious.

45 In short, with the feminization of power campaign we will change the debate and the faces of the 1988 elections and beyond.

46 The tour, beginning after Labor Day, will be produced by the Peg Yorkin Production Company, and will include feminist leaders, singers, entertainers, and a media campaign. We intend to reach out to millions, and to inspire feminists to action, to run for public office, and to get involved in NOW and the feminist movement. The tour will target the primary states. We intend to organize women and the feminist majority of those states to such a degree, the 1988 candidates will become "born again" feminists. We intend to expand the feminist movement and to create audiences larger than ever before. We are the majority and we intend to take the power.

47 Seventy-five percent of the nation supports the ERA (New York Times/CBS Poll, May 1987); the vast majority of Americans (88%) believe that abortion should be legal (54% always, 34% sometimes) (Harris, 1985). A majority of the nation supports pay equity; 67% oppose funding the Contras (Post/ABC, May/June 1987); 59% approve of cutting military spending (Gallup, January 1986); and 59% of the people believe President Reagan is lying to them.

48 The conventional wisdom that Ronald Reagan should be allowed to quietly serve out his term is wrong.

49 A President whose administration has brought disaster and dishonor to the Constitution he has sworn to uphold should not be allowed to appoint a Supreme Court justice who would provide the key point vote to dismantle human rights. This appointment could mean the reversal of *Roe v. Wade* which legalized abortion; the unraveling of affirmative action; the destruction of the Constitutionally-implied Right to Privacy; and the dismantling of the principle of one person, one vote. Bork, the man who carried out the order for the Saturday Night Massacre of Watergate, should not be further rewarded with a seat on this nation's highest court to carry out the Right Wing agenda of yet another failed Presidency.

50 Rather than the Senate Judiciary Committee preparing for hearings on a reactionary nomination, the House Judiciary committee should begin hearings to investigate *impeachment*. We should have around this nation not only "Save the Court" rallies, but impeachment rallies. What will the Constitution mean, in this its 200th year, if we allow this President and his men to be above the law, to go around Congress with impunity? We are not bored with this scandal, we are outraged, and it's about time Americans started showing it.

51 Our nation deserves a return to morality—real morality—where no person, no government official, no captain of industry, no self-proclaimed religious leader is above the law or beyond the reach for our system of jurisprudence.

52 In this Bicentennial year of our Constitution, the American people deserve no less—and demand no less.

53 And you can be certain that in the months ahead, the voices of We The Women will be heard loudly and clearly as we demand a return to morality, to decency and dignity, to justice and equality for all.

Truth and Tolerance in America
Edward M. Kennedy

For over three decades, Edward M. (Ted) Kennedy has been in the glare of the public spotlight as a major political figure. In a lengthy analysis of Kennedy's public and private life in *Time* magazine (April 29, 1991, pp. 24–27), political commentator Lance Morrow acknowledges that during this time period one public image of Kennedy has become, with some justification, the "Palm Beach boozer, lout and tabloid grotesque." But Morrow also convincingly argues: "He became one of the great lawmakers of the century, a Senate leader whose liberal mark upon American government has become prominent and permanent. The tabloid version does not do him justice. The public that knows Kennedy by his misadventures alone may vastly underrate him."

Due to a computer error, Edward Kennedy, the liberal Democratic U.S. Senator from Massachusetts, mistakenly was sent a membership card in the conservative Moral Majority political action organization founded by Rev. Jerry Falwell. Rev. Falwell also is a widely viewed television evangelist, founder of Liberty Baptist College, and pastor of the Thomas Road Baptist Church. After an exchange of communications between Kennedy and Moral Majority officials prompted by the error, Kennedy accepted an invitation to speak at Liberty Baptist College.

On the evening of October 3, 1983, Kennedy, a Roman Catholic, addressed over 5000 students, faculty, and townsfolk at the college in Lynchburg, Virginia. The attitude of most audience members toward Kennedy prior to the speech was distinctly unfriendly if not outright hostile. On previous occasions Rev. Falwell had attacked Kennedy's personal life, characterizing him as a womanizer and as often inebriated. And in Falwell's words, some Moral Majority members viewed Kennedy as "the devil incarnate" (*Chicago Tribune,* October 5, 1983, sec. 1, p. 4; *Newsweek,* October 17, 1983, pp. 30–31). According to the *Chicago Tribune,* the speech had "little of the stem-winding partisan rhetoric for which Kennedy is known." The audience greeted him politely and interrupted the 21-minute speech "16 times with light applause." In the judgement of *Newsweek,* Kennedy did not compromise his own convictions, did not "trim his rhetoric for the religious right." Indeed, said *Newsweek,* it was "one of the best speeches he has ever given."

Kennedy employs a number of approaches to reduce the hostility of the audience and to increase the chances of securing a fair hearing for his views. Humor is used, especially in the introduction (1–4, 28). Did it seem clear and relevant? He makes a request for a fair hearing of divergent viewpoints (7). He compliments Falwell's introduction of him (1) and the audience's courtesy to him (38). Perhaps most important, Kennedy himself sets an example of fairness. He defends Falwell against unjust criticism (9, 38) and uses both liberals and conservatives to illustrate abuses of the principle of respect for motives (38). But Kennedy does not pander to his audience. When he believes it is merited, he condemns Falwell and the Moral Majority (26–27, 37–38).

The *Chicago Tribune* (October 5, 1983) noted that "Kennedy clearly viewed the speech as an opportunity to make a major policy statement on religion and politics." In analyzing "whether and how religion should influence government," Kennedy advocates continuation of the historic national policy of separation of church and state (7, 10, 11, 21). It is a sound policy, in need only of being refined for application to the present. The policy is defended both by reliance on examples and quotations from the colonial and revolutionary eras in America (12–14) and by placing it in the larger cultural context of a pluralistic society (8, 9, 16). He warns of the dangers of breaking down the separation (11, 15, 16).

Kennedy advocates four "tests" to answer the need for principles or standards to guide the functioning of the separation policy (22–23, 25, 29, 36). These guidelines would nurture persuasive expression of moral judgments on appropriate public issues while thwarting the imposition of views and use of coercive government power (19–21). In developing each of the four tests, he provides examples, often through direct quotation, of where each principle recently has been violated. By implication there is a continuing need to teach and exercise these standards, thus maintaining the policy as effective.

To explain that separation does not mean "an absolute separation between moral principles and political power" (11), Kennedy distinguishes among three types of current controversial issues, only some of which are appropriate for mixture of moral judgment with public policy. How clear are his categories and how reasonable and appropriate are the examples of issues he places in each category? First, there are "uniquely personal," "inherently individual," matters where religion properly may try to influence individual conscience but not governmental policies (17). Second, there are questions "inherently public in nature" where ethical and religious value judgments are appropriate (18–21). Third, there are public issues that do not involve religious values (23–24).

Evaluate Kennedy's use of the following argumentative, structural, and stylistic tactics. He quotes from his assassinated brother, President John F. Kennedy (10, 21, 42) and frequently he employs biblical allusion or quotation (2, 7, 23, 24, 43). Alliteration (9, 15, 31, 33, 34), antithesis (17, 21, 29, 30–31), and parallel structure (30–32, 39–41, 44) are evident. Both overtly (15) and in a variation (28), he employs what argumentation and logic textbooks call the "slippery slope" line of reasoning. Here it is used to show his audience that, if today they approve of some violations of the separation policy, they someday may themselves be victims of similar violations.

Two excellent analyses of Kennedy's speech and its context are: Robert Brenham and W. Barnett Pearce, "A Contract for Civility: Edward Kennedy's Lynchburg Address," *Quarterly Journal of Speech,* 73 (November 1987): 424–443; Gary C. Woodward, *Persuasive Encounters: Case Studies in Constructive Confrontation* (Praeger, 1990), pp. 53–76.

The text of this speech was provided by Senator Kennedy's office in Washington, D.C.

---

1 Let me thank Dr. Jerry Falwell for that generous introduction. I never expected to hear such kind words from him. So, in return, I have an invitation of my own: On January 20, 1985, I hope Dr. Falwell will say a prayer—at the inauguration of the next Democratic president of the United States. Now, Dr. Falwell, I'm not sure exactly how you feel about that. You might not appreciate the president, but the Democrats certainly would appreciate the prayer.

2 Actually, a number of people in Washington were surprised that I was invited to speak here—and even more surprised when I accepted the invitation. They seem to think that it is easier for a camel to pass through the eye of a needle than for a Kennedy to come to the campus of Liberty Baptist College.

3 In honor of our meeting, I have asked Dr. Falwell, as your chancellor, to permit all the students an extra hour next Saturday night before curfew. In return, I have promised to watch "The Old Time Gospel Hour" next Sunday morning.

4 I realize that my visit may be a little controversial. But as many of you have heard, Dr. Falwell recently sent me a membership card in the Moral Majority—and I didn't even apply for it. I wonder if that means I am a member in good standing.

5 This is, of course, a nonpolitical speech—which is probably best under the circumstances.

6 Since I am not a candidate for president, it certainly would be inappropriate to ask for your support in this election—and probably inaccurate to thank you for it in the last one.

7 I have come here to discuss my beliefs about faith and country, tolerance and truth in America. I know we begin with certain disagreements; I strongly suspect that at the end of the evening some of our disagreements will remain. But I also hope that tonight and in the months and years ahead, we will always respect the right of others to differ—that we will view ourselves with a sense of perspective and a sense of humor. After all, in the New Testament, even the disciples had to be taught to look first to the beam in their own eyes, and only then to the mote in their neighbor's eye.

8 I am mindful of that counsel. I am an American and a Catholic; I love my country and treasure my faith. But I do not assume that my conception of patriotism or policy is invariably correct—or that my convictions about religion should command any greater respect than any other faith in this pluralistic society. I believe there surely is such a thing as truth, but who among us can claim a monopoly on it?

9 There are those who do, and their own words testify to their intolerance. For example, because the Moral Majority has worked with members of different denominations, one fundamentalist group has denounced Dr. Falwell for hastening the ecumenical church and for "yoking together with Roman Catholics, Mormons, and others." I am relieved that Dr. Falwell does not regard that as a sin—and on this issue, he himself has become the target of narrow prejudice. When people agree on public policy, they ought to be able to work together, even while they worship in diverse ways. For truly we are all yoked together as Americans—and the yoke is the happy one of individual freedom and mutual respect.

10 But in saying that, we cannot and should not turn aside from a deeper, more pressing question—which is whether and how religion should influence government. A generation ago, a presidential candidate had to prove his independence of undue religious influence in public life, and he had to do so partly at the insistence of evangelical protestants. John Kennedy said at that time, "I believe in an America where there is no (religious) bloc voting of any kind." Only twenty years later, another candidate was appealing to an evangelical meeting as a religious bloc. Ronald Reagan said to fifteen thousand evangelicals at The Roundtable in Dallas, "I know that you can't endorse me. I want you to know that I endorse you and what you are doing."

11 To many Americans, the pledge was a sign and a symbol of a dangerous breakdown in the separation of church and state. Yet this principle, as vital as it is, is not a simplistic and rigid command. Separation of church and state cannot mean an absolute separation between moral principles and political power. The challenge today is to recall the origin of the principle, to define its purpose, and refine its application to the politics of the present.

12 The founders of our nation had long and bitter experience with the state as both the agent and the adversary of particular religious views. In colonial Maryland, Catholics paid a double land tax and in Pennsylvania they had to list their names on a public roll—an ominous precursor of the first Nazi laws against the Jews. And Jews in turn faced discrimination in all the thirteen original colonies. Massachusetts exiled Roger Williams and his congregation for contending that civil government had no right to enforce the Ten Commandments. Virginia harassed Baptist preachers and also established a religious test for public service, writing into the law that no "Popish followers" could hold any office.

13 But during the revolution, Catholics, Jews, and nonconformists all rallied to the cause and fought valiantly for the American commonwealth—for John Winthrop's "city upon a hill." Afterwards, when the Constitution was ratified and then amended, the framers gave freedom for all religion—and from any established religion—the very first place in the Bill of Rights.

14 Indeed the framers themselves professed very different faiths—and in the case of Benjamin Franklin, hardly any at all. Washington was an Episcopalian, Jefferson a deist, and Adams a Calvinist. And although he had earlier opposed toleration, John Adams later contributed to the building of Catholic churches—and so did George Washington. Thomas Jefferson said his proudest achievement was not the presidency, or writing the Declaration of Independence, but drafting the Virginia Statute of Religious Freedom. He stated the vision of the first Americans and the First Amendment very clearly: "The God who gave us life gave us liberty at the same time."

15 The separation of church and state can sometimes be frustrating for women and men of deep religious faith. They may be tempted to misuse government in order to impose a value which they cannot persuade others to accept. But once we succumb to that temptation, we step onto a slippery slope where everyone's freedom is at risk. Those who favor censorship should recall that one of the first books ever burned was the first English translation of the Bible. As President Eisenhower warned in 1953, "Don't join the bookburners . . . the right to say ideas, the right to record them and the right to have them accessible to others is unquestioned—or this isn't America." And if that right is denied, at some future day the torch can be turned against any other book or any other belief. Let us never forget, today's Moral Majority could become tomorrow's persecuted minority.

16 The danger is as great now as when the founders of the nation first saw it. In 1789 their fear was of factional strife among dozens of denominations. Today there are hundreds—and perhaps thousands—of faiths and millions of Americans who are outside any fold.

Pluralism obviously does not and cannot mean that all of them are right; but it does mean that there are areas where government cannot and should not decide what it is wrong to believe, to think, to read, and to do. As Professor Laurence Tribe, one of the nation's leading constitutional scholars has written, "Law in a nontheocratic state cannot measure religious truth"—nor can the state impose it.

17 The real transgression occurs when religion wants government to tell citizens how to live uniquely personal parts of their lives. The failure of Prohibition proves the futility of such an attempt when a majority or even a substantial minority happens to disagree. Some questions may be inherently individual ones or people may be sharply divided about whether they are. In such cases—cases like Prohibition and abortion—the proper role of religion is to appeal to the conscience of the individual, not the coercive power of the state.

18 But there are other questions which are inherently public in nature, which we must decide together as a nation, and where religion and religious values can and should speak to our common conscience. The issue of nuclear war is a compelling example. It is a moral issue; it will be decided by government, not by each individual; and to give any effect to the moral values of their creed, people of faith must speak directly about public policy. The Catholic bishops and the Reverend Billy Graham have every right to stand for the nuclear freeze—and Dr. Falwell has every right to stand against it.

19 There must be standards for the exercise of such leadership, so that the obligations of belief will not be debased into an opportunity for mere political advantage. But to take a stand at all when a question is both properly public and truly moral is to stand in a long and honored tradition. Many of the great evangelists of the 1800s were in the forefront of the abolitionist movement. In our own time, the Reverend William Sloane Coffin challenged the morality of the war in Vietnam. Pope John XXIII renewed the Gospel's call to social justice. And Dr. Martin Luther King, Jr., who was the greatest prophet of this century, awakened our national conscience to the evil of racial segregation.

20 Their words have blessed our world. And who now wishes they had all been silent? Who would bid Pope John Paul to quiet his voice about the oppression in eastern Europe; the violence in Central America; or the crying needs of the landless, the hungry, and those who are tortured in so many of the dark political prisons of our time?

21 President Kennedy, who said that "no religious body should seek to impose its will," also urged religious leaders to state their views and give their commitment when the public debate involved ethical issues. In drawing the line between imposed will and essential witness, we keep church and state separate—and at the same time, we recognize that the city of God should speak to the civic duties of men and women.

22 There are four tests which draw that line and define the difference.

23 First, we must respect the integrity of religion itself. People of conscience should be careful how they deal in the world of their Lord. In their own history, religion has been falsely invoked to sanction prejudice and even slavery, to condemn labor unions and public spending for the poor. I believe that the prophecy "the poor you have always with you" is an indictment, not a commandment. I respectfully suggest that God has taken no position on the Department of Education—and that a balanced budget constitutional amendment is a matter for economic analysis, not heavenly appeals.

24 Religious values cannot be excluded from every public issue—but not every public issue involves religious values. And how ironic it is when those very values are denied in the name of religion. For example, we are sometimes told that it is wrong to feed the hungry, but that mission is an explicit mandate given to us in the twenty-fifth chapter of Matthew.

25 Second, we must respect the independent judgments of conscience. Those who proclaim moral and religious values can offer counsel, but they should not casually treat a position on a public issue as a test of fealty to faith. Just as I disagree with the Catholic bishops on tuition tax credits, which I oppose, so other Catholics can and do disagree with the hierarchy, on the basis of honest conviction, on the question of the nuclear freeze.

26 Thus, the controversy about the Moral Majority arises not only from its views, but from its name, which in the minds of many seems to imply that only one set of public policies is moral—and only one majority can possibly be right. Similarly, people are and should be perplexed when the religious lobbying group Christian Voice publishes a morality index of congressional voting records, which judges the morality of senators by their attitude toward Zimbabwe and Taiwan.

27 Let me offer another illustration. Dr. Falwell has written, and I quote, "To stand against Israel is to stand against God." Now there is no one in the Senate who has stood more firmly for Israel than I have. Yet I do not doubt the faith of those on the other side. Their error is not one of religion, but of policy, and I hope to persuade them that they are wrong in terms of both America's interest and the justice of Israel's cause.

28 Respect for conscience is most in jeopardy—and the harmony of our diverse society is most at risk—when we reestablish, directly or indirectly, a religious test for public office. That relic of the colonial era, which is specifically prohibited in the Constitution, has reappeared in recent years. After the last election, the Reverend James Robison warned President Reagan not to surround himself, as presidents before him had, "with the counsel of the ungodly." I utterly reject any such standard for any position anywhere in public service. Two centuries ago, the victims were Catholics and Jews. In the 1980s, the victims could be atheists; in some other day or decade, they could be the members of the Thomas Road Baptist Church. Indeed, in 1976 I regarded it as unworthy and un-American when some people said or hinted that Jimmy Carter should not be president because he was a born again Christian. We must never judge the fitness of individuals to govern on the basis of where they worship, whether they follow Christ or Moses, whether they are called "born again" or "ungodly." Where it is right to apply moral values to public life, let all of us avoid the temptation to be self-righteous and absolutely certain of ourselves. And if that temptation ever comes, let us recall Winston Churchill's humbling description of an intolerant and inflexible colleague: "There but for the grace of God—goes God."

29 Third, in applying religious values, we must respect the integrity of public debate. In that debate, faith is no substitute for facts. Critics may oppose the nuclear freeze for what they regard as moral reasons. They have every right to argue that any negotiation with the Soviets is wrong, or that any accommodation with them sanctions their crimes, or that no agreement can be good enough and therefore all agreements only increase the chance of war. I do not believe that, but it surely does not violate the standard of fair public debate to say it. What does violate that standard, what the opponents of the nuclear freeze have no right to do, is to assume that they are infallible—and so any argument against the freeze will do, whether it is false or true.

30 The nuclear freeze proposal is not unilateral, but bilateral—with equal restraints on the United States and the Soviet Union.

31 The nuclear freeze does not require that we trust the Russians, but demands full and effective verification.

32 The nuclear freeze does not concede a Soviet lead in nuclear weapons, but recognizes that human beings in each great power already have in their fallible hands the overwhelming capacity to remake into a pile of radioactive rubble the Earth which god has made.

33 There is no morality in the mushroom cloud. The black rain of nuclear ashes will fall alike on the just and unjust. And then it will be too late to wish that we had done the real work of this atomic age—which is to seek a world that is neither Red nor dead.

34 I am perfectly prepared to debate the nuclear freeze on policy grounds or moral ones. But we should not be forced to discuss phantom issues or false charges. They only deflect us from the urgent task of deciding how best to prevent a planet divided from becoming a planet destroyed.

35 And it does not advance the debate to contend that the arms race is more divine punishment than human problem, or that, in any event, the final days are near. As Pope John said two decades ago, at the opening of the Second Vatican Council, "We must beware of those who burn with zeal, but are not endowed with much sense . . . we must disagree with the prophets of doom, who are always forecasting disasters, as though the end of the Earth was at hand." The message which echoes across the years since then is clear. The Earth is still here; and if we wish to keep it, a prophecy of doom is no alternative to a policy of arms control.

36 Fourth, and finally, we must respect the motives of those who exercise their right to disagree. We sorely test our ability to live together if we too readily question each other's integrity. It may be harder to restrain our feelings when moral principles are at stake, for they go to the deepest wellsprings of our being. But the more our feelings diverge, the more deeply felt they are, the greater is our obligation to grant the sincerity and essential decency of our fellow citizens on the other side.

37 Those who favor E.R.A. are not "antifamily" or "blasphemers" and their purpose is not "an attack on the Bible." Rather we believe this is the best way to fix in our national firmament the ideal that not only all men, but all people, are created equal. Indeed, my mother—who strongly favors E.R.A.—would be surprised to hear that she is antifamily. For my part, I think of the amendment's opponents as wrong on the issue, but not as lacking in moral character.

38 I could multiply the instances of name-calling, sometimes on both sides. Dr. Falwell is not a "warmonger" and "liberal clergymen" are not, as the Moral Majority suggested in a recent letter, equivalent to "Soviet sympathizers." The critics of official prayer in public schools are not "Pharisees"; many of them are both civil libertarians and believers, who think that families should pray more at home with their children and attend church and synagogue more faithfully. And people are not "sexist" because they stand against abortion; they are not "murderers" because they believe in free choice. Nor does it help anyone's cause to shout such epithets or try to shout a speaker down, which is what happened last April when Dr. Falwell was hissed and heckled at Harvard. So I am doubly grateful for your courtesy here today. That was not Harvard's finest hour, but I am happy to say that the loudest applause from the Harvard audience came in defense of Dr. Falwell's right to speak.

39 In short, I hope for an America where neither fundamentalist nor humanist will be a dirty word, but a fair description of the different ways in which people of goodwill look at life and into their own souls.

40 I hope for an America where no president, no public official, and no individual will ever be deemed a greater or lesser American because of religious doubt—or religious belief.

41 I hope for an America where we can all contend freely and vigorously, but where we will treasure and guard those standards of civility which alone make this nation safe for both democracy and diversity.

42 Twenty years ago this fall, in New York City, President Kennedy met for the last time with a Protestant assembly. The atmosphere had been transformed since his earlier address during the 1960 campaign to the Houston Ministerial Association. He had spoken there to allay suspicions about his Catholicism, and to answer those who claimed that on the day of his baptism, he was somehow disqualified from becoming president. His speech in Houston and then his election drove that prejudice from the center of our national life. Now, three years later, in November 1963, he was appearing before the Protestant Council of New York City to reaffirm what he regarded as some fundamental truths. On that occasion, John Kennedy said, "The family of man is not limited to a single race or religion, to a single city or country. . . . The family of man is nearly 3 billion strong. Most of its members are not white—and most of them are not Christian." And as President Kennedy reflected on that reality, he restated an ideal for which he had lived his life, that "the members of this family should be at peace with one another."

43 That ideal shines across all the generations of our history and all the ages of our faith, carrying with it the most ancient dream. For as the apostle Paul wrote long ago in Romans, "If it be possible, as much as it lieth in you, live peaceably with all men."

44 I believe it is possible; the choice lies within us. As fellow citizens, let us live peaceably with each other; as fellow human beings, let us strive to live peaceably with men and women everywhere. Let that be our prayer—yours and mine—for ourselves, for our country, and for all the world.

Multiculturalism in the Public Schools
Diane Ravitch

At a meeting of the New Jersey School Boards Association on November 2, 1990, Diane Ravitch spoke on multiculturalism as an issue and policy for the public schools. She is an adjunct professor of history and education in the Teachers College of Columbia University in New York City. Diane Ravitch is author of several books, including *The Troubled Crusade: American Education, 1945–1980,* and the California State Board of Education called upon her to structure the state's K–12 history curriculum.

What persuasive function might be served by her introductory massing of examples of contemporary European racial, ethnic, and religious conflict and her reassurance that, unlike some European nations, America will not disintegrate (1–4)? Ravitch advocates the general policy of multiculturalism for public school curricula and she specifically advocates adoption of a "pluralist" program to implement that concept (5, 12). She spends little time proving that a need for multiculturalism exists—that there has been a problem requiring a solution (6–11). She seems to assume that her audience of school board members from throughout New Jersey already acknowledge such a need and that they recognize precedents already in place for such a general policy.

Ravitch's major argumentative strategy is to contrast the defining elements of a pluralist and an ethnocentric program of multiculturalism—the former desirable and the latter dangerous (13–15, 26–27)—and also to present the advantages of pluralism and the disadvantages of ethnocentrism (16–22). How clearly and reasonably does she explain and justify the basic components of the pluralist policy? What types of evidence does she use and how soundly does she use them? What values are embodied in pluralism and violated by an ethnocentric approach? Antithesis is a major language resource used to contrast the desirable and undesirable features of the two policies (17–19, 27). How effectively and fairly do you believe that she uses this resource?

At one point Ravitch mentions a "common American culture" embodied in "music, food, clothing, sports, holidays, and customs" that reflects multicultural influences (14). How clearly and adequately is the nature of this common culture demonstrated here and elsewhere in the speech? At another point she poses an either-or-choice with only one of the choices pictured as desirable (22). Must we be forced to choose as she describes? Cannot schools foster *both* pride in heritage *and* knowledge, creativity, and cooperation? Consider her massive accumulation of historical examples of hatred and violence stemming from extreme ethnocentrism (23–25). Does pride in and knowledge about ethnic heritage necessarily result in such barbarism?

Almost in passing, Diane Ravitch mentions Afrocentrism as a type of ethnocentrism and makes an analogy between Afrocentrism and earlier "whites-only" curricula (16). Does she develop this analogy fully and clearly enough to be reasonable? For example, what are the "flaws" and "wild inaccuracies"? Are they simply to be inferred from the following paragraphs? You will want to compare Ravitch's speech with the following speech by Molefi Asante on Afrocentrism. Is Afrocentrism ethnocentric in the major negative ways that Ravitch contends? For a much more complete and detailed defense of the pluralist approach and a more specific attack on the Afrocentric approach, see Diane Ravitch, "Multiculturalism: E Pluribus Plures," *The American Scholar,* 59 (Summer 1990): 337–354.

The text of this speech was provided by Diane Ravitch.

---

1 I recently returned from Eastern Europe, where nationalism and ethnicity are on the rise, in ominous ways. Czechoslovakia may split into two nations, the Czechs and the Slovaks. Armenians and Azerbaijanis are killing each other. The Romanians are unresolved about how to deal with their Hungarian minority; the Hungarians are unresolved about how to deal with their Romanian minority. Yugoslavia may disintegrate if Serbs, Croats, Albanians, Slovenians, Slavonians, and Montenegrens find it impossible to get along together.

2 And of course religious tension is also on the rise. The Poles are reintroducing religious education in their public schools. And ugly manifestations of anti-Semitism are again in the air. Throughout Eastern Europe there is the occasional and amazing phenomenon of anti-Semitism without Jews.

3 Here in United States, we too are preoccupied with tensions about race, ethnicity, and language. This is inevitable, because we are a multiracial, multiethnic society, and we have people in America who speak the languages of every other nation in the world.

4 And, unlike Yugoslavia, Czechoslovakia, and the Soviet Union, we are not going to disintegrate. First, because we have no territorial basis to our racial-ethnic differences; and second, because racial and ethnic and linguistic issues have been part and parcel of American history from our earliest days.

5 The issue that today confronts the schools is multiculturalism. It is the buzzword of the 1990s. What is it? Why has it become a major controversy? How should the schools respond? Why do some people find it threatening? How can it become a positive force in our schools and society?

6 Due to demographic changes and new immigration of the past generation, there is today widespread cultural diversity in our schools and in our society. Children in American classrooms represent all of the world's races, religions, and ethnic groups.

7 Our greatest concern as educators must be to educate all of these children so that they can enjoy productive lives as Americans citizens. All of our children must be equipped for the demands of the 21st century. In the past few years, demands have been made to change the curriculum to reflect the changing realities of American society.

8 These are not new issues in American education. Twenty years ago, black educators complained about the lily-white textbooks used in the schools. Their complaints were well-founded. The literature textbooks never included a black poet or writer. The history textbooks included slavery as a cause of the Civil War, but otherwise neglected the lives and experiences of black Americans and ignored the grim realities of racial segregation and discrimination.

9 A generation ago, the city of Detroit inaugurated the first multi-ethnic teaching materials, and other big-city districts began to demand changes in the textbooks. In higher education, scholars advanced the frontiers of knowledge, recovering the long-neglected history of blacks, women, Indians, and immigrants. The work of black leaders like W. E. B. Du Bois, Frederick Douglass, Harriet Tubman, James Weldon Johnson, and Ida B. Wells began to receive new attention. Based on years of solid research, the textbooks in our schools began to reflect a far more interesting America.

10 As a result, the textbooks in our schools today are dramatically different from the textbooks that I read as a child. The most widely used history textbook, Todd and Curti's *Triumph of the American Nation,* presents a picture of a pluralistic America, a nation that is multiracial and multiethnic, a nation built by men and women and people of all different origins.

11 And this approach has become commonplace among today's textbooks. Today our textbooks routinely illustrate children and adults of all races engaged in a variety of occupations, and routinely pay attention to the achievements of people from different backgrounds. Children's reading books include the writings of a wide variety of people, of diverse origins.

12 Given the rapid changes of the past generation, why is multiculturalism a controversial issue today? The controversy arises because the word multiculturalism means different things to different people, and it is being used to describe very different educational approaches. The two basic approaches are either pluralist or ethnocentric. One has the potential to strengthen public education, the other has the potential to harm it.

13 The pluralist approach recognizes that one of the purposes of public education is to create a democratic community and to expand children's knowledge beyond their own home and neighborhood to a larger world. In doing so, education must prepare children to live in a world of competing ideas and values, to be able to live and work with people from different backgrounds, and to learn to examine their own beliefs.

14 The pluralist approach to American culture recognizes that we have a common American culture that was shaped by the contributions of all of many different groups— by American Indians, by Africans, by immigrants from all over the world, and by their descendants. Consider American music, food, clothing, sports, holidays, and customs—all of them demonstrate the commingling of diverse cultures in one nation. We are many peoples, but we are one nation. Paradoxically, we have a common culture that is multicultural. It was shaped by all of us, and we reshape it in every generation.

15 The ethnocentric approach to American culture insists that there is no common culture, and that each of us must trace our origins to the land of our ancestors and identify only with people who have the same skin color or ethnicity. Each of us, by this definition, is defined by who our grandparents were. We must look only to people of the same group for inspiration, for it is they—and they alone—who can offer us role models of achievement. By this approach, I cannot be inspired by Harriet Tubman's bravery or by Zora Neale Hurston's moving prose or by Octavio Paz's eloquence because I am not from their racial/ethnic group. And black children, in turn, cannot be moved by the words of Abraham Lincoln or Elizabeth Cady Stanton or Robert Kennedy because they are of a different race. Ethnocentrism insists that each of us is defined by our race or ethnicity.

16 Some of our schools today have adopted the ethnocentric approach. Sometimes it is called Afrocentrism, and it is modeled on the whites-only curriculum that prevailed in American schools until a generation ago. It contains the same flaws and is equally subject to wild inaccuracies and pervasive bias.

17 What I would suggest to you is that these two approaches—pluralism and ethnocentrism—cannot both be multicultural, because they are completely opposite in purpose. One teaches children that they are part of a multiracial, multiethnic world, the other immerses them in a prideful version of their own race or ethnicity.

18 Pluralism teaches us that we are all part of the great American mosaic and provides us with the glue of civic knowledge that holds the mosaic together. Ethnocentrism teaches children to regard with respect only those of their own particular group.

19 Pluralism teaches that despite our surface differences, we are all human. Ethnocentrism teaches that our differences define us.

20 There is a significant difference in the methods by which these two very different approaches are taught. In the pluralist classroom, the teacher should stress critical thinking. Students should learn about every subject with a critical eye. They should be taught to ask questions, to wonder "How do we know what we know?" "What is the evidence for what we believe?" This is the very opposite of indoctrination. By this approach, it is possible to study the history of religion in a public school classroom, because the object is to learn about it, not to become a member of the faith.

21 By contrast, in the ethnocentric classroom, students are taught to believe in certain truths about their race or ethnic group. They are expected to believe what the teacher and the textbook believes, not to raise doubts or look for alternative explanations. The teacher offers up a pantheon of heroes and stories about the struggles of the faithful, and students are not supposed to disagree. The message of the ethnocentric classroom is, believe what you are told; do not question or doubt. In the same sense, the ethnocentric classroom resembles a sectarian approach to teaching.

22 Based on method alone, public education must reject ethnocentrism. The public schools do not exist to indoctrinate students into the faith of their ancestors or to instill ethnocentric pride—not for whites, or blacks, or Hispanics, or Asians, or American Indians.

The public schools must prepare the younger generation to live in the world of the 21st century, a world of global interdependence, a world of differences—where what will count is what we know, what we can do, and our ability to think creatively and work with others.

23 The history curriculum should not become a tool to build self-esteem or ethnic pride. It is a subject in which to learn about our society and the world, and sometimes the truth can be unpleasant. All of the peoples in the world have been guilty of terrible misdeeds: the Aztecs and Mayans practiced human slavery and human sacrifice; Germans and other Europeans committed genocide against millions of Jews and other Europeans during the Second World War; in Soviet Russia, millions of landowners and political dissidents were killed by their own government; the regime of Idi Amin slaughtered hundreds of thousands of Ugandans; in Nigeria, a million or more Biafrans were murdered by other Africans; in Cambodia, the Pol Pot regime killed more than a million of their fellow Cambodians; the Turks slaughtered hundreds of thousands of Armenians at the time of the first World War; the Chinese Communists murdered millions of Chinese during the 1950s and 1960s; the Iraqis killed thousands of Iraqi Kurds with poison gas in 1982; the Burmese military gunned down thousands of students in 1988.

24 The record of death and genocide and slavery and human suffering is truly universal. The more we learn about history, the more humble we should all become. Human beings, it seems, have always found plenty of reasons to hate and kill other human beings. Differences in the way we look, the way we dress, the god we worship, the language we speak—almost anything has provided grounds for hatred. And if you pick up the daily paper and read the news, you will see that the beat goes on, all over the world—in India, Pakistan, Armenia, Romania, Liberia, Ireland, Burma, China, South Africa, and Lebanon.

25 Given the dismal record of humankind, particularly during the 20th century, it would seem that we as educators should do whatever we can to discourage ethnocentrism and to promote a sense of respect for our common humanity. Ethnocentrism does not belong in public education. It undermines the very purpose of public education, which is to create a community to which we all belong.

26 How can you tell whether a curriculum is pluralist or ethnocentric? It requires thought—it requires intelligence. How can you tell the difference between objective reporting and propaganda? You have to think about it. How can you tell the difference between science and creation science? You have to think about it.

27 Here are some parameters: The pluralist curriculum stresses learning about a subject, while the ethnocentric curriculum indoctrinates students into the tribe or the ways of the elders. The pluralist curriculum promotes mutual respect among people from culturally different backgrounds, while the ethnocentric curriculum promotes feelings of anger, vengeance, bitterness, and hatred. The pluralist curriculum promotes a sense of mutuality and interdependence, while the ethnocentric curriculum promotes racial and ethnic separatism. The pluralist curriculum promotes the building of a community that crosses ethnic/racial/religious lines, while the ethnocentric curriculum builds separate communities based on race or ethnicity or religion.

28 My parents were immigrants, yet I feel that I too inherited Thomas Jefferson's claim that "All men are created equal." I am a woman, yet I feel that I too share Abraham Lincoln's call to rededicate ourselves to the proposition "that government of the people, by the people, for the people, shall not perish from the earth." I am white, yet I celebrate Martin Luther King Jr. as a role model of brevity, profundity, and eloquence.

29 We were not born knowing how to hate those who are different. As the song in South Pacific says, you have to be taught to hate, "you have to be carefully taught." It should be our goal as educators to teach respect and mutuality.

30 Culture is not skin color. Culture is history, tradition, and experience. Just as we need to know those experiences that make us different, we need to know the ideas and experiences that hold us together in community. We are all of us—black and white, Hispanic and Asian, American Indian and recent immigrant—in a common project. Education is the means that we have chosen to make it work. It is the spirit of interdependence, the spirit of mutuality, the spirit of respect for our many heritages, and the spirit of common purpose that we must build and cultivate in our schools.

Imperatives of an Afrocentric Curriculum
Molefi Kete Asante

"When a lot of people, especially white people, hear the word 'Afrocentricity,' they feel threatened, nervous, or both. They shouldn't." This is the reassuring view developed at length in a guest editorial in the *Washington Post National Weekly Edition* (November 26-December 2, 1990, p. 28) by Franklyn G. Jenifer, president of the historically black Howard University in Washington, D.C. In contrast, David Nicholson argues in a commentary essay on multicultural curricula in the *Washington Post National Weekly Edition* (October 8-14, 1990, pp. 23-24): "The question, though, is not whether the curriculum needs to be changed, but whose vision will prevail—that of the nationalists and the zealots, or that of more reasonable people who still believe in a common American culture and shared national values."

When Molefi Kete Asante addressed over two thousand listeners at the Detroit Public Schools Annual Teachers Conference in Cobo Hall in Detroit on February 4, 1991, clearly he was at the center of a national controversy. Asante is chair of the Department of African American Studies at Temple University in Philadelphia, has been a Fulbright professor at the Zimbabwe Institute of Mass Communications, and is chief consultant for the Baltimore public school system's Afrocentric Curriculum Project.

Asante intertwines his presentation of the problem and the proposed solution. The problem—the need to change from a Eurocentric to a truly multicultural curriculum—is described and explained at length (7, 9, 12, 16–17). Asante heightens concern for the problem through examples (10–11) and through an analogy that encourages whites to perceive the issue from an African American viewpoint (4–5). In analyzing this analogy, you are encouraged to apply the relevant standards for soundness of literal analogy discussed in the theory section of Chapter 4 on propositions of fact.

Asante advocates adoption of a multicultural public school curriculum based on the model of an Afrocentric curriculum. In describing the basic assumptions and components of the program, how clear are some of the key concepts (8, 19, 21). For example, what does he mean by hegemony (3), or by the subject-object distinction (6)? As another method of defending the components of an Afrocentric curriculum, Asante refutes criticisms by his opponents (4, 12, 18, 22–24). What arguments and evidence does he use in refutation and how reasonably does he use them? Again, consider the clarity of his key concepts. How well would his audience probably understand his criticism of the pluralist-particularist distinction (19)?

Although in this speech Asante does not mention Diane Ravitch by name, in other speeches he does so in refuting his opponents. On some occasions, Ravitch has distinguished her pluralist multicultural program from what she terms Asante's particularist multiculturalism. Without naming them in this speech, Asante characterizes the criticisms by his opponents as hysterical, strident, screaming, and mis-readings (perhaps intentional). Consider in what ways, if any, Ravitch's arguments in the previous speech warrant such labels. Note that like Ravitch, Asante, too, depicts for his audience a stark either-or choice. Here it is between "true multiculturalism" based on the Afrocentric model and "maintenance of the white hegemony" through Ravitch's "pluralist" approach (20). To what degree would you accept this either-or choice as reasonable? Why?

Does an Afrocentric approach to multiculturalism as proposed by Asante seem dangerously ethnocentric in the ways contended by Ravitch in the previous speech? What concrete evidence from Asante's speech would you cite to support your judgment? For example, what is Asante's view on pride and self-esteem, on devaluation of European-heritage contributions to culture, and on a pluralism of respect for all different cultures?

In response to Ravitch's initial article in *The American Scholar,* 59 (Summer 1990), Asante and Ravitch engage in a very heated and more detailed exchange in the same journal (Vol. 60, Spring 1991, pp. 267–276). You are urged to read this exchange with their speeches. Advocates of policies to solve societal problems often argue their cases through varied channels as part of a continuous persuasive campaign: speeches; articles in scholarly journals or popular magazines; books; television talk-show or news program interviews; guest editorials or letters to the editor in newspapers.

The text of this speech was provided by Molefi Kete Asante.

---

1 Since the publication of my first book on centering the educational experience in the child's reality, *Afrocentricity* in 1980 and subsequent works such as *The Afrocentric Idea* (1987) and more recently *Kemet, Afrocentricity, and Knowledge* (1990), there has been quite a lot of controversy about its relationship to the revitalization of curricula at every level of American education. Quite frankly, some of the more hysterical and strident voices against Afrocentricity seem to confirm what Alexander Thomas and Samuel Sillen wrote in their wonderful book, *Racism and Psychiatry,* about the interrelatedness of the idea of African American inferiority and African American pathology in the mainstream thinking.

2 The imperatives of an Afrocentric curriculum are found in three important propositions about education:

1. Education is fundamentally a social phenomenon.
2. Schools prepare children for society.
3. Societies develop schools suitable to the societies.

3 I have argued for an Afrocentric curriculum as a way to systematically augment the teaching of African American children and as a method of centering children in their own historical experiences. Since the primary mode of instruction and the basic design of curriculum are Eurocentric, we have never been in danger of losing the centeredness of white children. An Afrocentric curriculum has to be developed before a general multicultural curriculum can be implemented. If there is no organic presentation of scope and sequence information about the African American, then there can be no multicultural project because most Americans, including African Americans, are woefully ignorant of the African American experience. Educated in the same system of white hegemony as other students, the African American comes out of the experience of school knowing next to nothing about Africa or African Americans. White students, without the benefit of cultural hearsay, know even less.

4 Opposition to the idea of teaching children from the standpoint of their centeredness rather than marginality has reached screaming levels. Those who oppose a centric education for African American children seem to say that content does not matter, yet the same opponents would find it unthinkable to teach white children a curriculum that is not centered in their experiences. For the most part, what we have right this moment in American education is a self-esteem curriculum for white children. It would be interesting to test the theory that self-esteem does not matter in the curriculum by simply eliminating the Eurocentric basis of the present curriculum and replacing it with, say, an Asio-centric one. Would some white children master such a curriculum? Of course they would. But a larger number would simply find the information, accurate as it might be, about the Vedic Period, varuna, Mokska, Bodhisattva, and the Ulama, a rather dislocating experience for them.

5 Accustomed as they would be to their parents stories about King Henry VIII, Shakespeare, Goethe, Joan of Arc, and Homer, white children in an Asio-centric classroom would find it extremely troubling. Can one expect any less of children of African descent who are fed only Eurocentric information?

6 Across this dynamic nation there is a renewed sense of the possible in education. The reason for the excitement lies in a very simple proposition about education: children will learn with a greater sense of integrity if they view themselves as subjects rather than as objects. When a teacher places a child in the context of the information being taught the child gains a greater sense of self and more enthusiasm for learning. There are enough studies, including those of Dr. Faheem Ashanti of the North Carolina Central University, to demonstrate the value of this proposition.

7 Stated particularly, African American or Latino children should be taught in such a way that they are not alienated from the material they are supposed to be learning. Children of European ancestry do not have to be reinforced in this way because the manner of teaching and the curriculum itself perpetuate a Eurocentric hegemony in education. Furthermore, this view is promoted as a universal truth.

8 Education should reinforce students in their history and heritage as a matter of choice. This does not mean that students should only be taught information that is comfortable and accessible but rather that the teacher should be sensitive to the historical perspectives of the students in the classroom. Any good communicator seeks to know his or her audience.

9 When teachers teach information centered only on the European experience they do not have to make a case about the teaching of European dominance and supremacy; the structure of the curriculum is itself the message of Eurocentric hegemony. What we teach is normally considered what is important and since most schools teach Europe instead of Africa or Asia, students assume that Europe is not only significant but that it is more significant than it ought to be in a multicultural society.

10 When one teaches about Marco Polo, or William of Normandy, or Goethe, or Joan of Arc, one is essentially engaging in the process of transmitting information about a cultural heritage and legacy. The names of the Africans, Ibn Battuta, or King Sundiata of Mali, or Ahmed Baba, or Yenenga, are never spoken in high school classes, and under the current curricular structure, if they were heard, would lack credibility even though they are by world standards certainly the equal of the Europeans I have mentioned in contrast.

11 The African American child whose parents speak of Sojourner Truth or James Weldon Johnson will most likely never hear those names spoken in any respectable way in a classroom from kindergarten to 12th grade. Instead of being reinforced in cultural heritage, African American children are being placed in crisis. Those who remain in school often have to put up with the total disregard of their own history and heritage. This is not so for white children and should not be so for any children.

12 Our society is multicultural and multi-ethnic and the idea of teaching as if the African American has no historical legacy or to force the discussion of our history to the Enslavement is to teach incorrectly and inadequately. More than this, it reinforces the false notion of white superiority and the equally false notion of black inferiority. We cannot afford to continue to promote the idea that African Americans who demand that an Afrocentric curriculum be infused into the general curriculum are asking amiss. It is the path of folly not just for African Americans but for all of the children of this society who are depending upon us to transmit to them the proper tools for living in this global village.

13 Another point should be made about this project. It is a project about accuracy and fullness in education. The aim of Afrocentric education is not merely to raise self-esteem of African American children. Indeed we have found that few African American children have problems with self-esteem; the real problem is with self-confidence. One can have a good feeling about one's personal attributes but feel a deep lack of confidence brought on by a lack of knowledge. Thus, while self-esteem may be a by-product of the central objective of the Afrocentric method, which is to provide a wholistic, accurate interpretation of the world, self-confidence will certainly be improved by this method.

14 Such an approach will have an impact on white students as well as African American, Latino, and Asian students. For some students it will be the first time that they will have heard the ancient Egyptians discussed as Africans or discovered that Africans played a significant role in the Revolutionary War. It is a fact that we African Americans were here before the United States government and many of our families have lived on this land longer than the families of many presidents of this country.

15 Of course, none of these ideas will have a full impact on education until there are big changes in schools of education throughout the nation. I am not aware of any school of education that has grappled with this problem in any serious manner. In some of the training institutions for teachers it is still possible for a teacher who will eventually teach in an urban setting to complete a degree without ever having taken a course in African American studies! This is truly unbelievable, but it is at the heart of the matter. Certainly the Afrocentric idea ought to be among the perspectives taught in institutions of teacher training.

16 A few months ago I asked fifty principals to identify the names of five African ethnic groups from West Africa. I explained to them that there were no African Americans three hundred and seventy two years ago. Africans who were brought to America against their wills came from particular ethnic groups often with long and important histories. Who are the African Americans you see in your schools? What are some of the names of the groups that combined in the Americas to produce the present African American population?

17 Sadly, almost no one knew the name of an African ethnic group that had become a contributor to the African American gene pool. Names like Yoruba, Hausa, Fulani, Ibo, Baule, Congo, Angola, Serere, Wolof, Mandinka did bring something to mind for a few of the principals when I began to mention them. These are the names of the people, who along with Native Americans and some Europeans, contributed to the present day gene pool of African Americans.

18 Afrocentricity is not an ethnocentric view. While Eurocentric views are often promulgated as universal views, e.g., classical music as European concert music or classical dance as European ballet, etc., the Afrocentric view seeks no valorization of African-centeredness above any other perspective on reality. It is human centered in the sense that no one should be divested of his or her heritage or background. Normally, the only people asked to do so are those who do not hold physical or psychological power. Ethnocentric views valorize themselves and degrade others. Afrocentricity promotes pluralism without hierarchy.

19 To say that we are a multicultural and multi-ethnic society must not mean that we promote a view of these cultures only through the eyes of whites. A true multiculturalism presupposes that we know something about the cultures. Few of those who have spoken or written about multiculturalism seem to understand that the road to a true multiculturalism leads by the way of Afrocentricity. The development of a systematic, organic, wholistic portrayal of the African culture as opposed to a detached, episodic, personality-based version is necessary for a real multicultural project.

20 The idea of a pluralist multiculturalism and a particularist multiculturalism is a non-starter. This first idea is a redundancy and the second is an oxymoron. You either believe in a true multiculturalism or you believe in the maintenance of the white hegemony in education. As a nation we must choose between these positions, there is no other choice.

21 I have made my choice for multiculturalism which means that I need to know all I can about the cultures of the nation. Does it mean that we will now have to know more about Native Americans, Latinos, Asians? Yes, it does and we will be a better nation because of it. Does it mean that the enforcement of a white hegemony on information and process in education is over? Probably not. However, we will never be able to exercise the full potential of this nation until we realize the incredible beauty and value of the collective cultures of America.

22 Finally, Afrocentricity does not negate all Eurocentric views. It should, however, modify those views that are pejorative and stereotypical. By pointing to other perspectives including Native American, Asian, and Latino as well, Afrocentricity suggests a new compact among American peoples. Of course, this means that the Eurocentric idea will not control the structure of knowledge but become, as it should have been all along, one perspective besides many.

23 This should be welcomed in a society such as ours where we will have in fifty years a largely non-European population needing to be educated but needing to be turned on to education by having the same advantage European Americans have had all along, education which centers them in the experience being taught. No one has suggested that this cease being the case with European Americans. However, we have said that where the Eurocentric perspective has turned racist, ethnocentric, or sexist, it should eliminate those attitudes. Pejoratives and racist language should be removed and the curriculum infused with an Afrocentric curriculum. This step is absolutely necessary, otherwise there are those who say that they want multiculturalism without knowing anything about the African American culture. They say they favor multiculturalism and still want to retain the negative expressions about Native Americans or Latinos. The path to multiculturalism goes by the way of cultural respect. This is as true in the United States as it should be in Israel and South Africa, and any other nation where human beings of different heritages live together.

24 It is certainly a mis-reading, perhaps even a deliberate misreading, of the concept of Afrocentricity to say that it means a blacks-only curriculum. No one that I know has proposed we replace Shakespeare with Ahmed Baba or James Baldwin. We say let us share in the great diversity of everyone. Why not teach Maimonides alongside Frederick Douglass and Wendell Phillips? Why not discuss the contributions of Yenenga, or Yaa Asantewaa, or Nzingha, alongside those of Joan of Arc? If we learn about Marco Polo, what is wrong with learning about the African, Ibn Battuta who travelled farther than Marco Polo and was considered the greatest traveller of the medieval period? Why not alert students to the story of Abubakari II who is reported to have travelled to Mexico from his empire in West Africa in 1312? We must recognize that this nation is an incomplete project whose present is not its past and whose future will not be what we know now. Let us prepare all of our children for the multicultural future that is surely around the turn of the century.

Sacred Rights: Preserving Reproductive Freedom
Faye Wattleton

Legalized abortion—whether to allow it and, if so, under what restrictions, if any—continues to be a major political and moral issue at the national, state, and local levels. In this continuing debate, advocates of differing positions and policies struggle over fundamental distinctions and concepts: the competing values of life and of freedom of choice; the tension between legal rights and moral responsibilities; the definition of when ''life'' begins; the constitutional separation of church and state—of religious doctrine and public policy.

In 1973 in *Roe v. Wade,* the U.S. Supreme Court in a 7–2 decision held that a fetus is not a person in a legal sense of the term and that laws restricting women's access to legal abortion violate her constitutional right to privacy. The Court held that a woman had the right to terminate her pregnancy until the final three months of the pregnancy. In July 1989, in *Webster v. Reproductive Health Services,* a 5–4 decision by the U.S. Supreme Court agreed that Missouri had the right to prohibit use of public facilities and personnel to aid abortions that are not necessary to save the mother's life. Without overturning *Roe v. Wade,* the Court opened the option for states to consider more restrictive laws on abortion.

On June 25, 1990, Faye Wattleton accepted the ''Ministry to Women Award'' of the Unitarian Universalist Women's Federation at their meeting in Milwaukee, Wisconsin. Wattleton holds both Bachelor of Science and Master of Science degrees in nursing and since 1978 she has been President of the Planned Parenthood Federation of America. Planned Parenthood advocates contraception, abortion, sterilization, and infertility services as means of voluntary fertility regulation. In an analysis of Faye Wattleton as ''Ms. Family Planning,'' Paula Span (*Washington Post National Weekly Edition,* November 2, 1987, pp. 8–9) observes: ''Both supporters and foes go on at length about her articulateness, her presence, and her forcefulness.'' Indeed Faye Wattleton may be one of the most prominent and influential black women in America.

The Unitarian Universalist Women's Federation supports human rights for all, especially rights of women. The Federation supports the *Roe v. Wade* decision, quality in child care centers, concern for the family, and work for and with the aging. In accepting her award from this favorably disposed audience, Wattleton identifies points of commonality between herself, Planned Parenthood, and the Federation (1–4, 29, 33–34).

The policy that Faye Wattleton advocates and defends is legal protection for reproductive choice and for women's right to privacy (5). She advocates continuation of the *Roe* decision, constitutional protection of fundamental freedoms, and privacy from governmental intrusion (14, 28). She also advocates continued separation of church and state (9–10) and believes that morality should not be legislated (25). The *Webster* decision and the orientation of the current Supreme Court are problems that threaten the *Roe* constitutionally protected policy (6, 8). Through antithetical phrasing, she alludes to other policies advocated by Planned Parenthood: sex education in public schools; adequate adoption and child care; improved birth control methods (27).

Wattleton argues against opposing positions by reducing them to absurdities—by extending them to their logical but ridiculous extremes (11–12)—and by exposing contradictions (18). Evaluate how fairly and reasonably she develops these arguments. What persuasive function might be served by her references to positive political changes in Eastern Europe (15, 23)? She employs statistics to argue that the shepherd has inappropriately strayed from the flock (32). Within a religious context, what objections might there be to the logic of this argument?

Finally, consider some of the distinctive language resources that Wattleton employs. Frequently she uses alliteration to associate a series of positive items (4, 5, 31). Parallel structure is utilized effectively to reinforce a point through a series of examples (13, 14, 21, 25). Note the vivid negative images that Wattleton creates to characterize some of her opponents: under siege (5); zealots (6, 22); fanatics (21); obscene (25); oppressive tyrant, vicious and violent (30). How reasonable and appropriate are these labels for the people she describes? What is your evidence to support your judgment?

The text of this speech was provided by the national office of the Planned Parenthood Federation of America.

———————

1 As some of you know, I am a minister's daughter, so addressing a religious gathering always feels like coming home. I'm *especially* comfortable in a Unitarian setting: I've had the honor of speaking from the pulpit of All Souls Church in New York; I've joined Forrest Church in his "All Souls World of Ideas" discussion programs; and last fall I took part in a sunrise Unitarian service in Kennebunk, Maine.

2 I can honestly say that some of my *best friends* are Unitarian Universalists!—including Planned Parenthood's executive vice president David Andrews. David and I were chatting recently with one of our affiliate presidents, whose husband is the Episcopal bishop of New Mexico. She was telling David that she feels very warmly toward Unitarians. When she and her husband first moved to Albuquerque, their new Episcopal church wasn't ready for use. Since Unitarians don't have summer services, the Unitarian church facility was made available to them. At that point I asked David, "Why don't Unitarians go to church in the summer?" David said, "I don't know, I guess it's just too hot." To which the bishop's wife replied, "Not as hot as it's *gonna* be!"

3 Planned Parenthood's founder Margaret Sanger was herself a Unitarian. In fact, the Brooklyn Unitarian Church gave her both spiritual and financial support back in 1916, when she opened the nation's first birth control clinic—the tiny storefront that grew to become the nation's foremost public health movement.

4 Since that first auspicious alliance, Planned Parenthood has enjoyed a warm partnership with generations of Unitarians the world over. As individuals and as a church, you've shown your commitment to tolerance and compassion—to civil rights and civil liberties—to the free exercise of any religion or *no* religion. Your faith has been a *clarion call to conscience* for women and men in all walks of life.

5 And your uplifted voices have never mattered more than *now*. For one of our most precious, most personal freedoms is imperilled as never before. Reproductive choice—the right that makes all our *other* rights possible—is under siege. Last July—16 years after

Roe v. Wade recognized women's constitutional right to abortion—the Supreme Court retreated from that historic ruling. In *Webster v. Reproductive Health Services,* the Court severely curbed women's access to abortion—and invited an all-out attack on our cherished right to *privacy.*

6 Plainly put, *Webster* allows state governments to put *fetuses* first. And zealots in *every state* are trying to do just that. More than *450* anti-choice bills have been introduced in the past year in *44* state legislatures. Re-energized pro-choice forces have defeated most such efforts. But in Pennsylvania, Guam, and now Louisiana, legislatures have advanced bills that would virtually eliminate legal abortion.

7 When *Roe v. Wade* was decided in 1973, who could have *imagined* that Americans would be fighting this battle in *1990?* As Yogi Berra said, "It's like *deja vu* all over again!"

8 Historically, we have counted on the courts to *expand* rights that were not explicit in the Constitution—rights for women, minorities, children, the disabled. But *today's* Court interprets the Constitution the way fundamentalists interpret the Bible—with a stubborn literalism. If a right wasn't *spelled out* by that first quill pen, it doesn't exist! In other words, "If you don't see it on the shelf, we don't carry it—and we won't order it!"

9 One of the *most* troubling aspects of the *Webster* decision is the least-discussed. It concerns the preamble to the Missouri Constitution, which defines *human life* as *beginning at conception.* The Supreme Court refused to rule on this matter—and thus allowed Missouri to make a narrow, *religious* belief *the law of the land!*

10 Preferential treatment for *one* religion over *others* is blatantly unconstitutional. It's like that old bumper sticker from the '60s—"*Your kar*ma ran over *my dog*ma!" Since when is Roman Catholicism our national faith? The view of the Catholic Church—or any other denomination, for that matter—is valid for those who adhere to it. But Americans must *never* be *governed* by it—or by *any religious doctrine!*

11 We've already seen some *bizarre* legal outcomes of this religious definition of human life. Lawsuits have cropped up claiming fetuses as dependents for tax purposes—or charging "illegal imprisonment" of the fetuses of pregnant inmates—or seeking to reclassify juvenile offenders as adults by tacking an extra nine months onto their age!

12 What's *bizarre* today may turn *grim* by tomorrow. Compulsory pregnancy, forced Caesareans, surveillance and detention of pregnant women—these are the chilling, *logical* outcomes of laws that reduce women to *instruments of the state.*

13 We are *not* instruments of the state! We are *persons,* with human needs and human rights. It is nothing less than *evil* to deny our reproductive autonomy. Without it, our other rights are meaningless. Without it, our dignity is destroyed. And the first victims will be those among us who are already most vulnerable—those whose rights are *already* precarious—those whose access to health care is *already* limited—the young, the poor, and usually that means minorities.

14 But reproductive freedom is an issue that goes *beyond* the disadvantaged, *beyond* state boundaries, *far beyond* abortion itself. It goes to the heart of what this country stands for—to the principles embodied in our *Bill of Rights.* Our Constitution established powers

of government and majority rule—and the purpose of the Bill of Rights was to set clear *limits* on those powers. The authors of that great document knew that certain fundamental freedoms must be *guaranteed—insulated* from public debate, *immune* to partisan politics.

15 For over 200 years, America has been "a light unto the nations." How disgraceful, that in *1989,* the year the Berlin Wall came down and the Iron Curtain parted, the only barricade that started to crumble in *this* country was the precious wall protecting our private freedoms!

16 The crack in that wall may soon go even further—this time disenfranchising *teenagers.* Supreme Court rulings are pending in two cases involving mandatory parental notification for minors' abortions.

17 Most of us think parents *should* be involved in such a serious decision. And most pregnant teens *do* tell their parents. But laws that *force a family chat* can be *deadly*—not only for teens in unstable or violent homes—but also for teens with *loving* families. In Indiana, where parental notice is required, one teenager risked an illegal abortion rather than disappoint her parents—and it killed her.

18 It's true that parental involvement laws provide something called a judicial bypass. Minors who feel they *can't* confide in their parents may appear before a judge instead. But the judge is in a hopeless bind: by ruling that a minor is *too immature* to choose an abortion, the judge rules by implication that she is somehow *mature enough to become a mother!* Such a paradox would try the *wisdom of Solomon!*

19 The fact is, judges simply have *no business* making this decision for teens *or* adult women. Any female capable of *becoming* pregnant must have the ability to *prevent* or *end* a pregnancy. That right must never depend on age, race, state residence, wealth—*or* the vagaries of partisan politics. That right is as basic and as precious as our right to assemble here today.

20 Such fundamental freedoms are the proudest heritage of our nation. But our heritage of *Puritanism* also remains deeply rooted. My favorite description of the Puritans is this one, by a 19th century humorist: "The Puritans nobly fled from a land of despotism to a land of freedom—where they could not only enjoy their *own* religion, but where they could prevent everybody *else* from enjoying *theirs!*"

21 The flames of intolerance still burn brightly in this nation. And, like all religious fanatics, *today*'s Puritans subscribe to their own moral code—a code that embraces far more *brutality* than *morality.* To "save lives," they burn clinics. To "defend womanhood," they taunt and threaten pregnant women. To "strengthen the family," they invade our privacy. Blinded by their disregard for the *neediest* of women, they insist that making abortion *harder to get* will make it *go away.*

22 Haven't these zealots learned *anything* from history? Throughout time, women with unwanted pregnancies have *always ended them,* regardless of the law, regardless of the risk to our lives! Throughout the world, women and men equate *freedom* and *democracy* with the right to make private reproductive decisions, *free from government intrusion!*

23 The recent history of Romania is a perfect example. When Ceaucescu was over-thrown, two of the *first acts* of the *new* government were to decriminalize abortion—and to deregulate the private ownership of *typewriters.* The new regime clearly recognized that *reproductive choice* is as *fundamental* as *freedom of speech!*

24 If only *our own* government were so wise. On the contrary, our president has taken a *jackhammer* to the bedrock of our basic rights. He has repeatedly asked the Supreme Court to overturn *Roe v. Wade.* He has attacked the federal family planning program, which helps *prevent* half a million abortions each year. And in a recent Supreme Court brief, his administration attacked not only the right to *abortion,* but the very *concept of privacy* that underlies our right to *contraception!*

25 It's nothing short of *obscene* that women are forced to *expose ourselves* to politicians—to submit our *private* matters, our *private* decisions, and our *private* parts to *public* debate! Morality should be taught in the home—it should be preached from the pulpit—it should be practiced in our individual lives—but it must *never* be legislated by lawmakers.

26 *Surely,* America's politicians have more *important* things to do. Like house the homeless, feed the hungry, and educate the ignorant. Like tackle the *root cause* of the abortion issue: *unintended pregnancy.*

27 Instead of compulsory ignorance, we need comprehensive sexuality education—in every home and in every school, from grades K–12. Instead of laws that punish pregnant women, we need our government's commitment to develop better birth control. Instead of pontifications about the *un*born, we need proper care for the children *already* born.

28 Finally, instead of sermons on the stump, we need to be *left alone by the government.* We need to remove the abortion debate *forever* from the legislative arena. We need a universal recognition that our civil liberties are *off limits to partisan politics!* They are *fundamental* rights! *Indivisible* rights! *Non-negotiable* rights!

29 *Your* advocacy is essential to making these goals a reality. I learned a lot about organized religion from my minister mother. So I know that congregational life can have a profoundly positive impact—not only on our daily lives as individuals—but on the formation of our values and principles as a nation. The best possible wielding of that impact is exemplified by all of you today. You are ever aware that *your* right to freely practice your faith is only as secure as *other* people's right to believe differently. You are eternally *intolerant of intolerance.*

30 When the mechanism of religion goes awry, it is an *oppressive tyrant.* Some fanatics are merely self-righteous. Others are vicious and violent. For *all* those who seek to browbeat the rest of us, I have *these* words, by the folklorist Zora Neale Hurston: "I'll bet you, when you get down on them rusty knees and get to worrying God, He goes in His privy-house and slams the door. *That*'s what He thinks about *you* and *your* prayers!"

31 Those of us who lead spiritual lives have a special responsibility to combat fanaticism. We must remind Americans that *true* morality lies in the freedom to *make* choices—not in *prohibiting* them. We must lift up our voices for liberty—among our families and friends, our colleagues and communities, our pundits and politicians. We must preach from our pulpits that we hold our privacy *sacred!*

32 Happily, the "gospel" *we* are spreading *already* has millions of adherents. The Roman Catholic Church, however, is less fortunate. As I'm sure you've heard, the Church has launched a *$5 million* P.R. campaign to promote its anti-choice message. Questionable priorities aside, this is clearly an act of *desperation.* Has the Church examined its membership lately? Lay Catholics are overwhelmingly *pro-choice!* Three out of four use contraception—77% favor legal abortion in some or all situations—and 85% say a woman can have an abortion and still be a "good Catholic." Clearly, the *shepherd* has strayed from the *flock!*

33 In *this* flock, though, I sense great unity and strength. Maybe that's because you can support reproductive rights and still be a *good Unitarian!* In fact, from what I understand, to be a good Unitarian *by definition* is to support liberty, justice, equality, and a plurality of opinions—and *that's* what *pro-choice really means.*

34 Margaret Sanger, the good Unitarian, once said: "I have always known that it is not enough just to know one great truth. Truth must be *lived*—not merely passively accepted." I know all of you share that courage and that commitment. I am proud to count you among my friends. Thank you for your prestigious award—but much more, for your partnership in our shared faith.

Address on Abortion
Jerry Falwell

As a television evangelist, Jerry Falwell's "Old Time Gospel Hour" reached over 500,000 homes during the mid-1980s. His Moral Majority conservative political organization claimed four million members. Falwell is founder and pastor of the Thomas Road Baptist Church in Lynchburg, Virginia, with over 20,000 members. Also he is founder and chancellor of Liberty University in Lynchburg. In late 1987 Falwell stepped down as head of the Moral Majority to devote more time to his ministry. In the summer of 1989, Falwell announced that the Moral Majority was being dissolved although the key policies that it had advocated would continue on the public agenda for national debate.

At the Unity '90 Conference in Chicago on June 28, 1990, Falwell addressed a wide range of groups and individuals associated to one degree or another with the pro-life or anti-abortion movement. At such a conference, one natural goal of the speech was to promote social cohesion (8–10). He warns that conflict and bickering among pro-life groups only weakens the effort to reverse *Roe* and to make abortion illegal (4–7). Also he urges cooperation and compromise among the diverse groups in the service of the larger goal (52–54). And of the four "challenges" he describes facing them, the first two stress the social cohesion theme (10–11). Falwell's early massive accumulation of diverse statistics vividly reminds his listeners of the difficulties they still face (3).

But the bulk of Falwell's speech advocates instrumental courses of action that should be adopted to promote significantly the achievement of the ultimate policy—reversal of *Roe* and making abortion illegal. One major action urged by Falwell is opposition to development and distribution of RU 486, the so-called abortion pill (14–15).

Clearly, however, Falwell's primary focus is advocacy of reframing the public debate on the abortion issue and overcoming confusing and misapplied labels (12–13). He offers an extensive plan of argumentation to retake the initiative through refuting ten "myths and misconceptions" that have been "perpetuated for so long by our opponents and the media" (17–50).

Consider, now, the array of rhetorical choices that characterize his speech. Bear in mind that the unspoken definitional assumption that "life" (humanness) begins at conception undergirds his statistics on the "killing" of "innocent and defenseless children" (1, 3). For some of the statistics he uses, he specifies their sources (36, 39–41) while for other statistics he does not specify sources (3, 43). Why should he or should he not have supplied more information on the sources and methods from which the statistics stem? Note also the specifics on several research studies are lacking (18, 19).

You are urged to apply the relevant standard tests for soundness of use of testimony (discussed in Chapter 4 on propositions of fact) to his extensive reliance on various kinds of testimony. Falwell quotes respected religious figures (0, 14, 07, 55), medical experts (06), opponents to use their own words to convict them (15), and journalistic sources that combine judgments with examples (11, 30, 33, 45–46, 49). Especially evaluate the reasonableness of his pervasive use of "reluctant" testimony from persons normally identified with the opposition and normally not expected to say anything favorable to the pro-life cause (20–22, 29, 31–32, 46).

For example, no source is provided for the quotation from Tietze and Henshaw so that a listener might check its accuracy and context (20). The quotation from Dr. Hern's medical textbook (21) should be understood in the context of the chapter in which it appears, where he laments the inadequate training in safe abortion procedures of many surgeons, not that abortion procedures in themselves are unsafe. The quotation by Dr. Calderone (22) represents her personal position and understanding of psychiatric evidence as of 1959, is not an official position of the Planned Parenthood Federation, is part of a speech on the dangers of *illegal* abortion, and is in a context where Calderone advocates reduced need for abortion through increased sex education and contraception availability. (See Calderone, "Illegal Abortion as a Public Health Problem," *American Journal of Public Health,* July 1960, pp. 948–954; Paul K. B. Dagg, "The Psychological Sequelae of Therapeutic Abortion—Denied and Completed," *American Journal of Psychiatry,* May 1991, pp. 578–585.)

Assess, also, the responsibilities of Falwell's interpretation of public opinion poll evidence (24–28) and the soundness of his use of examples (6–7, 37, 42, 44, 48). He argues that morality and religion take precedence over law and human opinion (23, 28). To what extent should this be the case for public policy as well as for private morality? Falwell sometimes uses comparison, analogy, and simile to undercut an opposing argument (15, 21, 50). How fair, accurate, and well-founded are these comparisons?

Among the many books on the abortion controversy, one with special relevance for the rhetorical critic is Celeste Condit, *Decoding Abortion Rhetoric: Communicating Social Change* (University of Illinois Press, 1990).

The text of this speech was provided by Rev. Falwell's office at Liberty University.

---

1 January 22, 1973 stands out in my mind as if it were yesterday. I was just 39 years old on the day the United States Supreme Court, by a vote of 7 to 2, struck down state bans on abortion. What has happened "legally" in this country in the 17 years since that infamous decision is almost incomprehensible. The lives of nearly 25 million innocent and defenseless children have been needlessly and selfishly snuffed out.

2 During these 17 years, the debate on abortion has been raging. Dozens, perhaps hundreds of groups and organizations have been formed to fight this issue from both sides. Countless pieces of legislation have been drafted. Some have been passed, some have been defeated, and virtually all have been challenged. Hundreds of thousands of people have marched and picketed both in opposition to and support of abortion. Thousands have even spent time in jail in defense of their position on this volatile issue.

3 With the exception of preaching the Gospel of Jesus Christ, no single issue has captivated my attention for so long a period of time as has the issue of abortion. This is a good time to stop and take a careful look at this issue and to ask ourselves, "Are we winning or losing the abortion struggle?" Well, let us consider some statistics.

1. Since 1973, nearly 25 million unborn children have been killed in America by legalized abortion—that is 1.5 million annually and 4,100 daily.
2. There were 1,160,389 American casualties from the Revolutionary War, Civil War, World War I, World War II, Korean War and Vietnam War combined. We will kill that many unborn children legally in the next 283 days.
3. Nearly 30 percent of all pregnancies end in induced abortion. 81 percent of abortion patients are unmarried. 43 percent of women having abortions have already had one or more abortions.
4. Our national bird enjoys better protection than does an unborn child. To damage an eagle's nest or shoot a bird is a crime that carries a maximum penalty of one year in prison and a $250,000 fine.
5. 13,000 dolphins died in 1989 at the hands of tuna fisherman, prompting a successful consumer boycott of the three major tuna canners. While this issue received tremendous national media coverage, we will kill nearly that many unborn children in this country by the time we wake up on Monday morning.
6. While 1.5 million babies are aborted in this country every year, *50 million* are aborted worldwide every year.
7. According to the Allan Guttmacher Institute, *46 percent* of American women over the age of 45 have had an abortion.

4 While I believe we are making progress on many fronts, I must admit that it is difficult to claim that we are "winning" in the "fight for life." That is why I am excited about UNITY '90. I am proud to join with like-minded people from across the country for this unified strategy session.

5 Unfortunately, it was the call to unity that this conference sent forth which brought to mind the lack of unity within the pro-life ranks which so often besets us. I am ashamed to say that our opponents are publicly far more unified than we are.

6 For example, during debate in the Idaho legislature earlier this year on a bill that would have restricted abortions in that state, a nationally known pro-life organization actually sent a representative to the legislature to testify *against* that bill. That same group later claimed partial credit when Gov. Cecil Andrus vetoed the bill that the legislature had passed. That kind of self-defeating behavior can only drag us down. Whether or not you think that particular bill was the best possible legislation, the fact is that it would have saved lives.

7 Let me give another example. Recently the National Conference of Catholic Bishops announced a $5 million nationwide anti-abortion campaign. NEWSWEEK magazine, April 23, 1990 reported the following about this news, "But surprising criticism came from the non-Catholic anti-abortion activist groups the Bishops hoped to reach." One of our nationally recognized pro-life brothers was quoted as saying, "Christ was in the trenches. The Bishops are not committed to fighting abortion in the most effective way, which is confrontation." That kind of public bickering is at best, counter-productive. There is no room or time for that kind of in-fighting. Unfortunately, our opponents are wise enough to speak with one voice.

8 Let me pause for a few moments to thank many people and organizations who are working faithfully to make a difference in the fight for human life. These people could comprise a Human Life Hall of Fame.

[EDITOR's NOTE: At this point Falwell at length praises numerous anti-abortion organizations, their leaders, and other individuals. American Life Lobby; Americans United for Life; Focus on the Family; National Conference of Catholic Bishops; Annual March for Life; Operation Rescue; and Bethany Christian Services. Dr. Bernard Nathanson, producer of the films "Silent Scream" and "Eclipse of Reason." U.S. Senators Jesse Helms, Orin Hatch, Bill Armstrong, and Gordon Humphrey. U.S. Representatives Henry Hyde, Christ Smith, and Bob Doran. Vice-President Dan Quayle and President George Bush.]

9 As far as I am concerned, this is what UNITY '90 is all about—bringing together different people with different strategies for *one* purpose—bringing an end to this holocaust which we call abortion. We may not agree with every person here on every aspect of the abortion debate but we can and *must* agree *on one* thing—that we must use our collective energies and resources to discontinue this national sin. We should also pledge never to publicly disagree with each other. Dr. Bob Jones, Sr., now in heaven, used to say, "I'd cheer for a hound dog if he came through Greenville barking for Jesus." I feel that way about the abortion issue. I applaud *anyone* who is doing *something* to chip away at this abomination. I appreciate what **Cardinal O'Connor** of New York said last year in an open letter.

I continue to respect and admire every individual who participates in the Pro-Life Movement in any way—through quiet prayer, through discouraging others through quiet personal persuasion from having abortions, through joining the March for Life in Washington, or in whatever way seems best suited to their own conscience, way of life, or other responsibilities. There is room for all in the Pro-Life Movement. No one need follow the way of others nor should any of us criticize the way of others. United we stand; divided, babies die.

10 Well, what are the challenges that lie before us today? *First* of all, we must develop a unified strategy on every front of the abortion issue. Hopefully, we will begin to put aside our differences and work together with one heart, one mind, and one voice.

11 *Secondly,* we must realize that the Webster decision handed down by the Supreme Court last July and the Minnesota and Ohio decisions handed down Monday did not create an atmosphere in which we could relax but, rather, one in which we must work harder than ever. U.S. NEWS & WORLD REPORT in its April 2, 1990 edition analyzed abortion in this country since the Webster ruling. They reported that "at the time the Court announced its decision in Webster, both pro-life and pro-choice advocates predicted the ruling would mark the denouement of abortion." They went on to quote several prominent leaders on both sides of the issue before drawing this conclusion: "Notwithstanding the hyperbole, the fact is that the right to abortion is just as unencumbered today as it was before the Webster ruling." I say this, not to discourage you, but to challenge all of us to more fervent and diligent work in the months ahead.

12 *Thirdly,* we must re-frame public debate on this issue. We have allowed the debate on abortion to be sidetracked and hijacked from the real issues. Admittedly, we have been virtually helpless on much of this because we do not control the media, but we can do better. For example, we have watched the most basic terminology change before our very eyes. While we were once called "pro-life," we are now routinely referred to as "*anti*-abortion." Likewise, our opponents, rather than being called "pro-abortion," are conveniently referred to as "pro-*choice*." Now, rather than being in *favor* of life, we are "*opposed* to a woman's right to choose." And our opponents, rather than being in favor of abortion are merely in favor of "a woman's right to choose." Let's re-focus the debate—let's debate what abortion *is,* rather than who is for it and who is not. Let's focus on the number of lives that have been lost rather than the number of people who march at our respective rallies.

13 Two months ago, I was proud to be an observer at the "Rally for Life" in Washington, DC. For over three hours one speaker after another delivered an important message on this issue. Yet throughout the day and in the days that followed, the overriding news story was the running debate over the number of people in attendance. As important as it is to have a strong and public show of support for our cause, it is not nearly as important as spreading the message that abortion is wrong and we have a "better way."

14 *Fourth,* and perhaps our greatest challenge ever, is the development of RU 486— the abortion pill, and its inevitable distribution in this country. As Chuck Colson recently wrote,

> What RU 486 will eventually mean, I fear, is a dramatic shift in the rules of the abortion battle. It will mean that our fight against abortion will no longer focus on the clinic, the dumpster, the Supreme Court steps. It will be relational and educational: Christians persuasively pressing the point among their peers that a life conceived is precious to God and must not be poisoned by a pill. The struggle will no longer be focused on legislatures and suction machines, but on people and the individual values they hold, the values that create their choices. What it means is changing the hearts and minds of a self-centered, callous generation.

15 I recently read, in PEOPLE magazine, an interview with the French medical researcher, Dr. Baulieu who has developed this abortion pill. He talks about abortion as if he were talking about a cure for the common cold, saying, "There is no reason to make a moral debate out of it. If something works, there's no reason to stop it." He goes on to say "there is no reason to be against us. We didn't invent abortion." That is about as logical as a politician supporting the legislation of cocaine and marijuana because he didn't invent the drugs. Some say that Dr. Baulieu may eventually win the Nobel Prize. God help us. If the Nobel Prize is awarded to this Doctor, they might as well award one posthumously to Adolph Hitler.

16 I think you will agree that the task that lies before us is a difficult one. Let's put our heads and hearts together and be heard with one loud voice.

17 How then, can we capture and reframe public debate on the abortion issue? There are many myths and misconceptions about abortion that must be dispelled or corrected. Many of these myths have been perpetrated for so long by our opponents and the media that many people automatically assume them to be accurate. Let me briefly discuss ten of these myths and how we can respond to them.

18 Myth 1: Making abortion illegal will mean a return to "back alley" abortions. The fact is that legalized abortion has merely brought "back alley" abortionists to Main Street. In-depth study shows that maternal deaths resulting from legal abortions are replacing those due to illegal abortions almost one-for-one.

19 Another study comparing the year after Medicaid funding was cut off to the year before showed that the number of abortions decreased dramatically and the number of child births decreased slightly. Instead of abortion, many were exercising greater responsibility in avoiding pregnancy.

20 Abortions may have been safer *prior* to *Roe* than they are now. According to Tietze and Henshaw of the Guttmacher Institute, "it is entirely possible that the death-to-case ratio following illegal abortion in the United States is *higher,* not lower, than it was 15 to 20 years ago."

21 Myth 2: If abortion is legal, it is safe and uncomplicated. Dr. Warren M. Hern, an abortionist and author of a leading text on abortion procedures, has stated that "in medical practice there are few surgical procedures given so little attention and so underrated in its potential hazards as abortion." Abortions can be performed virtually any place someone chooses to perform the procedure. Over three-fourths of abortions are performed in non-hospital facilities.

22 In 1959, Dr. Mary Calderone, Medical Director of Planned Parenthood, made a speech before the American Public Health Association in which she said:

> I ask you not to assume that I am indiscriminately for abortion. Believe me, I am not, for, aside from the fact that abortion is the taking of life, I am mindful of what was brought out by our psychiatrists, that in almost every case, abortion, whether legal or illegal, is a traumatic experience that may have severe kickbacks later on.

23 Also, don't forget that just because something is legal does not mean it is a desirable thing to do. A woman has the legal right to smoke and drink heavily during pregnancy, but no one, including the doctors who perform abortions would recommend such irresponsibility.

24 Myth 3: Americans favor abortion on demand. The most important thing to consider when looking at public opinion polls is the wording of the questions. Simply changing two or three words can dramatically change the results. When worded in a fair and objective way, polls, in fact, reveal that an overwhelming majority of the American people oppose abortion in at least 95% of the cases in which abortion is obtained today. All the controversy we hear about maternal health, rape, and incest amount for less than 5% of the 1.5 million abortions performed annually in this country.

25 A January 1990 Wirthlin Survey asked under which circumstances abortion should be legal. *Only 11%* of Americans said abortion should be legal **"always"**, which is the current solution under Roe. A June 1989 CBS poll asked the question, "What if your state could pass a law that would only permit abortions in the cases of rape, incest, and to save the life of the mother. Would you favor or oppose that law?" 66% said they would favor such a law while only 29% would oppose that law.

26 In March, 1989, a BOSTON GLOBE/WBZ survey on abortion was released. Due to fairly worded questions, this poll showed that abortion for the reasons given by most women seeking abortions is opposed by an overwhelming majority of Americans. This poll listed common reasons for abortion with the percentage of people who opposed abortion in these cases.

Wrong time in life to have a child	82%
Fetus not desired sex	93%
Woman cannot afford a child	75%
As a means of birth control	89%
Pregnancy would cause too much emotional strain	64%
Father unwilling to help raise child	83%
Father absent	81%
Mother wants abortion father wants baby	72%
Father wants abortion mother wants baby	75%

27 It is also interesting to note how few people even know under what conditions abortion is legal today. Most people are surprised to learn that in all 50 states abortion is legal for *any* reason at *any* time including the ninth month of pregnancy.

28 I would be remiss if I did not go a step further and say that even if a majority of Americans favored or supported abortion for any reason, that would not make it right. Let us not lose sight of the fact that regardless of how abortion is considered in the hearts and minds of men, it is murder in the heart of God.

29 Myth 4: Abortion is a feminist issue—a question of women's rights. Modern day feminists either do not realize or simply ignore the fact that abortion is contrary to the original goals of the feminist movement. Early feminists such as Sarah F. Norton, Mattie Brinkerhoff, Susan B. Anthony, Mother Jones, Emma Goldman and Victoria Woodhull all denounced abortion as oppressive to women.

30 Syndicated columnist Steven Chapman said in a April, 1989 column,

> Most pro-choice people are libertarian only when it's personally convenient. Women's groups, while adamantly in favor of barring the Government from any role in abortions decisions, are equally insistent that the Government take a *bigger* role in just about everything else. One demonstrator [in a pro-choice march] carried a sign saying, 'My Body, My Baby, My Business.' That's the pro-choice view of abortion. But when a woman chooses to *have* a baby, the cherub suddenly becomes society's concern.
>
> Women's groups endlessly lobby to force taxpayers and employers to bear part of the cost of parenthood. Government subsidies for child care, laws requiring businesses to grant time off to new parents, programs to improve health and welfare of mothers and babies— you name it, they're for it.

31 Juli Loesch, the anti-nuclear activist at Three Mile Island, and now a member of "Feminists for Life," commented in the April, 1989 edition of the WASHINGTON MONTHLY, on her reconsideration of protests against the Vietnam War. She said she found herself being "inconsistent to the point of incoherence. We are saying that killing was not an acceptable solution to conflict situations, yet when we had our own conflict situation, we were willing to go straight to killing as a technical fix."

32 I think we let men off the hook too easily on the abortion issue. Abortion provides a climate that encourages men to abdicate their responsibility to their born, as well as pre-born children. Juli Loesch suggests that the acceptance of abortion actually encourages exploitation of women by men. She says "The idea is that a man can use a woman, vacuum her out, and she is ready to be used again." Men can help make the pro-choice position a responsible one by contributing to a process where the choice is made prior to conception.

33 Jo McGowan is a writer living in India where nearly all abortion cases involve a female fetus. McGowan discusses this in a 1989 NEWSWEEK column where she says:

> Feminists are speaking out of both sides of their mouths. When the issue is sex determination and the 'selective' abortion of girls, they call it female feticide. But when the issue is reproductive freedom and the abortion of male and female fetuses, they call it a 'woman's right to choose.' It won't work. They can't have it both ways. Either they accept abortion or they don't.
>
> She concludes by saying: Perhaps from the undeniable truth that it is wrong to kill a baby simply because she is a girl will emerge the larger truth that it is wrong to kill a baby at all.

34 Myth 5: Forcing women to carry pregnancies to term will only result in unwanted, abused children. Legalized abortion has not reduced child abuse problems in this country—in fact, such cases have skyrocketed. According to the U.S. Bureau of the Census, in it's 1988 *Statistical Abstract of the United States,* between 1978 and 1985, reported cases of child abuse and neglect rose from 607,000 to 1.3 million annually.

35 There is a lack of statistical research to prove any correlation between child abuse and unwanted pregnancies. Several years ago, Dr. Vincent Fontana, a professor of Clinical Pediatrics and a chairman of the Mayor's task force on Child Abuse and Neglect of the city of New York, stated that:

> Abortion is a 'sweeping and simplistic' solution that fails because the assumption that every battered child is an unwanted child, or that most or even a large proportion of abused children are unwanted children is totally false.

36 Myth 6: Pro-lifers care only about the baby and aren't extending any help to the pregnant women. The fact is, there are more crisis pregnancy centers than there are abortion clinics in the United States. The February, 1990 *National Catholic Register* estimates there are over 3,400 pro-life centers in this country, and that 400 new centers are being established each year.

37 I believe that the church of Christ has a better way. I remember 30 years ago, Bishop Fulton Sheen said that the church has no right to preach against abortion unless it is willing to say to that pregnant girl, we have a better way. It was that philosophy that led us through the Thomas Road Baptist Church to start the Liberty Godparent Home in Lynchburg, Virginia eight years ago. This ministry provides housing, medical care counselling, a licensed adoption agency, and an opportunity to continue education, all free of charge to unwed mothers. Through the residence program and the toll-free counselling service, over 3,000 abortions have been prevented since this ministry began in 1982.

38 While much is happening nationwide, much remains to be done. We must establish enough crisis pregnancy homes, adoption agencies, and counselling centers to accommodate the 1.5 million girls and women who, each year, face a traumatic dilemma.

39 Myth 7: If all the women who are currently seeking abortions were forced to carry their pregnancies to term, there would not be enough adoptive parents to care for these children. According to the National Committee for Adoption, there have been approximately 50,000 adoptions per year since 1974. However, there are also 2 million childless couples on agency waiting lists or at fertility clinics who would like to adopt. That means 40 couples are waiting to adopt every available baby. Most people wishing to adopt wait anywhere from three to seven years before a baby is available.

40 We need to begin to promote adoption as a viable alternative to abortion. An editorial in *The Wall Street Journal* last year referred to a study conducted by the U.S. Department of Health and Human Services which indicated that 40% of the time, pregnancy counsellors did not even *mention* adoption as an option during discussions with pregnant women.

41 The National Committee for Adoption cites the "legalization of abortion" as a factor that reduces the potential number of adopted children. For example, in 1972, the year before *Roe v. Wade*. there were 403,000 out-of-wedlock births and 65,000 unrelated adoptions; but, in 1982 there were 715,000 out-of-wedlock births and only *50,000* unrelated adoptions.

42 I believe there is enough love and care in this country to provide a good home for every baby brought into this world. Even the Spina-Bifida Association of America and the National Down's Syndrome Adoption Exchange report waiting lists for babies they are able to place for adoption.

43 Myth 8: What we really need is better education about birth control and safe sex. Rather than teaching young people how to have safe sex, we ought to teach them how to **save** sex for marriage. 81% of all abortion patients are unmarried. This is not how God intended for us to live.

44 There has been much debate in recent years about placing sex clinics in our public schools to make condoms and birth control pills readily available. As far as I am concerned, passing out birth control pills in a public school is like distributing cook books at a fat farm.

45 The April 30 issue of *Insight* magazine recounted an assignment that a *Washington Post* reporter named Leon Dash was given in 1984 to write about teenage pregnancy. He assumed that ignorance about reproduction was the main cause of teenage pregnancy and spent a year living in a neighborhood that had one of the highest numbers of teenage parents. During that year he interviewed his subjects more than 30 hours apiece and reported the following:

> They were all very well-versed in sex education, and those who didn't want children, didn't have them. These girls became mothers to be affirmed as women.
> Sixteen-year-old Tauscha Vaughn said 'Mr. Dash, will you please stop asking me about birth control? Girls out here know all about birth control. There's too many birth control pills out here. All of them know about it. Even when they're 12, they know what it is.'

46 The magazine went on to say that even the Guttmacher Institute, a leading proponent of education and contraception has been rethinking this issue. Jeannie Rosoff, the institute's president, says "Most of the programs we have had have been preaching sex education. We now know that increasing knowledge does *not* necessarily affect behavior." Finally, this article discussed morality.

Young people are supposed to find the very idea of morality laughable. But the best indicator these days for not getting pregnant as a teenager is membership in a fundamentalist Protestant church that teaches in no-nonsense fashion that sex outside of marriage is a sin. A study by Sandra Hofferth, an Urban Institute researcher, shows the direct correlation between weekly attendance at religious services and delayed sexual activity.

47 We need *less* sex education and *more* parents, pastors and teachers serving as role models and providing moral education.

48 Myth 9: You cannot be openly pro-life and win public office in this country. Contrary to popular opinion, certain pro-life candidates have not lost recent elections because they were pro-life, but rather because they handled the issue poorly. Jim Courter, the GOP gubernatorial candidate in New Jersey last year, did not lose because he was pro-life. He lost because he waffled on his pro-life position and record and eventually abandoned it altogether. Frankly, there really was no pro-life candidate in the New Jersey Governor's race. In the Virginia governor's race, republican Marshall Coleman attempted to hide from the abortion issue by not responding to the media campaign that Wilder and pro-abortion groups launched against him. He too, lost in what turned out to be the narrowest margin in Virginia gubernatorial history.

49 In the January issue of the *American Spectator,* columnist Fred Barnes explains why ducking this issue won't work. He says, "Pro-choice Democrats are unwilling to vote for pro-choice republicans over pro-life democrats. But pro-life Republicans will jump ship in a hurry. Better to stick with the pro-life stand." This is why I have so much respect for men like Ronald Reagan and Jesse Helms. These men and others like them, stand firmly in defense of the unborn without regard for public opinion polls. May God raise up more men and women who are more concerned with the next generation than with the next election.

50 Myth 10: It's OK to say "I am personally opposed to abortion *but,* I would never force my views on someone else." That rationale would be like saying in 1860, "I am personally opposed to slavery, but if my neighbor wants to own a few, that's OK." The fact is if abortion is wrong and if abortion is murder, we ought to have the guts to stand up and say so. Imagine the backlash if George Bush one day said during a Press Conference that he was personally opposed to Apartheid but if South Africa wanted to practice it, that was OK. He would be run out of office instantly. Yet, we continue to let politicians off the hook who use this warped logic on the abortion issue. Let's not let them get away with it any longer.

51 Where do we go from here? Perhaps more important than *where* we go is that we go *together.* If anything is obvious from our 17-year struggle, it is that there is no quick or easy solution to this problem.

52 Let's win this fight by changing one heart at a time—saving one baby at a time. Let's agree that preventing *some* abortions is better than preventing none. An "all or nothing" mentality will never succeed in this real world in which we live.

53 I remember appearing on ABC's 20/20 program in 1985 to discuss abortion. On that program I said that I would support *legislation* which would outlaw abortions except in the cases of rape, incest, or when the life of the mother is endangered. Judging from the mail and phone calls we received, you would have thought that I had opened an abortion clinic. I was accused of "selling out" and giving in too easily on this issue. My remarks did not mean that I approve of abortion in some cases and not in others but rather, for the purpose of achieving *some* legislative progress, I would support legislation that would legally prevent over 95% of all abortions. *Any* number of abortions we can prevent legally will be more than we are currently preventing.

54 Let's not argue with each other over anything that would save lives. As each day passes, over 4,000 precious babies are snatched away. Let's covenant together to use every available means—legal, political, and most importantly, spiritual, to reverse this terrible tide.

55 Chuck Colson in a recent column, eloquently articulates the challenge before us.

Even if we were to win in the battleground states, that will not be the end of the pro-life struggle. True, we will have brought human law into conformity to God's law—a good end, but not enough. While the law is a moral teacher, law alone cannot change peoples' moral choices. Women will still seek out illegal abortions.

So we must work on a more fundamental level than legislation alone, painting a fresh moral vision on our dingy national canvas, a vision of hope and human dignity. We must woo peoples' hearts towards righteousness.

But we cannot woo unless we love. It is more than the battle against abortion that suffers when Christians conduct themselves with anger and hate. We wound our witness of the truth and the Gospel and the love of Jesus Christ.

56 In my heart, I question how long God can continue to bless a nation that places as little value on human life as we do in America. It is my prayer that the 1990s will be the decade in which the unborn are emancipated. Let us all pray and work to that end.

Against Granting War Powers to the President
Sam Nunn

On August 2, 1990 military forces of Iraq invaded the small, oil-rich, Persian Gulf kingdom of Kuwait. In the days following, the United Nations Security Council passed resolutions condemning the invasion, calling for immediate and unconditional withdrawal, and approving mandatory economic and political sanctions by UN member nations.

On August 8 President George Bush, in a morning televised address to the nation and a noon news conference, announced deployment of American air force and airborne ground units, totaling 125,000 men and women, to "take up defensive positions in Saudi Arabia." There was growing international concern that Iraq also might invade equally oil-rich Saudi Arabia. The President stressed that the "mission of our troops is wholly defensive." During August, September, and October, the size of America's military force grew to over 200,000 and an international coalition of European, Mid-Eastern, African, and Asian nations committed either troops, medical personnel, or economic aid to bolster the defense. In an address to a Joint Session of Congress on September 11, the President declared that "we will not let the aggression stand" and that "Iraq will not be permitted to annex Kuwait."

Although the Bush Administration privately made a decision in late October to significantly increase American forces, the President delayed until several days after the national Congressional elections in early November to publicly announce the doubling of America's troops commitment to a total of over 400,000. America's military posture moved from a defensive one to an offensive one with capability of attacking Iraq and ejecting its forces from Kuwait. A mid-November *Washington Post*-ABC News Poll indicated that 70 percent of those polled favored calling Congress back into session to debate U.S. Persian Gulf policy. But both Bush and Democratic leaders were cool toward the idea (*Washington Post National Weekly Edition*, Nov. 26-Dec. 2, 1990, p. 37).

In late November the Senate Armed Services Committee, chaired by Sam Nunn, held hearings on America's Gulf policy and much of the testimony heard from former high ranking military and governmental officials cautioned against moving too quickly to war and advised continuation of the sanctions. However, at the end of November, the UN Security Council passed a resolution approving use of military force if necessary to eject Iraq from Kuwait and setting a January 15, 1991 deadline for voluntary withdrawal of Iraqi forces. On January 8, 1991 President Bush requested that Congress formally approve the use of military force against Iraq if necessary.

On January 10–11, 1991 the debates in the Senate and the House of Representatives essentially focussed on two resolutions—one granting the President the power to use military force to drive Iraq from Kuwait and the other insisting that economic sanctions be given significantly more time to work and that the President again must ask Congress for approval to use military force. That Congress was deeply divided is reflected in the fact that the resolution granting the President the power to use military force passed 250–183 in the House and by only 52–47 in the Senate. The other resolution was defeated by essentially the same vote. "Packed galleries in both houses watched as emotions were tested and voices broke during speeches in the debates" (*Chicago Tribune*, January 13, 1991, Sec. 1, pp. 7, 8). Cable Network News covered the entire debates. David Broder, respected political analyst for the *Washington Post* (*National Weekly Edition*, Jan. 21–27, p. 4) judged the quality of the debate: "The weekend debate was civil and somber, always serious and often eloquent. Senators and Representatives dealt respectfully with each other's arguments and showed compassion for the anguish even their opponents felt. The debate served superbly well the requirements of representative government, informing the public and reflecting the electorate's divided views." Broder added, "Never have I seen more of them retire to their offices to write their own speeches explaining how and why they reached their decision."

Sam Nunn, conservative Democratic Senator from Georgia, made his speech in the debate on January 10, 1991. Nunn was widely respected in both political parties as an expert on American military policy and national security and he was chair of the powerful Senate Armed Services Committee. Also Nunn was high among those Democrats frequently mentioned as potential presidential candidates for the 1992 election. After underscoring the seriousness of the occasion (4–6), Nunn quickly focuses on the choice of policies facing Congress (7).

Nunn advances two main arguments to support significant continuation of economic sanctions. First, the liberation of Kuwait *at this time* is not vital to American national security (8–15). Second, continuation of the sanctions is a reasonable alternative to war at this time (16–20). Nunn also strengthens his case by attempting to refute the major arguments opponents have offered against continuation of the sanctions (21–28).

We will center our attention on only some of his contentions and rhetorical choices. Note the lengthy analysis of how central the definition of "vital" interests is to the debate (10–14). Meanings of "vital" often are shifted too easily and explained too vaguely. And Nunn warns that often after America has used military force to protect its "vital" interests by protecting a nation, we have failed to follow up and fulfill our economic, political, and military responsibilities (13). This proved to be a prophetic warning. After the conclusion of the war with Iraq, President Bush was criticized increasingly for moving too indecisively to support Kurdish and Shiite Muslim rebels against Saddam Hussein and moving too slowly to aid refugees (*Newsweek* April 15, 1991, pp. 22–31).

In refuting major opposing arguments, Nunn stresses that probabilities, not certainties, are at issue (20, 28), employs expert testimony and statistics, questions the logic of contentions (23–24), and pinpoints internal inconsistencies (26). Evaluate how reasonably and fairly Nunn conducts his refutation. Nunn's characteristic use of expert testimony to support his arguments is to cite "reluctant" testimony from the Administration's own sources or from persons normally expected to favor military action (15–16, 21–22, 24). The assumed "reluctance" of such testimony often is seen as adding to its credibility. How adequately does Nunn's use of testimony meet the standards for soundness of expert testimony (see Chapter 4)? Finally, what persuasive purposes seem to be served by his use of questions and how adequately does he use them (2, 7, 8, 16, 27, 28)?

Among the consequences of this speech for Nunn personally were his being grouped by some Republicans with those Democrats who voted against the President and labeled as "appeasement-before-country liberals." In addition, Nunn's stock declined as a potential presidential candidate and the Pentagon limited his access to national security information that previously he routinely had gotten (*Chicago Tribune,* March 15, 1991, Sec. 1, p. 23; *Newsweek,* February 4, 1991, p. 10, March 18, 1991, p. 40).

The text of this speech was provided by Senator Nunn's office in Washington, D.C.

---

1 It is regrettable that because of Iraqi intransigence, the meeting in Geneva this week with Secretary Baker produced no diplomatic breakthrough and very little that was encouraging. I noted with interest—and I must say with almost complete amazement—that the Iraqi Foreign Minister refused to accept President Bush's letter to Saddam Hussein because the letter, according to the Foreign Minister, was supposedly not polite. I have not seen President Bush's letter. But I find that Iraqi protest both ironic and, indeed, repulsive.

2 Was it polite when Saddam Hussein used chemical weapons against his own people? And then, again, against Iran? Was it polite when Iraqi forces launched a brutal, unprovoked invasion of Kuwait? Was it polite when Iraqi forces used savage violence against innocent Kuwaiti civilians and took hostage innocent foreigners residing in that country?

3 Saddam Hussein and his top spokesmen do not have the standing in the court of world opinion to raise the issue of politeness.

4 Mr. President, I still believe there is room for some hope that diplomacy can succeed in avoiding war. But as January 15th approaches, as so many of my colleagues have already observed, the Congress must act. Article 1, section 8 of the Constitution provides that the Congress clearly has the authority and the duty to decide whether the Nation should go to war. In many past instances it was true that military actions have occurred without congressional authorization. Pursuant to the authority assumed by the President in his constitutional capacity as Commander-in-Chief in today's fast-moving, interconnected world with instant communications, a world plagued with nuclear weapons and international terrorism, there are certainly instances when United States military force must be used without congressional authorization.

5 There are many gray areas where the Congress, by necessity, has permitted and even encouraged and supported military action by the Commander-in-Chief without specific authorization and without a declaration of war. I do not deem every military action taken as war. I think there is always room for debate on definitions. But a war against Iraq to liberate Kuwait initiated by the United States and involving over 400,000 American forces is not a gray area.

6 In this case, I believe the Constitution of the United States is absolutely clear. It is essential, to comply with the Constitution and to commit the Nation, that Congress gives its consent before the President initiates a large-scale military offensive against Iraq. I think the founding Fathers had a great deal of wisdom when they put this provision in the Constitution. One of the main reasons, of course, was to prevent one person from being King. They did not want that. But I also believe that there was another purpose, and that is to make sure that when this Nation goes to war and asks its young men and, increasingly, young women also to put their lives on the line, the Nation must commit itself before we ask them to lay down their lives.

7 The President's January 8th request that Congress approve the use of military force presents Congress with an issue, simply stated, but profound in its consequences; not simply short term but also long term. Many of us strongly believe a war to liberate Kuwait should be the last resort and that sanctions and diplomacy combined with a threat—a continuing threat of force—should be given more time. Should we give the President—after all of these debates when the die is cast—should we give him blanket authority to go to war against Iraq to liberate Kuwait? This is the question we face. There are numerous questions that will have to be answered in the minds of each of us before casting our vote.

8 The first question I try to ask when it comes to matters of war and peace is the question of whether a particular situation is vital to our Nation's security. In this case, *is the liberation of Kuwait vital to our Nation's security?* We all agree with the goal of restoring Kuwaiti sovereignty; no doubt about that. But have we concluded here that the liberation of Kuwait in the next few weeks is so *vital* to our Nation's security that we must take military action *now* instead of waiting a few months—waiting a period of time to allow the economic embargo and blockage to take its toll?

9 Back in August and September when the embargo was successfully—and I'd say very skillfully brought about by President Bush, through what I think was his superb leadership—no one thought or predicted the embargo was going to be over by January. No one predicted we were going to be able to bring about the termination of Iraqi presence in Kuwait by January. None of the intelligence experts or other experts who testified felt the embargo was really going to have much effect before April or May of 1991 and almost all of them said it would take at least a year. There was no surprise about that. I'm absolutely amazed when people say well, we've waited four months and five months and the embargo is not working. They must not have been there at the beginning or they must not have talked to anybody at the beginning about how long it was going to take. It's very puzzling to me how someone could give up on the embargo after five months when nobody that I know of predicted that it was going to last less than nine months to a year, and most people said a year to eighteen months from the time of inception, which was August of last year.

10 When we talk about the question of vital—a lot of times we in Washington throw that word around as if it's just another word. Sometimes we use so many words in the course of debate that we don't think carefully about what we mean. I recall very clearly President Reagan's 1982 declaration that Lebanon was vital to the security of the United States. Shortly thereafter, following the tragic death of more than 200 Marines, we pulled out of Lebanon, we pulled out of a country that only a few weeks before had been declared vital. Today, as we debate this, eight years later, while pursuing our newly proclaimed vital interest in Kuwait. It was not vital before August 2nd. Nobody had said it was vital then. There was no treaty. In fact, when we were protecting Kuwaiti vessels coming out of the Gulf for several years during the Iran/Iraq war, the Kuwaitis didn't even let us refuel, as I recall. I'd have to be checked on that one but that's my recollection.

11 All of a sudden it's vital—vital. And while this embargo has been undertaken since August 2nd, and while we all seem to take for granted that the liberation of Kuwait is vital, not just in general but in the next 2 or 3 or 4 weeks—while that's been going on, our Government has watched passively, said very little if anything, while our former enemy, a nation on the terrorist list for years and years and I believe it still is—Syria—used its military power to consolidate its control over Lebanon, the same country that was our vital interest in 1982. So one of our so-called vital interests, Lebanon, eight years ago, is now under the control of Syria, while we have pursued another vital interest.

12 The point is, not all these things are simple. The point is we ought to be careful about defining vital. A lot of things are important, very important, that aren't vital. Vital in the sense of young men and young women being called to put their lives on the line.

13 In more recent history, we defined Panama and Nicaragua as vital, and we used force in the case of Panama directly. In the case of Nicaragua, we supported force. I supported both of those decisions. But after achieving our short-term goals in both these countries—we arrested Noriega and we cheered the election of President Chamorro—we seem to have forgotten their on-going economic and political agony. These were countries in which we used or supported force for one reason or the other. Again I supported it in both cases. And now, while we're pursuing another vital interest, they are going through economic and political wrenching experiences with the outcome being very uncertain. Both the Bush Administration and the Congress have unfulfilled responsibilities regarding those two countries.

14 My point is, Mr. President, we throw around the word "vital" very carelessly. When politicians declare an interest to be vital, our men and women in uniform are expected to put their lives at risk to defend that interest. They train for years to be able to go out and, if necessary, give their lives to protect what we declare to be vital. Sometimes when you see how quickly we come to use that term, it makes you wonder whether we are fulfilling our responsibility to those men and women in uniform. We have an obligation as leaders to distinguish between important interests which are worthy of economic, political, and diplomatic efforts and interests that are vital, that are worth the calling by the leaders of this Nation on our young men and women in uniform to sacrifice, if necessary, their lives.

15 Former Secretary of Defense and former CIA Director James Schlesinger spoke to this very point when he testified before our Committee. He testified that he did not think liberation of Kuwait "was a vital interest on the 2nd day of August, 1990." Dr. Schlesinger, however, went on to say, quoting him again:

> . . . the investment of the prestige of the President of the United States now makes it vital (he does not use the word "vital" lightly) for Iraq to withdraw from Kuwait. I do not think that it is necessary, to achieve that objective, for us to turn to war. I think that we can avoid war and still achieve the objective of Iraqi withdrawal from Kuwait.

16 This brings up the next question. Are there reasonable alternatives to war? What is the likelihood that sanctions will work? In testimony before the Congress, and in public and private statements as recently as January 3, the Bush Administration stopped short of saying that sanctions cannot get Iraq out of Kuwait. The Administration acknowledges the significant economic impact sanctions have had on Iraq but now says there is "no guarantee" whether or not they will bring about an Iraqi decision to withdraw from Kuwait. Last August, President Bush asserted himself, saying, quoting him "Economic sanctions, in this instance, if fully enforced, can be very, very effective. . . . and nobody can stand up forever to total economic deprivation." That is from President Bush.

17 The international sanctions are, indeed, having a devastating effect on Iraq's economy, for two basic reasons. The Iraqi economy is based on oil, which accounts for about 50% of the country's GNP and almost 100% of the country's hard currency earnings. Iraq is essentially landlocked, depending upon oil pipelines, foreign ports, and international highways for its imports and exports. As Georgetown University specialist on economic sanctions Dr. Gary Hufbauer testified before the Senate:

> On no previous occasion have sanctions attracted the degree of support they have in the Iraqi case. Never have they been so comprehensive in their coverage. Never have they imposed such enormous costs on the target country. Moreover, Iraq's economy, geographically isolated and skewed as it is toward oil, is far more vulnerable to economic coercion than other economies that have been the target of sanctions.

18 The net result to date is that the international sanctions have cut off more than 90% of Iraq's imports, almost 100% of Iraq's exports, including virtually all of Iraqi oil exports. Iraqi industrial and military plants are receiving from abroad virtually no raw materials, no spare parts, no new equipment, no munitions, no lubricants. Moreover, Iraq now has no way to earn hard currency to purchase desperately needed imports, even if they can be smuggled in spite of the embargo. "Amstel Light" beer may be available in Baghdad, but it is a very poor substitute for such essentials as motor oil and transmission fluid.

19 The key to a meaningful embargo is oil: so long as Iraq's oil exports are shut down—and no one disputes that they are shut down, no one; that is not in dispute—Saddam Hussein will be deprived of at least half of his country's GNP and essentially all of his hard currency income. So long as oil exports are shut down, he will become progressively weaker—there is no doubt about that. We worry about recession in the United States— we worry right now about a recession—we're talking about whether the economy of the United States is going down 3–5% of our GNP, and it's of great and legitimate concern. Saddam Hussein has to worry about a devastating reduction of approximately 70% of his GNP by the summer of this year. By the end of this summer, the country will be an economic basket case, and I mean Iraq and Saddam Hussein may be in jeopardy with his own people.

20 The question is: can anyone guarantee that Iraq will abandon Kuwait when their GNP goes down 70%? Can anybody guarantee that? The answer is no. We can't guarantee that. But the other options we have also must be held to the same standard. A sanctions policy is not perfect. There are no guarantees here. But it has to be weighed against the alternatives. The Bush Administration is correct when they point out that sanctions do not guarantee that Iraq will leave Kuwait. But the story does not end there. What guarantees do we have that the war will be brief and that American casualties will be light? No one can say whether a war will last five days, five weeks, or five months. We know we can win, and we will win. There is no doubt about that. There is no doubt about who wins this war. Our policy and our military planning, however, cannot be based on an expectation that the war will be concluded quickly and easily. In large measure, the scope and scale of the hostilities, once begun, will be determined by Iraq's willingness to absorb massive punishment and to fight on. A quick Iraqi military collapse is possible in days. We hope it will happen if war comes. But it cannot be assured.

21 The Administration argues that the coalition may crumble before Iraq withdraws from Kuwait. The Senator from Louisiana, my good friend, referred to that. Admiral William Crowe, the former Chairman of the Joint Chiefs of Staff, took this issue head-on during his testimony before the Armed Services Committee last November. Quoting Admiral Crowe, the immediate past Chairman of the Joint Chiefs, "It is hard to understand," he said, "why some consider our international alliance strong enough to conduct intense hostilities, but too fragile to hold together while we attempt a peaceful solution."

22 Mr. President, the Administration's position is that if we wait for sanctions to work, Kuwait and its citizens will be further victimized. Tragically, this is no doubt true. But to quote Admiral Crowe again: "War is not neat, not tidy; once you resort to it, war is uncertain and a mess." The additional cost to Kuwait of letting sanctions work must be weighed against the cost to Kuwait in terms of human lives, human suffering, as well as national resources, if the United States-led coalition launches a military offensive to liberate a country which is heavily fortified.

23 Mr. President, those who support prompt military action argue that delay will allow Iraq to strengthen its defensive positions in Kuwait, thereby adding to the eventual cost of forcing Iraq out of Kuwait. A couple of observations on this point. This would have been a better argument in September and October of last year than it is today. Iraq already has had five months to dig in and to fortify and they have done so in a major way. Kuwait has fortifications reminiscent of World War I. This argument also overlooks the costs to the Iraqi military of sitting in Kuwait with a 500,000-man force while logistical support degrades because of the sanctions.

24 Mr. President, I am aware Director Webster sent Congressman Les Aspin a letter on January 10 that addressed this issue. I read the Webster letter as confirming that the sanctions, if kept in place for six to twelve months, will severely degrade Iraq's armored forces, air force, and air defenses. I consider that good news. For some unexplained reason, and I'm sure people will have a reason, but I find it puzzling now because I don't understand what it is, Judge Webster implies that Iraq's tanks, its air defenses, and its over 700 combat aircraft will not play an important role in Iraq's defense of Kuwait. I would certainly hate to try to explain this to several hundred American pilots that are out there, the Air Force and Navy pilots, who have the job of putting their lives in their aircraft at risk to knock out these very targets at the beginning stage of any conflict. I don't understand the Webster letter, frankly. Perhaps we will get more from that later. But it's incredible to me that he seems to write off the importance of the tanks, the aircraft, and the air defenses. Everything I've heard is that we are going to have to make those the priority targets, among others. And to write those off and say that degrading them is really not going to play a big role to me is bewildering. But we'll wait and hear from Director Webster at a later point.

25 Supporters of prompt military action argue that our offensive military capability will degrade if our huge force sits for months in the Saudi desert. This is also true, and for several months I have suggested that we should institute a policy of unit rotation, commencing with quick reaction forces, such as the 82nd Airborne, that might be needed on short notice elsewhere in the world. We should take full advantage of the coalition's superiority in air and sea power, while establishing the capability of deploying additional ground forces to the region quickly if needed.

26 I find it puzzling, however, Mr. President, that proponents of our early military option voice concern about the degradation of our 400,000-strong force, fully backed by the United States and supported by numerous allies, yet at the same time, those favoring authorization of an early military offensive minimize the degradation of Iraq's 500,000-man force in the Kuwaiti theater, a force essentially supported by Iraq, totally lacking significant allies and subjected to a remarkably effective international embargo.

27 Mr. President, in weighing the costs of the military option, one must also consider our long-term interests in the region. Has there been any in-depth analysis in the Administration about what happens in the Middle East after we win? And we will win. The President's declared goals include establishing stability in the Persian Gulf and protecting U.S.

citizens abroad. Considering the wave of Islamic reaction, anti-Americanism and terrorism that is likely to be unleashed by a highly destructive war with many Arab casualties, it is difficult to conceive of the Middle East as a more stable region where Americans will be safe.

28 Finally, the Administration has argued there is no guarantee economic hardships will in the end compel Saddam Hussein to withdraw from Kuwait. Mr. President, I have attended Intelligence Community as well as Defense and State Department briefings for 18 years. I have been thinking back. I cannot recall one instance where I ever came out of those briefings with any guarantee of anything. For the Intelligence Community to say they can't guarantee that Iraq is going to get out of Kuwait because of the sanctions which is going to reduce his GNP by 70% and cut off all the hard currency, for them to say that is true. Nobody can guarantee it. But what else have they guaranteed? I haven't seen any guarantee on any subject from the Intelligence Community. It's not their fault. They're not in the business of guaranteeing. The CIA is not the FDIC. They give you the facts, then you use common sense to come to conclusions.

29 In summary, Mr. President, I believe that on balance there is a reasonable expectation that continued economic sanctions, backed up by the threat of military force and international isolation, can bring about Iraqi withdrawal from Kuwait. I believe that the risks associated with continued emphasis on sanctions are *considerably less* than the very real risks associated with war and, most importantly, the aftermath of war in a very volatile region of the world.

30 Many of my constituents in Georgia have written and called and asked me whether this is another Vietnam. Are we about to get into another Vietnam? No. I do not believe so. I agree with President Bush and other Administration spokesmen who assure us that a burgeoning Persian Gulf conflict will not be another Vietnam. I think they are right on that. The territory of Iraq and Kuwait is different in most respects from that of Vietnam, particularly in terms of geography and vulnerability to air attack and economic embargo. Iraq is vulnerable to air attack. The conditions of warfare will be vastly different from those in Vietnam.

31 Of course there are military lessons we should remember from Vietnam. We should hit military targets at the outset with overwhelming and awesome power, at the beginning of any conflict, as well as knocking out power and communications, nuclear, biological, and chemical facilities.

32 At the same time, we should not "overlearn" the Vietnam lesson. We in America like instant results. We want fast food and we want fast military victories. However, our Nation places a much higher value on human life, especially on the lives of our men and women in uniform. Depending upon developments after the first wave of air attacks, a short war may be possible and may save lives, but we must avoid an "instant victory" kind of psychology with demands and expectations in this Country that could cause a premature and high casualty assault on heavily fortified Kuwait by American ground forces. We don't want to create a psychology that puts pressure on our military commanders in the field to do things that are foolish because we think they should get it over with quickly. We hope they will be able to do it with a minimum loss of life.

33 But if war becomes necessary, we should not tell the military commanders to get it over with quickly, no matter what. No. The order should be to accomplish the mission with whatever force is required, but do so in a way that minimizes American casualties, even if it takes more time. Making continued Iraqi occupation of Kuwait untenable with air and naval bombardment plays to our strengths. Rooting out the Iraqi army with ground forces going against heavy fortification plays right into Iraq's hands.

34 Mr. President, in conclusion, a message to Saddam Hussein: You are hearing an impassioned debate emanating from the U.S. Capitol, both the House and the Senate. These are the voices of Democracy. Don't misread the debate. If war occurs, the Constitutional and policy debates will be suspended and Congress will provide the American troops in the field whatever they need to prevail. There will be no cutoff of funds for our troops while they engage Iraq in battle. President Bush, the Congress, and the American people are united that you must leave Kuwait. We differ on whether these goals can best be accomplished by administering pain slowly with an economic blockage or by dishing it out in large doses with military power. Either way, Saddam Hussein, you lose.

35 Mr. President, in concluding, and in closing, I can think of no better person to quote than General Norman Schwarzkopf, Commander of U.S. forces in the Gulf, who will bear the heavy responsibility of leading American forces into combat, if war should occur.

36 On the question of patience, General Schwarzkopf said in mid-November in an interview, quoting him:

> If the alternative to dying is sitting out in the sun for another summer, then that's not a bad alternative.

37 On the question of cost of waiting for sanctions to work, General Schwarzkopf also said in an interview in November, quoting him:

> I really don't think there's ever going to come a time when time is on the side of Iraq, as long as the sanctions are in effect, and so long as the United Nations coalition is in effect.

38 On the question of effect of sanctions, General Schwarzkopf said in October—and this is immediately prior to a major switch in the Administration's policy—immediately prior to it—quoting General Schwarzkopf:

> Right now, we have people saying, 'OK, enough of this business; let's get on with it.' Golly, the sanctions have only been in effect about a couple of months. . . . And now we are starting to see evidence that the sanctions are pinching. So why should we say 'OK, we gave them two months, they didn't work. Let's get on with it and kill a whole bunch of people.' That's crazy. That's crazy. (End quote, from the Commander in the field.)

39 Mr. President, in closing, I believe that before this Nation is committed to what may be a large-scale war, each of us in the Senate of the United States in reaching a decision which will be very personal and very difficult for all of us, we should ask ourselves a fundamental question: will I be able to look at the parents, the wives, the husbands, and children in the eye and say their loved-ones sacrificed their lives for a cause vital to the United States, and that there was no other reasonable alternative? Mr. President, at this time, I cannot.

War with Iraq
George Bush

On the day after the UN Security Council deadline for Iraq's withdrawal from Kuwait, January 16, 1991, President George Bush addressed the nation on evening television to announce and justify the attack by American and coalition forces against Iraq. In the prior months since his August 6, 1990 nationally televised speech announcing deployment of American troops to Saudi Arabia, President Bush utilized a variety of communication channels to present to the American public the reasons—the justifications—for American intervention. For example, he often used press conferences, such as the one on November 30, 1990, because he felt very comfortable and successful with the intimate format of a brief opening statement followed by questions and answers with reporters (*Washington Post National Weekly Edition,* June 4–10, 1990, p. 4; August 13–19, 1990, p. 7; *Newsweek,* December 10, 1990, p. 96).

Although not noted for the eloquence of his nationally televised public speeches, his addresses that included live audiences, such as the September 11, 1990 address to a Joint Session of Congress and his January 29, 1991 State of the Union message, also were important parts of his campaign to justify his policies (*Newsweek,* September 24, 1990, pp. 26–27; January 28, 1991, p. 34; *Chicago Tribune,* January 31, 1991, Sec. 1, p. 24; February 3, 1991, Sec. 4, p. 3). Speeches to favorable audiences but not televised in prime time by the major networks, such as the one to the National Religious Broadcasters printed in Chapter 4 of this book, played a significant role. Bush provided an essay on "Why We Are in the Gulf" exclusively for *Newsweek* (November 26, 1990, pp. 28–29). And in the week just prior to the launching of military action against Iraq, he sent a letter to editors of student newspapers at colleges and universities around the nation. In this letter, he previews some of the arguments used in his January speech, mentions his own World War II combat experience, and declares that the choice is not "washed in shades of gray": "It's black and white. The facts are clear. The choice is unambiguous" (Northern Illinois University *Northern Star,* January 14, 1991, p. 23).

But political analysts in the news media criticized President Bush and his Administration for not presenting a consistent and coherent rationale for American actions. They noted that at one time or another, and in varying combinations, one or another of the following reasons were used: protect the American way of life; thwart a modern-day Hitler; protect vital economic interests such as oil or jobs; punish naked aggression (*Washington Post National Weekly Edition,* November 19–25, 1990, p. 37; *Chicago Tribune,* November 25, 1990, Sec. 4, p. 3). In fact Jim Hoagland of the *Washington Post* (*National Weekly Edition,* November 12–18, 1990, pp. 23–24), criticizes Bush for calling "a news conference, where he enjoyed demonstrating mastery of detail before the press corps, rather than providing a sustained and coherent overview of his case directly to the public."

You are encouraged to compare this speech on January 16, 1991 with his January 28 "Just War" speech reprinted earlier in Chapter 4 and his January 29 State of the Union address (*Vital Speeches of the Day,* February 15, 1991, pp. 258–263) to assess the degree of coherence, completeness, and reasonableness of his justifications. Also compare and contrast this speech with that of Senator Sam Nunn reprinted just prior to it. For example, evaluate their evidence and arguments on whether the economic sanctions are working, on whether delay would hurt American forces and help Iraq's, and on whether it is in America's "vital interests" *now* to undertake military action.

In their analysis of genres of presidential rhetoric, *Deeds Done in Words* (Chapter 6), rhetorical critics Karlyn Kohrs Campbell and Kathleen Hall Jamieson contend that "presidential war rhetoric throughout U.S. history manifests five pivotal characteristics." In paraphrased form they are: (1) The decision to resort to force is the result of deliberate, thoughtful consideration; (2) military intervention "is justified through a chronicle or narrative from which argumentative claims are drawn"; (3) "the audience is exhorted to unanimity of purpose and total commitment"; (4) the rhetoric legitimizes "presidential assumption of the extraordinary powers of the commander in chief"; and (5) the address "evinces an unusual tendency to misrepresent the events therein" in order to foster "the president's desire to stifle dissent and unify the nation for immediate and sustained action." We will use only several of these characteristics as part of our analysis. You are encouraged to read their chapter and undertake your own complete application.

President Bush indicates that the decision to go to war was serious, deliberate, and thoughtful by mentioning the "months of constant and virtually endless diplomatic activity" and by stressing that "no president can easily commit our sons and daughters to war" (3, 20). The president exhorts to unity of purpose and totality of commitment by describing the crucial values at stake and nobility of America's motives (17–18). Of special interest is his citation of testimony from American troops (20–25). In their words we hear voiced some of Bush's justifications, especially not allowing brutal aggression to go unpunished. But the words of these troops also serve as an implicit exhortation to unity and commitment: Can American citizens believe in the cause any less fervently or cohesively than these men and women who are risking their lives?

According to Campbell and Jamieson (pp. 107, 110), the dramatic narrative from which argumentative claims are extracted in presidential war rhetoric typically depicts a "threat that imperils the nation, indeed civilization itself, which emanates from the acts of an identifiable enemy and which, despite patient search for an alternative, necessitates forceful, immediate response." And they note: "Despite exhaustive efforts to find other means to resolve conflicts, the threat persists; military intervention is unavoidable. In this rhetoric, aggressors have choices, but the United States acts out of necessity."

President Bush presents a lengthy narrative (2–14) from which he extracts claims that he contends justify immediate military action. Identify the justifications he offers and assess the reasonableness of their evidence and development. Note his use of parallel phrasing to underscore the negative consequences of further delay (7–12). Certainly Bush vividly depicts an identifiable enemy. Again, as we saw in his "Just War" speech, here images of savagery abound (2, 8, 21). And Saddam Hussein's attitudes toward peace efforts are contempt, intransigence, and arrogance (12–14).

The narrative also demonstrates that the enemy has choices (3, 12–14), but that America now has no choices (4). America and its allies have engaged in "last ditch efforts," "exhausted all reasonable efforts," and "exhausted every means" at their disposal (3, 11–12). Note that while failed efforts at diplomacy are described at some length, rather brief treatment is given to the contention that economic sanctions have failed (7). To what extent, if at all, do you believe that President Bush should have devoted more time and evidence to this contention? Why? And bear in mind the comment of Hobart Rowan, political analyst for the *Washington Post* (*National Weekly Edition,* January 28-February 3, 1991, p. 5): "Bush said 'the world could wait no longer.' That's something he can assert but will never be able to prove."

This speech is reprinted from *Weekly Compilation of Presidential Documents,* 27 (January 21, 1991): 50–52.

1 Just 2 hours ago, allied air forces began an attack on military targets in Iraq and Kuwait. These attacks continue as I speak. Ground forces are not engaged.

2 This conflict started August 2d when the dictator of Iraq invaded a small and helpless neighbor. Kuwait—a member of the Arab League and a member of the United Nations—was crushed; its people, brutalized. Five months ago, Saddam Hussein started this cruel war against Kuwait. Tonight, the battle has been joined.

3 This military action, taken in accord with United Nations resolutions and with the consent of the United States Congress, follows months of constant and virtually endless diplomatic activity on the part of the United Nations, the United States, and many, many other countries. Arab leaders sought what became known as an Arab solution, only to conclude that Saddam Hussein was unwilling to leave Kuwait. Others traveled to Baghdad in a variety of efforts to restore peace and justice. Our Secretary of State, James Baker, held an historic meeting in Geneva, only to be totally rebuffed. This past weekend, in a last-ditch effort, the Secretary-General of the United Nations went to the Middle East with peace in his heart—his second such mission. And he came back from Baghdad with no progress at all in getting Saddam Hussein to withdraw from Kuwait.

4 Now the 28 countries with forces in the Gulf area have exhausted all reasonable efforts to reach a peaceful resolution—have no choice but to drive Saddam from Kuwait by force. We will not fail.

5 As I report to you, air attacks are underway against military targets in Iraq. We are determined to knock out Saddam Hussein's nuclear bomb potential. We will also destroy his chemical weapons facilities. Much of Saddam's artillery and tanks will be destroyed. Our operations are designed to best protect the lives of all the coalition forces by targeting Saddam's vast military arsenal. Initial reports from General Schwarzkopf are that our operations are proceeding according to plan.

6 Our objectives are clear: Saddam Hussein's forces will leave Kuwait. The legitimate government of Kuwait will be restored to its rightful place, and Kuwait will once again be free. Iraq will eventually comply with all relevant United Nations resolutions, and then, when peace is restored, it is our hope that Iraq will live as a peaceful and cooperative member of the family of nations, thus enhancing the security and stability of the Gulf.

7 Some may ask: Why act now? Why not wait? The answer is clear: The world could wait no longer. Sanctions, though having some effect, showed no signs of accomplishing their objective. Sanctions were tried for well over 5 months, and we and our allies concluded that sanctions alone would not force Saddam Hussein from Kuwait.

8 While the world waited, Saddam Hussein systematically raped, pillaged, and plundered a tiny nation, no threat to his own. He subjected the people of Kuwait to unspeakable atrocities—and among those maimed and murdered, innocent children.

9 While the world waited, Saddam sought to add to the chemical weapons arsenal he now possesses, an infinitely more dangerous weapon of mass destruction—a nuclear weapon. And while the world waited, while the world talked peace and withdrawal, Saddam Hussein dug in and moved massive forces into Kuwait.

10 While the world waited, while Saddam stalled, more damage was being done to the fragile economies of the Third World, emerging democracies of Eastern Europe, to the entire world, including to our own economy.

11 The United States, together with the United Nations, exhausted every means at our disposal to bring this crisis to a peaceful end. However, Saddam clearly felt that by stalling and threatening and defying the United Nations, he could weaken the forces arrayed against him.

12 While the world waited, Saddam Hussein met every overture of peace with open contempt. While the world prayed for peace, Saddam prepared for war.

13 I had hoped that when the United States Congress, in historic debate, took its resolute action, Saddam would realize he could not prevail and would move out of Kuwait in accord with the United Nations resolutions. He did not do that. Instead, he remained intransigent, certain that time was on his side.

14 Saddam was warned over and over again to comply with the will of the United Nations: Leave Kuwait, or be driven out. Saddam has arrogantly rejected all warnings. Instead, he tried to make this a dispute between Iraq and the United States of America.

15 Well, he failed. Tonight, 28 nations—countries from 5 continents, Europe and Asia, Africa, and the Arab League—have forces in the Gulf area standing shoulder to shoulder against Saddam Hussein. These countries had hoped the use of force could be avoided. Regrettably, we now believe that only force will make him leave.

16 Prior to ordering our forces into battle, I instructed out military commanders to take every necessary step to prevail as quickly as possible, and with the greatest degree of protection possible for American and allied service men and women. I've told the American people before that this will not be another Vietnam, and I repeat this here tonight. Our troops will have the best possible support in the entire world, and they will not be asked to fight with one hand tied behind their back. I'm hopeful that this fighting will not go on for long and that casualties will be held to an absolute minimum.

17 This is an historic moment. We have in this past year made great progress in ending the long era of conflict and cold war. We have before us the opportunity to forge for ourselves and for future generations a new world order—a world where the rule of law, not the law of the jungle, governs the conduct of nations. When we are successful—and we will be—we have a real chance at this new world order, an order in which a credible United Nations can use its peacekeeping role to fulfill the promise and vision of the U.N.'s founders.

18 We have no argument with the people of Iraq. Indeed, for the innocents caught in this conflict, I pray for their safety. Our goal is not the conquest of Iraq. It is the liberation of Kuwait. It is my hope that somehow the Iraqi people can, even now, convince their dictator that he must lay down his arms, leave Kuwait and let Iraq itself rejoin the family of peace-loving nations.

19 Thomas Paine wrote many years ago: "These are the times that try men's souls." Those well-known words are so very true today. But even as planes of the multinational forces attack Iraq, I prefer to think of peace, not war. I am convinced not only that we will prevail but that out of the horror of combat will come the recognition that no nation can stand against a world united. No nation will be permitted to brutally assault its neighbor.

20 No president can easily commit our sons and daughters to war. They are the Nation's finest. Ours is an all-volunteer force, magnificently trained, highly motivated. The troops know why they're there. And listen to what they say, for they've said it better than any President or Prime Minister ever could.

21 Listen to Hollywood Huddleston, Marine lance corporal. He says, "Let's free these people, so we can go home and be free again." And he's right. The terrible crimes and tortures committed by Saddam's henchmen against the innocent people of Kuwait are an affront to mankind and a challenge to the freedom of all.

22 Listen to one of our great officers out there, Marine Lieutenant General Walter Boomer. He said: "There are things worth fighting for. A world in which brutality and lawlessness are allowed to go unchecked isn't the kind of world we're going to want to live in."

23 Listen to Master Sergeant J. P. Kendall of the 82d Airborne: "We're here for more than just the price of a gallon of gas. What we're doing is going to chart the future of the world for the next 100 years. It's better to deal with this guy now than 5 years from now."

24 And finally, we should all sit up and listen to Jackie Jones, an Army lieutenant, when she says, "If we let him get away with this, who knows what's going to be next?"

25 I have called upon Hollywood and Walter and J. P. and Jackie and all their courageous comrades-in-arms to do what must be done. Tonight, America and the world are deeply grateful to them and to their families. And let me say to everyone listening or watching tonight: When the troops we've sent in finish their work, I am determined to bring them home as soon as possible.

26 Tonight, as our forces fight, they and their families are in our prayers. May God bless each and every one of them, and the coalition forces at our side in the Gulf, and may He continue to bless our nation, the United States of America.

Dual Basing of American Military Forces
Patricia Schroeder

Since 1973 Democrat Patricia Schroeder has represented Colorado's First Congressional District in the U.S. House of Representatives. In the House she is a senior member of the Armed Services Committee. Although often characterized by the national press as a liberal primarily concerned with feminist issues and with nuclear and conventional arms control, the budget-minded National Taxpayers Union regularly gives her a moderate rating on fiscal policy (DeKalb, IL, *Daily Chronicle,* July 3, 1987, p. 4) A lawyer by profession, she earned her law degree from Harvard Law School.

For four months during 1987, Patricia Schroeder hit the political campaign trail to explore whether to enter the race for the Democratic nomination for President. Ultimately she decided against declaring her candidacy. Her political campaign speeches were characterized in the press as informal, free-wheeling, and full of pithy phrases and quotable TV "sound bites." Earlier she had coined the phrase "Teflon president" to capture President Reagan's ability to avoid criticism or blame sticking to him personally (*Washington Post National Weekly Edition,* August 17, 1987, p. 12; March 18–24, 1991, p. 34). In criticizing Schroeder's speaking style, conservative *Newsweek* columnist George Will concluded: "Schroeder is a rhetorical roughneck."

When Patricia Schroeder spoke to over 100 members and guests of the Cosmos Club in Washington, D.C., at a Noon Forum on September 27, 1990, she spoke as the senior woman in Congress and as the chair of the military installations and facilities subcommittee of the House Armed Services Committee. According to the club's descriptive literature, men and women are elected as members to recognize their "scholarship, creative genius, or intellectual distinction."

Schroeder argues that the need for her proposal stems both from drastically changed military circumstances in Europe (3–9) and from the necessity for increased burdensharing among nations (20–21). She clearly explains the nature and components of her policy of dual basing of American military forces (13–15). She attempts to demonstrate the workability of the policy in two ways. First, she uses the success of the Desert Shield deployment as an example of workability (7, 18). Second, through the use of antithetical phrasing, she asserts the efficiency of the policy (19). As part of her argument for the need for her policy, she wonders why no American troops were sent from Europe to Saudi Arabia. In November of 1990, President Bush did announce the transfer of 150,000 American troops from Europe as part of the massive build-up from a defensive to offensive posture. However, after the end of the war with Iraq, most of these troops were, over time, returned to their European bases.

To strengthen her case for adoption of her proposal, Schroeder refutes Bush Administration arguments about the Conventional Forces in Europe negotiations and refutes attacks on her policy (16–17). Her skepticism about the CFE negotiations is captured in her allusion to the Bertolt Brecht play, *Waiting for Godot,* in which Godot never arrives (11). Here she also predicts that the final CFE treaty would limit tanks, planes, and artillery but not troop levels. In fact the CFE agreement signed by NATO and Warsaw Pact representatives on November 19, 1990 limited only tanks, planes, and artillery but placed no limits on troops. On the same day, these representatives signed a joint statement proclaiming the end of the Cold War and that the two military alliances no longer were adversaries. Assess the adequacy of Schroeder's refutation of Administration charges that dual basing is anti-NATO and isolationist.

Throughout the speech, Schroeder shows flashes of her informal, quotable, biting use of language: get off the dime (15); wildly off the mark (16); this is silly (18); take a hike (20); and let Uncle Sucker do it (21). How effective and appropriate are these phrases in the context of the specific contentions in which they are embedded? Also, Schroeder employs parallel structure, especially to highlight examples as part of an argument (14, 22–23).

Finally, you are asked to compare and contrast Schroeder's speech with the one immediately following by General Colin Powell. Although Powell's speech ranges across a very broad spectrum of American foreign and military policy, and although it was presented six months prior to Schroeder's, and thus prior to the outbreak of Desert Shield, there are some fundamental points of disagreement. Assess the adequacy of the evidence they use and the soundness of their arguments on the degree of potential military threat still posed by the Soviet Union, on the role of NATO, on whether our European allies want our troops to remain in Europe, and on the size of American military forces that should remain permanently stationed abroad.

The text of this speech was provided by Representative Patricia Schroeder's office in Washington, D.C.

---

1 On August 2, when Iraq invaded Kuwait, President Bush decided to deploy a large contingent of American ground, air and naval forces to the Persian Gulf to deter further Iraqi expansion, to force Iraq to withdraw from Kuwait, to prevent Iraq from controlling a disproportionate share of the world's oil supply, and to tell other expansionist nations that the world will not tolerate strong nations invading and annexing weak neighbors.

2 At this point, we do not know whether President Bush's decision will prove successful or not. The American people have supported the President's action and most other nations have, at least, given political and diplomatic support to the embargo of Iraq. Yet, this action highlights some serious problems with the current defense posture of the United States. Simply put, we are set up to fight the Soviet Union in Europe at a time when others pose a far more serious threat and Europe is an unlikely battlefield.

3 For every one soldier we have in Saudi Arabia, we have three in Germany. Most Americans seem to have a pretty good idea why we are in Saudi Arabia today. But, why do we have 250,000 soldiers defending against a hostile attack across the inner-German border, when there is no longer an inner-German border? And, why was not a single soldier, tank, or plane sent from Europe to the Persian Gulf and, instead, personnel and equipment were transported from the United States?

4 Let me supply you with the official answers to each of these questions. As to why we still have 250,000 troops in Germany, the Administration says that it will reduce our European troop presence pursuant to and in accordance with a conventional arms limitation treaty, known as CFE. General Galvin, the Supreme Allied Commander in Europe, has been developing a reduction plan which will result in reducing our European troop strength from 305,000 to 225,000 over the next two years. This reflects President Bush's proposal of last year. The plan will be implemented if there is a CFE agreement this year.

5 Yesterday, DOD announced that American troop strength in Europe would be reduced by 40,000 during next year. And, Secretary Cheney last week released an anemic list of overseas base closures which probably was based on this sort of reduction. Administration officials say that the 225,000 troop level will surely come down, but that they want it reduced through arms control negotiations with the Soviets, rather than through bilateral American reduction.

6 The answer to the second question—why no US troops in Europe were sent to the Persian Gulf—is much the same. Administration officials say we have a commitment to NATO and that we did not want to renege on that commitment. They also claim, and some of them can keep a straight face while doing so, that our troops in Europe do not have the proper equipment for desert deployment.

7 Deploying our large expeditionary force to the Persian Gulf was a massive and largely successful operation. We were able to move 100,000 military personnel and their equipment half way around the world to one of the world's most hostile environments in about a month. But the costs of this move were higher than they should have been because all the equipment and personnel came from the United States. Our most modern tanks and anti-tank weapons are in Europe. Our best trained tank crews are in Europe. And, Europe is substantially closer to the Middle East than is Texas or California.

8 Something is very strange here. We cannot send our best and closest forces to the Persian Gulf because they are committeed to an alliance against which the threat has disappeared. The Soviet Union continues to possess modern and lethal strategic nuclear weapons. The Soviet Union remains the only nation on Earth that could inflict unacceptable damage to the continental United States. But, the Soviet Union no longer poses an imminent threat to Western Europe. A year or two ago, the Soviet Union could stage operations from Warsaw Pact nations bordering directly on NATO countries. These Warsaw Pact countries provided massive armies and modern conventional weapons of war. Today, Hungary, Czechoslovakia, and Poland not only are not contributing forces, they are kicking the Soviet troops out of their countries. And, there is serious question as to whether these countries would permit the Soviet army free passage during time of war.

9 East Germany next week will no longer exist. Soviet troops will remain in the former East Germany while the new German government builds housing for them back in the Soviet Union. We are no longer talking about a fighting force here. We are talking refugees. And, while liberalization of Bulgaria and Romania is not as advanced as in the northern countries of the old Warsaw Pact, anti-Soviet feelings may be even stronger. The internal disorder in Bulgaria and Romania makes any expansionism a very remote possibility.

10 Now, this snapshot of Eastern Europe may seem familiar and boring, but it is important to mention because there are those in the Administration, in the Pentagon, and in NATO headquarters who insist there remains a real and serious threat to the NATO alliance. And, this fantasy guides US policy, which is not to reduce troops in Europe except as part of an arms control agreement.

11 So you might ask, why not wait for an arms control agreement? I wish we could conclude the DFE talks in Vienna more quickly. The delays have been on both sides. These are not talks between the United States and the Soviet Union. They are talks between NATO and the Warsaw Pact. As one American negotiator told me, "It is easy to reach agreements in Vienna. It is harder to reach them in Brussels [NATO headquarters], and harder still in Washington." Also, the central thrust of CFE is to limit tanks, planes, and artillery. The personnel limitations are secondary and may drop out of the final treaty altogether. So, CFE negotiations are slow going. The final agreement, expected in November, is not likely to result in large troop reductions. Waiting for CFE to reduce troops may be like waiting for Godot to arrive.

12 While we are waiting for CFE, and maintaining our 305,000 troop presence in Europe, the Soviets are continually withdrawing their troops from Eastern Europe. They are doing so for precisely the same reasons we ought to be withdrawing troops from Europe:

1. There is no serious threat of the outbreak of hostilities between East and West. While ethnic conflicts could result in fighting, our being there doesn't stop these conflicts.
2. We are both going broke. We both face serious budget deficits which can only be reduced through cutting back on defense spending.
3. Our hosts in Europe are losing patience with our being there. The Hungarians and Czechs have told the Soviets to leave. The Germans have told us to stop low level flying and much of our ground training. How long will it be before we are told to leave?

13 My proposal is to cut our permanent troop presence outside the United States to a bare minimum. Units permanently stationed abroad should be limited to those gathering intelligence, securing and maintaining prepositioned war materials, providing liaison with allied governments, and receiving reinforcement troops. In Europe, I would guess that we should have about 25,000, rather than the 305,000 troops permanently stationed. In Japan, the number would be 10,000 not 50,000.

14 Light, mobile, and flexible combat troops would be permanently stationed in the United States, but forward deployed for short term assignments. Based on our threat analysis, agreements with allies, and world events, we could deploy small units, divisions, or even corps to foreign countries for training, exercises, or actual missions, like Desert Shield. The difference is that we would deploy fighting forces and essential combat support. No longer would we build and maintain little American cities abroad. No longer would spouses and dependents be forced to rotate to foreign bases every few years. No longer would we need all the butchers, barbers, bartenders, teachers, travel agents, and teen guides who we now employ abroad.

15 This proposal is known as dual basing. I added a provision to the defense authorization bill this year to require the Secretary of Defense to implement, over the next three years, a program of dual basing. Despite veto threats from the White House, the House of Representatives endorsed this plan by a vote of 249 to 174. The Senate has no similar provision and conference on this issue will not be easy. Whatever the legislative outcome, the Administration is being told to get off the dime and start withdrawing troops abroad.

16 In attempting to strike this dual basing proposal, the Administration claimed that it was anti-NATO and isolationist. Both of these charges are wildly off the mark. I am not NATO's worst enemy. Those in NATO who pretend that the world has not changed are

NATO's worst enemies. By refusing to adjust, they are undermining the consensus which has long supported NATO throughout Western Europe and the United States. They are trying to get American, Canadian, and European taxpayers to pay their hard-earned money to support a military force which has no mission, no enemy, and no reason for being. This is not a tenable situation. This is not likely to produce a continuation of NATO.

17 America has long protected Western Europe. Twice in this century, Americans did it with their lives. Our bonds to Europe remain strong. NATO can continue to serve as an institutional link among the member nations. But, this requires finding new goals and purposes for NATO. Interim goals could include cleaning up the environmental damage caused by the heavy military presence for the last forty years and monitoring and implementing the conventional arms control treaty. Perhaps, NATO could serve as a multinational military force for operations like the Persian Gulf. What NATO cannot survive as is the bulwark against a Warsaw Pact attack through the inner-German border, because there is no Warsaw Pact and there is no inner-German border.

18 The other charge raised against duel basing is that it is isolationist. This is silly. Whether dual basing proves isolationist or not depends on our foreign policy and our decisions on deploying troops. President Bush's widely supported decision to send troops to Saudi Arabia is the very antithesis of isolationism. And, it is an excellent example of dual basing at work. In Desert Shield, we have deployed a large combat force from bases in the US.

19 More importantly, isolationism, as a viable doctrine, died with the birth of the jet plane and radio communnication. Our continent nation is no longer immune from tensions and disputes elsewhere in the world. Civil wars in Cambodia, Namibia, and El Salvador, border disputes in the Arabian Penisula, Kashmir, and Africa all touch us directly. We cannot be isolationist. That does not mean that we have to send US troops to intervene in each and every crisis. It does mean that we have to be able to insert military force where we need to when we need to. With hundreds of thousands of US troops permanently stationed in foreign countries, that is very difficult. With dual basing, it is far easier.

20 Dual basing is not the only change we need in America's military posture in the world. The other side is that we can no longer do it all alone. The operation in the Persian Gulf demonstrates what we can expect from our allies. Britain and France are helpful, but not really pulling their weight. Japan has promised a very modest contribution, but only after legislative threats and public criticism. And, the Germans have told us to take a hike. Other countries are willing to support the UN embargo and send a ship or two. But, besides the United States, Saudi Arabia, Egypt, and Syria, nobody has sent any sizeable number of ground troops to the Persian Gulf.

21 Maybe this is just another example of the way defense burdensharing has worked since World War II. Maybe, once again, our allies have decided to let Uncle Sucker do the heavy lifting. Why should they tax their citizens or endanger their soldiers if the US is willing to do it alone?

22 But our allies may be saying something else. They may be telling us that they do not support military action to force Iraq out of Kuwait or to cripple Iraq's military. The problem may be less one of burdensharing and more one of power sharing. We cannot expect other nations to join us on military endeavors they do not support. On the other hand, they should not expect us to provide troops for their own territorial defense if they are unwilling to support us. If NATO nations do not want to send their own ground troops to the Persian Gulf, they ought to offer at least to meet US obligations to NATO so that we can deploy our European troops to the Middle East. If Germany is constrained by its constitution from sending the Bundeswehr to Saudi Arabia, Germany can offer to cover the missions of, say, five divisions of US troops in Germany.

23 We are entering a new world, where the Cold War between the communist nations and the West is giving way to different, less intense, more diffuse threats. We cannot address this new world with our old military posture. We cannot afford our old military posture. We need to design a new American military which is smaller, more flexible, less tied to any geographic area, quickly deployed, and aimed at avoiding, rather than promoting, conflict. The Bush Administration has resisted suggestions to move away from the Cold War defense structure. It will be up to Congress to force the needed changes.

U.S. Foreign Policy in a Changing World
Colin L. Powell

The Town Hall has, for over half a century, been Southern California's leading public issues forum. Because of its reputation for excellence, Town Hall attracts leaders in government, industry, and the arts and sciences from throughout the world. Town Hall's General Meetings are normally held at luncheon venues attended by leaders from across the professions who value dialogue on contemporary issues.

On March 23, 1990, General Colin L. Powell, chairman of the Joint Chiefs of Staff, addressed the Town Hall at the Sheraton Grande Hotel in Los Angeles, California. As a communicator, Powell has been characterized as physically impressive, extremely intelligent, supremely articulate, witty, amiable, and unflappable. In addition, he is highly qualified, by virtue of his position, to assess the impact of changes in East-West relations on United States international military policy. It must be recognized, of course, that General Powell is not an unbiased source; one would not expect the Chairman of the Joint Chiefs of Staff to advocate a major reduction in U.S. military involvement around the world—and he does not. One might expect him, however, to show recognition that his reaffirmation of the policy of global military supremacy is not universally acclaimed—and he does not. Should a speaker, addressing a forum on a matter of public policy, feel compelled to recognize and respond to opposing points of view as a means of advancing full consideration of issues? Or, from a pragmatic perspective, is it unwise for a speaker to pay lip service to the arguments of opponents? How would Patricia Schroeder respond to this speech if she were given the right of rebuttal?

Beginning with the usual social amenities (1–3), Powell presents his assessment of recent, electrifying changes in the world order, especially in Eastern Europe (4–19). In the process of discussing changes in East-West relations, the speaker uses personal illustration (12–13) to compare past and present circumstances. Is this an effective strategy?

Having recognized the reduction in the Soviet military threat, Powell then moves to the most potentially controversial portion of his speech (20–25). In six brief paragraphs, he argues that we must reaffirm our commitment to a global military presence. He does so by advancing three arguments: 1) The Soviet Union is still the major Eurasian military power and is still a threat to our homeland through its nuclear capability; 2) no one can accurately predict future changes in Soviet policy; 3) American interests are threatened by crises not directly involving the U.S.S.R. Do these arguments constitute sufficient justification for reaffirming our commitment to a global military presence?

After detailing more specific components of our military presence (26–57), General Powell advances a new general argument favoring the preservation of the U.S. military establishment: Our superpower status imposes responsibilities upon us (58–71). Do you find this argument persuasive? How would opponents challenge this line of thinking? Does paragraph 60 adequately address the call of opponents for reduction of U.S. military forces?

This speech is reprinted by permission of *Vital Speeches of the Day*, May 1, 1990, pp. 418–421.

---

1 Thank you for that most generous introduction, Jack [Dean Borsting]. Chairman Miscoll, President Medawar, members of the Town Hall of California, honored guests, ladies and gentlemen—I am pleased to be back in California. I came here frequently in my last job as Commander in Chief of the U.S. Army Forces Command—to Fort Ord to visit the 7th Infantry Division; to the Presidio of San Francisco to visit the U.S. 6th Army headquarters; and to Fort Irwin at Barstow to visit the fine young troops in training at our National Training Center.

2 I am especially pleased to have this opportunity to speak to such a prestigious group. For over half a century, Town Hall of California has provided a distinguished forum for the discussion of public issues. And your reach is more than local—*The Town Hall Journal* and your radio broadcast, "Town Hall on the Air," provide for wide dissemination of your discussions.

3 You provide a valuable service by informing the American public and increasing their knowledge of critical issues. In her letter of invitation to me, President Medawar wrote that the members of Town Hall of California "are firmly convinced that knowledge of international and national issues in today's world is not merely a social or intellectual asset— it is vital."

4 Today, such knowledge is indeed vital. Today, the world is changing with such dizzying speed that it demands the earnest involvement of every citizen if we are to shape and mold this change to the benefit of our nation—and, ultimately, to the benefit of the world.

5 The change is electrifying. Democracy is on the move everwhere. Free economies, responsive to market pressures, are being studied by yesterday's most ardent Marxists. Freedom of speech occurs between East and West German policemen talking over the rubble of the Berlin Wall that is now a monument to the past rather than a barrier to the future. The votes for self-determination fill ballot boxes in East Germany, in Nicragua, and, yes, even inside the Soviet Union.

6 These changes are a result of the power of ideas—the power of freedom, the power of democracy, the power of free economies, and the power of people in control of their own destinies. And ultimately the power of human dignity.

7 These changes are also a direct result of the steadfast commitment of America and her allies to the policies of collective security, peace through strength, and the rule of law. These policies created today's world in which freedom and democracy are now the dominant forces at work.

8 Almost half a century ago, George Kennan advocated a policy of containment. If we held firm, he said, the inherent weaknesses of communism would bring it down. We held firm. And the walls of communism are coming down.

9 Since 1945, the major threat to peace in the world has been the Soviet Union and its allies. Today, in what seems in the broad scope of history little more than the time required for a sound bite on CNN, the Soviet Union seems to have abandoned its aggressive foreign policy, encouraged several of its allies to do the same, and is increasingly focusing on its own critical internal problems.

10 Those Soviet client states who remain unmoved—such as Cuba and North Korea— are pariah nations in the world community. They are economic basket cases, and their leaders wait in great anxiety for the sunlight to shine suddenly on them and expose all the underlying rot. Fidel Castro, a pathetic, irrelevant, aging starlet, still shows up for casting calls carrying faded, dog-eared 8×10 glossies, and accompanied by a crew of body-guards that needs 10 tons of weapons to feel secure.

11 In the words of an old song, "What a difference a day makes!"

12 Only three and a half years ago I was a Corps Commander in Europe. My 72,000 young volunteers were positioned astride the Fulda Gap, one of the classic invasion routes into Germany from the East. We were poised to stop a Soviet invasion into West Germany. My corps had been there for almost forty years with virtually that same mission. In fact, I began my career in that same corps as a second lieutenant 28 years earlier.

13 Across that border, opposite my corps, was the Soviet 8th Guards Army that I knew could engage my corps with just a few days warning. I also knew that behind the 8th Guards Army was another Soviet Army—a tank army that could perhaps threaten my corps while I was engaged with the lead army. And there were other armies behind those two. It might take nuclear weapons to stop them all. For me and my soldiers this wasn't a game. It was for real. Every time I visited my border units at Fulda, I could look over the wire and see the enemy. This was before perestroika, glasnost, and Gorbachev took hold.

14 But what a difference a day makes.

15 Two months ago in Vienna, I met with my counterparts in the East European armed forces and my counterpart in the Soviet armed forces, General Moiseyev. One message I got loud and clear: Soviet armies were rolling all right but not west; they were rolling east, back into the Soviet Union. Within the past month, the Soviet armies in Hungary and Czechoslovakia continued their march home—125,000 more men to be gone by June of 1991. Soviet armies still in Poland and East Germany—430,000 troops—will also eventually start to go home.

16 These armies are withdrawing because they know they couldn't win, and they learned they could not intimidate us any longer. They leave empty-handed. Soviet strategy has failed. It failed because of the systemic strength of the Free World—our values, our resilient economies, our powerful political processes, our rule of law, our belief in human rights, and our strong and well-supported armed forces together in even stronger alliances. Our systemic strength has beaten the Soviet juggernaut before it could be unleashed on Europe.

17 I can visualize a small travel item in *The Los Angeles Times* in about 1993. Some reporter will have been to Germany and will end the travelogue piece with a description of a visit to the town of Fulda:

> And in this historic German city, lying at the foot of the Vogelsberg Mountains—once on the border, now situated in the heart of the new, unified Germany—I was caught up in a sense of history as I visited the second oldest church in Western Europe, and as I noted a bronze marker on a hill just outside of town, near what's referred to as the Fulda Gap. The marker was inscribed as follows: "Dedicated to the American men and women whose forty-year watch at this spot gave Eastern Europe her freedom and changed the course of history."

18 Throughout Europe dramatic change is the order of the day. In the Soviet Union, dramatic change seems to be the order of the hour—so much so that we know the Soviet Union will never be the same. The real question is what will it be? Will it become a real democracy, or will it become something else we cannot yet see clearly or define?

19 Irrespective of which future course the Soviets follow, East Europeans will be moving swiftly ahead toward democratically-elected, non-communist regimes.

20 As we try to analize all of this incredible change, we have to be careful. As Clausewitz said, "Beware the vividness of transient events." Amidst these incredible changes, we have to identify the principal factors that affect our interests and sort them out from the cascade of more glamorous but essentially transient events.

21 First, we must understand what is really happening to Soviet military capabilities. We know that right now their armed forces appear to be the instrument of a much more benign foreign policy. But we also know that while reductions and restructuring are in fact ongoing, the Soviets are not demobilizing or disarming. Mr. Gorbachev is making a virtue of necessity where he can. Yes, the Soviet army is going home. But it is not disbanding. When this is all over, the Red Army will still be modern and capable and several million strong—still the major Eurasian military power. Others may wish to ignore that or say it doesn't matter. I am charged not to ignore it; and it does matter.

22 And as far as their nuclear capacity is concerned, the Soviets are not giving up any capabilities that will be allowed under a new strategic arms agreement. The Soviet nuclear arsenal that threatens our very homeland is still intact, and it is being modernized to the state-of-the-art.

23 Second, we have no way of knowing what is in store for the Soviet Union. I am confident that even the Soviets don't know. It will take some years for them to sort out the mess that they have created over the past 70 years and to try to become an economic as well as a military superpower—to try to become a responsible, participating member of the world democratic community.

24 Third, the world has not ceased being a place where America's interests are sometimes threatened. We are not approaching Utopia. I have been involved in several crises using military force in the six months I have been Chairman. They have provided me with stark evidence of how dangerous the world remains and how on-guard we must remain.

25 These three factors remind us of the importance of the strength that brought the Free World this victory in the first place. One of the keys to that strength is our alliance structure.

26 We are an Atlantic nation, so I believe we need to stay in Europe—in a strong NATO. Our allies want our armed forces to stay in Europe. We are not an occupying power like the Soviets; they are being asked to leave, we are being politely asked to stay. So long as that invitation stands, I believe we must stay to insure the peace. Let no Soviet leader ever look back and not see us on guard.

27 Notwithstanding the momentous, riveting events in Europe and the Atlantic Community, we must never forget we are also a Pacific nation—we are in Pacific alliances as well.

28 In East Asia and the Pacific, more so than in Europe, our alliances were never based totally on a response to the Soviets. We have interests in the Pacific and East Asia that would remain even if the Soviets disappeared completely from the region. Not that I believe they will disappear; their Pacific Fleet alone dissuades me from that belief.

29 So we need to stay in East Asia and in the Pacific. Nature and politics can't tolerate a vacuum. Were we to depart from the region it would create one of the largest political vaccums in history—a vacuum we cannot afford to have.

30 As we remain involved in East Asia and the Pacific, we will adjust to the realities of a changing world. Strong regional security relationships will be crucial to our involvement, so let me briefly review our principal Pacific relationships.

KOREA

31 The security relationships we have with the Republic of Korea has kept the peace on the Korean peninsula for 37 years. The teeth in that relationship are the U.S. and Korean forces standing shoulder to shoulder on the ground in Korea. So far North Korea has felt none of the tremors that have rocked dictatorships in Eastern Europe and elsewhere. South Korea meanwhile has become an economically prosperous democracy.

32 I believe we can adjust our forward military presence in Korea to accommodate the realities of a mature and economically prosperous South Korea. But we should not leave South Korea entirely, or even disengage in a major way. To do so would be unwise. We did it once before to our regret.

33 What would not be unwise, and what we would dearly love to see, would be for Mr. Gorbachev to apply more pressure on the North Koreans to open up their closed society and to share in meaningful and productive dialog with the South. And, to submit immediately to the international inspection regime for nuclear facilities and the possible presence of weapons-grade nuclear material. However monolithic and reactionary the North Korean regime has been all these years, the historic winds of change will eventually reach Pyongyang.

AUSTRALIA

34 Down under, the U.S.-Australia bilateral relationship is alive, well, and kicking. And it is an important relationship particularly in the Southwest Pacific and in the Indian Ocean. I believe Australia will always be a solid member of the Free World's alliance structure—as those brave people were throughout World War II. Only now they participate in a rigorous peace rather than a bloody world war.

THE PHILIPPINES

35 Turning to the Philippines, you are aware that our security relationship there is undergoing some understandable tensions as we approach negotiations on the future of the U.S. military presence. Our principal objective in the Philippines is not the U.S. facilities, not the dollars involved, and not the contribution of those facilities to regional stability—though each of these things is important. Our principal objective is to support the Philippines as a democracy—a democracy firmly imbedded in the Free World's great system of nations.

36 We would like to keep our facilities in the Philippines. Our presence there contributes to stability in Southeast Asia and in the Southwestern Pacific and Indian Oceans. Other regional friends know this. That is why Singapore, for example, has offered publicly to help us stay in the area should we have to depart the Philippines.

37 These are decisions we cannot make alone. The Filipino people will tell us their decision and we will abide by that decision. But our fondest hope is that, irrespective of the outcome of the base negotiations, the Philippines remains a friend and an active participant in the regional alliance structure.

JAPAN

38 Our relations with Japan, one of our most important allies, are incredibly complex and multi-dimensional. The economic and security dimensions affect our interests most powerfully today. The interplay of these two dimensions frequently gives us cause for concern.

39 Let me give you a presidential statement of concern over our relationship with Japan:

40 "In common with other western powers," said the President of the United States, "our relations with Japan have been brought into serious jeopardy. . . . It is hoped, although not with entire confidence, that these difficulties may be peacefully overcome."

41 The President who spoke these words was not George Bush but Abraham Lincoln in 1863.

42 Lincoln's words fit perfectly our modern image of the economic problems a majority of Americans believes between our country and Japan. And the modern sound of the last of Lincoln's words—that we may lack complete confidence that we can solve our problems—fits our present situation too perfectly indeed.

43 And that perception of a lack of confidence in our ability to keep U.S.-Japan economic relations on an even keel affects the other dimensions of our relationship with Japan, whether we want it to or not. Let me concentrate for a moment on why it's important we understand this interplay between the economic and security dimensions of our relations with Japan.

44 First, as a military man, I must tell you that Japan is absolutely critical to our ability to keep the peace in the Pacific. Keeping the peace in the Pacific without Japan would be a burden very few Americans would want to bear—and rightfully so.

45 Second, again as a military man, I will tell you that in terms of sharing the defense burden of keeping the peace in the Pacific, no finer ally than Japan exists today.

46 Japan has the third largest defense budget in the world—second only to the Soviet Union's and our own. That budget has been increasing at an average rate of 5 to 6 percent per year for the past ten years. The Japanese pay 40 percent of the costs of keeping U.S. forces in Japan—2.5 billion dollars last year, a higher percentage than any of our other allies. The magnitude of Japanese burden-sharing is enormous—and the Japanese have indicated they are willing to do even more.

47 The Japanese are responsible for the air and land defense of Japan and for the security of sea lines of communications out to 1,000 nautical miles. They have embarked on an ambitious modernization program to expand their naval and air forces to meet these clearly defensive responsibilities.

48 In short, the U.S.-Japan security relationship is in good shape. In fact, as Secretary Cheney said in Tokyo last month, it "has never been better."

49 Our economic relations, on the other hand, need a great deal of work. Unfortunately, much of the trade squabble between the U.S. and Japan is a kabuki play, full of smoke and mirrors and a great deal of dancing in the dark. We need to clear the air of the smoke, remove the mirrors from the room, and deal with the real issues that divide us. The early March meeting in Palm Springs between President Bush and Prime Minister Kaifu, and the meeting between the President and former Prime Minister Takeshita in Washington two weeks ago, have energized the process of getting at the issues.

50 The United States and Japan are so economically intertwined that neither of us will be successful in the years ahead without the other. The people of both our great nations must come to understand this interdependence.

51 Just as the United States without California would be a much reduced country, America without her Japanese ally would find it difficult to continue being the leader the Free World depends on to keep alive the powerful global movement toward peace and prosperity.

52 We could do it without Japan. We could still be a superpower, but we would need to increase dramatically the cost to the American people and the investment they would have to make. And there is simply no necessity for us to expend so much of our national treasure in that manner, if we can keep collective security alive and well. And in the Pacific, the key to that collective security is the U.S.-Japan relationship—in all of its many dimensions.

53 We cannot permit any single dimension of our relations with Japan to compromise our friendship and our need for one another. We must solve our economic differences. It's as simple—and, as difficult—as that.

54 I would be remiss if in my quick sweep over the Pacific and East Asia I omitted the nation that holds almost a fourth of the world's population. Our national feelings about China have waxed and waned over the years between love and hate, between understanding and incomprehension. There is perhaps no better example of the desire for freedom than that vivid image of the young man standing alone near Tiananmen Square against a column of tanks. We want to see such a desire for freedom fulfilled; yet we understand that it may require time and patience.

55 I believe we can best assist the people of China to join the ranks of free peoples everywhere by the pressure of our example, and by our willingness to stay involved in the Pacific and Asia. I believe our current policies toward China—including military-to-military relations—reflect the right balance of this pressure, concern, commitment, and understanding.

56 One of the fascinating aspects of today's world, and especially of the Pacific region, is that we have so many friends without any formal treaty mechanisms.

57 In the Pacific we have friends like Thailand, Indonesia, Malaysia, and the South Pacific Island nations, Papua, New Guinea, and a host of others. There's a reason for this. That reason has many dimensions—among them our values, our economic system, and our altruism. Also, there is the dimension of power—in our case, of superpower.

58 We are a superpower. At the moment, in many respects, we are the only superpower in each of the critical aspects of power. The Soviet Union retains only the aspect of military power.

59 Superpower status imposes responsibilities on us. Our outlook must be global and it must encompass the strong alliances that are critical to the future peace of the world. America must invigorate these alliances. America must lead the world into the 21st century, if it is to be a century of peace.

60 If we are to stay a superpower, we must keep intact all the aspects of power—political, economic, technological, and, yes, military. We can take advantage of the incredible change in the world and the commensurate reduction in the threat to our interests. We can reduce the size of our military forces and prudently adjust our forward presence around the globe. We can cut our Defense Budget over time. President Bush, Secreary Cheney, I, the Joint Chiefs of Staff—we must do it carefully over time. But there is a bottom line; there is a base force which this country needs beneath which we dare not go.

61 Such a base force must provide for our forward presence in the Atlantic Community. It must provide for our forward presence in the Pacific and East Asia, and in the Persian Gulf Region when necessary. Moreover, it must provide a pool of contingency forces in the United States. And it must provide the needed mobilization and reinforcement capabilities to support our forward presence around the world, and to back up our contingency forces. We must have a Navy second to none. And we must insure that our strategic nuclear forces are strong enough to deter any nuclear threat to us.

62 We must find the balance between our superpower base force requirements and what the American people are willing to pay for. That is what the budget debate in Washington is all about. Secretary Cheney and I are determined to make sure that paying a peace dividend does not leave America weak and unable to lead.

63 Will Rogers spoke in 1932 on the anniversary of California's statehood. "Eighty-two years ago today," Rogers said, "California entered the Union—on a bet. The bet was that the country would eventually be called California and not America."

64 But we are America. We are America because our Union is greater than its individual states.

65 Today, we hear similar bets about the future world. We hear bets on the future world dominated by Japan. We hear bets on a future world dominated by a united Europe. And we hear bets on an American domination as well.

66 Well, I'll take those bets. Because I believe that as long as America leads the free world, there will be no dominating state or region. The peace of the future will be a peace of all the democracies and of all the free peoples in the world. In fact, I believe that is the only way to make it a true peace—a peace that is enduring, that brings equal opportunities for economic prosperity to all, and that at the same time establishes safeguards for the liberty of all free people.

67 And the proper safeguards are the same safeguards that have secured the Free World's liberties for over four decades—our strong values, our resilient democracies, our vibrant market economics, our strong alliances, and, yes, our proud and ready armed forces.

68 All of these things constitute our great systemic strength. That strength sustains the Free World, just as in America it sustains our great Union—of which California is such an important part.

69 And that strength will continue to add people to the Free World's ranks. From Prague to Managua and from Budapest to Brasilia, few dark corners remain—and it's only a matter of time until these few bastions of dark tyranny are consigned to the ashheap of history.

70 Now the task is keeping democracy alive, not fighting and containing communism. Now the task is helping the dozens of democracies that are just being born. Now the task is teaching the basics of government of the people, by the people, and for the people—to the people. Now the task, in the words of the playwright-turned-president Vaclav Havel, is to continue "approaching democracy"—to do so with hundreds of thousands of new recruits.

71 No one is better fitted for these tasks than America and her allies. If we stay strong and lead, the world will follow. Of that, I am sure.

72 Thank you very much.

Is Government Working?

Mario Cuomo

Among America's best known politicians and noted speakers is Governor Mario M. Cuomo of New York. A liberal Democrat who was elected in 1990 to a third four-year term as governor, Cuomo first gained national prominence as a speaker through his eloquent keynote address at the 1984 Democratic National Convention. (See his keynote address in *Contemporary American Speeches,* 6th ed., pp. 307–315.) In his keynote speech he castigated the programs of the Republican Reagan Administration as embodying a selfish, inhumane, survival-of-the-fittest philosophy. In contrast and at length Cuomo offered the image or story of America as a national "family"—an image embodying values such as mutuality, sharing, fairness, reasonableness, compassion, and idealism tempered with practicality. Throughout the late 1980s and early 1990s, Cuomo often has been mentioned in the press as a major potential candidate for the Democratic Party's nomination for president.

In 1987 in an attack on "Nine Great Myths About Mario Cuomo," Miriam Pawel (*Mother Jones* magazine, February/March 1987, pp. 27–35, 49) argued that while Cuomo's rhetoric "has made him a national hero to liberals" and that while New Yorkers have been moved by his speeches, New Yorkers also increasingly were finding his actions and programs unsatisfactory—indeed sometimes inconsistent with his rhetoric. In 1991 in the *Washington Post National Weekly Edition* (January 28-February 3, pp. 13–14), reporter Michael Specter observed: "Cuomo has gained a perplexing reputation in New York even as he carries his eloquent message of empowerment and compassion to Washington and beyond. Here [in New York], he is seen as a sort of domestic Mikhail Gorbachev, whose words are so charismatic and convincing to those he does not govern that his unpopularity at home is dismissed."

On September 10, 1990, Mario Cuomo spoke at the John F. Kennedy School of Government at Harvard University on the occasion of the dedication of the School's new Taubman Building. He used the occasion to assess the proper roles of federal, state, and local governments in dealing with society's current problems (2). More specifically he advocated adoption of the policy of "Progressive Federalism" to replace the Reagan era's "New Federalism."

The need for change from the present situation rests on multiple lines of argument reinforced with examples and statistics. First, the nation faces numerous unresolved national problems (8–9). Second, the Reagan policies of New Federalism and supply-side economics (10–11) have resulted in disasterous consequences for states, localities, and individual citizens (12–17). Third, we have forgotten lessons and principles learned by our nation's Founders (9, 18). Especially we have forgotten that the idea of confederation, with a weak federal government, was found unworkable. Cuomo implies an analogy between Reagan's program and the idea of confederation (3, 19). You are encouraged to apply the standard tests for soundness of cause-effect reasoning (see Chapter 4) to Cuomo's contentions concerning Reagan politics and disasterous consequences.

After foreshadowing it earlier in the speech (5, 18), Cuomo advocates at length the structure and principles of Progressive Federalism (22, 29), again undergirding them with examples and statistics. The program involves local responsibility for local problems (23), national responsibility for national problems (24), and shared responsibility for shared problems with leadership provided by the federal government (25). Any new taxes must be federal and progressive rather than regressive (26).

Is the policy that Cuomo advocates workable? The Governor argues on two grounds that it is workable. First, where there is a will there is a way. The federal government always can find money when it really wants to (28). To what degree is the Savings and Loan bailout a reasonable example here? Second, citizens can return to a potent fundamental American value or vision—the nation as a "family" (30, 33). Assess the strengths and weaknesses of this metaphor or figurative analogy. Draw out implications of the family metaphor in terms of how families actually do function, how they should function, and how sometimes they are dysfunctional.

As a stylistic device, alliteration involves repetition of the same sound, usually a consonant, in a series of words in proximity. Often it is used to make ideas memorable or to associate several positive or negative ideas. Note Cuomo's adept use of this language resource to associate a series of negative ideas (19, 28). Finally, consider that although Cuomo relies heavily on examples and statistics throughout the speech, he does not employ expert testimony. Why might he have made this choice? As a related consideration, what persuasive functions might be served by Cuomo's allusions to his own expertise and competence (2, 25)?

The text of this speech was provided by Governor Cuomo's office in Albany, New York.

---

1 I am pleased to be here for this dedication—and to express my admiration and respect for the man who made it possible, Alfred Taubman. As an internationally renowned businessman, a patron of the arts, a friend of academia—Al Taubman has benefitted *this* state, *mine,* and many others, with his courage, business acumen, and generosity. Now he does it again with this important addition to a great institution. The Taubman Center for the Study of State and Local Government has begun its life at an auspicious moment.

2 Today, state and local governments face new challenges that have prompted scholars and students to ask some fundamental questions: Is government working? Can we, in 1990, say—as Lincoln did in the last century—that "The legitimate object of government is to do for the people what needs to be done, but which they cannot, by individual effort, do at all, or do so well, for themselves"? If so, what role should the federal, state, and local governments have in that collective action? Are there options available? What has been tried? What has succeeded? What has failed? As the Governor of a large state who's been wrestling with these questions since 1983, I'd like to use this occasion to consider a few of them.

3 I should begin by noting that, while the challenges we face are new, obviously, the questions about government's role are not. No one in America knows better than this audience, that the geniuses who founded our nation were searching for answers to these basic questions 200 years ago. In 1781, thirteen disparate states—wanting not to be totally alone but concerned about sacrificing independence—had strung themselves together in loose confederation. But, as we recall, the desire to be separate and independent overwhelmed the instinct for cooperation. Walls went up between the states, fragmenting them, denying them the strength that comes from unity.

4 So the founders made a new judgment—to *nationalize*. To try to form a more perfect union whose basic understandings and principles would give the 13 governments a common cause and a cohesive strength. They wrote a constitution that created a new overarching government with greater central power, while reserving to the states significant rights and responsibilities. It was a unique document describing a unique idea. It was written in broad strokes with room left for application to the unseeable, unknowable developments of an indefinite future. The original blueprint of our national unity would be tested—and shaped—by being stretched and configured on the procrustean bed of reality. It has been. Through the early years of confusion—through years of growth by accession and conquest—through war and civil war—the national government it created has constantly moved America forward. Sometimes in fits and starts, but inexorably. After a miraculous journey of only 200 years, the United States of America—through the power of coming together—has become the most powerful single nation on earth.

5 In this century, the strength of our national government rescued the entire nation from the depths of the great depression. The *Social Security Act of 1935* created a covenant between generations to assure that senior citizens would live in dignity. The *Marshal Plan* turned the devastation of World War II into a new age for democracy; the *G.I. Bill of Rights* educated a generation of returning veterans; the *National Defense Education Act* and the space program that followed, put American footprints on the moon and made us first in technological advancement. Positive national strength, gave us *Medicaid, Medicare, the Civil Rights Act of 1964, the Voting Rights Act of 1965, the Clean Air* and

Clean Water Acts. We could not have succeeded as we have, if we had not responded to *national* challenges with *national* solutions. Make no mistake, *the loosely tied raft of Confederation would have broken up in the rough waters of our history.*

6 That familiar history is good to recall today when the whole nation faces a new series of challenges that raise disturbing questions about our future. Even before the stunning invasion of Kuwait by Iraq, our national interest had been under siege . . . by the largest annual federal deficit and the greatest accumulated debt in our history; by lagging productivity growth and stagnating wages. And by an astonishing plague of drugs and the violent crime it generates.

7 We have other national challenges. Roads and bridges crumbling from coast to coast; acid rain pouring across state and national borders; *AIDS:* homeless families living out of automobiles; 12 million children going to sleep hungry; 23 million Americans who can't read a job application; 37 million Americans living in fear of getting sick because they have no health insurance to pay their bills.

8 These are not isolated, local vulnerabilities. Surely, it would be a delusion to believe that if Florida or New York lose the drug battles raging in their states—Georgia and New Jersey can escape the consequences. Or that—if we fail to liberate children from poverty in Illinois or Arizona—Ohio or California will not suffer. And surely it would be folly to believe—as long as the winds carry pollutants across our borders from the west and south—that New York or Massachusetts alone can stop the corrosive, killing effects of acid rain.

9 The nation can no more leave it to the individual states to fight these national problems than it can expect the states' valiant militias and National Guard units to fight and win a war in the Middle East without the Federal Army, Navy, Marines, Air Force—and Treasury. Two hundred years of history have instructed us how to use national strength to deal with national challenges like these. But in the last 10 years, we seem to have forgotten—or ignored—those lessons.

10 About a decade ago, the federal government announced a different approach. It was called "The New Federalism." As the theory evolved it called for the federal government to withdraw from previous commitments to help the states meet national needs. The federal cutbacks over the decade were massive. Housing aid was cut 80 percent. Energy conservation, 67 percent. Job training, 65 percent. Revenue sharing, obliterated. Urban development grants, eliminated. Money for education, the environment, mass transit—all cut.

11 The states were told that we could fill these gaps and build a stronger nation, without the federal government using its hands—or its resources. We would, instead, be delivered to the promised land by a magical force called "supply-side economics." Supply side's magic started with huge income tax cuts, benefitting especially the richest Americans. The theory was that because the wealthy had so much money already, they would not consume this new bonanza but would invest it in the private economy. The private economy would then get so strong it would create enough new revenues to balance the federal budget in three years despite these huge tax cuts and an accompanying huge military buildup. There would be loaves and fishes enough for everyone. So robust would the new economy be that, with the states gathering huge amounts of new revenues at *their* level, the federal government could rationalize cutting back federal support for domestic programs. Well, supply side proved to be more myth than magic. Because the tax cuts didn't generate the revenues needed to pay our federal bills, today the nation borrows huge amounts from foreigners we used to sell to, to buy from them the things they used to buy from *us*— like cars, and steel, and electronics.

12 The effect of all this? Supply side has been such a palpable failure that even its most zealous high priests now shrink from acknowledging their worship at the altar of this false idol. In less than a decade we went from being the world's largest creditor nation to the world's largest debtor. The national debt—which has tripled to over $3 trillion since 1980—is now a great albatross around the nation's neck, dragging it into a sea of red ink. It costs us nearly $200 *billion* a year in *interest* alone, and seriously imperils the entire national economy.

13 There have been other effects. Together, the New Federalism and supply side have led to a massive, simultaneous, twin redistribution. They have redistributed a large part of the burden of national problems away from the national government and onto the states, separately. And they have simultaneously produced a massive redistribution of the nation's *wealth,* away from the middle class, and into the relatively small stratum of our wealthiest Americans.

14 The progressivity of our taxes—that is, their relationship to the amount of income and ability to pay—has been nearly destroyed. At the federal level, the top income tax rate for the wealthiest Americans was cut from 70 percent down to 28 percent. At the same time, the Social Security Tax, a blatantly *regressive* charge, increased for about 130 million American workers, and their employers. As the income tax went down, depriving the National Treasury of revenues it needed, this payroll tax went up, dramatically, and was used to fill the hole.

15 This regressivity trickled down to the state and local levels. While Washington politicians chanted boastful slogans about their income tax cuts, state and local governments were forced to raise revenues to assume national burdens Washington once carried. As a result, states and localities looked to the taxes they believed would least threaten their competitive position. That was sales and real estate taxes—taxes that also have *no* effective relationship to one's ability to pay. Nationally, sales and real estate taxes doubled in the 1980's.

16 In effect, the middle class and the working poor have been paying for the huge income tax cuts at the federal level. But the truth is that—at least until now—distracted by the increasingly harsh realities of day to day existence, few of the middle class and poor realized it. Those of us whose business it is to observe these things, do realize it, understand it, and resent it.

17 Now, to add further anxiety to already substantial injury, the federal government—desperate for ways to pay the bills resulting from fiscal miscalculation, and not willing to acknowledge its mistakes—is considering shifting still more of the obligation away from Washington and onto the states. They are once again threatening states, as they did in 1985 and 1986, with the disallowance of deductibility of state and local income and property taxes. To put it more clearly, Washington wants to tax, at the federal level, taxes already paid by Americans to state and local governments, at the same time, preserving the huge tax cuts for the wealthiest Americans and perhaps even adding a capital gains tax cut as a further sweetener. This disallowance of deductibility would be a new double tax further punishing the separate states already bearing the load of federal abandonment. Today, 37 states are in serious fiscal trouble, sixteen already in recession, many others on the edge, all being dragged down by the rapidly ebbing national tide. This proposal would take still more resources from children, from police, from firefighters, from hospital workers, from the people who perform the public services. And it would encourage more regressive taxation at the state and local level, and widen regional economic disparities among the states.

18 The New Federalism offered up in 1980—and the supply side miracle that was supposed to make it work—for a while, fooled the nation into believing we could overcome national challenges without a unified national response. And left us off balance as we struggle to regain our footing for the global economic competition. It happened because we forgot the lesson learned by our founding fathers 200 years ago.

19 Today, we have a "fend-for-yourself" federalism, which forces the states to try to go it alone. This creates a tension—between the needs of states to raise revenues for unmet problems, and their need to create congenial tax policies to attract and hold increasingly mobile businesses. States are pitted against each other in the kind of destructive competition that we sought to move away from 200 years ago when we tore up the Articles of *Confederation*. Ironically, this is occuring just as Europe moves toward *consolidation*— uniting—in order to make themselves *stronger*. In 1992, the European economic community will fuse itself into the largest economy—and the largest consumer market—in the world. They, getting stronger by uniting; *we* growing weaker—by *fragmentation*.

20 And so, we are at a crossroad in our history. We can allow a regressive federalism to push us back towards the idea of confederation, leaving our capacities unevenly distributed and weakened by the scattering among our several states or we can choose to forge a new *progressive federalism*—to consolidate our strength and thereby increase it. It seems clear to me that—before we choose a path—we need to remind ourselves of the truth that gave birth to this nation. We are not just a collection of individual communities. At our *best*—especially when we are being tested—we are a *National Community*.

21 Today, as we struggle to rethink what form the future of federalism in America should take, we should apply a simple test: does it strengthen or weaken our national community? The federalism that *best* suits our time, is one that recognizes our *inter*dependence and acts on it. Not by *dividing power,* but rather by *sharing it.* By pooling efforts between local, state and federal government—to forge a *progressive federalism* that directs our national strength toward achieving common national goals. The rest of the world is not wrong. Nor were we, 200 years ago.

22 A federalism for our times should return to the principles that made us strong. In place of the failed New Federalism, we should return to the recognition of *national* responsibility for *national* problems, *local* responsibility for *local* problems, and *shared* responsibility for *shared* problems.

23 State and local governments—those closest to the people—should continue to play a leading role in education; in maintaining their *local* infrastructure and their own amenities; and in designing, administering, and applying national programs to meet human needs, as efficiently and as effectively as possible. Successful programs, already in place on the state and local level, can serve as national models to solve national problems. But, at the same time that we reaffirm the unique role state and local governments play, we must acknowledge that without national leadership and national resources, innovative state programs in housing and job training and drug treatment will address only a small part of our major national challenges.

24 We need a *progressive federalism* that recognizes our national problems will not be solved by sporadic successes in scattered states. It has been established by no less a figure than the president himself that drugs—and the violence, destruction and terrible expense they create—are a *national* problem—even public enemy number one! How then can the White House declare war on drugs yet fail to give the states all the help they need to fight the battles raging in the streets of their cities? Even President Eisenhower acknowledged that the roads and bridges and infrastructure that tie the states together are so vitally national in their implications that they should forever remain high on the list of federal concerns. But now the funds collected by Washington to help the states maintain and improve their highways are purloined by the Federal Government to conceal the true dimensions of its fiscal debacle. We need to change that. The National Government must decide to do the things that *only* the National Government can do—like reducing the federal deficit to help reduce interest rates and jumpstart the national economy. Like negotiating with governments to open up foreign markets.

25 And where shared responsibility is needed, the Federal Government must lead, not abdicate its responsibility. Only a *shared* national effort will end hunger in America and rescue 12 million children at risk. Only a *shared* national effort can provide the necessary job training to prepare our work force and maintain our technological edge through renewed investments in research and development. While some states have made valiant efforts to build new transitional and affordable housing, we won't end homelessness without a renewed federal role. Only strong federal leadership will extricate the nation from its dependence on foreign oil. Some of the states—like my own—have extensive, carefully analyzed and constructed energy programs. But a patchwork of state efforts will not be enough to secure our energy supply, or to protect our air, land, and water for future generations.

26 And if there is a need for further revenues to do all these things, then they should be gathered from those best able to afford them. For ten years those taxes have been essentially state and local and regressive. Now, to restore some balance, *new* taxes should be *federal* and *progressive.*

27 Conceding the truth of what we say here certainly does not make it easier to deal with what has been, until now, an intractable federal budget problem. But trying to make a budget that ignores our national challenges, would be absurdly unrealistic. Of course it would be easier to balance the budget if Washington pretended the needs that are so obvious to every governor in America did not exist, but that would be like operating on the patient for ulcers and leaving a cancer in his stomach.

28 The threat will not go away because we find it difficult to deal with. And let's be honest with ourselves. The deficit is a hard problem, but we know that it is not the wallet Washington lacks, it is the will! We know Washington can make difficult choices—and find the wealth—when it chooses to. It will find *$500* billion to bail out banks and bankers that stole the people's money. Think about it; *$5* billion would allow us to reach nearly every child eligible for *head start.* and yet, we're told we don't have the resources. But when it comes to the S and L's, we are ready to commit 100 times that amount. How does that make sense? Are the savings and loans 100 times more important?

29 This is a challenging time. But it can be converted into the beginning of a whole new dynamic era, if it inspires a renewal of our commitment to a wisdom 200 years old. We should begin by replacing the failed federalism of the past decade with a *progressive federalism*—a bolder, sounder pooling of the strength and wisdom of *all* the states to realize our full potential as a nation. And that potential is vast. For all the wrong turns and meanderings our history has taken us on, we have always—in the end—moved toward the light.

30 Something in us survives all the temporary distractions. I think it is the power of the idea that lay at the core of the American story at its founding, and is resurrected throughout our history. Because I am more comfortable with simple notions, I've called it "family." But by whatever name it goes, it is something deep in our national psyche . . . something that rises to the surface in times of war or other national crisis . . . something we need now to tap into. It is that hard-to-define feeling, that sense, that while we cherish our own individuality, *we are also part of something bigger than ourselves,* bigger than any individual—and yes, bigger than any state.

31 Perhaps it is to this idea that we should dedicate the Taubman Building. Perhaps with *it* as our inspiration, we can excite the imaginations and rouse the hopes of young and old alike. I hope so.

32 I hope the graduates of the Kennedy School, and the Harvard freshmen assembled here today—and all those who will help build America's future—will be exhilarated by the bright prospects still ahead of us. I hope they will be believers and doers who will take what has been passed on to them and make it something better. Honoring us by their works, and by their desire to be more than we have been. That—after all—has been the story of our history. And it is a glorious story.

33 Despite our faults, in only 200 years, we have become the greatest nation on earth. With one hand tied behind our back, without yet fully realizing the potential of women, of African Americans, of a population disabled by social problems and failures. Imagine how much stronger we could be if all our people were truly free to use the opportunity of this miraculous place. Imagine how much more we could achieve if we could only remember— as we have when we had to in the past—that we are at our best *as a family,* coming together for common purposes. Imagine how much more we could achieve, if only we could remember that we are at our best as a *nation.*

34 May the Taubman Center and the Kennedy School, and our own best instincts, lead us.

The New Paradigm
James P. Pinkerton

A Deputy Assistant to the President for Policy Planning, James P. Pinkerton holds a relatively junior position on President Bush's White House staff. But Pinkerton has developed what he believes is a coherent, well-reasoned domestic policy for the Bush Administration—The New Paradigm—that he hopes the President will explicitly and completely embrace. Starting with the 1988 presidential campaign and continuing through Bush's first two years in office with his focus on international crises, Bush was criticized for lack of such a coherent domestic agenda—lack of what Bush himself had termed "the vision thing." Within the Bush Administration, opposition to Pinkerton's program was led by Richard Darman, Director of the Budget. (See *Washington Post National Weekly Edition,* December 3–9, 1990, p. 26; December 17–23, 1990, pp. 13–14; *Newsweek,* December 3, 1990, pp. 24–25.)

Although raised in a politically liberal family, Pinkerton's university education at Stanford led him toward libertarianism—a political philosophy that favors free-market economic principles widely applied and abolition of as much governmental regulation and bureauacracy as possible. On April 23, 1990, James Pinkerton addressed members of the Reason Foundation. The Reason Foundation promotes an individualist philosophy and free-market principles. Thus it is natural that Pinkerton acknowledges his favorably inclined audience with praise (2, 22, 54).

Pinkerton states two value judgments as facts that would go unchallenged by his audience but which have been challenged by contemporary political analysts: Lyndon Johnson's Great Society program was a failure (9) and President Reagan demonstrated as workable the concept of a social safety net of programs for the truly needy (12). Concerning such challenges see David Broder, "Removing Bush's Rose-Colored Glasses," *Chigago Tribune,* May 19, 1991, Sec. 4, p. 3; David Zarefsky, et al., "Ronald Reagan's Safety Net for the Truly Needy," *Central States Speech Journal,* 35(1985): 113–119. Also consider, how fair is Pinkerton's association of the Great Society with "tyranny" (8–9)?

As a prelude to explaining the New Paradigm and to increase audience understanding of that label, Pinkerton sketches the philosophical and historical context from which it stems (17–23). By doing so he also is able to characterize it as a "revolution" rather than simply an evolution or modification. Pinkerton describes the nature of the New Paradigm by identifying the five basic premises on which it rests and by illustrating each premise with one of President Bush's proposals: a cut in the capital gains tax (32); parental choice of public school for their children (33); tax credits for low-income parents to facilitate choice of child care (36); a market-oriented national transportation policy (45); and tenant control of their own public housing (57).

As evidence to support his advocacy of the New Paradigm, Pinkerton extensively employs testimony (7, 24, 41, 45, 52) and examples (34, 43, 51, 57, 61). Using the standard tests for soundness discussed previously (Chapter 4), evaluate the reasonableness of his usage. Pinkerton enhances the clarity of his arguments through summaries (49, 62), forecasting of points (11, 30), and verbal signposts (12, 14, 31, 33, 35, 39, 51). Especially noteowrthy is Pinkerton's frequent use of metaphors to illuminate and reinforce the strengths of the New Paradigm and weaknesses of the Old Paradigm (11, 15, 37, 43, 53). For each metaphor assess the degree to which it prompts special insight, reasonably implies similarities between two normally dissimilar items, and fairly and ethically makes its point.

Compare and contrast Pinkerton's speech with Mario Cuomo's "Is Government Working?" Identify the basic differences between the New Paradigm and Cuomo's Progressive Federalism. How do these differences reflect what Pinkerton characterizes as a "battle" of ideas (2–3)? Compare the ways in which each speaker utilizes examples of recent political and economic changes in Russia and Eastern Europe to bolster their arguments. Consider whether legitimate equations might be made between Progressive Federalism and the Old Paradigm and between Reagan's New Federalism and the New Paradigm.

Also compare Pinkerton's speech with President Bush's January 29, 1991 State of the Union address (*Vital Speeches of the Day,* February 15, 1991, pp. 258–261). Even though Bush does not employ the New Paradigm label, to what extent does his speech reflect the elements and coherency of the New Paradigm?

The text of this speech is reprinted with permission from *Vital Speeches of the Day,* September 1, 1990, pp. 711–715.

---

1 Thank You. I'm here to talk about George Bush, the first President to govern in the spirit of the New Paradigm. If the last decade will be remembered as the time when the New Deal model broke down, I believe this decade will be remembered as the time when a new order for the age was established not only in the U.S., but around the world.

2 Leaving D.C. for L.A. is like not having left at all. In both places temperamental egos dominate an atmosphere of overspending, hype, and make-believe. Both places have a small number of free marketeers, greatly outnumbered, who can occasionally win victories. I am reminded of Henry V, both King and movie. After all, when you're the underdog, you have to believe in leadership and new ideas! Henry had his St. Crispin's Day oration at Agincourt. You're not going to hear any Shakespeare from me, nor am I as articulate as Olivier or Kenneth Branagh, but I am armed with an idea: the New Paradigm. So I will address this talk to we few, we happy few, we band of brothers and sisters!

3 Some have said that the war of ideas is over, that we have reached the end of history. At one level that may be true. But in the streets of Watts, in the factories of the Heartland, and especially in the corridors of Washington, there is work to be done, history to be made. So once more into the breach! This is not the end of anything: this is the beginning of the New Paradigm.

4 Ironically, in the midst of all the change in the world, there are those who say that Washington has become "boring." I'm not sure that anyone outside the Beltway cares, but the consensus of elite opinion seems to be that at least in domestic politics, the thrill is gone.

Certainly compared with 1981 when I started working the then-new Reagan Administration, Washington is a quieter place. But I think that quiet times in Washington represent an *achievement,* not an indictment, of the Bush Administration.

5 The country is cynical about its capital. But that cynicism is not directed toward President Bush. The public's skepticism focuses on the centralized bureaucracies—the IRS, the Postal Service, the Pentagon, HUD, and, of course, Congress. Voters distrust those institutions that lack accountability to the people they serve. The electorate distinguishes between those parts of the government that function and those that don't. Think of a machine that works and a squeaky wheel that needs grease. One hums quietly, the other fails noisily.

6 In defiance of received opinion, *the President has kept his campaign promises of a Kinder, Gentler Nation, and No New Taxes.* Because of his policies, America stands at the horizon, ready for the dawning of the New Paradigm around the world. There is a new energy, a force that has cracked the Berlin Wall, dismantled the Soviet Empire, freed Nelson Mandela, and democratized Nicaragua. This new vitality has redefined how the world works. It is bringing a new peaceful integration of the international economy, with the prospect of a better life for all humanity.

7 The President has spoken of the "New Breeze" of peace and freedom. The New Breeze is a metaphor for the learning process that is teaching all of us what George Bush said nearly three years ago:

We know what works. Freedom works.

8 And we learned what does not work. After decades of collectivization and concentration camps, we have seen the truth about an ideology whose central premise is a war against human nature, a nature that includes the basic desire for voluntary market exchange. Socialism doesn't work, no matter what name it goes by: National Socialism, Stalinism, Sandinismo, Apartheid—all are synonyms for tyranny.

9 I'm laboring the obvious here only because we must realize that the same dream of centralized socialized bureaucracies has failed here at home in its lesser manifestations. As in the Third World, the biggest losers under what I call the *Old Paradigm* have been poor people. The Great Society has been a continuing, if well-intentioned, failure, because it falsely assumes that experts, wise bureaucrats in league with university professors and politicians, can somehow administer supply and demand, prosperity and equality, from an office building far away.

10 Having said all that, do I dismiss all attempts to solve social problems? No, I'm here to say just the opposite. Precisely because we care about helping people we seek new ideas. And that has led us to the *New Paradigm.* The New Paradigm is most compelling when it addresses homelessness, inner city education, the underclass, and equal opportunity for all. The Old Paradigm has clung to these dilemmas to justify its continued existence.

Ironically, these are also the issues where the centralized bureaucratic structures that define the Old Paradigm have spent the most money and hurt the most people.

11 The electricity of freedom and market forces around the world has jolted the status quo here at home. The contours of the new American political reality are shaped by *two areas* of emerging national consensus.

12 *First,* most people agree on the goals this country should achieve; whether we are Democrats or Republicans, black or white, male or female, all of us want an educated young generation, a roof over every head, racial and sexual equality, and a clean environment. It's a cliche that Ronald Reagan, the most conservative President in our lifetime, nevertheless ratified the concept of the social safety net.

13 So now the argument shifts away from *goals*—which we all agree upon—to *means.* That is, how do we do what needs to be done?

14 The *second consensus* is limits to the size of government. "Read my lips" is national policy and will be, certainly as long as people think that government, especially the federal government, is incompetent and wasteful.

15 Some think that these two consensuses that define the 90's are in conflict, that we are condemned to wander on a political darkling plain, stumbling over the rubble of demolished expectations, poking around for bits and pieces of past policies that at best will bring marginal improvements. They once dreamed of "Camelot." What we got was "Bladerunner." These people—I call them Old Paradigm Pessimists—pose a pathetic choice: either go back to the Great Society, they tell us, or fall into a Grim Society.

16 The New Paradigm is an attempt to light a candle of hope and optimism amid the cynicism and fatalism that pervade today's Washington. People of good will can seize this opportunity. We can restructure government. We can move away from insensitive monopolistic bureaucracies. We can welcome change, harnessing the power of the New Paradigm for decency, compassion, and propserity.

17 The use of the phrase New Paradigm is one I have adapted from Thomas S. Kuhn's classic work, *The Structure of Scientific Revolutions,* as a way of understanding the nature of today's social transformation. Indulge me a moment to review Kuhn's thesis.

18 Kuhn argues that all scientists work from models, or sets of assumptions about how things work. Kuhn calls those working assumptions "paradigms." His book describes the process of scientific "revolution" that overturns an old, discredited paradigm, replacing it with a new and more useful paradigm.

19 For example, in the third century A.D., the astronomer Ptolemy outlined the theory, or *paradigm,* that the sun revolved around the earth. This "geocentric" paradigm dominated astronomy for over a thousand years, until it was overturned by the "heliocentric" paradigm of Copernicus and Galileo.

20 The old medical paradigm, for example, postulated that disease was caused by "bad blood." The favored "cure" was bleeding! In the 19th century, that paradigm was successfully challenged by a new one, which asserted that many illnesses came from germs. We should all be grateful. If the old medical paradigm had survived, doctors would still be defining "progress" as bigger and better leeches!

21 Kuhn's insight into the evolution of science applies to society as well. In the 18th century, mercantilism—capitalism without freedom or competition—was the dominant paradigm. In 1776 Adam Smith's *Wealth of Nations* articulated a new paradigm. Smith's paradigm was widely, if imperfectly, applied, and the result has been the greatest period of progress and prosperity in human history.

22 Of course, as Galileo discovered, new ideas are not always welcome. In spite of the best efforts of the Inquisition, people have gotten used to the idea that the earth revolves around the sun. But even today, not everybody has gotten the word that freedom works best. That's why we need the Reason Foundation!

23 The crisis in our cities, the crisis of our roads, the crisis of our schools—these are all symptoms of a larger crisis, the terminal crises of the Old Paradigm. According to Kuhn, "the state of Ptolemaic astronomy was a scandal before Copernicus . . ."

24 And "scandal" is certainly the word for the corrupt bureaucratic welfare state that House Republican Whip Newt Gingrich describes so brilliantly. Gingrich said recently that the welfare state:

> means that in your mind you have two standards of time. You have the time you use when you go into a private business, like your hardware store or a McDonald's or a Sears and you have the time you use when you walk into a government office. The first is [measured] in minutes, the second in hours. There is a level of customer service you expect when you are paying for something in a private business and there is a level of customer service you expect when, as a taxpayer, you go to the government business. And they are different models. If any private enterprise in America treated you the way you routinely get treated by government, you would put them out of business.

25 The bureaucratic impulse turns the governance of *free people* into the administration of things. Kafka foresaw that bureaucracy would only get worse as new layers piled on the old, like sediment. The original mission was forgotten, as bureaucracy went from being a progressive new idea in the time of Max Weber into a reactionary bad idea today. Perhaps Kafka was lucky that he did not live longer, because the sheer scope of bureaucracy today would defy even *his* imagination! Waking up to find that you are a cockroach is nothing compared to waiting in line for a driver's licence in the District of Columbia!

26 A bit of folk wisdom: "if it ain't broke don't fix it." Because of the failures of the Old Paradigm, lots of things *are* broken—and we need to fix them.

27 But there's another adage: "you can't beat something with nothing." Or, in Kuhnian terms, people will not let go of the old, familiar paradigm, no matter how defective, until they can see an alternative paradigm that they are convinced will work better. This is the transition period we are going through—people around the world see that the Old Paradigm is failing. They see glimmers of the New Paradigm. Leaders have a duty to help bring those glimmers into focus.

28 It would not be worth it for the Reason Foundation to invite me to come all the way from Washington to talk about how people like us can escape from the labyrinth of obsolete bureaucracy. Looking around this room, my guess is that most people here can afford to send their kids to private schools, hire security guards, and so on. They pay twice for the same service, but at least they get something.

29 The *real* urgency here is the tragedy in the inner city, where people are literally dying because the Old Paradigm bureaucracies fail to deliver even minimum levels of police protection, education, housing, and so on.

30 Enough of the Old Paradigm. The *New Paradigm* has *five* characteristics:

31 *First, governments are now subject to market forces in a way they haven't been before.* The official who tinkers with the economy, who pushes the wrong policy button, will see the flow of capital and investiment re-route itself instantaneously across the nations and continents and oceans. I've used the metaphor of energy and electricity to describe the power of the New Paradigm. Here, it isn't just a metaphor, it's a literal description. Prices are signals. And nowadays, these signals are carried at the speed of light. In seconds, the circuits of the international economy can switch in response to new information.

32 This aspect of the New Paradigm is a function of *feedback* and the increasing sensitivity of the global market. A self-monitoring and self-correcting system leaves little room for the foolish social and economic experiments of the 60s and 70s. If you don't deal with reality, other people will! In this New Paradigm light, President Bush's determination to see a cut in the tax rate on capital gains seems all the more compelling. He knows that America's greatest economic competitors have little or no capital gains tax.

33 *Second, the New Paradigm is characterized by increasing individual choice.* The President's education program offers a concrete example. During the 1980s, real spending per student shot up nearly 30 percent. Spending in this country is now about $5200 for each public school student. Imagine a class of 20 to 25 students. Multiply that by $5,200. The result is over $100,000 in expenditures per classroom. If the teacher is getting, on average, $32,000, where is the rest of the money going? Meanwhile, SAT scores sink and we typically rank in the second decile internationally. In big cities, where students routinely graduate from high school without being able to read their diplomas, spending is often much greater. instead of pouring money into this existing leaky structure, *the President seeks to change that structure by letting parents choose the public school their children will attend.* In a changing world, the schools should change too!

34 Up to now, bureaucrats have been the ones to decide what makes a good public school. President Bush believes that parents should have a say—the final say. The New

Paradigm of choice in education is sweeping the country. It's been embraced in 20 states by Democrats and Republicans, liberals and conservatives, governors as different as Rudy Perpich and Kay Orr. But, the most significant leader of all is not a governor, but a former welfare mother. Polly Williams, now a Democratic state representative, has led a grass-roots movement of poor parents in Milwaukee. They have won the freedom to choose the schools, public *or* private, that their children will attend.

35 *Third, the New Paradigm is characterized by policies that empower people to make choices for themselves.* As the President said here in Los Angeles last Spring, "This is the age of empowerment."

36 *Empowerment* is the flip side of *choice:* one side provides options, the other side helps exercise those options. Take the Bush Administration's approach to child care: The President offered a tax credit for low-income working parents. He wanted to empower those parents to care for their children in the way that best suits them: at home, with a relative or neighbor, at a church- or synagogue-based child care program, or at a day-care center.

37 By contrast, the Old Paradigm method is bureaucracy, one-size-fits-all, whether you like it or not! The Old Paradigm would simultaneously subsidize and regulate, to the exclusion of other alternatives. The Old Paradigm is the ultimate in trickle-down economics! Tax money floods into Washington, irrigating the bureaucratic gardens. This wouldn't be so bad if the runoff did some good. In fact, what seeps back is so poisoned by toxic paperwork that parents and children are worse off.

38 The Old Paradigm focus on *input—quantity—*only gets us in deeper. If we want to get out of the mess we're in, we have to focus on *qualitative outcomes.*

39 *Fourth, the New Paradigm is characterized by decentralization.* Authority is dispersing as bureaucracy is devolving. Stalinist governments in Eastern Europe, stodgy corporations on Park Avenue, sclerotic city halls here at home, socialist ministries in the Third World—all are changing. Let's look particularly at the Third World, where the Old Paradigm has done the most damage.

40 Old Paradigm social scientists made the subtly racist presumption that the Third World was "backward." Their "solution" was socialism, which they thought would protect these allegedly lesser peoples from the rigors of the marketplace. This "help" was no help at all. In fact, it was devastating. There is no way out of the global market. Today, the language of the experts has changed to "lesser developed countries," but Old Paradigm thinking still dominates international agencies, and the losers are still the poor.

41 These paternalists missed the central insight of the great Peruvian economist Hernando de Soto: that people in the Third World are the same as us—with the same goals. President Bush described de Soto's discovery:

> By walking the streets of Lima, not analyzing official statistics, [de Soto] found that the poor of Latin America—who have never read Jefferson or Adam Smith—ran their affairs democratically, outside the formal economy, organizing their private, parallel economy in a free and unregulated manner . . . People everywhere want the same things. And when left alone by government, people everywhere organize their lives in remarkably similar ways.

42 But what about here? What about decentralization here at home? Here too, centralized bureaucracies have proven unable to translate our wealth and compassion into opportunity and a better life for every American. Public and private bureaucracies have not been able to adjust to the change of the last decade, not to mention the coming decade! Therefore, a new generation must look for *new ideas* and *new approaches* to achieve the old goals.

43 David Osborne's *Laboratories of Democracy* is a wonderful overview of the individual states' efforts to make life better. I don't agree with everything David says, but that's not the point. The New Paradigm does not rely on the wisdom of any one individual, it relies on diversity and innovation, an intellectual marketplace, spread out across the states like 50, or 1,000, points of light.

44 As Hayek pointed out, new ideas and new approaches have a special significance when they arise spontaneously, the result of millions of individual decisions. The President emphasized a particularly vivid example when he was last here in Los Angeles: *telecommuting*—working from home. No bureaucrat decreed that henceforth, millions of Americans should work via their telephones and computers, but that is exactly what is happening. According to some studies, one out of five of us work from home at least part of the time.

45 When he announced his innovative and market-oriented National Transportation Policy, the President said: "Millions have already found their productivity actually increases when they work nearer the people they're really working for—their families at home."

46 Aside from the obvious environmental benefits, telecommuting shows that decentralization does not atomize people, as some feared. Instead, it brings them together to work where and how they want.

47 Lacking exposure to the New Paradigm, the voters are frustrated by the failures of Old Paradigm monopolistic bureaucratic government. It does not help when the mandarins of the Old Paradigm scorn them for the views they hold and the candidates they elect. As Bob Samuelson recently wrote in *Newsweek,* Americans are not so much *stingy* as *skeptical.* This skepticism—this immunity to bureaucratic baloney is a healthy thing. It is the result of bitter experience, a cumulative learning process.

48 The Information Age empowers everyone with a greater sophistication. Knowledge is power. Awareness is more broadly distributed than ever. When people are information-empowered, centralized, top-down government will never recover its former authority. Big Brother was killed by the MacIntosh, but Uncle Sam finds that he too, is being watched more closely by an increasingly alert citizenry.

49 Accountabily and feedback are the essence of the New Paradigm. Instead of blind dedication to monolithic centralized government, the New Paradigm emphasizes flexibility and results. Achieving those results will require *first, market orientation, second, choice, third, empowerment,* and *fourth, decentralization.*

50 I would add that centralized government bureaucracies have a cognate in centralized *private* bureaucracies. That's why we must fight the natural tendency of Big Government to join with Big Business in a dangerous liaison, the results of which are monopoly, protectionism, and the strangulation of mobility and opportunity.

51 *Fifth, the New Paradigm implies an emphasis on what works:* Once we agree on the goals of a decent life for every American, the debate shifts to achieving those goals, as opposed to merely talking about them and spending money. In Old Paradigm New York City, three different bureaucracies had responsibility for building safety. And then there was the tragic fire at the Happy Land disco. Eighty-seven people lost their lives. How many bureaucrats lost their jobs? The point is that in crucial areas of public safety, we don't necessarily need *more* government, or *less* government. We need *capable* government, and the Old Paradigm structures have proven themselves utterly *in*capable of keeping us safe. Some will say that all we need is another round of piecemeal reform. I say we are buried in pieces. We need a new structure.

52 The Old Paradigm stresses *input*. It measures how well we do by how much we spend. Yet spending money is no substitute for common sense. Consider this: Donald Graham, publisher of the *Washington Post* who spent a year as a DC cop, recently described the sorry state of the District's police force. Listen to this:

> [A]mazingly, the department still has a promotion system in which effectiveness at a patrolman's job has nothing to do with promotion. Who makes sergeant is based partly on an exam and partly on a brief interview with two police officials and a citizen who are supposed to be unacquainted with the officer they're interviewing.

53 This defies common sense, but defiance of common sense is what the Old Paradigm is all about. Bureaucracy elevates Standard Operating Procedure and regulation above the practical. Like other cities trapped in the tar pit of the Old Paradigm, Washington DC is sinking, and its people are suffocating. Sprinkling money into the mire won't help. Dollar bills, in and of themselves, make a lousy lifeline.

54 As people learn that government does not know best, they will refuse to turn over decision-making power when they can decide better for themselves. Popular opinion now converges around the notion that instead of doing many things badly, the government should do a few things well. The public debate now focuses on qualitative, as opposed to quantitative, changes in government, to a restructuring that finally begins to put the government in tune with the society that changed so much in past decades. Bob Poole and the Reason Foundation have pioneered New Paradigm approaches to chronic problems, from pollution to traffic congestion to health care. More and more pople are listening.

55 President Bush holds office at a time of consensus: everyone wants an educated young generation, a roof over every head, racial and sexual equality, and a clean environment. And yet, we want limits on government power.

56 Do these two areas of consensus clash? If, for example, you believe that money alone will solve the problems of America's schools, if you believe that the best answer to the high cost of raising kids is bureaucratized, monopolized day care, if you believe that the answer to housing the public is public housing, then not only must you believe that our national aspirations are in conflict, you should join the *Old Paradigm Society.* But be advised, it will take them six-and-a-half years to process your application in triplicate!

57 On the other hand, if you believe that we ought to judge our schools by how well they perform, not by how much money they spend, if you believe that families should choose the child care that's best for themselves, if you think that Kimi Gray had the right idea when she liberated her home from the DC government and now runs Kenilworth-Parkside for the benefit of the people that live there, then you can see how the reality of the New Paradigm 1990s can work for the benefit of all Americans. You've been a member in good standing of the *New Paradigm Society* and didn't even know it!

58 The New Paradigm is not limited to the United States, nor should it be. The lessons of the New Paradigm are universal, and many around the world are applying them. In the global economy, it's up to us to compete. We only have the power to be our best, not a guaranteed First Place finish. However, American history reminds us that opportunity is all we've ever needed.

59 I've been speaking quite grandly of the planet. But what about the question that politicians will immediately ask themselves: What's in it for *me?* Why should practicing politicos be interested?

60 For Republicans, the answer should be obvious. Fighting taxes and Communists has brought us about as far as it can. Not taking anything away from those concerns, but the experience of the 10 years since Reagan's election tells us this is a formula for winning the White House and not much else, especially at the local level. The future growth of the Republican Party depends on our ability to address voters' concerns about other important issues, such as health, child care, education, and pollution. The New Paradigm enables the GOP to move forward in these areas and do good, without going back to the Great Society of nobel rhetoric and unintended consequences. But as Jack Kemp reminds us, people don't care that you know until they know that you care. And that's what George Bush was driving toward in his New Paradigm Acceptance Speech when he sought a mandate to lead a kinder, gentler nation, with no new taxes.

61 As for the Democrats, they need the New Paradigm even more. After all, their core constituents are suffering the most from the status quo. Democratic polls may be tempted to blame all problems on David Stockman. But eventually they will run out of scapegoats. They will be forced to account for the Old Paradigm failures they have created and sustained. Polly Williams called their bluff with her school voucher plan. In the course of overcoming the special interests, she found out that the liberal Democrats weren't nearly as interested in the well-being of poor black children in Milwaukee as they were in defending the bureaucratic monopolistic status quo. So she forged a coalition with the Republicans to enact a bill to help the kids get better schools, and the New Paradigm has come to Wisconsin. Representative Williams has made us realize that the challenge we face is not Left vs. Right, but Up vs. Down.

62 When we recognize the broad similarities in human aspirations in the *Third, Second,* and *First* Worlds, when we shift the focus of public policy to what works, when we judge programs qualitatively not quantitatively, when we expand individual choice, empower the poor, and create decentralized, flexible and adaptable institutions, then we make a world where there is no insurmountable conflict between our national goal of caring for our neighbors *and* enlarging our freedoms by limiting our government.

63 If this seems a lot to ask over lunch, think back to the challenge that Henry V had to overcome on St. Crispin's Day. Planning a victory against a foe that outnumbered him five to one, he said "All things are ready, if our minds be so."

Against a Constitutional Amendment Banning Flag-Burning

John Danforth

The American flag is a potent symbol for American citizens. For most citizens it represents the accomplishments of representative democracy, the heroism of America's wars, and the fundamental values at the core of the American way of life. The flag also has been the center of controversy—whether in deciding if the Pledge of Allegiance can be required of all public school students or in deciding the degree of Constitutional protection of persons who mutilate or desecrate it as part of social protest. For some citizens the flag primarily represents patriotism and thus should be protected as almost sacred. For other citizens the flag primarily represents freedom—even the freedom to use the flag in protest. (See *Newsweek,* July 3, 1989, pp. 18–20.)

In the summer of 1989, the U.S. Supreme Court in the case of *Texas v. Johnson* decided 5–4 that the First Amendment guarantee of freedom of speech protects persons who burn the flag in political protest. The U.S. Congress rapidly responded in two ways. An amendment to the Constitution was proposed in the Senate to give Congress and the states "the power to prohibit the physical desecration of the flag of the United States." After major debate in October 1989, the proposed amendment was defeated in the Senate. Congress also passed the Flag Protection Act of 1989 that criminalized the conduct of anyone who "knowingly mutilates, defaces, physically defiles, burns, maintains on the floor or ground, or tramples upon" an American flag. In the case of *United States v. Eichman* decided 5–4 in June of 1990, the U.S. Supreme Court ruled that Flag Protection Act unconstitutional because it was inconsistent with the First Amendment.

Republican Senator John Danforth of Missouri spoke on October 17, 1989 during the Senate debate on the amendment. Danforth was one of the original co-sponsors of the proposed constitutional amendment. Now he speaks against it. This is a rare occasion in American political life. Citizens are not accustomed to seeing prominent politicians publicly reverse a policy position and provide the arguments for their change of mind. An editorial in the *Chicago Tribune* (October 29, 1989, Sec. 4, p. 2) praised the Senate for its "courage and sanity" in defeating the amendment and urged that Danforth's speech "should be required reading for every school civics class."

By explaining why his mistaken judgment was a "mistake of the heart," Danforth reassures his colleagues of his profound respect for the flag and what it symbolizes (2–5, 22). To support his stance against adoption of the amendment, Danforth employs not only "practical" reasons (6–11) but also more significant philosophical/constitutional justifications. Note particularly two value judgments advocated by Danforth to support his position. First, the Bill of Rights ought to have priority over the flag (16–17, 28). Second, political expression is the most important right protected by the Constitution (21)—a right necessary to ensure freedom (29). Do you believe that these are reasonable value judgments? Why?

Danforth uses a number of argumentative strategies. Frequently he supports his position by refuting arguments of those favoring the amendment (12–14, 18–19, 26). Also he expresses agreement with the reasoning of the Supreme Court in *Texas v. Johnson* (19–20). And he uses a variation of the "foot-in-the-door" or "thin-entering wedge" argument. The amendment would open the door, he contends, to suppression of other less extreme but nevertheless "unpopular political expression" that merits protection (27). In other words, the amendment would be a dangerous first step toward eventual suppression of a wide range of political communication. To what extent is Danforth's refutation of opposing arguments adequate and how sound is his "foot-in-the-door" argument?

The text of this speech is reprinted from the *Congressional Record*, 101st Congress, 1st Session, Vol. 135, #140, pp. S13511–13512.

---

1 Mr. President, one reason it is good not to rush things is that sometimes on reflection you realize that views you have held are mistaken, and consideration gives you an opportunity to reflect and to change your mind. That is exactly what I have been doing with respect to the constitutional amendment which is now before us.

2 I rise this morning, Mr. President, for the purpose of admitting a mistake. It was a mistake of the heart, but nonetheless it was a mistake. If Senators will look at the resolution that is on their desks, they will see that my name appears as a cosponsor of this constitutional amendment. I rise now to state that I made a mistake in doing that, and I will not vote for this constitutional amendment. I will vote against it.

3 Mr. President, it was a mistake of the heart. Like all of us in the Senate, like all of us in our country, I was raised to revere our flag. I grew up during one of the great periods of patriotism in American history. I grew up during the Second World War. I grew up to recite the pledge of allegiance and to respect the flag and to take a keen interest in our war efforts. I remember both with pride and sadness the news that my cousin had been killed in north Italy fighting that war to protect our country.

4 When I go home to Missouri, one of the first things I do is raise the flag. I have a large flagpole outside my house. I might say it is the second flagpole I have had outside my house in Missouri. The first one I thought was just a little too flimsy to do the job. It started getting rusty, and it just did not look the way a flagpole should look. So I bought a much taller, sturdier, shinier flagpole from which to fly the flag outside my house.

5 The flag is dear to me as it is dear to every Member of the Congress and it is dear to every person in this country. So it was a mistake of the heart.

6 When the proposal came around to my office to cosponsor a constitutional amendment to protect the flag, my response was: If that is what is necessary to protect the flag, fine. I will do it. But on reflection, Mr. President, that decision was just plain wrong. I think it was wrong for a couple of practical reasons, and it was wrong for a much bigger reason as well.

7 One practical reason was touched on by the Senator from North Carolina, who said in effect that he believed if we were to so amend the Constitution, it might invite flag burning: it might serve as a waving of the red flag in front of those who would seek to be arrested. Maybe the best way to deal with these people is to ignore them. Maybe to outlaw desecration of the flag simply causes more desecreation of the flag. That is a practical thing to consider.

8 Then there is a question of the statute. It has been argued that the statue is unconstitutional. How do we know it is unconstitutional? We just passed it 2 weeks ago in the Senate. More than 90 Senators voted for it. Do you mean that more than 90 Senators voted for something at the time they knew was unconstitutional? I do not think so.

9 We do not know that a statute is unconstitutional until it goes through the courts, until it is held to be unconstitutional by the courts, and this is not even a statute yet. It is barely a bill. It was just passed. It was sent to the President.

10 I think, Mr. President, that if it is possible to accomplish something by a statute we should do it by a statute, not by amending the Constitution of the United States.

11 So I say why not give the statute a chance? Why do we have to rush it? Maybe if we give the statute a chance some more people will conclude as I have that to amend the Constitution of the United States is no trivial matter, that there is no more profound thing we as a country do than to amend the Constitution of the United States.

12 This, Mr. President, is an amendment to the Bill of Rights.

13 The Senator from Utah at the close of his very learned speech disputed this fact. He said this does not amend the Bill of Rights.

14 Mr. President, of course it amends the Bill of Rights. The decision of the Supreme Court of the United States was founded solely on the first amendment to the Constitution. The Supreme Court's decision in Texas versus Johnson was an interpretation of the first amendment. This constitutional amendment is put forward for the express purpose of cutting back on the first amendment to the Constitution as that amendment has been interpreted by the Supreme Court. Of course, this is an effort to amend the Bill of Rights, and if it succeeds, and it may well succeed, Mr. President, it will be a first. If it succeeds, and it has a good chance of succeeding, it will be unique, unique in the history of the United States of America.

15 I say "if it succeeds" because, Mr. President, I believe that if it is going to be stopped it will be stopped in the Senate. I can remember, very soon after the Supreme Court's decision, speaking with Senator Biden, and he said he believed that the constitutional amendment would go through this country like a hot knife through butter. This is such an emotional issue. Can you not see State legislatures rushing to act on constitutional amendment resolutions in their States?

16 The question of whether we are going to do this is going to be determined here in the Senate. So, Mr. President, this is not a throwaway vote. This is not just the kind of vote that you cast thinking, well, this is nothing, somebody else can act as the safety net. We are the decisionmakers. We will be responsible if our Constitution is amended. And if it is amended, it will be the first time in the history of our country that we have altered the Bill of Rights.

17 We are talking about the flag. The flag has been altered any number of times. But in the 200-year-plus history of our Constitution, the Bill of Rights has never been altered. Not even a comma has been changed.

18 Now we are told, well, the first amendment is too big, the first amendment is too broad. Let us act on a constitutional amendment to cut the first amendment down to size.

19 Mr. President, if there is anything that is protected by our Constitution it is political speech. Some say that the act involved in the Texas case was not speech, but the Supreme Court says that it was. The Supreme Court held that what this character Johnson did was political expression and therefore speech. Some Senators might disagree with that. But that is what the Supreme Court said, and as Charles Evans Hughes once noted, in this country the Constitution is what the judges say it is. I think in this case the judges were right.

20 What was it other than political speech? It took place at the time and at the place of the Republican National Convention in 1984. It involved a demonstration. It was part of a political demonstration. Pamphlets were being handed out. Speeches were being made. And Mr. Johnson burned the flag. He did not burn it because it was some kind of hobby. He did not burn it because he had an itch to burn the flag. He burned it because it was part of the expression of political views.

21 It is political speech. And political speech is the most important right to be protected by the Constitution of the United States.

22 Mr. President, was it nice speech? Was it attractive speech? Was it an agreeable speech? Absolutely not. It was totally abhorrent to everything we believe in. It was an affront to every American. It makes your blood boil to think about it—burning the flag of this country.

23 But, Mr. President, the first amendment to the Constitution does not protect only nice speech or only attractive speech or only popular speech. We would not need a Constitution for that purpose. The great thing about the United States of America is that our Constitution protects any crackpot who wants to stand on his soapbox and express any oddball point of view that pops into his mind.

24 Nor does the Constitution say that you can express whatever opinion you have provided that you do so in the official prescribed way.

25 Burning the flag was a terrible act. But it was within the protection of our Constitution.

26 Some say, well, there is some expression, some political expression that is so abhorrent, so awful that we just cannot take it anymore, so abhorrent that we cannot tolerate it. But that is not what the Constitution says. So then people say, well, then let us change the Constitution.

27 Well, Mr. President, if we change the Constitution to prevent this abhorrent, terrible kind of political expression, what other kind of unpopular political expression will we decide is outside the bounds of [propriety] and law? Where would we stop? I think, Mr. President, the answer is that we should never start. The answer is the same as it has been for 200 years, that we should never start to change the Bill of Rights.

28 Every country has a flag. But America has the Bill of Rights. It is the crowning glory of our country. It is what makes this place so special. This is not just a place where you hang your hat.

29 This is America, and this is the place where freedom does shine. Mr. President, the amendment before us would alter the first amendment to the Constitution of the United States. It would pare it down, and that is why I was mistaken to cosponsor this amendment in the first place. That is why I repudiate my cosponsorship and why I will vote against the amendment.

Influence Peddling: The Revolving Door of Government
Daniel J. Donnelly

Daniel Donnelly, a student at Northern Illinois University represented his university and the State of Illinois at the 114th Annual contest of the Interstate Oratorical Association. The contest was hosted by the Maryland Oratorical Association and was held at College Park, Maryland on May 8 and 9, 1987. Mr. Donnelly survived preliminary and semi-final rounds on his way to the final round where he won first place.

This speech advances a proposition of policy: that stronger ethics legislation should be enacted to eliminate influence peddling. In advancing this claim, Donnelly identifies the harmful effects of influence peddling, the reasons why influence peddling is so popular, and the means through which influence peddling may be reduced. In essence, his speech is organized around an effect/cause/solution pattern of organization. Is this an effective organizational strategy? By the time you arrive at paragraph 12 are you ready to conclude, as the speaker does, that it's time to replace current, toothless Ethics Laws with "a new pair of dentures"?

Mr. Donnelly attempts to convince audience members that they are victims of influence peddlers. A number of paragraphs conclude with the words: "The loser: the American citizen." What emotional impact does this strategy have on you as a reader? Do you feel angry or outraged as the speaker intended?

This speech is reprinted by permission of the Interstate Oratorical Association from *Winning Orations,* 1987, pp. 25–29.

1 January, 1986. Washington, D.C. You're in the very hectic office of a very busy Congressperson when a letter arrives from Mrs. Margaret T. Workman of Anywhere, U.S.A. One of the aides assigned to go through the thousands of pieces of incoming mail soon discovers that Mrs. Workman is displeased about U.S. support for Ferdinand Marcos. The aide tosses the letter on the pile entitled foreign affairs, and a form letter is soon dispatched. Halfway around the world Ferdinand Marcos is also writing, but he is not writing a letter. He is writing a check in the sum of $950,000 to the lobbying firm of Black, Manafort, and Stone—a firm comprised mainly of former Reagan Administration members, former Congresspeople, and close Reagan associates. Their goal is to use their influence with Reagan and lawmakers to keep the money flowing to Marcos. And the winner in Workman verses Marcos? Unfortunately, we already know who the winner was. But perhaps it was a mistaken victory or an isolated case. Unfortunately not, for the hot new game in Washington is influence peddling—selling who you know and where you can go. In large numbers, high level government personnel are shedding the shackles of public service for the profit of the private sector. In the process, the government that was once of, for, and by the people is now the government of, for, and by the rich. Senator Howard Metzenbaum of Ohio proclaims; "Washington has become a sinkhole of influence peddling. Many people believe victory goes to the well-heeled and the well-paid and they are right." For you see, influence peddling does not affect one in eight of us or one in twelve of us. It affects every one of us. It does not threaten our lives, but it does threaten our way of life. It is a slap on the face of fair and equal repres/ntation.

2 So in the next few minutes, tear down your no solicitation signs—for we will invite these peddlers of influence in. I will examine the problems that they present, the reasons for their recent emergence, and some ways to eliminate this problem and effectively slam the door on influence peddling.

3 Unfortunately, the door is not closing. The March 3, 1986 *Time* reports, "For many, government service has become a mere internship for a lucrative career as a hired gun for special interests." And in this flip-flop of positions, the power, knowledge, friendships and secrets that were acquired in government are now used against the government. And this is the key in understanding the distinction between lobbying and its evil offspring influence peddling. For in our society, lobbying plays an important part in the lawmaking process by both providing legislators with vital information and giving legitimate interests an avenue through which to be heard. However, when an individual has no expertise to offer, but only government-acquired influence, the fine line between lobbying and influence peddling has been crossed. And make no mistake, as the May 12, 1986 *U.S. News and World Report* points out, the only attribute of an influence peddler is access to former associates and a former department.

4 For example, ex-Congresspeople who have become lobbyists still have access to the floor of Congress and to the cloakrooms. Granted, they are not supposed to lobby in those areas. But as Senator David Pryor of Arkansas points out, "they don't call it lobbying; they call it visiting. But you know exactly what they're there for." They are there to promote the welfare of a special interest group because they have been paid a lot of money. For it seems that representation has become synonymous with wealthy and democracy synonymous with capitalism. And as long as influence peddlers continue to use their government-acquired influence to the advantage of only a few and the exclusion of a few too many, the losers in this market of influence will be those who cannot afford to buy the influence. The loser is the American citizen.

5 For example, former White House aide Michael Deaver used his influence to save tax breaks for companies that invest in Puerto Rico, even though every job created in Puerto Rico costs the U.S. treasury $22,000. Meetings with several top government officials and a ground-to-air call to Secretary of State George Schultz who was headed to Geneva aboard Air Force One had no small part in ensuring that these tax breaks would be maintained. The loser: the American citizen.

6 Yet don't be misled into believing that only highly publicized and top level government officials partake in influence peddling. The March 23, 1985 *Congressional Quarterly* reports that in 1981, the Social Security Administration awarded a $115 million computer contract to Paradyne Corporation which had passed several tests developed by the Office of Data Communications. But as it turned out, Paradyne was able to pass the tests only because it had hired Alfred Leung, who as Deputy Director of Data Communications had developed the tests. By incorrectly awarding the contract to Paradyne, the Social Security Administration received faulty equipment and the project was delayed three years. The loser: the American citizen.

7 In fact, our inability to match the influence of the special interest groups is so evident that Congressman Barney Frank of Massachusetts laments, "Sometimes I think the only people not represented up here are the middle class." Yet since nothing is ever lost or gained, it is only reshuffled, the rights that were at one time guaranteed to us are now guaranteed only to the highest bidder. And in a sad yet alarming commentary, the highest bidder is all too often a foreign government, a foreign corporation, or even one of our enemies. Our rights are now the rights of the foreign entities that spend $150 million yearly on advice from U.S. influence peddlers. In the past few years, our rights have become the rights of Taiwanese shoemakers, which hired National Security Advisor Richard Allen to head its lobbying effort. Our rights have become the rights of the Marxist regime of Angola, which hired former Reagan transition team member and close Reagan friend, Bob Gray. Our rights have become the rights of Nicaragua, which hired the firm of Reichler and Applebaum for $166,000. In commenting on the influence peddling situation, Senator David Boren of Oklahoma remarks, "It is no wonder that foreign aid has increased by 169 percent in the past six years, while education, agriculture, and other domestic programs have been drastically cut."

8 While the use of influence peddlers by foreigners to get a piece of the U.S. foreign aid pie is scary, the practice of influence peddlers divulging U.S. secrets to these foreigners is hideous. Yet according to the June 2, 1986 *Newsweek,* the revolving door between the

U.S. government and foreign entities has made it almost impossible to keep U.S. trade strategy secret. In fact, Congresswoman Marcy Kaptur of Ohio, pointing out the more than 100 former senior U.S. officials now working for Japan, believes that influence peddling is partly responsible for our expanding trade debt. The loser: the American citizen.

9 Having examined the problem of influence peddling, we must now answer the question: why is it that anyone who can muster any influence at all is looking to leave government and enter the private sector? Simply answered, it's that old dynamic duo of big bucks and loose laws. Listen to Ed Rollins, a former Reagan Adminnistration member: "I spent a lot of years doing things for love. Now I'm going to do things for money." And the money comes extra quick and extra green. With millions of dollars spent every year to buy influence, the self-proclaimed, underpaid legislators and government officials view influence peddling as their ticket on the gravy train. For example, former White House aides Deaver and Lyn Nofzinger became instant millionaires through their influence peddling schemes.

10 While it is the money that makes influence peddling hot, it is the laws that make it not. For under the current Ethics in Government Act, nearly all forms of influence peddling are legal. And if we don't question its legality, the influence peddlers certainly won't question its morality.

11 The current Ethics Law does not regulate ex-Congresspeople, does not deal with the problem of top officials working for foreign nations, and does not adequately cover all federal government employees. The March 3, 1986 *Time* called current Ethics Laws toothless.

12 Perhaps it's time for a new pair of dentures—for we have the ability to regulate the influence peddlers. Primarily, we can support legislation to further prohibit influence peddling. Now notice that I said support, and not write, your Congressperson. In the past, writing your Congressperson may have been a viable way to have your voice heard and a problem remedied. But as my speech has pointed out today, that is no longer the case. And until this problem is corrected, no other problems will be heard. But how can one support such legislation? The key is awareness and publicity.

13 First, you can either write editorials yourself or write to editors and syndicated columnnists urging them to speak out on this problem. Next, contact citizen lobby organizations such as Common Cause. This organization has continually stated its opposition to influence peddling, and your support would provide it with even more ammunition to carry on the fight. And if you really want to write a Congressperson, rather than write [to] your own write to either Senator Strom Thurmond or Senator Howard Metzenbaum, who have introduced eithics legislation in the past and are considering doing so again. By writing to these men, you will be providing them with a resource they can use to persuade your Congressperson to oppose influence peddling. At the same time, you will be sending a message that you have lost faith in the ability to gain access to your own legislator.

14 To regain our access, a more stringent ethics bill should be passed which includes: prohibiting all federal government employees, including Congresspeople, from lobbying the government for at least one year upon leaving; preventing all top officials from lobbying for a foreign entity; and imposing severe fines and/or penalties for those who violate the Ethics Act. Yet even further restrictions should be implemented. Administration officials should not be allowed to lobby until a new administration takes over, and former Congresspeople should lose some or all of their privileges.

15 In another area, simply by making a public issue of influence peddling, we can reinstill the mechanisms of public shame and stigma. Influence peddling is a back door industry. By locking the back door and forcing the industry to come to the front, we can weed out and ridicule those who are engaged in unlawful or unethical behavior. Just as Michael Deaver.

16 Today I examined influence peddling, the reasons for its recent emergence, and some ways to eliminate this problem. By following through, we can regain the rights that were at one time guaranteed to us. We can ensure fair and equal representation will be afforded to all. But in combating this problem, let us remember this: Freedom is not free. Our right to fair and equal representation was won on the battlefield. To regain those rights, we must return to the battlefield. But this time the enemy is not carrying a gun. He is carrying influence. Thus, for each of us, it is time to do battle once more.

Black American civil rights leader Jesse Jackson speaking at a news conference.

CHAPTER 8

SPEECHES THAT INTENSIFY SOCIAL COHESION

Social cohesion, any social order, rests on shared values, customs, and traditions which identify us in our roles as members of a society. We are disposed accordingly to empathy, cooperation, lawful behavior, and even altruistic acts. We understand each other, for we "speak the same language," that is, we share the same values, perceptions, identifications, ideals, reactions, and rules of action. A social order is both the effect and the source of shared values and beliefs.

Ernest van de Haag

THE NATURE AND IMPORTANCE OF SPEECHES THAT INTENSIFY SOCIAL COHESION

At the heart of any social order is a set of values that constitutes the basis for all social action. In recognition of the importance of values, Chapter 5 discussed the nature of speeches that seek to establish propositions of value. However, once values have been established, the perpetuation of social order demands that these values periodically be reaffirmed and intensified. A rhetorical critic, Ronald F. Reid, reminds us: "Building and maintaing social cohesion is an ever present need; for although individuals within society are obviously not all alike, they must transcend their differences if they are to function as a viable social unit."

There are numerous occasions in our society on which speeches that intensify social cohesion are given; church services, victory celebrations, awards convocations, retirement luncheons, funeral services, nominating conventions, fund-raising rallies, sales promotion meetings, and commencements are such occasions. At moments like these, speakers address audiences about the values that both share as members of a common group. The speeches given in such moments are noncontroversial for a specific audience. They do not urge adoption of new values or rejection of old values. Rather, they seek to reinforce and revitalize existing audience values. Speakers seek unity of spirit or a reenergizing of effort or commitment; they try to inspire, to kindle enthusiasm, or to deepen feelings of awe, respect, and devotion.

Among the types of speeches that intensify social cohesion are the following:

Sermons: A sermon articulates the tenets of a faith. It is designed to inspire stronger commitment to religious beliefs and values.

Eulogies: A eulogy pays tribute to the dead. It identifies, in the life of the departed, qualities which those who remain behind should value and emulate.

Dedication Speeches: A dedication speech marks the completion of a group project. It praises group achievement and stresses the importance of the object being dedicated to future group endeavors.

Commemorative Speeches: A commemorative speech marks the anniversary of an event. It demonstrates the significance of the event in the light of present group values, beliefs, and goals.

Commencement Speeches: A commencement speech signals the completion of a course of study. It praises those being graduated and speaks to the values that should be reflected in their future lives.

Keynote Speeches: A keynote speech serves as a preface to a meeting, conference, or convention. It stresses the social worth and importance of the work to be done by those assembled.

Welcoming Speeches: A speech of welcome extends a greeting to people who are new to a group. It expresses satisfaction with the presence of new members or visitors and relates the values of the group to the values of those joining or visiting the group.

Farewell Speeches: A farewell speech is given by a person who is leaving a group. The speaker usually reflects on the quality of the experiences that were shared with the group and the emotions he or she is experiencing at the moment of departure.

Presentation Speeches: A presentation speech accompanies the presentation of an award to a group member. It specifies the qualities the award is meant to symbolize and justifies the presentation of the award to the person being honored.

Nomination Speeches: A nominating speech places the name of a person before a group of voters as a candidate for an elective office. It describes the requirements of the office (abilities, personal qualities, duties, problems to be faced), praises the virtues, accomplishments, and experiences of the person being nominated, and depicts the success the group will have under the leadership of the nominee if he or she is elected.

Acceptance Speeches: An acceptance speech is given by the recipient of an award or honor. In accepting an award, a speaker is expected to express gratitude and to demonstrate the personal qualities the award is intended to symbolize.

Inaugural Addresses: An inaugural address is given by a person as he or she is about to assume a position of leadership in a group. The speaker normally acknowledges the passing of leadership, praises past group performance and achievements, and identifies the values and goals of future group activities.

Each of these types of speeches serves a different immediate purpose. However, all share the larger social purpose of intensifying social cohesion by paying tribute to the values of the group. By nature, the speech that intensifies social cohesion invites members to reaffirm their commitment to the values, customs, and traditions that are at the heart of group life.

Students often assign less importance to this form than to informative or persuasive communication. Drawing on their past experiences with ceremonial gatherings, they conclude that speeches that intensify social cohesion are often "flowery" and trite—given more to affected *or* artificial flourishes than to substantive issues. However, sociologist Robert Bellah warns against taking this speech form lightly. He observes:

> . . . we know enough about the function of ceremonial and ritual in various societies to make us suspicious of dismissing something as unimportant because it is "only a ritual." What people say on solemn occasions need not be taken at face value, but it is often indicative of deep-seated values and commitments that are not made explicit in the course of everyday life.[1]

1. Cited in Michael Novak, *Choosing Our King: Powerful Symbols in Presidential Politics* (New York: Macmillan, 1974), p. 142.

Careful students will recognize that ceremonial speeches often capture the essence of a social fabric. Such speeches help to illuminate the central values that undergird group traditions, procedures, and goals. In fact, many of the greatest speeches of recorded history have sought to intensify social cohesion.

CRITERIA FOR EVALUATING SPEECHES THAT INTENSIFY SOCIAL COHESION

Although one could devise discrete criteria for the evaluation of each type of speech discussed in the previous section, each type may be meaningfully considered by applying criteria common to them all.

1. Has the speaker satisfied the ceremonial purpose(s) of the gathering?

Because speeches that intensify social cohesion are usually given at ceremonial gatherings, the first question to be asked is whether the speech has satisfied the ceremonial purpose. For example, when one attends a dedication ceremony, it is expected that the speaker will praise the object being dedicated. When one attends a commencement, it is expected that the graduating seniors will be appropriately honored and advised. A welcoming ceremony calls for a tribute to both the person being welcomed and the institution extending the welcome. A presentation ceremony calls for a speech in praise of the person being awarded a tribute.

Whenever the speaker prepares a speech designed to intensify social cohesion, the audience's expectations at that moment must be considered. The Christian minister who on Easter Sunday ignores the meanings of the resurrection, the commencement speaker who ignores the graduating seniors assembled, and the eulogist who ignores or condemns the life of the departed all err in their omissions by failing to meet the ceremonial demands of the occasion. Whatever their personal reasons for speaking, speakers must conform to the particular expectations of their audiences on specific occasions if their speeches are to succeed.

2. Has the speaker selected group values worthy of perpetuation?

Although the ceremonial demands of the occasion strongly constrain the speaker's behavior when seeking to intensify social cohesion, the speaker should still be held responsible for the substantive worth of the message. Because speeches that intensify social cohesion attempt to strengthen group values, the speaker should be expected to identify values worthy of esteem and perpetuation by the audience.

In applying this criterion, the enlightened listener or reader will test the values selected by the speaker. Has the eulogist selected the finer values examplified by a person's life? Has the inaugural speaker identified the most significant and worthy values as guides for future group action? Has the commencement speaker identified relevant and meaningful values for his audience of graduates? In evaluating Douglas MacArthur's speech "Farewell to the Cadets," reprinted later in this chapter, the reader should ask, "Are 'duty, honor, country' the finer values to which a soldier should subscribe in a free society?" In evaluating Martin Luther King's speech "I Have a Dream," also reprinted later, the reader should question whether the values of creative suffering and nonviolent resistance were those most relevant and wise for the black minority in a "white" America in 1963.

3. Has the speaker given impelling expression to the values selected?

Many critics have condemned speeches of this type because they tend to reexpress the commonplace values of our social order. For example, many critics have condemned the commencement speech as a genre. Such speeches, they claim, are seldom more than dull rearticulations of established truths. Born of truisms, these speeches are infrequently more than trite reexpressions of the public mind. Although such charges are too often justified, they are not inherent indictments of the speech form. Rather, they are criticisms made valid by speakers who are incapable of giving impelling expression and redefinition to the values that bind our society together.

Because speeches that intensify social cohesion must by definition treat shared values, speakers must exercise special skill in giving new meaning and purpose to old values. Speakers have succeeded in accomplishing this difficult task. Through incisive analysis and amplification and through vivid and compelling language, gifted speakers succeed in gaining renewed audience commitment to old values without seeming trite.

Through the process of analysis, speakers must determine the particular relevance of cherished values to contemporary events and problems. Through the process of amplification, speakers must select those anecdotes, comparisons, contrasts, descriptions, examples, restatements, and definitions that make their contemporary analyses come alive. In the process, they must also demonstrate that their analyses are appropriate to the emotions that the nature of the occasion naturally evokes—whether elation, hope, gratitude, affection, pride, sympathy, anger, hate, shame, remorse, or grief. Speakers must also select vivid and compelling language to clothe their ideas. Through such stylistic devices as metaphor, vivid imagery, alliteration, parallelism, antithesis, hyperbole, and personification, gifted speakers can find ways for language to give new excitement and meaning to old values.

CONCLUSION

Many situations call for speeches that urge audience recommitment to social values. Among the common types of speeches that intensify social cohesion are sermons, eulogies, dedication speeches, commemorative speeches, commencement speeches, keynote speeches, welcoming speeches, farewell speeches, presentation speeches, acceptance speeches, and inaugural speeches.

In evaluating speeches of this form, the critic must consider *whether the speaker has met the ceremonial purpose of the gathering, whether the speaker has selected group values worthy of perpetuation, and whether the speaker has given impelling expression to the values selected.*

For further reading

Allen, R. R., and McKerrow, Ray E. *The Pragmatics of Public Communication.* 3rd ed. Kendall/Hunt Publishing Company, 1985. Chapter 9 examines ceremonial speaking and offers guidelines for building social cohesion.

Carlile, Clark S. and Daniel, Arlie V. *A Project Text for Public Speaking.* 6th ed. Harper/Collins, 1991. Some projects involve speeches that aim primarily at social cohesion, including farewell, eulogy, dedication, anniversary, and nomination acceptance.

Condit, Celeste. "The Function of Epideictic: The Boston Massacre Orations as Exemplar." *Communication Quarterly,* 33 (Fall 1985): 284–298. Describes the functions of epideictic/ceremonial discourse as definition/understanding, shaping/sharing community, and display/entertainment. Suggests "communal definition" as the aim of a "complete" epideictic speech.

Gronbeck, Bruce, et al. *Principles and Types of Speech Communication.* 11th ed. Scott, Foresman, 1990. Ch. 18 discusses varied types of speeches for ceremonial purposes, many of which seek social cohesion.

Gronbeck, Bruce E. *The Articulate Person.* 2nd ed. Scott, Foresman, 1983. Chapter 7 discusses speeches that reinforce existing audience values and beliefs. Pages 248–257 describe the cultural functions of speeches at public ceremonies. Chapter 12 examines speeches for various special occasions.

Hart, Roderick P. "The Functions of Human Communication in the Maintenance of Public Values." In Carroll Arnold and John Bowers, eds. *Handbook of Rhetorical and Communication Theory,* Allyn and Bacon, 1984, Chapter 12.

Osborn, Michael, and Osborn, Suzanne. *Public Speaking.* 2nd ed. Houghton Mifflin, 1991. Chapter 15 examines various types of ceremonial speaking and their functions in reinforcing existing values and promoting group and cultural cohesion. Pages 256–259 illustrate language techniques that create cohesion.

Perelman, Chaim, and Olbrechts-Tyteca, L. *The New Rhetoric.* Trans. John Wilkinson and Purcell Weaver. University of Notre Dame Press, 1969. Pages 47–54 discuss types of discourse that "establish a sense of communion centered around particular values recognized by the audience."

Reid, Ronald F. *The American Revolution and the Rhetoric of History.* Speech Communication Association, 1978. Ch. 3 analyzes ways in which present societal values are reinforced through appeals to noble Revolutionary forebearers and to noble Revolutionary principles.

Rosenfield, Lawrence W. "The Practical Celebration of Epideictic." In Eugene White, ed. *Rhetoric in Transition.* Pennsylvania State University Press, 1980, pp. 131–155. A scholarly reinterpretation of the nature and function of speeches in honor of excellence, speeches that acknowledge goodness, grace, and intrinsic excellence rather than merely praise achievements and accomplihsments.

Walter, Otis M. *Speaking Intelligently.* Macmillan, 1976. Pages 185–92 examine the nature of discourse which seeks to intensify social cohesion and offer specific strategies for increasing group pride and identity.

Inaugural Address
John F. Kennedy

On January 20, 1961, the late John Fitzgerald Kennedy delivered his Presidential inaugural address to a large outdoor audience before the nation's Capitol on a cold, clear day. In contrast to his rapid-fire delivery during the campaign, Kennedy spoke slowly, giving careful emphasis to special phrases and the cadence of his prose.

An inaugural address by an American President typically reflects some now-traditional expectations and characteristics. Multiple audiences are addressed directly or indirectly: the inaugural crowd, Americans everywhere, world heads-of-state, and the people of the world. One major function is to set the general tone of the new administration. On social, economic, and military matters domestically and internationally, the President usually outlines in broad strokes some intended stances. But advocacy of specific, detailed policies and programs is not expected and abstract language may be more acceptable here than in other kinds of political discourse. A second major function is to promote social cohesion. The President seeks to heal the wounds and antagonisms of the recent political campaign, to urge reenergized commitment to central societal values and goals, and to promote a feeling of national unity. In an inaugural address, the President frequently will cite or adapt the words and wisdom of revered past Presidents and leaders. And such a speech may praise noble elements of America's heritage and applaud America's destiny. Both the introductions and conclusions of inaugural addresses typically call upon the blessings of God.

Kennedy's address demonstrates that effective style is not bombast or artificial ornament. Perhaps the most important stylistic quality of his speech is his sentence construction. Observe that his sentence length varies widely and that he employs many abstract and few concrete words. Is abstractness perhaps a natural quality of an inaugural address? What role do antithesis, parallelism, rhythm, and energy and movement play in this speech? Kennedy utilizes numerous metaphors, some rather hackneyed, but some fresh and subtle. Can you identify metaphors of each type?

The passage most frequently quoted from this speech is "Ask not what your country can do for you—ask what you can do for your country." Examine the context in which this sentence is used. Does it appear to be a natural outgrowth from the flow of ideas in the speech? Notice also phrases that echo passages in speeches by Abraham Lincoln (paragraphs 6 and 22) and by Franklin D. Roosevelt (10 and 25). Kennedy uses Biblical allusions (19 and 23) and images reflecting his Navy days in the South Pacific (20).

For a detailed analysis of the functions and techniques of American Presidential inaugural addresses, see Karyln Kohrs Campbell and Kathleen Hall Jamieson, *Deeds Done In Words: Presidential Rhetoric and the Genres of Governance* (University of Chicago Press, 1990), Ch. 2.

The text of this speech was taken from a recording of the address.

1 *Vice President Johnson, Mr. Speaker, Mr. Chief Justice, President Eisenbhower, Vice Presdient Nixon, President Truman, Reverend Clergy, Fellow Citizens:* We observe today not a victory of party but a celebration of freedom—symbolizing an end as well as a beginning—signifying renewal as well as change. For I have sworn before you and Almighty God the same solemn oath our forebears prescribed nearly a century and three quarters ago.

2 The world is very different now. For man holds in his mortal hands the power to abolish all forms of human poverty and all forms of human life. And yet the same revolutionary beliefs for which our forebears fought are still at issue around the globe—the belief that the rights of man come not from the generosity of the state but from the hand of God.

3 We dare not forget today that we are the heirs of that first revolution. Let the word go forth from this time and place, to friend and foe alike, that the torch has been passed to a new generation of Americans—born in this century, tempered by war, disciplined by a hard and bitter peace, proud of our ancient heritage—and unwilling to witness or permit the slow undoing of those human rights to which this nation has always been committed, and to which we are committed today, at home and around the world.

4 Let every nation know, whether it wishes us well or ill, that we shall pay any price, bear any burden, meet any hardship, support any friend, or oppose any foe to assure the survival and the success of liberty.

5 This much we pledge—and more.

6 To those old allies whose cultural and spiritual origins we share, we pledge the loyalty of faithful friends. United, there is little we cannot do in a host of cooperative ventures. Divided, there is little we can do—for we dare not meet a powerful challenge at odds and split asunder.

7 To those new states whom we welcome to the ranks of the free, we pledge our word that one form of colonial control shall not have passed away merely to be replaced by a far more iron tyranny. We shall not always expect to find them supporting our view.

8 But we shall always hope to find them strongly supporting their own freedom—and to remember that, in the past, those who foolishly sought power by riding the back of the tiger ended up inside.

9 To those people in the huts and villages of half the globe struggling to break the bonds of mass misery, we pledge our best efforts to help them help themselves, for whatever period is required—not because the Communists may be doing it, not because we seek their votes, but because it is right. If a free society cannot help the many who are poor, it cannot save the few who are rich.

10 To our sister republics south of our border, we offer a special pledge—to convert our good words into good deeds—in a new alliance for progress—to assist free men and free governments in casting off the chains of poverty. But this peaceful revolution of hope cannot become the prey of hostile powers. Let all our neighbors know that we shall join with them to oppose aggression or subversion anywhere in the Americas. And let every other power know that this hemisphere intends to remain the master of its own house.

11 To that world assembly of sovereign states, the United Nations, our last best hope in an age where the instruments of war have far outpaced the instruments of peace, we renew our pledge of support—to prevent it from becoming merely a forum for invective—to strengthen its shield of the new and the weak—and to enlarge the area in which its writ may run.

12 Finally, to those nations who would make themselves our adversary, we offer not a pledge but a request: That both sides begin anew the quest for peace, before the dark powers of destruction unleashed by science engulf all humanity in planned or accidental self-destruction.

13 We dare not tempt them with weakness. For only when our arms are sufficient beyond doubt can we be certain beyond doubt that they will never be employed.

14 But neither can two great and powerful groups of nations take comfort from our present course—both sides overburdened by the cost of modern weapons, both rightly alarmed by the steady spread of the deadly atom, yet both racing to alter that uncertain balance of terror that stays the hand of mankind's final war.

15 So let us begin anew—remembering on both sides that civility is not a sign of weakness, and sincerity is always subject to proof. Let us never negotiate out of fear. But let us never fear to negotiate.

16 Let both sides explore what problems unite us instead of belaboring those problems which divide us.

17 Let both sides, for the first time, formulate serious and precise proposals for the inspection and control of arms—and bring the absolute power to destroy other nations under the absolute control of all nations.

18 Let both sides seek to invoke the wonders of science instead of its terrors. Together let us explore the stars, conquer the deserts, eradicate disease, tap the ocean depths, and encourage the arts and commerce.

19 Let both sides unite to heed in all corners of the earth the command of Isaiah— to "undo the heavy burdens . . . [and] let the oppressed go free."

20 And if a beachhead of cooperation may push back the jungle of suspicion, let both sides join in creating a new endeavor: not a new balance of power, but a new world of law, where the strong are just and the weak secure and the peace preserved.

21 All this will not be finished in the first one hundred days. Nor will it be finished in the first one thousand days, not in the life of this administration, nor even perhaps in our lifetime on this planet. But let us begin.

22 In your hands, my fellow citizens, more than mine, will rest the final success or failure of our course. Since this country was founded, each generation of Americans has been summoned to give testimony to its national loyalty. The graves of young Americans who answered the call to service surround the globe.

23 Now the trumpet summons us again—not as a call to bear arms, though arms we need—not as a call to battle, though embattled we are—but a call to bear the burden of a long twilight struggle, year in and year out, "rejoicing in hope, patient in tribulation"— a struggle against the common enemies of man: Tyranny, poverty, disease and war itself.

24 Can we forge against these enemies a grand and global alliance, North and South, East and West, that can assure a more fruitful life for all mankind? Will you join in that historic effort?

25 In the long history of the world, only a few generations have been granted the role of defending freedom in its hour of maximum danger.

26 I do not shrink from this responsibility—I welcome it. I do not believe that any of us would exchange places with any other people or any other generation. The energy, the faith, the devotion which we bring to this endeavor will light our country and all who serve it—and the glow from that fire can truly light the world.

27 And so, my fellow Americans: Ask not what your country can do for you—ask what you can do for your country.

28 My fellow citizens of the world: Ask not what America will do for you, but what together we can do for the freedom of man.

29 Finally, whether you are citizens of America or citizens of the world, ask of us here the same high standards of strength and sacrifice which we ask of you. With a good conscience our only sure reward, with history the final judge of our deeds, let us go forth to lead the land we love, asking His blessing and His help, but knowing that here on earth God's work must truly be our own.

Inaugural Address as Mayor of the District of Columbia
Sharon Pratt Dixon

In November of 1990, Sharon Pratt Dixon, a lawyer, was elected Mayor of the District of Columbia—thus becoming the first black woman elected mayor of a major American city. Among the candidates that she defeated in the Democratic Party primary the previous September was long-time incumbent mayor Marion Barry, whose political viability was damaged by a conviction for cocaine possession. On January 2, 1991, in Washington, D.C., Sharon Pratt Dixon delivered her inaugural address as mayor.

In evaluating this speech, recall that an inaugural address normally acknowledges the transition of leadership, praises past performances and achievements of the electorate, remembers the group's praiseworthy heritage, and identifies the central values and goals for the future. Also, apply the suggested criteria for evaluating speeches that intensify social cohesion. Has the speaker satisfied the ceremonial purpose of the occasion? Has the speaker selected group values worthy of perpetuation? Has the speaker given impelling expression to the values selected?

Throughout the speech, the refrain of "Yes, We Will" underscores her vision of an attitude or ethic of confidence and determination that will guide her administration (3, 7, 17–19). Quite naturally for her inaugural, Dixon stresses unity and cooperation. She seeks legislative cooperation with the District Council (11) and with Congress (16–17). She urges the united effort of all citizens (2) and uses parallel structure to reinforce that plea (19).

Central to her message is Dixon's call for a return to and reenergizing of the "time-honored values" (4, 7, 12). These values include commitment, excellence, service, honesty, appreciation of diversity, and a sense of community. She itemizes problems that at least partially stem from forgetting those values (4), describes a city heritage reflective of those values (5), and recounts personal experiences illustrative of the values (6).

Antithesis is the phrasing of two opposing or competing items into sharp, terse contrast, with one item of the pair given clear preference. Dixon utilizes antithesis as a major language resource. Early in the speech she says (3): "We must cease defining our city by her problems. We must begin defining our city by her potential." Later she illustrates this potential (15). Antithesis is used to highlight the need for changes (10). And at length she uses antithetical phrasing to sharpen necessary value commitments (12): titles and perks versus good ideas and solid solutions; values and character versus rank and station; who you are versus who you want to help; grandness of rank versus greatness of service; quantity of worldly possessions versus significance of contributions.

The text of this speech was provided by Mayor Sharon Pratt Dixon.

---

1 When I first announced that I would run for office I quoted Ecclesiastes, "there is a time and a season for everything and everyone." So it is with our great city. In their time and in their season Mayor Walter Washington and Marion Barry, each in his own way, made a telling contribution to the progress and growth of our community.

2 Now, today, we begin a new time, a new season of coming together. A season where the international city, the federal city, the many neighborhoods, the many constituents, move to become one. For in this togetherness we have the power to meet the staggering challenges we face and do more—to allow this city to become all of what she was meant to be—a great cosmopolitan community—a beacon for a 21st century America. To achieve great things means we must first envision what we can be. We must envision how we can make a difference—how it is within each of our grasp to make Washington, D.C., a city of hope, humanity and excellence.

3 So "YES WE WILL" is more than a theme for a day. It is an attitude and an ethic we must embrace to move beyond a city troubled by drugs and crime, racial polarization, and mounting financial problems. We must cease defining our city by her problems. We must begin defining our city by her potential. "Yes, We Will" is an affirmation of our striving; an assertion that every intractable problem, however stubborn, can yield to a solution. And, "Yes, We Will" must resonate from Congress Heights to Wesley heights—from Shepherd Park to LeDroit Park—from Capitol Hill to the District Building. "Yes, We Will" must resonate in the hearts and minds of each and every one of us—and with this pledge and in this bond anything is within our reach. The mere fact that I am speaking to you now as your Mayor is a testament to the power of the ethic—"Yes She Can—Yes We Will." In spite of the political pundits, the powerbrokers, and the pollsters—together we beat the odds—a partnership that brought us to this moment.

4 Throughout the campaign you heard me say "clean house." And I said it meant many things. One thing it clearly means is rediscovering time-honored values; pulling the dust and cobwebs off values that were set aside too easily in the fast paced "Let's have it all today world." We, as a community, have paid a handsome price for setting aside these values: the value of commitment; of making an investment in the future; the value of excellence; and serving others. We cannot afford to set them aside again. And no quarter is more illustrative of this point than the pain and trouble that have beset our children. A generation of young people has been lost. Lost to drugs, instant gratification, and violence; to the overwhelming sense that they have no place in our lives. And, we are in danger of losing the next generation unless we act now to reclaim our heritage and values.

5 We are a community with a rich tradition of excellence. This is the city created by Washington, laid out by Benjamin Banneker, engineered into a splendid reality by L'Enfant. We are the poetry of Paul Lawrence Dunbar, the freedom cry of Frederick Douglass, the jazz of Edward "Duke" Ellington, and the constitutional voice of Charles Hamilton Houston. Decade after decade the people of this city have contributed their talent to this community and nation: Sterling Brown, Billy Eckstein, and Julia West Hamilton. Natives all. Mordecai W. Johnson, Melvin Grosvenor, and David Lloyd Kreeger.

6 I know in the most direct and personal way the great strength that abides in Washington, D.C. For I was reared, disciplined, and loved by three of her products—my father, grandmother, and aunt. All of whom are here today. And, I was encouraged to pursue my dreams by my home room teacher from Roosevelt— a teacher who made all of the difference Mrs. Helen Blackburn. So, I remember Washington D.C., when she was still a sleepy, Southern town. A town where government was the only real employer; and summer fashion meant seer sucker suits. And yet in spite of the lack of wealth and opportunity, we were in many ways richer than we are today. For we had a sense of community, a deep commitment to one another, and an uncompromising devotion to excellence and making way for a better tomorrow.

7 Now, in this new season, we need to re-kindle these values and recapture this ethic. Where we pledge to commit ourselves to one another, to be one community, and to give ourselves—to invest in a better tomorrow for the sake of our children. To this we must say: "Yes We Will!"

8 Our Washington—Our Washington of the 90's—is no longer a sleepy, Southern town where success is measured by our GS rating. The economic landscape and profile of our city has changed. Today, the primary source of employment in Washington, D.C. is the private sector. Washington has become a cosmopolitan city of research and law, science and education. In the last two decades, we have become the hub and magnet for one of the great metropolitan regions of this country.

9 We are also a community of diverse cultures and many hues. To walk down 18th Street in Adams-Morgan is to see the richness of a hundred different cultures at play. We are African-American and Latino, Irish-American and Italian, Ethiopian and Vietnamese. We hail from San Salvador, Managua, Asmara, and Lagos. We speak Spanish, Korean,

Hebrew, and Farsi. We dance the Electric Slide and sing in the Gay Men's Choir. We worship in synagogues and storefronts, in great cathedrals of Christianity and mosques dedicated to Allah. We are a community reflecting the new diversity that is America. We come from every region of the country and every nation on the globe—yet all of us call Washington, D.C. home.

10 Our city has changed and continues to change—but our city government has been left behind. We have a system of governing for the 1970's striving to serve a city that has already moved into the 1990's. We have too few people in the right jobs and too many people in jobs that shouldn't even exist.

11 Our immediate responsibility is to give the people of this city the government they deserve and expect. I know that this mission is uppermost in the minds of Chairman John Wilson and the new District Council. So, I extend my hand to every member of the Council and say—let us build a true partnership to make this city work again, to return the government to the people again, to make this city great!

12 To make good on this commitment means returning to some time honored values. To rekindle that sense that quality service and to serve the public good are cherished things. To remember again that titles and perks are less important than good ideas and solid solutions: that values and character take precedence over rank and station. So, I say to every civil servant on the front-line—paramedic and policemen—computer operator and teacher— let this be the first rule of this new season—it's not who you are that's important but who you want to help that matters; it's not how grand your rank, but how great your service; its not how manifold your worldly possessions, but how significant your human legacy.

13 What the people of Washington want most is an honest deal. We have lived through a decade of national excess, ignoring all the while the fundamental truth of our condition. There has been a corruption of the public estate; a disregard by those on top for those fundamental values that hold us together. Our situation is not unique. All across America, in every statehouse and city hall, the same issues that beset this city are being confronted. What will be unique will be our determination to give our citizens that honest deal—to reclaim our values—to streamline our government—to balance our books—and then, together, to affirm that which is indicative of our potential.

14 It will not be easy. Our fiscal posture is not sound while taxpayers are demanding a government that minds their money. And it would be foolish to ignore the wealth of good advice offered by the Rivlin Commission. It is an informative and instructive guidepost, a contribution of many concerned citizens. Above all, it is a message that old ways of doing business must yield to a new order.

15 However difficult the immediate future, we need to envision our city by its full potential. A great city where the youth enjoy a promising future. Where a quality educational system is the order of the day. Where senior citizens can walk the streets safe and secure. Where African-Americans and Latinos are captains of commerce. All of this potential lies latent in the horizon of our future. And the energy that will carry us lies within us all. We need to harness, galvanize, and meld the ideas, vitality, and strength of this community; to find new anchors of hope and promise for our children. Every neighborhood is rich with Ph.D.s in survival skills; men and women who are engineers and architects of hope. It's Eugene Hughes at the Midtown Youth Academy; the Latin American Youth Center and Ernest White's mentor program; the House of Ruth and Martha's Table; Yvonne Vega at AYUDA and the Organization of Concerned Black Men. What they need is our full support; a public-private partnership that says we are all part of the same family; a partnership that gives them the green light to use their ingenuity. So I say to each and everyone of them today—give us your best ideas and we will find a way to make it happen.

16 And there is nothing in my book that says good ideas stop at the edge of the Potomac because our problems don't either. The gridlock on our roads, our transportation problems, the shortage of affordable housing, the growth of air pollution, matching jobs-to-workers—these issues are regional in scope and demand a stronger regional response. It is a partnership to which I am committed; to find new solutions that help us all.

17 As we rebuild our city we ask the Congress for its support and confidence. We know where we are going and what needs to be done. We hope that the Congress will re-examine old arrangements that hinder our ability to be effective. For some time, now, the District has carried an unequal financial burden. No matter how prized the relationship—that is an arrangement we can no longer afford. We need a U.S. Congress who pays her fair share and her full share. We have much to be proud of as we enter the 1990s and we will be prouder still when we are the State of New Columbia. Home rule for all of us is a half-way mark on a long journey; a statement that we have not yet gained the absolute full measure of our equality. Not stopping until we achieve our goal of full freedom is another way in which we must say, "Yes we will."

18 So, to all the naysayers, we must say, "Yes, we will"! Naysayers are famous for outlining the problems as if there were no solutions. They will go on and on about fiscal problems, the drug problem, and the health problem—as if it were preordained that we would all drown in a sea of insurmountable concerns. Well, I am here to tell you that nothing is beyond our reach, especially, if we really reach out to one another—creating an anchor and a bridge to a great city of hope and promise.

19 Together, we can plant strong and lasting anchors in every neighborhood in this community. Together, we can put back hope in the hearts of our children. Together, we can give the people of this great city the honest deal they deserve and expect. This is our purpose and this is our quest. To this we must say, "Yes, We Will."

20 Now, let us begin.

State of the Mille Lacs Band of Chippewas
Arthur Gahbow

The State of the Union Address delivered annually to Congress by the President of the United States has become a firm tradition in our governmental process of representative democracy. In *Deeds Done in Words: Presidential Rhetoric and the Genres of Governance* (Ch. 4), Karlyn Kohrs Campbell and Kathleen Hall Jamieson identify three traditional elements of this form of public address. First, through public meditation on fundamental American values, social cohesion is promoted. A collectivity of individuals comes to view itself as a community or nation with "an identity that unifies its members and distinguishes them as a group." A national ethos or character is developed through narratives of the values and actions of the past that emphasize shared experience and provide a link to the future. Second, in addition to emphasizing accomplishments, presidents define problems facing the nation through assessing "enduring national issues, such as foreign affairs, commerce, civil rights, or immigration." Also they link their addresses to those of past presidents. Third, whether as a broad general outline, lengthy undeveloped list, or well-developed legislative program, presidents recommend and justify "specific legislative initatives" as solutions to the nation's problems. Typically a cooperative and conciliatory tone toward Congress is expressed.

The tradition of the State of the Union address has become so powerful that it has spread to other levels of government. Governors of most states present an annual State of the State message. An increasing number of mayors, especially mayors of large cities, also present State of the City addresses.

In his essay, "Between Myth and History: Enacting Time in Native American Protest Rhetoric," *Quarterly Journal of Speech,* 77 (May 1991): 123–151, Randall Lake makes two observations especially relevant for an understanding of Arthur Gahbow's speech. First, although the Native American social protest movement of the 1960s and 1970s has been largely inactive more recently, "tribal localities everywhere perennially confront the issues of land, sovereignty, and cultural integrity. . . . Thus, conditions are perpetually ripe for activism and, if today represents a downturn in the cycle of resistance, inevitably a resurgence will occur." Second, unlike the European-American conception of time as linear and sequential, the Native American conception of time is circular and cyclical. The cycle of life and of the ages provides confidence and patience that inevitably, some day, Native American culture will be re-established if only Native Americans will return to traditional values and ways.

On January 14, 1989, Chief Executive Arthur Gahbow delivered the annual State of the Band address concerning the Mille Lacs Band of Chippewas. The Mille Lacs Reservation comprises about 4000 acres in central Minnesota and the Mille Lacs band has about 2,350 members (*Chicago Tribune,* February 14, 1991, Sec. 1A, p. 31). Arthur Gahbow does devote much of his speech to assessing the current situation both by emphasizing band accomplishments (29–30, 40, 55–58, 63) and by defining unresolved problems (32–35, 41). And he does itemize proposed policies and actions to work toward solution of the problems (42–54).

But it seems to us that promotion of social cohesion is Gahbow's primary purpose and he seeks to accomplish this through a variety of rhetorical choices and resources. A lengthy opening historical narrative provides a shared background of events and value judgments necessary for assessing the present and future (3–17). Throughout the speech, Gahbow praises traditional Chippewa values that should be recaptured, reinforced, and re-energized: Honesty/promise-keeping (5–15, 25); courage (15–16, 28, 35, 65–66); determination/patience (19, 28, 36, 65); optimism (3, 10, 60); peacefulness (15); hard work (25); and sovereignty (34). In contrast he stresses a cluster of negative American traits: lying/promise-breaking (5–6, 62); greed (24, 26, 60); and ignorance (25, 27, 33, 60).

To foster social cohesion through reinforcement of traditional values, Gahbow uses several distinctive stylistic resources. His antithetical phrasing in two paragraphs allows for concentrated contrast between desirable Chippewa values and undesirable American traits (5, 15). Parallel phrasing (15, 25) and use of a refrain (65) also reinforce commitment to values. Following the moral "high road" is emphasized (25, 64). One function of the opening narrative that fosters social cohesion is to allow for celebration of past successes (11–14). Gahbow makes overt pleas for unity of effort (16, 50–51, 64). Finally, evaluate the appropriateness and possible rhetorical functions of Gahbow's paraphrase in his concluding paragraph (66) of a paragraph from John Kennedy's Inaugural Address (3) printed earlier in this chapter on social cohesion.

The Chippewa conception of time also seems apparent. Time is on their side and eventually, ultimately, they will succeed. The pendulum of justice is swinging their way (18, 26). A 100 year time-frame is used within which success will be achieved (19, 64). And it is the Chippewa's "destiny" to succeed (28). Thus there is sound reason for the Mille Lacs' optimism, patience, and determination.

The text of this speech is reprinted with permission from *Vital Speeches of the Day*, April 15, 1989, pp. 409–413.

---

1 Madame speaker, Honorable members of the Band Assembly, Madame Chief Justice, Honorable Justices of the Court of Central Jurisdiction, Commissioners, honored guests and fellow Band members, I welcome you. It is my great honor and privilege today to deliver the State of the Band Address.

2 Before beginning I must point out that this tribal government suffered a great loss last year. Harry Simons, our good friend and commissioner of Finance, passed away. Harry put in many years of faithful service to the Mille Lacs Band. His accomplishments will not be forgotten. I speak for the Band when I say he will be greatly missed.

3 Today is a significant date in the history of this Reservation. I chose this date for the State of the Band Address because on this day 100 years ago, the Nelson Act was enacted. The Nelson Act provided for allotments within the Mille Lacs Reservation boundaries. Because of the Nelson Act, we lost about half of our land on the Reservation. In spite of this fact, today is not a sad day, today is a day for optimism.

4 In the past 100 years we have lost our land, we have lost some of our jurisdiction, we have lost our loved ones to alcoholism and despair. In short, somewhere along the line we began to lose hope.

5 We have come to view ourselves as a defeated nation. We have forgotten our own history. We forget that in 1855 the United States made a treaty with us. We promised to remain peaceful and they promised we could have this Reservation of 61,000 acres forever. We kept our promise, the government did not keep their promise. We forget that in 1864, we were told that so long as we were peaceful, we could not be compelled to be removed from these lands. We kept our promise. They did not keep theirs. We forget that in 1884, we were promised that no lands within the reservation could be taken. They did not keep their promise. Starting in the 1870's and until 1889, white people came to the Reservation and took lands for timber and homesteads. This was in violation of the 1884 Act. These lands taken prior to the Nelson Act were never paid for. 29,000 acres were taken illegally and we still haven't seen a dime for these lands. They did not keep their promises.

6 We forget that in 1889, the Nelson Act took the rest of the lands within the Reservation boundaries. The Nelson Act was the biggest lie of all. The United States promised that the Band members could take an allotment on this Reservation first, before anyone else. The United States promised all of us allotments, it would have been 1500 allotments. Again they failed to keep their promise. The United States appointed a commission to deal with the Band. Much to the disbelief of Band members, the commission refused to grant allotments to Band members.

7 You see, the real agenda of the commission was to compel Mille Lacs people to move to White Earth. In fact, two men on the commission got more money if they kept Mille Lacs people from taking allotments at Lake Mille Lacs. So, how many allotments of the 1500 promised in 1889 did Band members get? ONE! There was one 80 acre allotment which was obtained by Me gee zee. Of the 60,000 acres possible for allotment we got 80.

8 So let me review for you. First, the Reservation was formed in 1855. We were promised we could hold the lands forever. Second, in 1864 we were told we could not be removed from these lands if we remained peaceful. Third, in 1884 we were told no one could take lands within the Reservation boundaries. This in spite of the fact that 29,000 acres were taken around this time. Fourth, in 1889, the Nelson Act, promised us we could take 1500 allotments on this land. We got ONE.

9 We started with 12 ½ million acres. In 1855 we were reduced to 61,000 acres. In the 1870's and 1880's 29,000 acres were taken illegally and we were never paid for them. After the Nelson Act, we lost over 30,000 acres. That left us with 80 acres in 1901. A scholar from the Indian Rights Association of Philadelphia stated that of all the Indian tribes in the United States, the rights of the Mille Lacs Band were the most abused in the history of the country.

10 We must not forget our history, we must not forget the past. But we must not despair about the past. Despite this long history of abuses, we still remain optimistic. We have many things on our side.

11 First, in spite of the fact that the United States tried to remove us, we are still here. One hundred years later, the Mille Lacs Band still occupies these hallowed grounds.

12 Second, since the Nelson Act we have been in court trying to get paid for the lands wrongfully taken. In the 1920's, we got some land back and many Band members were given 5 acre allotments. Other lands came under the jurisdiction of the Mille Lacs Band in the 1930's: Lake Lena, East Lake, and Sandy Lake.

13 Third, in the past 20 years, we have improved our government and our sovereign status. Part of this is because the era of self-determination began in 1968. But we have also improved internally.

358 CONTEMPORARY AMERICAN SPEECHES

14 Today, we look back at the past 100 years and we say *yes* there was a great injustice done. We might say yes, we might have some reason to lose hope.

15 But when I look at our history I see this: I see a people who were honorable. The Mille Lacs Band never broke any of its agreements. I see a people who remained peaceful when they could have gone to war with the United States in 1862 as did the Dakota. I see a people who stayed on their land after the Nelson Act tried to move them to White Earth. I see a people who stayed on their land in spite of the burning of their homes by the County Sheriff in the 1920's. I see a people who are proud and strong.

16 In your veins is the blood of Shaw Bosh Kung and Sha Go Bay. In your hearts there is a spirit of the warriors who moved the Dakota from these lands in the 18th century. You are the final line of defense. You are the Non-Removable Mille Lacs Band. Non-Removable. No other Reservation in the country has been deemed Non-Removable. By treaty of 1864, the people of Mille Lacs and Sandy Lake were deemed Non-Removable. We cannot and *will not* be removed.

17 Since January 14, 1889, ours has been a history of defensive strategy. We have tried to hang on to what little we have left. We have done well on the defensive. We have held on. But it is no longer enough.

18 The pendulum of justice will swing our way. In this universe there is a sense of divine justice which we have been denied. It occurred to me recently that there must be some reason why this Band was treated as it was. There must be some divine plan the Great Spirit has for us as a people. From the time I took office 16 years ago until recently, I was not sure what that plan was. But I don't think it was divine intervention, it was more common sense and a sense of injustice that made me arrive at this conclusion about the land.

19 That conclusion is this: We will take it back! We have been on the defensive for 100 years. I tell you this day, this hour, this moment in history we are no longer just holding our ground. As of right now we are on the offensive. We are on the attack. To state simply, we will take it back. Our forefathers were lied to and their land was taken illegally. For them we will take it back. We will not get the entire 61,000 acres in my lifetime. In fact, my plan will not see its completion until one hundred years from this date.

20 My plan has several phases. Phase one is the creation of a Land Purchase Trust Fund. This fund will be created this year. For the next 25 years, this trust fund will build. By its terms, it will not be allowed to be touched for any reason for 25 years. The only contact we will have with this account will be to make deposits. The account will be built with our tax revenues, private donations, and above all, monies we obtain from Band economic enterprises. Each year for the next 25 years, the Chief Executive of the Band will announce to the people the amount of money in the trust account.

21 Phase two is after 25 years, the money from the account will be used for land purchases. The goal is to get back the original Mille Lacs, Sandy Lake, and Rice Lake Reservations. The Lake Lena area will also be expanded.

22 Phase three, in one hundred years, we want to have a complete restoration of the original Reservations. Those who were removed to White Earth will be given the opportunity to return. Right now we also want to examine the title of lands not held by the Band which exist within the original 1855 treaty boundaries. These boundaries run from Isle up to Garrison and include Onamia. If title is vested in the Mille Lacs Band, we will take it back.

23 Those who own lands around the Lake, fear not. We want to pay you for the land. But if your title is no good, we will take the appropriate steps. One way or the other, we will take it back. The non-Indian people who live within our reservation boundaries are not our enemies. The United States and the State of Minnesota are not our enemies either.

24 The true enemies of the Mille Lacs Band are those aspects of humanity that ruin the world: greed and ignorance. We lost our land because of greed. Greed caused the injustice of the last century. Mainly it was the greed of timber companies, but it was also the greed of America itself. Our enemy in this century is ignorance. The United States forgets what it did to us. The State of Minnesota does not understand that we are a sovereign government. Of the two enemies, ignorance is the more dangerous.

25 To combat these enemies, greed and ignorance, we must always take the high road. We must fight for our rights, but we must do so in a decent, honest, and legal manner as our ancestors taught us. We must follow the principles of the Midewewin. We must be honest, we must respect others, and we must be hard working. The high road.

26 I believe in their heart of hearts, the United States and the State of Minnesota know they have done a grave injustice to us. They have taken our land and tried to break our spirit. They abused us in different ways. Sending our children to boarding schools. Allowing our land to be stolen. Participating in the theft of our land. Burning our houses. They know they were wrong. They also have to know that a day would come when the pendulum of justice would one day begin to swing the way of the Mille Lacs Band. They fear that day because they will be held accountable for their misdeeds.

27 To the United States and the State of Minnesota, I say this—learn about our past. Educate yourselves. Once you know the truth, you will understand why I can stand here today and talk about injustice. Because of the injustice of the last one hundred years, the Mille Lacs Band must work for the next one hundred years to restore our spirit.

28 We will not retreat, we will not surrender. You will try to stop us and you will fail. It is our destiny to get these lands back. With this in mind, I will discuss the events of the last year and our plan for the immediate future.

STATE RELATIONS

29 We won a major victory this year in the State Legislature. As you recall, the Mille Lacs Band went for two years without state contracts. We did this because the State of Minnesota required us to deny our sovereign status when entering into contracts with them. We took a stand on this point. To us, sovereignty is nearly sacred. Sovereignty is the right and ability of the Band to govern our own affairs. If we lose sovereignty, we lose our ability to preserve and protect our culture. So we took a stand. It paid off.

30 In 1988 thanks to lobbying efforts by Mille Lacs Band officials the law of the state was changed. Band officials met with Senator Chuck Davis and his assistant Pat Decker about a year ago. They listened to our problems and introduced a Bill which prohibited the State from requiring tribes and bands to deny their sovereignty. A companion bill was introduced in the House by Jerome Peterson. Mille Lacs representatives gave testimony on the bill and it ended up passing by an overwehlming majority because once the legislature was shown the light, they understood. We finally were heard.

31 Today, I want to officially thank Senator Davis, Pat Becker, and Representative Peterson for their efforts. This law has worked well with the State Department of Human Services. Most of our contracts with that Department have been signed for this year, I commend the efforts of Commissioner Gardebring and her staff. We now have intergovernmental agreements with the State Department of Human Services and we deal with them on a government to government basis.

32 Not so with the State Department of Jobs and Training. Unfortunately, they refuse to respect our sovereign status. Because of this we could not get an energy assistance contract with the State. I have met with the Commissioner of the Department of Jobs and Training, Joe Samargia, to attempt to resolve our differences. We had frank talks but we failed to resolve our differences. The Commissioner suggested that we resolve our issues in court and we are currently exploring that possibility. My wish is that the Department of Jobs and Training would take a lesson from the Human Services Department.

33 The State does not understand why we fight so hard when we negotiate contracts. You see after we sign the contracts they go into our archives for future generations. My staff spends a great deal of time studying documents from the past. They know that a word in a treaty from 150 years ago might mean that a reservation boundary is expanded or diminished. They know that executive orders from the last century are scrutinized in 20th century courts to see what the precise legal status of the Band was. They know that in the 21st century, contracts and intergovernmental agreements will be scrutinized in some lawsuit the Band will incur in the future. The State contracts for this year. The Band asserts its sovereign status in its agreements for the future generation. Therefore, every word in every contract and agreement we sign is important.

34 The State hates to negotiate with us and we know it. The people sometimes go without services and we know that, too. Sovereignty is not easily defended, sacrifices must be made so our children will have the land, the resources, the treaty rights. Lose sovereignty and we lose all that.

35 It is hard on my staff. They want to provide services to the people. They are sometimes tempted to sign contracts without thinking of the future. But they won't sign a bad contract. They won't sell us out. We will sacrifice to preserve this Band for the next 100 years and after that.

36 State of Minnesota, I say this to you, we were a self-governing people before your ancestors thought of coming here. Will we continue to defend our sovereign status in contract negotiations? You bet we will! Be on notice State of Minnesota, your arguments with Mille Lacs will continue.

FEDERAL RELATIONS

37 I have just returned from Washington D.C. where we had a meeting on the Self-Governance Demonstration Project. Last year Mille Lacs was chosen as one of ten tribes in the United States to participate in this Demonstration Project. The goal of this project is to try to gradually eliminate the Bureau of Indian Affairs from administering tribal monies.

38 In September, we submitted our report to Congress. The report suggested that we submit yearly budgets to the House Appropriations Committee and they fund us directly. The Bureau and the Minnesota Chippewa Tribe would not be involved in this process. We propose to eliminate the middle men who usually take the lion's share of our money. While we do not know if this will ever come about, we drew up a substantial plan for how it could work.

39 The other part of our report dealt with the establishment of Community Advisory Councils for the outlying Districts as well as this District. These Advisory Councils would take on the governmental functions they feel they could handle. They would then submit a budget to the Band Assembly to carry out their plans. I believe that this Advisory Council part of the plan we submitted to Congress could actually be put into effect in the very near future. I am requesting that the Band Assembly study our plan and work with East Lake, Sandy Lake, and Lake Lena on establishing these Community Advisory Councils.

40 As for federal legislation in the past year, it was a good year and a bad year. House Concurrent Resolution 331 passed as did the bill called House Resolution 5. These firmly state that the era of terminating tribes is out and the era of government to government relations is in.

41 On the negative side, the recent gaming legislation is an infringement on our sovereign rights. This gaming bill is a wrongful extension of federal power. The federal government says it has plenary power over tribes. I say no, and I am not alone. The Alliance of American Indian Leaders agrees with me as do a growing number of legal scholars including law professors Milner Ball and Robert Williams. We will continue this fight as well.

EXECUTIVE BRANCH

42 I commend the commissioners of my executive branch. They are underpaid and overworked. I give them the following directives for 1989.

43 Commissioner of Administration David Aubid. I want you to draft legislation for the development of the Community Advisory Councils for the outlying districts and introduce it to the Band Assembly for their enactment.

44 Commissioner of National Resources Don Wedll. I want to have our 1837 treaty litigation underway within the next six months. We applied for litigation monies to the Bureau of Indian Affairs four years ago. They have been sitting on it in spite of the fact they think we will surely win. So pressure them. When we get these treaty rights, we will have the right to hunt, fish, and regulate our treaty rights off-reservation similar to the Wisconsin tribes.

45 Commissioner of Public Works Ray Kegg. We need housing. I want you to work with the Housing Authority as closely as possible to try to get HUD to fund some new housing projects on the Reservation.

46 Commissioner of Human Services Mabel Smith. We need to have a chemical dependency treatment center on this reservation. Use your $10,000 state grant to explore that possibility.

47 We have two new Commissioners. Polly Williams is our new Commissioner of Finance. She has worked for us for many years and we have great confidence in her ability. My direction to finance is to develop financial controls to keep our governmental budget balanced. Doug Twait is our new coprorate commissioner. Doug is a graduate of the University of Minnesota Law School and has a Master's degree from the Humphrey Institute. For six months he has been our Economic Development Planner.

48 My two biggest initatives for the next few years have to do with my Corporate Commissioner and my Commissioner of Education. As we lay the foundation for the future, your two positions are the most crucial.

49 First, to my new Corporate Commissioner, I say welcome to the fight. You are needed here. You are the field general in our war on poverty. We need economic development. We need jobs. We need you to coordinate our new museum. For my one hundred year plan to work, we need you to fill the jar with money. This will not be an easy job. But I also have confidence in your abilities.

50 And to my Commissioner of Education. Yours is the most important job of all. I need you to instill in our students a sense of confidence and pride. Every student in this Band is a genius in one area, as I believe every person is. Your difficult task is to find out what area each child is best in. I want you to concentrate on that. Have your teachers reward each student for what they are truly good at. The true power of this Band resides in our students. They have the power of new ideas. The students of Vineland, Isle, East Lake, Sandy Lake, and Lake Lena must be encouraged. They are the future of this Band.

51 Tell them they can be doctors, lawyers, engineers, nurses, writers or anything they want to be. I know they can do anything. I need them to know it. Tell them that the Band needs them. Tell them how important they are. They are our most precious resource. As with the Band, it is time for the school to take the offensive. From now on, we are no longer just existing as a school. From now on, we shall advance and strive for excellence.

52 Finally, once the Band Assembly passes the new criminal code, a new Department will be created under the executive branch, the Department of Justice. This Department will be headed by our Solicitor General Tadd Johnson. Chief Law Enforcement officer Jim Bankey will also be in this Department.

53 Once the criminal code is in place, I want this Department to work to retrocede Public Law 280. This will give us exclusive criminal jurisdiction over Band members. I urge the Band Assembly to go ahead with this criminal code. Once it passes, our sovereign status will be enhanced.

54 I also request that the Solicitor General work to reassume jurisdiction under the Indian Child Welfare Act. I would like to see this done within the next three months.

SEPARATION OF POWERS

55 We are now in our eighth year of the separation of powers form of government. I can say without hesitation that it is working. Our court is growing stronger and handles 40–50 cases each month. Our appellate court is separate from that of the Minnesota Chippewa Tribe and the tribe acknowledged this by resolution. We now have a full time legal aid attorney on the reservation to represent Band members in tribal and state court. Two years ago we didn't have any lawyers working at the government center. Now we have three. This sudden influx of legal knowledge has improved the court system as well as the other two branches.

56 The legislative branch makes the laws that we in the executive branch carry out. They too are growing stronger and more independent. Our government is different from other bands in Minnesota which is why we continue to see a separation from the Minnesota Chippewa Tribe. We have contacted Senator Boschwitz on this matter and are discussing the reintroduction of our separation bill into Congress. We are also exploring ways to amend the Tribal constitution for the improvement of our government.

PLANS FOR 1989

57 There are several exciting projects on the Reservation this year. Ground will be broken for the new 4 million dollar museum this year. Along with the museum will be other retail stores, a restaurant, and shops which will provide employment opportunities.

58 The Opportunities Industrialization Centers Incorporated of America is getting started on the reservation. It is the first O.I.C. on a reservation in the country. For two decades, O.I.C's have been training inner-city youth. The Anishenabe O.I.C. exists to bring training to our people and teach them employable skills. Their long range goals are to teach our people skills while renovating the Marina. A coordinator has been hired and one building has been renovated.

59 There is a possibility of a large scale bingo operation in Hinkley which would be principally operated by the Lake Lena people. So there is a great deal of economic development in the works and it is getting started this year.

CONCLUSION

60 Today is a day for great optimism. We begin our recovery from the Nelson Act. It was a bad law. It was a law based on greed and enforced with ignorance. The United States knows that because we have been in their courts trying to straighten out our payments under the Nelson Act off and on for 100 years. In fact, right now we are litigating in the Courts of claims for lands taken during that period.

61 We have been on the defensive for too long. For too long we have fought to hold on to small pieces of land. For too long we have forgotten that our ancestors were honorable people who kept their promises. For too long we have forgotten that every promise made to us by the government in the 19th century was broken. For too long we have lived without hope.

62 Today, we begin our war on poverty. Today, we begin our economic recovery. Today, we begin to take the offensive. Today, we begin to take it back.

63 We begin this quest from a position of strength and financial health. For the past eight years, we operated on a deficit. One of the last legacies Harry Simons left this reservation was a balanced budget. For the first time in almost a decade, we are in the black. From here we must be cautious in our investments. We must be prudent in our financial dealings.

64 We must now build for the future. Not just our immediate future, but for the next 100 years. We must be moral in our business transactions. We must always take the high road. We must keep our long range goal in mind at all times. All work hours, all business transactions, all contract negotiations will be aimed at one goal: Restoration of the Reservation lands.

65 29,000 acres were taken illegally by timbermen and farmers. We will take it back. We lost 30,000 acres under the Nelson Act. We will take it back. We lost some of our jurisdiction under Public Law 280. We will take it back. Somewhere along the line we lost our hope for the future. We will get it back.

66 For now let the word go forth from this time and place, the state of this Band is sound and let friend and foe alike know that we are on the offensive. We will not back down. We are on the attack. There is no retreat. There is no surrender.

I Have a Dream
Martin Luther King, Jr.

Late in August 1963, more than 200,000 people held a peaceful demonstration in the nation's capital to focus attention on Negro demands for equality in jobs and civil rights. The marchers assembled at the Washington Monument on the morning of the 28th and filed in two columns down to the Lincoln Memorial. A little later, 10 civil-rights leaders met with President Kennedy at the White House and subsequently returned to the Lincoln memorial, where each of them addressed the assembled throng. As measured by crowd reaction, this speech by Martin Luther King was the high point of the day. In the months prior to his assassination in April, 1968, King broadened his advocacy to include the rights of poor people of all races and ethnic groups and to condemn continued American involvement in the Vietnam War.

One way to assess this speech would be to apply the criteria suggested at the start of this chapter for evaluating speeches that intensify social cohesion. Has the speech satisfied the cermonial purpose(s) of the gathering? Has the speaker selected group values worthy of perpetuation? Has the speaker given impelling expression to the values selcted? Or this speech might be examined as a particular type of social cohesion speech, namely a *rally speech* that arouses enthusaism for tasks ahead through uplifting sagging spirits and through deepening of commitments. Rally speeches occur on various occasions, such as keynote addresses at political and professional conventions, sales promotion speeches at meetings of company sales personnel, and speeches to civic action groups. Speakers at rallies typically utilize some combination of the following approaches: (1) Stress the importance, the value, of the work the group has been doing. (2) Promote group self-confidence by praising their past success, dedication, and sacrifice and by praising their basic values, principles, and goals. (3) Outline the tasks, opportunities, and challenges ahead. (4) Use vivid imagery and emotionally stimulating language to paint word pictures of the better future achievable through united, sustained group effort.

In this speech, King urges rededication to the black non-violent civil rights movement and reinforces values central to this view of that movement: courage, faith, hope, freedom, justice, equality, non-violence, sacrifice, dignity, and discipline. He sees these values as rooted in the traditional American Dream. Early in the speech, King balances pleas for non-violence and for cooperation between blacks and whites with a strong sense of urgency to achieve results. Perhaps to blunt the charges of gradualism and over-moderation made by some black leaders such as Malcolm X, King stresses the "fierce urgency of now."

King's audience on this occasion would have attributed to him a very high level of ethos, a very positive degree of speaker credibility. His followers saw him as an expert, trustworthy, dynamic leader of their movement. In the speech and setting themselves, echos of Abraham Lincoln further reinforce his high ethos with this particular audience. As the Lincoln Memorial provides the physical setting, echos of the Gettysburg Address come through the structure of the speech (past, present, future) and in paragraphs two and five.

King utilizes varied language resources to lend power, motivation, and inspiration to his message. Consider where, for what possible functions, and how effectively he uses such stylistic devices as repetition, parallelism, and refrain. Consider especially the "I have a dream" and "Let freedom ring" passages. In the same manner, examine his use of antithetical phrasing, including "meeting physical force with soul force," "heat of oppression. . . oasis of freedom and justice," and "jangling discords . . . beautiful symphony." How appropriate to the occasion and to King as a Southern Baptist minister was his frequent use of imagery, paraphrases, and direct quotations from the Bible? Finally, assess his heavy use of metaphors throughout the speech. Would the audience probably experience them as natural to the topic, as artificial, as fresh and stimulating, as trite and dull, or as familiar and reassuring? What functions might have been served by parrticular metaphors? Note especially the early extended metaphor (figurative analogy) of cashing a check.

Rhetorical scholar Keith D. Miller has explored the ways in which King in his speeches, as one thoroughly exposed to the heritage of black folk preaching, reflected the tradition of "voice merging." In voice merging, black ministers created their own identities "not through original language but through identifying themselves with a hallowed tradition"—often by "borrowing homiletic material from many sources, including the sermons of their predoooooooro and peers."

In his speeches King typically both explicitly capitalized on revered biblical and national traditions with which his audiences agreed and "borrowed without acknowledgement from the sermons of both black and white Protestant ministers." In this way much of King's rhetoric had "been tested—often repeatedly tested—with both listeners and readers before King employed it." After extensive analysis, Miller argues that rhetorical critics should reconsider their "unqualified remonstrations against plagiarism and the use of cliches." See Keith D. Miller, "Voice Merging and Self-Making: The Epistemology of 'I Have A Dream'," *Rhetoric Society Quarterly,* 19(Winter 1989): 23–32; Miller, "Martin Luther King Borrows a Revolution: Argument, Audience, and Implications of a Second Hand Universe," *College English, 48(March 1986):*

This speech is reprinted by permission of Joan Daves Agency, Copyright 1963 by Martin Luther King, Jr.

---

1. I am happy to join with you today in what will go down in history as the greatest demonstration for <u>freedom</u> in this history of our nation.

2 Five score years ago, a great American, in whose symbolic shadow we stand today, signed the Emancipation Proclamation. This momentous decree came as a great beacon light of hope to millions of Negro slaves, who had been seared in the flames of withering injustice. It came as a joyous daybreak to end the long night of their captivity.

3 But one hundred years later, the Negro is still not free. One hundred years later, the life of the Negro is still sadly crippled by the manacles of segregation and the chains of discrimination. One hundred years later, the Negro lives on a lonely island of poverty in the midst of a vast ocean of material prosperity. One hundred years later, the Negro is still languished in the corners of American society and finds himself an exile in his own land. So we have come here today to dramatize a shameful condition.

4 In a sense, we've come to our nation's Capitol to cash a check. When the architects of our republic wrote the magnificent words of the Constitution and the Declaration of Independence, they were signing a promissory note to which every American was to fall heir. This note was a promise that all men—yes, black men and well as white men—would be guaranteed the unalienable rights of life, liberty, and the pursuit of happiness.

5 It is obvious today that America has defaulted on this promissory note insofar as her citizens of color are concerned. Instead of honoring this sacred obligation, America has given the Negro people a bad check; a check which has come back marked "insufficient funds." But we refuse to believe that the bank of justice is bankrupt. We refuse to believe that there are insufficient funds in the great vaults of opportunity of this nation. So we've come to cash this check—a check that will give us upon demand the riches of freedom and the security of justice. We have also come to this hallowed spot to remind America of the fierce urgency of *now*. This is no time to engage in the luxury of cooling off to take the tranquilizing drug of gradualism. *Now is the time* to make real the promises of Democracy. *Now is the time* to rise from the dark and desolate valley of segregation to the sunlight of racial justice. *Now is the time* to lift our nation from the quicksands of racial injustice to the solid rock of brotherhood. *Now is the time* to make justice a reality for all of God's children.

6 It would be fatal for the nation to overlook the urgency of the moment. This sweltering summer of the Negro's legitimate discontent will not pass until there is an invigorating autumn of freedom and equality. Nineteen sixty-three is not an end, but a beginning. Those who hope that the Negro needed to blow off steam and will now be content will have a rude awakening if the nation returns to business as usual. There will be neither rest nor tranquility in America until the Negro is granted his citizenship rights. The whirlwinds of revolt will continue to shake the foundations of our nation until the bright day of justice emerges.

7 But there is something that I must say to my people who stand on the warm threshold which leads into the palace of justice. In the process of gaining our rightful place we must not be guilty of wrongful deeds. Let us not seek to satisfy our thirst for freedom by drinking from the cup of bitterness and hatred.

8 We must forever conduct our struggle on the high plane of dignity and discipline. We must not allow our creative protest to degenerate into physical violence. Again and again we must rise to the majestic heights of meeting physical force with soul force. The marvelous new militancy which has engulfed the Negro community must not lead us to a distrust of all white people, for many of our white brothers, as evidenced by their presence here today, have come to realize that their destiny is tied up with our destiny. And they have come to realize that their freedom is inextricably bound to our freedom. We cannot walk alone.

9 And as we walk we must make the pledge that we shall always march ahead. We cannot turn back. There are those who ask the devotees of civil rights, "When will you be satisfied?" We can never be satisfied as long as the Negro is the victim of the unspeakable horrors of police brutality. We can never be satisfied as long as our bodies, heavy with the fatigue of travel, cannot gain lodging in the motels of the highways and the hotels of the cities. We cannot be satisfied as long as the Negro's basic mobility is from a smaller ghetto to a larger one. We can never be satisfied as long as our children are stripped of their selfhood and robbed of their dignity by signs stating "For Whites Only." We cannot be satisfied as long as a Negro in Mississippi cannot vote and a Negro in New York believes he has nothing for which to vote. No, no, we are not satisfied, and we will not be satisfied until justice rolls down like waters and righteousness like a mighty stream.

10 I am not unmindful that some of you have come here out of great trials and tribulations. Some of you have come fresh from narrow jail cells. Some of you have come from areas where your quest for freedom left you battered by the storms of persecution and staggered by the winds of police brutality. You have been the veterans of creative suffering. Continue to work with the faith that unearned suffering is redemptive.

11 Go back to Mississippi, go back to Alabama, go back to South Carolina, go back to Georgia, go back to Louisiana, go back to the slums and ghettos of our Northern cities knowing that somehow this situation can and will be changed. Let us not wallow in the valley of despair.

12 I say to you today, my friends, so even though we face the difficulties of today and tomorrow, I still have a dream. It is a dream deeply rooted in the American dream.

13 I have a dream that one day this nation will rise up and live out the true meaning of its creed: "We hold these truths to be self-evident; that all men are crated equal."

14 I have a drcam that one day on the red hills of Georgia the sons of former slaves and the sons of former slaveowners will be able to sit down together at the table of brotherhood; I have a dream—

15 That one day even the state of Mississippi, a state sweltering with the heat of injustice, sweltering with the heat of oppression, will be transformed into an oasis of freedom and justice; I have a dream—

16 That my four little children will one day live in a nation where they will not be judged by the color of their skin but by the content of their character; I have a dream today.

17 I have a dream that one day down in Alabama with its vicious racists, with its governor having his lips dripping with the words of interposition and nullification, one day right there in Alabama little black boys and black girls will be able to join hands with little white boys and white girls as sisters and brother; I have a dream today.

18 I have a dream that one day every valley shall be exalted, every hill and mountain shall be made low, and rough places will be made plane and crooked places will be made straight, and the glory of the Lord shall be revealed, and all flesh shall see it together.

19 This is our hope. This is the faith that I go back to the South with. With this faith we will be able to hew out of the mountain of despair a stone of hope. With this faith we will be able to transform the jangling discords of our nation into a beautiful symphony of brotherhood. With this faith we will be able to work together, to pray together, to struggle together, to go to jail together, to stand up for freedom together, knowing that we will be free one day.

20 This will be the day. . . . This will be the day when all of God's children will be able to sing with new meaning. "My country 'tis of thee, sweet land of liberty, of thee I sing. Land where my fathers died, land of the pilgrim's pride, from every mountainside, let freedom ring," and if America is to be a great nation—this must become true.

21 So let freedom ring—from the prodigious hilltops of New Hampshire, let freedom ring; from the mighty mountains of New York, let freedom ring—from the heightening Alleghenies of Pennsylvania!

22 Let freedom ring from the snowcapped Rockies of Colorado!

23 Let freedom ring from the curvaceous slopes of California!

24 But not only that; let freedom ring from Stone Mountain of Georgia!

25 Let freedom ring from Lookout Mountain of Tennessee!

26 Let freedom ring from every hill and molehill of Mississippi. From every mountainside, let freedom ring, and when this happens. . . .

27 When we allow freedom ring, when we let it ring from every village and every hamlet, from every state and every city, we will be able to speed up that day when all of God's children, black men and white men, Jews and Gentiles, protestants and Catholics, will be able to join hands and sing in the words of the old Negro spiritual, "Free at last! free at last! thank God almighty, we are free at last!"

Democratic Convention Keynote Address
Barbara Jordan

On July 12, 1976, Barbara Jordan, U.S. Congresswoman from Texas, delivered this nationally televised keynote address to the Democratic National Convention in New York City. A lawyer, Jordan was the first black woman elected to the Texas state senate. She came to national public prominence on July 25, 1974, with her eloquent and impassioned defense of the Constitution as a committee speaker during the televised hearings of the U.S. House of Representatives committee on President Nixon's impeachment. Her 21 minute speech at the 1976 Democratic convention followed a comparatively lackluster keynote speech by Sen. John Glenn, the astronaut hero. She was introduced via a film biography of her life and career and was greeted by the convention audience with a three minute standing ovation. In keeping with her reputation as an excellent public speaker, Jordan delivered the speech in a clear, forceful, and dramatic manner. A *New York Times* reporter (July 13, 1976, p. 24) describes the audience reaction: "Time and again, they interrupted her keynote speech with applause. And, after it was all over . . . she was brought back for a final curtain call and for the loudest ovation of all."

Clearly a political convention keynote address seeks to mold social cohesion. Typically the keynote speaker stresses the importance of the convention and the deliberations of the delegates, castigates the opposing party, praises the heritage, values, and policies of their own party, and exhorts the convention delegates and all party members to unite in a vigorous, successful campaign. A keynote speaker attempts to inspire and reenergize members by setting a theme, a tone, a *key note,* for the convention.

Throughout the speech Jordan develops the central theme of a people in search of a national community, in search of the common good. This note of cohesiveness is reflected in her choice of phrases: one nation; common spirit; common endeavor; common ties; each person do his or her part. Frequently she justifies a position or judgment as harmonious with the will or interests of "the people." She attributes to "the people" such values as common sense and generosity. (For an analysis of the socially cohesive function served by appeals to "the people" in political discourse, see Michael C. McGee, "In Search of 'The People'," *Quarterly Journal of Speech,* October 1975.)

In a major section of the speech, Jordan utilizes parallel phrasing (we believe, we are, we have) to outline the Democratic Party's concept of governing—its basic beliefs that reflect its view of human nature. She metaphorically ("bedrock") stresses the fundamental nature of these beliefs and claims that they are not negotiable. The beliefs have explicit or implicit values imbedded in them: equality (note the double antithetical phrasing of the first belief); opportunity; government of, by, and for the people; activity; innovativeness; adaptability; sacrifice for a good cause; optimism.

Note that Jordan frequently repeats words, rephrases ideas, and in vocal delivery overenunciates the pronunciation of words (gov-er-ning; hyp-o-crit-i-cal). She may have intentionally used such techniques of redundancy and emphasis to overcome the physical noise and listener inattention typical of political conventions. Some in the audience, most likely the television audience, may have felt that her attitude toward them was one of superiority, as if they were simpleminded folk who needed everything spelled out and overemphasized for comprehension.

In at least two ways, Jordan's address differs slightly from the expectations or traditions associated with political convention keynote speeches. First, she makes virtually no direct attacks on the Republicans. Her apparent attacks are implied. By metaphorically characterizing past Democratic mistakes as those "of the heart," she may be indirectly asserting calculating, devious mistakes by the Nixon Administration. By arguing that no President can veto the decision of the American people to forge a national community, she indirectly may be attacking President Ford's heavy use of the veto to block Congressional legislation.

In a second departure from tradition, she does criticize her own party, but in such a moderate way as to freshen the speech without weakening her praise of party principles or generating negative audience reaction. She admits the Democratic Party has made past mistakes, but they were in behalf of the common good and the Party was willing later to confess them. Metaphorically she underscores the point by saying that Party "deafness" to the will of the people was only temporary. Her warning that the Democratic Party at times has attempted to be "all things to all people" may be indirect criticism of Jimmy Carter who was faulted during the primaries for making that kind of appeal. As a final analytic consideration here, assess whether this warning against being "all things to all people" is to some degree inconsistent with her point earlier in the speech that the Democratic Party is an inclusive party ("Let everybody come").

Two prominent rhetorical critics have said of Jordan's speech: "Many critics who watched and heard her speak will have recognized a recurrent rhetorical form, a reflexive form, a form called 'enactment' in which the speaker incarnates the argument, *is* the proof of the truth of what is said." (Karlyn Kohrs Campbell and Kathleen Hall Jamieson, *Form and Genre, Shaping Rhetorical Action* (Falls Church, VA: The Speech Communication Association, n.d., p. 9.) Discuss the speech from this perspective of rhetorical enactment by the speaker. Does it help you to understand the power of Jordan's words?

Reprinted by permission from *Vital Speeches of the Day,* August 15, 1976, pp. 645–46.

---

1 One hundred and forty-four years ago, members of the Democratic Party first met in convention to select a Presidential candidate. Since that time, Democrats have continued to convene once every four years and draft a party platform and nominate a Presidential candidate. And our meeting this week is a continuation of that tradition.

2 But there is something different about tonight. There is something special about tonight. What is different? What is special? I, Barbara Jordan, am a keynote speaker.

3 A lot of years passed since 1832, and during that time it would have been most unusual for any national political party to ask that a Barbara Jordan deliver a keynote address . . . but tonight here I am. And I feel that notwithstanding the past that my presence here is one additional bit of evidence that the American Dream need not forever be deferred.

4 Now that I have this grand distinction what in the world am I supposed to say?

5 I could easily spend this time praising the accomplishments of this party and attacking the Republicans, but I don't choose to do that.

6 I could list the many problems which Americans have. I could list the problems which cause people to feel cynical, angry, frustrated: problems which include lack of integrity in government; the feeling that the individual no longer counts; the reality of material and spiritual poverty; the feeling that the grand American experiment is failing or has failed. I could recite these problems and then I could sit down and offer no solutions. But I don't choose to do that either.

7 The citizens of America expect more. They deserve and they want more than a recital of problems.

8 We are a people in a quandary about the present. We are a people in search of our future. We are a people in search of a national community.

9 We are a people trying not to solve the problems of the present—unemployment, inflation—but we are attempting on a larger scale to fulfill the promise of America. We are attempting to fulfill our national purpose: to create and sustain a society in which all of us are equal.

10 Throughout our history, when people have looked for new ways to solve their problems, and to uphold the principles of this nation, many times they have turned to political parties. They have often turned to the Democratic Party.

11 What is it, what is it about the Democratice Party that makes it the instrument that people use when they search for ways to shape their future? Well I believe the answer to that question lies in our concept of governing. Our concept of governing is derived from our view of people. It is a concept deeply rooted in a set of beliefs firmly etched in the national conscience of all of us.

12 Now what are these beliefs?

13 First, we believe in equality for all and privileges for none. This is a belief that each American regardless of background has equal standing in the public forum, all of us. Because we believe this idea so firmly, we are an inclusive rather than an exclusive party. Let everybody come.

14 I think it no accident that most of those emigrating to America in the 19th century identified with the Democratic Party. We are a heterogenous party made up of Americans of diverse backgrounds.

15 We believe that the people are the source of all governmental power; that the authority of the people is to be extended, not restricted. This can be accomplished only by providing each citizen with every opportunity to participate in the management of the government. They must have that.

16 We believe that the government which represents the authority of all the people, not just one interest group, but all the people, has an obligation to actively, underscore actively, seek to remove those obstacles which would block individual achievement . . . obstacles emanating from race, sex, economic condition. The government must seek to remove them.

17 We are a party of innovation. We do not reject our traditions, but we are willing to adapt to changing circumstances, when change we must. We are willing to suffer the discomfort of change in order to achieve a better future.

18 We have a positive vision of the future founded on the belief that the gap between the promise and reality of America can one day be finally closed. We believe that.

19 This my friends, is the bedrock of our concept of governing. This is a part of the reason why Americans have turned to the Democratic Party. These are the foundations upon which a national community can be built.

20 Let's all understand that these guiding principles cannot be discarded for short-term political gains. They represent what this country is all about. They are indigenous to the American idea. And these are principles which are not negotiable.

21 In other times, I could stand here and give this kind of exposition on the beliefs of the Democratic Party and that would be enough. But today that is not enough. People want more. That is not sufficient reason for the majority of the people of this country to vote Democratic. We have made mistakes. In our haste to do all things for all people, we did not foresee the full consequences of our actions. And when the people raised their voices, we didn't hear. But our deafness was only a temporary condition, and not an irreversible condition.

22 Even as I stand here and admit that we have made mistakes I still believe that as the people of America sit in judgment on each party, they will recognize that our mistakes were mistakes of the heart. They'll recognize that.

23 And now we must look to the future. Let us heed the voice of the people and recognize their common sense. If we do not, we not only blaspheme our political heritage, we ignore the common ties that bind all Americans.

24 Many fear the future. Many are distrustful of their leaders, and believe that their voices are never heard. Many seek only to satisfy their private work wants. To satisfy private interests.

25 But this is the great danger America faces. That we will cease to be one nation and become instead a collection of interest groups: city against suburb, region against region, individual against individual. Each seeking to satisfy private wants.

26 If that happens, who then will speak for America?

27 Who then will speak for the common good?

28 This is the question which must be answered in 1976.

29 Are we to be one people bound together by common spirit sharing in a common endeavor or will we become a divided nation?

30 For all of its uncertainty, we cannot flee the future. We must not become the new puritans and reject our society. We must address and master the future together. It can be done if we restore the belief that we share a sense of national community, that we share a common national endeavor. It can be done.

31 There is no executive order: there is no law that can require the American people to form a national community. This we must do as individuals and if we do it as individuals, there is no President of the United States who can veto that decision.

32 As a first step, we must restore our belief in ourselves. We are a generous people so why can't we be generous with each other? We need to take to heart the words spoken by Thomas Jefferson:

33 "Let us restore to social intercourse that harmony and that affection without which liberty and even life are but dreary things."

34 A nation is formed by the willingness of each of us to share in the responsibility for upholding the common good.

35 A government is invigorated when each of us is willing to participate in shaping the future of this nation.

36 In this election year we must define the common good and begin again to shape a common future. Let each person do his or her part. If one citizen is unwilling to participate, all of us are going to suffer. For the American idea, though it is shared by all of us, is realized in each one of us.

37 And now, what are those of us who are elected public officials supposed to do? We call ourselves public servants but I'll tell you this: we as public servants must set an example for the rest of the nation. It is hypocritical for the public official to admonish and exhort the people to uphold the common good if we are derelict in upholding the common good. More is required of public officials than slogans and handshakes and press releases. More is required. We must hold ourselves strictly accountable. We must provide the people with a vision of the future.

38 If we promise as public officials, we must deliver. If we as public officials propose, we must produce. If we say to the American people it is time for you to be sacrificial; sacrifice. If the public official says that, we (public officials) must be the first to give. We must be. And again, if we make mistakes, we must be willing to admit them. We have to do that. What we have to do is strike a balance between the idea that government should do everything and the idea, the belief, that government ought to do nothing. Strike a balance.

39 Let there be no illusions about the difficulty of forming this kind of a national community. It's tough, difficult, not easy. But a spirit of harmony will survive in America only if each of us remembers that we share a common destiny. If each of us remembers, when self-interest and bitterness seem to prevail, that we share a common destiny.

40 I have confidence that we can form this kind of national community.

41 I have confidence that the Democratic Party can lead the way. I have that confidence. We cannot improve on the system of government handed down to us by the founders of the Republic, there is no way to improve upon that. But what we can do is to find new ways to implement that system and realize our destiny.

42 Now, I began this speech by commenting to you on the uniqueness of a Barbara Jordan making the keynote address. Well I am going to close my speech by quoting a Republican President and I ask you that as you listen to these words of Abraham Lincoln, relate them to the concept of a national community in which every last one of us participates: "As I would not be slave, so I would not be master. This expresses my idea of Democracy. Whatever differs from this, to the extent of the difference is no Democracy."

Opportunities for Hispanic Women: It's Up to Us
Janice Payan

A keynote speech serves as a motivational preface to a meeting, conference, or convention. Typically it stresses the social importance of the work to be done by those assembled. A keynote speaker attempts to inspire and re-energize the audience by setting a theme, a tone, a *key note,* for the meeting. Janice Payan, a Vice President of U.S. West Communications, presented this keynote address on May 19, 1990 at the Adelante Mujer (Onward Women) Conference in Denver, Colorado. U.S. West Communications specializes in telecommunications products and services, includiing cellular telephones.

One of the most noteworthy features of this speech is Payan's pervasive use of personal narrative—the telling of personal stories (19–20, 22–24, 26–36). What are some of the persuasive functions that these stories seem to aim at accomplishing? How well do they accomplish those functions? In what ways do they reflect the values she stresses in the speech? Payan frequently relates personal stories that serve the special function of enhancing identification between her audience and herself; these stories emphasize experiences that she and the audience have in common (1, 10–13, 15, 17, 21). How well do you think they accomplish this purpose of identification?

The key values that Payan attempts to reinforce and re-energize in her audience are hard work/perseverance (4, 21, 32); self-confidence (6, 28, 30, 32); united effort (20, 31, 34, 36); cooperation (33); pride in heritage (20); fulfilling ones potential (10, 16, 26, 38); and taking action (6). To further underscore hard work and perseverance as values, she tells stories of three Hispanic women as examples or role models of success due to determination (7–9). She reassures her listeners that these examples are representative ones (10): "Virtually every Hispanic woman in America started with a similar slate." To emphasize taking action as a value, Payan uses a refrain to motivate action (29, 32, 33, 36): "What are you going to do about it?"

Two additional aspects of Payan's speech invite comment. First, consider her use of humor—both obvious and subtle (3–4, 16, 22, 24, 31). For any particular instance, to what extent does the humor seem a natural part of the point she is making and seem to flow naturally from the subject matter? Does any of the humor seem artificial, irrelevant, or "tacked-on"? How much does the humor add to or detract from her point? Are there other places where humor is used that we have overlooked? Second, of the "five things I wish I had known," Payan clearly enumerates the first four. What, specifically, is the fifth one? Should she have enumerated it for clarity and completeness? Why or why not?

The text of this speech is reprinted with permission from *Vital Speeches of the Day,* September 1, 1990, pp. 697–700.

---

1 Thank you. I felt as if you were introducing someone else because my mind was racing back 10 years, when I was sitting out there in the audience at the Adelante Mujer conference. Anonymous. *Comfortable.* Trying hard to relate to our "successful" speaker, but mostly feeling like Janice Payan, working mother, *glad for a chance to sit down.*

2 I'll let you in on a little secret. I *still am* Janice Payan, working mother. The only difference is that I have a longer job title, and that I've made a few discoveries these past 10 years that I'm eager to share with you.

3 The first is that keynote speakers at conferences like this are *not* some sort of alien creatures. Nor were they born under a lucky star. They are ordinary *Hispanic Women* who have stumbled onto an extraordinary discovery.

4 And that is: *Society lied to us.* We *do* have something up here! We *can* have not only a happy family but also a fulfilling career. We *can* succeed in *school* and *work* and *community life,* because the key is not supernatural powers, it is *perseverance.* Also known as *hard work! And God knows Hispanic women can do hard work!!!* We've been working hard for centuries, from sun-up 'til daughter-down!

5 One of the biggest secrets around is that successful Anglos were not born under lucky stars, either. The chairman of my compnay, Jack MacAllister, grew up in a small town in eastern Iowa. His dad was a teacher; his mom was a mom. Jack worked, after school, sorting potatoes in the basement of a grocery store. Of course I realize, *he could have been hoeing them,* like our migrant workers. Nevertheless, Jack came from humble beginnings. And so did virtually every other corporate officer I work with. The major advantage they had was living in a culture that allowed them to *believe* they would get ahead. So more of them did.

6 It's time for *Hispanic women* to believe we can get ahead, *because we can.* And because *we must.* Our families and work-places and communities and nation need us to reach our full potential. There are jobs to be done, children to be raised, opportunities to be seized. We must look at those opportunities, choose the ones we will respond to, and *do something about them.* We must do so, for others. And we must do so, for ourselves. *Yes,* there are barriers. You're up against racism, sexism, and too much month at the end of the money. *But so was any role model you choose.*

7 Look at Patricia Diaz-Denis. Patricia was one of nine or ten children in a Mexican-American family that had low means, but high hopes. Her parents said Patricia should go to college. But they had no money. So, little by little, Patricia scraped up the money to send herself. Her boyfriend was going to be a lawyer. And he told Patricia, "You should be a lawyer, too, because *nobody can argue like you do!*" Well, Patricia didn't even know what a lawyer was, but she became one—so successful that she eventually was appointed to the Federal Communications Commission in Washington D.C.

8 Or look at Toni Pantcha, a Puerto Rican who grew up in a shack with dirt floors, no father, and often no food. But through looking and listening, she realized the power of *community*—the fact that people with very little, when working together, can create much. Dr. Pantcha has created several successful institutions in Puerto Rico, and to me, *she* is an institution. I can see the wisdom in her eyes, hear it in her voice, wisdom far beyond herself, like Mother Teresa.

9 Or look at Ada Kirby, a Cuban girl whose parents put her on a boat for Miami. Mom and Dad were to follow on the next boat, but they never arrived. So Ada grew up in an orphanage in Pueblo, and set some goals, and today is an executive director at U.S. WEST's research laboratories.

10 Each of these women was Hispanic, physically deprived, but *mentally awakened to the possibilities of building a better world,* both for others and for themselves. Virtually every Hispanic woman in America started with a similar slate. In fact, let's do a quick survey. If you were born into a home whose economic status was something *less than rich* . . . please raise your hand. It's a good thing I didn't ask the *rich* to raise their hands. I wouldn't have known if anyone was listening. All right. So you were not born rich. As Patricia, Toni, and Ada have shown us, it doesn't matter. It's the choices we make from there on, that make the difference.

11 If you're thinking, "that's easy for *you* to say, Payan," then I'm thinking: "little do you know. . . ." If you think I got where I am because I'm smarter than you, or have more energy than you, you're wrong. If I'm so smart, why can't I parallel park? If I'm so energetic, why do I still need eight hours of sleep a night? And I mean *need.* If I hadn't had my eight hours last night, you wouldn't even want to *hear* what I'd be saying this morning!

12 I am more like you and you are more like me than you would guess. I'm a third-generation Mexican-American . . . born into a lower middle-class family right here in Denver. My parents married young; she was pregnant. My father worked only about half the time during my growing-up years. He was short on education, skills, and confidence. There were drug and alcohol problems in the family. My parents finally sent my older brother to a Catholic high school, in hopes that would help him. They sent me to the same school, to *watch* him. That was okay.

13 In public school I never could choose between the "Greasers" and the "Soshes." I wanted desperately to feel that I "belonged." *But did not like feeling that I had to deny my past to have a future.* Anybody here ever feel that way?

14 Anyway, the more troubles my brother had, the more I vowed to avoid them. So, in a way, he was my inspiration. As Victor Frankl says, there is meaning in every life. By the way, that brother later died after returning from Vietnam.

15 I was raised with typical Hispanic female expectations. In other words: If you want to *do* well in life, you'd better . . . can anybody finish that sentence? Right! *Marry well.* I liked the idea of loving and marrying someone, but I felt like he should be more than a "meal ticket." And I felt like *I* should be more than a leech. I didn't want to feel so dependent. So I set my goals on having a marriage, a family, *and* a career. I didn't talk too much about those goals, so nobody told me they bordered on *insanity* for a Hispanic woman in the 1960s.

16 At one point, I even planned to become a doctor. But Mom and Dad said "wait a minute. That takes something like 12 years of college." I had no idea how I was going to pay for *four* years of college, let alone *12.* But what scared me more than the cost was the *time:* In 12 years I'd be an *old woman.* Time certainly changes your perspective on that. My advice to you is, if you want to be a doctor, go for it! It doesn't take 12 years, anyway. If your dreams include a career that requires college . . . go for it! You may be several years older when you finish, but by that time you'd be several years older if you *don't* finish college, too.

17 For all my suffering in high school, I finished near the top of my graduating class. I dreamed of attending the University of Colorado at Boulder. You want to know what my counselor said? You already know. That I should go to a business college for secretaries, at most. But I went to the University of Colorado, anyway. I arranged my own financial aid: a small grant, a low paying job, and a *big* loan. I just thank God that this was the era when jeans and sweatshirts were getting popular. That was all I had!

18 I'm going to spare you any description of my class work, except to say that it was difficult—and worth every painful minute. What I want to share with you is three of my strongest memories—and strongest learning experiences—which have nothing to do with books.

19 One concerns a philosophy professor who, I was sure, was a genius. What I liked best about this man was not the answers he had—but the questions. He asked questions about the Bible, about classic literature, about our place in the universe. He would even jot questions in the margins of our papers. And I give him a lot of credit for helping me examine my own life. I'm telling you about him because I think each of us encounter people who make us think—sometimes painfully. And I feel, very strongly, that we should listen to their questions and suffer through that thinking. We may decide everything in our lives is just like we want it. But we may also decide to change something.

20 My second big "non-book" experience was in UMAS—the United Mexican American Students. Lost in what seemed like a rich Anglo campus, UMAS was an island of familarity: people who looked like me, talked like me, and *felt* like me. We shared our fears and hopes and hurts—and did something about them. We worked hard to deal with racism on campus, persuading the university to offer Chicano studies classes. But the more racism we experienced, the angrier we became. Some members made bombs. Two of those members died. And I remember asking myself: "Am I willing to go up in smoke over my anger? Or is there another way to make a difference?" We talked a lot about this, and concluded that two wrongs don't make a right. Most of us agreed that working *within* the system was the thing to do. We also agreed not to deny our Hispanic heritage: not to become "coconuts"—brown on the outside and white on the inside—but to look for every opportunity to bring *our* culture to a table of many cultures. That outlook has helped me a great deal as a manager, because it opened me to listening to all points of view. And when a group is open to all points of view, it usually chooses the right course.

21 The third experience I wanted to share from my college days was the time they came nearest to ending prematurely. During my freshman year, I received a call that my mother had been seriously injured in a traffic accident. Both of her legs were broken. So was her pelvis. My younger brother and sister were still at home. My father was unemployed at the time, and I was off at college. So who do you think was elected to take on the housework? Raise your hand if you think it was my father. No??? Does anybody think it was *me?* I am truly amazed at your guessing ability. Or is there something in our Hispanic culture that says the women do the housework? Of course there is. So I drove home from Boulder every weekend; shopped, cleaned, cooked, froze meals for the next week, did the laundry, you know the list. And the truth is, it did not occur to me until some time later than my father could have done some of that. I had a problem, but I was part of the problem. I *did* resist when my parents suggested I should quit school. It seemed better to try doing everything, than to give up my dream. And it was the better choice. But it was also very difficult.

22 Which reminds me of another experience. Would it be too much like a soap opera if I told you about a personal crisis? Anybody want to hear a story about myself that I've never before told in public? While still in college, I married my high school sweetheart. We were both completing our college degrees. My husband's family could not figure out why I was pursuing college instead of kids, but I was. However, it seemed like my school-work always came last.

23 One Saturday night I had come home from helping my Mom, dragged into our tiny married-student apartment, cooked a big dinner for my husband, and as I stood there washing the dishes, I felt a teardrop trickle down my face. Followed by a flood. Followed by sobbing. *Heaving.* If you ranked crying on a scale of 1 to 10, this was an 11. My husband came rushing in with that . . . you know . . . that "puzzled-husband" look. He asked what was wrong. Well, it took me awhile to figure it out, to be able to put it into words. When I did, they were 12 words: "I just realized I'll be doing dishes the rest of my life."

24 Now, if I thought you'd believe me, I'd tell you *my husband finished the dishes.* He did not. But we both did some thinking and talking about roles and expectations, and, over the years, have learned to share the domestic responsibilities. We realized that we were both carrying a lot of old, cultural "baggage" through life. *And so are you.*

25 I'm not going to tell you what to do about it. But I am going to urge you to realize it, think about it, and even to cry over the dishes, if you need to. You may be glad you did. As for me, *What have I learned from all this?* I've learned, as I suggested earlier, that Hispanic women have bought into a lot of myths, through the years. Or at least *I* did. And I want to tell you now, especially you younger women, the "five things I wish I had known" when I was 20, 25, even 30. In fact, some of these things I'm *still* learning—at 37. Now for that list of "five things I wish I had known."

26 First: I wish I had known that I—like most Hispanic women—was under-estimating my capabilities. When I first went to work for Mountain Bell, which has since become U.S. WEST Communications—I thought the "ultimate" job I could aspire to, would be district manager. So I signed up for the courses I knew would help me achieve and handle that kind of responsibility. I watched various district managers, forming my own ideas of who was most effective—and why. I accepted whatever responsibilities and opportunities were thrown my way, generally preparing myself to be district manager.

27 My dream came true. But then it almost became a nightmare. After only 18 months on the job, the president of the company called me and asked me to go interview with *his boss*—the president of our parent company. And the next thing I knew, I had been pro-moted to a job *above* that of district manager. Suddenly, I was stranded in unfamiliar ter-ritory. They gave me a big office at U.S. WEST headquarters down in Englewood, where I pulled all the furniture into one corner. In fact, I sort of made a little "fort." From this direction, I could hide behind the computer. From that direction, the plants. From over here, the file cabinet. Safe at last. *Until,* a friend from downtown came to visit me. She walked in, looked around, and demanded to know: *"What is going on here?* Why was your door closed? Why are you all scrunched up in the corner?" I had all kinds of excuses. But she said: "You know what I think? I think you're afraid you don't deserve this office!"

28 As she spoke, she started dragging the plants away from my desk. For a moment, I was angry. Then afraid. Then we started laughing, and I helped her stretch my furnish-ings—and my confidence. And it occurred to me that had I pictured, from the beginning, that I could become an executive director, I would have been better prepared. I would have pictured myself in that big office. I would have spent more time learning executive public speaking. I would have done a lot of things. And I began to do them with my new, expanded vision of becoming an officer—which subsequently happened.

29 I just wish that I had known, in those early years, how I was underestimating my capabilities. I suspect that *you are, too.* And I wonder: *What are you going to do about it?*

30 Second: I wish I had known that power is not something others give you. It is something that comes from *within yourself.* . . and which you can then share with others.

31 In 1984, a group of minority women at U.S. WEST got together and did some arithmetic to confirm what we already knew. Minority women were woefully under-represented in the ranks of middle and upper management. We had a better chance of winning the lottery! So we gathered our courage and took our case to the top. Fortunately,

we found a sympathetic ear. The top man told us to take our case to *all* the officers. We did. But we were scared. And it showed. We sort of "begged" for time on their calendars. We apologized for interrupting their work. Asked for a little more recognition of our plight. And the first few interviews went terribly. Then we realized: we deserve to be on their calendars as much as anyone else does. We realized that under-utilizing a group of employees is not an interruption of the officers' work—it *is* the officers' work. We realized that we should not be asking for help—we should be *telling* how *we could help*. So we did.

32 And it worked. The company implemented a special program to help minority women achieve their full potential. Since then, several of us have moved into middle and upper management, and more are on the way. I just wish we had realized, in the beginning, where power really comes from. It comes from within yourself . . . and which you can then share with others. I suspect *you* need to be reminded of that, too. And I wonder: *What are you going to do about it?*

33 Third: I wish I had known that when I feel envious of others, I'm really just showing my lack of confidence in myself. A few years ago, I worked closely with one of my co-workers in an employee organization. She is Hispanic. Confident. Outgoing. In fact, she's so likeable I could hardly stand her! But as we worked together, I finally realized: She has those attributes; I have others. And I had to ask myself: do I want to spend the time it would take to develop her attributes, or enjoy what we can accomplish by teaming-up our different skills? I realized that is the better way. I suspect that you may encounter envy from time to time. And I wonder: *What are you going to do about it?*

34 Fourth: I wish I had realized that true success is never something you earn single-handedly. We hear people talk about "networking" and "community" and "team-building." What they mean is an extension of my previous idea: We can be a lot more effective working in a group than working alone.

35 This was brought home to me when I was president of our Hispanic employees' organization at U.S. WEST Communications. I wanted my administration to be the best. So I tried to do everything myself, to be sure it was done right. I wrote the newsletter, planned the fund-raiser, scheduled the meetings, booked the speakers, everything. For our big annual meeting, I got the chairman of the company to speak. By then, the other officers of the group were feeling left out. Come to think of it, they *were* left out. Anyway, we were haggling over who got to introduce our big speaker. I was determined it should be me, since I so "obviously" had done all the work.

36 As it turned out, I missed the big meeting altogether. My older brother died. And I did a lot of painful thinking. For one thing: I was glad my team was there to keep things going while I dealt with my family crisis. But more important: I thought about life and death and what people would be saying if *I* had died. Would I prefer they remember that "good ol' Janice sure did a terrific job of arranging every last detail of the meeting?" Or that "we really enjoyed working with her?" "Together, we did a lot." All of us need to ask ourselves that question from time to time. And I wonder: *What are you going to do about it?*

37 Hispanic women in America have been victims of racism, sexism, and poverty for a long, long time. I know, because I was one of them. I also know that when you stop being a victim is largely up to you. I don't mean you should run out of here, quit your job, divorce your husband, farm out your kids, or run for President of the United States.

38 But I *do* mean that "whatever" you can dream, you can become. A couple of years ago, I came across a poem by an Augsburg College student, Devoney K. Looser, which I want to share with you now.

"I wish someone had taught me long ago
"How to touch mountains
"Instead of watching them from breathtakingly safe distances.
"I wish someone had told me sooner
"That cliffs were neither so sharp nor so distant nor so solid as they seemed.
"I wish someone had told me years ago
"That only through touching mountains can we reach peaks called beginnings, endings or exhilarating points of no return.
"I wish I had learned earlier that ten fingers and the world shout more brightly from the tops of mountains
"While life below only sighs with echoing cries.
"I wish I had realized before today
"That I can touch mountains
"But now that I know, my fingers will never cease the climb."

Please, my sisters, never, ever, cease the climb.

39 Adelante Mujer!

The Rainbow Coalition
Jesse Jackson

On July 17, 1984, the evening following Mario Cuomo's eloquent keynote speech, candidate Jesse Jackson addressed the Democratic National Convention. Although now it was clear that Walter Mondale would receive the nomination for president, the convention audience was very uncertain what the tone and substance of Rev. Jackson's message might be. His campaign rhetoric often was characterized by the press as confrontative and divisive. During the campaign Jackson won seven presidential primaries, brought some prisoners home after visiting Fidel Castro in Cuba, and secured freedom for an American naval pilot shot down over Syria. Delegates and viewers on national television would recall his early ethnic slur against Jews ("Hymies") and his refusal for much of the campaign to reject the support and views of Louis Farrakhan, the Black Muslim leader.

But Jackson's speech in San Francisco was one of conciliation rather than division. *Newsweek* (July 30, 1984, p. 23) observed that "without departing from the dictates of his conscience, he said nearly all the things party leaders had hoped for." *Newsweek* also contended that his speech "brought a new music to the mainstream of American oratory, stirring the spirit and wrenching the emotions in a way more reminiscent of the revival tent than the convention hall." Flordia's Governor Bob Graham, according to *Newsweek,* declared: "If you are a human being and weren't affected by what you just heard, you may be beyond redemption."

Clearly Jackson's general purpose was social cohesion. He sought to re-energize the commitment of his followers in the Rainbow Coalition, to heal divisive wounds that he and others had inflicted during the campaign, and to unite all Democrats around shared values and against a common enemy, Reaganism. Justifiably his address also could be analyzed as an unofficial keynote speech (see introduction to speech by Barbara Jordan in this chapter) or as a rally speech (see introduction to Martin Luther King, Jr. speech in this chapter).

Throughout the speech he stresses the need for unity (6, 12, 14–16, 25–26, 31–33, 39, 76, 84), even to the extent of setting a personal example through apology (20–21). Fundamental values shared by Democrats are emphasized: justice, fairness, humaneness, sharing, conscience, and inclusiveness. Jackson depicts the role of diversity and competition as healthy (12, 25) and describes the inclusiveness of the Rainbow Coalition and of the Democratice Party (27–28, 34–38, 71, 86).

To demonstrate that he has a firm command of political and economic realities, both domestic and foreign, Jackson relies heavily on two forms of support for his contentions. He employs statistics to quantify the seriousness of problems (42, 44–51, 61–67). Often he supports a judgment or defines a concept by itemization of examples or qualities (2, 6, 9, 18, 22, 56, 63, 76). To what extent are his uses of statistics and examples appropriate and reasonable?

In a very real sense, Jackson's speech can be characterized as a political sermon. Much more so than is typical of American political discourse, Jackson overtly preaches. He frequently describes God's nature and role. Allusions are made to the Bible (10, 12, 34, 76, 81) and religious concepts are employed (6, 24, 79, 85), including being called to redemption and to a mission. Search Jackson's address for additional illustrations of these, or other, sermonic features. For purposes of clarity and emphasis, Jackson often structures a series of ideas in parallel sequence (33, 34–38, 44–50, 77). Indeed parallelism in the form of repetition (54, 71, 73) and refrain provide stress on some central themes, such as the need to "dream" and his veiw that "our time has come" (78–79, 80–84).

Metaphorical imagery is a stylistic tactic important to the power of Jackson's message. The cumulative metaphorical image, developed in different ways at various points, is of movement upward and into the light (10, 22, 32, 71, 76–77). This movement takes the form of a journey (10, 69), a rising boat (10, 42–43), and progress to higher ground (32–33, 84). In paragraph 26 Jackson vividly captures his theme of unity-in-diversity through the metaphors of the rainbow and the quilt. Alliteration is used to associate in a memorable way clusters of things or ideas, either all positive or all negative (4, 5, 20, 37, 62–63, 72). Antithesis is the phrasing of two opposing or competing items into sharp, terse contrast with one item of the pair given clear preference over the other. Jackson frequently employs antithesis to crystalize value judgements (2, 8, 18, 20–21, 37–38, 52, 54, 69, 73, 77, 79, 84–85). Pervasive antithesis is such a marked feature of the speech that the rhetorical critic cannot ignore assessing the appropriateness, clarity, and persuasive functions of specific usages.

Parts of this analysis of Jackson's speech are indebted to two insightful essays: Martha Cooper and John Makay, "Political Rhetoric and the Gospel According to Jesse Jackson," in Charles W. Kneupper, ed., *Visions of Rhetoric* (Rhetoric Society of America, 1987), pp. 208–218; Leslie A. DiMare, "Functionalizing Conflict: Jesse Jackson's Rhetorical Strategy at the 1984 Democratic National Convention," *Western Journal of Speech Communication,* 51 (Spring 1987): 218–226.

With some corrections added based on a recording of the speech, the text is reprinted with permission from *Vital Speeches of the Day,* November 15, 1984, pp. 77–81.

1. Tonight we come together bound by our faith in a mighty God, with genuine respect for our country, and inheriting the legacy of a great party—a Democratic Party—which is the best hope for redirecting our nation on a more humane, just, and peaceful course.

2 This is not a perfect party. We are not a perfect people. Yet, we are called to a perfect mission: our mission, to feed the hungry, to clothe the naked, to house the homeless, to teach the illiterate, to provide jobs for the jobless, and to choose the human race over the nuclear race.

3 We are gathered here this week to nominate a candidate and write a platform which will expand, unify, direct, and inspire our party and the nation to fulfill this mission.

4 My constituency is the damned, disinherited, disrespected, and the despised.

5 They are restless and seek relief. They've voted in record numbers. They have invested the faith, hope, and trust that they have in us. The Democratic Party must send them a signal that we care. I pledge my best not to let them down.

6 There is the call of conscience: redemption, expansion, healing, and unity. Leadership must heed the call of conscience, redemption, expansion, healing, and unity, for they are the key to achieving our mission.

7 Time is neutral and does not change things.

8 With courage and initiative leaders change things. No generation can choose the age or circumstances in which it is born, but through leadership it can choose to make the age in which it is born an age of enlightenment—an age of jobs, and peace, and justice.

9 Only leadership—that intangible combination of gifts, discipline, information, circumstance, courage, timing, will, and divine inspiration—can lead us out of the crisis in which we find ourselves.

10 Leadership can mitigate the misery of our nation. Leadership can part the waters and lead our nation in the direction of the Promised Land. Leadership can lift the boats stuck at the bottom.

11 I have had the rare opportunity to watch seven men, and then two, pour out their souls, offer their service, and heed the call of duty to direct the course of our nation.

12 There is a proper season for everything. There is a time to sow and a time to reap. There is a time to compete, and a time to cooperate.

13 I ask for your vote on the ballot as a vote for a new direction for this party and this nation: a vote for conviction, a vote for conscience.

14 But I will be proud to support the nominee of this convention for the president of the United States of America.

15 I have watched the leadership of our party develop and grow. My respect for both Mr. Mondale and Mr. Hart is great.

16 I have watched them struggle with the cross-winds and cross-fires of being public servants, and I believe that they will both continue to try to serve us faithfully. I am elated by the knowledge that for the first time in our history a woman, Geraldine Ferraro, will be recommended to share our ticket.

17 Throughout this campaign, I have tried to offer leadership to the Democratic Party and the nation.

18 If in my high moments, I have done some good, offered some service, shed some light, healed some wounds, rekindled some hope, or stirred someone from apathy and indifference, or in any way along the way helped somebody, then this campaign has not been in vain.

19 For friends who loved and cared for me, and for a God who spared me, and for a family who understood, I am eternally grateful.

20 If in my low moments, in word, deed, or attitude, through some error of temper, taste, or tone, I have caused anyone discomfort, created pain, or revived someone's fears, that was not my truest self.

21 If there were occasions when my grape turned into a raisin and my joy bell lost its resonance, please forgive me. Charge it to my head and not to my heart. My head is so limited in its finitude; my heart is boundless in its love for the human family. I am not a perfect servant. I am a public servant. I'm doing my best against the odds. As I develop and serve, be patient. God is not finished with me yet.

22 This campaign has taught me much: that leaders must be tough enough to fight, tender enough to cry, human enough to make mistakes, humble enough to admit them, strong enough to absorb the pain, and resilient enough to bounce back and keep on moving. For leaders, the pain is often intense. But you must smile through your tears and keep moving with the faith that there is a brighter side somewhere.

23 I went to see Hubert Humphrey three days before he died. He had just called Richard Nixon from his dying bed, and many people wondered why. And, I asked him.

24 He said, "Jesse, from this vantage point, with the sun setting in my life, all of the speeches, the political conventions, the crowds, and the great fights are behind me now. At a time like this you are forced to deal with your irreducible essence, forced to grapple with that which is really important to you. And what I have concluded about life," Hubert Humphrey said, "when all is said and done, we must forgive each other, and redeem each other, and move on."

25 Our party is emerging from one of its most hard-fought battles for the Democratic Party's presidential nomination in our history. But our healthy competition should make us better, not bitter. We must use the insight, wisdom, and experience of the late Hubert Humphrey as a balm for the wounds in our party, this nation, and the world. We must forgive each other, redeem each other, regroup, and move on.

26 Our flag is red, white, and blue, but our nation is rainbow—red, yellow, brown, black, and white—we're all precious in God's sight. America is not like a blanket—one piece of unbroken cloth, the same color, the same texture, the same size. America is more like a quilt—many patches, many pieces, many colors, many sizes, all woven and held together by a common thread.

27 The white, the Hispanic, the black, the Arab, the Jew, the woman, the Native American, the small farmer, the businessperson, the environmentalist, the peace activist, the young, the old, the lesbian, the gay, and the disabled make up the American quilt.

28 Even in our fractured state, all of us count and fit somewhere. We have proven that we can survive without each other. But we have not proven that we can win or make progress without each other. We must come together.

29 From Fannie Lee Hamer in Atlantic City in 1964 to the Rainbow Coalition in San Francisco today; from the Atlantic to the Pacific, we have experienced pain but progress as we ended American apartheid laws; we got public accommodations; we secured voting rights; we obtained open housing; as young people got the right to vote; we lost Malcolm, Martin, Medgar, Bobby and John and Viola.

30 The team that got us here must be expanded, not abandoned. Twenty years ago, tears welled up in our eyes as the bodies of Schwerner, Goodman, and Chaney were dredged from the depths of a river in Mississippi. Twenty years later, our communities, black and Jewish, are in anguish, anger, and pain.

31 Feelings have been hurt on both sides. There is a crisis in communication. Confusion is in the air. We cannot afford to lose our way. We may agree to agree, or agree to disagree on issues; we must bring back civility to these tensions.

32 We are co-partners in a long and rich religious history—the Judeo-Christian traditions. Many blacks and Jews have a shared passion for social justice at home and peace abroad. We must seek a revival of the spirit, inspired by a new vision and new possibilities. We must return to higher ground. We are bound by Moses and Jesus, but also connected to Islam and Mohammed.

33 These three great religions—Judaism, Christianity, and Islam—were all born in the revered and holy city of Jerusalem. We are bound by Dr. Martin Luther King, Jr. and Rabbi Abraham Heschel, crying out from their graves for us to reach common ground. We are bound by shared blood and shared sacrifices. We are much too intelligent; much too bound by our Judeo-Christian heritage; much too victimized by racism, sexism, militarism, and anti-Semitism; much too threatened as historical scapegoats to go on divided one from another. We must turn from finger-pointing to clasped hands. We must share our burdens and our joys with each other once again. We must turn to each other and not on each other and choose higher ground.

34 Twenty years later, we cannot be satisfied by just restoring the old coalition. Old wine skins must make room for new wine. We must heal and expand. The Rainbow Coalition is making room for Arab-Americans. They too know the pain and hurt of racial and religious rejection. They must not continue to be made pariahs. The Rainbow Coalition is making room for Hispanic-Americans who this very night are living under the threat of the Simpson-Mazzoli bill, and farm workers from Ohio who are fighting the Campbell Soup Company with a boycott to achieve legitimate workers rights.

35 The Rainbow is making room for the Native Americans, the most exploited people of all, a people with the greatest moral claim amongst us. We support them as they seek the restoration of their ancient land and claim amongst us. We support them as they seek the restoration of land and water rights, as they seek to preserve their ancestral homelands and the beauty of a land that was once all theirs. They can never receive a fair share for all that they have given us, but they must finally have a fair chance to develop their great resources and to preserve their people and their culture.

36 The Rainbow Coalition includes Asian-Americans, now being killed in our streets—scapegoats for the failures of corporate, industrial, and economic policies. The Rainbow is making room for the young Americans. Twenty years ago, our young people were dying in a war for which they could not even vote. But 20 years later, Young America has the power to stop a war in Central America and the responsibility to vote in great numbers. Young America must be politically active in 1984. The choice is war or peace. We must make room for Young America.

37 The Rainbow includes disabled veterans. The color scheme fits in the Rainbow. The disabled have their handicap revealed and their genius concealed; while the able-bodied have their genius revealed and their disability concealed. But ultimately we must judge people by their values and their contribution. Don't leave anybody out. I would rather have Roosevelt in a wheelchair than Reagan on a horse.

38 The Rainbow is making room for small farmers. They have suffered tremendously under the Reagan regime. They will either receive 90 percent parity or 100 percent charity. We must address their concerns and make room for them. The Rainbow includes lesbians and gays. No American citizen ought be denied equal protection under the law.

39 We must be unusually committed and caring as we expand our family to include new members. All of us must be tolerant and understanding as the fears and anxieties of the rejected and of the party leadership express themselves in many different ways. Too often what we call hate—as if it were deeply rooted in some philosophy or strategy—is simply ignorance, anxiety, paranoia, fear, and insecurity. To be strong leaders, we must be long-suffering as we seek to right the wrongs of our party and our nation. We must expand our party, heal our party, and unify our party. That is our mission in 1984.

40 We are often reminded that we live in a great nation—and we do. But it can be greater still. The Rainbow is mandating a new definition of greatness. We must not measure greatness from the mansion down, but the manger up.

41 Jesus said that we should not be judged by the bark we wear but by the fruit that we bear. Jesus said that we must measure greatness by how we treat the least of these.

42 President Reagan says the nation is in recovery. Those 90,000 corporations that made a profit last year but paid no federal taxes are recovering. The 37,000 military contractors who have benefited from Reagan's more than doubling the military budget in peacetime, surely they are recovering. The big corporations and rich individuals who received the bulk of the three-year, multibillion tax cut from Mr. Reagan are recovering. But no such recovery is under way for the least of these. Rising tides don't lift all boats, particularly those stuck on the bottom.

43 For the boats stuck at the bottom there is a misery index. This administration has made life more miserable for the poor. Its attitude has been contemptuous. Its policies and programs have been cruel and unfair to working people. They must be held accountable in November for increasing infant mortality among the poor. In Detroit, one of the great cities of the Western world, babies are dying at the same rate as Honduras, the most underdeveloped nation in our hemisphere.

44 This administration must be held accountable for policies that contribute to the growing poverty in America. Under President Reagan, there are now 34 million people in poverty, 15 percent of our nation. Twenty-three million are white, 11 million black, Hispanic, Asian, and others. Mostly women and children. By the end of this year, there will be 41 million people in poverty. We cannot stand idly by. We must fight for change, now.

45 Under this regime we look at Social Security. The 1981 budget cuts included nine permanent Social Security benefit cuts totaling $20 billion over five years.

46 Small businesses have suffered under Reagan tax cuts. Only 18 percent of total business tax cuts went to them—82 percent to big business.

47 Health care under Mr. Reagan has been sharply cut.

48 Education under Mr. Reagan has been cut 25 percent.

49 Under Mr. Reagan there are now 9.7 million female-head families. They represent 16 percent of all families, half of all of them are poor. Seventy percent of all poor children live in a house headed by a woman, where there is no man.

50 Under Mr. Reagan, the administration has cleaned up only 6 of 546 priority toxic waste dumps.

51 Farmers' real net income was only about half its level in 1979.

52 Many say that the race in November will be decided in the South. President Reagan is depending on the conservative South to return him to office. But the South, I tell you, is unnaturally conservative. The South is the poorest region in our nation and, therefore, has the least to conserve. In his appeal to the South, Mr. Reagan is trying to substitute flags and prayer cloths for food, and clothing, and education, health care, and housing. But President Reagan who asks us to pray, and I believe in prayer—I've come this way by the power of prayer. But, we must watch false prophecy.

53 He cuts energy assistance to the poor, cuts breakfast programs from children, cuts lunch programs from children, cuts job training from children and then says, to an empty table, "let us pray." Apparently he is not familiar with the structure of a prayer. You thank the Lord for the food that you are about to receive, not the food that just left.

54 I think that we should pray. But don't pray for the food that left, pray for the man that took the food to leave. We need a change. We need a change in November.

55 Under President Reagan, the misery index has risen for the poor, but the danger index has risen for everybody.

56 Under this administration we've lost the lives of our boys in Central America, in Honduras, in Granada, in Lebanon.

57 A nuclear standoff in Europe. Under this administration, one-third of our children believe they will die in a nuclear war. The danger index is increasing in this world.

58 With all the talk about defense against Russia, the Russian submarines are closer and their missiles are more accurate. We live in a world tonight more miserable and a world more dangerous.

59 While Reagonomics and Reaganism is talked about often, so often we miss the real meaning. Reaganism is a spirit. Reaganomics represents the real economic facts of life.

60 In 1980, Mr. George Bush, a man with reasonable access to Mr. Reagan, did an analysis of Mr. Reagan's economic plan. Mr. Bush concluded Reagan's plan was "voodoo economics." He was right. Third-party candidate John Anderson said that the combination of military spending, tax cuts, and a balanced budget by '84 could be accomplished with blue smoke and mirrors. They were both right.

61 Mr. Reagan talks about a dynamic recovery. There is some measure of recovery, three and a half years later. Unemployment has inched just below where it was when he took office in 1981. But there are still 8.1 million people officially unemployed, 11 million working only parttime jobs. Inflation has come down, but let's analyze for a moment who has paid the price for this superficial economic recovery.

62 Mr. Reagan curbed inflation by cutting consumer demand. He cut consumer demand with conscious and callous fiscal and monetary policy. He used the federal budget to deliberately induce unemployment and curb social spending. He then waged and supported tight monetary policies of the Federal Reserve Board to deliberately drive up interest rates—again to curb consumer demand created through borrowing.

63 Unemployment reached 10.7 percent; we experienced skyrocketing interest rates; our dollar inflated abroad; there were record bank failures; record farm foreclosures; record business bankruptcies; record budget deficits; record trade deficits. Mr. Reagan brought inflation down by destablizing our economy and distrupting family life.

64 He promised in 1980 a balanced budget, but instead we now have a record $200 billion budget deficit. Under President Reagan, the cumulative budget deficit for his four years is more than the sum total of deficits from George Washington to Jimmy Carter combined. I tell you, we need a change.

65 How is he paying for these short-term jobs? Reagan's economic recovery is being financed by deficit spending—$200 billion a year. Military spending, a major cause of this deficit, is projected over the next five years to be nearly $2 trillion, and will cost about $40,000 for every taxpaying family.

66 When the government borrows $200 billion annually to finance the deficit, this encourages the private sector to make its money off of interest rates as opposed to development and economic growth. Even money abroad—we don't have enough money domestically to finance the debt, so we are now borrowing money abroad, from foreign banks, government, and financial institutions—$40 billion in 1983; $70 to $80 billion in 1984 (40 percent of our total); over $100 billion (50 percent of our total) in 1985.

67 By 1989, it is projected that 50 percent of all individual income taxes will be going to pay just for the interest on that debt. The U.S. used to be the largest exporter of capital, but under Mr. Reagan we will quite likely become the largest debtor nation. About two weeks ago, on July 4, we celebrated our Declaration of Independence. Yet every day, supply-side economics is making our nation more economically dependent and less economically free. Five to six percent of our gross national product is now being eaten up with President Reagan's budget deficit.

68 To depend on foreign military powers to protect our national security would be foolish, making us dependent and less secure. Yet Reaganomics has us increasingly dependent on foreign economic sources. This consumer-led but deficit-financed recovery is unbalanced and artificial.

69 We have a challenge as Democrats: to point a way out. Democracy guarantees opportunity, not success. Democracy guarantees the right to participate, not a license for either the majority or a minority to dominate. The victory for the Rainbow Coalition in the platform debates today was not whether we won or lost; but that we raised the right issues. We can afford to lose the vote; issues are non-negotiable. We cannot afford to avoid raising the right questions. Our self respect and our moral integrity were at stake. Our heads are perhaps bloodied but now bowed. Our backs are straight. We can go home and face our people. Our vision is clear. When we think, on this journey from slaveship to championship, we've gone from the planks of the boardwalk in Atlantic City in 1964 to fighting to have the right planks in the platform in San Francisco in '84. There is a deep and abiding sense of joy in our soul, despite the tears in our eyes. For while there are missing planks, there is a solid foundation upon which to build. Our party can win. But we must provide hope that will inspire people to struggle and achieve; provide a plan to show the way out of our dilemma, and then lead the way.

70 In 1984, my heart is made to feel glad because I know there is a way out. Justice. The requirement for rebuilding America is justice. The linchpin of progressive politics in our nation will not come from the North; they in fact will come from the South. That is why I argue over and over again—from Lynchburg, Va., down to Texas, there is only one black congressperson out of 115. Nineteen years later, we're locked out of the Congress, the Senate, and the governor's mansion. What does this large black vote mean? Why do I fight to end second primaries and fight gerrymandering and annexation and at large. Why do we fight over that? Because I tell you, you cannot hold someone in the ditch unless you linger there with them. If we want a change in this nation, reinforce that Voting Rights Act—we'll get 12 to 20 black, Hispanic, female, and progressive congresspersons from the South. We can save the cotton, but we've got to fight the boll weevil—we've got to make a judgment.

71 It's not enough to hope ERA will pass; how can we pass ERA? If blacks vote in great numbers, progressive whites win. It's the only way progressive whites win. If blacks vote in great numbers, Hispanics win. If blacks, Hispanics, and progressive whites vote, women win. When women win, children win. When women and children win, workers win. We must all come up together. We must come up together.

72 I tell you, with all of our joy and excitement, we must not save the world and lose our souls; we should never short-circuit enforcement of the Voting Rights Act at every level. If one of us rises, all of us must rise. Justice is the way out. Peace is a way out. We should not act as if nuclear weaponry is negotiable and debatable. In this world in which we live, we dropped the bomb on Japan and felt guilty. But in 1984, other folks also got bombs. This time, if we drop the bomb, six minutes later, we, too, will be destroyed. It's not about dropping the bomb on somebody; it's about dropping the bomb on everybody. We must choose developed minds over guided missiles, and think it out and not fight it out. It's time for a change.

73 Our foreign policy must be characterized by mutual respect, not by gunboat diplomacy, big stick diplomacy, and threats. Our nation at its best feeds the hungry. Our nation at its worst will mine the harbors of Nicaragua; at its worst, will try to overthrow that government; at its worst, will cut aid to American education and increase aid to El Salvador; at its worst our nation will have partnership with South Africa. That's a moral disgrace. It's a moral disgrace. It's a moral disgrace.

74 When we look at Africa, we cannot just focus on apartheid in southern Africa. We must fight for trade with Africa, and not just aid to Africa. We cannot stand idly by and say we will not relate to Nicaragua unless they have elections there and then embrace military regimes in Africa, overthrowing Democratic governments in Nigeria and Liberia and Ghana. We must fight for democracy all around the world, and play the game by one set of rules.

75 Peace in this world. Our present formula for peace in the Middle East is inadequate; it will not work. There are 22 nations in the Middle East. Our nation must be able to talk and act and influence all of them. We must build upon Camp David and measure human rights by one yardstick. In that region we have too many interests and too few friends.

76 There is a way out. Jobs. Put Americans back to work. When I was a child growing up in Greenville, S.C. the Rev. Sample who used to preach every so often a sermon linked to Jesus. He said, if I be lifted up, I'll draw all men unto me. I didn't quite understand what he meant as a child growing up. But I understand a little better now. If you raise up truth, it's magnetic. It has a way of drawing people. With all this confusion in this convention—the bright lights and parties and big fun—we must raise up the simple proposition: if we lift up a program to feed the hungry, they'll come running. If we lift up a program to study war no more, our youth will come running. If we lift up a program to put America back to work, an alternative to welfare and despair, they will come working. If we cut that military budget without cutting our defense, and use that money to rebuild bridges and put steelworkers back to work, and use that money, and provide jobs for our cities, and use that money to build schools and train teachers and educate our children, and build hospitals and train doctors and train nurses, the whole nation will come running to us.

77 As I leave you now, and we vote in this convention and get ready to go back across this nation in a couple of days, in this campaign, I'll try to be faithful to my promise. I'll live in the old barrios, and ghettos and reservations, and housing projects. I have a message for our youth. I challenge them to put hope in their brains, and not dope in their veins. I told them like Jesus, I, too, was born in a slum, but just because you're born in a slum, does not mean the slum is born in you, and you can rise above it if your mind is made up. I told them in every slum, there are two sides. When I see a broken window, that's the slummy side. Train that youth to be a glazier, that's the sunny side. When I see a missing brick, that's the slummy side. Let that child in the union, and become a brickmason, and build, that's the sunny side. When I see a missing door, that's the slummy side. Train some youth to become carpenter, that's the sunny side. When I see the vulgar words and hieroglyphics of destitution on the walls, that's the slummy side. Train some youth to be a painter, an artist—that's the sunny side. We need this place looking for the sunny side because there's a brighter side somewhere. I am more convinced than ever that we can win. We'll vault up the rough side of the mountain; we can win. I just want young America to do me one favor. Just one favor.

78 Exercise the right to dream. You must face reality—that which is. But then dream of the reality that ought to be, that must be. Live beyond the pain of reality with the dream of a bright tomorrow. Use hope and imagination as weapons of survival and progress. Use love to motivate you and obligate you to serve the human family.

79 Young America, dream! Choose the human race over the nuclear race. Bury the weapons and don't burn the people. Dream of a new value system. Teachers, who teach for life, and not just for a living, teach because they can't help it. Dream of lawyers more concerned about justice than a judgeship. Dream of doctors more concerned about public health than personal wealth. Dream of preachers and priests who will prophesy and not just profiteer. Preach and dream. Our time has come.

80 Our time has come. Suffering breeds character. Character breeds faith. And in the end, faith will not disappoint.

81 Our time has come. Our faith, hope, and dreams will prevail. Our time has come. Weeping has endured for the night. And, now joy cometh in the morning.

82 Our time has come. No graves can hold our body down.

83 Our time has come. No lie can live forever.

84 Our time has come. We must leave racial battleground and come to economic common ground and moral higher ground. America, our time has come.

85 We've come from disgrace to Amazing Grace, our time has come.

86 Give me your tired, give me your poor, your huddled masses who yearn to breathe free, and come November, there will be a change because our time has come.

87 Thank you and God bless you.

Farewell to the Cadets
Douglas MacArthur

General Douglas MacArthur became a national hero during World War II as the Supreme Allied Commander in the Pacific. Perhaps his greatest moment was when he successfully returned to Manila after the Japanese early in the war had driven American forces from the Phillippines. Upon leaving Manila, MacArthur had vowed, "I shall return." At the close of the war, he commanded the Allied occupational forces in Japan, and his skillful supervision of the restoration of the Japanese nation was widely acclaimed, even by the Japanese. When President Truman ordered American forces into Korea in 1950 to stop the invasion of the South by the North, General MacArthur was again placed in command of the expedition. However, he became an outspoken critic of the administration's Korean policy, and, as a consequence, President Truman relieved General MacArthur of his command in 1951. MacArthur returned to America to a hero's welcome. He accepted an invitation to address a joint session of Congress, and his concluding remarks on the ballad of the "Old Soldier" captured the imagination of the American people. He died on April 5, 1964.

In leaving formal, active association with a group or position, persons sometimes deliver farewell speeches; at times the farewell is combined with an acceptance of an award from the group for outstanding service. In such a situation a critic could assess the ways in which the speaker satisfies various expectations probably held by audiences on such occasions: (1) Expression of gratitude for the award presented and/or for the cooperation and opportunities provided by the group. (2) Expression of sadness and other emotions on leaving the group or position. (3) Recollection of praiseworthy accomplishments or memorable events shared with the group. (4) Praise for the group's values, principles, and goals, along with urging rededication to their continuation. (5) Discussion of the speaker's reasons for leaving: sometimes this even may mean discussion of disagreements or conflicts with superiors or others that led to the departure. (6) Description of the future in broad, sometimes vivid, terms if the group's values and efforts are perpetuated.

On May 12, 1962, General MacArthur, an honor graduate of the United States Military Academy at West Point, went there to receive the Sylvanus Thayer award for service to his nation. The Old Soldier, then 82, accepted the award and, despite failing health, made a moving and inspirational farewell speech to the cadets of the academy, an institution he had served earlier as superintendent. He sought to reinforce and defend the cadets' commitment to the values of "duty, honor, country," the motto inscribed on the academy coat of arms. Although MacArthur originally was gifted with an exceptionally rich and resonant voice, it was now hoarse and often faint. He spoke slowly and deliberately, gaining intensity with phrases such as "faint bugles blowing reveille" and "the strange, mournful mutter of the battlefield."

MacArthur had employed many of the key ideas and vivid phrases in this speech repeatedly in varied contexts in earlier speeches throughout his career. And parts of two paragraphs (9, 25) were derived, without acknowledging the sources, from the previously published words of other people.[1] Although his powers of rhetorical invention might be criticized as being limited, an ability to combine rhetorical elements for moving impact nevertheless is reflected in this address.

As you analyze this speech, you should focus upon several important rhetorical factors. The first is credibility of source. MacArthur, a legendary war hero, doubtlessly enjoyed high ethos with the cadets. Moreover, the text of the speech reveals that MacArthur was fully aware of ethos factors. Second, MacArthur

---

1. Stephen Robb, "Pre-Inventional Criticism: The Speaking of Douglas MacArthur," in G. P. Mohrmann et al., eds., *Explorations in Rhetorical Criticism* (University Park: Pennsylvania State University Press, 1973), pp. 178–90.

was a conscious speech stylist, a fact readily apparent in this address; imagery, metaphor, antithesis, parallelism, and elegance of language are pronounced. Do any of his images seem strained, or are any of his metaphors mixed? Third, note his strategy of linking "duty, honor, country" with desirable consequences (paragraphs 7–10) and with valiant men (11–18). And in paragraph 6 he promotes these values by asserting that blameworthy men consistently downgrade them. Finally, to what higher values does MacArthur relate "duty, honor, country" in order to defend the worth of the cadets' motto?

This speech was taken from a recording of the address and is printed by permission of the Mac-Arthur Memorial Foundation.

---

1 As I was leaving the hotel this morning, a doorman asked me, "Where are you bound for, General?" And when I replied, "West Point," he remarked, "Beautiful place. Have you ever been there before?"

2 No human being could fail to be deeply moved by such a tribute as this, coming from a profession I have served so long and a people I have loved so well.

3 It fills me with an emotion I cannot express. But this award is not intended primarily to honor a personality, but to symbolize a great moral code—the code of conduct and chivalry of those who guard this beloved land of culture and ancient descent. That is the animation of this medallion. For all eyes and for all time it is an expression of the ethics of the American soldier. That I should be integrated in this way with so noble an ideal arouses a sense of pride and yet of humility, which will be with me always.

4 Duty, honor, country: those three hallowed words reverently dictate what you want to be, what you can be, what you will be. They are your rallying points to build courage when courage seems to fail, to regain faith when there seems to be little cause for faith, to create hope when hope becomes forlorn.

5 Unhappily, I possess neither that eloquence of diction, that poetry of imagination, nor that brilliance of metaphor to tell you all that they mean.

6 The unbelievers will say they are but words, but a slogan, but a flamboyant phrase. Every pedant, every demogogue, every cynic, every hypocrite, every troublemaker, and, I am sorry to say, some others of an entirely different character, will try to downgrade them even to the extent of mockery and ridicule.

7 But these are some of the things they do. They build your basic character. They mold you for your future roles as the custodians of the nation's defense. They make you strong enough to know when you are weak and brave enough to face yourself when you are afraid.

8 They teach you to be proud and unbending in honest failure, but humble and gentle in success; not to substitute words for action; not to seek the path of comfort, but to face the stress and spur of difficulty and challenge; to learn to stand up in the storm, but to have

compassion on those who fall; to master yourself before you seek to master others; to have a heart that is clean, a goal that is high; to learn to laugh, yet never forget how to weep; to reach into the future, yet never neglect the past; to be serious, yet never take yourself too seriously; to be modest so that you will remember the simplicity of true greatness, the open mind of true wisdom, the meekness of true strength.

9 They give you a temper of the will, a quality of the imagination, a vigor of the emotions, a freshness of the deep springs of life, a temperamental predominance of courage over timidity, of an appetite for adventure over love of ease.

10 They create in your heart the sense of wonder, the unfailing hope of what next, and the joy and inspiration of life. They teach you this way to be an officer and a gentleman.

11 And what sort of soldiers are those you are to lead? Are they reliable? Are they brave? Are they capable of victory? Their story is known to all of you. It is the story of the American man-at-arms. My estimate of him was formed on the battlefields many, many years ago, and has never changed. I regarded him then, as I regard him now, as one of the world's noblest figures—not only as one of the finest military characters but also as one of the most stainless.

12 His name and fame are the birthright of every American citizen. In his youth and strength, his love and loyalty, he gave all that mortality can give. He needs no eulogy from me or from any other man. He has written his own history and written it in red on his enemy's breast.

13 But when I think of his patience under adversity, of his courage under fire, and his modesty in victory, I am filled with an emotion of admiration I cannot put into words. He belongs to history as furnishing one of the greatest examples of successful patriotism. He belongs to posterity as the instructor of future generations in the principles of liberty and freedom. He belongs to the present—to us—by his virtues and by his achievements.

14 In twenty campaigns, on a hundred battlefields, around a thousand campfires, I have witnessed that enduring fortitude, that patriotic self-abnegation, and that invincible determination which have carved his statue in the hearts of his people.

15 From one end of the world to the other, he has drained deep the chalice of courage. As I listened to those songs, in memory's eye I could see those staggering columns of the First World War, bending under soggy packs on many a weary march, from dripping dusk to drizzling dawn, slogging ankle-deep through the mire of shell-shocked roads; to form grimly for the attack, blue-lipped, covered with sludge and mud, chilled by the wind and rain, driving home to their objective, and, for many, to the judgment seat of God.

16 I do not know the dignity of their birth, but I do know the glory of their death. They died unquestioning, uncomplaining, with faith in their hearts, and on their lips the hope that we would go on to victory.

17 Always for them: duty, honor, country. Always their blood, and sweat, and tears, as we sought the way and the light and the truth. And 20 years after, on the other side of the globe, again the filth of murky foxholes, the stench of ghostly trenches, the slime of dripping dugouts, those boiling suns of relentless heat, those torrential rains of devastating storms, the loneliness and utter desolation of jungle trails, the bitterness of long separation from those they loved and cherished, the deadly pestilence of tropical disease, the horror of stricken areas of war.

18 Their resolute and determined defense, their swift and sure attack, their indomitable purpose, their complete and decisive victory—always victory, always through the bloody haze of their last reverberating shot, the vision of gaunt, ghastly men, reverently following your password of duty, honor, country.

19 The code which those words perpetuate embraces the highest moral law and will stand the test of any ethics or philosophies ever promulgated for the uplift of mankind. Its requirements are for the things that are right and its restraints are from the things that are wrong. The soldier, above all other men, is required to practice the greatest act of religious training—sacrifice. In battle and in the face of danger and death he discloses those divine attributes which his Maker gave when he created man in his own image. No physical courage and no brute instinct can take the place of the divine help, which alone can sustain him. However horrible the incidents of war may be, the soldier who is called upon to offer and to give his life for his country is the noblest development of mankind.

20 You now face a new world, a world of change. The thrust into outer space of the satellite spheres and missiles marks a beginning of another epoch in the long story of mankind. In the five-or-more billions of years the scientists tell us it has taken to form the earth, in the three-or-more billion years of development of the human race, there has never been a more abrupt or staggering evolution.

21 We deal now, not with things of this world alone, but with the illimitable distances and as yet unfathomed distances of the universe. We are reaching out for a new and boundless frontier. We speak in strange terms of harnessing the cosmic energy; of making winds and tides work for us; of creating synthetic materials to supplement or even replace our old standard basics; to purify sea water for our drink; of mining ocean floors for new fields of wealth and food; of disease preventatives to expand life into the hundreds of years; of controlling the weather for a more equitable distribution of heat and cold, of rain and shine; of space ships to the moon; of the primary target in war no longer limited to the armed forces of an enemy, but instead to include his civil populations; of ultimate conflict between a united human race and the sinister forces of some other planetary galaxy; of such dreams and fantasies as to make life the most exciting of all times.

22 And though all this welter of change and development your mission remains fixed, determined, inviolable. It is to win our wars. Everything else in your professional career is but corollary to this vital dedication. All other public purposes, all other public projects, all other public needs, great or small, will find others for their accomplishments; but you are the ones who are trained to fight.

23　Yours is the profession of arms, the will to win, the sure knowledge that in war there is no substitute for victory, that if you lose the nation will be destroyed, that the very obsession of your public service must be duty, honor, country.

24　Others will debate the controversial issues, national and international, which divide men's minds. But serene, calm, aloof, you stand as the nation's war guardians, as its lifeguard from the raging tides of international conflict, as its gladiator in the arena of battle. For a century-and-a-half you have defended, guarded, and protected its hallowed traditions of liberty and freedom, of right and justice.

25　Let civilian voices argue the merits or demerits of our processes of government: whether our strength is being sapped by deficit financing indulged in too long; by federal paternalism grown too mighty; by power groups grown too arrogant; by politics grown too corrupt; by crime grown too rampant; by morals grown too low; by taxes grown too high; by extremists grown too violent; whether our personal liberties are as firm and complete as they should be.

26　These great national problems are not for your professional participation or military solution. Your guidepost stands out like a tenfold beacon in the night: duty, honor, country.

27　You are the leaven which binds together the entire fabric of our national system of defense. From your ranks come the great captains who hold the nation's destiny in their hands the moment the war tocsin sounds.

28　The long, gray line has never failed us. Were you to do so, a million ghosts in olive drab, in brown khaki, in blue and gray, would rise from their white crosses, thundering those magic words: duty, honor, country.

29　This does not mean that you are warmongers. On the contrary, the soldier above all other people prays for peace, for he must suffer and bear the deepest wounds and scars of war. But always in our ears ring the ominous words of Plato, that wisest of all philosophers: "Only the dead have seen the end of war."

30　The shadows are lengthening for me. The twilight is here. My days of old have vanished—tone and tints. They have gone glimmering through the dreams of things that were. Their memory is one of wondrous beauty watered by tears and coaxed and caressed by the smiles of yesterday. I listen vainly, but with thirsty ear, for the witching melody of faint bugles blowing reveille, of far drums beating the long roll.

31　In my dreams I hear again the crash of guns, the rattle of musketry, the strange, mournful mutter of the battlefield. But in the evening of my memory always I come back to West Point. Always there echoes and reechoes: duty, honor, country.

32　Today marks my final roll call with you. But I want you to know that when I cross the river, my last conscious thoughts will be of the Corps, and the Corps, and the Corps.

33　I bid you farewell.

Eulogies for the *Challenger* Astronauts
Ronald Reagan

On January 28, 1986, at 11:39 A.M. EST, only 70 seconds after lift-off from Cape Canaveral, Florida, flying at almost 2000 miles per hour, the space shuttle, *Challenger,* exploded and all seven crew members were killed. The flight was being shown live on national television and the tragedy stunned the nation. President Ronald Reagan delivered two eulogies in response to the disaster.

Speeches of tribute, such as testimonials for living persons and eulogies for the dead, typically reflect rather traditional rhetorical resources to praise accomplishments and acknowledge virtues. The speaker may remind us that the person being paid tribute possesses various qualities of character, such as courage, justice, wisdom, temperance, concern for others, faith, charity, generosity, courtesy, dedication, honesty, industriousness, or humility. The speaker could describe qualities of the person's accomplishments: bravery: extreme difficulty; acknowledgement of excellence by others; personal harm incurred; a "first"; the "best"; the unexpected; the "only"; frequency of achievement; a "last" time ever. Immediate and longterm influences could be stressed, perhaps by describing the "debts" that society owes the person and how we can continue to "repay" that indebtedness through our attitudes and actions, how we can carry on the person's values and commitments. Speakers frequently emphasize the praiseworthy values, ideals, motives, and life goals held by the person. Among the kinds of rhetorical supporting materials typically used in speeches of tribute are factual examples, testimony from notables, experts, or literary sources, narration of incidents, comparison to other persons, Biblical quotations or allusions, and quotations or paraphrases of the person's own words.

By summarizing and slightly modifying the extensive research of Kathleen Jamieson, we can describe four characteristic functions of eulogies in European-American cultures.[1] First, by publicly confirming the person's death, the eulogy helps us overcome our temporary denial of the reality of the death; we overcome our initial reaction of "I just don't believe it." Second, the uneasy realization of our own eventual death is lessened by descriptions of ways in which the deceased "lives on" in history, in heaven, through good works, through followers, or through the person's family. Third, a recounting of the life and virtues of the person *in the past tense* allows us to reorient our own relationship with the deceased from present to past and from physical encounter to memory. Finally, by expressing community solidarity and social cohesion, the eulogy reassures us that our community or group will survive the death. To promote such social cohesion, audiences expect that the eulogist will not "speak ill of the dead," although some eulogists may mentioned modest "faults" in order to "humanize" the person. Sometimes the eulogist provides a rationale for the death so that we do not feel the death was in vain or due to pure chance. Such reasons might include God's will, fulfillment of destiny, evil conditions in society, or even a conspiratorial plot. Another study of eulogies describes three major purposes of the eulogistic form: (1) to express appropriate personal and audience grief; (2) to deepen appreciaton and respect for the deceased; and (3) to give the audience strength for the present and inspiration for the future.[2]

At 5:00 P.M. on the same day of the *Challenger* tragedy, the day on which he was scheduled to present his annual State of the Union address, President Ronald Reagan offered a brief eulogy nationally televised from the oval Office at the White House. At the outset he expresses appropriate personal grief (1–2) and grief on behalf of the audience (3–4). He deepens respect and appreciation for the dead by praising their courage (3–4) and by depicting them as pioneers (5) and explorers (6). He promotes solidarity in the "community" of space program employees by expressing faith and respect for the program (7) and

[1]Kathleen M. Jamieson, *Critical Anthology of Public Speech* (Chicago: Science Research Associates, 1978), pp. 40–41.
[2]Paul C. Brownlow and Beth Davis, " 'A Centainty of Honor': The Eulogies of Adlai Stevenson,: *Central States Speech Journal,* 25 (Fall 1974), 217–24.

by praising their dedication and professionalism (9). Reagan reassures American citizens that in a sense the astronauts' example and efforts will "live on" through the continuation of a vigorous manned space program; they will not have died in vain (8).

Reagan mentions two coincidences, one directly (10) and one indirectly (3). They place the tragedy in a larger historical context of exploration. They may even imply that fate or destiny was at work. The conclusion (11) is a moving and poetic confirmation of the astronauts' death. The quotation is paraphrased from "High Flight," a sonnet by John Gillespie Magee, Jr., a World War II American airman who died in the service of the Royal Canadian Air Force.

Peggy Noonan, a member of Reagan's speechwriting staff, wrote most of the January 28 eulogy. For her account, see Peggy Noonan, *What I Saw at the Revolution* (Random House, 1990), pp. 252–259. For an extensive analysis of the January 28 eulogy, see Steven M. Minter, "Reagan's Challenger Tribute: Combing Generic Constraints and Situational Demands," *Central States Speech Journal,* 37 (Fall 1986): 158–165.

Shortly before noon on January 31, 1986, President Reagan delivered a second and longer eulogy (10 minutes) at the formal memorial service for the *Challenger* astronauts. The scene was the mall in front of the Avionics Building at the Johnson Space Center in Houston, Texas, and the audience was estimated at 10,000, including 2000 space program employees, 90 members of the House and Senate, and 200 relatives of the astronauts. The memorial service was nationally televised.

Reagan's introductory sentence succinctly reflects two purposes of any eulogy: to express personal and collective grief and to give the audience strength for the present and hope for the future. Use of the parallel structure, "we remember" (6–12), forcefully confirms the reality of their deaths, a reality made more emotionally moving through the personal details provided about each of their lives. The President praises values and virtues exemplified in the way "they led . . . and lost their lives" (3), especially perseverance (10, 12) and heroism (7–8, 13, 15). As in the first eulogy, he honors the astronauts' achievement by comparison to the explorations of American pioneers (16). Again Reagan reassures Americans that the astronauts will continue to live in several ways: in heaven (21); through our following their example of courage and character (17); and through continuation of the space shuttle program (10, 18–20).

These eulogies are reprinted from *Weekly Compilation of Presidential Documents,* 22 (February 3, 1986), pp. 104–105, 117–119.

Address to the Nation. January 28, 1986

1 Ladies and gentlemen, I'd planned to speak to you tonight to report on the state of the Union, but the events of earlier today have led me to change those plans. Today is a day for mourning and remembering.

2 Nancy and I are pained to the core by the tragedy of the shuttle *Challenger.* We know we share this pain with all of the people of our country. This is truly a national loss.

3 Nineteen years ago, almost to the day, we lost three astronauts in a terrible accident on the ground. But we've never lost an astronaut in flight; we've never had a tragedy like this. And perhaps we've forgotten the courage it took for the crew of the shuttle; but they, the *Challenger* Seven, were aware of the dangers, but overcame them and did their jobs brilliantly. We mourn seven heroes: Michael Smith, Dick Scobee, Judith Resnik, Ronald McNair, Ellison Onizuka, Gregory Jarvis, and Christa McAuliffe. We mourn their loss as a nation together.

4 For the family of the seven, we cannot bear, as you do, the full impact of this tragedy. But we feel the loss, and we're thinking about you so very much. Your loved ones were daring and brave, and they had that special grace, that special spirit that says, "Give me a challenge and I'll meet it with joy." They had a hunger to explore the universe and discover its truths. They wished to serve, and they did. They served all of us.

5 We've grown used to wonders in this century. It's hard to dazzle us. But for 25 years the United States space program has been doing just that. We've grown used to the idea of space, and perhaps we forget that we've only just begun. We're still pioneers. They, the members of the *Challenger* crew, were pioneers.

6 And I want to say something to the schoolchildren of America who were watching the live coverage of the shuttle's takeoff. I know it is hard to understand, but sometimes painful things like this happen. It's all part of the process of exploration and discovery. It's all part of taking a chance and expanding man's horizons. The future doesn't belong to the fainthearted; it belongs to the brave. The *Challenger* crew was pulling us into the future, and we'll continue to follow them.

7 I've always had great faith in and respect for our space program, and what happened today does nothing to diminish it. We don't hide our space program. We don't keep secrets and cover things up. We do it all up front and in public. That's the way freedom is, and we wouldn't change it for a minute.

8 We'll continue our quest in space. There will be more shuttle flights and more shuttle crews, and yes, more volunteers, more civilians, more teachers in space. Nothing ends here; our hopes and our journeys continue.

9 I want to add that I wish I could talk to every man and woman who works for NASA or who worked on this mission and tell them: "Your dedication and professionalism have moved and impressed us for decades. And we know of your anguish. We share it."

10 There's a coincidence today. On this day 390 years ago, the great explorer Sir Francis Drake died aboard ship off the coast of Panama. In his lifetime the great frontiers were the oceans, and an historian later said, "He lived by the sea, died on it, and was buried in it." Well, today we can say of the *Challenger* crew: Their dedication was, like Drake's, complete.

11 The crew of the space shuttle *Challenger* honored us by the manner in which they lived their lives. We will never forget them, nor the last time we saw them, this morning, as they prepared for their journey and waved goodbye and "slipped the surly bonds of earth" to "touch the face of God."

Remarks at the Johnson Space Center in Houston, TX. January 31, 1986

1 We come together today to mourn the loss of seven brave Americans, to share the grief that we all feel, and perhaps in that sharing, to find the strength to bear our sorrow and the courage to look for the seeds of hope.

2 Our nation's loss is first a profound personal loss to the family and the friends and the loved ones of our shuttle astronauts. To those they left behind—the mothers, the fathers, the husbands and wives, brothers and sisters, yes, and especially the children—all of America stands beside you in your time of sorrow.

3 What we say today is only an inadequate expression of what we carry in our hearts. Words pale in the shadow of grief; they seem insufficient even to measure the brave sacrifice of those you loved and we so admired. Their truest testimony will not be in the words we speak, but in the way they led their lives and in the way they lost their lives—with dedication, honor, and an unquenchable desire to explore this mysterious and beautiful universe.

4 The best we can do is remember our seven astronauts, our *Challenger* Seven, remember them as they lived, bringing life and love and joy to those who knew them and pride to a nation.

5 They came from all parts of this great country—from South Carolina to Washington State; Ohio to Mohawk, New York; Hawaii to North Carolina to Concord, New Hampshire. They were so different; yet in their mission, their quest, they held so much in common.

6 We remember Dick Scobee, the commander who spoke the last words we heard from the space shuttle *Challenger*. He served as a fighter pilot in Vietnam earning many medals for bravery and later as a test pilot of advanced aircraft before joining the space program. Danger was a familiar companion to Commander Scobee.

7 We remember Michael Smith, who earned enough medals as a combat pilot to cover his chest, including the Navy Distinguished Flying Cross, three Air Medals, and the Vietnamese Cross of Gallantry with Silver Star in gratitude from a nation he fought to keep free.

8 We remember Judith Resnik, known as J.R. to her friends, always smiling, always eager to make a contribution, finding beauty in the music she played on her piano in her off-hours.

9 We remember Ellison Onizuka, who as a child running barefoot through the coffee fields and macadamia groves of Hawaii dreamed of someday traveling to the Moon. Being an Eagle Scout, he said, had helped him soar to the impressive achievements of his career.

10 We remember Ronald McNair, who said that he learned perseverance in the cottonfields of South Carolina. His dream was to live aboard the space station, performing experiments and playing his saxophone in the weightlessness of space. Well, Ron, we will miss your saxophone, and we *will* build your space station.

11 We remember Gregory Jarvis. On that ill-fated flight he was carrying with him a flag of his university in Buffalo, New York—a small token, he said, to the people who unlocked his future.

12 We remember Christa McAuliffe, who captured the imagination of the entire nation; inspiring us with her pluck, her restless spirit of discovery; a teacher, not just to her students, but to an entire people, instilling us all with the excitement of this journey we ride into the future.

13 We will always remember them, these skilled professionals, scientists, and adventurers, these artists and teachers and family men and women; and we will cherish each of their stories, stories of triumph and bravery, stories of true American heroes.

14 On the day of the disaster, our nation held a vigil by our televison sets. In one cruel moment our exhilaration turned to horror; we waited and watched and tried to make sense of what we had seen. That night I listened to a call-in program on the radio; people of every age spoke of their sadness and the pride they felt in our astronauts. Across America we are reaching out, holding hands, and finding comfort in one another.

15 The sacrifice of your loved ones has stirred the soul of our nation and through the pain our hearts have been opened to a profound truth. The future is not free; the story of all human progress is one of a struggle against all odds. We learned again that this America, which Abraham Lincoln called the last, best hope of man on Earth, was built on heroism and noble sacrifice. It was built by men and women like our seven star voyagers, who answered a call beyond duty, who gave more than was expected or required, and who gave it little thought of worldly reward.

16 We think back to the pioneers of an earlier century, the sturdy souls who took their families and their belongings and set out into the frontier of the American West. Often they met with terrible hardship. Along the Oregon Trail, you could still see the gravemarkers of those who fell on the way. But grief only steeled them to the journey ahead.

17 Today the frontier is space and the boundaries of human knowledge. Sometimes when we reach for the stars, we fall short. But we must pick ourselves up again and press on despite the pain. Our nation is indeed fortunate that we can still draw on immense reservoirs of courage, character, and fortitude—that we're still blessed with heroes like those in the space shuttle *Challenger*.

18 Dick Scobee knew that every launching of a space shuttle is a technological miracle. And he said, "If something ever does go wrong, I hope that doesn't mean the end to the space shuttle program." Every family member I talked to asked specifically that we continue the program, that that is what their departed loved one would want above all else. We will not disappoint them.

19 Today we promise Dick Scobee and his crew that their dream lives on, that the future they worked so hard to build will become reality. The dedicated men and women of NASA have lost seven members of their family. Still, they, too, must forge ahead with a space program that is effective, safe, and efficient, but bold and committed.

20 Man will continue his conquest of space. To reach out for new goals and ever greater achievements—that is the way we shall commemorate our seven *Challenger* heroes.

21 Dick, Mike, Judy, El, Ron, Greg, and Christa—your families and your country mourn your passing. We bid you goodbye; we will never forget you. For those who knew you well and loved you, the pain will be deep and enduring. A nation, too, will long feel the loss of her seven sons and daughters, her seven good friends. We can find consolation only in faith, for we know in our hearts that you who flew so high and so proud now make your home beyond the stars, safe in God's promise of eternal life.

22 May God bless you all and give you comfort in this difficult time.

A Bird Outside Your Window
Dolores M. Bandow

A returning adult student at the University of Wisconsin-Madison, Dolores Bandow delivered this speech in a public speaking course during the 1986 fall semester. The speech was given in response to an assignment calling for a ceremonial speech emphasizing values.

Ms. Bandow commemorates the ninth anniversary of a most significant event in her life—the birth of a child with a genetic anomaly. While celebrating the life of her child, Elizabeth, the speaker is, at the same time, identifying the essence of what it means to live. What values constitute that essence? Do these values require periodic reaffirmation?

Speeches that intensify social cohesion often contain vivid and memorable language. Why do you suppose this is true? Consider the speaker's word choice and use of figurative language as you read this speech. How many different kinds of figurative language are used? What role does figurative language play in the emotional impact of this speech?

It is difficult to read this speech without growing admiration and respect for the speaker. As you read this speech, try to identify the aspects that most contribute to your positive perceptions of the speaker. What conclusions may be drawn about speaker ethos?

This speech is published by permission of Dolores Bandow.

1 I am here today to celebrate life. I am here to celebrate a particular life which began nine years ago this month. The day I gave birth to our third child, Nov. 2, 1977, I thought was the bleakest day one could experience. My hopes for a healthy baby were snuffed away. Of two children born at the hospital that hour, both had birth defects. The other child died. For one dreadful, fleeting moment, I thought it would be easier if ours had.

2 To admit such a transient thought and regret such a thought is sobering. How selfish; how self-pitying; how wrong I was. I had wanted a "perfect" baby. But by shattering our illusion of perfection with her birth, she has been perfecting our reality with her life.

3 Elizabeth's life has taught me compassion, unconditional love, humility; and has set me on a path to wisdom. The Greek philosophers said, "Wisdom begins when you realize that you don't know what you thought you knew." I thought I knew sadness; I hadn't. I thought I knew happiness; I thought I knew love; not all kinds. I thought I knew compassion; I thought I knew humility; I hadn't. In her book, Judith Viorst views life as a series of "Necessary Losses" that people must give up in order to grow up. Here was one of those losses—the loss of an ideal that was being traded for humanity.

4 As I lay in the hospital bed those days following her birth, reading medical genetics textbooks instead of Dr. Spock, I learned that humans need 46 chromosomes—precisely. Any more or any fewer can result in abnormalities of every cell. Overwhelmed by the data, unable to sleep, I would steal down to the nursery in the wee hours of the morning where I had to scrub my arms and hands with betadine and don a surgical gown and mask before entering. Elizabeth was caged in an isolet with tubes and wires reaching out from every orifice like guy wires holding her down. Electronic blips marched across oscilloscopes. Rapid high pitched beeps competed with babies' cries for attention. But when my hands found their way through the maze to stroke her face, she nuzzled against me in her suckling instinct. At that moment, I saw her not as a syndrome but as my infant daughter. She made me peer beyond the "accidentals" to the "essence" of human life.

5 Later, at the age of seven months, Elizabeth was in heart failure, fighting for life. Before I took her to the hospital for heart surgery, I prepared to say "good-by" to her. Unable to make myself cross the threshold with her, I turned around and saw the flowers. I carried her over and let her breathe the fragrance. I pointed up to the clouds; I lifted her up to the trees and told her to look at it all—see it. But it was I who was seeing it as never before.

6 Standing there I remembered a poem I had heard over and over again in my child-hood from an old family phonograph record. The poem included the words of a sad old Negro preacher addressing a couple in Savannah who were mourning their child. He said, "Now, Father didn't give you that baby by a hundred thousand miles. He just thinks you need some sunshine and he lent him for a while. And he let you love and keep him till your hearts were bigger grown. And these silver tears you're sheddin' are just interst on a loan . . . " Sunshine is indeed what Elizabeth brought us in the form of illumination and en-lightenment. She still casts her light.

7 Recently I've been grumpy over turning 40. When I was bemoaning my greying hair, sagging skin, and aching joints, Elizabeth said, "Mom, you should be glad to be living a long, long time. Celebrate!" With that piece of advice, once again she helped me peer beyond the superficial to realize the privilege of a healthy life despite sagging jowls and greying hair.

8 Elizabeth has been to me the bird that sings too early outside your window and rouses you from that dream state—she sang her song. Like that uninvited bird that sings incessantly, while you wish it would whistle its tune outside someone else's window—she sang her song to me. And like that bird's tune, I harked, heard, and hummed it back.

9 My song is this: keep in mind that children with birth anomalies are not the pitiful. Not they, but we with our attitude, ignorance, and insensitivities are pitiful. Just consider, "There but for the grace of God go I."

10 Yes, there was a brief moment at her birth when her unwelcome song jarred me awake. Sometimes the thing we welcome least is a blessing which, disguised, knocks boldly on our door; then rejected, sneaks quietly in the back door of the heart and establishes residence before being recognized—quietly working magic—quietly transforming.

11 So, Elizabeth, I thank you for singing your song outside my window and forcing me to look through that window beyond the "accidentals" to the "essence." Thank you for allowing me to glimpse through that window and see the flowers through your eyes. Thank you for showing me my reflection in that window—for making me realize that the alternative to growing old is not being alive. And thank you, Elizabeth, for making growing old worthwile.

To you, Elizabeth:

L'Chaim

INDEX OF RHETORICAL PRINCIPLES